K

NOV 2 5 1986			
NOV 2 1 1992			
FEB - 9 1993			
JUN 2 3 1995			
JAN 2 5 1992			
APR 1 1 1999			
OCT 3 1			
REG - 10097326			
Reg - 10251327			

The Social Transformation
of American Medicine

THE
SOCIAL
TRANSFORMATION
OF AMERICAN
MEDICINE

PAUL STARR

Basic Books, Inc., Publishers   New York

To the Memory

of My Father

Library of Congress Cataloging in Publication Data

Starr, Paul, 1949–
  The social transformation of American medicine.

  Includes bibliographical references and index.
    1. Medical care—United States—History. 2. Social
medicine—United States—History. 3. Physicians—
United States—History. I. Title. [DNLM: 1. History
of medicine, Modern—United States.   WZ 70 AA1 S7s]
RA395.A3S77 1982   305'.961'0973   81-68412
ISBN 0-465-07934-2

CONTENTS

BOOK ONE

A SOVEREIGN PROFESSION
The Rise of Medical Authority and
the Shaping of the Medical System

BOOK TWO

THE STRUGGLE FOR MEDICAL CARE
Doctors, the State, and the Coming
of the Corporation

PREFACE

I HAVE DIVIDED this history into two books to emphasize two long movements in the development of American medicine: first, the rise of professional sovereignty; and second, the transformation of medicine into an industry and the growing, though still unsettled, role of corporations and the state. Within this framework I explore a variety of specific questions, such as:

why Americans, who were wary of medical authority in the early and mid-nineteenth century, became devoted to it in the twentieth;

how American doctors, who were bitterly divided and financially insecure in the nineteenth century, became a united and prosperous profession in the twentieth;

why hospitals, medical schools, clinics, and other organizations assumed distinctive institutional forms in the United States;

why hospitals became the central institutions in medical care;

why public health did not;

why there is no national health insurance in the United States;

why Blue Cross and commercial indemnity insurance, rather than other types of health plans, dominated the private insurance market;

why the federal government in recent years shifted from policies that encouraged growth without changes in the organization of medical care to policies that encouraged reorganization to control growth;

why physicians long escaped from the control of the modern corporation, but are now witnessing and indeed taking part in the creation of corporate health care systems.

This last question became more salient while this book was in progress. When I began work in 1974, it was widely thought that medical schools, planners, and administrators were emerging as the chief counterweight to private physicians. Government seemed to be assuming a major, perhaps dominant role in the organization of medical care. Decisions that had formerly been private and professional were becoming public and political. Eight years later this is no longer clearly the direction of change, but neither is the status quo ante being restored. Private corporations are gaining a more powerful position in American medicine; if leading members of the Reagan administration have their way, the future may well belong to corporate medicine. However, the origins of this development precede the current administration; the force behind it is more powerful than the changing fashions in Washington. Precisely because of what is now taking place, it has become more necessary to understand medicine as a business as well as a cultural phenomenon—and perhaps most important, to understand the relation between the two.

Many of the chapters dealing with these and other problems can be read almost as self-contained studies. However, my primary intention in writing this volume has been to provide an integrated account of the social and economic development of medicine in America. I have tried to present an interpretation that makes sense in terms of the broader historical patterns in our culture, economy, and politics.

All the chapters refer back, moreover, to the arguments adumbrated in the Introduction about the relation of knowledge and power and the nature and uses of authority. The opening theoretical passages, I recognize, may be a barrier rather than an invitation to some readers. I ask their patience. My aim in the Introduction is to place the analysis in the context in which I think it belongs; to define my terms; and to provide an analytical map that may serve as a guide through the chief turns of the argument, at least in Book One. But should the reader find this map too sketchy and abstract, I suggest skipping to Chapter One, where the journey begins. The point of my concern with authority and economic power will, I hope, shortly become clear.

In writing this volume, I have not assumed the reader would necessarily be acquainted with the history, economics, or sociology of medicine. Therefore, I have tried to provide as much background as necessary to make the story clear and to enable the analysis to stand on its own, without leaving gaps that could only be filled by reading further in the literature. But should the reader wish to learn more, the notes provide references to additional sources. The notes also, of course, identify the extent of my debts to other scholars as well as some of my differences with them. In the interests of straightforward exposition, I have tried to leave the text relatively unencumbered with polemic.

The reader who expects to find a political program here will be disappointed. This omission is not a reflection of any indifference on my

part, nor a pose of neutrality. I have written elsewhere on more immediate questions of policy, and it will scarcely require a cryptographer
to decipher my sentiments, especially in some of the final chapters. But
history does not provide any answers about what should be done. Were
I to take up problems of political choice, it would require me to speak
here in a different voice and, indeed, to write another book. My hope
is that this historical analysis may help to illuminate our present predic-
ament, even for people of divergent sympathies. I have sought to trace
not only the origins of the institutions and policies that are with us
today, but also the fate of those that failed or were defeated or stunted
in their development. I would not be sorry if these analyses of roads not
taken served as a reminder that the past had other possibilites, and so
do we today.

Cambridge, Mass.
August 1982

ACKNOWLEDGMENTS

THIS BOOK was written in the old-fashioned way: the lone scholar pecking away at his word processor. But like many solo practitioners, I had the benefit of consultations with colleagues and the resources of some large institutions at my disposal. Without them my work would have been impossible.

For any serious research and reflection, there is no substitute for time —time left wholly to one's own organization. Without the three years provided to me by the Society of Fellows at Harvard between 1975 and 1978, this book could not have been written. I am also indebted to the Commonwealth Fund for support while I was a Fellow in Law, Science, and Medicine at Yale Law School in 1974–1975, when I was beginning this work; and to the John Simon Guggenheim Memorial Foundation for support while I was a visitor at Yale's Institution for Social and Policy Studies in 1981–1982, when the final editorial work was, belatedly, completed. And to those who were my teachers and are now my colleagues in the Department of Sociology at Harvard, I am also obliged—for their advice, confidence, and encouragement. To Daniel Bell I owe a special debt, for the example that his range of knowledge constantly provides, as well as for the line-by-line attention he paid some time ago to an earlier draft of what is now Book One.

Over the years more people than I can now faithfully recall gave me counsel, criticized drafts of chapters, or simply heard me out while I carried on about my research. I would particularly like to thank Joan Lidoff, Michael Schudson, Jerry Avorn, Peter Temin, Kenneth Ludmerer, John Harley Warner, Morris Vogel, Mark Blumberg, John Simon, George Silver, and Daniel Fox.

An earlier version of Chapter Two appeared in the *Journal of Social History* 10 (Summer 1977) under the title "Medicine, Economy, and

Society in Nineteenth-Century America." There are also some fragments here from an essay, "Medicine and the Waning of Professional
Sovereignty," which appeared in *Daedalus* (Winter 1978). I would like
to thank the editors of those publications for our initial agreements that
permitted me to use that work in the present volume.

I also would like to thank Martin Kessler of Basic Books for his confidence and tolerance and Maureen Bischoff for her painstaking labors
in the production of the book. I owe a debt to Scott Bradner, for making
possible the direct publication of this book from Harvard computers.
Stephen Holmes and Nancy Maull provided delightful hospitality as the
end drew near, and it drew near many, many times. My daughter
Rebecca thoughtfully waited to leave her mother's womb until the
manuscript had left mine. And, most important, my wife Sandra gave
me the benefit of her wisdom, her own considerable knowledge of the
subject, and her patience. There is no way I can convey here the measure of my love.

BOOK ONE

A SOVEREIGN PROFESSION

*The Rise of Medical Authority
and the Shaping
of the Medical System*

INTRODUCTION

The Social Origins of Professional Sovereignty

THE DREAM of reason did not take power into account.

The dream was that reason, in the form of the arts and sciences, would liberate humanity from scarcity and the caprices of nature, ignorance and superstition, tyranny, and not least of all, the diseases of the body and the spirit. But reason is no abstract force pushing inexorably toward greater freedom at the end of history. Its forms and uses are determined by the narrower purposes of men and women; their interests and ideals shape even what counts as knowledge. Though the works of reason have lifted innumerable burdens of hunger and sorrow, they have also cast up a new world of power. In that world, some people stand above others in knowledge and authority and in control of the vast institutions that have arisen to manage and finance the rationalized forms of human labor.

Modern medicine is one of those extraordinary works of reason: an elaborate system of specialized knowledge, technical procedures, and rules of behavior. By no means are these all purely rational: our conceptions of disease and responses to it unquestionably show the imprint of our particular culture, especially its individualist and activist therapeutic mentality. Yet, whatever its biases and probably because of them, modern science has succeeded in liberating humanity from much of the burden of disease. Few cultural relativists, suffering from a bad fever or a broken arm, would go so far to prove a point as to trade a modern physician for a traditional healer. They recognize, in behavior if not always in argument, that in medicine the dream of reason has partially come true.

But medicine is also, unmistakably, a world of power where some are more likely to receive the rewards of reason than are others. From a relatively weak, traditional profession of minor economic significance, medicine has become a sprawling system of hospitals, clinics, health plans, insurance companies, and myriad other organizations employing a vast labor force. This transformation has not been propelled solely by the advance of science and the satisfaction of human needs. The history of medicine has been written as an epic of progress, but it is also a tale of social and economic conflict over the emergence of new hierarchies of power and authority, new markets, and new conditions of belief and experience. In America, no one group has held so dominant a position in this new world of rationality and power as has the medical profession. Its rise to sovereignty in the late nineteenth and early twentieth centuries is the first part of the story I have to relate; the emergence in our own time of a bureaucratic and corporate regime is the second.

Power, at the most rudimentary personal level, originates in dependence, and the power of the professions primarily originates in dependence upon their knowledge and competence. In some cases, this dependence may be entirely subjective, but no matter: Psychological dependence is as real in its consequences as any other kind. Indeed, what makes dependence on the professions so distinctive today is that their interpretations often govern our understanding of the world and our own experience. To most of us, this power seems legitimate: When professionals claim to be authoritative about the nature of reality, whether it is the structure of the atom, the ego, or the universe, we generally defer to their judgment.

The medical profession has had an especially persuasive claim to authority. Unlike the law and the clergy, it enjoys close bonds with modern science, and at least for most of the last century, scientific knowledge has held a privileged status in the hierarchy of belief. Even among the sciences, medicine occupies a special position. Its practitioners come into direct and intimate contact with people in their daily lives; they are present at the critical transitional moments of existence. They serve as intermediaries between science and private experience, interpreting personal troubles in the abstract language of scientific knowledge. For many people, they are the only contact with a world that otherwise stands at a forbidding distance. Physicians offer a kind of individualized objectivity, a personal relationship as well as authoritative counsel. The very circumstances of sickness promote acceptance of their judgment. Often in pain, fearful of death, the sick have a special thirst for reassurance and vulnerability to belief. The therapeutic definition of the profession's role also encourages its acceptance: Its power is avowedly enlisted solely in the interests of health—a value of usually unambiguous importance to its clients and society. On this basis, physicians exercise authority over patients, their fellow workers in health care, and even the public at large in matters within, and sometimes outside, their jurisdiction.

In clinical relations, this authority is often essential for the therapeutic process. The sick are ordinarily not the best judge of their own needs, nor are those who are emotionally close to them. Quite aside from specialized knowledge, professionals possess an advantage in judgment. Furthermore, effective therapeutic measures frequently require not only difficult and even repellent tasks, such as violating the integrity of the body, but also rechanneling the unconscious urges of some patients to be sick and to be cared for. Their families often cannot handle, indeed may be responsible for such urges—hence the need for some outside party to mediate recovery. Professionals are ideally suited for this role because they can refuse to indulge such tendencies in patients without threatening their relationships with them. And so professional authority facilitates cooperation in recovery besides compensating for the often impaired and inadequate judgment of the sick.

The dominance of the medical profession, however, goes considerably beyond this rational foundation. Its authority spills over its clinical boundaries into arenas of moral and political action for which medical judgment is only partially relevant and often incompletely equipped. Moreover, the profession has been able to turn its authority into social privilege, economic power, and political influence. In the distribution of rewards from medicine, the medical profession, as the highest-paid occupation in our society, receives a radically disproportionate share. Until recently, it has exercised dominant control over the markets and organizations in medicine that affect its interests. And over the politics, policies, and programs that govern the system, the profession's interests have also tended to prevail. At all these levels, from individual relations to the state, the pattern has been one of professional sovereignty.

How the medical profession rose to this position of cultural authority, economic power, and political influence; how, together with other powerful social forces, it shaped the institutional structure of medical care;

and how that system has now evolved, so as to put the profession's autonomy and dominance in jeopardy—these are the questions that this book addresses.

Some may think the sources of professional sovereignty too obvious to be worth pursuing. For haven't healers always been esteemed and powerful? And doesn't the growth of science make inevitable the high value and position attached to medicine? And isn't there something about American culture, particularly our preoccupation with health and well-being, that makes us especially inclined to give doctors a high status?

The answer to each of these questions is no.

It is simply not true, as some might have it, that physicians have always occupied positions of honor and comfort ever since the first medicine man had the good fortune to recite an incantation immediately before his patient's spontaneous recovery. There are numerous historical counter-examples. Under the Romans, physicians were primarily slaves, freedmen, and foreigners, and medicine was considered a very low-grade occupation. In eighteenth-century England, while ranking above the lowlier surgeons and apothecaries, physicians stood only at the margins of the gentry class, struggling for the patronage of the rich in the hope of acquiring enough wealth to buy an estate and a title. In nineteenth- and early twentieth-century France, doctors were mostly impecunious, and the successful among them, conscious that medicine was an inadequate claim to status, pursued an ideal of general cultivation rather than mere professional accomplishment.[1]

In the world today, not all societies with scientifically advanced medical institutions have powerful medical professions. To take a conspicuous case, in the Soviet Union the average earnings of physicians are reported to be less than three-quarters of the average industrial wage. Not coincidently, 70 percent of the doctors are women.[2] Even in a Western society quite similar to ours, Great Britain, most general practitioners are only moderately well paid, and they work within a national health service whose budget and overall policies they do not control. In Britain and other European countries, there is a powerful upper stratum of consultants within the medical profession, but such sharp internal differences also tend to distinguish their medical professions from ours. Hardly anywhere have doctors been as successful as American physicians in resisting national insurance and maintaining a predominantly private and voluntary financing system. The growth of science, while critically important in the development of professionalism, does not assure physicians broad cultural authority, economic power, or political influence, as they have achieved in the United States.

The explanation for professional sovereignty in medicine also cannot be found in any ingrained peculiarities of American culture. Doctors in America were not always the powerful and authoritative profession that they are today. A century ago they had much less influence, income, and prestige. "In all of our American colleges," a professional journal commented bitterly in 1869, "medicine has ever been and is now, the most despised of all the professions which liberally-educated men are expected to enter."[3] Although a few eminent doctors made handsome fortunes, many before 1900 could hardly scrape together a respectable living.

To be sure, many observers, beginning with de Tocqueville, have remarked that Americans are singularly concerned with their individual well-being. Since the 1830s, when de Tocqueville visited America, the United States has been swept by a series of popular movements concerned with improving health variously through diet, exercise, moral purity, positive thinking, and religious faith. Today, were a revived de Tocqueville to observe Americans jogging in parks, shopping in health food stores, talking psychobabble, and reading endless guides to keeping fit, eating right, and staying healthy, he would probably conclude that, if anything, the obsession is now more pronounced.

But a concern with health has not always produced faith in doctors. On the contrary, many of those most disposed to take health "into their own hands" are skeptical of physicians. The advocates of popular health fashions, even when they are doctors, frequently see themselves at war with the medical profession. Intensified religious feeling does not always benefit established churches; similarly, a therapeutic awakening may lead to a proliferation of health sects rather than deference to professional authority.

These plausible, yet mistaken explanations for the high status and power of physicians have the same general problems. They cannot explain comparative and historical variations in the position of the profession, and they assume that popular attitudes—whether toward healing, science, or health—translate directly into status and power. The analysis here begins with several contrary premises.

First, the problem of professional sovereignty in American medicine is historical; there is no necessary and invariant relation to social structure of a function such as caring for the sick. Social structure is the outcome of historical processes. To understand a given structural arrangement, like professional sovereignty, one has to identify the ways in which people acted, pursuing their interests and ideals under definite conditions, to bring that structure into existence. In the nineteenth century, the medical profession was generally weak, divided, insecure in its status and its income, unable to control entry into practice or to raise the standards of medical education. In the twentieth century, not only did physicians become a powerful, prestigious, and wealthy profession, but they succeeded in shaping the basic organization and financial structure of American medicine. More recently, that system has begun to slip from their control, as power has moved away from the organized profession toward complexes of medical schools and hospitals, financing and regulatory agencies, health insurance companies, prepaid health plans, and health care chains, conglomerates, holding companies, and other corporations. Understanding these changes requires an analysis that is simultaneously structural and historical: structural in its identification of the underlying patterns of social and economic relations that explain observed events; historical in its tracing of those patterns to the human actions that brought them about. I do not want to deny the value of narrative history without structural analysis, nor even of structural analysis without history (though the former is certainly more entertaining). But the two, it seems to me, go further in each other's company than either can go alone.

My second premise is that the organization of medical care cannot be understood with reference solely to medicine, the relations between doctors and patients, or even all the various forces internal to the health care sector. The development of medical care, like other institutions, takes place within larger fields of power and social structure. These external forces are particularly visible in conflicts over the politics and economics of health and medical care. In the twentieth century, the costs of illness and medicine have become critical concerns of governments and political parties because of their implications for social welfare, overall economic efficiency, and political conflict. In the United States, private foundations play a critical role in financing medical education and research. Employers, unions, and insurance companies are centrally involved as intermediaries in the financing of services. Some of these external agents are mainly interested in profit in the narrow sense. But often, by providing medical care or paying costs associated with it, governments, political parties, foundations, employers, unions, and voluntary agencies hope to derive a different sort of benefit: good will, gratitude, loyalty, solidarity, dependence. The prospect of advantages of this kind makes medical care an especially strategic arena of political and economic conflict.

My third premise is that the problem of professional sovereignty calls for an approach that encompasses both culture and institutions. Consequently, this study goes back and forth between consciousness and organization in attempting to understand both the growth of the cultural authority of the medical profession and the conversion of that authority into the control of markets, organizations, and governmental policy. This is not to put either cultural analysis or political economy ahead of the other. For it is not possible, as I see it, to understand the origins of the power of the medical profession, in the face of all the other political and economic forces at work in health care, without reference to its cultural authority. Nor is it possible to understand the rise of its cultural authority without reference to underlying changes in material life and social organization.*

THE ROOTS OF AUTHORITY

Dependence and Legitimacy

If, as I argue, the rise of the medical profession depended on the growth of its authority, we need to understand more precisely what authority is.

Authority, in its classical sense, signifies the possession of some status, quality, or claim that compels trust or obedience.[4] As part of this ability to compel trust or obedience, authority signifies a potential to use force or persuasion, though paradoxically authority ends when either of these is openly employed. The use of force, as Hannah Arendt observes, signifies the failure of authority; so does resort to persuasion, which, she points out, "presupposes equality and works through a process of argumentation. Where arguments are used, authority is left in abeyance."[5] Authority calls for voluntary obedience, but holds in reserve powers to enforce it. Behind political authority ultimately stands the threat of violence or imprisonment; behind managerial authority, the threat of dismissal from work. These reserve powers make subordinates dependent upon such authorities for their life, liberty, and livelihood; they create a strong basis for compliance, apart from any belief that subordinates may hold about the authorities' claim to obedience.

Authority, therefore, incorporates two sources of effective control: legitimacy and dependence. The former rests on the subordinates' accep-

*Some readers may wish at this point to proceed to the beginning of Chapter One and to return to this Introduction only after having finished the final section of Chapter Three on "the retreat of private judgment." I recommend this alternative route especially to the general reader, who may find the following abstract discussion more useful after having seen how I develop the idea of a struggle for cultural authority specifically in relation to the history of medicine.

tance of the claim that they should obey; the latter on their estimate of the foul consequences that will befall them if they do not.

Authority relations are not fixed and untroubled. Often they go through periods of distress, as when children fight with their parents, students disagree with their teachers, or workers protest against their employers' policies. In such periods, the legitimacy of authority may be in doubt, but the ongoing dependence of subordinates maintains authority. Conversely, when the governing authorities may, for one reason or another, be weak and incapable of carrying out their reserve threats, their legitimacy may assure continuity of control. Thus the twin supports of dependence and legitimacy introduce a stability into authority relations: When one is weak, the other may take over, and so authority, as a mode of control, is stronger and more reliable than either force or persuasion.[6]

Authority may also gain compliance from different people for different reasons. In a firm, for example, the authority of the owners and directors is likely to be followed at the highest levels because the managers accept the rights of ownership and share a commitment to the enterprise; often the workers do, too. However, in some countries with large Communist and Socialist parties, the workers may accord little legitimacy to the firm, but feel much dependence upon it for jobs. The probability of compliance with managerial authority may still be great. Similarly, the upper strata in a society may support the ruling political authority because they believe it to represent the highest values, whereas the basis of compliance among subordinate castes or classes, ethnic or religious groups may be adherence to legality or sheer dependence. From childhood they may have learned that resistance to authority brings swift reprisal. Once again, the twin supports of legitimacy and dependence add to the overall effectiveness of authority as a mode of control.

The acceptance of authority signifies "a surrender of private judgment." However, even in surrendering private judgment, one may still believe that the words of authority can be persuasively elaborated.[7] For authority usually has a reserve of reasons as well as powers. The advantage of authority, however, is that it makes it unnecessary to elaborate the reasons for the believing subject, just as it dispenses with the use of force on the recalcitrant. This is its essentially economic value. From the viewpoint of a client independently seeking out professional advice, authority may be "a shortcut to where reason is presumed to lead,"[8] while for the professional using authority to control an involuntary inmate, authority may be a shortcut to where coercion would be presumed to lead.

If authority may be generally said to have reserves of both persuasion and force, the reserve strength of professional authority—when separate from bureaucratic office—consists primarily of persuasion. For it is almost always to argument, rather than coercion, that independent professionals turn when their authority fails. In the case of a voluntary client, they cannot draw on reserve powers that compare in coerciveness with the threats of violence or imprisonment and dismissal from work that rulers and bosses can employ. The chief basis of dependence upon professionals is their superior competence, but it would be a gross violation of their own ethical codes if in attempting to enforce compliance they threatened to use their skills to harm their clients. A professional can threaten to withdraw from a case, and under some conditions, such as in the midst of a trial or therapy, clients may find this prospect perfectly terrifying.[9] Such threats are probably rare, but they suggest the importance of yet another, nonrational basis of power—psychological dependency.

Although independent professionals may lack the formal power of enforcement possessed by rulers and employers, they often derive power from the dependent emotional condition of their clients. Even when voluntary clients have the option of going to another professional, they may be unable to bear the disruption of long-standing relations. The deeply emotional crises that often lead people to consult professionals over prolonged, anxious periods of their lives create greater possibilities for emotional dependency than exist between many other authorities and their subordinates. This emotional dependency may not be entirely positive; dependency relations are often marked by ambivalence. But the formation of dependency, even when it gives rise occasionally to resentment, helps strengthen the hand of professional authority apart from its claims to superior competence.[10]

Dependence, moreover, plays a major role in strengthening authority in all those encounters between professionals and clients that are not voluntary. In the modern state, professionals often stand between people and benefits they desire or penalties they fear. Social workers, teachers, and doctors certify those who come before them as eligible or ineligible to receive welfare payments, graduate from school, or gain exemption from military service. As gatekeepers into and out of various institutions, professionals acquire means of ensuring compliance quite independent of any belief in the moral basis of their authority. However, in such situations, the basis of trust may be corroded by a silent mutual suspicion: Clients may wonder whether their welfare really comes first, and professionals may feel manipulated by clients who have reason not to be entirely honest with them. The more administrative uses the state and other institutions find for professionals, the more they may simultaneously expand and undermine their authority.[11]

Clients from different social classes tend to have contacts with professionals that vary in dependency, power, and trust. The wealthier and better educated see professionals under circumstances that are more often voluntary than coerced, and they are more likely to pay for sessions in private settings than receive them in public institutions paid for by the state. They are also more than likely to share the same cultural framework as the professionals they consult. Sharing the same assumptions, they can speak openly with them and will regard the competence that professionals claim as valid. On the other hand, when poor and working-class people encounter professionals, they often experience difficulties in communication because of differences in linguistic and cultural background. Not sharing the same assumptions, they are more likely to be guarded in their communication and to feel alien and hostile. Many of their contacts with professionals are involuntary or take place in public institutions, and they do not have the control that private financial means provide. Under these conditions in schools, hospitals, offices, and agencies, individuals from the lower and working classes may comply, if at all, more for reasons of dependence than for reasons of belief. They may simply have few alternatives.

The encounters of the poor with doctors are probably less marked by ambivalence than their contacts with social workers, teachers, lawyers, and judges. But there are still many alienated—and alienating—encounters with physicians, such as psychiatrists in institutional settings. The cultural differences, difficulties in communication, and sense of powerlessness and dependency may be even greater with physicians than with other professionals because of the doctors' wealth and high social status. In some cases, this gulf may actually enhance the authority of physicians because of the association of therapeutic competence with a high and esoteric art. But these are not the grounds on which scientific medicine urges compliance.

Doctors and other professionals have a distinctive basis of legitimacy that lends strength to their authority. They claim authority, not as individuals, but as members of a community that has objectively validated their competence. The professional offers judgments and advice, not as a personal act based on privately revealed or idiosyncratic criteria, but as a representative of a community of shared standards. The basis of those standards in the modern professions is presumed to be rational inquiry and empirical evidence. Professional authority also presumes an orientation to specific, substantive values—in the case of medicine, the value of health. Insofar as a practitioner violates those values or the standards of practice upheld by the professional community, the exercise of authority is understood to be illegitimate—in the extreme case, malpractice.

The authority of the professions is distinctive in another regard. Professionals not only advise actions but also evaluate the nature of reality and experience, including the "needs" of those who consult them. Like the sovereign in Hobbes' Leviathan, their authority extends to the meaning of things. This point requires that we rethink what authority regulates.

Cultural Authority and Occupational Control

Most conceptions of authority emphasize the regulation of action. In the classic definition of Max Weber, for example, *Herrschaft* (variously translated as authority or domination) is the probability that people will obey a command recognized as legitimate according to the prevailing rules in their society.[12] But authority, as we commonly use the term in English, involves more than the giving of commands. A scientific treatise, a sacred text, and even a book of grammar embody authority. Institutions like the church make authoritative judgments about the nature of the world. In modern societies, such judgments become increasingly specialized, as different professional communities become sovereign over different aspects of reality. Authority, then, also refers to the probability that particular definitions of reality and judgments of meaning and value will prevail as valid and true. I will call this form of authority *cultural authority* to distinguish it from the social authority that Weber had in mind. This is in keeping with a familiar (though always troubling) distinction between culture, the realm of meaning and ideas, and society, the realm of relationships among social actors.[13]

Social and cultural authority differ in several basic ways. Social authority involves the control of action through the giving of commands, while cultural authority entails the construction of reality through definitions of fact and value. Whereas social authority belongs only to social actors, cultural authority may also reside in cultural objects, including products of past intellectual activity, such as religious texts (the Bible), recognized standards of reference (dictionaries, maps, mathematical tables), scholarly or scientific works, or the law. Authority, in this particular form, may be used without being exercised; typically, it is consulted (even by people in authoritative positions), often in the hope of resolving ambiguities.

Though they are often combined, social authority need not entail cultural authority. Subjects may obey a government while privately rejecting its claims as untrue or unjust. And cultural authority need not always entail authority over conduct. The priest or scientist may be authoritative about morals or nature, but may be restricted by convention from addressing, much less regulating, specific choices and actions.

The authority that physicians exercise over nurses, technicians, and other subordinates in the medical hierarchy is primarily social authority; physicians aim to regulate their actions. Insofar as doctors give patients instructions or advice, they are also exercising social authority. But prior to making any recommendations, physicians have to define and evaluate their patients' condition. Patients consult physicians not just for advice, but first of all to find out whether they are "really" sick and what their symptoms mean. "What have I got, doc?" they ask. "Is it serious?" Cultural authority, in this context, is antecedent to action. The authority to interpret signs and symptoms, to diagnose health or illness, to name diseases, and to offer prognoses is the foundation of any social authority the physician can assume. By shaping the patients' understanding of their own experience, physicians create the conditions under which their advice seems appropriate.

Of course, not all patients who accept doctors' judgments as authoritative also take their advice. A doctor may tell a patient that if he does not stop smoking and lose weight, he will not have long to live. The patient may very well take this as an authoritative judgment of the facts but decline to follow the advice. Here the physician's cultural authority exceeds his social authority; this is quite commonly the case. Physicians, insofar as they deal with voluntary patients, generally do not have the coercive powers of the state to enforce either their definitions of reality or their instructions. Judges rule; physicians usually advise. But the authority of the doctor is very much like the definition that the German historian Mommsen once gave of authority in general: "more than advice and less than a command, an advice which one may not safely ignore."[14] One may not safely ignore medical advice, not usually because of any threat of force by the physician, but because of the consequences that the doctor predicts will ensue if the advice is rejected. Insofar as one accepts the physician's cultural authority, one takes those predictions seriously.

There is, however, an entire class of functions carried out by physicians in which patients are more or less forced to accept the doctors' cultural authority. For purposes of certification, patients often have no choice but to submit to professional examination. In their capacity as cultural authorities, doctors make authoritative judgments of what constitutes illness or insanity, evaluate the fitness of persons for jobs, assess the disability of the injured, pronounce death, and even assess, after people have died, whether they were competent at the time they wrote their wills. These professional judgments carry implications for courts, employers, and other social authorities. In such situations, the physician is supposed to give the facts alone; others will decide what to do about them. This separation of cultural from social authority is quite common throughout modern society, and it is often encouraged as a means of protecting the mutual interest of potentially antagonistic parties in obtaining a fair and objective assessment of the "facts." Thus the search for legitimation by other agencies in society often promotes dependence upon the cultural authority of medicine. In this regard, medical authority is a resource for social order as well as for the profession and its clients.

The kind of authority claimed by the professions, then, involves not only skill in performing a service, but also the capacity to judge the experience and needs of clients. Professional authority can be defined, in part, by a distinctive type of dependency condition—the dependence on the professional's superior competence. Dependence also arises at times from the emotional needs of clients and the administrative functions of the professions, created especially by the welfare state. And, as I've indicated, the legitimation of professional authority involves three distinctive claims: first, that the knowledge and competence of the professional have been validated by a community of his or her peers; second, that this consensually validated knowledge and competence rest on rational, scientific grounds; and third, that the professional's judgment and advice are oriented toward a set of substantive values, such as health. These aspects of legitimacy correspond to the kinds of attributes—collegial, cognitive, and moral—usually cited in definitions of the term "profession." A profession, sociologists have suggested, is an occupation that regulates itself through systematic, required training and collegial discipline; that has a base in technical, specialized knowledge; and that has a service rather than profit orientation, enshrined in its code of ethics.[15]

Professional claims, of course, should not be taken simply at face value. The rewards of professional status encourage would-be and even established professions to invent or elaborate credentials, sciences, and codes of ethics in bids for recognition. Rather than as indicators of professional status, such features should be seen as the means of legitimating professional authority, achieving solidarity among practitioners, and gaining a grant of monopoly from the state. Occupations may or may not succeed, depending on their means of collective organization and the receptivity of the public and the government. In this sense, professionalism represents a form of occupational control rather than a quality that inheres in some kinds of work.[16] But professionalism is also a kind of solidarity, a source of meaning in work, and a system of regulating belief in modern societies.

Part of the historical task here is to explain how this complex developed in the case of medicine—how the various forms of dependence and claims to legitimacy became established, how they took institutional form, how the boundaries of medical authority expanded, and how authority translated into economic power and political influence.

The rise of medical authority is so intimately related to general changes in the bases of belief in modern cultures and the growth of the welfare state that it would be misleading to suggest that doctors somehow created it out of whole cloth. Much recent writing on the medical profession portrays it as a cartel, which for a while it became. But this was only a secondary part of its success. Moreover, the problem is to explain how the profession's power was generated in the first place; it does no good to explain the cause by one of its results.

Undoubtedly the most influential explanation for the structure of American medicine gives primary emphasis to scientific and technological change and specifically attributes the rise of medical authority to the improved therapeutic competence of physicians.[17] The role of science is necessarily an element in any account. However, the advance of science and technology did not necessarily guarantee that physicians would remain in control. Quite the opposite result might have occurred: The growth of science might have reduced professional autonomy by making doctors dependent upon organizations. Modern medical practice requires access to hospitals and medical technology, and hence medicine, unlike many other professions, requires huge capital investments. Because medical technology demands such large investments, it makes the medical profession vulnerable to control by whoever supplies the capital. Often the demands of technology are cited as the reason other self-employed artisans lost their independence. Medicine offers a case in point for those who wish to argue that technology is far from imperative in its demands for submission to organizational control.

Another view, put forward by Marxists, suggests that the structure of medicine can be more adequately explained as a mirror of the development of the capitalism. In this account, physicians succeeded in realizing their professional ambitions because capitalists found it in their interest and congruent with their ideological needs to underwrite the transformation. The difficulty here is that capitalism is compatible with many diverse systems of medical care, and it is not entirely clear whether the development of American medicine followed the "objective" interests of the capitalist class or the capitalist system. Although foundations set up originally by capitalists have made repeated efforts to rationalize medical care, it is impressive how little these efforts have succeeded. So even Marxists need to account for the success of the profession in long maintaining its sovereignty.

STEPS IN A TRANSFORMATION

The Growth of Medical Authority

The rise of the professions was the outcome of a struggle for cultural authority as well as for social mobility. It needs to be understood not only in terms of the knowledge and ambitions of the medical profession, but also in the context of broader changes in culture and society that explain why Americans became willing to acknowledge and institutionalize their dependence on the professions. The acceptance of professional authority was, in a sense, America's cultural revolution, and like other revolutions, it threw new groups to power—in this case, power over experience as much as power over work and institutions.

In a society where an established religion claims to have the final say on all aspects of human experience, the cultural authority of medicine clearly will be restricted. But this was no longer the principal barrier to medicine in the early nineteenth century. Many Americans who already had a rationalist, activist orientation to disease refused to accept physicians as authoritative. They believed that common sense and native intelligence could deal as effectively with most problems of health and illness. Moreover, the medical profession itself had little unity and was unable to assert any collective authority over its own members, who held diverse and incompatible views.

Authority, as I've indicated, involves a surrender of private judgment, and nineteenth-century Americans were not willing to make that surrender to physicians. Authority signifies the possession of a special status or claim that compels trust, and medicine lacked that compelling claim in nineteenth-century America. The esoteric learning, knowledge of Latin, and high culture and status of traditional English physicians were more compelling grounds for belief in a hierarchically ordered society than in a democratic one. The basis of modern professionalism had to be reconstructed around the claim to technical competence, gained through standardized training and evaluation. But this standardization of the profession was blocked by internal as well as external barriers—sectarianism among medical practitioners and a general resistance to privileged monopolies in the society at large.

The forces that transformed medicine into an authoritative profession involved both its internal development and broader changes in social and economic life. Internally, as a result of changes in social structure as well as scientific advance, the profession gained in cohesiveness toward the end of the nineteenth century and became more effective in asserting its claims. With the growth of hospitals and specialization, doctors became more dependent on one another for referrals and access to facilities. Consequently, they were encouraged to adjust their views to those of their peers, instead of advertising themselves as members of competing medical sects. Greater cohesiveness strengthened professional authority. Professional authority also benefited from the development of diagnostic technology, which strengthened the powers of the physician in physical examination of the patient and reduced reliance on the patient's report of symptoms and superficial appearance.

At the same time, there were profound changes in Americans' way of life and forms of consciousness that made them more dependent upon professional authority and more willing to accept it as legitimate. Different ways of life make different demands upon people and endow them with different types of competence. In preindustrial America, rural and small-town communities endowed their members with a wide range of skills and self-confidence in dealing with their own needs. The division of labor was not highly developed, and there was a strong orientation toward self-reliance, grounded in religious and political ideals. Under these conditions, professional authority could make few inroads. Americans were accustomed to dealing with most problems of illness within their own family or local community, with only occasional intervention by physicians. But toward the end of the nineteenth century, as their society became more urban, Americans became more accustomed to relying on the specialized skills of strangers. Professionals became less expensive to consult as telephones and mechanized transportation reduced the cost of time and travel. Bolstered by genuine advances in science and technology, the claims of the professions to competent authority became more plausible, even when they were not yet objectively true; for science worked even greater changes on the imagination than it worked on the processes of disease. Technological change was revolutionizing daily life; it seemed entirely plausible to believe that science would do the same for healing, and eventually it did. Besides, once people began to regard science as a superior and legitimately complex way of explaining and controlling reality, they wanted physicians' interpretations of experience regardless of whether the doctors had remedies to offer.

At a time when traditional certainties were breaking down, professional authority offered a means of sorting out different conceptions of human needs and the nature and meaning of events. In the nineteenth century, many Americans, epitomized by the Populists, continued to believe in the adequacy of common sense and to resist the claims of the professions. On the other hand, there were those, like the Progressives, who believed that science provided the means of moral as well as political reform and who saw in the professions a new and more advanced basis of order. The Progressive view, always stated as a disinterested ideal, nevertheless happily coincided with the ambitions of the emerging professional class to cure and reform. The cultural triumph of Progressivism, which proved more lasting than its political victories, was inseparable from the rise in status and power of professionals in new occupations and organizational hierarchies. Yet this was no simple usurpation; the new authority of professionals reflected the instability of a new way of life and its challenge to traditional belief. The less one could believe "one's own eyes"—and the new world of science continually prompted that feeling—the more receptive one became to seeing the world through the eyes of those who claimed specialized, technical knowledge, validated by communities of their peers.[18]

The growth of medical authority also needs to be understood as a change in institutions. In the nineteenth century, before the profession consolidated its position, some doctors had great personal authority and they pronounced on all manner of problems, by no means restricted to physical illness. Indeed, in the small communities of early American society, where the number of educated men was relatively small, some physicians may have possessed even broader personal authority than do most of their counterparts today. What I am talking about here, on the other hand, is authority that inheres in the status of physician because it has been institutionalized in a system of standardized education and licensing. The establishment of such a system reproduces authority from one generation to the next, and transmits it from the profession as a whole to all its individual members. Before the profession's authority was institutionalized in the late nineteenth and early twentieth centuries, physicians might win personal authority by dint of their character and intimate knowledge of their patients. But once it was institutionalized, standardized programs of education and licensing conferred authority upon all who passed through them. The recognition of authority in a given doctor by laymen and colleagues became relatively unambiguous. Authority no longer depended on individual character and lay attitudes; instead, it was increasingly built into the structure of institutions.

"Built-in" dependence on professional authority increased with such developments as the rise of hospitals. I do not mean only the development of mental hospitals and procedures for involuntary commitment, though the asylum is obviously an important and radical form of institutionalized medical authority. Even the voluntary shift of seriously ill patients from their homes to general hospitals increases the dependent condition of the sick. At home, patients may quite easily choose to ignore the doctor's instructions, and many do; this is much more difficult in a hospital. For the seriously ill, clinical personnel subordinate to the doctor have, in effect, replaced the family as the physician's vicarious agent. They not only administer treatment in the doctor's absence, but also maintain surveillance, keep records, and reinforce the message that the doctor's instructions must be followed.

Other institutional changes have also made people dependent on medical authority regardless of whether they are receptive or hostile to doctors. As the various certifying and gatekeeping functions of doctors have grown, so has the dependence of people seeking benefits that require certification. Laws prohibiting laymen from obtaining certain classes of drugs without a doctor's prescription increase dependence on physicians. "The more strategic the accessories controlled by the profession," Eliot Freidson writes, "the stronger the sanctions supporting its authority."[19] In the twentieth century, health insurance has become an important mechanism for ensuring dependence on the profession. When insurance payments are made only for treatment given by physicians, the beneficiaries become dependent on doctors for reimbursable services. A doctor's authorization for drugs and prosthetics has become necessary for a host of insurance and tax benefits. In all these ways, professional authority has become institutionally routine, and compliance has ceased to be a matter of voluntary choice. What people think about doctors' judgments is still important, but it is much less important than it used to be.

In their combined effect, the mechanisms of legitimation (standardized education and licensing) and the mechanisms of dependency (hospitalization, gatekeeping, insurance) have given a definite structure to the relations of doctors and patients that transcends personalities and attitudes. This social structure is based, not purely on shared expectations about the roles of physicians and the sick, but on the institutional-ized arrangements that often impose severe costs on people who wish to behave in some other way.*

The institutional reinforcement of professional authority also regu-lates the relations of physicians to each other. The doctor whose per-sonal authority in the nineteenth century rested on his imposing char-acter and relations with patients was in a fundamentally different situation from the doctor in the twentieth century whose authority de-pends on holding the necessary credentials and institutional affiliations. While laymen have become more dependent on professionals, profes-sionals have become more dependent on each other. Both changes have contributed to the collective power of the profession and helped physi-cians to convert their clinical authority into social and economic privi-lege.

From Authority to Economic Power

The conversion of authority into high income, autonomy, and other rewards of privilege required the medical profession to gain control over both the market for its services and the various organizational hier-archies that govern medical practice, financing, and policy. The achievement of economic power involved more than the creation of a monopoly in medical practice through the exclusion of alternative practitioners and limits on the supply of physicians. It entailed shaping the structure of hospitals, insurance, and other private institutions that

---

*Role expectations are the heart of what was once the most influential schema in the sociology of medicine—that of Talcott Parsons. According to Parsons, the social structure of medical practice can be defined by the shared expectations about the "sick role" and the role of the doctor. On the one hand, the sick are exempt from normal obligations; they are not held responsible for their illness; they must try to get well; and they must seek competent help. On the other, the physician is expected to be "universalistic," "functionally specific," "affectively neutral," and "collectivity-oriented." These comple-mentary normative rules have a functional relation to the therapeutic process and the larger society.[20]

While useful as a point of departure for understanding doctor-patient relations, Par-sons' model is open to severe objections as a model of medical practice. It fails to convey the ambivalence of doctor-patient relationships and the contradictory expectations with which each party must contend.[21] It also accepts the ideological claims of the profession—for example, to be altruistic ("collectivity-oriented")—and ignores evidence of contrary rules of behavior, such as tacit agreements to ignore colleagues' mistakes.[22] Parsons' ap-proach concentrates almost entirely upon the system of norms in purely voluntary doctor-patient relations. That such relations are not wholly voluntary both because of depen-dency conditions and the historical process that lies behind professional dominance is a point Parsons simply overlooks. The distribution of power, control of markets, and so on do not enter significantly into his analysis. Parsons also neglects other relations important to medical practice, such as those among doctors and between doctors and organizations. The more important these collegial and bureaucratic relations become, the less useful Parsons' approach appears.

impinge on medical practice and defining the limits and proper forms of public health activities and other public investment in health care. In the last half century, these organizational and political arrangements have become more important as bases of economic power than the monopolization of medical practice.

The emergence of a market for medical services was originally inseparable from the emergence of professional authority. In the isolated communities of early American society, the sick were usually cared for as part of the obligations of kinship and mutual assistance. But as larger towns and cities grew, treatment increasingly shifted from the family and lay community to paid practitioners, druggists, hospitals, and other commercial and professional sources selling their services competitively on the market. Of course, the family continues even today to play an important role in health care, but its role has become distinctly secondary. The transition from the household to the market as the dominant institution in the care of the sick—that is, the conversion of health care into a commodity—has been one of the underlying movements in the transformation of medicine. It has simultaneously involved increased specialization of labor, greater emotional distance between the sick and those responsible for their care, and a shift from women to men as the dominant figures in the management of health and illness.

What sort of a commodity is medical care? Do doctors sell goods (such as drugs), advice, time, or availability? These questions had to be worked out as the market took form. To gain the trust that the practice of medicine requires, physicians had to assure the public of the reliability of their "product." A standardized product, as Magali Sarfatti Larson points out about the professions, requires a standardized producer.[23] Standardization of training and licensing became the means for realizing both the search for authority and control of the market.

Through most of the nineteenth century, the market in medical care continued to be competitive. Entry into practice was relatively easy for untrained practitioners as well as for medical school graduates; as a result, competition was intense and the economic position of physicians was often insecure. Toward the end of the century, although licensing laws began to restrict entry, many doctors felt increasingly threatened by the expansion of free dispensaries, company medical plans, and various other bureaucratically organized alternatives to independent solo practice. In the physicians' view, the competitive market represented a threat not only to their incomes, but also to their status and autonomy because it drew no sharp boundary between the educated and uneducated, blurred the lines between commerce and professionalism, and threatened to turn them into mere employees.

The contradiction between professionalism and the rule of the market is long-standing and unavoidable. Medicine and other professions have historically distinguished themselves from business and trade by claiming to be above the market and pure commercialism. In justifying the public's trust, professionals have set higher standards of conduct for themselves than the minimal rules governing the marketplace and maintained that they can be judged under those standards only by each other, not by laymen. The ideal of the market presumes the "sovereignty" of consumer choices; the ideal of a profession calls for the sovereignty of its members' independent, authoritative judgment. A professional who yields too much to the demands of clients violates an essential article of the professional code: Quacks, as Everett Hughes once defined them, are practitioners who continue to please their customers but not their colleagues. This shift from clients to colleagues in the orientation of work, which professionalism demands, represents a clear departure from the normal rule of the market.

When fully competitive, markets do not obey the organized judgment of any group of sellers. A market is a system of exchange in which goods and services are bought and sold at going prices. In the ideal case cherished by economists, each buyer and seller acts independently of every other, so that prices are set impersonally by levels of supply and demand. There are no relations of dependency in the ideal market: Any individual buyer is supposed to have a free choice of sellers, any seller a free choice of buyers, and no group of buyers or sellers is supposed to be able to force acceptance of its terms. Nor are there supposed to be any relations of authority in the market, except those necessary to provide rules of exchange and the enforcement of contracts. Whereas the household and the state both allocate resources according to decisions made by governing authorities, the distinctive feature of a market is the absence of any such authoritative direction. The absence of power is, paradoxically, the basis of order in a competitive market. Collectively, sellers might wish to keep the prices of commodities higher than their marginal cost, but so long as they act individually, they are driven to bring them down into equilibrium to secure as large as possible a share of the market for themselves.

This is not a prospect that sellers usually enjoy and, whenever the means are available, it is one they quickly subvert. Power abhors competition about as intensely as nature abhors a vacuum. Professional organization is one form resistance to the market may take. Similarly, concentrations of ownership and labor unions are other bases of market power. These cases are parallel. Just as property, manual labor, and professional competence are all means of generating income and other rewards, so they can be used by a monopolistic firm, a strong guild or union, or a powerful, licensed profession to establish market power. This was what the medical profession set about accomplishing at the end of the nineteenth century when corporations were forming trusts and workers were attempting to organize unions—each attempting, with varying success, to control market forces rather than be controlled by them.

Doctors' increasing authority had the twin effects of stimulating and restricting the market. On the one hand, their growing cultural authority helped draw the care of the sick out of the family and lay community into the sphere of professional service. On the other, it also brought political support for the imposition of limits, like restrictive licensing laws, on the uncontrolled supply of medical services. By augmenting demand and controlling supply, greater professional authority helped physicians secure higher returns for their work.

The market power of the profession originated only in part from the state's protection. It also arose from the increasing dependence of patients on physicians. In the ideal market no buyer depends upon any seller, but patients are often dependent on their personal physicians, and they have become more so as the disparity in knowledge between them has grown. The sick cannot easily disengage themselves from relations with their doctors, nor even know when it is in their interests to do so. Consequently, once they have begun treatment, they cannot exercise that unfettered choice of sellers which characterizes free markets.

One reason that the profession could develop market power of this kind was that it sold its services primarily to individual patients rather than organizations. Such organizations, had they been more numerous, could have exercised greater discrimination in evaluating clinical performance and might have lobbied against cartel restrictions of the physician supply. The medical profession, of course, insisted that salaried arrangements violated the integrity of the private doctor-patient relationship, and in the early decades of the twentieth century, doctors were able to use their growing market power to escape the threat of bureaucratic control and to preserve their own autonomy.

Strategic Position and the Defense of Autonomy

When we speak of the "health care system" today, we usually have in mind a great array of organizations: hospitals and medical centers, public health and planning agencies, professional associations, health insurance and pharmaceutical companies, and so on. Although some of these organizations have distant historical antecedents, they did not really constitute an interdependent system, even in a loose sense, before the late nineteenth century. While there were precursors of organized medical services and health insurance, they were of minor importance. A few hundred hospitals had been built as of 1870, but until the 1880s and 1890s they had closer connections to charity than to medicine and played a small part in medical practice. Similarly, public health had originated in concerns that were not medical so much as sanitary and statistical. Only at the end of the nineteenth century, as hospitals and public health activities expanded and became more directly related to medical care, did an interconnected system begin to take form.

The rise of bureaucratic organizations represented two types of threats to the medical profession. First, organizations employing physicians and providing medical services might enter into competition with independent practitioners. And, second, organizations that provided facilities or financing for medical care, such as hospitals and insurance companies, might subject physicians to unfavorable terms of exchange and reduce their autonomy in fee setting and decision making. Doctors sought to eliminate entirely the first kind of organization—the free dispensary, the company or fraternal medical program, later the prepaid group practice plan—on the grounds that such arrangements were an unconscionable violation of their professional ethics. The second kind of organization—the hospitals and insurance companies—physicians attempted to shape to their own interests, particularly their interests in controlling their own work and setting their own prices.

In both these efforts, physicians were, at least until recently, eminently successful. They have been one of the few occupational groups in the twentieth century able to resist the current that has drawn self-employed artisans and craftsmen of all kinds into the orbit of industrial and bureaucratic organization. In fact, in the late nineteenth and early twentieth centuries, doctors were able to reverse the history that other occupations experienced. While many skilled crafts were losing monopoly power, the physicians were establishing theirs. In the same period as the crafts were being subordinated to large corporations, the medical profession was institutionalizing its autonomy. The doctors escaped becoming victims of capitalism and became small capitalists instead.

The profession's success in maintaining autonomy has had both material and psychological dimensions. Had doctors been subject to the hierarchical control and monopsonistic power of insurance companies, hospitals, and large medical practice organizations, their income would probably have suffered. They would have lost freedom in choosing their hours, their clients, their fields of specialization—all the advantages that come with "being one's own boss." For many physicians, these concerns about autonomy have outweighed strictly financial considerations. Even though universal health insurance, for example, would have boosted many physicians' incomes by covering unpaid bills, private doctors have generally resisted the idea for fear that their independence might eventually be compromised.

Yet the same forces that have led industrial firms to draw in the self-employed might well have led medical care organizations to draw in physicians. By employing workers directly, an organization generally gains greater control over their behavior as well as the whole system of production. It can monitor worker performance more closely and exact greater compliance with its own goals. It can reorganize the process of production, de-emphasizing highly paid skilled crafts in favor of less skilled and lower-paid labor.[24]

The organizations that developed as part of the health system had to resolve whether to integrate physicians into their hierarchies. Hospitals, for example, could have hired physicians on salary to perform necessary medical work. Insurance companies might have hired doctors to perform the services for which beneficiaries were covered. Some health plans of this type did develop. But it was not the approach typically followed.

Hospitals and insurers generally allowed physicians to remain independent entrepreneurs, though there can be little doubt that leaving doctors outside of the organizational structure of these institutions increased the costs of medical care. The difficulties in monitoring physicians are enormous; insurance companies, in particular, face severe information problems. As independent entrepreneurs, doctors are unlikely to be sensitive to any organizational interest in conserving resources. Hence, for the same reasons that firms incorporated independent artisans, the insurance companies and hospitals had clear incentives to seek control over physicians. But doctors were able to block this type of control, and the hospitals and insurers instead developed financial arrangements that allowed them to pass through the higher costs that professional autonomy produces.

The collective political organization of the profession was vital in defeating private health plans that incorporated physicians as employees. But perhaps most important in the defense of autonomy was the role of authority in creating economic power. The gatekeeping authority of doctors gives them a strategic position in relation to organizations. In effect, the profession's authority puts at its disposal the purchasing power of its patients. From the standpoint of the solvency of a health insurance company, the authority to prescribe is the power to destroy.

So, too, the physicians' authority to decide whether and where to hospitalize patients gives doctors great leverage over hospital policy. And, similarly, the authority to prescribe drugs and other supplies obliges pharmaceutical companies and other producers to court the profession's good will, to finance its journals, and thereby to subsidize its professional associations and political activities.

By the mid-twentieth century, the strategic position of the medical profession in relation to hospitals, health insurance, and the pharmaceutical industry became pivotal in sustaining the profession's economic position, superseding the earlier role played by their monopolization of practice. If licensing laws were completely eliminated today, the effect on physicians' incomes would probably be small. Their cultural authority would enable them to keep their patients, and the structure of the insurance system would enable them to maintain their fees.

Throughout the medical system, the profession was able by 1920—and for the next half century—to establish organizational structures that preserved a distinct sphere of professional dominance and autonomy. To critics, the lack of unified organization in hospitals, medical practice, and insurance, along with the separation of public health from medical care, has seemed irrational. But even disorganization is sometimes systematic. Hospitals, public health, and medical practice were only partially integrated; no powerful coordinating authority was permitted to emerge because it would have threatened professional autonomy and control of the market. This loose structure has set the stage for the struggle in recent decades in which the profession has been trying to defend its prerogatives against the drive to rationalize the organization of medical care. The organizations that the profession once defeated or restricted have re-emerged as threats to its sovereignty. Again, the threats are of two related kinds—competition and control. Prepaid health plans, now called "health maintenance organizations," represent a competitive form of bureaucratic organization in medical care. Insurance companies, under pressure to control medical costs, search for methods to regulate medical decisions. Hospitals and other organizations merge into larger and more powerful corporate systems. And beyond private bureaucratic organizations looms the regulatory power of the state and federal governments.

Professionalism serves, among other functions, as a basis of solidarity for resisting forces that threaten the social and economic position of an occupational group. In the nineteenth century, professionalism served physicians as a basis for resisting competition from other practitioners. Late in the nineteenth century, it began to serve doctors and others as a means of resisting corporate competition and control. And in the twentieth century, in addition to these two earlier functions, it has become the ground for resistance to government.

The medical profession has not, of course, opposed all government intervention. It actively sought licensing protection. Most doctors have advocated at least some public health programs. Nor have they strenuously objected to public investment in hospitals and medical research. Few have questioned the use of state power to support the role of medicine in the control of deviant behavior, as in involuntary confinement of the insane. In the nineteenth century, physicians were prominent advocates of legislation penalizing various kinds of sexual behavior. The medical reform of moral behavior went hand in hand with the extension of state power into private life.[25] So professional opposition to government intervention does not exactly follow the lines of a philosophically pure libertarianism.

The profession's chief concerns about government parallel its concerns about corporate and bureaucratic organizations. It has been worried about both competition and control. Private physicians have sought to keep government from competing with them, regulating their practice, or, worst of all, incorporating medical care into the state as a public service like education. Their struggle to limit the boundaries of public health, to confine public medical services to the poor, and to prevent the passage of compulsory health insurance all exemplify these concerns.

Thus, from the standpoint of the profession, the challenge was initially to establish its authority and control of the market, then to keep it as large organizations and government threatened to intervene. In the next three chapters, I trace the rise of professional authority and the decline of a competitive market from the early nineteenth to the early twentieth centuries. In the last three chapters of Book One, I turn to the institutions—hospitals, public health, and private corporations—whose development, especially toward the end of this period, potentially threatened professional autonomy. Book Two takes up the defense of autonomy in relation to health insurance and the struggles over the politics and business of health care in the twentieth century.

The modern economy is dominated everywhere by large corporations or by the state. Most professionals today, like other people, derive their income and much of their self-regard from organizations where they went to school and where they work. Doctors also depend on large organizations, such as hospitals, but they have held out against the usual organizational demands for control. Among the professions, medicine is both the paradigmatic and the exceptional case: paradigmatic in the sense that other professions emulate its example; exceptional in that none have been able to achieve its singular degree of economic power and cultural authority. But if medicine is an exceptional case, it is also an instructive one for understanding why American society—once distrustful of guilds and claims of expertise—has become so hospitable to professionalism in the organization of work and belief.

CHAPTER ONE

Medicine in a
Democratic Culture
1760–1850

BEFORE the twentieth century, American physicians found the path to professional status blocked by popular resistance, internal division, and an inhospitable economic environment. Their quest for special recognition as a profession began in the late colonial period. Beginning in the 1760s, some educated doctors took the initial steps to reproduce in America the professional institutions that in England gave physicians a distinct and exclusive status. They succeeded in organizing medical schools, and in some fields of work, such as obstetrics, doctors gained ground against rival practitioners. But they failed in their larger effort to establish themselves as an exclusive and privileged profession. The licensing authority doctors secured had little more than honorific value, and during the Jacksonian period in the 1830s and 1840s, their claims to privileged competence evoked a sharp backlash that crippled their ambitions for the next half century. State legislatures voted to do away with medical licensure entirely. No profession was being allowed, Oliver Wendell Holmes told the graduating class at Harvard in 1844, "to be the best judge of its own men and doctrines."[1] Lay practitioners, using native herbs and folk remedies, flourished in the countryside and towns, scorning the therapies and arcane learning of regular physicians and claiming the right to practice medicine as an inalienable liberty, comparable to religious freedom.

This tension between the aspirations of physicians to privileged status and popular resistance to their claims reflected a more general conflict in American life between a democratic culture and a stratified society. Between the colonial period and the early nineteenth century, America became, it now seems correct to say, more egalitarian and less equal. Democratic ideas, manners, and institutions became more widely and firmly established, while in the towns and cities, the distribution of wealth and power grew more highly concentrated.[2] The second tendency does not disprove the first. Democracy, de Tocqueville observed, did not eliminate differences between rich and poor or master and servant; it changed their mutual relations. Traditional distinctions of rank broke down; men no longer considered their status in society preordained and permanent. Deference to age declined. In new settlements and on the frontier, the conditions of material life made special demands for self-direction; forced to improvise, Americans developed a stubborn confidence in their own common sense. As a corollary of their political and religious convictions, they believed that in their private affairs, as in those of the community, men had free and equal rights to judgment. It was in this sense that American culture was democratic. At the same time, a nascent capitalist economy was creating new concentrations of wealth and power. In the Jacksonian era, partly in response to fears that privilege would be monopolized, the rhetoric of political and cultural life became more emphatically egalitarian. And not only the rhetoric: The franchise, public education, and the popular press expanded, and the contrast between a democratic culture and class inequality grew sharper.[3]

Medicine shared these contrary tendencies. While some physicians were seeking to make themselves into an elite profession with a monopoly of practice, much of the public refused to grant them any such privileges and asserted their own rights to judgment in managing sickness. Furthermore, the profession also faced challenges within its own ranks. Some leading physicians called into question whether medicine had any effective therapies to offer; many thought that the best doctors could do was to assist the healing powers of nature. The failure of self-confidence and growth of therapeutic dissension within the profession further contributed to its weakness; by 1850 the disaffection from the profession, which was initially concentrated among the less educated, had spread to the higher levels of society as well.

Medical care is never solely a matter of professional practice. Even today, much treatment of the sick takes place outside of the doctor's sphere in the home or under alternative practitioners. Before the late nineteenth century, the conditions of agrarian life did not permit dependence on medical authority, and popular skepticism about professional claims did not encourage it. There were three spheres of practice relatively equal in importance—the medicine of the domestic household, the medicine of the physicians, and the medicine of lay healers. And each sphere exhibited, in a distinctive way, the continuing conflict in American life between the democratic respect for common sense and professional claims of special knowledge.

DOMESTIC MEDICINE

The family, as the center of social and economic life in early American society, was the natural locus of most care of the sick. Women were expected to deal with illness in the home and to keep a stock of remedies on hand; in the fall, they put away medicinal herbs as they stored preserves. Care of the sick was part of the domestic economy for which the wife assumed responsibility. She would call on networks of kin and community for advice and assistance when illness struck, in worrisome cases perhaps bringing in an older woman who had a reputation for skill with the sick.

Although colonial newspapers and almanacs offered medical advice, their circulation was limited, and domestic practice was informed mostly by oral tradition. But the distance of domestic from professional medicine began to narrow in the late eighteenth and nineteenth centuries, as physicians published guides to domestic practice. The most widely read of these domestic medical manuals had a remarkably self-conscious political as well as practical character. The two aspects were inseparable. Written in lucid, everyday language, avoiding Latin or technical terms, the books set forth current knowledge on disease and attacked, at times explicitly, the conception of medicine as a high mystery.

The best known of these works was William Buchan's *Domestic Medicine*, described in its subtitle as "an attempt to render the Medical Art more generally useful, by showing people what is in their own power both with respect to the Prevention and Cure of Diseases." Published originally in 1769 in Edinburgh and two years later in Philadelphia,

Buchan's *Domestic Medicine* remained popular throughout the mid-1800s, going through at least thirty editions (reprintings) in America, where it was probably the most influential book of its kind. It had numerous American imitators, who borrowed Buchan's format and occasionally his prose. The book had two sections: a general exposition of the causes and prevention of disease, and a detailed description of the symptoms and treatment of specific disorders. Buchan himself was a member of the Royal College of Physicians of Edinburgh, though he was highly critical of the medical profession of his day. "No discovery can ever be of general utility while the practice of it is kept in the hands of a few," he wrote in his discussion of smallpox inoculation, which he argued never became widespread in England until "men not bred to physic" took it up. "The fears, the jealousies, the prejudices, and the opposite interests of the faculty [that is, the elite physicians], are, and ever will be, the most effectual obstacles to the progress of any salutary discovery."[4]

Though Buchan did not dismiss the value of physicians when they were available, he upheld the view that professional knowledge and training were unneeded in treating most diseases. It would not be difficult to prove, he asserted, "that every thing valuable in the practical part of medicine is within reach of common sense, and that the Art would lose nothing by being stripped of all that any person embued with ordinary abilities cannot comprehend." Most people, he assured his readers, "trust too little to their own endeavors." Physicians should be consulted when needed, but they should be needed very rarely.[5]

This belief that ordinary people were fully competent to treat illness had been expounded before by John Wesley, the founder of English Methodism, in a book of medical advice called *Primitive Physic*, originally published in 1747 and widely reprinted in the eighteenth century. Bernard Semmel has argued that the rise of Methodism was part of a shift in English society toward an emphasis on greater personal autonomy and self-direction.[6] As that interpretation suggests, Wesley compiled his book of remedies expressly to encourage greater autonomy in caring for illness. Unlike Buchan, however, he did not provide a reasoned explanation of the symptoms and causes of disease, only an inventory of what he thought to be ancient cures; and he denounced doctors much more vehemently than did Buchan. In former times, thought Wesley, people had treated themselves, but the physicians then concocted complicated theories to confuse ordinary people. "Physicians," he wrote, "now began to be had in admiration, as persons who were something more than human. And profit attended their employ as well as honour: so that they had now two weighty reasons for keeping the

bulk of mankind at a distance, that they might not pry into the myster-
ies of the profession. To this end . . . [t]hey filled their writings
with abundance of technical terms, utterly unintelligible to plain
men . . . ."[7]

The guides to domestic medicine usually emphasized an intention to
simplify the language of medicine. They argued that medicine was
filled with unnecessary obscurity and complexity, and should be made
intelligible and practicable. John C. Gunn's *Domestic Medicine*, which
appeared in 1830 and by mid-century replaced Buchan's work as the
popular favorite, was described on the title page as written "In Plain
Language, Free from Doctor's Terms . . . Intended Expressly for the
Benefit of Families . . . Arranged on a New Simple Plan, By Which the
Practice of Medicine is Reduced to Principles of Common Sense."
Gunn maintained that Latin names for common medicines and diseases
were "originally made use of to *astonish the people*" and aid the
learned in deception and fraud. "The more nearly we can place men
on a level in point of *knowledge*, the happier we would become
in society with each other, and the less danger there would be of
tyranny . . . ."[8]

In their advice, the books also generally emphasized the virtues of
simplicity. Elaborate and unnecessarily complex prescriptions, Wesley
argued, were one of the principal forms of mystification in medicine.
Buchan, too, recommended only simple medicines, usually made with
readily available ingredients. But more important, unlike many of the
other popular medical advisors, he offered a general skepticism about
the value of drugs altogether. "No doubt," Buchan wrote, "[this book]
would have been more acceptable to many, had it abounded with
pompous prescriptions, and promised great cures in consequence of
their use; but this was not my plan: I think the administration of medicines always doubtful, and often dangerous, and would much rather
teach men how to avoid the necessity of using them, than how they
should be used."[9]

This skepticism about the effectiveness and safety of medicine, which
pervades Buchan's work, led him to emphasize diet and simple preventive measures. He counseled repeatedly that exercise, fresh air, a simple
regimen, and cleanliness were of more value in maintaining health than
anything medicine could do. "Proper attention to AIR and CLEANLI-
NESS would do more to preserve the health of mankind than all the
endeavors of the faculty." However, bloodletting occupied a central
place in his therapeutics, and many of the later books, like Gunn's, despite an antiprofessional tone, recommended still more of the "heroic"
measures that entailed copious bleeding, purging, and blistering. In

these respects, they reflected the professional practice of their day.[10]

The importance of guides to domestic medicine, however, consists not in any originality of ideas, but in their popularity and what that discloses about the culture that embraced them. Buchan and those who imitated him treated disease in a fundamentally naturalistic and secular fashion. There was no suggestion of magic or witchcraft; incantations and charms did not figure among their remedies. They were materialistic in their conception of the universe. Buchan's description of epilepsy had no moral or superstitious overtones. "This disease," he noted, "from the difficulty of investigating its causes, and its strange symptoms, was formerly attributed to the wrath of the gods, or the agency of evil spirits. In modern times it has often, by the vulgar, been imputed to witchcraft or fascination. It depends however as much upon natural causes as any other malady . . . ."[11] A naturalistic view of disease perfectly complemented Buchan's desire to democratize medical knowledge: In neither diseases nor therapies did he see anything that common sense could not firmly grasp. In neither the causes nor treatment of sickness was there anything supernatural or occult.

Although this naturalistic outlook was widespread, it was often joined to a moral interpretation of the causes and incidence of disease. Protestant culture had firmly rejected the use of magic in healing the sick. However, clerics frequently warned and many of the laity believed that immorality and sin were a "predisposing" cause of illness and that prayer was an appropriate, although not sufficient response. These attitudes had their origins in the Reformation. As the English historian Keith Thomas has shown, Protestantism repudiated the magical practices permitted by the medieval Church, such as the invocation of saints and images, visits to sacred shrines, and the use of holy water and holy relics. At a time when science had not yet provided adequate explanations of disease, much less means of preventing it, Protestantism nonetheless promoted "the disenchantment of the world" by recognizing only one supernatural force, divine providence. And so, contrary to common opinion, it was the development of religious thought, rather than medical progress, that first brought about the decline of magic in healing and other spheres of life.[12]

Yet while Protestantism banished magical practices from religion and the supernatural from healing, it initially encouraged a moral view of misfortune. In sixteenth- and seventeenth-century England, according to Thomas, the proper reaction to an accident or illness was to search one's soul for moral error. "The incidence of sickness was particularly liable to be viewed theologically. The Elizabethan Prayer Book required the clergy when visiting a sick parishioner to begin by reminding him that whatever form the sickness might take he must realize that it was God's visitation. Of course a doctor should try to cure the patient by natural means. But such remedies were to be employed cautiously, with the recognition that they could only work if God permitted. It was lawful to take physic, but unlawful to trust in it too much. . . . Health came from God, not from Doctors."[13]

Even though, by the late eighteenth and early nineteenth centuries, naturalistic conceptions of disease had become more prevalent, they still coexisted uneasily with moral views of misfortune. Most Americans thought the world was governed by natural forces, but they also often took illness to be a sign of God's displeasure and a warning to the dissolute. Charles Rosenberg has traced the complex interplay of these ideas in American responses to three nineteenth-century cholera epidemics. In 1832 clergymen, like most of the laity, believed that although cholera obeyed natural laws, it was sent by God to punish sin. One editor warned Sunday school students, "The cholera is not caused by intemperance and filth, in themselves, but it is a scourge, a rod in the hand of God. . . ." But when those who saw God's hand in the epidemic called for officially sponsored prayer, President Andrew Jackson rejected the proposal as unconstitutional. During a second epidemic in 1849, clerical attacks on science were more common, but religious authority no longer figured prominently in the response to a third cholera epidemic in 1866. By then, public health methods and organizations were assuming more effective authority.[14]

It is difficult to know what meaning individuals privately attributed to disease in the early nineteenth century. But if the domestic medical advisors are any indication, the naturalistic conception was already widely current. This is not to say scientific in the sense we might understand science today. The means of distinguishing different diseases were not yet available; physicians no less than the public were prey to what may seem outlandish theories. The "natural" properties that were attributed to plants and other objects were often derived from ancient symbolic doctrines that had little to do with their physical properties. But an orientation was being established that regarded illness as a natural phenomenon not subject to magical or moral forces. The domestic medical guides, together with popular lectures on health and physiology, were one of many ways that rationalist ideas about disease and medicine were transmitted to the public and converted into attitudes and practices.

So while the domestic medical guides were challenging professional authority and asserting that families could care for themselves, they were also helping to lay the cultural foundations of modern medical practice—a predominantly secular view of sickness. They were altering domestic care even as they flattered it. In seeking to spread medical knowledge, Buchan and his imitators were also extending the perimeters of medical authority. The American guides often announced they were for farmers and their families, planters and their slaves, or men at sea who could not secure a physician's advice. Previously confined to those who could consult a physician, the authority of medicine now reached the far larger number who could consult a physician's book. Increasing the autonomous competence of the public helped prepare the ground for its later acceptance of professional authority.

PROFESSIONAL MEDICINE

From England to America

Like domestic medicine, professional medicine felt the effects of America's democratic culture. A profession, by its nature, is an inegalitarian institution; it claims to enjoy a dignity not shared by ordinary occupations and a right to set its own rules and standards. These claims go against the democratic grain. They are also exceptionally hard to establish and enforce in a fluid, rapidly expanding society with little centralized government and no effective gatekeepers of status, such as an aristocratic elite. Nineteenth-century America did not readily provide the political and institutional means to guard entry to professional status. Minimally, the members of an aspiring profession need to fix boundaries to separate them from other practitioners. In the first half of the nineteenth century, American physicians could not gain the power or legitimacy to accomplish even this minimal task. The boundaries they tried to erect by means of education, licensing laws, and professional societies were rapidly eroded by competition, dissension, and contempt.

In eighteenth-century England, which doctors in colonial America took as a model, the social structure of medicine reflected the hierarchical character of the society. Physicians, members of a learned profession, formed a small elite, distinct from the lower orders of surgeons, who practiced a craft, and apothecaries, who followed a trade. Each of these "medical estates" had its own guild organization and its defined functions and privileges, though the boundaries were not always religiously observed. As gentlemen, physicians declined to work with their hands and only observed, speculated, and prescribed. Surgeons, who until 1745 were members of the same guild as barbers, engaged in manual tasks, though in many cases they, too, prescribed. After 1703 apothecaries, the most numerous of the three, had the right to attend patients and prescribe as well as compound medicine, but they could charge only for drugs, not for advice. Beneath these three orders were diverse empirics and lay healers.

The English physicians represented what has been called a "status profession" rather than an "occupational profession," which is to say, the profession was defined by its privileged rank rather than its role in the division of labor. It consisted only of the small number of men concentrated in London who held membership in the Royal College of Physicians. Between 1771 and 1833 the college admitted only 168 fellows; it included about the same number of licentiates, its lower rank. No doctor could gain admission to the college as a fellow unless he had graduated from Oxford or Cambridge, even though neither university provided a medical education. At Oxbridge physicians studied the classics; at the London hospitals they acquired more practical experience. This system, poorly adapted for advancing science, was well adapted for advancing careers, for professional success depended on acquiring the proper social graces and connections.[15]

Though more prestigious than surgeons and apothecaries, English physicians were less powerful than the aristocratic patients whose patronage they courted. The physicians emulated the style and bearing of the upper class, sought entry to "society," and made every effort to attract attention to themselves by cultivating distinctive manners and fashionable dress. The English sociologist N. D. Jewson points out that just as fashion allowed them to advertise themselves while demonstrating membership in "society," so they continually devised new theoretical systems of medicine that varied in particulars while sharing the same conceptual foundations. These theories, derived from the classical Hippocratic texts, had been modified by Newtonian influences and the special demands of their social situation. In the classical view, illness had no local origin in the body; it was a general disturbance caused by an imbalance of the four humors (blood, phlegm, yellow and black bile). After the Newtonian revolution in physics, new medical theories attributed disease to disturbances of solid entities in the body, such as the blood vessels, but the basic model remained the same. Disease was the result of a single, underlying condition that affected the entire constitution; however, in any given patient, the factors that brought on this condition were individual. The entire focus of treatment was on the patient's symptoms, which were regarded, not as signs of the disease, but as the disease itself. This orientation to symptoms, suggests Jewson, reflected a consultative relationship in which the patient was the more powerful figure.[16]

The American medical profession, though influenced by the same monistic theories of disease, did not develop along the same lines as the English. The elite English physicians had no reason to migrate to America. In the seventeenth and eighteenth centuries, the trained practitioners in the colonies were the equivalent of surgeons and apothecaries. However, since American doctors did not serve a society as highly and rigidly stratified, the guild titles, like the guilds themselves, had no force in the colonies. Americans came to regard all those who practiced medicine as doctors, abandoning the linguistic forms that reflected traditional class distinctions in medical practice.[17] As in the books of domestic medicine, ordinary language was the most immediate expression of democratic conditions.

All manner of people took up medicine in the colonies and appropriated the title of doctor. The physician's role did not exist in a completely separate and independent form. In the seventeenth and eighteenth centuries, it was common for the clergy to combine medical and religious services to their congregations (an "angelical conjunction" Cotton Mather called it). Men and women of lower rank also served as doctors. The boundaries between profession and trade, so assiduously preserved in Britain, became blurred in America. In eighteenth-century Virginia, one historian records a Dr. John Payras, "who besides drugs, sold tea, sugar, olives, grapes, anchovies, raisins and prunes"; another, Jean Pasteur, described as a surgeon in a newspaper obituary but only as a wigmaker in his will; and a Mrs. Hughes, who advertised in 1773 that besides practicing midwifery, she cured "ringworms, scald heads, piles, worms" and also made ladies' dresses and bonnets in the newest fashion. A traveler passing through Fredericksburg in 1732 wrote, "I must not forget Mrs. Levistone, who Acts here in the Double Capacity of a Doctoress and Coffee Woman."[18]

In such circumstances, medicine could have little collective consciousness or organization. But gradually those who practiced medicine began to practice it as a primary role (if not always full-time), and by the mid-eighteenth century, they had emerged as a corporate group. Increasingly, Americans who had served an apprenticeship with a colonial practitioner sought a medical education in Europe in such cities as Leyden, London, and Edinburgh, The ones who returned home brought back with them the ambition to create in America a profession with the standards and dignity that physicians in Europe possessed. A similar process occurred in law. America's "first wave of professionaliza-

tion" began around 1750 as the usages and forms of the British professions were adopted by Americans of lower rank. The movement toward
professionalism in medicine found expression in the creation of the first
medical schools and medical societies and agitation for protective medical legislation. These developments all began to occur at the same time.
The first medical school was chartered in Philadelphia in 1765; the first
provincial medical society was organized in New Jersey in 1766; and
the first licensure law calling for prospective examination of doctors was
passed in New York City in 1760. At the time of the Revolution, there
appear to have been about 3,500 or 4,000 physicians; 400 of them had
formal medical training, perhaps half as many held medical degrees.[19]
This professional elite was concentrated almost entirely in the larger
cities.

One aspect of these first steps toward the formation of a profession
was the growing separation of medicine from religion. The early medical society in New Jersey provides some evidence on this point. Its first
president in 1766 was a clergyman; similarly, the first president of the
College of New Jersey was both a physician and minister. In the society's first ten years, six of its thirty-six members were "pastor-
physicians." Objections to this dual role came from some parishioners
who believed the two functions of doctor and pastor were incompatible.
By 1796 the medical society had ninety-one members, but only seven
were clergymen, and out of the last fifty-five to join, only one had been
a minister.[20] Pastoral practice continued into the nineteenth century,
but clerical practitioners (that is, clergymen primarily involved in medicine) became increasingly rare.

Professional Education on an Open Market

By establishing medical schools on American soil, physicians hoped
to create a profession in the European image. Apprenticeship served
as the principal form of medical training in the colonial period, however, and it remained central even after the advent of medical schools,
which were at first only supplemental. Successful practitioners took in
young men to serve as their assistants, read their medical books, and
take care of household chores. They were fed, clothed, and at the end
of their term, typically three years, given a certificate of proficiency and
good character. An apprentice's education might be as good as his preceptor's library and personal commitment; there were expectations as
to what had to be learned but no firm standards. From the perspective
of physicians, apprenticeship had definite cultural limitations. It could
not provide a basis for professional status, which in European society

belonged only to men with an education in the liberal arts, nor could it instill the proper demeanor and bearing that physicians required if they were to receive the respect due professional men. From apprenticeship, a young man might get a certificate of proficiency, but from a school of medicine he could get a warrant of authority. If physic was to be a learned profession, it had to have a seat of professional learning.

The University of Pennsylvania, then called the College of Philadelphia, opened the first medical school in the colonies in 1765 on the initiative of a young physician, John Morgan, who had recently returned from Europe. In an introductory lecture, Morgan called for the separation of physic from surgery and pharmacy and the establishment of the proper professional hierarchy in medicine. The proposal aroused opposition, and so in a preface to the published version of the speech, Morgan defended the hierarchy that existed in every "wise and polished" country. "The general of an army," he noted, "should be acquainted with every part of military science, and understand the whole detail of military duty, from that of colonel down to a private sentinel. But there is no need that he should act as a pioneer and dig in a trench. . . . No more then is a physician obliged, from his office, to handle a knife with a surgeon. . . ." Morgan himself tried to confine his work to physic, refusing all "manual operation," and it reduced his practice accordingly.[21] Few other doctors were able to practice in such purity. Many continued to make their own drugs and almost all practiced both medicine and surgery. To have supported an aristocracy of physicians would have required aristocratic patronage and legal protection; the social and political basis of the British professional system did not exist in America.

Nor was there the cultural basis for adopting the manners of an aristocratic profession. The aristocratic personality invests the sense of rank and authority in every detail of dress, speech, and carriage. We have a good picture of the traditional physician in a description by a contemporary of Adam Kuhn, one of the leading practitioners of colonial Philadelphia:

He was, by far, the most highly and minutely furnished specimen of old-school medical production I have ever beheld. . . . His hand and bosom-ruffles were full and flowing, his breeches were black, his long-skirted waist-coat white or buff, and his coat snuff-colored. In his hand he carried a gold-headed cane, in his waistcoat pocket a gold snuff-box, and his knee and shoe-buckles were of the same metal. When moving from house to house, in his professional business, so sternly and stubbornly regular were his steps, in both extent and repetition, that he could scarcely be induced to quicken or lengthen them . . . [even] to save the life of the most meritorious of his patients.[22]

On the other hand, the revolutionary leader and physician Benjamin Rush—a republican in manners as well as politics, who greatly influenced future generations of physicians at the University of Pennsylvania—counseled his students to shun all aristocratic affectation as "incompatible with the simplicity of science, and the real dignity of physic."[23]

Yet while shunning aristocratic manners, Rush devised a therapeutic system that reflected the same quest for novelty and bondage to tradition that characterized English medical thought. "I have formerly said that there was but one fever in this world," he told his students in 1796. "Be not startled, gentlemen; follow me and I will say there is but one disease in the world."[24] The one disease was a "morbid excitement induced by capillary tension," and it had one remedy. This was to deplete the body by letting blood with the lancet and emptying out the stomach and bowels with the use of powerful emetics and cathartics. These stringent therapies were to be used with courage. Patients could be bled until unconscious and given heavy doses of the cathartic calomel (mercurous chloride) until they salivated. Heroic therapy of this kind dominated American medical practice in the first decades of the nineteenth century.

After the War of 1812, medical schools began to proliferate through the country. The new institutions had only tenuous connections, if any, with universities. Between 1810 and 1820 new schools were established in Baltimore, Lexington, and Cincinnati, and even in rural communities in Vermont and western New York. Over the next three decades the growth continued, until by 1850 there were forty-two schools in the United States at a time when there were three in all of France. Most of the growth after 1820 occurred in the West, and many schools were founded in rural areas, where costs could be kept low, although there were no hospitals or other clinical facilities.

The initiative for new medical schools came from their professors. Typically, a group of physicians approached a local college with a proposal for a school. From the doctors' perspective, the college would lend their enterprise legitimacy and the legal authority to grant degrees. From the college's perspective, a medical school meant added prestige without any investment, since the schools were all self-financed out of students' tuition. Sometimes, the physical facilities consisted of as few as two rooms, one for lectures and one for dissections. There were no laboratories and in many only limited libraries. Clinical instruction in hospitals was spotty even in urban schools.[25]

A faculty usually consisted of five to seven professors, all unsalaried. They received compensation directly from student fees for classes and private tutorials, and indirectly from the advantages that professorial appointments gave them in private practice. The term of study for a year of medical school lasted only three to four months, generally from the end of November to the beginning of March. Two years were required for a degree, and the second year consisted in repeating the courses of the first. The "graded curriculum," in which distinct courses were offered in the first and second years, was introduced after 1850 and considered a great reform.

Originally, in the eighteenth century, medical schools offered both a bachelor's and a doctoral degree in medicine. It was soon learned that students who took a bachelor's degree after one year rarely came back for the doctorate; a certificate of any sort sufficed for them to be considered graduates and thereby competent physicians. So in 1789 the medical school at the College of Philadelphia, which then set the standard, eliminated the bachelor's and required as the only prerequisite for the M.D. one course in natural and experimental philosophy, or the equivalent. As the designation of the degree went up, the requirements came down. The inflation of the medical degree, from bachelor's to doctorate, paralleled the earlier inflation of occupational titles from surgeon-apothecary to physician. It might be supposed that this was evidence of the profession's rising status. But quite a different cause was responsible. The inflation of titles and degrees in medicine was a result of the inability of its elite to prevent the diffusion and degradation of emblems of status.

Nominally, the requirements for an M.D. in the eighteenth century were a knowledge of Latin and natural and experimental philosophy; three years of tutelage as an apprentice; the attendance of two terms of lectures and passing of all examinations; and a thesis. To graduate a student also had to be at least twenty-one years of age. These requirements were not well enforced. Latin was neglected; many schools failed to require certificates for the three years' apprenticeship; the theses were generally unoriginal and occasionally barely literate. The examinations were less rigorous in part because professors were paid by a student only if he passed. Periodically, reformers made attempts to stiffen requirements, but these failed for want of cooperation among medical schools. An institution that raised its standards stood the risk of losing its students and its income.

Medical schools were originally conceived by physicians who wanted to raise the American profession to the dignity and privileges that medical men had in Europe. But they had no means of preventing other doctors elsewhere in the country from creating medical schools for their own advantage, too. The result was unrestrained competition in which the length of the term was kept at a minimal level, requirements were sacrificed, and student fees were driven down. In seeking to raise their status individually, physicians undermined it collectively.

The Frustration of Professionalism

Medical societies and medical licensure could also serve to draw boundaries around the profession and enhance its status and authority. In England the two were combined: Professional societies had the power to license. The aspiration of some leading American physicians was to achieve the same. When John Morgan proposed founding a medical school at Philadelphia, he also suggested chartering a medical society with licensing authority. In 1763 physicians in Norwich, Connecticut, requested their colonial legislature "to Distinguish between the Honest and Ingenious Physician and the Quack or Empirical Pretender" by allowing doctors to found societies with licensing power. Both these bids for authority were rejected.[26]

Some licensing did take place, but it was primarily honorific. It conferred approval on the recipient without excluding anyone else from practicing medicine, too. In the 1600s, legislatures would now and then bestow licenses on worthy doctors, but the acts themselves indicate that these men had already been in practice for years. The clear assumption was that not all medical care would come from licensed physicians; most would necessarily remain in the hands of domestic and lay practitioners. An early Massachusetts law, reflecting those realities, stated that no one ought to engage in healing "without the advice and consent of such as are skillful in the same Art, (if such may be had) or at least some of the wisest and gravest then present."[27]

When, in 1760, New York City passed the first law that called for examining and licensing prospective doctors and placing a fine on the unlicensed, it vested authority in city officials. The law exempted anyone already practicing medicine. There is no evidence that the statute was ever enforced against unlicensed practitioners, who seem, in fact, to have increased over the next few decades.[28]

After independence, as medical societies were organized in many states, legislatures began to extend licensing authority to them. Yet these licensure powers also turned out to be ineffective. Typically, no standard was set for education or achievement, no power was given to rescind a license once awarded, no provision was made for enforcement against unlicensed practitioners, and no serious penalties were imposed for violating the law. The only restriction usually placed on the unlicensed was that they were blocked from using the courts to recover

debts. It was sometimes said that this only supplied the unlicensed practitioners with a good argument for demanding payment in advance. If
the law included a fine for unlicensed practice, its imposition required
a jury trial, and juries would not convict. The laws usually exempted
apothecaries, midwives, and botanics; unlicensed practitioners who
identified themselves as one of these avoided legal sanctions. Licensing
boards also suffered from the same structural problems that plagued
medical schools. Just as schools were reluctant to flunk students and lose
their graduation fees, so boards of censors hesitated to turn down applicants and lose their licensing fees.[29]

The reasons why licensing persisted, in spite of its ineffectiveness,
were the same as the reasons why medical schools multiplied: They
were both in the immediate interests of the parties to the transaction.
The doctors who received the licenses could use them as a form of official certification that was perhaps more convincing than a preceptor's
letter of commendation. The collective interest of practicing physicians
was to keep entry into the profession restricted, but the particular interests of the doctors involved in medical education and licensing conspired to keep the field open. The profession had as yet no means of
asserting its collective interests over more narrow ones.

The weakness of the medical societies, moreover, was aggravated by
the proliferation of the medical schools, for their diplomas were considered licenses to practice in and of themselves. The two institutions were
in competition with each other, offering alternative means of certification. Neither held definitive authority, since it was possible to enter
medical practice without the approval of one or the other, or both. The
medical societies occasionally expressed dismay at the spread of medical schools; the medical schools' professors occasionally expressed dismay at the laxness of licensing. But neither was in a position to alter
the other's behavior.

The medical societies were unable to maintain effective boundaries
for the profession in other ways besides licensing. Through their codes
of ethics, the societies sought to isolate "quacks" by denying them all
consultations with regular physicians; anyone who conferred with them
was supposed to be subject to penalties, such as expulsion. The societies
also tried to develop uniform fee schedules to discourage price competition. Yet it appears that they failed in both of these efforts: Their rivals
were not isolated, nor were the fee schedules observed.

The societies faced a fundamental problem. If they insisted on high
standards, their membership would be small, and they would be unable
either to isolate quacks or control price cutting by competitors. If, on
the other hand, they admitted the larger number of practitioners to

help isolate quacks and impose fees, they would be unable to insist on high standards for professional status. Neither alternative could greatly elevate the profession's social and economic condition; there were no means to induce compliance and participation. So membership was low, dues were often unpaid, rules were ignored, and some early societies lapsed completely into inactivity for long periods.[30]

Even in a relatively successful organization, the difficulties in maintaining exclusiveness and authority were evident. The Massachusetts Medical Society, incorporated in 1781, was established, according to its founders, so "that a just discrimination should be made between such as are duly educated, and properly qualified for the duties of their profession, and those who may ignorantly and wickedly administer medicine. . . ." The society tried to reproduce the structure of the Royal College of Physicians by maintaining two separate ranks, fellows and licentiates, and by limiting to seventy the number of fellows. This closed corporate structure proved impossible to maintain. Though the society could give "letters testimonial" to those passing an examination, doctors could practice without its endorsement, and any graduate of Harvard had as official a license by virtue of his medical degree. Limited in its power, the society found it difficult to induce many physicians to seek its approval or accept its authority. In 1803 it ceased to be a closed corporation. The limit on the number of fellows was removed, and anyone who passed an examination and practiced for three years in good repute was admitted. The society became less exclusive in much the same way that medical education became more accessible.[31]

The boundaries defining the medical profession might have been drawn on any of three lines: graduates versus nongraduates of medical schools; members versus nonmembers of medical societies; licensed versus unlicensed practitioners. None of these worked. The preferred statuses—medical school graduate, society member, licensed practitioner—were continually invaded by the lower ranks of the profession as schools multiplied, societies became less exclusive, and licenses became easier to acquire. Eventually, the boundaries would be drawn so that education and licensure coincided: Only graduates could be licensed and only the licensed could practice. All licensed physicians, therefore, would have strong inducements to join their local medical society. But these developments were decades away. The attempt to set boundaries in the early nineteenth century only blurred them further. Daniel Drake, one of the early notable physicians of the Midwest, wrote of licensing: "Laws which admit to the practice of medicine, those who have not graduated, give many young men a passport to the confidence of the public, who do not deserve that confidence, and could not easily have acquired it without a license. Those, moreover, who are rejected by boards of censors are, in most cases, sustained by the society on that very account." It is difficult, Drake continued, for these bodies to establish an authority "that society or even the profession will recognize." The state, Drake believed, should only license graduates, but he opposed penalties against those without a diploma. "Such laws are never carried into effect."[32]

THE MEDICAL COUNTERCULTURE

Popular Medicine

Democratic ideology received its sharpest expression in lay medicine. Lay, or popular, medicine was not merely an improvised substitute for professional medicine; it became an active rival with a coherent structure of its own. Lay healers in the early nineteenth century saw the medical profession as a bulwark of privilege, and they adopted a position hostile to both its therapeutic tenets and its social aspirations.

Beneath this antagonism, however, was hidden a deeper resemblance. Folk medicine and lay healing typically include ideas and practices taken over from professional and authoritative sources. Popular culture develops partly by a process of "cultural sedimentation." Like a residue of the past, the theories and remedies of learned traditions filter down to the lower classes, where they remain even after the learned have abandoned them.[33] Moreover, not every rebellion in thought implies a radical change in its structure; often the elements of the old theories are only rearranged. The major popular medical movement in the early nineteenth century, Thomsonian medicine, showed precisely this pattern; so, too, did another popular heresy, homeopathy. But the filtering down and rearrangement of received ideas is only half the story. The transfers between professional and lay medicine went in both directions. Some important remedies used by regular physicians, such as smallpox inoculation and cinchona (quinine), were borrowed from folk cultures. In the nineteenth century, lay competition created much of the pressure against the medical profession to abandon "heroic" practices. So while professional and lay medicine often regarded each other with hostility and contempt, they bore one another a considerable though little acknowledged debt.

Lay medical practice may be imagined as occupying the ground between domestic and professional medicine. In its simplest form, informal practice is an extension of domestic care into the community; somewhat more developed is the adoption of lay healing as an occupation, but still without any standardized training or group organization. Conducted as part of a movement, lay medical practice may become an organized and self-conscious alternative to the dominant profession. In American history, several movements of lay practitioners have developed this kind of organization and then been either absorbed into the medical profession, like botanic medicine, or kept on its margins, like osteopathy and chiropractic.

The autobiography of one lay doctor suggests how easily medical practice might be entered. In 1844 James Still, a free Negro in New Jersey, bought a book of "medical botany" and began preparing remedies for his family. One day, in return for some sassafras roots, he agreed to cure a neighbor of the "piles" (hemorrhoids) and borrowed a little wooden mortar and a long stone to pound the herbs. "Having prepared the remedy, I took it to him, and it had the desired effect. In a few days he was well. I was pleased, and so was he. It did not occur to me at this time, however, that I was practicing medicine. I thought I was but doing a friendly service to a fellow-being."[34] Self-taught, Still eventually took up healing as a practical vocation.

Botanic practitioners and midwives were probably the most numerous of the lay therapists, but there were also uncounted cancer doctors, bonesetters, inoculators, abortionists, and sellers of nostrums. Many were itinerant and moved freely into and out of various trades. Though the categories are not neat, two classes may be distinguished: those like midwives, bonesetters, and inoculators who claimed a specific skill, and those like botanics and nostrum venders who claimed as generalized a competence as physicians.

In early pioneer communities, Indian doctors were one source of popular medical treatment. Some were "held in quite as high repute as regular white doctors."[35] From the period of the first settlements in America, many colonists took a strong interest in the medicine of the Indians. The natives initially seemed free of all the dread diseases that afflicted Europeans, and their good health was understandably thought to be a product of their special knowledge of indigenous medicinal herbs. An early historian of North Carolina reported in 1714 that cures performed by the Indians were "too many to repeat"; he even advocated intermarriage with the natives partly to obtain "a true Knowledge of all the Indian's Skill in Medicine and Surgery." Cotton Mather also thought the Indians did "cures many times which are truly stupendous." God, he believed, had carefully placed remedies around the earth wherever they were needed; the Indians had been in America a long time, and so might well have already discovered them. After visiting America in the 1730s, John Wesley wrote of the natives that their diseases were "exceedingly few" and their medicines "quick, as well as generally infallible."[36] The popular image of the Indian as a healer led to the appearance of white or mulatto "Indian doctors." These were men who claimed to have been tutored by the natives in their herbal lore, or who ostensibly used the same methods. Many of their medicines were actually of their own devising, but the adoption of Indian identity is suggestive of the reputation the natives enjoyed.

Among the most remarkable of the various lay practitioners were the natural bonesetters, who specialized in treating fractures and dislocations. Basically artisans without formal education, they represented a kind of mechanical craftsmanship applied to medicine. The most famous were the Sweet family of Rhode Island, whose members were bonesetters from the seventeenth to the early twentieth centuries. Practicing only part-time, they were, according to a local historian, "for the most part industrious farmers, mechanics, laborers, and fishermen, all in humble circumstances, but none in poverty." Their skill was legendary. While popular belief ascribed to them a "natural gift" for repairing injuries, they were actually trained in the craft from early childhood, according to the account of one of several descendants who became physicians. Though accused of ignorance by some doctors, they were widely respected and even received occasional referrals from regular practitioners.[37]

In colonial America, as I indicated earlier, most medical care was routinely provided by women in the home. Women were also prominent as lay practitioners. According to Joseph Kett, medical practice in New Jersey as late as 1818 belonged almost entirely to women.[38] But by the Jacksonian period, women no longer held as dominant a position as they had earlier. The decline of midwives began in the late 1700s. Until then, pregnant women had called in a circle of female relatives and friends, sometimes even returning to their mothers' homes during their confinement. The midwife offered emotional and practical support in the management of childbirth. However, in the eighteenth century, medical knowledge of anatomy and professional skill in using forceps to shorten labor were developing rapidly. When Dr. William Shippen took up obstetric practice in 1763, he was the first physician in the colonies to do so. The shift from midwives to doctors, Catherine Scholten has found, started among women in the urban middle classes. While the Philadelphia city directory in 1815 listed twenty-one women and twenty-three men as practicing midwifery, four years later the numbers had

changed to thirteen women and forty-two men, and by 1824 only six
women remained. No licensing laws compelled the shift, and though
physicians had economic motives to take over midwifery, they were in
no position to force women to accept them. There was, in fact, some
moral opposition to male physicians attending childbirth. Not the least
probable explanation is that well-to-do women had come to accept the
physicians' claims of superior skill. No protests were registered at the
time physicians took over obstetrical practice. "American midwives,"
Scholten notes, "ceased practice among women of social rank with few
words uttered in their defense."[39]

The more general decline of women as lay practitioners paralleled
developments in other fields. Women had been shopkeepers during the
colonial period, but public opinion in the early nineteenth century assigned them, once married, a more strictly domestic role. (School teaching, however, was a major exception.) Gerda Lerner argues that while
the Revolution and its aftermath overturned the hierarchical ideology
of colonial life, the new democracy did not include women, whose role
became more narrow. She singles out medical practice as a case in point
and suggests that the rise of medical colleges and licensing requirements were the reasons for women's exclusion.[40] But, as Mary Walsh
has pointed out, this reflects a misunderstanding of licensure, which was
only honorific, and of the earlier role of women in healing, which was
never the equivalent of male physicians'. Women practiced primarily
where male doctors were absent. As the number of male doctors increased, the women practitioners were displaced. In fact, Walsh argues,
the rise of professionalism offered women the first real chance to practice medicine on an equal basis with men. As a result of popular prejudice against women physicians, they especially needed the credentials
of medical education. In the 1840s, encouraged by the women's rights
movement, the first women secured formal medical training in America; the New England Medical College, founded in Boston in 1848, was
the first medical school exclusively for women in the world.[41]

Nearly all regular physicians, however, were decidedly opposed to
the admission of women into the profession. The policy of medical societies was strict ostracism. Women found more sympathy among the
irregulars who practiced with roots and herbs. In the 1830s, women also
became prominently involved in the popular movement stirred by the
health reformer Sylvester Graham. (Now best remembered for the
crackers that were part of his dietary regimen, Graham advocated a
lighter, vegetarian diet, regular bathing, abstention from alcohol and
coffee and the popularization of knowledge about physiology and hygiene.[42]) As a result, there was a broad alliance linking women's rights

and protests against the regular profession and its stringent remedies. But within this "popular health movement" was another movement that reflected the problems of the medical profession in its protests against it.

The Thomsonians and the Frustration of Anti-Professionalism

The major organized alternative to the medical profession in the early nineteenth century emerged in the radical movement of botanic medicine led by the New Englander Samuel Thomson. Thomson, who had no formal education, began practicing in the years after 1800, arousing jealousy, according to his own account, from regular physicians because of his success. In 1809, after a patient died, he was accused of murder by a doctor, but was tried and acquitted. The trial attracted public attention to his ideas. Four years later, he managed to obtain a patent from the federal government for his system of botanic medicine, enabling him both to sell rights for use of his methods and to claim official endorsement. His followers, mostly rural, spread from New England through the Mohawk Valley to western New York, following the same route as a wave of religious enthusiasm. The Thomsonians had all the appurtenances of a movement: They were organized into "friendly botanic societies," held conventions, and published journals. Their bible was Thomson's *New Guide to Health*, published in 1822. By 1839 Thomson claimed to have sold 100,000 family rights to his system; presumably others made use of it as well, since control was impossible. Thomson boasted half of Ohio's population were adherents; his critics said only a third.[43]

Thomson's system revolved around a few simple principles. All disease was the effect of one general cause and could be removed by one general remedy. Cold was the cause; heat, the remedy. All "animal bodies" were composed of four elements: earth, air, fire and water. Earth and water were the solids; air and fire, or heat, the cause of all life and motion. The way to produce health was to restore heat, either directly by clearing the system of all obstructions, so the stomach could digest food and generate heat, or else indirectly by causing perspiration.[44] Hence Thomson's principal medications: a violent emetic known as Indian tobacco, or *lobelia inflata*; red pepper; and steam and hot baths. Thomson vigorously opposed all the "mineral" remedies of the medical profession: Since minerals came from the ground, they were deadly; herbs grew toward the sun and were, therefore, life-giving.

Political ideology formed an integral part of Thomson's thought. Like the books of domestic medicine, his writing contrasted common sense with arcane, professional learning and evinced a supreme faith in the simplicity and accessibility of valid knowledge. Thomson believed that the study of medicine was "no more necessary to mankind at large, to qualify them to administer relief from pain and sickness, than to a cook in preparing food to satisfy hunger."[45] Medicine, like religion and government, had been shrouded in unnecessary obscurity, but was easily understood. "Let mystery be stripped of all pretence [*sic*]," ran an epigraph over the *Thomsonian Recorder*, "And practice be combined with common sense." In an article in the journal in 1832, one writer commented, "Learning and property are the elements of political power. These elements combined, and put in operation, are the most efficient means for the elevation of the few and the subjugation of the many." There was in all countries "a literary aristocracy, a privileged order" hostile to ordinary men, and it was the aim of the Thomsonians, whose declared sympathies were with the laboring classes, to overthrow this tyranny of priests, lawyers, and doctors.[46]

These ideas, medical and political, must be seen not only as related but as homologous. What they lack in originality, they make up in consistency. Thomson's system was largely borrowed from the dominant authorities. Pathology was systemic rather than local. Like Rush, he claimed there was but one disease and one remedy, which was to deplete the body. The substitution of botanic for "mineral" drugs only rearranged one element in an otherwise familiar structure. To that extent, his system contained the "sediment" of a culture molded by learned traditions. But this peculiar mixture of ideas had its own structural unity, built around simple and parallel binary oppositions. The therapeutic system can be expressed as follows: Disease is to life, as cold is to heat, as minerals are to herbs. The political ideology shares the same pattern: Learning is to common sense, as aristocracy is to democratic government, as physicians are to popular healers. The genius of the Thomsonian system was to express a protest against the dominant order in its therapeutic as well as its political ideas.

This protest was directed, however, not at science, but at a particular way in which knowledge was controlled. The theme echoes through Thomsonian writings. Many doctors, said Thomson, "have learned just enough to know how to deceive people, and keep them in ignorance, by covering their doings under a language unknown to their patients."[47] The Thomsonians spurned "superstition" and denounced "quackery" as vigorously as regular physicians; they thought of themselves as belonging to the tradition of reason. The "natural" remedies of botanic medicine stood at the system's heart; there were no supernatural powers, no laying on of hands. One must not mistake Thomsonianism to be a vestige of magical belief; it was a creative misreading of the Enlightenment. In a regular column on quackery, one writer inveighed against secret nostrums, noting, "There can be no good reason for keeping us ignorant of the medicines we are compelled to swallow."[48] The Thomsonians adapted rationalism to their own situation. The defenders of knowledge have always treated it as an interest of society; the Thomsonians viewed knowledge as an element in class conflict.

Despite its wide appeal, the Thomsonian movement suffered from a series of contradictions. It professed to have nothing but the interests of the people at heart, yet it was conducted by its founder for his own profit and under the protection of a patent. Thomson sold rights to his system at $20 apiece. The instruction booklet omitted key ingredients from the recipes, which agents filled in only after the buyers swore themselves to secrecy. When one of his disciples betrayed him and offered the system at only $5, Thomson accused him of trying to take the "whole business" for himself.[49]

A second and related contradiction pitted the social aspirations of botanic doctors against the democratic ideology of the movement. Probably for the same reasons that motivated physicians, some botanics wanted to separate themselves from the ill qualified by raising requirements and standards. In November 1835, the Philadelphia branch of the Thomsonian society urged "greater restrictions . . . on the qualifications of practitioners, so as to secure not only the better success of the practice, but the respect and confidence of the public at large." They suggested at least one year of study with an authorized practitioner, followed by a qualifying examination. Others drew up plans to found a Thomsonian medical school, but Thomson himself repudiated the idea and was ready only to consider establishing a hospital and infirmary, where instruction would be practical, as in a carpenter's shop.[50]

The conflict brought into the open the internal weaknesses of his position. "You seem to think, Doctor," answered one of his followers, "that all the owners of family rights ought to understand your book as well as you do. But, if you could travel through the country and see what bungling work many make of your practice, you would cheerfully subscribe to the establishment of schools to teach the application of that practice. . . ."[51]

The Thomsonian movement divided over this issue. Medical schools represented a way for Thomson's followers to solidify their own social position. The disciples of a charismatic leader need mechanisms to stabilize their situation. The leader himself may fail to recognize that need; his role and thought may even be incompatible with its satisfac-

tion. This was the case with the Thomsonian movement. When Samuel
Thomson died in 1843, his faction of the movement went into decline.
The independent Thomsonians, who founded a medical college at Cincinnati, prevailed among his followers for a while, before being absorbed into another botanic sect, the Eclectics.[52] The medical counterculture gradually underwent its own professionalization. In the second
half of the nineteenth century, the opposition between popular and
professional medicine was less central; the major conflict became the
struggle among rival schools of physicians, each contending for public
favor.

THE ECLIPSE OF LEGITIMATE COMPLEXITY

Nineteenth-century medicine took its unique character in America
from the dialectic between professionalism and the nation's democratic
culture. Physicians tried to raise their standards, dignity, and privileges
through medical schools, societies, and licensing, but the openness of
the society and the ambitions of their fellows subverted their efforts.
Standards for degrees and licenses were soon compromised rather than
strengthened; distinctions between qualified and unqualified practitioners became blurred rather than clarified; entry into practice was
opened up rather than tightened. The position of doctors arguably became less secure.[53] Yet just as professional medicine was unable to resist
democratizing influences, so popular medicine, in the form of the
Thomsonian movement, proved susceptible to the temptations of professionalism. Neither the ideals of John Morgan nor those of Samuel
Thomson governed the movements they initiated; in both cases, the results were nearly antithetical to their aims. By the mid-1800s, the ambitions of professionalizers and democratizers were equally frustrated.

The deepening of therapeutic confusion in the first half of the nineteenth century came, paradoxically, at a time of great progress in medical science. In France after the Revolution, the conservative order had
been swept aside in medicine; reformers of medical education and
practice called for an end to metaphysical abstractions and an emphasis
on clinical observation. In the large hospitals that arose in Paris, physicians were placed in closer contact with surgeons, and the surgical
viewpoint began to influence their views, encouraging an emphasis on
localized rather than systemic pathology. The decades between 1800
and 1830 mark the decisive break with the vague "systems" of classical

medicine and the formation of modern clinical methods. Combining clinical observation with pathological anatomy, the French physicians correlated the signs and symptoms of patients with the internal lesions disclosed at autopsy. In 1816 Laennac introduced the first crude stethoscope; auscultation allowed the physician to penetrate behind the externally visible to "see" into the living. As is often said, doctors previously observed patients; now they examined them. And, in a further critical step, the Paris school began to evaluate the effectiveness of therapeutic techniques statistically.[54]

This new orientation was not simply a rearrangement of the elements within the traditional structure of medical thought; it transformed the structure itself. The nature of debate also changed. Empirical evidence rather than dogmatic assertions of personal or traditional authority became the grounds for assessing truth. The early empirical investigations showed that accepted techniques had no therapeutic value, yet there were no effective alternatives available to replace them. Medicine had reached that difficult point in its history when leading scientists knew its limitations, but as yet lacked the means to advance beyond them. Ironically, as Richard Shryock writes, "the most hopeful period in the history of medicine was the one in which the public looked to medicine with least hope."[55]

These developments led in two directions. On the one hand, the emphasis on localized pathology called attention to specific organs; this aroused interest in medical instrumentation and provided foci for the development of medical specialties.[56] On the other hand, the growth of therapeutic skepticism directed attention to the value of preventive hygiene. During the middle decades of the century, before the rise of bacteriology, some European and American physicians began to stress the importance of social conditions in the causation of disease.[57] The French revolution in medicine was, to use the phrase that Marx borrowed from Hegel, "a labor of the negative" that released two kinds of possibilities. One became modern clinical medicine; the other, social medicine. Their relative priority was ultimately to become a political question.

In the 1820s and 1830s, Americans who went to Europe to study medicine increasingly went to Paris and brought back with them the therapeutic skepticism of the French. In an influential address in 1835 on "self-limited diseases," Jacob Bigelow of Harvard acknowledged the therapeutic poverty of contemporary medicine. It was, Bigelow maintained, "the unbiased opinion of most medical men of sound judgment and long experience" that "the amount of death and disaster in the world would be less, if all disease were left to itself." Bigelow called upon physicians to recognize nature as "the great agent of cure" and to use art only as an auxiliary. This, for him, was "rational medicine." Others called it "therapeutic nihilism," but a complete rejection of medical intervention was rare. However, by the 1850s many regular physicians had subscribed to what Oliver Wendell Holmes referred to as the "nature-trusting heresy." Bloodletting and other practices of heroic medicine were in decline, and Rush was repudiated. Sectarian challenges to medical orthodoxy may have encouraged the shift toward less violent remedies. Doctors themselves preferred to explain the change on the basis of scientific advance or a decline in their patients' constitutions that made them less able to withstand the rigors of heroic treatment.[58]

Popular resistance to professional medicine has sometimes been portrayed as hostility to science and modernity. But given what we now know about the objective ineffectiveness of early nineteenth-century therapeutics, popular skepticism was hardly unreasonable. Moreover, by the nineteenth century in America, popular belief reflected an extreme form of rationalism that demanded science be democratic. The democratic ideal in the sphere of knowledge, Karl Mannheim has argued, calls for the greatest possible accessibility and communicability. "Democratic cultures," Mannheim notes, "have a deep suspicion of all kinds of 'occult' knowledge cultivated in sects and secret coteries."[59] We have seen how pervasive an influence this was in medicine. It had become an article of faith in America that every sphere of social life— law, government, religion, science, industry—obeyed principles of natural reason that were intelligible to ordinary men of common sense. Insofar as medicine was valid and useful, it also ought to be plain and simple. The appearance of complexity was an imposition by a self-interested class; it was the result of mystification and deception, not of any intrinsic difficulty. There was this much to be said for the Thomsonians' doctrine, declared a writer in the *New York Evening Star* in 1833: "That *medicine*, like every useful science, should be thrown open to the observation and study of all. It should, in fact, like law and every important practical science, be made a part of the primary education of the people. . . . We should at once explode the whole machinery of mystification and concealment—wigs, gold canes, and the gibberish of prescriptions—which serves but as a cloak to ignorance and legalized murder!"[60]

These are standard sentiments of the period. Perry Miller has written that a majority of the people in early American society "simply hated the law as an artificial imposition on their native intelligence" and believed it was "a gigantic conspiracy of the learned against their helpless integrity."[61] Andrew Jackson said of the duties of public office that they "are, or at least admit of being made, so plain and simple that men of intelligence may readily qualify themselves for their performance,"[62] and this was almost exactly what people said of medicine.

The Thomsonian movement and other developments in medicine were a relatively minor expression of a much larger cultural and political upheaval. As old state constitutions in New York, Massachusetts, and Virginia were set aside, property and religious qualifications for suffrage and office holding were reduced or eliminated. The nation's political life was convulsed by attacks on the power of monopolies and the central bank. At a local level, the Masons were accused of being a monopolistic clique that won unjust advantages and influence for its members through secret organization.[63]

But while antagonistic to traditional forms of privilege, the democratic impulse was not necessarily anticapitalist. Much of the early resentment of lawyers and courts in America came from the commercial and middle classes because of the cost and length of litigation and vestiges of preindustrial rules that businessmen felt were obstructing enterprise. In education, there were attacks on classical learning, but at the same time demands for universal public education, public control of the schools, and training in practical skills. In politics, the special privileges of monopolies were denounced, but reformers replaced special corporate charters with general incorporation statutes, which facilitated economic development. The response to corruption in government was to increase bureaucratic regulation: formal rules replaced personal organization. So the desire to remove mystery, personal control, and special privileges resulted not in disorder or a leveling of inequalities, but in the development of a new order that was simultaneously capitalist, bureaucratic, and culturally and politically a democracy.[64]

The professions offended Jacksonian ideology primarily because of their attempts to establish exclusive privileges. In the demands of insurgent parties, the abolition of "licensed monopolies" had a high priority, and though this referred mainly to business corporations with special privileges, the professions were included. The number of states and territories requiring professional study to practice law fell from three quarters in 1800 to a third in 1830 and then to one quarter by 1860.[65] The decline of licensing in medicine was even more dramatic.

While medical licensure had never been strictly enforced, it caused sufficient discomfort to irregular practitioners to encourage them to organize for its repeal. The Thomsonian botanic societies led this effort. Just as physicians had formed societies to distinguish themselves from irregular practitioners, so the irregulars organized to resist that distinction. The issue was defined by the regular physicians as science versus quackery; by the irregulars, as free competition versus monopoly. It is a measure of the profession's meager authority that its terms did not prevail. The physicians said they feared the danger quacks and pretenders posed to the innocent public; the irregulars said they trusted the good sense of the public, which ought to be free to make its own choice. At a later date, regulation would be thought of as a "progressive" measure, protecting the public interest; not so in the 1830s and 1840s. "A people accustomed to govern themselves and boasting of their intelligence are impatient of restraint," declared a New York legislator introducing a bill for repeal of licensure. "They want no protection but freedom of inquiry and freedom of action."[66]

State legislatures were still enacting licensing laws in the 1820s; then they began rescinding them in quick succession. Illinois empowered medical societies to issue licenses in 1817, modified the law in 1825, and abolished licensing the next year. In Ohio, licensing was introduced in 1811 and repealed in 1833. Licensing laws, or penalties for the unlicensed, were dropped in Alabama in 1832, Mississippi in 1836, South Carolina, Maryland, and Vermont in 1838, Georgia in 1839, New York in 1844, and Louisiana in 1852. Several states, including Pennsylvania, never had any licensing.[67] In some, like New York, the battle was prolonged, but by mid-century, the legislative verdict was unmistakable.

Yet public opinion had never allowed licensing to become exclusive, and repeal only ratified a judgment passed by society at large. In 1837 the president of the New York State Medical Society noted that in trials for unlicensed practice, the testimony of physicians as prosecution witnesses was "received with suspicion and disfavor by juries," making laws against irregular practitioners "almost a dead letter." He confessed that the accused almost always had the public's sympathy, "while nothing but odium has fallen to the share of the medical profession, for aiding the prosecution."[68]

What fundamentally destroyed licensure was the suspicion that it was an expression of favor rather than competence. A license was useful as a means of establishing authority only if it was accepted as evidence of objective skill. But the belief that medical societies and boards of censors were merely closed corporations, like the banks and monopolies, utterly subverted their value as agencies of legitimation.

The spirit of rationalism had only encouraged this suspicion, for it brought into question all the traditional forms of mystification that medicine and other professions had relied upon. Yet the same spirit would also help reestablish professional authority. From the perspective of democratic thought in the early nineteenth century, the seeming complexity of medicine was artificial; if properly understood, medicine could be brought within reach of "common sense." The development of science broke that confidence. It helped establish the cultural authority of medicine by restoring a sense of its *legitimate complexity*. The attempts by physicians to recreate English institutions in America were futile efforts to restore outdated bases of legitimacy. Science would provide a much more stable foundation.

Science shares with the democratic temper an antagonism to all that is obscure, vague, occult, and inaccessible, but it also gives rise to complexity and specialization, which then remove knowledge from the reach of lay understanding. For a time in the first half of the nineteenth century, the democratic claim of accessibility and universality prevailed in medicine. But the public, through its legislators and its own private decisions, gradually relinquished that claim as it became convinced of the growing complexity of medical science and the limits of lay competence. Every man, it became clear, could not be his own physician. The democratic interregnum of the nineteenth century was a period of transition, when the traditional forms of mystification had broken down and the modern fortress of objectivity had not yet been built.

CHAPTER TWO

The Expansion
of the Market

ECONOMIC obstacles also blocked the professional development of medicine in the nineteenth century. Medical practice offered too small a financial return for many doctors to invest in a lengthy professional education or for state legislatures to require one. Only in part were the meager economic rewards the result of competition with lay practitioners. The more fundamental reason was that the market for physicians' services was limited by economic conditions that encouraged most families to care for themselves. These conditions are typical of preindustrial societies; they arise from the low level of real incomes and the geography of rural life. As these conditions changed in the nineteenth century, the economic opportunities of the medical profession expanded dramatically.

In early American society, medicine was relatively insignificant as an economic institution. Insofar as care of the sick remained within the family and communal circle, it was not a commodity: It had no price in money and was not "produced" for exchange, as were the trained skills and services of doctors. But when people in sickness and distress resorted to physicians, paid for hospital care, or bought patent medicines instead of preparing their own remedies, medical care passed from the household into the market. The shift of medical care into the market altered the social and economic relations of illness, yet the rule of market forces could never be complete. The public, as well as physicians, resisted treating medicine purely as a commodity and giving free rein to commercial impulses. And so the social history of medicine in the nineteenth century is a history of both the extension of the medical market and its restriction.

Nineteenth-century society, Karl Polanyi has written, was governed by just such a "double movement": The market expanded continuously, reaching into almost every sphere of social life, but was met by a countermovement restraining its action. On one side, the principles of economic liberalism called for the release of the market from all constraint. On the other, the forces of "social protectionism" attempted to curb the devastating effects of the market on traditional institutions, nature, and even the economic system itself.[1]

These two political responses had their counterparts in medicine. The advocates of economic liberalism believed that in the care of the sick, as in other activities, private choice should prevail—hence their support for the abolition of all medical licensing. They thought people should be able to contract for treatment with whomever they wished; the market, in other words, could best regulate itself. On the opposing side of the issue, seeking protection from an unconstrained market, medical societies tried to limit entry into practice and commercial behavior, like price cutting and advertising. The countermovement was also evident in medical aid to the indigent and, after the turn of the century, government and professional regulation of the drug industry. In different ways, professionalism, charity, and government intervention were efforts to modify the action of the market, without abolishing it entirely.

THE EMERGING MARKET BEFORE THE CIVIL WAR

In one respect, the commercial nature of professional practice was more forthrightly acknowledged in America than in England. Under an ancient legal fiction, English law regarded the services of physicians as wholly philanthropic. While surgeons and apothecaries could sue for their fees, physicians could not. Similarly, the low-ranking English attorneys could sue clients for payment, but the elite barristers were presumed to be above material motives. Like the gradations of status among practitioners, these presumptions never successfully crossed the Atlantic.[2] The only doctors ever barred from suing for fees in the United States were unlicensed practitioners. To be placed outside the market was an honor in an aristocratic culture, but a penalty in a democratic and commercial one.

In the late eighteenth and early nineteenth centuries, the state relinquished control over the market for professional services in what was perhaps the most crucial area—the determination of professional fees. Before the rise of laissez faire ideology in the nineteenth century, government played an active, explicit, and direct role in economic life that included the regulation of prices. In 1633 in Massachusetts the charging of extortionate prices was made punishable by law, and in 1639 the Virginia Assembly passed the first of several medical practice acts specifically providing for judicial action against "griping and avaricious" doctors levying exorbitant charges.[3] In 1736, the House of Burgesses enacted a lengthy fee schedule for physicians. Whereas later schedules consisting of minimum fees would be issued by medical societies hoping to prevent price cutting, the earliest consisted of maximum fees aimed at preventing price gouging. Yet state determination of medical prices was short-lived. In 1766 the Chief Justice of Massachusetts ruled that "Travel for Physicians, their Drugs and Attendance have as fixed a Price as Goods sold by a Shopkeeper," but this decision was reversed four years later when a physician was permitted to sue in *quantum meruit* (for the reasonable value of his services).[4] State determination of lawyers' fees eroded more slowly, the last traces finally disappearing around 1850.[5] The price-setting mechanism shifted from law and custom to contract.

Thus the expansion of market forces in medicine originated in diminished state involvement as well as the attenuated role of the household in the treatment of the sick. In the mid-nineteenth century, particularly after the collapse of licensure in the 1830s and 1840s, the state had almost nothing to do with the private transactions between medical practitioners and their patients, except insofar as it guaranteed the sanctity of contracts and provided a means for determining and redressing negligence (malpractice). Some communities paid for medical treatment of the poor and maintained hospitals and pesthouses for contagious disease; some states gave small subsidies to medical schools, and by 1860 all the older states had constructed at least one mental asylum. The federal government maintained a limited system of compulsory hospital insurance for merchant seamen.

But these functions were the extent of state intervention in the economics of medicine before the Civil War.

Medical societies tried to assume some functions the state had abandoned. "The law nowhere settles the precise value of professional opinion or advice," noted an article in the *New England Journal of Medicine and Surgery* in 1825. "A fee table settles this . . ."[6] Yet the fee bills often went unobserved and had, as one writer put it, "little importance as authorities." A Philadelphia journal, publishing a fee schedule of the local College of Physicians in 1861, noted that this would be the first time most practitioners in the city had ever seen it, as charges had "not been guided by any fee-bill" at all. "Like literary labor," the journal observed, "medical attendance is worth in the market what it will bring."[7]

Most physicians were paid by a fee per service or a fee per case. Some were retained for a fixed fee per annum to provide all needed care to a family, a plantation, or the indigent members of a community. Called "contract practice," this method—actually a primitive form of insurance—was frowned upon by many doctors, who believed they were exploited under the system because of the unlimited services they might be asked to provide. Indeed, such arrangements did place the entire burden of risk on the individual physician; the existence of such contracts testifies to the weak bargaining position of many doctors. However, despite its name, contract practice was no more or less contractual than other forms; the contract was just explicit, rather than implied. The legal system presumed a contract between doctor and patient (or someone acting on the patient's behalf) even where none was expressly made.[8]

Much medical care was provided on credit. Physicians tried to collect their fees quarterly or annually, but they lost a substantial portion of their income through unpaid bills. The credit system, like contract practice, was a source of much irritation to doctors, but they were in no position to eliminate it. As probate records for New England doctors in the early 1800s indicate, many were enveloped in a tangled web of debt and credit relationships until their deaths. Practitioners in New England in the 1830s rarely received more than $500 a year in gross income. Much of this was paid in kind rather than money.[9]

The supply of physicians in the early and mid-nineteenth century was unrestricted by significant institutional barriers to entry. Because of the proliferation of medical schools, offering easy terms and quick degrees, the cost of medical education, in both money and time, was kept relatively low. Nor was an education beyond an apprenticeship always necessary. In five New England counties during the period from 1790 to

1840, the proportion of medical school graduates among practicing physicians ranged from 20 to 35 percent.[10] In eastern Tennessee in 1850, according to a doctor of the era, there were 201 physicians, only 35 of whom (or 17 percent) were graduates of a school; 42 other practitioners claimed to have taken a course of lectures.[11] The total investment necessary to enter medical practice in 1850, including direct expenses and opportunity costs, probably ranged between $500 and $1,300, depending on the degree of schooling.[12] By contrast, the cost of establishing a farm in the West during the same period was likely to be larger, in the range of $1,000 to $2,000.[13] And since neither licensing requirements nor a limit on the number of places in medical schools impeded entry into medicine, the supply of practitioners grew. Between 1790 and 1850, the number of physicians in the United States rose from five to forty thousand, a rate of growth faster than that of the population. As a result, the number of people per doctor dropped from about 950 to 600 during the same period.[14] Doctors complained continually about overcrowding in the profession.

As a result of unrestricted entry into practice, doctors were apparently well distributed through rural areas. "Physicians, even in surplus quantity, were available to the most remote New England towns, but the competition was keen and not always amiable. The most common problems of new practice were the dearth of patients and lack of rapport with established doctors."[15] This pattern was repeated elsewhere. Preceptors often suggested to their students that they seek "stands" (practices) in the frontier communities in the West and South, but according to a recent study, "Wherever and whenever they went, acceptable stands were difficult to find." In 1836 a young Vermont doctor thinking of settling in Georgia was told that the "only way to get practice would be to underbid those already practicing"; another, who graduated from Dartmouth in 1832, moved to a small village in Virginia because the best Virginia locations were already taken.[16]

Had educational and licensing requirements for medicine been more rigorous, physicians would undoubtedly have been more scarce, especially in rural areas. The money to be made in small towns and rural communities was too meager to recoup the investment in a lengthy education. The limited training of nineteenth century doctors was not so much an expression of ignorance as it was a response to economic realities—the limits of effective demand.[17]

THE CHANGING ECOLOGY OF MEDICAL PRACTICE

The Local Transportation Revolution

Low use of professional services was the fundamental constraint on medicine in early American society. Many physicians found it extremely difficult to support themselves solely from medical practice. A second occupation, usually farming, often proved necessary. "The resources of a farm," Benjamin Rush observed in his advice to medical students, "will prevent your cherishing, even for a moment, an impious wish for the prevalence of sickness in your neighborhood."[18] Later, many doctors, especially in small town and frontier areas, ran drug stores; and druggists, if they were not previously doctors, often took up medical practice as part of their work. (One historian records a doctor who, "not satisfied with his practice, robbed stagecoaches on the side" before he was captured in 1855 and sent to prison.[19] But he may have been looking for excitement.) Starting out in practice frequently meant protracted underemployment and hardship. "The fact is," stated the *Boston Medical and Surgical Journal* in 1836, "there are dozens of doctors in all great towns, who scarcely see a patient from christmas-time to christmas-coming."[20]

This pattern, Ivan Waddington has shown, is typical of medical practice in preindustrial societies. In eighteenth- and early nineteenth-century France and England, as in the United States, the demand for professional advice was limited by the inability of the great mass of the population to afford services and the persistence of traditional and domestic forms of treatment. Doctors had difficulty setting themselves up in practice and many abandoned the occupation entirely.[21] The structural problem everywhere was the same: Given the limited extent of the market, physicians could not lucratively monopolize the medical work available in the society. In Europe, a small elite of physicians confined itself to practice among the rich and separated itself from other practitioners. This "status professionalism" had broken down in America. The more numerous American physicians, scattered among small communities or overcrowded in the towns, struggled on under modest circumstances.

The inadequacy of local markets stemmed partly from Americans' ingrained self-reliance, their disbelief in the value of professional medicine, and the ease with which competitors entered the field. Some may wish to argue that all these factors were ultimately reducible to the ineffectiveness of contemporary therapeutics. It is not clear, however, that doctors' economic problems would have been resolved if they had the scientific knowledge of 1920 under the economic and cultural conditions of 1850 or even 1880. I leave aside, for the moment, the question of whether such knowledge would have been as widely recognized as authoritative. The basic problem would have remained the same: Most families could not have afforded to rely on physicians' services.

The heart of the economic problem was not that the physicians' fees were so high, but that the real price of medical care was so much higher than their fees. The price of medical services consists not only of the direct price (the physician's fee, the charge for a hospital room) but also of the indirect price—the cost of transportation (if the patient travels to the doctor or sends another person to summon one) and the foregone value of the time taken to obtain medical care. In most discussions, only the direct price is taken into account, but this bias is unwarranted.[22]

In the early and mid-nineteenth century, the indirect price of medical services probably outweighed the direct price. Dispersed in a heavily rural society, lacking modern transportation, the great majority of the population was effectively cut off from ordinary recourse to physicians because of the prohibitive opportunity cost of travel. For a farmer, a trip of ten miles into town could mean an entire day's lost work. Contemporary observers and historians have continually drawn attention to the isolation of rural life and most small communities before the twentieth century. This was as much an economic as a psychological fact.

The self-sufficiency of the household in early American society was never complete, but it was quite extensive, particularly in the frontier, back-country, and rural communities where most Americans lived. Families produced not only food for their own consumption, but also clothes, furniture, household utensils, farm implements, building materials, and many other necessities. After 1815 household manufacturers rapidly declined in New England; according to Rolla Tryon, the transition to shop and factory-made goods there was nearly accomplished by 1830. Elsewhere it took longer; the presence of a large frontier population through mid-century meant that the transition was "always taking place but never quite completed" in the country as a whole. "As soon as manufactured goods could be supplied from the sale or barter of the products of the farm, the home gave up its system of manufacturing, which had been largely carried on more through necessity than desire. Generally speaking, by 1860 the factory, through the aid of improved means of transportation, was able to supply the needs of the people for manufactured commodities."[23]

A similar, but slower transition from the household to the market economy took place in the production of personal services. For rural families, the time it took to procure specialized services outside the household greatly increased their cost. The growth of cities, the advent of modern means of transportation, and the building of hard roads radically altered the structure of prices. By reducing the opportunity and transportation costs for services, urbanization and improved transportation generally promoted the substitution of paid, specialized labor for the unpaid, unspecialized labor of the household or local community. Getting a haircut, visiting a prostitute, and consulting a doctor all became, on the average, less expensive because of reduced costs of time.

Data contained in nineteenth-century fee tables provide a basis for estimating the relation between direct and indirect prices. The fee bills published by medical societies may be poor indicators of average charges, but they are probably reliable as indicators of the relative value of different services. In addition to a basic fee for a physician visit, almost all nineteenth-century fee schedules list a charge per mile if the doctor needed to travel out of town. The charge for mileage represents an estimate of the foregone value to the doctor of the time spent in traveling, plus the expense of his personal transportation (a horse, or horse and buggy). We may assume that time had about the same value for patients as for their physicians. (This assumption probably holds for the nineteenth century, though it would be untenable today because of the high median income of physicians relative to the population at large.) Thus the monetary value doctors assigned to travel may give us an estimate of the indirect prices faced by patients when they called on the doctor.

Nineteenth-century fee bills vary from one region to another, especially between urban and rural areas, but the importance of indirect prices is evident everywhere. A few examples will suffice to make the point. In 1843 in Addison County, Vermont, the fee for each visit by a doctor was 50 cents at less than half a mile; $1.00 between a half mile and two miles; $1.50 between two and four miles; $2.50 between four and six miles and so on. In Mississippi the same year, according to a report in a Boston journal, a visit cost $1, while the charge for travel was $1 per mile during the day ($2 at night).[24] These ratios between charges for service and mileage are typical. Even at relatively short distances, the share of the total price due to traveling and opportunity costs exceeded the physician's ordinary fee; at a distance of five or ten miles, the mileage charges typically amounted to four or five times the basic fee for a visit.[25]

For major services, the indirect price became less significant; the fee for serious operations could overshadow the charge for mileage. So indi-

rect prices especially limited use of physicians' services in routine illness. In rural areas, many families would not think of calling in a doctor
except under the most grave conditions.

When patients were treated at home, before the advent of the telephone, the doctor had to be summoned in person. So the costs of travel
were often doubled, as two people, the physician and an emissary, had
to make the trip back and forth. Furthermore, since the doctor was
often out on calls, there was no guarantee that he would be found when
someone went in search of him. A doctor from the District of Columbia,
observing that no physician in Washington during the 1840s or 1850s
kept regular office hours, later recalled, "Patients and other persons
wishing to consult [a doctor] waited at irregular times for indefinite periods, or went away and came back, or followed in pursuit in the direction last seen, and sometimes waited at houses to which it was known
the doctor would come. . . . The only certain time at which one could
be found was when [one was] in bed and had not instructed the servant
to deny the fact."[26]

Before the construction of hard roads, according to one Illinois practitioner, "The doctor did not often go more than ten miles from his
home."[27] Within that radius were a limited number of patients. The size
of the market might be enough to keep village practitioners hard at
work, but not enough to enable them to set the terms of business and
limit their practice to an office. The doctor of the early and mid-
nineteenth century passed much of his day (and many of his nights)
traveling along back country roads. Autobiographies of nineteenth-
century doctors dwell on these long periods of solitude and the weari-
ness that often came over them on their rides. As one doctor put it, he
spent "half of his life in the mud and the other half in the dust."[28] In
several nineteenth-century fee schedules, a fee for an entire day's attendance by a doctor is given as $5 or $10. (The average daily income
for doctors, depending on locality, probably fell within or below this
range.) These same fee schedules list the charge for an office visit at
$1.00 or $1.50.[29] It seems likely, therefore, that doctors in the early and
mid-1800s were seeing no more than an average of five to seven patients
a day (in urban areas perhaps more, in rural areas less).

The high costs of travel contributed to the individualism and isolation
of medical practice. The country practitioner had to rely on his own
devices; consultations were not readily available. Practitioners might
be long out of touch with new developments; or if apprised of them,
completely on their own in carrying them out. "The first appendec-
tomy many a doctor saw was the first he himself performed after this

operation came into use in the late 1880s and the 1890s," remarks a historian of medicine in Oregon.[30]

As more Americans and more physicians began to live in larger towns
and cities, they came in closer contact with both their patients and their
colleagues. The proportion of Americans living in towns of 2,500 or
more increased from just 6 percent in 1800 to 15 percent by 1850; it then
jumped to 37 percent in 1890 and 46 percent in 1910.[31] In the late nineteenth century, doctors moved to cities even more rapidly than the
population as a whole. Between 1870 and 1910, the number of physicians
per 100,000 people grew from 177 to 241 in the large cities, while it fell
from 160 to 152 in the rest of the country—this during a time when the
overall ratio of doctors to population was still increasing.[32]

The rise of cities was brought about partly by the building of canals
and the development of steamboats and railroads. This "transportation
revolution" widened the markets of cities and enabled the larger and
stronger producers to penetrate what were previously fragmented local
markets. On a more modest scale, the railroads and the telegraph
helped widen doctors' markets by expanding the territory they could
cover. This proved a boon especially to consultants; one mentions log-
ging ten thousand miles of railroad travel in a half year.[33] If the railroad
did not take physicians all the way to their destination, a carriage might
be waiting for them when they alighted. Doctors were such frequent
users of railroads that some treated injuries to railroad workers in exchange for a travel pass. The railroads also brought in patients from a
distance and naturally doctors wanted to be in towns along the routes
to enjoy the benefits. In cities, they had a similar incentive to locate
along the routes followed by streetcars.[34]

The transportation revolution of the nineteenth century has generally been considered from the standpoint of regional and long-distance
flows of commodities, information, and even disease. But there was also
a revolution in local travel. One historian remarks, "The automobile
and the telephone did not greatly lower the cost of transportation as
had been the case with the railroad in the 19th century."[35] Though this
may be true of inter-city transportation between two points along main
routes, it does not apply to local travel.

The telephone made it less costly to reach a physician by greatly reducing the time formerly spent tracking down the peripatetic practitioner on foot. Phones first became available in the late 1870s. Curiously,
the first rudimentary telephone exchange on record, built in 1877, connected the Capital Avenue Drugstore in Hartford, Connecticut, with
twenty-one local doctors.[36] (Drugstores had often served as message

centers for physicians.) The first telephone line in Rochester, Minnesota, set up in December 1879, connected the farmhouse of Dr. William Worrall Mayo with Geisinger and Newton's drugstore downtown.[37] As telephones became more widespread, families could, of course, keep continually in touch with the doctor without a visit. In an apt analogy, one manual for medical practice in 1923 commented that the telephone had become as necessary to the physician as the stethoscope.[38]

As automobiles, first produced in the 1890s, became more reliable after the turn of the century, they further reduced time lost in travel. Doctors were among the earliest to buy cars. Physicians who wrote to the *Journal of the American Medical Association*, which published several supplements on automobiles between 1906 and 1912, reported that an auto cut the time required for house calls in half. "It is the same as if the day had forty-eight hours instead of twenty-four," a doctor from Iowa rejoiced.[39] "Besides making calls in one-half the time," wrote a physician from Oklahoma, "there is something about the auto that is infatuating, and the more you ride the more you want to ride."[40] In a 1910 survey of readers that drew 324 replies concerning automobiles, three out of five doctors said they had increased their income; answering a slightly different question, four out of five agreed that it "pays to own a car." The survey asked physicians using either automobiles or horses to give their annual mileage and costs, including maintenance and depreciation. The 96 physicians still using horses reported costs that work out to 13 cents a mile; for the 116 who owned low-priced cars (under $1,000), the cost per mile was 5.6 cents. It came to 9 cents for 208 doctors who owned cars priced over $1,000. However, the initial investment in purchasing a car was greater than in buying a horse.[41] "To assert that it costs no more to run a car than to keep up a team is absurd," insisted one physician. "But if one considers the time saved on the road, and the consequent additional business made possible, to say nothing of the lessened discomfort, a busy practitioner will find a large balance on the side of the motor car."[42]

Besides saving time, the automobile, like the railroad, widened the doctors' market geographically. In 1912, a Chicago physician noted that the residential mobility of patients required doctors to drive a car. "Chicago today is a city of flats [apartments], and people move so, that a patient living within a block today may be living five miles away next month. It is impossible to hold one's business unless one can answer calls quickly, and this is impossible without a motor car. I have not only held my own, but have increased my business by making distant calls promptly . . . [averaging] about 75 miles a day . . ."[43]

Just as telephones, automobiles, and hard roads enabled physicians to cut down on traveling costs, so they enabled patients to do the same in visiting doctors' offices. Reduced traveling time in both directions cut the cost of medical care and raised the supply of physicians' services, by increasing the proportion of doctors' time available for contact with patients.

The reduction of indirect prices from the local transportation revolution and the rise of cities put medical care within the income range of more people; in this way, it had the same effect as cost reductions from new technology in manufacturing. Underlying the shift from household to market in manufactured goods were radical changes in productivity that drastically altered relative prices. In the production of textiles, for example, family manufacture was virtually eliminated in a remarkably short period. In 1815 the power loom was introduced in Massachusets; by 1830 the price of ordinary brown shirting had fallen from 42 to 7.5 cents a yard. A woman at home could weave 4 yards of the cloth in a day; one worker in a factory, tending several power looms, could turn out 90 to 160 yards daily. There was no way women at home could compete.[44]

In medicine, no radical or sudden change in technology drastically cut the cost of producing physicians' services; there was only the gradual erosion of indirect prices that came from more rapid transportation and more concentrated urban life. Though difficult to measure, the "productivity" of physicians (measured simply as services to patients per day) significantly increased. I mentioned before that physicians probably averaged no more than five to seven patients a day in the mid-nineteenth century. In contrast, by the early 1940s, the average load of general practitioners, rural and urban, was about eighteen to twenty-two patients daily.[45] Such figures suggest a gain in productivity for practicing doctors on the order of 300 percent. For surgeons, the gains have been much larger, considering the infrequency of surgery before antisepsis.

The local transportation revolution also improved the efficacy of treatment by reducing the isolation of medical practice. It made possible more rapid intervention in emergencies, and the ambulance was meant to accelerate that process. Reduced distances may also have had a psychological effect: Increasingly, one came to expect the doctor's intervention. Improved access ultimately brought greater dependency.

WORK, TIME AND THE SEGREGATION OF DISORDER

A second development also contributed to the saving of professional time and the expansion of professional opportunities. This was the growing concentration of patients in institutions. I have already mentioned that the development of large hospitals in Paris in the early nineteenth century was a factor in the emergence of modern clinical investigation. For both economic and scientific reasons, the rise of hospitals was a key precondition for the formation of a sovereign profession. In the case of psychiatry, hospitals constituted the basic framework of professionalism. There was no private practice in psychiatry in the early nineteenth century. The mental asylum created not only a new institutional market for doctors, but also a new sphere in which they could exercise authority.

In the early nineteenth century, there was little demand for the services of general hospitals in America. Almost no one who had a choice sought hospital care. Hospitals were regarded with dread, and rightly so. They were dangerous places; when sick, people were safer at home. The few who became patients went into hospitals because of special circumstances, which generally had to do with isolation of one kind or another from the networks of familial assistance. They might be seamen in a strange port, travelers, homeless paupers, or the solitary aged— those who, traveling or destitute, were unlucky enough to fall sick without family, friends, or servants to care for them. Isolation was also related, but in a converse fashion, to the kindred institutions of pesthouse and asylum. There, isolation (or respite) from the community was the intent rather than the occasion of removal to an institution.

The rise of mental hospitals followed closely upon the rise of cities in America. In the colonial period, the mentally ill, along with other classes of dependents, were treated as a local responsibility, primarily within their own or other families. The growth of cities in the early nineteenth century changed the character of the problem. An increase in scale brought higher concentrations of the insane, the breakdown of informal controls, and a greater demand for order and security. The first of the new institutions for the mentally ill in America were philanthropic. Originally intended to serve the entire community, they gradually became oriented to the more affluent, as their resources proved inadequate to make available free care to the indigent. Beginning in the 1820s, some purely proprietary asylums were also opened for the insane from prosperous families. In the late 1820s, studies of public welfare recommended a general shift from "outdoor" relief (in homes) to "indoor" relief (in institutions); the expansion of asylums under state authority began in the next decade. By the 1840s a psychiatric profession had begun to appear. As Gerald Grob suggests, the institutions played a greater role in shaping psychiatry in the nineteenth century than psychiatry played in shaping the institutions.[46]

The explanation for the emergence of specialized institutions for the mentally ill is not, of course, strictly demographic. The need for urban security might have been met by other means, such as the expansion of almshouses. But the changes in material life in the late eighteenth and early nineteenth centuries took place against the backdrop of greater optimism about the plasticity of human nature. During the French Revolution, reforms introduced into the treatment of the mentally ill expressed a new conviction that the insane could be cured rather than simply restrained. The new "moral treatment" of Pinel in France was introduced independently by Tuke in England. Americans were acquainted with these efforts, and the broader religious and ideological currents in American society favored the same kind of positive effort to cure. Although the new treatment in all three countries was as much moral as medical, the leading figures were physicians.[47]

For American doctors, mental asylums offered important opportunities. Superintendents received between $1,000 and $2,000 a year.[48] Moreover, asylums offered the physician the chance to exercise judgment and control in a sphere where there was relatively little resistance to his authority. Some of the superintendents also used their positions as platforms from which they lectured the public on the relationship of mental illness, vice, and the disorders of modern civilization. Although, by the 1840s, most superintendents were doctors, they kept aloof from other physicians. And, increasingly, as mental hospitals shifted from therapeutic to custodial functions, psychiatry became primarily an administrative rather than a medical specialty.[49]

Although the earliest general hospitals predate mental asylums, the period of most rapid growth occurred about a half century later. In 1873 a government survey counted fewer than 200 hospitals. By 1910 over four thousand were counted, and by 1920 more than six thousand.[50]

Changes in both the family and the hospital affected their relative capacity to manage treatment of the sick. The separation of work from residence made it more difficult to attend the sick at home. With industrialization and high geographic mobility in America, the conjugal family also became more isolated from the threads of kinship, and so fewer relatives were close by in case of illness. To say, however, that there was a shift from an extended to a nuclear family in the nineteenth century may exaggerate the degree of change. Average household size declined from 5.7 persons in 1790 to 4.8 in 1900. On the whole, family structure seems to have had a "modern" shape in America even before industrialization.[51] But significant change did take place in the size of upper-class households. In 1790 in Salem, Massachusetts, the households of merchants averaged 9.8 persons, master carpenters 6.7, and laborers 5.4. By the end of the nineteenth century, families in different classes were equally small.[52] Well-to-do households diminished in size because of the decline in the number of domestic servants as well as children. Also, urban growth led to higher property values, forcing many families to abandon private houses for apartments in multi-family dwellings, which limited their ability to set aside rooms for sickness or childbirth. A 1913 analysis of the decline of home care of the sick noted, "Fewer families occupy a single dwelling, and the tiny flat or contracted apartment no longer is sufficient to accommodate sick members of the family. . . . The sick are better cared for [in hospitals] with less waste of energy, and their presence in the home does not interrupt the occupations and exhaust the means of wage earners . . . The day of the general home care of the sick can never return."[53]

Industrialization and urban life also brought an increase in the number of unattached individuals living alone in cities. In Boston between 1880 and 1900, boarding and lodging house keepers rose in number from 601 to 1,570, almost double the rate of population growth for the city. An array of new establishments—laundries, eating places, tailors—sprang up to meet the needs of this class. The hospital, as Morris Vogel points out, was one of these "corollary" institutions. In England and America, many of the first hospitals to care for private patients were built with lodgers and apartment-house dwellers especially in mind.[54]

All these changes meant less labor power and physical space at home to handle the acutely ill. Talcott Parsons and Renée Fox have further speculated that the modern urban family lost some of its emotional capacity to deal with illness. They argue that the small size and increased isolation of the conjugal family make it peculiarly vulnerable to strains created by illness: One member of the family cannot be attended at home without draining emotional support and attention from the others. When one becomes ill, others are often likely to be overly indulgent, inviting perpetuation of sickness, or possibly overly severe, disrupting recovery. Illness, they suggest, has become an increasingly attractive "semi-legitimate channel" of withdrawal from daily routines. And so the growth of hospitals can be explained as the emergence of an alternative mechanism to handle these motivational problems to encourage recovery and the resumption of normal obligations.[55]

Working-class households did not undergo the changes in size and structure that this line of argument presumes. They were small even before the nineteenth century because of high infant mortality and the early departure of children into the labor force. But the Parsons-Fox hypothesis seems more plausible when restricted to the middle and upper social strata. One newspaper account in 1900, emphasizing that hospitals were "A Boon Not Only to the Poor But to the Well-to-do," describes them as affording "great relief to the family from physical as well as mental strain." Observed a hospital director, "It can be put down as one of the advantages of a hospital that the relatives and friends do not take care of the patients. It is much better for them not to be under the care of anyone who is overconcerned for them."[56]

From the beginning of the industrial era, changes in work and family structure probably created a growing disposition in favor of extra-familial care. However, the dangers of infection in general hospitals led families to manage physical illness at home if they could possibly do so. The reforms in hospital hygiene and the advent of antiseptic surgery both came after the Civil War and probably account for the delay in the growth of general hospitals until after the mental asylum had become widely accepted. General hospitals were also more directly affected by changes in transportation. In an unmechanized rural society, the general hospital is inaccessible in most cases of short-term acute illness, but use of a mental hospital depends less on quick access. Because of its relation to broad cultural concerns over the stability of the social order, the mental asylum has had a different history from the general hospital. The asylum could serve the public functions of the control and confinement of mental disorder when the general hospital was still unsuitable for illnesses of a more purely physical character.

Both institutions relieved the household of obligations that interfered with employment in the market economy. The segregation of sickness and insanity, childbirth and death was part of a rationalization of everyday life—the exclusion from daily experience of disturbances and strains that made difficult participation in the routine of industrial society. The segregation of disorder also reflected the growing tendency to exclude pain from public view. As John Stuart Mill once remarked, "One of the effects of civilization (not to say one of the ingredients in it) is, that the spectacle, and even the very idea of pain, is more and more kept out of the sight of those classes who enjoy in their fullness the benefits of civilization."[57]

Yet this very deep-run current to segregate pain and illness as private events reinforced the desire of more prosperous families to receive physicians in the privacy of their own homes, rather than go to the more public setting of the office or hospital. The different loci of medical care had different moral connotations. Treatment in offices and hospitals was generally regarded as a mark of lower status. It is a measure of the changing position of the profession and medicine's success in overcoming the feelings of delicacy accentuated by the Victorian sensibility that this stigma was gradually overcome. By the turn of the century, the office and the hospital were losing their traditional moral taint, and the home was in decline as a place for physicians' services. Again, economic considerations were partly at work. The telephone made it much easier for patients to see physicians at their offices at a prearranged time, reducing the risk of dropping in while the doctor was out on call; it also made office practice more attractive to doctors, who could now make orderly appointment hours and see more patients than when relying on an uneven stream, or trickle, to their door. As physicians' incomes rose relative to the population at large, patients had an increased incentive to substitute their own travel time for that of the doctors. The shift from home to office was also encouraged by the growing use of clinical equipment and ancillary personnel. And as the doctors' social position rose, they increasingly expected the patient not to waste their time, which had become so much more valuable.

The concentration of patients in hospitals and offices (and the relocation of physicians' offices next to hospitals) added to the effects of urbanization and improved transport: The space in which the physician worked became steadily more compressed. The doctor of the nineteenth century was a local traveler who knew the interior of his patients' homes and private lives more deeply than did others in the community. By the early twentieth century, many physicians went to work at hospitals or offices and had little contact with the homes or living conditions of the patients they treated. These radical changes in the ecology of medical practice enabled physicians to squeeze unproductive time out of their working day. This had obvious advantages. One physician commented in 1909 that "as a matter of dollars and cents I can attend ten patients in a hospital at less cost to myself than I can attend to perhaps three cases outside, because in a few minutes I can go through the whole hospital list, whereas, in the three cases outside, no two of them might be nearer together than two or three miles."[58]

The local transportation revolution, urbanization and the rise of hospitals widened the medical market and created new opportunities for physicians. Among these was specialization. The division of labor, as Adam Smith pointed out in his key discovery in *The Wealth of Nations,* varies according to the extent of the market. As the medical market grew, so did the opportunity and the incentive to specialize. Specialization gives producers partial relief from competition and enables them to take advantage of whatever comparative advantage they may enjoy. The specialist typically gives up those services offering the lowest return and concentrates on those offering the highest. In medicine, these are often services performed in hospitals because of the indirect savings in time to the physician and the standard of higher fees for procedures that are or were at one time complex.

The changing ecology of medical practice thus had tremendous economic significance in enabling physicians to reduce their unit costs, to increase the volume of their practice, and to specialize. But these were not the only effects of changes in the market. The same changes that brought increased opportunities also brought greater competition.

THE MARKET AND PROFESSIONAL AUTONOMY

The expansion of the market made possible a transformation of the profession but did not guarantee it. While demand for services grew, so did the supply of professional time. Not only did doctors continue to become more plentiful, but each doctor represented more medical service as a result of the squeezing of wasted time from the professional working day. Furthermore, midwives and other practitioners who specialized in tasks claimed by physicians could potentially share in the growth of the medical market. The concentration of patients in hospitals might give hospitals control of doctors. Physicians stood to benefit only if they could control the supply of practitioners, the division of labor, and their own relation to organizations.

The effect of improved transportation was also to expose doctors to more competition from nearby colleagues. The practitioner in a small town who formerly enjoyed a monopoly, albeit a small one, now had to worry that his patients might use a practitioner or a hospital in another town. As improvements in transportation and communication put a larger market within reach of the practitioner, they also put the practitioner within reach of competition from his peers and distant institutions.

The same processes were at work throughout the economy in the nineteenth century. Local businessmen continually found their markets invaded by outsiders. The widening of industrial markets brought about by the railroads was analogous to the increased radius of medical practice brought about by railroads, automobiles, and telephones. As the local businessman struggled to survive the rise of the big corporation, so the small-town general practitioner had to contend with the increased accessibility of the urban specialist and hospital.

The expansion of the market affected the development of medicine in Europe as well as America, but the impact was somewhat different. In England, the rise of a middle-class market for medical care contributed to a decline in the dependence of doctors on aristocratic patrons. "The widening of the market for professional services," writes the S. W. F. Holloway in an account of changes in English medicine between 1830 and 1858, "had a profound effect upon the relationship between the practitioner and his clients. As the demand for medical care increased, the importance for the doctor's livelihood of any one patient declined. Instead of a small group of wealthy and aristocratic patients, the market now comprised a large and growing section of society. . . . In the eighteenth century the patient was the dominant figure in the relationship; in the nineteenth century the power positions were reversed."[59]

The traditional hierarchy of English medicine broke down in the mid-nineteenth century as a consequence of these economic developments and the impact of new scientific advances that began in France. By the 1830s the leading surgeons were no longer confining themselves to manual operation, but were also practicing as physicians. At the same time, the emergence of concepts of localized pathology and modern techniques of clinical examination made it difficult for physicians to continue refusing to perform any manual procedures. An increasing number of physicians and surgeons began engaging in "general practice" (as it was now being called) among the growing middle classes. The line between these general practitioners and the apothecaries became unclear, especially as apothecaries could now receive a higher education at University College London. In fact, two out of every five members of the College of Surgeons also held a license from the Society of Apothecaries. The preface to a medical directory in 1847 noted that the traditional system of classification had become "almost obsolete." Physicians, surgeons, and apothecaries were "by the force of a public convenience they cannot withstand, being gradually classed into Consulting and General Practitioners."[60] In 1858 Parliament created a a single register for all medical practitioners and a council to coordinate all medical education in the United Kingdom. This was the key step in the emergence of an autonomous and unified medical profession in Great Britain. American doctors would wait another half century for an analogous breakthrough in medical education and state support.

CHAPTER THREE

The Consolidation of Professional Authority 1850–1920

MOST studies of social mobility follow the movement of individuals or families through the socioeconomic order. They generally take for granted the relative positions of occupations and classes, as if the structure of society remained fixed and only the fate of individuals varied. For many purposes, this is a convenient fiction. But it obscures the movements that classes and occupational groups themselves have made through social hierarchies. These instances of collective social mobility reshape the structure of society and set new terms for the realization of personal ambition. Just as behind the apparently fixed contours of a landscape lie great historic shifts and upheavals in the earth, so behind the seeming permanence of a social order lie the past struggles of classes and other groups negotiating for advantage.

The rise of medicine, and of the professions more generally, represents one of the more striking instances of collective mobility in recent history. The historical success of a profession rests fundamentally on the growth of its particular source of wealth and status—its authority. Acknowledged skills and cultural authority are to the professional classes

what land and capital are to the propertied. They are the means of securing income and power. For any group, the accumulation of authority
requires the resolution of at least two distinct problems. One is the internal problem of consensus; the other is the external problem of legitimacy. These are necessary but not sufficient conditions for success. Consensus facilitates the articulation of common interests and the
mobilization of group effort, while respect and deference, especially
from the more powerful classes, open the way to resources and legally
sanctioned privileges.

A profession, as I earlier suggested, differs from other occupations in
part by its ability to set its own rules and standards. But it cannot do
so unless its members agree, first, on criteria for belonging to the profession and, second, on what its rules and standards ought to be. Before
convincing the public and the state of the legitimacy of their claims to
self-regulation, physicians had to reach some agreement among themselves. Perhaps the foremost obstacle to the collective authority of the
medical profession in mid-nineteenth-century America arose within its
ranks. Mutual hostility among practitioners, intense competition, differences in economic interest, and sectarian antagonisms held the medical
profession in check. Internally divided, it was incapable of mobilizing
its members for collective action or of winning over public opinion.

While individual practitioners enjoyed autonomy, not to say isolation,
they prospered—or more likely coped—according to their own wits:
The profession of medicine did not endow its members automatically
with public respect. In the early nineteenth century, as we have already
seen, physicians had failed to establish clear boundaries marking off
members of the profession from untrained and "irregular" practitioners. Internecine hatreds were rife. When Samuel Gross, later a famous
surgeon, took up practice in the town of Easton, Pennsylvania, in the
early 1830s, he found the local practitioners busy with enmity. "Every
man seemed to live in and for himself. Hardly any two could be found
willing to meet each other in consultation. Jealousy and ill-feeling were
the order of the day."[1]

The failure of doctors to establish any effective authority within the
profession or in the society at large profoundly affected their relationships with patients. The doctor in America was more a courtier than
an autocrat. Arpad Gerster, a scholarly and perceptive young Hungar-
ian physician arriving in New York in the 1870s, was struck by the way
American practitioners treated their patients:

As I soon found [he later wrote], physicians in America were more concerned
with establishing a feeling of confidence and trust, hence of comfort in patients,

than were our colleagues abroad. To a great extent, this was a natural consequence of the difference between the status of the physician in the United
States and in Europe. Abroad, the medical degree *per se* invested the physician
with a social standing and authority unknown in America, where, in 1874, the
meager educational requirements made it easy to secure a diploma after "two
sessions of so many weeks a year." With some exceptions, the rank and file of
the profession were—as far as general education went—little, if any, above the
level of their *clientèle*. And the *clientèle* not only felt this, but knew it. Hence
the medical man had to be more than modest; he had to be circumspect, even
deferential, in facing ignorance, absurd pretensions, and ill manners—
especially where they abounded most, among a certain class of the self-made,
uncultured wealthy.[2]

One way of looking at the changes that took place between the 1870s
and the early 1900s is that the social distance between doctor and patient increased, while the distance among colleagues diminished as the
profession became more cohesive and uniform. The state, which had
been indifferent to physicians' claims since the Jacksonian era, finally
embraced the profession's definition of a legitimate practitioner. All
these developments reflected a movement toward the strengthening
of professional status and the consolidation of professional authority.

PHYSICIANS AND SOCIAL STRUCTURE IN MID-NINETEENTH-CENTURY AMERICA

Class

Before the twentieth century, the role of doctor did not confer a clear
and unequivocal class position in American society. There was considerable inequality among those who practiced medicine, perhaps as much
as in the communities where they lived. Instead of locating medicine
at a particular point in a hierarchy of occupations, it might be more accurate to say that the inequalities among doctors paralleled the class
structure. To the wealthier families, there corresponded an elite of the
medical profession; to the poor, practitioners of lower status and less
training. The social position of the majority of doctors was not low, but
it was insecure and ambiguous. A physician's standing depended as
much on his family background and the status of his patients as on the
nature of his occupation. Education, too, was a salient though probably
secondary criterion of social distinction (secondary because higher education depended on family background). The men at the top of the pro-

fession had graduated from medical schools—the most prestigious having gone to Europe for part of their training—while practitioners in the
lowest ranks were often no more than autodidacts. In the middle were
the rank and file, the great majority of doctors, who had served apprenticeships and perhaps taken a course of lectures or a two-term medical
degree, but who had little general education. The transformation the
profession eventually underwent consisted not so much in raising the
status of those at the top, as in raising the middle and eliminating the
bottom altogether. And achieving some uniformity within the profession helped to make the practice of medicine itself, apart from one's
family origins or clientele, a sufficient condition for high social position.

From the Jacksonian period through the end of the nineteenth century, a medical career did not carry the prestige and guaranteed security
it does today. In 1832 J. Marion Sims, who would later become one of
America's foremost surgeons, returned home to his family in South Carolina after graduating from college. His mother, who had recently died,
had wanted him to become a clergyman; his father hoped he would become a lawyer. Sims wanted to be neither, and felt that if he had to
take up a profession, medicine would make the fewest demands on his
frail talents. "If I had known this," his father exclaimed in an outburst
that might amuse parents today, "I certainly should not have sent you
to college. . . . it is a profession for which I have the utmost contempt.
There is no science in it. There is no honor to be achieved in it; no reputation to be made."[3] A similar story comes from S. Weir Mitchell, a leading neurologist and genteel novelist, who, as a young man, first thought
of entering chemical manufacturing. His father, a physician, suggested
commerce, and Mitchell might well have entered an English cousin's
trading firm had not the cousin died in a shipwreck. "After a while my
father more distinctly insisted on a choice, and I at last decided to be
a doctor, much to his disgust."[4]

Perhaps both Sims and Mitchell, savoring the irony, embellished their
father's reactions, but the incidents were not implausible. Many people
thought of medicine as an inferior profession, or at least as a career with
inferior prospects. In 1851 a committee of the recently formed American Medical Association (AMA) reported the results of a study it had
made of the careers followed by 12,400 men who had graduated between 1800 and 1850 from eight leading colleges (Amherst, Brown,
Dartmouth, Hamilton, Harvard, Princeton, Union, and Yale). While 26
percent became clergymen and a similar proportion were thought to
have entered law, under 8 percent became physicians. Furthermore,
the proportion going into medicine was lower among students who
graduated with honors than among students in general. The committee

thought these figures indicative of a general distaste for medicine among the "educated talent" of the country.[5] As late as 1870 a medical journal remarked that when a young man of merit and ability chose to become a doctor "the feeling among the majority of his cultivated friends is that he has thrown himself away."[6]

This may exaggerate the picture. Physicians were often influential figures in their communities. The elite of the medical profession may well have had more civic importance in the earlier periods of American history than it does today. Of the first one hundred members of the Medical Society of New Jersey, organized in 1766, seventeen eventually became members of Congress or the state legislature.[7] Four medical practitioners—Benjamin Rush, Josiah Bartlett, Lyman Hall, and Matthew Thornton—signed the Declaration of Independence; twenty-six other doctors were members of the Continental Congress. Historically, the number of Congressmen trained as physicians was actually highest in the earliest years of the Republic. Between 1800 and the Civil War, at least seven and usually twelve to eighteen physicians served in Congress. In the early decades of the twentieth century, the number ranged between six and ten. In recent decades, there have been at most four or five, in spite of the singularly high income and status of the medical profession in our day.[8]

The explanation for this decline seems relatively clear. In the earlier years, professional roles were much less specialized, and professional training was not as long and arduous as it is now. It was common for professional men, whether in law, medicine or divinity, to take on many roles. The educated were few and physicians a relatively high proportion of them. Since medicine was much less remunerative, the incentive to become politically engaged was relatively greater. Today, the demands of professional careers no longer permit the same easy interchange of roles that characterized a less industrialized and less differentiated society. The educated are more numerous and more specialized. The status of physicians has risen, but their prominence has diminished. They are less evident in politics and public affairs, which cannot easily offer them the economic rewards and security of medical practice.

The social and political fortunes of the professional elite should, in any event, not be confused with the situation of the larger body of medical practitioners. The prominence of a few notables says no more about a profession than the wealth and prestige of a handful of celebrated painters and musicians says about the general condition of artists in a society. Yet the distance between the middle and the top of a profession is itself a fact of interest, and among nineteenth-century physicians that distance was so great that doctors cannot be said to have belonged to a single social class.

Medicine then rarely offered a path to wealth. Physicians who were rich typically had inherited fortunes or made money from commercial enterprises. Even at the close of a successful career, noted a writer in 1831, professional fees "hardly compare with the profits of one fortunate voyage, or the successful operations of a single day on the exchange."[9] J. Marion Sims, even after some years as a doctor, was ready to abandon the field should a good opportunity open up "because I knew that I could never make a fortune out of the practice of medicine."[10] Data from Rochester, New York, suggest the financial position of physicians in that community was actually declining in the mid-nineteenth century. In 1836, when two thirds of Rochester practitioners were property owners, their property was worth an average of $2,400, while the average value of all property per voter was $1,420. But in 1860 the proportion of property-owning physicians fell to one third, and their property averaged out at $1,500, the same as for all voters. Among 455 Rochester men who reported income of more than $1,000 in 1865, there were only eleven physicians and, among these, only four regular practitioners.[11]

Estimates of physicians' incomes, while scattered and fragmentary, present a relatively consistent picture. The few physicians who counted their incomes in the thousands were clearly atypical. In 1850, in a much noted report on public health, Lemuel Shattuck wrote that the average Massachusetts practitioner had billings of about $800 and earned about $600 in income.[12] By way of comparison, the budget for a working family of five, printed in the *New York Daily Tribune* in 1851, gave its annual expenditures as $538.44.[13] This level of expenditure, however, was probably within the reach only of skilled workers; the average annual earnings of nonfarm employees for 1860 were an estimated $363.[14] One economist suggests that incomes in the working class around 1860 ranged from $200 to $800, in the middle class from $800 to $5,000, and among the rich between $5,000 and $10,000.[15] This would put most doctors at the lower end of the middle class. In 1861 the city physician of Chicago, then a city of 134,000, was paid an annual salary of $600.[16] In 1871 a Detroit journal estimated that the average doctor earned $1,000 a year.[17](Prices that year, however were 40 percent above 1860 levels, still showing the residual effects of Civil War inflation.) In 1888 a doctor ruefully observed, "Even with continued health and strength, a physician in this country can never possibly acquire by his toil the incomes readily made in other occupations now recognized as professions."[18] In 1901 a financial handbook for doctors put the earning of an average city physician at $730 and those of a country doctor at $1,200.[19] Another guide, in editions from 1890 to 1905, estimated the average physician's income at between $1,000 and $1,500, and noted that every older physician knew it was impossible to get rich by practicing medicine, except in a money-making specialty.[20] In 1904 the *Journal of the American Medical Association* observed that an average income for a doctor was about $750, though this may have been a self-serving underestimate.[21]

That same year, average earnings in all occupations, excluding farm labor, were $540; federal employees averaged just over $1,000; ministers, $759.[22] A magazine article in 1903 commented that doctors often earned less than an "ordinary mechanic."[23] This no doubt understated their average income, but it reflected a widespread perception that doctors were not particularly well off. It seems unlikely they earned more than other professionals.

Status

Whatever a physician earned, even in the 1800s he was still a professional man and this lent him a higher status than manual workers. Two dimensions of social ranking need to be kept separate: differences in wealth and income (objective access to scarce resources) and differences in honor, deference, and prestige (favorable or unfavorable social evaluations). The former corresponds roughly to the concept of class; the latter to that of status. Property and income should not necessarily be taken as accurate indicators of honor and prestige. The status of the medical profession, though insecure, was probably higher than its objective economic situation might suggest. This incongruity created a distinctive strain. On the one hand, physicians felt a need to maintain an image of a cultivated, respectable, learned profession; on the other, the reality was that many doctors had little education and often, when starting out in practice, could barely support themselves. In the face of financial pressures, the American physician was obliged to take on various kinds of work, like pharmacy and midwifery, that many of his European counterparts would have regarded as beneath their dignity. The village doctor was not above looking after his farmer's livestock as well as his family. He pulled teeth, sat up all night with patients, and embalmed the dead—functions later spun off to dentists, nurses, and undertakers.

Like many people whose position in society is somewhat precarious, physicians were much concerned to maintain a front of propriety and respectability. There is perhaps no more acute testimony to the status anxieties of late nineteenth-century doctors than the popular manual for medical practice by D. W. Cathell, *The Physician Himself*, which

ran through numerous editions beginning in 1881. Cathell gave elaborate attention to the establishing of a proper distance between doctors
and their clients. Physicians could not allow people to get overly familiar with them. Conviviality, he warned, "has a levelling effect, and di-
vests the physician of his proper prestige." Appearing in public in shirts-
leeves, unwashed and unkempt, was unwise because it would "show
weakness, diminish your prestige, detract from your dignity, and lessen
you in public esteem, by forcing on everybody the conclusion that you
are, after all, but an ordinary person."[24]

Manuals of personal advice generally come in two varieties: vague,
uplifting, moralistic treatises filled with tedious pieties; and no-
nonsense, amoral guidebooks to getting on in the world. Cathell's manual fell into the second category, and consisted fundamentally of rules
for what Erving Goffman has called "impression management." In the
interests of presenting an idealized image of the physician, it attached
paramount importance to his manner and appearance. "If one is especially polished in manner and moderately well versed in medicine,"
wrote Cathell, "his politeness will do him a great deal more good with
the public than special acquaintance with histology, embryology, and
other ultra-scientific acquirements."[25]

Here as elsewhere, Cathell's standard for judging the value of any
aspect of a physician's behavior or personality was the effect it would
have on public opinion. This concern reflected the situation of the average doctor, who depended for his livelihood on public favor, rather than
the judgment of his professional brethren or bureaucratic superiors. Because most physicians were independent general practitioners, doing
basically the same kinds of work, they acquired business through a lay
referral network, rather than from colleagues, as do specialists, or from
organizational affiliations, as do physicians employed by institutions. Cathell's physician was basically on his own, at the mercy of lay judgment
and anxious to curry good will.

The result was a preoccupation with the image that physicians projected to clients rather than to colleagues. This frame of reference affected the psychology of medical work. All people, as Goffman says, are
obliged not only to carry out their tasks and routines, but also to *express*
their competence in doing so. Only in some cases, however, does the
expression become more important than the activity itself. Some students so concentrate on appearing attentive, with their eyes open and
pens poised, that they miss everything being said.[26] This is one of the
more familiar pathologies of everyday life, and it appears abundantly
in Cathell's manual. Cathell advises the physician to concern himself
first with expressing his competence and only secondarily with actually

being competent. "Errors of diagnosis and prognosis," he writes in an altogether typical passage, "are ordinarily far more damaging to the physician than errors of treatment. Very few people can discover whether or not your diagnosis and treatment are correct . . . but if you say a patient will recover and he dies, or that he will die and he gets well . . . everybody will see that you are wrong . . . and they will naturally seek out some one with more experience or deeper thought."[27]

For the same reason, a doctor had to be bold and prompt. Simulated spontaneity helps to dramatize social performance. "The public," Cathell wrote, "love to see a physician appear to understand his business fully and to know things intuitively; therefore you must study and practice to be quick in diagnosis and ever ready in the treatment of the ordinary diseases and emergencies that will constitute nine-tenths of your practice."[28] This premium on quick and bold response suggests why doctors were drawn to active and "heroic" intervention, especially when medical knowledge was uncertain.

Cathell's guide portrays physicians as facing a hostile, skeptical, and treacherous world. They had to take precautions against colleagues who might steal their patients and be on guard against "jealous midwives, ignorant doctor-women and busy neighbors," who spread malicious rumors about physicians.[29] Even patients were a threat as potential competitors. At one point, Cathell suggests various ways for physicians to conceal the contents of their prescriptions. "By employing the terms ac. phenicum for carbolic acid, secale cornutum for ergot, kalium for potassium, natrum for sodium, chinin for quinia, etc., you will debar the average patient from reading your prescriptions. . . . You can also further eclipse his wisdom by transposing the terms. . . ." There is some revealing advice about what to do with people who thought they could treat themselves:

Especially avoid giving self-sufficient people therapeutic points that they can thereafter resort to. . . . It is not your duty to cheat either yourself or other physicians out of legitimate practice by supplying this person and that one with a word-of-mouth pharmacopoeia for general use. If compelled to give a person remedies under a simple form, study to do so in such a way as not to increase his self-conceit and make him feel that he knows enough to practice self-medication and dispense with your services; use whatever strategy is necessary to prevent such persons from taking unfair advantage of your prescriptions.

The physician ought to do tests at his office, not at patients' homes, lest they "begin to do tests for themselves—think they know more than they really do, and give you trouble."[30]

Deliberate artifice is the weapon, not of a powerful profession, but of a weak one, which has no confidence in its own authority. Cathell's guide reflects the exceptional insecurity of nineteenth-century doctors, their complete dependence on their clients, and their vulnerability to competition from laymen as well as colleagues. Uncertain of their authority, they were inclined to dissemble and cajole. "The American physician of those days," Gerster recalled of the 1870s, "wielded less authority over his patients than did his European colleagues; he had to endure too much quizzing, and had to waste time in arguing patients into acquiescence."[31] In 1888 one physician, writing in a medical journal about the depressed state of the profession, recounted a futile attempt to explain the importance of color-blindness to the board of directors of a railroad:

They could not or would not understand or admit it. One otherwise pleasant old gentleman sank back in his arm-chair, and with almost a snarl of doubt and derision exclaimed, "Why Dr. Jeffries, I have been railroading more than forty years, now if any such thing as color-blindness existed, I must know all about it."[32]

The inability to command deference was the root of the profession's trouble. Cathell noted that physicians would very likely meet up with "many a presumptuous patient or his keen friend" who would question prescriptions and argue about treatment. "You will be often harrassed and cross-examined by such self-constituted Solomons, and compelled to resort to various expedients to satisfy or foil them, and avoid collisions with their whims, insinuations and prejudices. In fact, from this cause, the good effects of mystery, hope, expectation and will-power are of late almost entirely lost to regular physicians; all special confidence is sapped. . . ."[33] And here Cathell may have had a point. Diminished authority may have cost doctors therapeutic effectiveness as well as social status.

Powerlessness

The stresses and insecurities of nineteenth-century medicine were particularly acute for young physicians. Consider the contrast between a professional career in medicine today and in the 1800s. Now a medical career follows a virtually fixed course. In America, becoming a doctor means four years of liberal arts education, followed by four years of medical school, and an average of four years of supervised hospital training. Standardized national tests must be taken first to get into medical school, then to get through it, and finally to qualify as a certified specialist. The entire process, aptly called "contest mobility," emphasizes academic competition and meritocratic achievement. It has a strong semblance of legitimacy. The students who fail generally believe it is their fault; those who do well interpret their success as the result of ability and hard work. The prolonged training imparts a strong sense of common identity as well as technical skills. The training is difficult, but the social and economic rewards are fairly certain.

The nineteenth century could hardly offer a more vivid contrast. A professional career had no fixed pattern. Whether or not a physician went to medical school and if he did, for how long and with what general education, were all variable. Apprenticeships had no standard content. A medical education was neither as long nor as peer oriented; organized professional socialization was minimal. Few training positions were available in hospitals, and those were not awarded competitively; social connections weighed heavily in selecting candidates. Most young physicians had to strike out on their own, gradually building up a practice. At that early point in a professional career when doctors now spend sleepless nights as overworked interns and residents, their counterparts in the nineteenth century were waiting for their first patients to show up. Often a first location might not work out because of an unfavorable reception or a surplus of local practitioners. Everything depended on the successful courting of patients. The process was difficult, and the social and economic rewards were uncertain.

For the ambitious, status competition in medicine revolved around two major contingencies: the acquisition of socially prominent patients and appointments to medical colleges, hospitals, and dispensaries. Often the two were related, as the socially prominent held positions as trustees of medical institutions and could open the necessary channels of influence. The elite of the profession, even in a fair-sized city, was ordinarily small enough so that its members knew each other. Admission to the group was not easy; the wrong ethnic background was often a categorical disqualification. Family ties could be crucial. The same surnames tend to appear in succeeding generations as the leading doctors of a city: Bigelows, Warrens, Minots, and Jacksons in Boston; or Peppers, Chapmans, and McClellans in Philadelphia.

The professional elite did not necessarily identify its interests with those of ordinary practitioners. On the contrary, they were often scornful of their abilities and character, and anxious to dissociate themselves from their less favored colleagues. The profession in New York City in the years after the Civil War was organized in a series of concentric circles. At the center was the small Medical and Surgical Society, whose thirty-four members held about half the consulting and attending positions at city hospitals and dispensaries. They were known, appropriately enough, as the "hospital men." Next in exclusiveness was the New York Academy of Medicine, with 273 members; last, the county medical society, open to all regular practitioners, of whom there were about eight hundred. The elite played a role in the academy but none in the county society.[34]

Neither the top ranks of physicians nor the bottom had a strong interest in effective medical licensing. The less educated practitioners, who had never been to medical school or had never graduated or held degrees of doubtful quality, feared the laws would be used to exclude them. The elite, on the other hand, stood to gain very little from their enactment. "These physicians," John Shaw Billings pointed out, "whose positions are fairly assured, and who, as a rule, have all the practice they desire, are not usually active leaders in movements to secure medical legislation, although they passively assent to such efforts, or at least do not oppose them; and their names may sometimes be found appended to memorials urging such legislation. They are clear-headed, shrewd, 'practical' men, who know that their business interests are not specifically injured by quacks."[35]

In England, according to W. J. Reader, the impulse for protection in the professions came, not from the highest ranks, but rather from the practitioners just beneath them. The elite was quite content with its gentlemanly, informal way of co-opting members to the royal colleges. It was the men at the edges of the elite who most wanted formal examinations and formal standards.[36] This may also have been the case in America. Billings suggested that the competition of irregular and untrained practitioners was felt most strongly among "young men who have not yet acquired local fame," who accordingly had the "more decided views about the importance of diplomas."[37] When, in 1846, after several false starts, a convention met in New York to plan a national medical association for the United States, it was composed, as its chief organizer, then only twenty-nine, later recalled, "of the younger, more active, and, perhaps, more ambitious members of the profession." This initial session of what would become the leading organization of the profession—the American Medical Association—failed to attract many of the men who customarily took leading roles in professional affairs.[38]

If the AMA owed its impetus to the discontent felt by younger, less established doctors, it nonetheless had a very traditional program. It aimed primarily to raise and standardize the requirements for medical degrees. It also enacted a code of ethics that denied fraternal courtesy to "irregular" practitioners. Several immediate considerations prompted the founding of the association. The call for a convention emerged from discussions of educational reform in the New York State

Medical Society, which concluded that local efforts would inevitably be frustrated. If the schools in New York raised their requirements, students would simply move elsewhere, and only the schools and their professors would suffer. Consequently, a national approach was necessary. Second, because of the repeal of licensing statutes, which had come in New York in 1844, only two years earlier, the orthodox profession could no longer look to the state for protection against what it viewed as the degradation of its standards. Instead, regular physicians would have to turn inward and rely on their own system of regulation. This was the impetus for the AMA's adoption of a code of professional ethics, with its concern for excluding sectarian and untrained practitioners. Denied the state's authority, the orthodox doctors were obliged to rely on their own.

Whatever the objectives of the AMA, it turned out to have little impact during its first half century. The "irregular" physicians accused it of attempting to monopolize medical practice and drive them from the field, and the AMA did have some success in keeping them out of the few medical positions in the federal government. But while monopoly was doubtless the intent of the AMA's program, it was not the consequence. The "irregulars" thrived. The efforts of the AMA at voluntary reform of medical education failed miserably, as the schools would not comply. The AMA had scant resources at its disposition. Its membership was small, it had no permanent organization, its treasury was bare. Its authority was questioned even within the profession. The association met once a year, and then for all practical purposes disappeared. It had an amorphous system of representation, at first drawing delegates from hospitals and medical schools as well as medical societies; once elected, delegates became permanent members, so long as they paid the dues. "A purely voluntary organization," one prominent doctor called it, "without any chartered privileges and with no authority to enforce its own edicts."[39]

The association became so embroiled in political squabbles that the more scientifically minded members split off to form a separate learned society. "We want," said Francis Delafield, the first president of the Association of American Physicians, at its first meeting in 1886, "an association in which there will be no medical politics and no medical ethics; an association in which no one will care who are the officers, and who are not. . . . We want an association composed of members, each one of whom is able to contribute something real to the common stock of knowledge and where he who reads such a contribution feels sure of a discriminating audience."[40] There was no mistaking which group Delafield intended to criticize.

The failure of physicians to generate strong collective organization reflected a deeper structural weakness in the profession. It is all too easy to assume, as some analysts do, that because doctors, or any other group, share some imputed common interest, say, in obtaining a monopoly, they will act coherently to support and defend that interest. Yet any number of factors—competing loyalties; internal conflicts; the inability of the members of a group or class to communicate with one another; the active hostility of the state, church, or other powerful institutions— can prevent the effective articulation of common interests. At a minimum, collective action requires some mechanism for inducing individuals to lay their private affairs aside and devote effort, time, and resources to the group. Paradoxically, the collective ends pursued by organizations usually are not sufficient inducement. Interest-group organizations tend to produce generalized benefits, like favorable public opinion or friendly legislation, that members of a group can enjoy regardless of whether they personally contribute to the organization's activities. Such collective goods encourage individuals to take a "free ride" on others' efforts. To counteract this tendency, organizations have to be able to provide some benefit or penalty, apart from the collective good, that will induce participation. Mancur Olson has called these sanctions "selective incentives."[41]

Selective incentives for participation in professional organization were precisely what nineteenth-century medical societies were missing. Had licensing been placed in their hands, and had a license been essential to practice, they would have had a very powerful inducement. In depriving the medical societies of licensing powers, the states had deprived them of the power to organize and discipline their natural constituency. To be a member of a medical society helped certify the practitioner's social status, but a diploma from a medical college could do the same. Professional organizations languished because they had no leverage over individual doctors.

The medical practitioners of the nineteenth century could get by pretty much on their own. They did not need access to hospital facilities, since very little medical care took place there. The natural inclination of physicians then was to solve their problems individually. They advertised themselves, either by their manner or in the press, or through what economists call "product differentiation" (that is, by offering a distinctive brand of medicine). The orientation of the profession, in short, was *competitive* rather than *corporate*. The forces pulling its members apart prevailed over the common interests that might have held them together.

MEDICINE'S CIVIL WAR AND RECONSTRUCTION

The Origins of Medical Sectarianism

Nothing weakened the medical profession more than the bitter feuds and divisions that plagued doctors through the late nineteenth century. Partly, the hatreds were sectarian; partly, they were personal. They were open and acrimonious, and as common in the high tiers of the profession as in the low. Philadelphia, the center of early American medicine, was a maelstrom of professional ill will. The animosity between John Morgan and William Shippen, Jr., the first two medical professors in the city, was especially notorious. It divided the country's first medical school and then split the medical department of the Continental Army during the Revolutionary War, as the two physicians conspired against each other for control. During the yellow fever epidemic in Philadelphia in 1793, Benjamin Rush and his rivals took to the press to denounce each other's treatment. "A Mahometan and a Jew," Rush wrote, "might as well attempt to worship the Supreme Being in the same temple, and through the medium of the same ceremonies, as two physicians of opposite principles and practice, attempt to confer about the life of the same patient."[42]

Medical colleges were a particularly rich source of fraternal hatred. Since an appointment had great value in increasing the size of a physician's practice, there was inevitably resentment among those excluded. Often the faculty at one school could not abide the faculty of another. Even within the same school professors sometimes refused, as one noted, "to hold any communication with each other except such as their official position as teachers peremptorily demanded, in faculty meeting."[43] The history of medical schools in the nineteenth century is a tale of schisms, conspiracies, and coups, often destroying the institutions in the process. Daniel Drake, who wrote an essay on professional quarrels listing ten different causes, founded a medical college in Ohio, then helped remove some of his colleagues on the faculty, only to find himself ousted in the equivalent of a palace revolt. One of the more colorful imbroglios occurred in 1856 at the Eclectic Medical Institute of Cincinnati, where the professors and their allies among the students split into two factions over the financial management of the school and the introduction of new "concentrated" medications. One party seized control of the school building and locked out its opponents, who then massed outside the doors. "This was the declaration of war," writes the school's historian. "Knives, pistols, chisels, bludgeons, blunderbusses, etc. were freely displayed." The battle was finally settled when one side brought in a six-pound cannon![44]

Physicians were not exactly supposed to behave this way. Professional tradition insisted that doctors present a unified front to the public, no matter how divided they were in private. The AMA's code of ethics, like others before it, prescribed a "peculiar reserve" toward the public in all professional disputes. The code enjoined consulting physicians to discuss cases entirely in secret and to present patients with a single opinion. If two practitioners disagreed, they were supposed either to let the decision rest with the regular attending doctor or to call in a third physician, so patients would never know there had ever been a difference of opinion in their case. Only in hopeless deadlocks were physicians to let patients make a choice.[45] The etiquette of consultations called for the regular attendant to precede the consultant in entering the sick room and to follow him in leaving it, thereby allowing the outsider no time to impugn the regular doctor's ability. Especially during a first consultation, the consultant was supposed to suggest as few changes in treatment as possible to avoid embarrassment. He was to say nothing that might jeopardize the impression of competence the regular doctor was trying to project.[46]

A concern for fostering professional solidarity guided the formulation of professional ethics. Under the code, physicians were to avoid any behavior that might smack of patient stealing, even in their daily activities. So, for example, they were supposed to avoid visiting any sick friends who were under the care of another doctor since that might arouse suspicions; and if they did make such a visit, they were to skirt any discussion of the treatment. Doctors were to give free care to one another and fill in for sick or traveling colleagues. When taking over a case, they were to justify, as far as honesty would permit, the previous doctor's conduct of the case. A wealthy doctor, according to the code, was never to give free advice to the affluent, for this was to deplenish the "common funds" available for support of the profession.

These rules had only mixed success. Bedside controversies among consulting physicians were apparently not unusual. It was a standing joke that no two doctors could ever agree. And the ethical code itself exacerbated divisions because it excluded sectarian physicians from professional courtesy and association.

Of all the divisions that rent the profession, sectarianism was the most virulent. According to the usual explanation, medical sects grew in the mid-nineteenth century because of the inadequacy of contemporary medicine, particularly the disastrous errors of "heroic therapy," which emphasized bleeding, heavy doses of mercury, and other modes of treatment now believed to range from the ineffective to the lethal. No doubt the inadequacy of therapeutics was one reason why physicians disagreed. It fails to explain, however, why disagreements led to sectarian organization. The shortcomings of medical treatment in earlier epochs were grievous, but they did not always produce antagonistic sects. Practitioners who severely disagree do not necessarily read each other out of a profession. Every field of thought or work is subject to great differences of opinion, sometimes violent ones, but only under certain circumstances do those differences generate organized factions.

Sectarianism also has a rather special meaning. A sect, religious or professional, is a dissident group that sets itself apart from an established institution—a church or a profession; its members often see themselves as neglected and scorned apostles of truth. As Troeltsch and Weber point out in distinguishing a sect from a church, sects typically originate in charismatic leadership and have a fundamentally voluntary character. One joins a sect, but one may be born into a church (or graduated into a profession).[47] Medical and religious sects resemble each other in their stipulation of certain definite ideas as requirements for membership, while churches and professions often accept members without closely inquiring into their beliefs. Religious sects, however, typically offer their members a complete way of life, while medical sects are more circumscribed in their concerns.

More than a qualified analogy links religious and medical sects; they often overlap. In the 1830s, the Millerites, a radical perfectionist Protestant sect, had strong leanings toward Thomsonian medicine. The Swedenborgians were inclined toward homeopathic medicine. And the Christian Scientists originated in concerns that were medical as well as religious. In America various religious sects still make active efforts to cure the sick, while the dominant churches are more or less reconciled to the claims of the medical profession and have abandoned healing as part of pastoral care.[48]

For both medicine and religion, the nineteenth century in America was a period of growing sectarianism. The society was not just pluralist, as many have described it, but "pluralizing": It created new divisions as well as incorporating traditional ones. To attribute this tendency to the sheer tolerance and diversity of American life would be ingenuous. Religious denominations multiplied, especially among the less privileged, along the lines of class, sectional, and ethnic antagonisms, as well as differences of theology.[49] Sectarianism intensified not only because American society was open, but also because it was closed. This was probably as true in medicine as in religion. The cliquishness of medical politics encouraged excluded practitioners to generate countermovements to improve their position. A sect, as one analyst points out, serves as a competing "reference-group" for its members, allowing them to seek status and prestige on more favorable terms than are available in the wider society.[50] For the less educated medical practitioner, or for educated immigrant physicians denied access to hospital and medical school appointments, sectarian organization provided an avenue for asserting their claims against the dominant profession. Moreover, because of the competitive conditions of medical practice, doctors had every incentive to differentiate themselves, to make their services distinctive, and to appeal to changing currents of public sentiment.

In the second half of the nineteenth century, after the decline of Thomsonianism, the principal medical sects in America were the Eclectics and homeopaths. The Eclectics, who had absorbed most of the Thomsonian movement, were botanic doctors, though they professed, as their name suggests, to take the best from various schools. They were followers of a New Yorker named Wooster Beach, who like Samuel Thomson had mixed radical politics with herbal medicine (a combination not unknown today). Unlike the Thomsonians, the Eclectics neither denied the importance of scientific training nor hesitated to create their own schools, although they also did not hesitate to destroy them by fighting with one another. The Eclectics accepted and taught most conventional medical science, except that in the area of therapeutics they carried on a vigorous campaign against the excessive drugging and bleeding of the regular profession. All but one Eclectic college accepted women. In number, the Eclectics were the third largest group of practitioners, following the regulars and homeopaths; they probably also stood third in the social status of their adherents. The Eclectics were distinguished mainly by their adversarial stance against the regular profession, their claim to be reformers, their empiricism, and their indigenous American roots.

The homeopaths were an entirely different breed. They had a highly elaborated, abstruse philosophical doctrine, drew many of their number from German immigrant physicians, and had much of their appeal among the urban upper classes. The founder of homeopathy was Samuel Hahnemann (1755-1843), a German physician. Hahnemann and his followers saw disease fundamentally as a matter of spirit; what occurred inside the body did not follow physical laws. The homeopaths had three central doctrines. They maintained first that diseases could be cured by drugs which produced the same symptoms when given to a healthy person. This was the homeopathic "law of similars"—like cures like. Second, the effects of drugs could be heightened by administering them in minute doses. The more diluted the dose, the greater the "dynamic" effect. And third, nearly all diseases were the result of a suppressed itch, or "psora." The rationale for homeopathic treatment was that a patient's natural disease was somehow displaced after taking a homeopathic medicine by a weaker, but similar, artificial disease that the body could more easily overcome.[51]

The first homeopathic practitioner in America was a Dutch immigrant who settled in New York in 1825. Before 1840 homeopathy had only a few proponents in a few states, but it became better known in the next decade, and in 1850 a homeopathic college was founded in Cleveland. Before 1860 the majority of homeopathic practitioners had been recruited from the orthodox profession and still considered themselves regular physicians. Converts to homeopathy seem to have prospered; for many practitioners, it may have served as a route to public favor.[52]

Part of the appeal of homeopathy apparently lay in the kind of relationship it encouraged between doctor and patient. Homeopathic doctrine insisted that symptoms were the only perceptible aspect of disease and that they had to be learned from the uninterrupted report of the patient. Consequently, homeopathy stressed the need for sympathetic attention by the physician and individualized diagnosis and treatment of patients. (The parallel with certain schools of modern psychiatry will be obvious.) Moreover, because homeopathy called for reduced dosages, it provided an alternative to the pharmacological excesses of orthodox physicians. Homeopathic treatment was probably more pleasant than were the ministrations of the conventional doctor of the epoch. Additionally, Hahnemann's notion that diseases could be cured by drugs producing similar symptoms led him and his followers to take an interest in experimental tests, or "provings," of drugs on healthy subjects. Because homeopathy was simultaneously philosophical and experimental, it seemed to many people to be more rather than less scientific than orthodox medicine.[53]

The significance of this appeal should not be missed. No longer were the main challengers to medical orthodoxy claiming that all useful medical knowledge was simple. They, too, now accepted that medicine was legitimately complex. The two leading dissident sects both believed in scientific training; most of their curriculum was indistinguishable from that of orthodox schools. The three groups shared a wide common ground, even though they disagreed about therapeutics. Much of the public, in fact, may have been unaware of the doctrinal differences that divided them.

As homeopathy won increasing numbers of adherents in the 1850s, a countermovement against it took shape among regular physicians.

The orthodox insisted that homeopaths had to be expelled from the profession not because their doctrines were wrong, but because they violated professional ethics in heaping abuse on their colleagues, basing their practice on an "exclusive" dogma, and actively proselytyzing among both physicians and the lay public. A report to the Connecticut Medical Society in 1852 accused homeopathy of waging "a war of radicalism against the profession" and observed, "Very different would have been the profession's attitude toward homeopathy if it had aimed, like other doctrines advanced by physicians, to gain a foothold among medical men alone or chiefly, instead of making its appeal to the popular favor and against the profession."[54] Whatever the justice of these and other charges, the homeopaths were forced to leave the company of the orthodox. They did not secede; the regulars threw them out. Although the AMA had not been formed primarily with homeopathy in mind, it quickly turned to the challenge. In 1855 the organization insisted that state and local societies desiring representation accept its code of ethics, including the bar from membership of doctors subscribing to an exclusive dogma, of which homeopathy was a chief example. A showdown came in the early 1870s. A committee of the AMA recommended that the Massachusetts Medical Society, which continued to harbor homeopaths among its members, lose representation until it purged itself of heretics. The Massachusetts society at first demurred, then faced a court battle over its legal right to expel dissenters, but finally removed them, to great public consternation. While the AMA did not cripple the advance of homeopathy, it did prevent regular physicians who adopted homeopathy from remaining in orthodox societies.

Between 1850 and 1880, the battle raged between the two camps, as the regulars sought to deny the homeopaths all official positions as well as all association with the profession. The avoidance of contact with homeopaths took on all the gravity of a pollution taboo. In 1878 a physician in Norwalk, Connecticut, Dr. Moses Pardee, was expelled from his local medical society under suspicion of having consulted with a homeopath—his wife, Dr. Emily Pardee. (The state society later annulled the decision for want of evidence.) A New York doctor was expelled for buying milk sugar at a homeopathic pharmacy. The Surgeon General of the United States was denounced for having taken part in the treatment of Secretary of State William Seward, the night he was stabbed and President Lincoln was shot, because Seward's personal physician was a homeopath. (Seward survived, and the AMA graciously held back from censoring the Surgeon General for having helped save the life of the Secretary of State.) The orthodox doctors righteously refused to serve with homeopaths on hospital staffs and for thirty years were able to exclude them from municipal institutions in major cities like New York and Chicago. During the Civil War, the regulars dominated the military medical boards, and the homeopaths, in spite of congressional support, were unable to gain approval for military service.[55]

Despite these attacks, homeopathy enjoyed wide popularity in the two decades after the Civil War. It was especially strong in cities like Boston and New York and had the support of many prominent social figures. In 1870 Congress approved a charter for a homeopathic medical society in Washington, D.C., which, unlike the regular society, was willing to admit blacks. When Boston University formed a medical school in 1873, it asked homeopaths to form the faculty. Homeopathy fought itself to a position almost of parity with the regular profession in legal entitlements and public respectability, though not in numbers of practitioners.

While unorthodox practitioners multiplied, they were still greatly outnumbered by members of the regular profession. Between 1835 and 1860, according to Kett, sectarians represented roughly 10 percent of the total number of physicians. By 1871 they represented 13 percent (nearly 6,000 sectarians compared to 39,000 regulars) according to statistics gathered by J. M. Toner and published by the AMA. Toner, however, was unable to classify 4,800 doctors and seems to have undercounted the total size of the profession by ten to fourteen thousand. As of 1870, the sectarians operated fifteen out of seventy-five medical schools, and during the next few decades their share of the market seems to have stabilized at around one fifth. In 1880 the regulars conducted seventy-six medical schools, the homeopaths fourteen, the Eclectics eight. Ten years later, the respective totals were 106, 16 and 9. (During both decades, two schools belonged to a fourth group, the "physiomedicals," direct descendants of the Thomsonians.) These figures suggest a fairly stable distribution of strength among the rival groups, with the irregulars at roughly 20 percent, or slightly lower.[56]

Conflict and Convergence

The sectarian challenge had an effect on the profession that cannot be measured in numbers. The mere existence of competing parties in medicine was a standing rebuke to the claims of orthodoxy to represent a science. As long as physicians were divided, any move by the regulars to bring back licensing or reform medical education seemed like a narrow maneuver on their part aimed at winning advantage over the dissenters. "[T]o-day our profession is regarded by the State," one orthodox practitioner pointed out, "as only a numerically strong medical sect."[57] This judgment was not wholly undeserved. The sectarians, following Hahnemann, had dubbed the regular doctors "allopaths," insisting that they, too, had an exclusive dogma, cure by opposites, the reverse of homeopathy. While leaders of the profession had insisted the designation was inaccurate, many regular practitioners apparently accepted it and believed it to be correct, thereby reducing themselves to nothing more than an orthodox sectarianism.[58]

For most of this period, the attitude of the press, the courts, and state legislatures was predominantly agnostic. They neither believed nor disbelieved in the claims of the competing groups and tried, when possible, to avoid becoming embroiled in their partisan disputes. When the regulars attacked the divergent practitioners, the press often took the side of the persecuted and called for tolerance. This was not so much an indication that they approved sectarian ideas; they wanted a generous pluralism to prevail. In the aftermath of the expulsion of the Massachusetts homeopaths, *The New York Times* commented that while the medical society "meant to disgrace the heretical physicians . . . we have little doubt that in the minds of all intelligent persons they have only succeeded in bringing disgrace upon themselves."[59] Many saw diversity in medical practice as a counterpart to religious differences. When the orthodox sought control of medical practice, they bridled: One could no more have boards of orthodox doctors passing on homeopaths than Protestant boards ruling on the acceptability of Catholic priests.

Slowly, the regular profession faced up to the unhappy fact that it had been fought to a draw. Public resistance to orthodox claims eventually brought concessions. An early sign of compromise came in Michigan, where the state legislature required the incorporation of homeopathy into the University of Michigan Medical School. The regulars were aghast but finally yielded. Once the school added a homeopathic division in 1875, professors of the two camps taught there together. Homeopathic students took the same basic courses as their classmates, except for materia medica (pharmacology) and the practice of medicine, which were given separately. The arrangement put orthodox faculty members in the awkward position of teaching future homeopaths in basic science courses, but the AMA declined to expel them on that account.[60] Acting through the state legislature, the public was forcing the regulars and homeopaths to come to terms with each other.

The movement toward convergence and compromise now came from both sides. By the late 1870s and early 1880s, there was growing restlessness among many regular physicians who wanted to work out some modus vivendi with the sectarians. It soon became apparent that wherever sectarians practiced, even in relatively small numbers, the regular physicians were unable to obtain licensing legislation over their opposition. Moreover, specialists, especially in the larger cities, were increasingly unhappy with the professional restriction on consultations. Referrals from homeopathic and Eclectic general practitioners represented a potentially significant source of income for them. At the same time, many homeopathic practitioners began moving toward an accommodation with orthodox medicine. While the purists among them held to Hahnemann's faith in extreme dilutions of drugs and believed in treating symptoms individually, the moderates, who were the dominant group, accepted concentrated medicines and thought in terms of treating diseases, as did allopathic physicians. The moderates also rejected as unscientific Hahnemann's belief in a "vital force." In 1880, as the internal disputes among homeopaths intensified, their national organization, the American Institute of Homeopathy, split as the purists left to form their own International Hahnemannian Association.[61]

An analogous division then opened up in the regular profession between doctors who wanted an accommodation with the homeopaths and others who wanted to maintain the AMA's hard line against them. Disenchantment with the AMA's position first surfaced in New York, where the state medical society voted in 1882 to abolish the clause in the code of ethics that forbade consultations with sectarians. The leaders of the revolt were among the most eminent New York physicians; many of them were specialists with important hospital connections. They argued that the AMA's strategy against the sectarians had failed. Rather than stigmatizing them, the denial of fraternal courtesies had only made the profession seem narrow-minded and monopolistic. In any event, the code was continually being violated: Consultations between regulars and homeopaths were increasingly common and the code was only selectively enforced. Doctrinal differences, furthermore, were diminishing as homeopaths abandoned Hahnemann's more extreme ideas. "We all know that the majority of sectarian physicians of the present day have a regular medical education, and avail themselves 'of the accumulated experience of the profession, and of the aids actually furnished by anatomy, physiology, pathology and organic chemistry,'" wrote one physician, referring to the language of the AMA code.[62]

This was by no means a majority viewpoint among orthodox doctors. The New York society was quickly expelled from the AMA, and a newly formed New York Medical Association replaced it as the state's national representative. Even in New York most doctors seem to have opposed the state society's decision to seek peace with homeopathy. In a survey taken at the time, support for the repeal of the code was greatest in the largest cities. The majority of doctors in New York City, Brooklyn, Albany, and Rochester favored the change, while small-town doctors generally were opposed.[63]

But the minority of the 1880s represented a future majority. The profession would become more urbanized, more specialized, more like the physicians who opposed the hard line against sectarians in the 1880s. The growth of specialization increased interdependence in the professions. In particular, it made specialists dependent upon homeopathic and Eclectic general practitioners for referrals. Conversely, the growth of hospitals made the sectarian general practitioners dependent upon the "hospital men" for access to the increasingly important facilities that the specialists controlled. Only in some areas could the sectarians create their own institutions. In the eighties, homeopaths gained entry to the municipal hospitals in Boston and Chicago that previously had been closed to them. The incentive to differentiate oneself was now counterbalanced by an incentive to conform and accommodate. At the same time, the development of medical science provided an increasingly firm basis for convergence. The sectarians shared most of the fundamentals of medical science in common with the regular profession; as scientific knowledge advanced into the area of therapeutics, their differences tended to diminish. The growth of science thus reinforced the effect of new institutional relations, laying the ground for a new professional consensus.

Licensing and Organization

Probably the most important sign of convergence between the competing groups was their common support, beginning in the 1870s and 1880s, for the restoration of medical licensing. Recognizing their inability to secure legislation on their own, many educated regular physicians accepted collaboration with sectarians to win licensing laws that would protect all of them against competition from untrained practitioners. Once united behind these measures, doctors were able to win favorable action, though the initial statutes enacted at their behest set rather minimal licensing requirements, usually no more than a medical diploma. This was acceptable to homeopaths and Eclectics because they had medical colleges under their own control. Moreover, any doctor who had been in practice for a given number of years, regardless of education, was typically allowed to continue.

It would be a mistake to take these new licensing laws as evidence that physicians were now a powerful interest group. The licensing movement of the late nineteenth century was by no means restricted to doctors or even to what are customarily regarded as professions. Plumbers, barbers, horseshoers, pharmacists, embalmers, and sundry other groups sought and were granted licensing protection. Historically, as Lawrence Friedman has pointed out, there have been two kinds of occupational licensing. Some statutes, like those requiring licenses of peddlers, have been clearly hostile in intent. They have set high, if not prohibitive, licensing fees and have been administered by local government officials. In the case of peddlers, the principal aim has been to limit competition with local tradesmen. Other licensing laws, sought by members of the regulated occupations, have set moderate fees and placed enforcement in the hands of the practitioners themselves. While hostile licensing had been common in America as far back as colonial times, "friendly" licensing developed on a large scale only in the late nineteenth century.[64]

The origins of this new pattern lay in the changed circumstances of the society, which put occupational licensing in a substantially new light. Increasingly, large corporations dominated the economic landscape, dwarfing independent professionals and small businessmen. Struggling to hold their own, these groups struck back under the banners of various movements. Support for antitrust legislation was one expression of their effort to survive; trade and professional organizations were another. Licensing, rather than being identified with power and privilege, as it had been in the 1830s, became part of the resistance of a threatened petite bourgeoisie.

The occupations that pursued their interests through licensing were distinguished less by their political power than by their distinctive structural position within the economy. Predominantly self-employed, most of their members worked out of small shops requiring little capital to establish. Their trades and professions were easy to enter and consequently beset by competition. Where an occupation included some members who were employers and some who were employees, as was the case among barbers, the differences in status were slight, mobility was common, and conflict was rare. Most important, none of the occupations faced any organized buyers or employers who stood to lose by the monopoly that licensing would create. They generally sold their goods and services to individuals rather than corporations. These features helped minimize coherent political opposition to licensing bills. The people whose interests would most immediately be sacrificed by licensing were relatively unorganized and unskilled competitors. And by stipulating that anyone in business at the time be able to qualify under the statutes, the laws disarmed much of the potential opposition within the trade.[65]

The initial medical practice acts, which required only diplomas and made exceptions for long established practitioners, generally followed this pattern. Only gradually were the requirements stiffened and enforced. One major landmark was an 1877 law passed by Illinois, which empowered a state board of medical examiners to reject diplomas from disreputable schools. Under the law, all doctors had to register. Those with degrees from approved schools were licensed, while others had to be examined. Of 3,600 nongraduates practicing in Illinois in 1877, 1,400 were reported to have left the state within a year. Within a decade, three thousand practitioners were said to have been put out of business.[66] In many states licensing developed incrementally. First, a minimal statute was enacted requiring only a diploma; then the principle was established that diplomas could be examined and candidates rejected if the school they had attended was judged inadequate; and finally, all candidates were required both to present an acceptable diploma and to pass an independent state examination. By 1901 twenty-five states and the District of Columbia were in this last category, while only two states were in the first. No jurisdiction was without a licensing statute of some sort.[67]

Missouri exemplifies the gradual extension of licensing control. The state passed an initial law in 1874, but it required a doctor only to register a degree from a legally chartered medical school with a county clerk. The statute had little effect. Since lax incorporation laws permitted anyone to start a school merely by applying for a charter, Missouri soon had more medical colleges than anyone could keep track of. Many were simply diploma mills. The state's doctors were too disorganized to do anything about the situation. According to a survey by the state medical society, nearly five thousand people practiced medicine in Missouri in 1882; only about half of them were graduates of "reputable" schools. At its highest point during the previous thirty years, the medical society had a membership of only 140; this gravely weakened its claim to speak for the profession. Its resources were meager. Between 1850 and 1900, its treasury never had more than $500 in it at any one time. Most physicians had no interest in regulation, and those who did were divided, since physicians who ran substandard schools had no interest in seeing licensing requirements stiffened. The lack of unity within the profession kept it almost powerless. Finally, in 1894, the state board of health, which was nominally in charge of licensing, tried to insist that medical schools set as a prerequisite for admission a college or high school degree, or an equivalent certificate. When the proprietary medical schools then began manufacturing certificates, the board announced that medical students would have to pass a state test to demonstrate their preliminary education. But the medical schools sought judicial relief, and the Supreme Court of Missouri ruled that in raising premedical requirements, the board of health had exceeded its authority. Not until 1901 was a definitive medical practice act approved empowering the board of health to act as a board of medical examiners. By then, physicians had finally united behind effective legislation, and they had the support of the Presbyterian and Methodist churches, which were alarmed at the growing popularity of Christian Science and Weltmerism, a local mind-cure cult.[68]

Missouri was particularly slow to regulate medicine and long remained a festering sore to the AMA, but its history illustrates a common irony. Even after the co-optation of the sectarians, the main resistance to strong licensing laws originated within the profession. "Practically the only opposition to effective medical legislation in the country," remarked a vice president of the AMA in 1887, "comes from the profession itself," and he was referring specifically to the numerous, quick-degree proprietary colleges.[69] The physicians who operated the schools had, in effect, acquired a strong interest in maintaining the profession's weakness: They profited from more medical graduates, while the profession was flooded. The first licensing acts had increased the demand for diplomas, even bogus ones, thereby promoting the commercial medical colleges and diploma mills rather than putting them out of business. But as the requirements were tightened, barring the graduates of the lesser schools from practice in an increasing number of states, those schools faced extinction. Their owners opposed stricter licensing in self-defense.

On more ideological grounds, some liberals and populists also opposed medical licensure. Social Darwinists, following the English social theorist Herbert Spencer, thought all such regulation unwise. "Very many of the poorer classes *are* injured by druggists' prescriptions and quack medicines," Spencer willingly conceded. But there was nothing wrong in that; it was the penalty nature attached to ignorance. If the poor died of their own foolishness, the species would improve. The physicians, Spencer and others warned, meant to set themselves up as a clergy. The opposition to licensing also found a voice in William James, who appeared before the Massachusetts legislature in 1898 to argue that licensing would interfere with freedom of research in medicine. James had personally tried an assortment of healers and was pursuing his own research into psychic cures. At a time when Christian Science was a great subject of controversy, he defended the right of "mind curers" to test out their new modes of therapy. "I well know," he wrote to a friend shortly thereafter, "how my colleagues at the Medical School .

.. will view me and my efforts. But if Zola and Col. Picquart can face
the whole French army [in the Dreyfus case], can't I face their disap-
proval? Much more easily than that of my conscience!"[70]

Such protests had little effect. The courts as well as the legislatures
had swung behind the medical profession. The crucial test of the legitimacy of medical licensing occurred in 1888, when the issue came before
the U.S. Supreme Court in the case of *Dent* v. *West Virginia*. Frank
Dent, an Eclectic physician in practice for six years, had been convicted
and fined under an 1882 West Virginia statute requiring a physician to
hold a degree from a reputable medical college, pass an examination,
or prove that he had been in practice in the state for the previous ten
years. The State Board of Health deemed unacceptable Dent's degree
from the American Medical Eclectic College of Cincinnati. Delivering
the Supreme Court's unanimous opinion upholding the law, Justice Stephen Field noted that every citizen had the right to follow any lawful
calling, "subject only to such restrictions as are imposed upon all persons of like age, sex and condition." But the state could protect society
by imposing conditions for the exercise of that right, as long as they
were imposed on everyone and were reasonably related to the occupation in question. "Few professions," he continued, "require more careful preparation . . . than that of medicine." It had to deal with "all those
subtle and mysterious influences upon which health and life depend"
and required knowledge not only "of vegetable and mineral substances,
but of the human body in all its complicated parts, and their relation
to each other, as well as their influence upon the mind." Everyone
might have occasion to consult a doctor, but "comparatively few can
judge of the qualifications of learning and skill which he possesses." Reliance had to be placed on the assurance given by a license. Reasonable
considerations, therefore, might prompt a state to exclude people without licenses from practicing medicine.[71] In a later case, *Hawker* v. *New
York* (1898), the Court extended the grounds for denying a medical license, noting that in a doctor "character is as important a qualification
as knowledge."[72] At the state level, courts also supported medical practice laws. After the Supreme Court decision, there never seems to have
been any serious question about the matter.

As boards of medical examiners were established, two patterns predominated. The less frequent was to set up separate boards for regular
physicians, homeopaths, and Eclectics, each having the right to license
physicians of its own persuasion. The more common pattern was to give
representation on the same board to sectarians as well as to regulars.
Sometimes statutes assigned to the various groups the right to fill a designated share of the seats; though this amounted to giving private orga-

nizations control of agencies of the state, it was upheld by the courts. Despite their historic efforts to avoid contact with sectarians, the regular physicians now found that a single integrated board worked better than multiple separate boards in controlling entry into the profession. Accordingly, they set aside their scruples about consorting with heretics and made common cause with them.

This collaboration between regular physicians and sectarians clearly violated the AMA's code of ethics, but none of the doctors who served on joint state licensing boards suffered excommunication. The code was simply ignored. By the turn of the century, prominent leaders in the AMA conceded the code was an anachronism and were anxious to put the issue of sectarianism behind them.[73] So in 1903 the AMA adopted a revised code of ethics that said little about irregular practitioners. While noting that it was inconsistent with scientific principles for physicians to designate their practice as exclusive or sectarian, the new code elided any reference to the kind of medicine doctors actually practiced. Within a few years, orthodox societies were seeking out members among sectarian physicians. In New York State the two competing regular medical organizations reunited after having been at odds for two decades over their relationships with sectarians. Homeopaths and Eclectics were admitted to the merged organization. D. W. Cathell, who had been a fierce antagonist of the sectarians, wrote in a medical journal that the new code would "have a great and far-reaching effect on our material interests; it will everywhere promote and foster professional unity; and, far above all else, by putting an end to partisan agitations it will increase the good repute of every worthy medical man in America."[74]

The myth persists today that homeopaths and herbal doctors were suppressed by the dominant allopathic profession. Yet the sequence of events suggests otherwise. Both the homeopaths and Eclectics won a share in the legal privileges of the profession. Only afterward did they lose their popularity. When homeopathic and Eclectic doctors were shunned and denounced by the regular profession, they thrived. But the more they gained in access to the privileges of regular physicians, the more their numbers declined. The turn of the century was both the point of acceptance and the moment of incipient disintegration. Enrollment at Eclectic schools peaked at one thousand in 1904; by 1913 it was down to 256. In 1900 there were twenty-two homeopathic schools, but ten years later there were only twelve, fewer than in any year since 1880; by 1918 only six remained and these all ceased to be homeopathic institutions within the next several years.[75] Homeopathy had one foot in modern science, the other in pre-scientific mysticism; this became

an increasingly untenable position. While regular medicine was producing important and demonstrable scientific advances, homeopathy
generated no new discoveries. The contrast was not lost on many in the
group. They edged further away from Hahnemann; the final dissolution
came of itself. The Eclectics also succumbed to quiet co-optation; they
were only too glad to be welcomed into the fold.

In part, the old sects gave way to new ones. The 1890s had seen the
appearance of two new groups representing almost diametrically opposed positions. One was purely mechanistic in conception; the other,
purely spiritual. The first, osteopathy, was founded by a rural Missouri
doctor, Andrew Still, who maintained that the human body, when sick,
had to be repaired by placing its parts back in their proper relationship.
"Quit your pills and learn from Osteopathy the principle that governs
you," Still declared. "Learn that you are a machine, your heart an en-
gine, your lungs a fanning machine and a sieve, your brain with its two
lobes an electric battery." In 1891 he began teaching his principles in
the town of Kirksville in Missouri; the following year he obtained a state
charter and created a school. Patients flocked there in hundreds, the
school flourished, and in 1897 osteopathy won legal protection from the
Missouri legislature.[76]

Christian Science, the second of the new sects, was born in the East,
near Boston, and like homeopathy picked up adherents in urban areas
among the well-to-do classes. Mary Baker Eddy, an obscure New England mystagogue who founded the group, altogether denied the reality of matter and claimed that disease, like all else, was purely a function
of mind and spirit. Christian Science was, in a sense, homeopathy taken
to the final dilution, the point where the world dissolved into idea. But
while Mrs. Eddy thought medicine and nourishment of no use ("We
have no evidence of food sustaining life, except false evidence"), she
did not, as her biographer Edward Dakin points out, deny the value
of money. Like osteopathy, Christian Science was run in a very business-like fashion and earned its founder a substantial fortune.[77]

The fate of these later sects turned out to be quite different from the
earlier ones. While homeopathy and Eclecticism were assimilated into
the medical profession, osteopathy and Christian Science remained independent and survived on their own. So, too, did chiropractic, which,
like osteopathy, originated as a commercial enterprise in the Midwest
in the 1890s, and was based on similarly mechanistic principles. Oddly
enough, the homeopaths and Eclectics no longer exist as well organized
groups because they were strong at a time when regular physicians
needed their political support for licensing legislation. Their price for
cooperation was acceptance into the profession. Osteopathy later also

became professionalized and sought integration into the medical profession. But lacking any point of leverage with physicians, it failed to gain entry.

The AMA's gesture of accommodation toward its old adversaries, the homeopaths and Eclectics, was part of a more general effort around the turn of the century to unify and strengthen the profession. As of 1900 the AMA had only eight thousand members. The total membership of all medical societies, local and state as well as national, was approximately 33,000; another 77,000 physicians belonged to no association whatsoever. As a writer who reported these figures wrote, the profession was in "wretched condition" as a political force.[78] In 1901 the AMA revised its constitution, creating a new legislative body, the House of Delegates, with representatives drawn primarily from state medical societies in proportion to their membership. Previously, a hodgepodge of county and regional organizations, as well as state societies, had been entitled to send delegates to AMA conventions in the ratio of one representative for every ten members. Some local societies had more delegates than did their state associations. By the late 1800s, the number of delegates had become unmanageable; virtually anyone showing up at the AMA's annual meeting could take part in its business, as it was impossible to check credentials. Besides being unwieldy, this arrangement gave inordinate influence to physicians who happened to live near the site of an annual convention, and cost the association authority and continuity in its decision-making. Under the new constitution, the House of Delegates had a fixed membership of 150, to be periodically reapportioned as in the U.S. House of Representatives. The AMA would be a confederation of the state medical societies, which in turn would be confederations of the county organizations in the states. The county medical societies, as the reorganization committees explained, would be "the foundation of the whole superstructure."[79] Henceforth, no doctors could be members of any higher professional association unless they first joined their own county organization. Membership at the county level would then carry with it membership in the state society and the obligation to pay state dues. The organizational structure thus neatly forced all physicians who wanted to belong to their county medical society or to the national AMA to become dues-paying members of their state association.

A rapid transformation quickly took place at the state level. Most of the state medical societies had been no more than nominal organizations, scarcely functioning, with only a small proportion of the profession as members. Since so many vital political decisions, like the enactment of licensure laws, were then being made by state governments, this had been a serious point of weakness. Now, between 1900 and 1905, in line with the requirements of the new AMA constitution, all but three of the state and territorial medical associations were reorganized on a uniform plan. They turned previously independent county societies into local chapters, gave their members representation in statewide decision-making bodies and assessed them for membership dues. Many of the state organizations began publishing their own monthly journals and employing paid rather than volunteer staff. The results were immediate and positive. The Michigan State Medical Association, reorganized in 1902, within two years increased its membership from 452 to 1,772 and its income from $1,615 to $4,813. The Missouri association, reorganized in 1903, saw its membership rise in one year from 258 to 1,600 and its revenues grow from $774 to $3,200. Between 1902 and 1904, membership in the Ohio Association jumped from 992 to 2,640 and in Tennessee from 386 to 1,097.[80] And so it went. In a remarkably short period, physicians began to achieve the unity and coherence that had so long eluded them. From a mere eight thousand members in 1900, the AMA shot up to seventy thousand in 1910, half the physicians in the country. By 1920 membership had reached sixty percent.[81] From this period dates the power of what came to be called "organized medicine."

The gathering movement in the medical profession was by no means unique at the time. The rise of labor unions and corporations, trade associations, and trusts in the late nineteenth and early twentieth centuries all point to a broader current pulsing in the society. In part, physicians were responding to the same developments that facilitated organization in other fields. As railroads and automobiles, telegraphs and telephones promoted national markets and broke down local isolation, groups of all kinds found it at once easier and more necessary to organize nationwide. (The federal structure the AMA adopted in 1901 was, in fact, copied from other national associations.) The growth of national corporations, Richard Hofstadter has suggested, radically altered the distribution of power and status in America, overshadowing local elites and engendering among the professions an acute resentment at their lost influence.[82] This may overstate the power that professionals had earlier. Yet the physicians of the Progressive era do seem to show a sharpened anger and militance, some of it directed at corporate hegemony. "The members of the profession," wrote an Ohio doctor to the AMA's *Journal* in 1902, "are constantly humiliated and insulted by wealthy corporations, state, county and city officials." Doctors, he complained, had no power compared to organized business or labor. Physicians like himself were forced to work on contract for big corporations for pitifully low fees; a local steel manufacturer had just refused to pay more than about 60 percent of his bill for emergency services. "As it is, if I do not accept the fees the company offers, the work will go to another physician and the company knows it can get plenty of doctors to do their work for whatever they are willing to pay. What the medical profession needs is a leader, to take it out of the valley of poverty and humiliation, a Mitchell, as the miners have, or a Morgan, as the trusts have."[83]

Yet the replacement of a competitive orientation with a corporate consciousness required more than common interests. It required a transfer of power to the group, and this was what began to happen in medicine around 1900 with changes in its social structure. Physicians came increasingly to rely on each other's good will for their access to patients and facilities. I have already alluded to the instrumental role of the rise of hospitals and specialization in creating greater interdependence among doctors. Physicians also depended more on their colleagues for defense against malpractice suits, which were increasing in frequency. The courts, in working out the rules of liability for medical practice in the late nineteenth century, had set as the standard of care that of the local community where a physician practiced. This limited possible expert testimony against physicians to their immediate colleagues. By adopting the "locality rule," the courts prepared the way for granting considerable power to the local medical society, for it became almost impossible for patients to get testimony against a physician who was a member. Medical societies began to make malpractice defense a direct service. Shortly after the turn of the century, doctors in New York, Chicago, and Cleveland organized common defense funds. The Massachusetts Medical Society began handling malpractice suits in 1908. During the next ten years, it supported accused physicians in all but three of the ninety-four cases it received. Only twelve of these ninety-one cases went to trial, all save one resulting in a victory for the doctor. For its first twenty years, the defense fund of the medical society of the state of Washington won every case it fought. Because of their ability to protect their members, medical societies were able to get low insurance rates, while doctors who did not belong could scarcely get any insurance protection.[84] This provided the sort of "selective incentive" that medical societies needed to help them attract members. Professional ostracism carried increasingly serious consequences: denial of hospital privileges, loss of referrals, loss of malpractice insurance, and, in extreme cases, loss of a license to practice. The local medical fraternity became the arbiter of a doctor's position and fortune, and he could no longer choose to ignore it. By making the county societies the gatekeeper to membership in any higher professional group, the AMA had recognized and strengthened the position of the local fraternity, as well as bolstering its own organizational underpinnings.

Yet the AMA still had to address the problem that originally motivated its formation, control of medical education. The key source of physicians' economic distress in 1900 remained the continuing oversupply of doctors, now made much worse by the increased productivity of physicians as a result of what I referred to in the previous chapter as the squeezing of lost time from the professional working day. The enactment of licensing laws had not cut down the production of doctors: It had only changed its character, promoting the expansion of medical colleges. Toward the end of the nineteenth century, the proliferation of medical schools had accelerated. Between 1850 and 1870, the number had grown from 52 to 75; ten years later, it jumped to 100, in another decade to 133, and by 1900 to 160. This was reflected in a great increase in students, who more than doubled from 11,826 in 1880 to 25,171 twenty years later. While the population of the United States grew 138 percent between 1870 and 1910, the number of physicians increased 153 percent.[85] The immediate beneficiaries of this expansion in supply were the proprietors and professors of the schools, who garnered income and prestige from their positions. But by producing more doctors, the medical colleges exacerbated the competitive relations among physicians. The weakness of the profession was feeding on itself; ultimately, help had to come from outside. The profession could not get off the treadmill it was on until other institutions intervened. That process had already begun in the universities, where educational reformers had a concurrent agenda of their own.

MEDICAL EDUCATION AND THE RESTORATION OF OCCUPATIONAL CONTROL

Reform from Above

Reform of medical education began around 1870 as part of the coming-of-age of American universities. The two developments are historically inseparable. They had their inception at the same institutions and were led by some of the same people, notably Presidents Charles Eliot of Harvard and Daniel Coit Gilman of Johns Hopkins. Before the Civil War, American colleges were intellectual backwaters whose poorly paid professors had little claim to original thought or research. A variety of forces combined in the wake of the war to infuse some colleges with new life and larger ambitions. Money, leadership, and ideas appeared almost simultaneously. The economy was now producing enough of a surplus to generate the capital necessary to underwrite the development of universities, and there were wealthy men—not many at first, but a few—sufficiently concerned about education to leave them with large endowments. When the Baltimore merchant Johns Hopkins died in 1873, he left $7 million to build a hospital and university—at that time, the largest single endowment in the country's history. Meanwhile, at some established institutions an older generation of college educators passed from power. Since taking command in the 1820s and 1830s, these men had viewed education as a matter of moral and mental discipline, best inculcated by a prescribed, classical curriculum in which modern languages and modern science had little place. This traditional orientation, while not wholly abandoned, gradually lost ground among their successors, as the conviction grew that higher education ought to have practical value in fitting students for the "real" world. The colleges had long been ridiculed precisely for their irrelevance to contemporary life and work; now their trustees and presidents began to converse in the language of utility. Higher education would satisfy the needs of an expanding economy. For some, this meant greater emphasis on teaching useful skills; for others, a new departure in encouraging research and the development of scientific knowledge. The universities would become worthy of respect; professors would be relieved of petty disciplinary responsibilities, paid better, and given freer rein in their work. For a model, reformers looked to Germany, which had developed a tradition of secular learning and strong universities, and sought to make their own institutions in every way the equal of those in Europe.[86]

In the eyes of reform-minded American educators like Eliot and Gilman, medicine epitomized both the backward state of higher education and the degraded state of the professions in America. "The ignorance and general incompetency of the average graduate of American Medical Schools, at the time when he receives the degree which turns him loose upon the community, is something horrible to contemplate," Eliot wrote. "The whole system of medical education in this country needs thorough reformation."[87] The deficiencies had remained the same for decades. Students came to professional schools with minimal preparation; even at the best universities, young men without high school diplomas could easily find admission to study medicine. Students followed medical courses in any order they pleased; the brief two-year program had no regular sequence. In Germany the laboratory sciences of physiology, chemistry, histology, pathological anatomy, and, somewhat later, bacteriology, were revolutionizing medicine, but American medical schools had no laboratories to speak of, let alone a tradition of original research. Didactic lectures remained the principal form of instruction. Students were supposed to learn the art of medicine through apprenticeships, but the medical faculty had no control over their preceptors, who might be completely inadequate. Educational standards were none too strict. To graduate from Harvard Medical School, students needed only to pass a majority of their examinations, no matter if they failed the rest.

When Eliot, who had been trained as a chemist, became president of Harvard in 1869, reorganization of the professional schools was a leading item on his agenda; breaking precedent, he personally presided at meetings of the medical faculty. Before 1869 Harvard Medical School had only a faint connection with the university. As in any proprietary medical college, the faculty collected fees directly from the students, paid the school's expenses, and divided what was left among themselves. They elected a dean and conducted their own affairs. A few professors favored upgrading the curriculum and standards of admission, but a conservative majority, led by the venerable Henry Bigelow, opposed any change. Bigelow thought higher requirements might keep out a natural genius in the art of healing, and considered training in the related biological sciences useful but not essential. Medical discoveries, he believed, were never made in laboratories. How was it, Bigelow asked at one meeting, that the medical faculty had for eighty years been "managing its own affairs and doing it well," and now, abruptly, when all was prosperous, great changes were being proposed? After a dead silence, Eliot quietly replied, "I can answer Dr. Bigelow's question very easily; there is a new President."[88] By the fall of 1871, Eliot could report that the medical faculty had "resolved to venture upon a complete revolution of the system of medical education." The school's finances were placed under the control of the Harvard Corporation, the system of dividing up fees was eliminated, and the professors were given salaries. The academic year was extended from four months to nine; the length of training needed to graduate rose from two years to three. In physiology, chemistry, and pathological anatomy, laboratory work was added to or replaced didactic lectures. Students henceforth would have to pass all their courses to graduate.[89]

The argument long invoked against higher standards in medical education was that they would drive students away and schools into bankruptcy. The reforms at Harvard initially did cause a sharp drop in enrollment, but the faculty held firm through a few difficult years. From a low of 170 students in 1872, attendance climbed steadily, reaching 263 by 1879; this was still beneath the pre-reform level of 330 ten years earlier, but because tuition had been increased, the school was momentarily in the black. Moreover, the quality of the students improved. The proportion with bachelor's degrees jumped from 21 percent in the fall of 1869 to 48 percent in 1880. Writing that same year, Eliot remarked that a decade earlier medical students had been "noticeably inferior" in bearing and manner to other students at the university, but now were their equals.[90]

If competition had once held medical schools in check, preventing any one institution from risking reform, it now began to have the reverse effect. Rivals could not afford to fall behind. In the mid-1870s, fearing a decline in reputation, the trustees of the University of Pennsylvania decided, against the wishes of a conservative dean of the medical faculty, to follow Harvard's lead and lengthen medical training from two to three years. Previously, in 1847, Penn had tried to extend its terms from four to six months but fell back after losing students to nearby Jefferson Medical College. This time, enrollment fell 22 percent, but as at Harvard, the changes stuck.[91] Over the next decade, other leading institutions moved in the same direction. When the more advanced schools formed a national association in 1890, the new group set a minimum standard for member institutions of three years of training, six months a year, with required laboratory work in histology, chemistry, and pathology.* In the nineties, this organization—now the Association of American Medical Colleges (AAMC)—represented a little more than a third of the nation's medical schools, but these were firmly in the ascendancy. As licensing boards began to impose more stringent requirements, the two-year medical degree faded into obscurity. By 1893 more than 96 percent of the schools required three or more years of work.[92]

The most radical departure from the old regime took place at Johns Hopkins University, which opened its medical school in 1893 with a four-year program and the unprecedented requirement that all entering students come with college degrees. From the outset, Johns Hopkins embodied a conception of medical education as a field of graduate study, rooted in basic science and hospital medicine, that was eventually to govern all institutions in the country. Scientific research and clinical instruction now moved to center stage. The faculty, rather than being recruited from local practitioners, as had always been the pattern in America, were accomplished men of research, wooed from outside Baltimore. Students were also drawn from a distance and carefully cho-

---

*This was not the first such effort. A predecessor organization had existed between 1876 and 1882, collapsing as a result of its effort to require a three-year program of its members.

sen; they spent their first two years studying basic laboratory sciences and their last two on the wards, personally responsible for a few patients under the watchful eyes of the faculty. A hospital was built in connection with the school, and the two were conducted as a joint enterprise. Advanced residencies in specialized fields were created. (It was at Hopkins that the term "residency" was first used to describe advanced specialty training following an internship.) Here were the glimmerings of the great university-dominated medical centers of the next century.[93]

The significance of Johns Hopkins Medical School lay in the new relationships it established. It joined science and research ever more firmly to clinical hospital practice. While apprentices had learned the craft of medicine in their preceptor's office and the patient's home, now doctors in training would see medical practice almost entirely on the wards of teaching hospitals. Hopkins also stood for a new synthesis of medicine and the larger culture—a union vividly represented by the two major figures at the school, William Welch and William Osler. Welch, who had done important work in pathology as a young man, and Osler, the great clinician, were both dedicated to research, but they were also broadly educated and had a lively interest in the history and traditions of their profession. Though Hopkins accentuated science, it did not stand for a narrowly technical vision of medicine; this was the secret of its special éclat. It radiated cultural as well as scientific assurance, especially in the person of Osler, whose learning and urbanity made him the profession's favorite doctor. Welch became its authoritative voice in public affairs. The influence of Johns Hopkins extended far beyond Baltimore. It sent its graduates to medical institutions all over the country and abroad, where, as professors and scientists, they took a major part in shaping the character of medical education and research in the twentieth century.[94]

Consolidating the System

Sharp contrasts characterized medicine by 1900. The changes in progress at Harvard, Johns Hopkins, and other universities were counterpointed by the continuing growth of commercial medical colleges. In 1850 there had been no example of an alternative in medical education; fifty years later, the alternative had begun to take shape but was yet to prevail. Despite the new licensing laws, the ports of entry into medicine were still wide open, and the unwelcome passed through in great numbers. At proprietary schools and some of the weaker medical departments of universities, the ranks of the profession were being recruited from workingmen and the lower-middle classes, to the dismay of professional leaders, who thought such riff-raff jeopardized efforts to raise the doctor's status in society. From the viewpoint of established physicians, the commercial schools were undesirable on at least two counts: for the added competition they were creating and for the low image of the physician that their graduates fostered. Medicine would never be a respected profession—so its most vocal spokesman declared—until it sloughed off its coarse and common elements.[95]

Among those who entered medicine in increasing numbers were women. In the second half of the nineteenth century, seventeen medical colleges for women were founded in the United States. A long struggle for admission to the elite medical schools finally brought victory in 1890. Strapped for funds, Johns Hopkins agreed to accept women into to its medical school in return for a half million dollars in endowment money contributed by wealthy women. In effect, American women were forced to buy their way into elite medical education. Many of those who had fought to establish separate women's medical colleges now thought their function was unnecessary. The women's schools began to close or merge as women gained entry to schools that trained men. By 1893-94, women represented 10 percent or more of the students at 19 coeducational medical schools. Between 1880 and 1900, the percentage of doctors who were women increased nationally from 2.8 to 5.6 percent. In some cities the proportion of women was considerably higher: 18.2 percent of doctors in Boston, 19.3 percent in Minneapolis, 13.8 percent in San Francisco. With more than 7,000 women physicians at the turn of the century, the United States was far ahead of England, which had just 258, and France, which had only 95. The increasing numbers of women in American medicine, however, brought in their train a growing reaction from men in the field.[96]

After its own reorganization, the American Medical Association made reform of medical schools a top priority. Since there was no chance of intervention by the federal government, any national action would have to be undertaken by the association itself, via the state licensing boards, which its members controlled. In 1904 the AMA established a Council on Medical Education, composed of five medical professors from major universities, with a permanent secretary, a regular budget, and a mandate to elevate and standardize the requirements for medical education. As one of its first acts, the council formulated a minimum standard for physicians calling for four years of high school, an equal period of medical training, and passage of a licensing test; its "ideal" standard stipulated five years of medical school (including one year of basic sciences, later pushed into the "premedical" curriculum in college) and a sixth of hospital internship. In an effort to identify and pressure weaker institutions, the AMA council began grading medical schools according to the record of their graduates on state licensing examinations; later it extended the evaluation to include curriculum, facilities, faculty, and requirements for admission. In 1906 it inspected the 160 schools then in existence and fully approved of only 82, which it rated Class A. Class B consisted of 46 imperfect, but redeemable, institutions, while 32, beyond salvage, fell into Class C. The results of the survey were disclosed at an AMA meeting, but were never published for fear of the ill will they would create. Professional ethics forbade physicians from taking up cudgels against each other in public; it would have been unseemly for the AMA to have violated its own code. Instead, the AMA council invited an outside group, the Carnegie Foundation for the Advancement of Teaching, to conduct a similar investigation.[97] The foundation agreed, and chose for the task a young educator, Abraham Flexner, who had taken a bachelor's degree at Johns Hopkins and whose brother Simon was a protégé of William Welch and president of the Rockefeller Institute for Medical Research.

Well before Flexner's report was published in 1910, the number of medical schools had begun to decline, dropping from a high point of 162 in 1906 to 131 four years later, a loss of almost one fifth. The turnabout came as the steadily rising requirements set by state licensing boards and other authorities gradually altered the economics of medical education for students and schools alike. The new requirements extending the length of medical training imposed increasingly large opportunity costs on prospective physicians. The academic year, time almost wholly lost for earnings, went from four to eight or nine months, and the total period of training from two years, possibly without high school, to four, then five, and eventually more than eight years beyond high school. Under the emerging system, young doctors could scarcely hope to be making a living on their own before age thirty. Higher tuition fees added to the change. The combined rise in indirect and direct costs produced a long-term decline in the number of medical students. This was especially evident among many schools of the second and third rank that later became extinct.[98] They could ill afford losses of enrollment. Medical schools were then facing greatly increased expenses under the new requirements for modern laboratories, libraries, and clinical facilities. No institution could defray all these costs out of their tuition charges, and since the commercial schools had no other source of income, they went under. These changing economic realities, rather than the Flexner report, were what killed so many medical schools in the years after 1906.

The proprietary medical colleges faced a Hobson's choice. If they ignored the new standards for medical education, their diplomas would cease to be recognized by state licensing boards and students would lose any incentive to enroll. If, on the other hand, they tried to comply with the standards, they would be rewarded with fewer students and higher costs because of the more stringent preliminary requirements, longer period of training, and more expensive facilities and equipment. Only a few courses of action were available to them. One option was to seek a merger with the medical school of a private or state university, which could draw on income from endowments or state assistance. Many second-rank schools did exactly that. Another option was, quite simply, fraud—to pretend to comply with the new standards without following through and incurring the expense. Many did that too. The commercial schools that resisted merger or bankruptcy were almost inevitably forced into misrepresentation.

This was the setting for the Flexner report. Accompanied by the secretary of the AMA Council on Medical Education, Flexner visited each of the nation's medical schools. As a representative of the Carnegie Foundation, thought to be on a scouting mission for the philanthropist, he no doubt had doors opened to him that otherwise would have been closed. To desperate deans and professors, the name Carnegie must have called up dancing visions of endowment plums. If so, the daydreams must have quickly vanished on publication of Flexner's famous *Bulletin Number Four*. Though a layman, he was much more severe in his judgment of particular institutions than the AMA had been in any of its annual guides to American medical schools. The association was constrained by possible suspicion of its motives; Flexner felt no such compunctions. Repeatedly, with a deft use of detail and biting humor, he showed that the claims made by the weaker, mostly proprietary schools in their catalogues were patently false. Touted laboratories were nowhere to be found, or consisted of a few vagrant test tubes squirreled away in a cigar box; corpses reeked because of the failure to use disinfectant in the dissecting rooms. Libraries had no books; alleged faculty members were busily occupied in private practice. Purported requirements for admission were waived for anyone who would pay the fees. None of this was really new. But while the problems were ancient, they now had a different meaning. In the 1800s, medical schools did not need to pretend to have all the facilities that were being demanded in 1910. (Even Harvard, after all, had no physiology laboratory before 1870.) Now many of the schools claimed to be what they clearly were not; and in doing so, they implicitly acknowledged the legitimacy of the standards that Flexner was exacting of them and made themselves more vulnerable to public exposure and embarrassment.

As Flexner saw it, a great discrepancy had opened up between medical science and medical education. While science had progressed, education had lagged behind. "Society reaps at this moment but a small fraction of the advantage which current knowledge has the power to confer." America had some of the world's best medical schools, but also many of the worst. Flexner's recommendations were straightforward. The first-class schools had to be strengthened on the model of Johns Hopkins, and a few from the middle ranks had to be raised to that high standard; the remainder, the great majority of schools, ought to be extinguished. America was oversupplied with badly trained practitioners; it could do with fewer but better doctors.[99] This was also the view of professional leaders, but it would be mistaken to dismiss Flexner as an agent of the AMA. He was a man of strong intellectual commitments, which guided him in a long career of educational reform. The closing of medical schools greatly enhanced the market position of private physicians, but Flexner himself had an aristocratic disdain for things commercial. And precisely because of this high-minded, unmercenary spirit, his report more successfully legitimated the profession's interest in limiting the number of medical schools and the supply of physicians than anything the AMA might have put out on its own.

So much credit—and blame—has been awarded to Flexner for the demise of small medical colleges in the first decades of the century that it may be somewhat difficult to put his report in perspective. The schools were condemned primarily by the changes in licensing rather than by *Bulletin Number Four*. At most, Flexner hastened the schools to their graves and deprived them of mourners. He himself recognized the primacy of economic considerations. Nearly half of the medical schools, he reported, had an annual income below $10,000; their existence was precarious. They were unable to comply, as he wrote, "even in a perfunctory manner with statutory, not to say scientific, requirements and show a profit."[100] The schools were at the end of their tether; at that point, it was relatively easy to strangle them.

The process of consolidation in medical education moved apace in the decade after 1910. By 1915 the number of schools had fallen from 131 to 95, and the number of graduates from 5,440 to 3,536. Mergers were common among Class A and B schools; Class C schools were often disbanded for want of students. In five years, the schools requiring at least one year of college work grew from thirty-five to eighty-three, or from 27 percent of the total in 1910 to 80 percent in 1915. Licensing boards demanding college work increased from eight to eighteen. In 1912 a number of boards formed a voluntary association, the Federation of State Medical Boards, which accepted the AMA's rating of medical schools as authoritative. The AMA Council effectively became a national accrediting agency for medical schools, as an increasing number of states adopted its judgments of unacceptable institutions. In the fall of 1914, a year of college work as a prerequisite for admission became essential for a Class A rating from the AMA; two years of college were required in 1918. By 1922 thirty-eight states were requiring two years of college in preliminary work, the number of medical schools had fallen to 81, and graduates to 2,529.[101] Even though no legislative body ever set up either the Federation of State Medical Boards or the AMA Council on Medical Education, their decisions came to have the force of law. This was an extraordinary achievement for the organized profession. Only a few decades earlier, many people had believed that the decentralized character of American government precluded any effective regulation of medical education. If one state raised its requirements, students would simply gravitate to schools elsewhere. Short of federal intervention, control seemed impossible. But the medical profession had carried its effort to every state, and its success was a measure of how far it had come since the mid-1800s.

The consolidation never went as far as Flexner or the AMA wanted it to go. *Bulletin Number Four* recommended that the number of medical schools be reduced to thirty-one; actually, more than seventy survived. Flexner would have left about twenty states without any medical schools, but this proved politically unacceptable. Legislatures stepped in to maintain at least one institution in their state. Had the United States been as centralized in its educational system as European countries, there might well have been fewer survivors.

Whatever its influence on public opinion, the Flexner report crystallized a view that proved immensely important in guiding the major foundations' investments in medical care over the next two crucial decades. In a sense, the report was the manifesto of a program that by 1936 guided $91 million from Rockefeller's General Education Board (plus millions more from other foundations) to a select group of medical schools. Seven institutions received over two thirds of the funds from the General Education Board. Though the board represented itself as a purely neutral force responding to the dictates of science and the wishes of the medical schools, its staff actively sought to impose a model of medical education more closely wedded to research than to medical practice. These policies determined not so much which institutions would survive as which would dominate, how they would be run, and what ideals would prevail.[102]

State legislatures wanted medical schools to supply local needs for physicians, but they generally could not be persuaded to invest in research or in building national institutions. Their purposes were limited—and quite understandably so: Research in medicine is typically a "public good," and an individual state, like a particular corporation, is unlikely to recover enough of the gains to society at large to justify the costs to itself. Hence state legislatures and private corporations will almost always rationally underinvest in basic scientific research. The situation of philanthropists, on the other hand, was entirely different. Their interest lay in legitimating their wealth and power by publicly demonstrating their good works. Medical research and education advertised their moral responsibility in ways congruent with the cultural standards of an age that increasingly revered science. As they did business on a national scale, so they did philanthropy.[103]

The assimilation of medical education into the universities drew academic medicine away from private practice. During the nineteenth century, the medical schools had been organizations of the dominant practitioners in a community. In the twentieth century, academic and private physicians began to diverge and represent distinctive interests and values. A pivotal step in the differentiation of the two groups was the creation of the first full-time academic positions in clinical medicine. Beginning in the 1870s, the laboratory sciences at Class A medical schools had been placed on a full-time basis, but clinical instruction had continued in the hands of physicians who also maintained private practices. This arrangement had one notable advantage for the medical schools: It held down costs. At the University of Pennsylvania in 1891, while professors in the laboratory sciences were receiving $3,000 a year, the senior clinical professors were paid only $2,000. Under the old system of dividing up student fees among the faculty, they would have taken in three or four times as much. But their incomes from private practice had risen because, as specialists, they were able to command higher fees for consultations. Clinical professorships had now become desirable almost entirely for their indirect value in augmenting private consulting practices, rather than for their direct income.[104] However, the time and attention these professors diverted to their private patients disturbed those who wanted to improve clinical teaching and research. Why, Simon Flexner and others asked, should academic positions in clinical medicine require less commitment than positions in the laboratory sciences? In 1907 Dean Welch of Johns Hopkins gave his support to full-time clinical professorships; Osler, now at Oxford, dissented, warning that teacher and student might become wholly absorbed in research and neglect "those wider interests to which a great hospital must minister." It would be "a very good thing for science, but a very bad thing for the profession."[105] But prodded by the General Education Board, some medical schools made clinical teaching full-time. Chicago, Yale, Vanderbilt, and Washington University in St. Louis restructured their clinical departments to meet the board's condition for grants. However, the board's insistence on full-time appointments aroused resentment, and the policy was dropped in 1925.[106]

As American medical education became increasingly dominated by scientists and researchers, doctors came to be trained according to the values and standards of academic specialists. Many have argued that this was a mistake. They would have preferred to see only a few schools like Johns Hopkins training scientists and specialists, while the rest, with more modest programs, turned out general practitioners to take care of the everyday ills that make up the greater part of medical work. But this was not the course that American medical education followed; the same curriculum and requirements were established for all students. The emphasis on the basic sciences initially ran counter to the inclinations of many in the profession. Bigelow's initial reaction to Eliot's reforms at Harvard in 1870 was typical of a widespread aversion to basic science among physicians. Even after 1900 the traditionalists did not give up without a fight. At schools like the University of Pennsylvania and Washington University, there were intense and occasionally bitter struggles for control between the old-line practitioners and the insurgent party of research scientists.[107] The foundation-sponsored victory of the Johns Hopkins model prevented American medicine from remaining as practical in its orientation as might have been its natural tendency. On the other hand, Flexner would have preferred medical education to have more of the flexibility of graduate education in the arts and sciences; he felt that the uniformity of medical education stifled creative work. In the years after his report was published, he became increasingly disenchanted with the rigidity of the educational standards that had become identified with his name.[108]

The Aftermath of Reform

The new system greatly increased the homogeneity and cohesiveness of the profession. The extended period of training helped to instill common values and beliefs among doctors, and the uniformity of the medical curriculum discouraged sectarian divisions. Under the old system of apprenticeships with solo practitioners, doctors acquired more idiosyncratic views of medicine and formed personal attachments with their preceptors rather than their peers. Hospital internships generated a stronger sense of shared identity among contemporaries. In 1904, when the AMA first investigated internships, it estimated that about 50 percent of physicians went on to hospital training; by 1912 75 to 80 percent of graduates were estimated to be taking internships. The AMA published its first listing of internships in 1914, and by 1923, for the first time, there were enough openings to accommodate all graduates.[109]

The profession grew more uniform in its social composition. The high costs of medical education and more stringent requirements limited the entry of students from the lower and working classes. And deliberate policies of discrimination against Jews, women, and blacks promoted still greater social homogeneity. The opening of medicine to immigrants and women, which the competitive system of medical education allowed in the 1890s, was now reversed.

The influx of women into the medical profession had already begun to ebb before publication of the Flexner report. By 1909 only three women's medical colleges still existed; the total number of women medical students, including those at coeducational schools, had dropped to 921 from 1,419 fifteen years earlier. The growing number of women doctors in the late nineteenth century may have been partly a product of Victorian concerns about the propriety of male physicians examining women's bodies. Conversely, the fall in their number may have stemmed partly from the waning of the Victorian sensibility. In his 1910 report, Flexner thought the declining numbers of women reflected declining demand for women doctors or declining interest among women in becoming physicians. Others, however, have since pointed to the active hostility of men in the profession. As places in medical school became more scarce, schools that previously had liberal policies toward women increasingly excluded them. Administrators justified outright discrimination against qualified women candidates on the grounds that they would not continue to practice after marriage. For the next half century after 1910, except for wartime, the schools maintained quotas limiting women to about 5 percent of medical student admissions.[110]

Before the Flexner report, there had been seven medical schools for blacks in the United States; only Howard and Meharry survived. Blacks also faced outright exclusion from internships and from hospital privileges at all but a few institutions. The scarcity of opportunities for training and practice had a material impact. In 1930 only one of every 3,000 black Americans was a doctor, and in the Deep South, the situation was even worse—in Mississippi, blacks had one doctor for every 14,634 persons.[111]

In the controversy over the reform of medical education, one objection frequently raised against eliminating the proprietary medical colleges was that they provided poor communities with doctors and poor children with an opportunity to enter medicine. Flexner denied in his report that the "poor boy" had any right to enter medicine "unless it is best for society that he should," and he made no allowance for the inability of low-income communities to pay for the services of highly trained physicians. From a medical school in Chattanooga, Tennessee, one doctor responded, "True, our entrance requirements are not the same as those of the University of Pennsylvania or Harvard; nor do we pretend to turn out the same sort of finished product. Yet we prepare worthy, ambitious men who have striven hard with small opportunities and risen above their surroundings to become family doctors to the farmers of the south, and to the smaller towns of the mining districts." The graduates of the larger schools, he added, could never be expected to settle in these communities. "Would you say that such people should be denied physicians? Can the wealthy who are in a minority say to the poor majority, you shall not have a doctor?"[112]

But that was, implicitly, what they did say.

Flexner insisted in his report that a kind of "spontaneous dispersion" would spread the graduates of the top medical schools to the four winds.[113] On this matter, he proved quite wrong. Doctors gravitated strongly to the wealthier areas of the country. A 1920 study by the biostatistician Raymond Pearl showed that the distribution of physicians by region in the United States was closely correlated with per capita income. Doctors, Pearl concluded, behaved the way all "sensible people" might be expected to. "They do business where business is good and avoid places where it is bad."[114]

The declining output of medical schools aggravated shortages of physicians in poor and rural areas, but regional inequalities in the availability of physicians had actually been increasing since the Civil War. Between 1870 and 1910, the poorer states lost physicians relative to population, while the wealthier states gained them. For example, in 1870 for every doctor in South Carolina there were 894 persons, compared with 712 persons per doctor in Massachusetts; by 1910, the number of people per doctor had risen to 1,170 in South Carolina and fallen in Massachusetts to 497. The disparities between cities and rural areas were also growing.[115]

These widening inequalities reflected the changing economic realities of medical practice I discussed in the previous chapter. Where local transportation improved, the market for medical services expanded. The development of hard roads and public transportation and the spread of telephone systems were far more rapid in the wealthier, more urban states. On the basis of such strictly ecological considerations, these areas could support a higher population of doctors. As railways and autos became common in rural areas, the village physician who formerly enjoyed a quiet local monopoly was exposed to the competition of doctors and hospitals in nearby towns and cities. The shift in distribution that began in the late nineteenth century was a response to these underlying changes in the market.

The increasing cost of medical education ensured that many small towns and rural areas would lose the services of any physician. In the twenties, articles began to appear in the popular press about the "vanishing country doctor." A study by AMA President William Allen Pusey showed that more than a third of 910 small towns that had physicians in 1914 had been abandoned by doctors by 1925. "As you increase the cost of the license to practice medicine you increase the price at which medical service must be sold and you correspondingly decrease the number of people who can afford to buy this medical service," wrote Pusey. He expressed particular concern about data he had collected showing that irregular practitioners were settling in the counties abandoned by physicians.[116]

In the twenties, even Flexner became convinced that the distribution of physicians was a more serious problem than he had originally anticipated. Through the General Education Board he supervised a study that showed a growing gap in medical service between town and city. In 1906 small towns (population 1,000 to 2,500) had 590 people per doctor, while large cities (population over 100,000) had 492. By 1923 the small towns had 910 people per doctor, the large cities 536: The small towns' deficit had grown from about 20 to 70 percent.[117] The study insisted, however, that there was still an overall surplus of doctors since many physicians were underemployed.

After the turn of the century, the supply of physicians did not keep pace with the population as a whole. According to Census data, in 1900 there were 173 physicians per 100,000 population, but only 164 in 1910. (Somewhat different AMA statistics give lower figures, 157 and 146 respectively.) By 1920 the ratio of doctors to population was down to 137 per 100,000 and ten years later to 125 per 100,000, where it bottomed out for the next two decades.[118]

Though physicians had succeeded in controlling their own numbers, they could not prevent rival practitioners from winning legal protection and staying in business. Despite vehement medical opposition, osteopaths and chiropractors were able to obtain licensing laws in nearly every state. Even where the chiropractors were unsuccessful in gaining statutory approval, they practiced openly, sometimes in greater numbers than in states where they were licensed. At the end of the twenties, there were an estimated 36,000 sectarians in practice,[119] compared to about 150,000 physicians—or about the same ratio as homeopaths and Eclectics bore to regular physicians fifty years earlier. However, the sectarian practitioners of the twentieth century were in a vastly different situation from their forerunners. In winning licensing privileges, the new sectarians were usually unable to win access to hospitals or the right to prescribe drugs. Unlike the homeopaths in the mid-nineteenth century, they did not represent a serious challenge to the profession. According to a survey of nine thousand families carried out over the years 1928 to 1931, all the non-M.D. practitioners combined— osteopaths, chiropractors, Christian Scientists and other faith healers, midwives, and chiropodists—took care of only 5.1 percent of all attended cases of illness.[120] Physicians finally had medical practice pretty much to themselves.

THE RETREAT OF PRIVATE JUDGMENT

Authority over Medication

Medical practitioners, of whatever kind, were not the only source of treatment available on the market in the nineteenth century. The patent medicine makers, whose advertisements were ubiquitous in the popular press, also offered therapy and advice. Since nineteenth-century practitioners often prepared their own medicines, the patent medicine companies were their direct competitors. The companies, furthermore, not only sold drugs, but also distributed guides to health and invited the puzzled and the sick to write them for advice about their medical problems. From the standpoint of financial resources, they were a more formidable alternative to regular physicians than were the medical sects. The money they spent on advertising assured a wide distribution to their propaganda and induced many newspapers to defend them.

The nostrum makers were the nemesis of the physicians. They mimicked, distorted, derided, and undercut the authority of the profession. While they often claimed to be doctors themselves, or to operate health institutes or medical colleges, or to have the endorsement of eminent physicians, they also frequently insinuated that the profession was jealously conspiring to suppress their discoveries. The contrasts they drew were vivid. Doctors wanted to cut people up or give prolonged treatment, while their "sure cure" would instantly provide relief. Physicians charged high fees; their remedies were cheap. When new scientific ideas appeared, the patent medicine makers were quick to exploit them. In the late 1880s, an ingenious Texan, William Radam, promoted a Microbe Killer that played upon public misunderstanding of the recent discoveries of Pasteur and Koch. Consisting nearly entirely of water—except for traces of red wine, hydrochloric and sulphuric acid— Microbe Killer was supposed to cure all diseases by destroying germs inside the body. By 1890 Radam had seventeen factories producing the Killer. Doctors, he explained, tried to deceive the public by doing elaborate and useless diagnoses: "Diagnosing disease is simply blindfolding the public." Reflecting on Radam's success, the historian James Harvey Young notes the irony that the age in which physicians could for the first time accurately explain much disease "was the very age in which patent medicines reached their apogee."[121]

The patent medicine makers played upon the changing forms of discontent with physicians. Advertising for such popular remedies as Lydia Pinkham's Vegetable Compound—introduced in 1876 for "FEMALE WEAKNESSES," "All Weaknesses of the generative organs of either Sex," and "all diseases of the Kidneys"—frequently appealed to fears of medical treatment, especially surgery. In 1879, as Sarah Stage reports in her history of the Pinkham company, the firm began inviting readers to "Write Mrs. Pinkham" about their medical complaints (a practice that continued even after Lydia Pinkham died in 1883). One woman suffering from a prolapsed uterus wrote, "Dr. tells me I can have the trouble removed but thought I would write and ask you if the Compound would do it before I submitted to an operation with *Doctor's tools*, a thing I have not much faith in." The company replied, "By all means avoid instrumental treatment for your trouble. Use the Compound as you have been using it—faithfully and patiently—and it will eventually work a cure. . . ." In the late 1890s the Pinkham company began increasingly to appeal to Victorian modesty to draw women away from doctors. "Do you want a strange man to hear all about your particular diseases?" asked one advertisement with the headline, "The Doctor Did No Good." And the company promised, "Men NEVER See Your Letters."[122]

From its founding, the AMA was at odds with the patent medicine business. It divided drugs into "ethical" preparations of known composition advertised only to the profession, and patent medicines of secret composition sold directly to the public. (Most "patent" medicines were actually not patented since a patent required disclosure of the formula; technically, they were "proprietary" drugs whose trademarks were protected by copyright.) Initially, the AMA rejected as unethical any secret formula or any private appropriation of medical knowledge or techniques, which it maintained ought to belong collectively to the profession. However, the AMA was powerless to enforce these views. In 1849 the association resolved to create a board to evaluate nostrums but proved unable to do so for lack of resources. In the late nineteenth century, proprietary drugs became more widely used, and professional concern about them intensified. Advertisements for such drugs filled the medical journals as well as the newspapers, and doctors, though often ignorant of their composition and effects, increasingly prescribed them. A survey of New York drugstores showed a steady increase in nostrums and machine-made tablets, as a proportion of physician prescriptions, from less than 1 percent as late as 1874 to 20 to 25 percent by 1902.[123] In 1900 the AMA launched a campaign to make the "legitimate" proprietary remedies "respond to the ethics of medicine" by forcing their manufacturers to disclose all formulae and cease public advertising. Its *Journal* announced that it would stop publishing all notices of offending drugs when current advertising contracts expired. And it urged physicians not to prescribe, nor other medical journals to advertise, either secret preparations or drugs "advertised directly to the laity."[124] However, no major campaign materialized, and the drug companies continued to advertise in many medical journals, which, like newspapers, depended on them for revenues.

Between 1900 and 1910, three changes enabled the medical profession to wrest control of the flow of pharmaceutical information. First, and perhaps most important, muckraking journalists and other Progressives joined physicians in a crusade for regulation of patent medicines as part of a more general assault on deceptive business practices. Second, as a result of its growing membership, the AMA finally acquired the financial resources to create its own regulatory apparatus and to mount a major effort against the nostrum makers. And, third, the drug makers were forced to recognize that they depended increasingly on doctors to market their drugs because of the public's increased reliance on professional opinion in decisions about medication.

Public reliance on professional opinion may have been stimulated by muckraking revelations about how dangerous many patent medicines were. Beginning about 1903, domestic magazines like the *Ladies' Home Journal* continually warned women about the imprudence of self-medication. Edward Bok, the journal's editor, pointed to drugs and syrups containing opium, cocaine, and alcohol, which unsuspecting mothers used themselves or gave to their children. "The physician's fee of a dollar or two, which the mother seeks to save, may prove to be the costliest form of economy which she has ever practiced."[125]

Probably the most famous investigations of the drug industry in American history began appearing in *Collier's Weekly* in October 1905. In two series—the first on patent medicines, the second on medical quacks—the muckraking reporter Samuel Hopkins Adams explored the cynical deceptions of medicine makers and medicine men who sold dangerous and addictive drugs. Adams attacked 264 individuals and companies by name, giving detailed evidence, such as laboratory reports showing drugs were worthless and burial notices of people who gave testimonials to drug companies and then died from the diseases that were supposed to have been cured. In an article on headache powders containing the deadly drug acetanilid, Adams listed people who had taken them and died soon after, and he warned, "There is but one safeguard in the use of these remedies; to regard them as one would regard opium, and to employ them only with the consent of a physician who understands their true nature."[126] The message underlying the exposés was that commercial interests were dangerous to health and that physicians had to be trusted. In the first article of the series, *Collier's* reprinted a poster from a Chicago drugstore showing two figures: a healthy workingman "before using" and a skeleton "after using" "Hoodwink's Sarsaparilla or any other old 'Patent Medicines.'" Below was written:

MORAL

Don't Dose Yourself with secret Patent Medicines, Almost all of which are Frauds and Humbugs. When sick Consult a Doctor and take his Prescription: it is the only Sensible Way and you'll find it Cheaper in the end.

The muckrakers utterly discredited the claims of the patent medicine companies to provide personal medical advice. In the *Ladies' Home Journal*, a young reporter, Mark Sullivan, wrote about "How the Private Confidences of Women Are Laughed At" and "How the Game of Medical Advice Is Worked." With devastating effect, Bok reprinted notices indicating that the patent medicine makers rented the letters of women seeking confidential advice to companies that compiled mailing lists. Next to a copy of an advertisement urging women to write Lydia Pinkham, he published a picture of her tombstone showing she had been dead twenty years.[127] "The whole 'personal medical advice' business," wrote Samuel Hopkins Adams, "is managed by rote, and the letter that you get 'special to your case' has been printed and signed before your inquiry ever reached the shark who gets your money."[128]

The second part of Adams' series, dealing with quack physicians, portrayed them as fakes and parasites on human misery, promising illusory cures for tuberculosis, cancer, and drug addiction. Some of these doctors, Adams suggested, used addictive drugs themselves. "How shall the public protect itself against quackery?" Adams asked.

Any physician who advertises a positive cure for any disease, who issues nostrum testimonials, who sells his services to a secret remedy, or who diagnoses and treats by mail patients he has never seen, is a quack. . . . Shut your eyes to the medical columns of the newspapers, and you will save yourself many forebodings and symptoms. Printer's ink, when it spells out a doctor's promise to cure, is one of the subtlest and most dangerous of poisons.[129]

The AMA distributed over 150,000 copies of "The Great American Fraud" over the next five years. Adams' series was to the proprietary drug makers and advertising doctors what the Flexner report five years later would be to the proprietary medical schools: a withering investigation of deceit by commercial interests that contributed to the consolidation of professional authority.

In 1906, on the heels of "The Great American Fraud" and Upton Sinclair's novel *The Jungle* exposing adulteration in the meat-packing industry, Congress passed the Pure Food and Drug Act. The act marks the beginning of federal drug regulation, but the law affected only the most arrant fakes. It did not require the disclosure of all contents, except in the case of narcotics; it only banned statements on the label of a drug about its composition that were "false and fraudulent." This rule did not initially apply to claims about the effectiveness of drugs, nor to statements made in newspaper advertisements. After some initial caution, drug makers discovered they could resume making bold claims, even intimating that their drugs now met a federal standard of purity and effectiveness. But although the law initially amounted to little, another regulatory system was also being established at the time that would, for the next several decades, be more consequential.

In 1905, after definitively closing its *Journal* to patent medicine advertisements, the AMA established a Council on Pharmacy and Chemistry to set standards for drugs, evaluate them, and lead the battle against nostrums. As part of this effort, it set up a laboratory and maintained close contact with the federal Bureau of Chemistry, which tested products under the food and drug law. This was one of several new undertakings the AMA's growing financial strength permitted. The council's publication *New and Nonofficial Remedies* became widely used by medical journals in setting advertising policies and by doctors in prescribing. When one company refused to submit its products for examination, a member of the council remarked that its work would be simplified if it could "induce all the objectionable manufacturers to commit this form of suicide."[130]

To have its drugs accepted, a company had to comply with the AMA council's rules. Not only were drugs forbidden whose manufacturers made false advertising claims or refused to disclose their drugs' composition. The council also would not approve any drug that was directly advertised to the public, or whose "label, package or circular" listed the diseases for which the drug was to be used. Companies would have a choice of markets: If they wished to advertise a drug to doctors, they could not advertise it to the public or instruct laymen in its use. For such drugs, the public would have to turn to physicians.

The AMA also institutionalized the work of the muckrakers. It set up an office to pursue fraudulent drugs and shame publishers of journals and newspapers into dropping all advertisements of patent medicines. The association denied that any distinctions could be made among patent medicines: "[T]here is no such thing as an unobjectionable 'patent medicine' advertisement in a newspaper," the editor of its journal declared.[131] The struggle to suppress such advertising put the profession in the position of demanding that newspapers sacrifice a lucrative source of income for the sake of public health and public respectability. It is a measure of the profession's new authority that, despite the financial loss, many newspapers began to censor patent medicine advertisements and rule out those listed as frauds by the AMA. A few states passed laws making it illegal for newspapers to publish any advertisements for doctors. The magnitude of the AMA's achievement was evident by 1919, when the U.S. Public Health Service sent out a circular to 20,000 periodicals and found that more than 19,000 refused to carry any advertisements for doctors.[132]

Neither federal regulation nor the AMA prevented proprietary drug companies from marketing drugs to the public; nor did they bar people from self-treatment. But the drug companies now labored under more rigid constraints about the claims they could make. The federal law was amended in 1912 to cover fraudulent claims of effectiveness and administratively extended in the 1920s to cover newspaper advertising as well as labels. In this period, the patent medicine makers beat a steady retreat. By 1915 the Pinkham company, for example, omitted any reference to prolapsed uterus in its advertising, and ten years later all mention of female disorders disappeared. The label now said it was "Recommended as a Vegetable Tonic in conditions for which this preparation is Adapted." The AMA official in charge of the nostrum campaign suggested it might just as well read, "For Those Who Like This Sort of Thing, This is the Sort of Thing That Those People Like."[133] Before regulation, scientific medicine had to compete with the claims of patent medicine companies, and amid this cacophony its voice was not always audible. Drug regulation turned down the volume of patent medicine claims and allowed scientific medicine to be heard more clearly.

Recognizing that public opinion had shifted, the patent medicine companies became more deferential to the medical profession. In the 1919 edition of *The People's Common Sense Medical Advisor*, Dr. R. V. Pierce, who had been one of the targets of Adams' investigations, conceded that he was not so "presumptuous" as to claim his book could make "every man his own physician." Urging his readers to consult a physician immediately in serious illness, he wrote, "No man can with advantage be his own lawyer, carpenter, tailor and printer; much less can he hope to artfully repair his own constitution."[134]

As physicians became more authoritative, many drug companies found it wiser to address their appeals for new products to the profession. But to do so, they were obliged to comply with the AMA's terms and withdraw advertising for those products from the public. In 1924 the AMA Council on Pharmacy and Chemistry ruled that a drug could be denied approval if a company derived much of its earnings from other products that were not in compliance with AMA guidelines.[135] The council did not want to let companies play both sides of the street with different drugs. Consequently, companies had to opt entirely for one side or the other.

The AMA's regulatory system did not merely augment the federal effort. The logic of the 1906 law was to improve the functioning of the market by making consumer information more accurate.[136] The logic of the AMA's regulatory system was to withhold information from consumers and rechannel drug purchasing through physicians. This shift meant a structural change in the market rather than simply an improvement in its functioning, and it gave physicians a larger share of the purchasing power of their patients.

The profession also extended its authority into other markets related to health. When manufacturers introduced infant food preparations in the late 1800s, they advertised widely in newspapers and magazines as well as in the medical press. The directions were simple: To prepare Nestlé's Milk Food, introduced in the United States in 1873, a mother had only to add water. Like the patent medicine companies, the infant food producers represented an alternative to physicians in an area of decision making that doctors and reformers believed required professional rather than commercial control. "The proper authority for establishing rules for substitute feeding," wrote a noted pediatrician in 1893, "should emanate from the medical profession, and not from non-medical capitalists."[137]

The shift to dependence on physicians in infant feeding followed the same pattern as in the use of drugs. Increasingly, the child-care literature counseled parents to consult a physician about their baby's diet. In the 1910s manufacturers discovered that advertising exclusively to the medical profession on its terms could be a more efficient way to market their products than by attempting to reach a far more diffuse public. When Mead Johnson began selling a milk modifier called Dextri-Maltose in 1912, it advertised it only to physicians; no directions were enclosed for the mother. The success of Dextri-Maltose and another such product, writes Rima Apple, "demonstrated to other companies that such advertising policies could result in a satisfactory compromise between the needs of the manufacturers to sell their products, and the desire of the physicians to control the distribution and use of the infant foods."[138] Introducing a new product in 1924, Nestlè advertised in the AMA's *Journal* that it would be "sold only on the prescription or recommendation of a physician. No feeding instructions appear on the trade package." Mead-Johnson put the point directly in its medical advertising: "When mothers in America feed their babies by lay advice, the control of your pediatric cases passes out of your hands, Doctor." Since Mead-Johnson advertised only to doctors, it shared the same interest as physicians in persuading mothers to follow professional advice.

Medical authority in prescribing drugs and other products enabled the AMA to stand between the manufacturers and their markets. This strategic gatekeeping role permitted the AMA, in effect, to levy an advertising toll on the producers. Revenues from journal advertisements became the principal source of funds for the association. In 1912 the AMA set up a cooperative advertising bureau, which channeled advertisements to state medical journals. The bureau gave the AMA considerable financial leverage over the state medical societies and helped bind the national association even more tightly together. Once again, cultural authority was being converted into economic power and effective political organization.

Ambiguity and Competence

The campaign against patent medicines reflected the extraordinary new confidence and authority that the medical profession enjoyed in the Progressive era. This confidence did not stem specifically from the development of effective therapeutic agents, which were still few in number. Even if they had been more numerous, new drugs alone could not explain the retreat of private judgment in their use. The growth of medical authority was related more to the success of science in revolutionizing other aspects of medicine and the growing recognition of the inadequacy of the unaided and uneducated senses in understanding the world.

Nineteenth-century medical science had its earliest successful applications in public hygiene. The key scientific breakthroughs in bacteriology came in the 1860s and 1870s in the work of Pasteur and Koch. The 1880s saw the extension and diffusion of these discoveries, and by 1890 their impact began to be felt. The isolation of the organisms responsible for the major infectious diseases led public health officials to shift from the older, relatively inefficient measures against disease in general to more focused measures against specific diseases. These new efforts made a particularly notable difference in the control of water-borne and food-borne diseases. Sand filtration of the water supply, introduced in the 1890s, was far more effective in preventing typhoid than was earlier sanitary reform; regulation of the milk supply dramatically cut infant mortality.

The other early successful use of bacteriology was in surgery. The advent of antiseptic surgery in the late nineteenth century sharply reduced the mortality from injuries and operations and increased the range of surgical work.* But, as the historian Erwin Ackerknecht points out, the rest of therapeutics lagged behind; this was preeminently "an era of public health."[139] One physician commented in 1893 that bacteriology had "rendered great service to the art by adding to the power of preventive medicine. It has not done much for the drug treatment of disease."[140] Pasteur had discovered a vaccine against rabies (which could be given after the bite of a rabid dog because the virus progresses slowly to the brain), but rabies was a relatively uncommon disease.

The first major therapeutic application of bacteriology—diphtheria antitoxin—did not come until the mid-1890s. In 1910 Paul Ehrlich discovered salvarsan ("606") for use against syphilis. Though the first major contribution of chemotherapy, Ehrlich's "magic bullet" was only partially effective, and there was no important successor for the next two and a half decades until the sulfa drugs.

Major advances, to be sure, were made in immunology. The vaccines against typhoid and tetanus date from the turn of the century. These helped raise great hopes for preventive medicine. In 1909 a *Report on National Vitality* by the economist Irving Fisher, surveying the means to extend life expectancy, gave equal weight to public hygiene, "semipublic hygiene" (medical research, medical practice), and personal hygiene. Sponsored by the Committee of One Hundred on National

*On surgery, see Book One, Chapter 4.

Health, a Progressive group concerned with health and efficiency, this was one of the earliest attempts to define priorities in health services. Of "semi-public" hygiene, Fisher noted, "Antiseptic surgery has in the last century been the greatest triumph of the medical profession and has given it a greater prestige than ever before." But in medical practice, he continued, physicians were giving up drugs and depending more on hygiene. "The number of medicines used by physicians is decreasing and will, if the predictions of experts in the field may be trusted, ultimately be reduced to a small fraction of the present pharmacopoeia."[141]

Public health and surgery, as the two great successes of scientific medicine, enjoyed greatly increased prestige in the late nineteenth century. Internal medicine lagged somewhat behind in public estimation. A 1912 report of the AMA Judicial Council, attempting to explain why physicians engaged in "fee-splitting" with surgeons, noted that physicians' fees were "practically the same" as twenty-five years earlier, while surgical fees were "enormously greater." It suggested that while surgery was "a concrete service of a visible, definite kind easily appreciated," medicine "concerns itself with the more abstract problems of inoperable disease and has cared for the nagging ailments of daily life and the intangible struggle against unseen infections, and it has shown its greatest triumph in the prevention of disease."[142]

Though curative agents were few, new diagnostic techniques were strengthening the authority of internal medicine and radically altering the doctor-patient relationship. At the beginning of the nineteenth century, physicians depended in diagnosis primarily on their patients' account of symptoms and their own superficial observation; manual examination was relatively unimportant. In the mid-1800s a series of new diagnostic instruments—the stethoscope, ophthalmoscope, laryngoscope—began to expand the physicians' sensory powers in clinical examination. The use of the stethoscope, as Stanley J. Reiser has observed, required the physician, at least momentarily, to "isolate himself in a world of sounds, inaudible to the patient," and encouraged him to "move away from involvement with the patient's experiences and sensations, to a more detached relation, less with the patient but more with the sounds from the body."[143] These sounds the patient could neither hear nor interpret. Similarly, the other instruments that gradually assumed a place in the doctor's bag reduced dependence on the patients' statement of symptoms and increased the asymmetry of information.

A second set of diagnostic technologies—the microscope and the X-ray, chemical and bacteriological tests, and machines that generated data on patients' physiological condition, such as the spirometer and electrocardiograph—produced data seemingly independent of the physician's as well as the patient's subjective judgment. These developments had uncertain implications for professional autonomy: They further reduced dependence upon the patient, but they increased dependence on capital equipment and formal organizations. Nonetheless, from the patients' standpoint, these detached technologies added a highly persuasive rhetoric to the authority of medicine. They also made it possible to remove part of the diagnostic process from the presence of the patient into "backstage" areas where several physicians might have simultaneous access to the evidence. As Reiser points out, while the ophthalmoscope and laryngoscope "could be used by only one person at a time" and were "thereby prone to the subjective distortions of the viewer," the X-ray enabled several doctors "simultaneously to view and discuss what they saw."[144] The collegial exercise of authority strengthened the claim to objective judgment.

The new diagnostic technologies also figured in the expanding role of physicians as gatekeepers to positions and benefits in the society. With the new apparatus of medical measurement, doctors could set standards of human physiology, evaluate deviations, and classify individuals. In the 1840s, the English physician John Hutchinson, who devised the spirometer to measure lung capacity, announced that it would allow doctors to judge physical fitness for military service. Physicians also began in the mid-1800s to study quantitatively the pulse, blood pressure, body temperature, and other physiological indicators, though simple and practical instruments to take the temperature and blood pressure were not devised until the end of the century. The use of more precise measurements in diagnosis only became standard in medical practice in the early 1900s. Standardized eye tests, standard weight-height tables, and IQ tests were all part of a movement to identify statistical norms of human physiology and behavior. With these new techniques, doctors claimed a progressively greater role in social classification.

Specific chemical and bacteriological tests for disease emerged rapidly at the turn of the century. In the 1880s, the organisms responsible in tuberculosis, cholera, typhoid, and diphtheria were isolated, and by the mid-1890s laboratory tests had been introduced to detect these diseases. The spirochete that causes syphilis was identified in 1905; the Wasserman test for syphilis was introduced in 1906. In the nineteenth century, advances in the analysis of the urine and the blood gave physicians additional diagnostic tools for such diseases as diabetes.

These innovations were not serendipitous. They were the result of progress in basic science that made it possible to duplicate successful applications more rapidly than ever before. The earlier advances in immunization, like smallpox vaccination, had been purely empirical discoveries and were not quickly repeated. Microbiology for the first time permitted physicians to link causes, symptoms, and lesions systematically. The principles that Pasteur demonstrated in the development of anthrax and rabies vaccines now provided a rational basis for developing vaccines against typhoid, cholera, and plague.[145]

Whether many people at the time understood the power of these principles is unlikely; it was probably not until the 1910s and 1920s that the momentum they imparted to scientific medicine was clearly evident. In the late nineteenth century, the picture continued to be confused. There was hardly an advance of medical science whose introduction into medical practice was not initially marred by uncertainty and disillusionment because of errors in application or failures of quality control. This was true of antiseptic surgery, rabies' vaccine, diphtheria antitoxin, and salvarsan. False starts also muddied the picture. Koch's mistaken announcement of a cure for tuberculosis in 1890 was a severe reverse in the clinical application of bacteriology.

But by the late 1890s, medicine was making a difference in health, primarily through its contributions to public hygiene. The role of physicians, however, should not be disparaged. In recent years it has become the fashion to argue that the great drop in mortality in the late nineteenth and early twentieth centuries was due to changes in the standard of living or to general public health efforts. Typically, evidence is cited showing that reductions in mortality from specific diseases occurred before effective prophylactics or therapies were in the hands of physicians.[146] But this is to draw an exaggerated distinction between medicine and public health during this period and to assume that the effectiveness of medicine depended solely on the possession of "magic bullets." By providing more accurate diagnosis, identifying the sources of infection and their modes of transmission, and diffusing knowledge of personal hygiene, medicine entered directly into the improved effectiveness of public health. In two diseases, diphtheria and tetanus, the introduction of antitoxins was followed by a rapid decline in mortality. In a third, typhoid, the introduction of a vaccine accounted significantly for the fall in mortality. Diphtheria and typhoid were two of the major causes of death whose declines figured in the general rise of life expectancy in this period.[147]

In any event, the impact on social behavior of vaccines and serums was not proportionate to their epidemiological effects. Diphtheria and tetanus, like rabies, were dreaded diseases with high case fatality rates, and medical intervention in these instances was dramatically effective.

Diphtheria antitoxin reduced the case fatality rate from 50 to 31 percent. The value of diphtheria antitoxin depended on early and accurate diagnosis; medical expertise in a case might mean the difference between life and death. For understanding the growth of medical authority, it may be irrelevant that doctors could not cure most sore throats. Informed parents would still want a physician to take a look at a child's sore throat even if the probability of diphtheria was only small. Moreover, it is not difficult to understand how this dependence could become generalized into areas in which physicians claimed expertise on less justifiable grounds.

Medical authority was not necessarily weaker for being objectively incorrect. The case of infant feeding offers a good example. Many of the proprietary infant foods of the late nineteenth century were, in fact, deleterious; some contained no milk at all, and babies who were fed artificially had much higher mortality rates than breast-fed infants. Some physicians advised against any artificial foods; others thought some were acceptable. Most knew little about nutrition and their recommendations were unreliable. A few made a valuable contribution by galvanizing public health authorities into regulating the milk supply. But the claim made by eminent authorities that feeding babies was so complicated it required medical supervision was based on a misreading of the medical evidence. Physicians had found that cow's milk had more protein than human milk, less sugar, and about the same proportion of fat. They believed that these differences accounted for indigestion and disease among babies who were not breast-fed. Consequently, they thought cow's milk had to be altered according to a complicated formula. Thomas Morgan Rotch, an influential pediatrician of the period, thought that minute variations in the composition of the milk, as little as 0.1 percent, would make all the difference. Doctors also believed that a baby would have trouble if it were fed more than its tiny stomach could accommodate; not knowing how rapidly milk is digested, they advised a regular and limited schedule of feeding. Rotch insisted, moreover, that what was good for one baby might not be good for another; hence individual medical supervision was crucial. Ironically, many pediatricians at the time also felt that heating milk made it less suitable for babies because it further altered its condition from the natural state. As a result, though they supported efforts to get a clean milk supply, they were ambivalent about pasteurization. Reviewing the previous forty-five years of pediatric opinion about infant feeding, a prominent pediatrician noted in 1935 that what was "most striking" was "that, barring the discovery of the vitamins and the recognition of their importance in nutrition, in spite of all the advances in biochemistry during this time, all the innumerable investigations which have been carried out . . . babies are now fed in almost the same way that they were at the beginning of this period."[148] In 1979 another pediatrician reviewing Rotch's theories concluded with Oliver Wendell Holmes' remark that, in feeding babies, two substantial mammary glands are more useful than the two hemispheres of a professor's brain.[149]

So cultural authority need not be based on competence. Ambiguity may suffice. In the case of public hygiene and the treatment of some infectious diseases, the professional claim to special competence had a rational foundation; in the case of infant feeding, it probably did not. Yet an item-by-item evaluation of medical knowledge is unlikely, it seems to me, to yield an understanding of the growth of medical authority. The change in social behavior was not limited to those decisions in which dependence on professional authority was prudent. On the shoulders of broad historical forces, private judgment retreated along a wide frontier of human choice.

The Renewal of Legitimate Complexity

Between the Jacksonian and the Progressive eras, American politics and culture had undergone a deep change. The American faith in democratic simplicity and common sense yielded to a celebration of science and efficiency. Yet one need not overdraw the contrast between the two periods. Both saw vehement attacks on the power of big corporations, and both witnessed further growth of corporate and bureaucratic organization. In each period, the continuing, unresolved tensions between the nation's democratic culture and its capitalist economy became particularly acute. Both the Jacksonians and the Progressives esteemed science, but they understood it in different ways: The Jacksonians saw science as knowledge that could be widely and easily diffused, while the Progressives were reconciled to its complexity and inaccessibility. So, for the professions, the contrast between the two eras was striking. In the Jacksonian era, professional monopolies were assailed in the same spirit as business monopolies. In the Progressive period, reformers and muckrakers crusading against business interests held up professional authority as a model of public disinterestedness.

Unlike the Jacksonians, Progressives of varying persuasions supported the drive of the medical profession for control of its domain, joining in moves for strict professional licensing and drug regulation. The crusade against medical quackery brought the muckrakers and the AMA together in common cause. Socialists and the Rockefeller philanthropies were equally committed to the extension of scientific medicine. So were women's organizations and antifeminists.

The assumptions of radicals, reformers and conservatives reflected the more general decline of confidence in the ability of the laymen to deal with their own physical and personal problems. The home medical advisors of the early twentieth century, unlike their predecessors a half century earlier, concentrated mainly on everyday hygiene and first aid. By the Progressive era, to call for popular autonomy in healing was to endanger one's own credibility. The public granted the legitimate complexity of medicine and the need for institutionalized professional authority.

Doctors saw the change in their own lifetimes. "Our work in the past ten years has changed tremendously," commented a Minnesota physician in 1923. "Ten years ago no parent brought a child to the physician for examination to make sure that nothing was wrong. Today, I venture to say that the greatest part of the work a pediatrician has is in preventive medicine." The same was true of older patients. "A man comes to the doctor and tells him he wants to be examined, and to be told what to do to increase his span of life."[150]

Few comparisons illustrate more clearly the growth of medical authority than do the differences in physicians' experiences in the Spanish American and First World Wars. Victor C. Vaughan, long the dean of the University of Michigan Medical School, recalled in 1923:

> I served in the war with Spain in 1898, and I went time and again to a division officer and made certain requests or offered certain advice. As a rule, I was snubbed and told by action, if not by words, that I was only a medical officer, and that I had no right to make any suggestions, and it was impudent of me to do so.
>
> The commanding general at Chickamauga [an army camp], when we had an increasing number of cases of typhoid fever, would every day ostentatiously ride up to a well which had been condemned and drink of this water to show his contempt. But in the late war I had a different experience. I never went to a line officer with a recommendation but that he said, "Doctor, it will be done". . .

"There was never a war in which the medical profession received the authority and won the credit as it did in the last war," Vaughan observed, ". . . and there never was a time when the medical profession had the honor and credit that it has today . . ."[151]

Christopher Lasch argues that the loss of autonomy and competence by laymen to professionals in the Progressive era was a result of the same forces as were responsible for the loss of autonomy and competence by workers to capitalists and engineers.[152] But the mechanisms involved were so different that the analogy is highly misleading. The power that employers derived from their control of jobs enabled them to carry out changes unwanted by their workers; professionals did not have an equivalent basis of power to deprive the laity of their autonomy. To put it simply, bosses can fire their workers, but doctors cannot fire their patients. Except where doctors were given legal authority or institutional power as gatekeepers, clients became dependent upon physicians only as they sought out professional consultation. That act cannot be explained as pure coercion or false consciousness. Professionals might, as Lasch suggests, "ridicule" the capacity of people to care for themselves, but it seems more reasonable to look for the origins of increased resort to professional advice in the new conditions of life at the end of the nineteenth century than in the self-serving exhortations of professionals.

The pervasive changes in everyday experience brought about by revolutions in technology and social organization altered perceptions of the value of specialized knowledge. The new order of urban life and industrial capitalism generally required people to rely more on the complementary skills of others and less on their own unspecialized talents. Professional medicine drew its authority in part from the changing beliefs people held about their own abilities and understanding. While professionals capitalized on these new conditions, they did not create them. As the main emissaries of science, physicians benefited from its rising influence. The continuing growth of diagnostic skills and therapeutic competence was sufficient to sustain confidence in their authority. And with the political organization they achieved after 1900, doctors were able to convert that rising authority into legal privileges, economic power, high incomes, and enhanced social status.

Physicians' incomes increased substantially in the early twentieth century. Around 1900, according to admittedly imprecise estimates cited earlier, average doctors' incomes ranged from about $750 to $1500. Since prices roughly doubled between 1900 and 1928, comparable incomes in the latter year would have increased to between $1,500 and $3,000. But according to data collected by the AMA from a sample of more than six thousand doctors, physicians in 1928 had an average net income of $6,354 and a median net income of $4,900. In 1929, according to Commerce Department statistics, the average net income of physicians in independent practice was $5,224, while their median net income was $3,758. For the same year, a survey of five thousand doctors conducted by the Committee on the Costs of Medical Care reported that the average net income of all physicians, salaried and non-salaried, was $5,304 and the median $3,827. Doctors' earnings fell with the Great Depression but remained high relative to other occupations. In a study for the National Bureau of Economic Research, Simon Kuznets and Milton Friedman found for the years 1929 to 1934 that the average annual net income of physicians was $4,081, about four times the average earnings of gainfully employed workers ($991). Median family incomes of the two groups were somewhat closer: Those of physicians were merely two to three times as large as those of the gainfully employed. To compensate for higher costs of education, professional incomes might have needed to be, at most, 70 percent higher than nonprofessional incomes, but the actual difference was much greater. After examining various possible explanatory factors, Kuznets and Friedman concluded that the excess was due to monopolistic barriers to entry into the professions.[153]

In prestige as well as income, the medical profession gained enormously in the first decades of the twentieth century. Medicine became a highly desirable career choice. By the thirties nearly twice as many people were applying to medical schools as were being accepted. The overall rejection rate—after taking into account unsuccessful applicants from one year who were admitted later on—stood at 45 percent.[154] Highly selective admissions had come with the demise of profit-making schools; before 1900 rejections had been virtually unheard of. In an empirical study of occupational prestige published in 1925, based on a survey primarily of high school seniors and school teachers, the physicians' average rank was third, behind bankers and college professors and just ahead of clergymen and lawyers. In a second study, conducted in 1933, medicine uniformly ranked first among people in varying occupations and communities of different size. Later studies have placed doctors ahead of every other occupational category, except for Justice of the U.S. Supreme Court.[155]

In explaining social hierarchies, two lines of thought have been especially conspicuous. One calls attention to differences in the *functional* importance to the society as a whole of its various roles and occupations. A second stresses variations in *power* available to people in different structural positions. Theories of change in social hierarchies—theories, that is, of collective mobility—follow the same general pattern. The functionalist view emphasizes changes in the needs of society or in the capacity of different groups to meet them. The contrasting position looks to changes in the power of classes or occupational groups because of increased resources or diminished resistance. These views suffer from complementary difficulties. The functionalist attributes too much to the society as a whole, while the power theorist attributes too much to particular organized groups. The functionalist view contemplates only social needs; the power theorist only private interests. Neither sees any way to transcend its own one-sidedness.

The two points of view and their limitations are apparent in interpretations of the rise of the professions. The functionalist ascribes their advance to the growing importance of professional skills and technical knowledge, while the power theorist cites the monopolistic practices of the professions. In the case of medicine, the former sees the growth of valid medical knowledge as the key to the advance of the profession, while the latter finds an explanation in the profession's monopolization of that knowledge.[156]

In the Introduction, I said that the advance of science, while vitally important, could not explain the comparative and historical variations in the position of the professions. Science may improve the efficacy and productivity of a profession without making it rich or revered; knowledge must be transformed into authority, and authority into market power, before the gains from scientific advance can be privately appropriated by a profession. On the other hand, monopolistic practices alone are an insufficient explanation. Many occupations seek monopolistic power; to cite the impulse is no explanation of why some succeed and others fail. The exponents of the monopolization thesis tend to presume the capacity of a group to articulate its collective interests over its competing interests. What must first be explained is how the group achieves consensus and mobilization.

If the medical profession were merely a monopolistic guild, its position would be much less secure than it is. The basis of its high income and status, as I have argued all along, is its authority, which arises from lay deference and institutionalized forms of dependence. The private interests of physicians alone would be insufficient to sway the society had they been unable to satisfy the felt needs of others. The strength of classes, as Polanyi has written, depends "upon their ability to win support from outside their own membership, which again will depend upon their fulfillment of tasks set by interests wider than their own."[157] This was exactly so for physicians, who, alone, had little power. With widespread support, which they received because of complex changes overtaking the entire society, physicians were able to see social interests defined so as to conform with their own. This was the essence of their achievement.

CHAPTER FOUR

The Reconstitution
of the Hospital

FEW institutions have undergone as radical a metamorphosis as have hospitals in their modern history. In developing from places of dreaded impurity and exiled human wreckage into awesome citadels of science and bureaucratic order, they acquired a new moral identity, as well as new purposes and patients of higher status. The hospital is perhaps distinctive among social organizations in having first been built primarily for the poor and only later entered in significant numbers and an entirely different state of mind by the more respectable classes. As its functions were transformed, it emerged, in a sense, from the underlife of society to become a regular part of accepted experience, still an occasion for anxiety but not horror.

The moral assimilation of the hospital came at the end of the nineteenth century with its scientific redefinition and incorporation into medicine. We now think of hospitals as the most visible embodiment of medical care in its technically most sophisticated form, but before the last hundred years, hospitals and medical practice had relatively little to do with each other. From their earliest origins in preindustrial societies, hospitals had been primarily religious and charitable institutions for tending the sick, rather than medical institutions for their cure. While in Europe from the eighteenth century they played an important part in medical education and research, systematic clinical instruction and investigation were neglected in America until the founding of Johns Hopkins. Before the Civil War, an American doctor might contentedly spend an entire career in practice without setting foot on a hospital ward. The hospital did not intrude on the worries of the typical practitioner, nor the practitioner on the routine of the hospital.

But in a matter of decades, roughly between 1870 and 1910, hospitals moved from the periphery to the center of medical education and medical practice. From refuges mainly for the homeless poor and insane, they evolved into doctors' workshops for all types and classes of patients. From charities, dependent on voluntary gifts, they developed into market institutions, financed increasingly out of payments from patients. What drove this transformation was not simply the advance of science, important though that was, but the demands and example of an industrializing capitalist society, which brought larger numbers of people into urban centers, detached them from traditions of self-sufficiency, and projected ideals of specialization and technical competence. The same forces that promoted the rise of hospitals also brought about changes in their internal organization. Authority over the conduct of the institution passed from the trustees to the physicians and administrators. Nursing became a trained profession, and the division of medical labor was refined and intensified, as conceptions of efficient and rational organization prevailing elsewhere in the economy were applied to care of the sick. The sick began to enter hospitals, not for an entire siege of illness, but only during its acute phase to have some work performed upon them. The hospital took on a more activist posture; it was no longer a well of sorrow and charity but a workplace for the production of health.

The effects of this change rippled outward, altering the relationship of doctors to hospitals and to one another and shaping the development of the hospital system as a whole. Once the hospital became an integral and necessary part of medical practice, control over access to its facilities became a strategic basis of power within the medical community. The tight grip that a narrow elite long held over hospitals no longer seemed tolerable to other physicians, who responded by forming their own institutions or pressing for access to established ones. Under financial pressures and the threat of increased competition, the older hospitals gradually opened their doors to larger numbers of practitioners, creating a wider network of associations stratifying and linking together the profession in new and unexpected ways.

The access that private practitioners gained to hospitals, without becoming their employees, became one of the distinctive features of medical care in America, with consequences not fully appreciated even today. In Europe and most other areas of the world, when patients enter a hospital, their doctors typically relinquish responsibility to the hospital staff, who form a separate and distinct group within the profession. But in the United States, private doctors follow their patients into the hospital, where they continue to attend them. This arrangement complicates hospital administration, since many of the people making vital decisions are not the institution's employees. Yet it also may encourage more private relationships between doctors and patients than exist where patients are attended solely by salaried hospital physicians.[1]

The terms "public" and "private" refer both to individual experience (its visibility to other people) and to the structure of institutions (their relation to the state). In both of these senses, hospital care in America has generally had a more private character than it has elsewhere. American hospitals not only have private doctors; their architecture creates more private space for the treatment of patients. Hospitals in Europe and elsewhere typically offer more of their care in large open wards, while American hospitals tend to be smaller in size, with more private accommodations. The economic organization of hospitals in the United States also reflects a less public conception of their function. Instead of a centralized system of hospitals under state ownership, America developed a variety of institutional forms—a kind of "mixed economy" in hospitals—with both public and private institutions of several kinds under independent management. The institutional transformation of the late nineteenth century did not lead to any higher-level coordination. Both internally and as a system, American hospitals have had a relatively loose structure because of the autonomy of physicians from hospitals and of most hospitals from the government. While hospitals changed radically, private interests, as well as the interests of privacy, were preserved and even strengthened.[2]

THE INNER TRANSFORMATION

Hospitals Before and After 1870

The reconstitution of the hospital involved its redefinition as an institution of medical science rather than of social welfare, its reorganization on the lines of a business rather than a charity, and its reorientation to professionals and their patients rather than to patrons and the poor. I state the changes rather sharply for emphasis; they need to be qualified in some particulars. Well before 1870 private voluntary hospitals in America emphasized active medical treatment and received some paying patients; well after 1910 they remained legally under the control of trustees as charities rather than profit-making firms. But as hospital care turned into a sizeable industry at the end of the nineteenth century, medical activism, professional dominance, and an orientation to the market became much more pronounced and widespread, even in voluntary institutions. And large numbers of new hospitals were established, the majority as business enterprises.

The late nineteenth century in America was a period of economic expansion and rapid institutional development that saw not just an increase in the number of organizations of all kinds, but also a renovation in their structure. The growth of business corporations, as Alfred Chandler has pointed out, was accompanied by the emergence of a salaried management and the multiunit firm. The rise of hospitals, as of universities, offers a study in the penetration of the market into the ideology and social relations of a precapitalist institution. As the university became more actively concerned with preparing students for practical careers, it moved from gentlemanly to utilitarian values and accorded more prominence and autonomy to its professors. As the hospital advanced in its functions from caretaking to active treatment, it shifted in its ideals from benevolence to professionalism and accorded its physicians greater power. In orienting their efforts to newly marketable services, both institutions became less concerned with moral supervision and turned more squarely to professionals to carry out their new productive functions.[3]

Set in a wider historical frame, the reconstitution of the hospital belongs to the general movement in social structure from "communal" to "associative" relations. As Weber made the distinction, communal relations refer to the bonds of families and brotherhoods and other ties of personal loyalty or group solidarity; associative relations involve economic exchanges or associations based on shared interests or ends.[4] The shift from the communal to the associative has taken place in two ways. Not only have the household and community given up functions to formal organizations; the organizations themselves have also changed. Institutions that were once primarily communal have become increasingly associative. This has been true historically even of corporations. The concept of the corporation was originally applied to monasteries, towns, and universities, where members were related to each other not by owning things in common but by living and working together. Corporations were communities. Only later did the corporation take on an abstract existence as an entity for doing business.[5] This same evolution took place in the development of hospitals, which include some of the oldest corporations in continuous existence. Medieval hospitals were conducted by religious or knightly orders and had a strong communal character; those who worked there were bound together in a common identity and belonged to a common household. "Even when hospitals were taken over from the ecclesiastical authorities by municipalities in the later Middle Ages," writes George Rosen, "they were not secularized. Essentially, the hospital was a religious house in which the nursing personnel had united as a vocational community under a religious rule."[6] In a different way, the almshouses of colonial America, which were the first institutions here to care for the sick, retained a communal character. The colonial almshouse, David Rothman writes, provided a "substitute household" for people without a home who were poor or sick. "The residents were a family, not inmates." Even the architecture of the colonial almshouse, which resembled an ordinary residence, reflected its conception as a household. In the language of architectural historians, its social structure, as well as its architectural form, was "derived" rather than "designed."[7]

Later almshouses and hospitals, with a distinctly public architecture, became more bureaucratic than familial in their internal organization. Early hospitals had a fundamentally paternalistic social structure; their patients entered at the sufferance of their benefactors and had the moral status of children. The staff, who often resided as well as worked within the hospital, were subject to rules and discipline that extended into their personal lives. A steward and matron, who might be husband and wife, presided over the hospital family. As the hospital has evolved from household to bureaucracy, it has ceased to be a home to its staff, who have come to regard themselves as no different from workers in other institutions. In their relation to patients and the public, hospitals have come to rely less on charity and more on payments for services. The modern history of the hospital has seen a steady stripping away of its communal relations as it has more closely approached the associative structure of business organizations.

The development of American hospitals, Henry Sigerist once suggested, recapitulates in shorter time the historical phases of European hospitals.[8] First came the almshouses and similarly unspecialized institutions, serving general welfare functions and only incidentally caring for the sick. Founded as early as the seventeenth century in America, they received dependent persons of all kinds, mixing together promiscuously the aged, the orphaned, the insane, the ill, the debilitated. Next appeared hospitals serving the sick but still limited to the poor; finally, in the nineteenth century, hospitals serving all classes of society emerged. In other words, the almshouse metamorphosed into the modern hospital first by becoming more specialized in its functions and then by becoming more universal in its use. In 1752 the Pennsylvania Hospital in Philadelphia became the first permanent general hospital in America built specifically to care for the sick; it was followed by New York Hospital, chartered in 1771, but not opened until twenty years later, and the Massachusetts General Hospital, opened in Boston in 1821. These were later to be called "voluntary" hospitals—voluntary because they were financed by voluntary donations rather than by taxes.

The establishment of these first hospitals did not signal the decline of the almshouse. On the contrary, almshouses became more important in the nineteenth century than they had been in the eighteenth. In the colonial period, the almshouse was a secondary response to poverty and illness. As I indicated earlier, the colonists preferred to provide relief to the poor in their own homes, or to pay neighbors for taking care of the feeble and the sick. Institutions were a last choice, to be used for strangers or especially onerous cases. But after about 1828, there was a shift in policy as states abolished home relief (generally reinstating it only during periods of economic distress). By making the almshouse the only source of governmental aid to the poor, legislatures hoped to restrict expenditures for public assistance. Often squalid and overcrowded, a place of shame and indignity, the almshouse offered a minimal level of support—its function as a deterrent to poverty and public assistance ruled out any amenities. Deterioration and neglect were common. Reformers, especially after the Civil War, devoted much of their effort to splitting up the undifferentiated almshouse and sending orphaned children, the insane, the blind, and the sick to institutions specifically concerned with their problems. In a number of cities, public hospitals evolved out of almshouse infirmaries. The Philadelphia Almshouse became Philadelphia General Hospital; Manhattan's Bellevue Hospital grew out of the New York Almshouse; the Baltimore County Almshouse became part of the Baltimore City Hospitals.[9]

Early American charity hospitals developed in a complementary relation to previously established almshouses and public hospitals. They were an attempt not only to separate out some of the sick from the poor and dependent, but also to provide a somewhat better alternative for the more respectable poor with curable illnesses, as well as a haven for occasional well-to-do people in special circumstances. Voluntary institutions, like the Pennsylvania and Massachusetts General Hospitals, were generally kept cleaner and better maintained and had less of a moral stigma than the almshouse, although they were still not widely used by members of the middle and upper classes.[10] Anxious to give these hospitals a more attractive identity and to make them safer and more acceptable, their managers and physicians excluded dangerous or morally reprehensible cases. The contagiously ill they sent to the pesthouse, and the incurable and chronically ill, as well as those whom they thought wicked and undeserving, they sent to the almshouse. Such exclusions enabled the hospitals to restrict the number of patients they admitted and to keep down the reported mortality rates, since the hopelessly ill could be directed or transferred elsewhere before they became a blot on the hospital's good name. This practice was encouraged by the medical staff, since the hospital would be less useful as a source of instruction to students if it filled up with chronic cases.

But, most of all, the exclusion of undesirable cases served to combat the traditional image of the institution as a house of death. Early hospitals were considered, at best, unhappy necessities. Reflecting on his experience during the Revolutionary War, Benjamin Rush had called them "the sinks of human life in an army" and hoped that the progress of science would go so far "as to produce an abolition of hospitals for acute diseases." Many early attempts to build hospitals aroused public opposition, especially from those who lived in the vicinity. Skepticism about their value was far from irrational. Mortality after surgery, according to data from English hospitals published around 1870, was not only higher in hospitals than at home, but it rose with the size of the hospital. In an essay awarded a prize by Harvard University in 1876, Dr. W. Gill Wylie could write that civilization had not yet reached "that state of perfection where hospitals can be dispensed with." Accident casualties, victims of contagious epidemics, soldiers, homeless paupers, and the insane required hospital care. But to extend hospitals any further was to encourage pauperism, idleness, and the breakup of the family. Hospitals, Wylie thought, "tend to weaken the family tie by separating the sick from their homes and their relatives, who are often too ready to relieve themselves of the burden of the sick."[11]

Up to the time Wylie wrote, hospitals had been formed mainly to take care of people who did not fit into the system of family care. The earliest hospitals were built chiefly in ports or river towns—Philadelphia, New York, Boston, New Orleans, Louisville—centers of commerce where strangers were likely to be stranded sick or where people were likely to be found working and living alone. Institutional charters and appeals for funds alluded to the needs of such people. In 1810, when Doctors James Jackson and John C. Warren circulated a letter to some of the "wealthiest and most influential citizens" of Boston to interest them in a hospital, they mentioned, as cases in need, journeymen mechanics living in boarding houses, widowed or abandoned women, servants, and others who had no adequate housing or kin to care for them. While only scattered figures are available, isolated individuals seem to have been disproportionately represented among patients in general hospitals.[12]

The impulse for founding the early hospitals typically came from physicians who struck up alliances with wealthy and powerful sponsors. Doctors had an interest in creating hospitals as a means of developing medical education and as a source of prestige. The status and influence they derived from hospital positions were of such value to them that they gave their services to the hospitals without pay. In fact, at the founding of the Pennsylvania Hospital in 1751, three doctors were so eager to serve as its staff that they volunteered to provide all medicines for three years at their own expense, as well as free services.[13] But in spite of the advantages doctors derived from hospitals, they could not establish them independently under their own control, for lack of funds and because of distrust of their motives. Particularly distrustful were the sick poor, who feared they might be used for surgical experiments or, in the event of death, turned over to medical students for dissection. Needing capital and legitimacy, the doctors were obliged to seek out the sponsorship of merchants, bankers, lawyers, and political leaders, who could contribute money and lead subscription campaigns. As a result, there developed an organizational structure in which boards of managers, trustees, governors, or commissioners, rather than physicians, retained the final decision-making power in private as well as public hospitals. This arrangement had its direct antecedents in England, but it would not have been reestablished in American communities unless strong forces continued in its favor. So long as doctors could not get hospitals to yield a return on the needed investment, their dependence on sponsors was unavoidable. In Reading, Pennsylvania, in the late 1860s, local physicians interested in founding a dispensary and hospital quickly realized, according to a history of the Reading Hospital, "the importance and necessity of obtaining the cooperation of certain citizens representative of the professional and business interests" of the city. Exercising great care, they chose representatives of "bench and bar, banking, the iron, lumber, publishing and brewing industries, as well as railroad and navigation, and of course, the political representatives of city, state and federal government." The local historian who describes these choices then perspicaciously remarks, "The men engaged in these pursuits—because of their wealth and professional standing—were bound up with the interests of the community in innumerable other ways. Churches, schools, charitable organizations, and all the intricate network of communal intercourse found expression through these leading and responsible citizens."[14] Such are the advantages of having a ruling class.

For the sponsors of hospitals, the benefits were various. As so often happens to the rich and successful, by serving a social interest, they could advance their own. No doubt, hospitals helped to satisfy a genuine sense of religious obligation to the helpless; the institutions might also bring about an improved standard of medical practice by giving young physicians experience working under supervision with the poor; and they might even prove a sound investment for the community by restoring to productive labor people who might otherwise become public charges. These were the kinds of considerations—the manifest functions, as sociologists say—that dominated the rhetoric of motivation. At another level, not to be overlooked but not to be exaggerated either, hospitals also conferred a certain amount of power on their trustees through management of the endowment, the letting of contracts, patronage in appointments, and even the admission of patients. In the nineteenth century, the trustees or managers entered directly into the detailed operation of hospitals, including decisions that now would be seen as strictly medical. To gain entry to a "free bed"—one that was privately endowed and required no payment—a patient generally needed a letter from a trustee or subscriber who previously had contributed to the hospital. Thus the links between the donor and recipient of charity were sometimes quite explicit and personal. The sponsorship of hospitals gave legitimacy to the wealth and position of the donors, just as the association with prominent citizens gave legitimacy to the hospital and its physicians. Hospital philanthropy, like other kinds of charity, was a way to convert wealth into status and influence. George Templeton Strong, a Wall Street lawyer active in founding St. Luke's Hospital, noted in his diary in May 1852, after John Jacob Astor had decided to donate $13,000, "If he and Whitney and the other twenty or thirty millionaires of the city would do such things oftener, they would never feel the difference, and in ten years would control the course of things in New York by the public confidence and gratitude they would gain."[15] An exaggeration without question, but not without some truth to it: witness the later philanthropy of the Rockefellers. Charity, too, pays dividends. Besides softening public hostility toward accumulated wealth, it also helps secure status within an upper class, which is likely to be the chief reference-group of the donor. Membership on the boards of hospitals and other private institutions became an important index of social position. In New York City, according to a historian of its Jewish community, Jews' Hospital (later Mt. Sinai) developed within a few years after its founding in 1852 into "the most important Jewish organization in the city." The hospital's annual public dinners were the most lavish ever held among New York Jews, and the success of the city's rising German Jews in securing seats on the hospital's board soon after it was created signaled the end of their subordination to the more established English and Portuguese Jewish elite.[16]

Despite the various indirect incentives to contribute, donations and bequests generally did not cover the costs of voluntary hospitals. The institutions turned instead to their patients for funds, requiring them to pay at least part of the cost of their treatment. At the Pennsylvania Hospital between 1751 and 1850, according to one study, 70 percent of the mental patients had their treatment paid for, compared with 39 percent of the medical patients and none of the maternity cases.[17] These figures may not have been typical, but the pattern probably reflects the diminishing proportion of persons in each category from middle-class, or at least self-supporting, families. Perhaps the presence of paying patients took away some of the traditional odium that had hung about the hospital. In America, the identification of hospitals with the pauper class was never as absolute as in Europe. On hospital wards, paying and free patients were treated together, while some wealthier individuals paid for private rooms apart from the rest. However, even these few private patients paid no fees to physicians. A tradition had been established in both public and voluntary hospitals that physicians were not supposed to take money for work there. As a charity, the hospital lay outside the theater of production and exchange.

The Making of the Modern Hospital

Primarily because of increased concern for cleanliness and ventilation, hospitals began to emerge from obloquy and disrepute even before any major technological advances had been made. During the Civil War, hospitals were no longer the sinks of human life that Benjamin Rush had mourned during the Revolution. The Union built a vast system of over 130,000 beds by the last year of the war and treated more than a million soldiers with a mortality of only eight percent. While the germ theory of disease was yet to be fully formulated, hospital authorities had heeded some of the lessons of Florence Nightingale, who through improved hygiene had reduced the death rate from forty to two percent at the British military hospitals in Scutari during the Crimean War.[18]

Two developments after the Civil War—one in organization, the other in medical knowledge—furthered the tendencies toward order and cleanliness already at work. The first was the professionalization of nursing, beginning with the establishment in 1873 of three training schools in New York, New Haven, and Boston. The second was the advent of antiseptic surgery, first announced by Joseph Lister in 1867 but not generally adopted for another ten or fifteen years. Together with the growth of demand from the middle and upper classes because of urbanization and changes in family structure, these developments helped to produce a deep change in the character of hospitals as well as an increase in their number.*

Before the 1870s, trained nurses were virtually unknown in America. Hospital nursing was a menial occupation, taken up by women of the lower classes, some of whom were conscripted from the penitentiary or the almshouse. The movement for reform originated, not with doctors, but among upper-class women, who had taken on the role of guardians of a new hygienic order. In New York, the impetus came from women in the State Charities Aid Association, who in 1872 formed a committee to monitor the conduct of public hospitals and almshouses. They represented, in the association's own humble words, "the best class of our citizens as regards enlightened views, wise benevolence, experience, wealth, influence, and social position." At Bellevue, the women found patients and beds in "unspeakable" condition; the one nurse for a surgical ward slept in the bathroom, the hospital laundry had not had any soap for weeks, and at night no one attended the patients except the rats that roamed the floors. Though some doctors approved of the ladies' desire to establish a nurses' training school, which would attract the wholesome daughters of the middle class, other medical men were opposed. Plainly threatened by the prospect, they objected that educated nurses would not do as they were told—a remarkable comment on the status anxieties of nineteenth-century physicians. But the women reformers did not depend on the physicians' approval. When resisted, as they were at Bellevue in efforts to install nurses on the maternity wards, they went over the heads of the doctors to men of their own class of greater power and authority.[19] (Florence Nightingale, who had friends high in the English government, had followed exactly the same course in reforming her country's military hospitals.) Professional nursing, in short, emerged neither from medical discoveries nor from a program of hospital reform initiated by physicians; outsiders saw the need first. Eventually, of course, physicians came not only to accept but to rely on trained nurses, who proved essential in carrying out the more complex work that hospitals were taking on. The new

*For the impact on hospitals of urbanization and changes in the family, see Chapter 2.

nurses' training schools also provided a source of cheap labor in the form of unpaid student nurses, who became the mainstays of the hospital's labor force. (Graduates went into private nursing, if they found work.) The three training schools of 1873 became 432 by 1900, and 1,129 by 1910.[20]

Like nursing, but even more so, surgery enjoyed a spectacular rise in prestige and accomplishment in the late 1800s. Before anesthesia, surgery was brutal work; physical strength and speed were at a premium, so important was it to get in and out of the body as fast as possible. After Morton's demonstration of ether at the Massachusetts General Hospital in 1846, anesthesia came quickly into use, and slower and more careful operations became possible. But the range and volume of surgery remained extremely limited. Infections took a heavy toll in all "capital operations," as major surgery was so justly called: The mortality rate for amputations was about 40 percent. Very rarely did the surgeon penetrate the major bodily cavities, and then only in desperation, when every other hope had been exhausted. Operations were so infrequent that a surgeon's colleagues considered it a privilege to be brought along to help out even in the minor chores. Surgery had a small repertoire and it stood far behind medicine in the therapeutic arsenal.[21]

Change came slowly after Lister's work on antisepsis was published in 1867 because it was inherently difficult to reproduce. Many surgeons tested out his carbolic acid spray but found they were still plagued by fatal infections; carrying out antiseptic procedures demanded a strictness—an "antiseptic conscience" it would later be called—they could not at first appreciate. Lister's method was not generally adopted until around 1880, soon after which it was superseded by aseptic techniques. (While antisepsis called for use of disinfectants during surgery to kill microorganisms, asepsis relied on sterile procedure to exclude them from the field of operation.) With control over infection, surgeons could begin to explore the abdomen, chest, and skull, but before they could do much good, a variety of new techniques had to be developed and mastered by the profession. It was not actually until the 1890s and early 1900s that surgery began to take off. Then, in a burst of creative excitement, the amount, scope, and daring of surgery enormously increased. Improvements in diagnostic tools, particularly the development of X-rays in 1895, spurred the advance. Surgeons began to operate earlier and more often for a variety of ills, many of them, like appendicitis, gallbladder disease, and stomach ulcers, previously considered medical rather than surgical cases. At the turn of the century, the main field of surgical invention was the abdomen. The Midwestern virtuosos William and Charles Mayo, who had done only 54 abdominal operations between 1889 and 1892, recorded 612 in 1900 and 2,157 five years later. A report by William Mayo on 105 gallbladder operations was rejected by a prominent medical journal in 1899 because the total was thought implausible; five years later the same journal reprinted an article by Mayo describing the results of a thousand such operations.[22] In the early 1900s, surgery continued to expand, as thoracic surgery and surgery of the nervous and cardiovascular systems developed.

Growth in the volume of surgical work provided the basis for expansion and profit in hospital care. But first certain impediments to the use of hospitals had to be removed. Before 1900 the hospital had no special advantages over the home, and the infections that periodically swept through hospital wards made physicians cautious about sending patients there. Even after the danger of cross-infection had been reduced, the lingering image of the hospital as a house of death and its status as a charity interfered with its growth. Both patients and physicians had grounds to be wary of hospitals. Many people objected to losing the privacy and control that they might have had at home; as ward patients, the poor had no say in choosing their physicians. And though practitioners might have liked to refer more patients to hospitals, they were often afraid that doing so would mean losing the fee, and perhaps the case, because the staff might offer treatment without charge on the hospital ward. It took time to establish new understandings about professional fees and control over patients. So at first, ether and antisepsis were adapted to the home and "kitchen surgery" continued. But performing surgery in the home became steadily more inconvenient for both the surgeon and the family, as the procedures became more demanding and more people moved into apartments. And the more busy surgeons became, the more costly was the lost time in traveling to the patient's home. To accommodate desires for privacy and fears of the hospital, many surgeons first moved their operations to private "medical boarding houses," which provided hotel services and nursing. In the suburbs and small towns, doctors built small hospitals under their own ownership; surgery had now made hospital care profitable and permitted them to open institutions without upper-class sponsorship and legitimation. After 1900, as the old prejudice died out, most surgery moved inside hospitals.[23]

With greater pressure for admission, hospitals began to limit care to the more acute periods of illness, rather than the full course. Although from their beginnings American hospitals had concentrated their efforts on curable patients rather than chronic invalids, average stays had typically been long, as much as a month or more. At the Massachusetts General Hospital, the average stay for free patients dropped below four

weeks for the first time in 1886; ten years later, the hospital began reporting the average length of hospitalization in days rather than weeks.
At Boston City Hospital, the average stay fell from 27 days in 1870-71
to 17.8 days thirty years later. At the Bridgeport Hospital in Connecticut, it dropped from 32 to 13 days between 1900 and 1920. By 1923 general hospitals in America had an average length of stay of 12.5 days; a
half century later they would average about 7.[24]

The growing emphasis on surgery and the relief of acute illness
brought about a redefinition of purpose in some of the older charity hospitals. Active medical and surgical treatment supplanted religious and
moralistic objectives and became the overriding mission. In New York
City, a charitable society of wealthy ladies concerned abut the "unob-
trusive sufferings" of former slaves opened a Home for Worthy, Aged,
Indigent Colored People in 1842. In 1882, "in view of the thoroughly
organized medical department," the home changed its name to the
Colored Home and Hospital. It became the Lincoln Hospital and Home
in 1902 as it opened its doors to white patients and local physicians, and
simply Lincoln Hospital in 1925 when it was turned over to the city.
From a paternalistic charity providing custodial care to poor and deserving blacks, it had turned into a general hospital providing acute
care to the poor of all descriptions.[25]

A similar shift from moralistic to medical objectives took place at
Children's Hospital in Boston, whose evolution Morris Vogel has described. When the hospital was founded in 1869, its managers announced that "while endeavoring to cure, or, at least to alleviate" the
diseases of poor children, they also desired "to bring them under the
influence of order, purity and kindness." The hospital was initially concerned not so much with medical intervention as with providing an alternative home for children who were neglected, a salubrious haven
where they would be nursed, fed, kept clean and safe, and receive what
its managers at one point referred to as a "positively Christian nurture."
So anxious were they to isolate the children from outside influences that
they restricted visiting hours to one relative at a time, between eleven
and twelve o'clock, weekdays only, thereby judiciously barring working
parents from frequent contact with their children. Medical concerns
became steadily more important during the 1870s, when an outpatient
department was opened, but the real turn toward medical activism
came the following decade, as orthopedic surgery advanced. In 1883
the number of surgical patients exceeded medical patients for the first
time. Moral uplift disappeared from official statements of the hospital's
objectives as the treatment of disease and injury became the chief con-

cern. And instead of treating the poor only, the institution began to admit children from all classes.[26]

As hospitals became more generally accepted, the social origins of their patients changed. We have no systematic socioeconomic data, although scattered statistics for particular hospitals suggest that by the early twentieth century the occupational distribution of their adult patients became more nearly like that of the population. Perhaps the clearest evidence of the shift came in the architecture of hospitals. The changing ratio between wards and private rooms reflected the changing social balance. Few class distinctions could be more sharply delineated. While ward patients were attended by the hospital staff, private patients were attended by doctors of their choice. Ward and private patients usually received two different kinds of food, and ward patients were often not permitted to see friends and relatives as frequently as were private patients. General hospitals built before 1880 consisted almost entirely of wards, with only a few private rooms. Large wards, as Florence Nightingale pointed out in her influential book *Notes on Hospitals*, permitted more efficient nursing: A single night nurse could attend forty patients in one ward but not four wards of ten patients each. Large wards, Nightingale also argued, improved ventilation, simplified discipline and reduced construction costs.[27] But despite these advantages, by 1908 large wards had declined to only 28 percent of the beds in hospitals designed that year, while single rooms now accounted for nearly 40 percent. These trends continued over the next two decades.[28] New intermediate accommodations, semi-private rooms, were built for the middle classes, who were widely believed to have been neglected by hospitals. Hospitals had gone from treating the poor for the sake of charity to treating the rich for the sake of revenue and only belatedly gave thought to the people in between.

As hospitals came to use more of their beds for surgery and the treatment of acute illness, they had less room for recuperating patients, who were discharged earlier, sometimes to newly built convalescent homes. As a result, the boundary between staff and patients in hospitals, once crossed by convalescents and the less seriously ill, now became more fixed. In the almshouse, the inmates had taken care of each other; the original rules of the Pennsylvania Hospital, as of many others, required patients to help in nursing, washing and ironing, and cleaning the rooms. But as general hospitals became more strictly devoted to acute illness, such functions were taken over completely by employees of the institutions. By 1907, in an essay on "The Social Function of the Hospital," a writer could complain, "At no point in his hospital career is [a patient] looked upon as anything but a medical subject. He enters the hospital because he is sick, he is treated as a phenomenon of medicine and surgery, and is discharged 'cured,' 'improved,' or 'no hospital case.' His social status, one might say, is studiously ignored." The patient's role was being reduced to Parsons' "sick role." Not considered responsible for their infirmities, the sick are released from daily obligations in exchange for which they are obliged to submit to treatment and try to get well.[29] These presumptions did not obtain in almshouses, where the sick were often seen as responsible for their infirmities, not released from all obligations, and not expected to get well. A complete dispensation from all duties came only in the fully bureaucratized hospital. This meant nigher costs, since attendants had to be employed to do the work previously done by patients.

As the functions and standards of hospitals changed, construction and operating costs both increased. The typical hospital of 1870, S. S. Goldwater wrote in 1905, had cost about 15 cents per cubic foot and allowed, if liberal in its proportions, about 6,000 cubic feet per patient. It had only rudimentary heating and plumbing and usually was not fireproof. In 1905, such a hospital, Goldwater estimated, could be built at 20 cents per cubic foot, or $1,200 per bed. But because of new technological and legal requirements for hospitals, the prevailing costs per cubic foot actually ran about 40 cents and the number of cubic feet per patient had risen to 11,000. As a result, the cost per bed was now $4,400 instead of $1,200.[30] In addition, the greater emphasis on acute care intensified hospital work, requiring more employees and higher operating costs per patient. Hospital budgets soared beyond the capacity of charity to meet them.

Because of the higher costs it brought, the intensification of hospital care required charitable institutions to put their finances on a new foundation. A crisis in hospital finance in New York City in 1904 brought the problem to public notice, forcing the press, the makers of policy, and the institutions themselves to explore the available alternatives.[31] The private hospitals could turn to the government for more aid, but the city was already facing increased costs for its own hospitals, and no one, in those days, proposed going hat in hand to Albany or Washington. They could also turn to the public for more voluntary contributions and organize a concerted fund drive, but this source, too, proved insufficient. A third response was to call for greater efficiency and stricter business methods in hospital management. The old charity hospitals had been managed on an almost informal basis. Now they had become large organizations and there was a demand for more careful accounting, more specialized labor, and better coordination of the various auxiliary hotel, restaurant, and laboratory services that a hospital maintained. The old rhetoric of charitable paternalism was superseded by a new vocabulary of scientific management and efficiency. While much of this may have been more talked about than acted upon, the ideological change was one further signal of the hospital's transition from household to bureaucracy.[32]

The principal answer to the hospitals' financial difficulties proved to be greater payments by patients. New conditions brought on the increase in costs, but they also enlarged the potential for income. Many people were now coming to hospitals who could afford to pay, and since the real value of hospital care had increased, charges would not drive them away. The hospitals were also encouraged to impose fees by physicians who objected to the free services being given patients who could afford to pay a doctor at home, but avoided all charges by going to a hospital. Between 1911 and 1921 in New York, ward paying patients increased from 18 to 45 percent of the total number and private patients rose from 20 to 24 percent, while charity cases declined. By the twenties, according to a survey sponsored by the New York Academy of Medicine, hospital finances in the city had become secure; two fifths of the hospitals were even reporting budget surpluses.[33] For the United States as a whole in 1922, receipts from patients amounted to 65.2 percent of the income of general hospitals. Public appropriations accounted for 17.7 percent; endowment income, 3.6 percent; donations, 5.7 percent; and all other sources, 7.8 percent.[34]

Changes in organization and financing gradually altered the distribution of power and authority in hospitals. The trustees' sphere of control diminished, while the physicians' sphere expanded. The shift was apparent in control over admissions. Originally, at voluntary hospitals the trustees as well as the doctors took part in deciding who of the deserving poor to accept, but as hospitals became more strictly medical institutions, the trustees' role in admitting declined. In 1875, as part of a continuing conflict, five members of the medical staff at Presbyterian Hospital in New York resigned because of opposition to the trustees' power of approval in admissions. The Boston City Hospital in 1897 dropped the provision that trustees might admit patients. Elsewhere the power of trustees and donors to nominate patients to free beds was quietly forgotten.[35]

The devolution of decision-making power to physicians reflected the more general change (to which I have already alluded) in the structure of organizations in the late nineteenth century—the growing importance of a salaried management in corporations, of administrators and professors in universities, of salaried editors and professional reporters on newspapers, of civil servants in government. In hospitals, the trustees could no longer enter into the details of management; the more common pattern was for the executive of the hospital to resolve all ordinary questions and to turn to the board only at intervals on major matters of policy.[36] Unlike corporations, however, hospitals saw authority devolve more upon outside professionals, the medical staff, rather than upon its own salaried management. This peculiarity of organization arose because of the special role that outside doctors came to play in the prosperity of the institution: They had replaced the trustees as the chief source of income. When hospitals relied on donations, the trustees were vital. But as hospitals came to rely on receipts from patients, the doctors who brought in the patients inevitably became more important to the organization's success.

THE TRIUMPH OF THE PROFESSIONAL COMMUNITY

The growing importance of hospitals to medical practice posed a severe problem for most members of the profession. While the few physicians who held hospital appointments were gaining a more decisive role, most practitioners were cut off from access to hospitals. In 1873, when the first national survey of hospitals was undertaken, the total number of visiting physicians was estimated at 580; the data were doubtlessly incomplete.[37] If, however, there were twice as many, the proportion of American physicians with hospital privileges would still have come to only about 2 percent. In the 1870s, this narrow monopoly was of relatively small consequence to most doctors since the few hospitals then in existence were used almost entirely by the poor. But as late as 1907, after hospitals had grown enormously in number and importance, a physician surveying his colleagues in the Bronx and Manhattan found that only about 10 percent held hospital positions. "The rest," he wrote, "are entirely excluded without rhyme or reason from hospital practice, and cannot enjoy even a share of the benefits derived from such a connection." Exclusion now "seriously handicapped" a physician. Moreover, it was unfair to patients to deny them the choice of their own family doctor when they entered a hospital. "On the one hand we have a public educated to avail itself of the facilities of a hospital in severe illness, and on the other hand a cast-iron regulation which closes the doors of the hospital to the majority of practitioners. This 'system' has made such striking inroads on the earning capacity of physicians in cities where it flourishes as to entail enormous pecuniary losses."[38]

While patterns of organization varied, the medical staff of late nineteenth-century hospitals was typically arranged in four distinct groups: a consulting staff, composed of older and distinguished physicians, who had no regular duties; a visiting or attending staff, made up of the active physicians who supervised treatment; a resident or house staff of young doctors in training who carried out the details of treatment; and a dispensary staff that saw outpatients. Of these groups, the visiting physicians were the most important. They generally served for rotating periods of three or four months a year, a system that reduced the burden on each physician, while allowing, as one surgeon pointed out in 1885, "a much larger number of medical men to derive whatever advantage there may be from the name of being connected with the institution.[39]

Hospitals paid none of these doctors for their work. The house physicians gave their services for a year or eighteen months in exchange for room, board, and experience; the dispensary staff gave theirs in the hope of obtaining appointments as visiting physicians and to make themselves known to patients, who might then come to their private offices. The visiting staff provided its labor in return for access to surgical facilities, opportunities to specialize, prestige, the use of capital that the community invested in hospitals, and regular contacts with colleagues, which might open the way to referrals, consultations, and professional recognition.[40] During the period between 1870 and 1910, hospital appointments became more valuable as hospitals became indispensable for surgical practice and specialization advanced.

But while their economic value increased, hospital appointments remained concentrated among a small professional elite. Among general practitioners resentment of hospitals was widespread. In an editorial in 1894, the *Medical Record* noted that most doctors looked upon the growth of hospitals "critically, not to say coldly." They resented the "arbitrary" treatment they received at the hands of hospital managers who took advantage of their desire for hospital affiliation "to get as much out of them with as little return as possible." The hospitals were killing private surgical work. Even well-to-do patients might enter hospitals, "paying perhaps nothing," because the hospital rules permitted no private fees to be taken. "The spread of the hospital is thus tending to throw a larger amount of medical work every year into the hands of corporations . . . [making] the few skilful, the many unskilful and dependent."[41]

The widely resented rule forbidding physicians to take fees from private patients, which had been established at the older voluntary hospi-

tals, began to die out at the turn of the century. In 1880, according to
Henry Burdett, no American hospitals permitted fees. But by 1905 a
writer in the *Boston Medical and Surgical Journal* could report that
of 52 hospitals surveyed in New England, only five, among them the
Massachusetts General Hospital, continued to deny physicians the right
to charge for services to private patients. In general, hospitals were now
permitting physicians to charge patients in private rooms, but still
barred fees for ward patients. Increasingly, they were also allowing physicians not on their staff to treat paying patients in unused private
rooms. But ambiguities and difficulties persisted; in 1904 a hospital journal reported that whether patients in private rooms had to compensate
physicians for their services was still "not clearly defined." In a typical
situation, "a doctor who is not on the staff sends a patient to the hospital,
and, perhaps before he has made his first visit the hospital authorities
have intimated to the patient that if she will accept the services of a
member of the staff she can have such without charge. It makes no difference how well able the patient may be to pay, the staff physician
makes no charge, and the physician who had previously been in charge
loses the patient and the fee which would have been his had the patient
been treated at home."[42]

Private practitioners protested vehemently against this sort of "pa-
tient-stealing" by the hospital staff, insisting that hospital authorities
abide by the profession's code of ethics and guard their proprietary interests. They also wanted adherence to the professional vow of silence
and noninterference. Without such cooperation, patients might hear
disparaging remarks about their doctor's ability, or members of the staff
might revise the diagnosis and plan of treatment. In sending patients
to hospitals, private doctors risked not only losing the fee, but possibly
discrediting the image of competence they were trying to maintain.
From their viewpoint, unless the staff cooperated, the management of
impressions was much more vulnerable in the hospital than in the
home.

Physicians started asking why they did not completely control hospitals. "Is it not about time the professional mind began to dominate in
the control of these institutions?" asked a physician in the *Journal of
the American Medical Association* in 1902. "Fairly estimated, do not our
services justly entitle us to a voice in all professional questions in and
out of the hospital, second to none, even to that of those benevolent
individuals, charitable organizations or religious societies that founded
these institutions?" Bayard Holmes, a prominent Chicago physician and
socialist, also writing in the AMA's *Journal*, formulated "the hospital
problem" for his colleagues in the following terms:

When the industrial revolution of the seventeenth century began it found Europe peopled with independent tradesmen. . . . Now we find the homeless, tool-less dependent machine operators far removed from the people who furnish a market for the standardized product of their toil. The hospital is essentially part of the armamentarium of medicine. . . . If we wish to escape the thralldom of commercialism, if we wish to avoid the fate of the tool-less wage worker, we must control the hospital.[43]

Oddly enough, proprietary hospitals were one of the main ways of resisting corporate domination and establishing professional control. Some small private hospitals were built by individual surgeons for their own cases; others were joint ventures. To supply enough patients to make the hospitals profitable, competing doctors often had to combine their efforts. "No other profession," wrote the leader of a group of eight physicians who incorporated a hospital in a town in upstate New York, "has had such cruel jealousies and such costly strifes. These differences are being abandoned and must be to make the . . . hospital . . . a success." The creation of doctor-controlled hospitals was easiest in small towns throughout the country and in the cities of the West, where trustee-dominated institutions had never been founded. In the early years of the century, more proprietary than charitable hospitals were being built. They were opened mainly by physicians who had no hospital privileges elsewhere, or who had positions but felt the hospitals were not providing adequate accommodations for their private patients. The increased competition from these new enterprises catering to the middle and upper classes forced the older voluntary hospitals to make adjustments because of the threatened loss of clients and revenue. The private hospital, a writer noted in 1903, had "taught the larger hospital that it must open its doors to all reputable physicians."[44]

By 1907 there was a movement—"none too strong, perhaps," commented the editor of the *National Hospital Record*, "but enough to show in which direction the current is moving"—to open up hospitals to doctors not formerly on their staffs. "Experience has proved conclusively that 'the open door' to the hospital is a benefit, not only to the rank and file of doctors, but to the hospital. It pays in dollars and cents." Not everyone was convinced; a few voices even urged movement in the opposite direction. A number of critics had long maintained that American hospitals were, if anything, too loose for the good of their patients and their own budgets. European hospitals, conducted by a small, permanent medical staff, stood as an example of more disciplined and economical organization. In American hospitals, observed Arpad Gerster, with a rotating staff of visiting physicians and changes every year in the house staff and student nurses, "you can only wonder that chaos and waste are no greater than they actually are." Since the services of the visiting staff were gratuitous, there was no way to regulate their hours or make sure they gave each patient adequate attention. "Medical men who complain that the hospitals are not converted into a free and general stamping ground for every one having a doctor's diploma," Gerster declared, "will naturally be disgusted by further restricting the number of those who will have charge of hospital facilities. They must be shown, however, that the hospitals do not exist mainly for the indiscriminate benefit of the medical profession, but are here, first, for the benefit of the patients, and secondly for that of the community. Restriction of the number of those who attend at our hospitals is the condition sine qua non of economic reform."[45]

General practitioners naturally saw closed staffing as a way to maintain privilege rather than quality. Physicians excluded from city hospitals in Louisville and Cincinnati petitioned against the "unjust and undemocratic" control of the institutions by a "ring" of monopolists; in New York, a number of them organized "physicians' economic leagues" to fight on their behalf. "We all know, only too well, the great scramble for hospital association," a doctor told a meeting of one such league in 1915. "A physician not in the coterie of a hospital staff pulls every wire to get one and not succeeding, starts another coterie to establish another hospital. A crooked politician would blush with shame to be seen in the company of some of our physicians did he know to what extent of knavery they have gone to get on a hospital staff." Partisans of the excluded noted that hospitals served to educate doctors and advocated extending privileges to all members of the profession on the grounds that those isolated from hospitals could not keep up with new advances.[46]

The decisive consideration proved to be financial. Voluntary hospitals had multiplied in great numbers and many had fallen seriously into debt. As the industry trade journal explained, hospitals would fail without support from local physicians. "If favorably disposed toward the hospital, the physician can very frequently recommend that a patient be transferred to the hospital even where the distinct need of this transfer does not exist." A 1909 guide to hospital administration noted, "The income from private patients depends largely upon the medical staff." If the staff had "large and profitable" practices, "then a sufficient amount of money can easily be realized to defray the entire running expenses of the institution, supplying the care not only for the private patients, but also for the charity inmates."[47]

With that hope in mind, hospital boards expanded the number of positions for doctors who could serve as "feeders" to fill their beds. In

Brooklyn, New York, according to a study of physician directories by David Rosner, the big change came between 1900 and 1910, when the proportion of hospital-affiliated practitioners rose from 15.6 to 42.3 percent. Many of Brooklyn's hospitals were in financial trouble because of rising costs and opened their doors to new physicians to increase their revenues. In New York City, other studies indicate, the proportion of hospital-affiliated physicians climbed from 36.8 to 52 percent between 1921 and 1927. Moreover, no hospitals, except for research institutions, were totally "closed," since they all generally had a courtesy staff with the privilege of attending patients in private rooms. On the other hand, no hospitals were totally "open" either, since even hospitals with large courtesy staffs limited their access to the charity wards. Nationally, almost two thirds of physicians in 1928 held staff appointments—90,903 out of about 150,000 doctors. By 1933 the number of affiliated physicians climbed to 126,261, leaving one doctor in six without any privileges.[48]

While doctors' access to hospitals expanded, professional associations sought ways to tighten the medical organization of hospitals. In 1919, as part of a campaign to assure minimum standards for hospital care, the recently established American College of Surgeons adopted a requirement that hospitals wishing to receive its approval organize their affiliated physicians into a "definite medical staff." The staff could be "open" or "closed," with as many "active," "associate," and "courtesy" members as desired, so long as they were restricted to competent and reputable physicians, engaged in no fee splitting, abided by formal bylaws, and held monthly meetings and reviews of clinical experiences. Also in 1919, the AMA's Council of Medical Education set minimum standards for hospital internships, the next year changing its name to the Council on Medical Education and Hospitals. Though compliance with these normative bodies was voluntary, they pushed hospitals toward a more formally structured, hierarchical organization.[49]

Even if more doctors gained entry to a hospital in their community, they did not necessarily gain access on the same footing as other physicians or to hospitals of equivalent status and quality. In Cleveland, according to a study published in 1920, 25 percent of the medical profession held control of 80 percent of the hospital beds. Blacks and foreign-born doctors, particularly Italians and Slavs, were almost completely unrepresented on hospital staffs. These kinds of inequalities persisted. When doctors from lower-status ethnic backgrounds obtained positions, they did so at the lower levels of the system. Studying the informal organization of medical practice in Providence, Rhode Island, about 1940, Oswald Hall found that appointment decisions depended largely on nontechnical considerations, such as personality and social background.

"In the earlier days," a hospital administrator told Hall in regard to the selection of interns, "we had competitive examinations, but we had to discontinue those. The person who did best on an examination might not show up well in the intern situation. He might lack tact; he might not show presence of mind in crises; or he might not be able to take orders. And more than likely the persons who did best on the written examinations would be Jewish."[50]

The continued dependence of practitioners on hospitals throughout their careers made them dependent on what Hall identified as the "inner fraternity" of the profession. "The freelance practitioner," he wrote, "has gradually been supplanted by one whose career depends on his relationship with a network of institutions." Access to favored positions in that network came through "sponsorship" by a community's established physicians, who could advance or exclude aspirants at various stages of their careers by influencing professional school admissions, dispensing hospital appointments, referring patients, and designating protégés and successors. Because the hospital was essential to successful practice, its various grades could be used as delicately calibrated rewards to signal the progress of a career.[51] Although opening up hospitals to more doctors weakened the elite's traditional monopoly over hospitals, it brought greater control over the profession.

"Paradoxically," writes William Glaser, "the integration of private and hospital practices in America produces a more diffuse staff structure inside the hospital and a more orderly structure in the community of private practitioners. Since the majority of doctors in most countries practice outside the public and voluntary hospitals, rank in these institutions cannot be used to arrange a hierarchy in the medical profession generally. Granting or withdrawing hospitalization privileges cannot be used to regulate professional and personal behavior; in fact, this use of hospitalization privileges makes America one of the few countries with any controls over the quality of private practice."[52]

It is unclear whether the use of this power in the early twentieth century did raise the quality of private practice in America. But there can be no doubt it was used to exclude doctors unacceptable to the organized profession. By the twenties, membership in the local medical society had become an informal prerequisite for membership on the staff of most local hospitals. In 1934 the AMA tried to institutionalize its control over hospital appointments by requiring all hospitals accredited for internship training to appoint no one to their staff except members of the local medical society. Black doctors, who were excluded from the local societies, could be kept out of hospital positions on those grounds.[53] So could anyone else who threatened to rock the boat. The private practitioners, who had first seen hospitals as a threat to their position, had succeeded in converting them into an instrument of professional power.

THE PATTERN OF THE HOSPITAL SYSTEM

Class, Politics, and Ethnicity

The rapid rise in the reported number of hospitals from 178 in 1872 to more than 4,000 in 1910 stemmed only in part from the growth of hospitalization. After all, more hospital beds might have been accommodated in fewer institutions by increasing their average size. Mental hospitals in America developed in this way, enlarging their capacity rather than feverishly multiplying in number. By 1920, when there were some 4,013 general hospitals with an average size, in beds, of 78, there were 521 mental hospitals with an average size of 567.[54] The contrast between the two kinds of hospitals developed because they had quite different functions. General hospitals became a necessary local adjunct of medical practice, while mental institutions did not. Physicians who were excluded from the staff of existing general hospitals formed new ones; doctors in small towns opened hospitals to prevent their big-city colleagues from drawing away their patients. No similar incentives promoted the establishment of mental institutions. While communities wanted to have general hospitals readily accessible, they were quite prepared to have the mentally ill removed to a distance. Small general hospitals also multiplied because many of them were sponsored by competing religious groups, while the more burdensome and unremunerative long-term institutional care of the mentally ill fell almost entirely to the states, which centralized facilities to save money.

The hospital system in America—leaving mental institutions aside—emerged in a series of three more or less coherent phases. The first of these, running roughly for a century after 1751, saw the formation of two kinds of institutions: voluntary hospitals, operated by charitable lay boards, ostensibly nondenominational but in fact Protestant; and public hospitals, descended from almshouses and operated by municipalities, by counties, and, in the case of merchant marine hospitals, by the federal government.

In the second phase, beginning about 1850, a variety of more "particularistic" hospitals were also formed. These were primarily religious or ethnic institutions and specialized hospitals for certain diseases or categories of patients, such as children and women. Hospitals were also opened by medical sects, mainly homeopaths.

The third phase of development, running from about 1890 to 1920, saw the advent and spread of profit-making hospitals, which were operated by physicians, singly or in partnership, and by corporations.

This pattern of development was not accidental. The formation of denominational hospitals after 1850 reflected the arrival of large numbers of Catholic immigrants; the growth of proprietary hospitals after 1890 reflected the new potential for profit due to the progress of surgery. An internal dialectic was also at work. Once general hospitals had been established, physicians interested in creating institutions appealed for funds and patients on more partial axes—ethnic affiliations, special categories of diseases, sectarian medical ideas. Like the proprietary hospitals, these institutions were established in response to the changing structure of opportunities.

This sequence of development unfolded in major cities with variations and exceptions, depending on the time a community was formed, its size, the ethnic makeup of its inhabitants, and its economic development. In cities emerging after 1850, the first and second phases were superimposed. While municipal and nonsectarian voluntary hospitals generally preceded denominational institutions in the older cities of the East, they emerged simultaneously in the Midwest; in some Midwestern cities, Catholic hospitals were actually built first. In those areas of the country that built their institutions last—the Far West and the South, where the growth of hospitals had been stunted by the economic aftereffects of the Civil War—the profit-making sector took on more importance than elsewhere. By the early 1900s, in comparison with national averages, the Eastern states showed more nondenominational voluntary hospitals, the Middle West a disproportionate number of church hospitals, and the South and West an excess of proprietary hospitals.* These regional variations reflect their successive development and associated economic differences. Because the Eastern cities grew up first, they had an edge as centers of banking and commerce. The greater accumulation of capital there aided the creation of the early voluntary hospitals, as well as private colleges, museums, and other non-

*The differences are striking. In 1923, according to a federal census, nonsectarian voluntary institutions represented 49 percent of hospitals in the Mid-Atlantic states, compared with 25 percent in the East North Central states, and only 12 percent on the Pacific Coast. Hospitals with religious sponsorship rose from a low of 8 percent in New England to 23 percent in the Midwest, but fell to just 13 percent in the Pacific states. More than half of the Pacific states' hospitals were proprietary (52 percent), compared with 17 percent in the Mid-Atlantic and 30 percent in the East North Central states. The pattern in the South resembled the West.[55]

profit institutions. Because the South and the West had less private capital available for philanthropy, they relied more on the profit-making sector in hospital care and on the state in higher education.

Despite these regional variations, metropolitan hospital systems across the country fell into a fairly standard pattern. At their core were the largest institutions, the elite voluntary and the municipal hospitals. The ethnic, religious, and special hospitals were somewhat smaller and less central (both functionally and geographically), while the proprietary and medical sectarian institutions were typically the smallest and furthest on the fringe of the system. Each group of hospitals had its characteristic functions, organizational structures, patients, and methods of finance.

The elite voluntary hospitals concentrated on acute care; they had relatively closed medical staffs and the closest ties to university medical schools. Their patients were the very poor (for teaching purposes) and the very rich (for revenue and, one hoped, bequests). They had the largest endowments, enjoyed the most prestige as centers for medical training and treatment, and were generally old and stable.

The municipal and county hospitals, usually the largest local institutions in number of beds, cared for the full range of acute and chronic illness. The organization of their medical staffs varied by region—the further west the city, the more likely its hospitals were to be open. Public hospitals generally treated the poor, relied on government appropriations rather than fees, and were plagued periodically by scandals over graft and neglect. Some were important teaching institutions.

The religious and ethnic hospitals were a mixed and intermediate group. In size, they were on the average smaller than the elite voluntary or municipal hospitals, but larger than the profit-making establishments. They rarely had large endowments and consequently relied on fees from patients, who were predominantly from the working and middle classes. Most treated short-term illness. Compared with elite voluntary hospitals, their medical staffs were more open and they had less frequent and less close ties to medical schools.

The profit-making hospitals were mainly surgical centers; they were usually small and had no ties to medical schools. They relied on fees exclusively, and their patients were from the middle and upper classes. Their rate of institutional survival was the lowest. In this regard they were typical of small businesses; they opened and closed with the vicissitudes of personal fortune.

The hospital system had no design since it was never planned, but it had a pattern because it reflected a definite system of class relations. The elite voluntary hospitals brought together the top and bottom of the society under one roof because their physicians simultaneously wanted to have poor patients for teaching and to save time by treating their wealthy patients in the same location. The mix of social classes was also thought to have some educational value. One hospital director candidly explained that in their training doctors and nurses tended to deal with ward patients "so much as cases, and not as persons," while "the personalities of the patients and the friends come in very largely in the care of patients in private rooms."[56] When the superintendents of several major hospitals in New York were asked in a 1904 survey whether hospitals ought to be divided into two classes—private hospitals for people who could pay and public hospitals for people who could not—they unanimously rejected the idea. If all poor patients were cared for by municipal hospitals, charitable donations would dry up, requiring higher rates in private rooms.[57]

Thus the split between public and private hospitals did not become a straightforward class boundary. Both kinds of hospitals treated poor patients, but they treated them in different ways. "[P]ublic hospitals," wrote S. S. Goldwater in 1906, "are conducted at a low rate of expenditure, which implies a low grade of efficiency; hospitals supported by voluntary contributions, on the other hand, aim at a higher grade of service and are unashamed of expense accounts relatively vast." New York City was a prime example. "Here, on the one hand, are the public hospitals, Bellevue, City, Metropolitan and Kings County, conducted at an average expense of $1.00 per capita per day or less; and on the other hand a large number of private institutions of the highest grade, supported mainly by the gifts of the benevolent and conducted at a daily per capita cost which approximates $2. Throughout the country, in Philadelpia, Cincinnati, St. Paul, Milwaukee, Chicago, St. Louis, San Francisco, New Orleans, etc., contrasts of this sort are found. . . ."[58]

The relation between public and private hospitals had been foreshadowed by the complementary roles of the almshouses and early voluntary hospitals. While voluntary hospitals admitted poor patients, the public institutions received the less desirable poor, the overflow of mostly chronic cases. Other state welfare institutions, such as mental hospitals and homes for the deaf, the blind, and the retarded, likewise provided long-term care of the poor at low average daily expenditures per person. The government accepted responsibility for the residual problem cases other institutions would not take.

In addition to operating their own hospitals, most state and local governments gave subsidies to private hospitals for their charitable services. In 1904 one quarter of all public funds spent for hospital care supported private institutions.[59] Such assistance, however, promoted a pattern of uneven development in medical services. In the District of Columbia, the secretary of the Board of Charities noted in 1906 that government subsidies had created "too many comparatively small hospitals for acute medical and surgical services, and . . . utterly failed, thus far, to provide the necessary accommodations for chronic, convalescent, tubercular, inebriate, and generally undesirable cases." Only one hospital was under the city's direct control. "The result is that this hospital is constantly overcrowded with general chronic cases, which are not desired and which will not be received by institutions not under the immediate control of the city."[60] This pattern became a standard feature of American medicine—a highly developed private sector for acute treatment and an underdeveloped public sector for chronic care. Private hospitals for acute illness would be running well below capacity, while overcrowded public institutions were teeming with the victims of tuberculosis, alcoholism, mental disorder, and other diseases of social disorganization.

The public and private hospitals also functioned as alternative systems of patronage and sponsorship. At elite private hospitals, as we have already seen, wealthy patrons sponsored the admission of patients to free beds, and staff appointments went to physicians from established families, while Catholics and Jews were passed over. Correspondingly, public officials used municipal hospitals to dispense jobs and contracts and secure the timely admission of their friends and constituents as patients. Such intervention was roundly criticized by physicians and upper-class reformers, who demanded that these and other municipal institutions be run on a strictly disinterested basis. But as many people have argued, the urban political machines, while frequently corrupt, were also more responsive to pressures from lower-status groups. In Boston, Brahmin families dominated the medical staffs of the private hospitals, but after Boston City Hospital was opened in 1864, Catholic and Jewish doctors were able to get staff appointments there through the intervention of their representatives.[61]

Discrimination was a principal reason for the formation of separate religious and ethnic hospitals. Except against blacks, outright prejudice was rare, though the Massachusetts General Hosital initially refused to admit Irish patients on the grounds that their presence would deter other people from entering the hospital. The early moralistic aims of hospitals gave religious minorities reasons for anxiety. Catholics were afraid they might not be given last rites, and Jews feared they would have to eat nonkosher food and face ridicule for their appearance and rituals. Both religious communities worried that efforts might be made to convert some of their members in moments of personal crisis. Enter-

ing a hospital necessarily involved encounters with strangers at times
of weakness and vulnerability, but the encounters might be less threatening if the hospital authorities and staff were of the same faith or, even
better, of the same ethnic background. For even within religious
groups, there were sharp differences, as a Russian Jew in New York in
1894 found out when visiting Mr. Sinai Hospital and other "uptown"
institutions controlled by the then dominant German Jews:

> In the philanthropic institutions of our aristocratic German Jews you see
> beautiful offices, desks, all decorated, but strict and angry faces. Every poor man
> is questioned like a criminal, is looked down upon; every unfortunate suffers
> self-degradation and shivers like a leaf, just as if he were standing before a Rus-
> sian official. When the same Russian Jew is in an institution of Russian Jews, no
> matter how poor and small the building, it will seem to him big and comfort-
> able. He feels at home among his own brethren who speak his tongue, under-
> stand his thoughts and feel his heart.

From the other side of the encounter with immigrant Jewish patients
comes a confession of the gentile doctor's prejudice by Richard Cabot,
a medical professor at Harvard and physician at the Massachusetts General Hospital:

> [T]he chances are ten to one that I shall look out of my eyes and see, *not*
> Abraham Cohen, but *a Jew* . . . I do not see *this* man at all. I merge him in
> the hazy background of the average Jew. But if I am a little less blind than usual
> today . . . I may notice something in the way his hand lies on his knee, something
> that is queer, unexpected. That hand . . . it's a muscular hand, it's a prehensile
> hand; and whoever saw a Salem Street Jew with a muscular hand before . . .
> I saw *him*. Yet he was no more real than the thousands of others whom I had
> seen and forgotten, forgotten—because I never saw *them*, but only their ghostly
> outline, their generic type, the racial background out of which they emer-
> ged.[62] (emphases in original)

Besides providing a haven from prejudice for the sick, the ethnic and
religious hospitals also offered material advantages to the sponsoring
communities and their physicians. They furnished opportunities for internships and residencies that Jewish, Catholic, and black doctors were
denied elsewhere and staff appointments so that they could attend patients of theirs needing hospitalization. As Oswald Hall discovered, the
most important dividing lines among hospitals were ethnic and religious, not technical. The ethnic and religious hospitals were part of a
chain of institutions that served doctors in each group at successive
stages of their careers. While the upper-class Yankee would go to an
expensive undergraduate college, elite medical school, and prestigious
hospital for his internship, the young Italian doctor would almost cer-

tainly find those gateways blocked. "However," Hall noted, "there are other chains of institutions (in this case Catholic) which provide an alternative route, and not only open a road to a medical career for him, but also shelter him in some degree from the competition of those [with more] advantages . . . ." [63]

It might seem, from the role played in relieving discrimination, that the denominational hospitals would have attracted discrete groups of patients. But this was not so. The hospitals illustrate the tendency in America first to assert and then to submerge religious differences. While specific groups sponsored hospitals, they took pride in serving patients of all faiths—though not all races—without prejudice. The clientele of a Protestant hospital might well include more Catholics than any other group. Jews' Hospital in New York originally accepted gentiles only in cases of accident or emergency, but soon changed its name to Mt. Sinai to signify that it served the community at large. Catholic hospitals were not only open to the general community, but in some places took responsibility for public hospital service. In Rochester, Minnesota, the Mayo brothers came to rely exclusively on a Catholic hospital, St. Mary's, even though neither they nor the majority of their patients were Catholic.

Denominational hospitals exemplified a broader pattern in American society. In some countries, where cultural divisions run much deeper than in the United States, the various groups create separate institutions to meet a broad range of social needs. The Dutch call this phenomenon *verzuiling*, or "pillarization," evoking the image of independent pillars supporting a common roof. "Each denominational bloc," writes Johan Goudsblom about the Netherlands, "has set up a whole array of organizations encompassing practically every sphere of social life. Schools and universities, radio and television corporations, trade unions, health and welfare agencies, sports associations, and so on, all fit into the *zuilen* system." [64] This pattern of "segmented integration" has developed only partially in America. Protestants, as by far the largest group, have generally felt little need to define their institutions on religious lines; the denominations that do build their own schools and hospitals tend to be those that see themselves as deeply at odds with the dominant culture. Among the major religious groups, only Catholics have organized an elaborate network of separate institutions—schools, colleges, hospitals, community associations. Blacks, too, have created separate institutions, at least in the South, but perhaps more out of necessity than desire. Jews have been more eager to join the common institutions of the society than to build their own. In education, for example, Jews have generally preferred to remain within the established system at all levels (the first

Jewish university, Brandeis, was formed only after the Second World War).[65] Jews made an exception of hospitals—every Jewish community of any size built its own hospital, often much larger than the community required—possibly because of the special place that medicine occupied in Jewish aspirations. Medicine was thought the ideal career for Jews because of the professional autonomy of private practice, which made it possible to escape most institutional antisemitism. But because of the discrimination in hospitals, special Jewish institutions had to be established to supply positions as house, attending, and consulting physicians. Nevertheless, in the long run, the assimilationist pattern prevailed. Many of the Jewish hospitals later became major teaching and research institutions and fell into the orbit of medical schools. In a sense, the assimilation and upward mobility of Jewish hospitals paralleled the larger experience of the Jewish community in America.

Cultural heterogeneity has been one of the chief factors inhibiting consolidation of hospitals in a state-run system. Ethnic and religious groups have wanted to protect their own separate interests. For the upper-class Protestants, voluntarism offered a way to exercise direct control without the mediation of state and local governments, which immigrant groups began to influence in the later nineteenth century. For the ethnic communities of lower status, private sponsorship offered a defense against discrimination. In culturally homogeneous societies, the administration of hospitals seems to gravitate sooner or later to the state. In a cross-national study of hospitals, William Glaser found that in all countries with one prevalent religion, hospitals were run by the government. Even where hospitals originated as religious organizations, the church had found the expense of running them too irksome and had chosen to use its resources for activities that more directly affected religious observance and belief. But where competition existed among religious groups, they retained control of hospitals to protect and extend their sphere of influence. As a general proposition, Glaser suggested that the greater the number of religions in a society, the more diffused the ownership and management of hospitals and the smaller their average size.[66]

That there were too many small hospitals in America was a complaint already being heard soon after 1900, and it became a steady part of criticism of the hospital system. "If many hospitals in each city could pool their interests," wrote a hospital superintendent in 1911, "the result would be greater efficiency and greater economy—and yet nothing is more unlikely than that independent, privately controlled hospitals will pool interests." Especially after the Depression began in 1929, private hospitals faced serious underutilization. A medical school professor in

1937, noting the large number of hospitals in debt running at 50 percent capacity, suggested that their financial troubles could be alleviated if some hospitals closed, raising the occupancy rates of the rest to 75 or 80 percent. "The trouble, of course, is that the hospitals are sectarian, or partially endowed, or are run for the individual benefit of some surgeon or staff."[67]

The Peculiar Bureaucracy

While corporations at the end of the nineteenth century became multi-unit operations, hospitals remained at an earlier stage of industrial development because of the parochial interests that sustained them. Despite the possible advantages of integrated organization, none was achieved. The early efforts to reform hospitals mounted by the American College of Surgeons had the goal of "standardization": the imposition of minimum requirements for medical record keeping, the performance of autopsies, and various other aspects of hospital organization. Hospitals participated in such voluntary efforts partly to preempt demands for more thorough government regulation. Emulating one another, hospitals became more standardized than might have been desirable, offering the same services regardless of the overall needs of their communities. They came to present the familiar American paradox of a system of very great uniformity and very little coordination. The absence of integrated management made it incumbent upon individual hospitals to develop a more elaborate administration than hospitals in other countries where administrative functions are more centralized. In America each voluntary hospital had to raise its own funds for capital expenditures, set its own fees, do its own purchasing, recruit staff, determine patients' ability to pay, collect bills, and conduct public relations efforts. All these activities required staff, money, and space. At the same time, the American system of attending physicians also created demands for more administration. The stable medical staff typical of foreign hospitals can resolve many problems through face-to-face discussions. But in the United States, large numbers of practitioners circulate through the hospital at different times, delegating tasks to its employees and requiring more coordination to make things run smoothly. Various internal responsibilities that in foreign hospitals are controlled by powerful chiefs of service fall to administrators in American hospitals. Abroad, because of greater centralization of functions in the society and greater decentralization within the hospital, administrators have been weak in authority and low in status. In America, however, hospital administration became more important and prestigious because there was little centralization of functions in the society and much within the hospital.[68]

So, paradoxically, as a result of the independence of both hospitals and doctors from higher bureaucratic authority, hospital administration became professionalized more rapidly in America than it did elsewhere. In Europe hospital administrators generally had no professional degrees and were clearly subordinate in status and authority to the leading clinicians. But in America physicians themselves were attracted to hospital administration, and university degree programs in hospital administration began in the 1920s. In 1899 the administrators had founded an Association of Hospital Superintendents, which in 1908 changed its name to the American Hospital Association; in 1933 the American College of Hospital Administrators was formed.

Medical domination of hospitals began to weaken in the thirties and forties, as challenges from administrators to the authority of physicians became more common. Much of the mid-twentieth century American sociological literature on hospitals reflects this development, emphasizing the split between "two lines of authority," the clinical and administrative, a much more salient issue in American hospitals because of the somewhat stronger position of the administration. The two groups held two different conceptions of the hospital. The private physicians continued to regard hospitals as "doctors' workshops," that is, as auxiliaries to their office practices, while the administrators tended to see them as "medical centers," serving the community as the main coordinators of health services. They frequently divided over administrators' efforts to expand outpatient care, increase medical research and education, hire full-time physicians in specialized services, and add administrative personnel to run those various activities.[69]

Authority in American hospitals, Charles Perrow argues, has passed successively from the trustees to the physicians and finally to the administrators, a development he explains as resulting from the changing technology and needs of hospitals. The domination of the trustees was rooted in the need for capital investment and community acceptance. Doctors then assumed control because of the increasing complexity and importance of their skills. Finally, there has been a trend toward administrative domination because of the complexity of internal organization and relations with outside agencies.[70] This argument suggests virtually an immanent process of change in organizations, depending entirely on their functional needs. Yet as we have seen, the changing structure of authority was related to specific historical conditions. The growing power of physicians at the turn of the century rested in large part on their new ability to bring in revenue because of the increasing use of hospitals by paying patients; the rising influence of hospital administrators depended in part on the resistance to both centralized coordination of the hospital system and full-time responsibilities for physicians practicing in hospitals. These were the results, not of functional necessities, but of a particular configuration of interests.

While the general trend in the twentieth century has been toward more administrative control and more structure in the organization of hospitals, they remain loosely coordinated, as does the system as a whole. Within the hospital, there continue to be three separate centers of authority—trustees, physicians, and administrators—posing a great puzzle to students of formal organizations. Sociologists have wanted to know why the hospital departs from the standard model of a bureaucracy in lacking a single, clear line of hierarchical authority. Economists have wanted to know what the hospital maximizes if it does not maximize profit. From the viewpoint of each discipline's paradigm, the hospital has been an anomaly. It seems much less so historically. Hospitals began as caretaking charities under the sponsorship of wealthy patrons. Their reconstitution as centers of active medical treatment made private practitioners anxious to gain access to their precincts. The practitioners were able to gain access in America because of the financial needs of voluntary hospitals that could not adequately draw on taxes as a source of revenue. The interests of private practitioners, together with those of different ethnic and religious groups, led to the multiplication of relatively small hospitals and blocked their integration under the state. In turn, the absence of integrated management led to more competition among hospitals, more emphasis on business functions, and more administration. All of which left, instead of a single governing power, three centers of authority held together in loose alliance. Hospitals remained incompletely integrated, both as organizations and as a system of organizations—a case of blocked institutional development, a precapitalist institution radically changed in its functions and moral identity but only partially transformed in its organizational structure.

This same pattern of blocked development was evident throughout the medical system. Integrated organization was limited in public health and almost entirely absent from what we now call "ambulatory" care. The rise of bureaucracy has been taken as an inexorable necessity in modern life, but in America the medical profession escaped, or at least postponed its capitulation.

CHAPTER FIVE

The Boundaries of
Public Health

THE MAINTENANCE of the public's health allows—some would say demands—concern with almost every aspect of life. Breathtaking definitions of public health, offered by some of the field's own leaders, suggest how far claims of its jurisdiction may reach. In 1920, Charles-Edward Amory Winslow, professor of public health at Yale, defined public health as "the science and art of preventing disease, prolonging life, and promoting physical health and efficiency through organized community efforts for the sanitation of the environment, the control of community infections, the education of the individual in principles of personal hygiene, the organization of medical and nursing service for the early diagnosis and preventive treatment of disease, and the development of the social machinery which will ensure to every individual in the community a standard of living adequate for the maintenance of health."[1] So broad—and downright subversive—a conception, if taken seriously, is an invitation to conflict. Public health cannot make all these activities its own without, sooner or later, violating private beliefs or private property or the prerogatives of other institutions. Much of the history of public health is a record of struggles over the limits of its mandate. On one frontier, public health authorities have met opposition from religious groups and others with moral objections to state intervention on behalf of the officially sponsored conceptions of health and hygiene. On another frontier, public health has met opposition from business and commerce, anxious to protect their economic interests. At the end of the nineteenth century, both the moral and the economic boundaries of public health were at issue as public health agencies intruded into activities that the medical profession believed to be rightfully its own.

This conflict has long antecedents, but it was intensified by an historic convergence between medicine and public health. In mid-nineteenth-century America, public health was mainly concerned with sanitary reform and affiliated more closely with engineering than with medicine. The efforts of the early sanitarians against disease were directed primarily at cleansing the environment of filth: To them, what was offensive was dangerous; disease emanated from impurity. But with the development of bacteriology in the late 1800s, the theory and practice of public health and its relation to medicine greatly changed. Public health authorities gradually developed a more precise conception of the sources and modes of transmission of infectious disease and concentrated on combatting particular pathogenic organisms. Shifting attention from the environment to the individual, they increasingly relied on the techniques of medicine and personal hygiene.[2] This development was partly a response to the discovery that a number of diseases were transmitted by human carriers. For if the sick are the source of infection, one way to prevent the spread of disease (a recognized function of public health) is to diagnose and cure the people who are ill (recognized functions of medicine). Extending the boundaries of public health to incorporate more of medicine seemed necessary and desirable to some public health officials, but as one might imagine, private practitioners regarded such extensions as a usurpation. Doctors fought against public treatment of the sick, requirements for reporting cases of tuberculosis and venereal disease, and attempts by public health authorities to establish health centers to coordinate preventive and curative medical services.

PUBLIC HEALTH, PRIVATE PRACTICE

The Dispensary and the Limits of Charity

One early conflict between public health and private practice concerned the role of public dispensaries in treating the sick poor. As a separate institution, the dispensary is now extinct, but its disappearance is itself a fact of some significance. Like hospitals, dispensaries were originally established as charities for the poor, but unlike hospitals, they failed to make the transition to serving society as a whole. Had different forces shaped the system, the dispensary rather than the hospital might have become the nucleus for community medical services, but this was not the direction events took.

The first dispensaries were founded in the late eighteenth century in the country's leading commercial centers: Philadelphia (1786), New York (1791), Boston (1796), and Baltimore (1800). They grew slowly in number through the mid-nineteenth century and remained concentrated in the East. As the name "dispensary" suggests, they mainly dispensed medicines—"medical soup kitchens" they were sometimes called. Operating on small budgets, their main resource was the free service of part-time physicians, who used them to teach medical students, gain experience in diagnosis, and advance their careers. The relation to medical education was central: The more medical students in need of opportunities for training, the more dispensaries were established. As medical schools increased in number during the late nineteenth century, dispensaries did, too. By 1900 there were an estimated one hundred in the country.[3]

The growth of dispensaries disturbed private practitioners and charity reformers who objected to the alleged abuse of dispensaries by people who could pay for private care. "Think of it!" wrote one physician. "If a doctor attends a clinic three times a week for fifty-two weeks, treating daily on an average five patients, every one of whom could pay a moderate fee, say $1.00 (yet this is a small average), what has he done? Simply deprived the profession of $780 in one year." Many doctors felt put upon by the poor. "It is simply not true," Dr. George Shrady, editor of the *Medical Record*, told the readers of the monthly magazine *The Forum*, "that poor people suffer for want of skilled medical attendance. On the contrary, they obtain vastly more than they have a right to expect. . . . Vast sums of money are wasted yearly on worthless and undeserving persons." And, of course, such charity would do the poor no good. Charity reformers claimed it would weaken their self-reliance and drag them down into further degradation. As a remedy for this "parasitism," the dispensaries introduced social workers to investigate patients to make certain they were genuinely destitute. In 1899 New York State made it a misdemeanor to visit a dispensary under false pretenses, though there was never any prosecution under the law.[4]

The concept of "dispensary abuse" epitomizes the role played by class bias in the definition of social problems. So preoccupied were reformers and physicians with misrepresentation by patients that little else about dispensaries received attention. As Michael Davis and Andrew Warner noted in 1918, the chief question discussed in articles about dispensaries, as well as their annual reports, had not been the needs of patients and how they might be met most efficiently, but instead, "How shall we keep people from getting treatment?"[5]

It is doubtful whether dispensary abuse was as widespread as private practitioners and upper-class reformers believed. Several studies indicated that the proportion of dispensary patients who could afford to pay was quite small—perhaps as little as 2 or as much as 12 percent. Though no fees were charged at dispensaries, the services were by no means free: Long waiting times imposed significant indirect costs in lost wages. Patients also paid an indirect cost in allowing themselves to be used for lectures and demonstrations to students. This was, W. S. Thayer observed, "often, indeed, usually, *very time taking*, and there are very few of the poor and ignorant who do not prefer to avoid the waste of time and the lengthy examination by seeking the services of a private physician when they can afford it." As for "pauperization," the social worker Mary Richmond noted that in fifteen years she had been unable to detect "any such downward tendency" among people who accepted free dispensary care. Just the opposite: Timely medical assistance often kept people out of poverty.[6]

Though a few patients may have abused dispensaries, it was also true that some dispensaries abused their patients, treating them without care or civility. In New York City, a 1913 door-to-door survey of a district on the Lower East Side found that well over half the sick were getting no treatment, partly because they were afraid of dispensaries. Those who came to them for help had to wait hours for hasty and superficial examinations. "In some of the dispensaries many patients, sometimes as high [*sic*] as fifteen or twenty, are crowded into one small room, and the physician hurries from one to the other dispensing prescriptions. At the apothecary's window the patients very often wait two or three hours before the prescriptions are filled. One experience of this kind usually serves to prevent the return of the timid ones, or of those who are unable to spend half a day on a dispensary visit."[7]

The controversy over dispensary abuse was, in large measure, a conflict between two segments of the medical profession: the economically insecure general practitioners who saw the dispensary as depriving them of income; and the more privileged specialists, or would-be specialists, who used the dispensary for teaching, research, and the acquisition of professional connections. The former wanted charity limited and the private market kept as large as possible. The latter wanted no limit on their prerogative to accept "interesting" cases, even if that meant occasionally taking patients who might be able to afford private treatment. While the hard-pressed general practitioners complained of unfair competition, some of the illustrious leaders of the profession, professors like William Osler and Austin Flint, defended dispensaries in the name of science and the interests of the poor.

The fate of the dispensary, at least in its traditional form, was linked to reform in medical education. The "abuses" of the dispensary system, as Henry Hurd, superintendent of Johns Hopkins Hospital, noted in 1902, stemmed from the proliferation of medical schools. "If there were fewer graduates," Hurd suggested, "there would not be the need of so many dispensaries"—implying that those who really needed dispensaries were the doctors, not the patients. "Until we get rid of the competition of medical schools, we shall not be able to remedy these abuses." After the profession was able to rid itself of many of its schools during the first two decades of the twentieth century, the pool of free labor for dispensaries dried up. Now, too, the postgraduate experience required for medical practice came from hospital internships. Dispensaries disappeared as freestanding institutions; many were absorbed into hospitals as outpatient departments, which by the twenties were imposing charges on patients from whom a fee could be collected.[8]

Health Departments and the Limits of Government

The ambivalent relation of private practitioners to public health was also a key factor in shaping the development of local and state health departments. Health departments were developed on a firm, bureaucratic basis after the Civil War. Earlier in the century, cholera and yellow fever epidemics and concern about the squalid living conditions of the "dangerous classes" had stimulated the organization of citizens' sanitary or hygiene associations to clean up the cities. Physicians were active in these groups, but they did not monopolize the leading positions. Although new epidemics periodically excited public interest, the United States did not establish government health agencies as rapidly as European countries did. Louisiana created the first state board of health in 1855, but it proved ineffective. More significant landmarks were the establishment of the Metropolitan Board of Health in New York City in 1866 and the first effective state board in Massachusetts in 1869. In 1870 the federal government centralized the direction of its marine hospitals under a Surgeon General in the Marine Hospital Service. In April 1878, after new cholera and yellow fever outbreaks, Congress gave the service authority to quarantine vessels that might be carrying contagious disease, but it also gave local authorities power to override any quarantine decision. When yellow fever struck New Orleans later that year, other public health reformers used the opportunity to induce Congress in March 1879 to establish a National Board of Health. This move, however, antagonized the Surgeon General, who four years later succeeded in persuading Congress to terminate the board. Thereafter, public health remained almost entirely a state and local responsibility.

In the late nineteenth century, while physicians were seeking licensing protection, they had a positive view of state intervention. Doctors supported efforts to extend the regulatory powers of health departments. When the American Public Health Association was founded in 1872 under the leadership of Stephen Smith of New York, its members were primarily physicians who served as local and state health officials. The AMA itself agitated for a Cabinet-level department of health throughout the Progressive era. But just as doctors did not want hospitals or dispensaries to steal patients from them, so they did not want public agencies to interfere in their business. While they favored public health activities that were complementary to private practice, they opposed those that were competitive. This opposition became even more strenuous in the early twentieth century.[9]

The range of professional response, from cooperation to resistance, is well illustrated by developments in New York City around the turn of the century. The city health department introduced laboratory diagnosis of communicable diseases, the production and free distribution to the indigent of vaccines and serums, mandatory registration of all cases of tuberculosis and venereal disease, an active program of health education, and physical examinations and treatment of school children. New York City was no microcosm of America. In many regions, particularly the South and the West, public health often barely reached the stage of sanitary reform, if it went that far. The underdevelopment of public health was the more characteristic pattern in the United States. The experience in New York is significant precisely because, as an exceptional case, it discloses some of the political constraints limiting public health at its boldest.[10]

The great contribution of the New York City Health Department was to translate the new bacteriology into practical use. Its major innovation was the diagnostic bacteriological laboratory, originally established in 1892 under the leadership of Hermann M. Biggs and his assistant William H. Park. Park was able to show that nearly half of the cases thought to be diphtheria at one of the city's hospitals were actually "pseudo diphtheria"; placing these patients in contact with the real disease endangered their lives. By testing suspected cases of diphtheria, the department could reduce the death rate and save the city the cost of many unnecessary fumigations. In the interests of health and economy, the city authorized the laboratory to make diagnostic tests available for free to physicians. A doctor could pick up a "culture outfit" left by the health department at a local pharmacy, inoculate and return it, and receive the laboratory verdict by mail within twenty-four hours.

From the outset doctors readily made use of the new service. The health department, as its annual report for 1893 noted, was doing for practitioners what they would have found "difficult, if not impossible to do for themselves." It provided them with "an absolutely certain diagnosis" and discovered for itself where the diphtheria cases were located, so that it could enforce proper isolation and disinfection to stop the outbreak of epidemics.[11] The next year it moved to assist physicians in treatment. Immediately upon learning of Emile Roux's method of producing diphtheria antitoxin from horses, Park's laboratory became the first outside Europe to make the serum, which it put on sale in drugstores and made available to physicians for free for patients in hardship. And since the health department was able to produce more than it could use in New York, it sold the surplus to other towns and cities across the country, generating enough income to pay the salaries of many of its own employees.

These measures brought about a marked reduction in the case fatality rate from diphtheria and were soon imitated by other cities. Biggs and Park earned the New York City Health Department an international reputation. It has been said that while Europeans made the major theoretical advances in bacteriology, Americans made some of the major practical applications. By refining the technique for producing antitoxin, the New York department brought down the cost of the serum from $12 to $1 a vial. It also began producing large quantities of serum for tetanus, performing the Widal test for typhoid, and offering rabies' vaccine to people bitten by dogs.

But despite international acclaim these achievements soon excited protests from local manufacturing chemists and doctors, who denounced the health department's activities as "municipal socialism" and unfair competition with private business. "Is there any more reason," asked one critic, "why Boards of Health should manufacture their own antitoxin and vaccine virus than that they should prepare ordinary drugs?"[12] In 1898, after the election of a new mayor, antitoxin production was reduced to deter overproduction and sale of the surplus. "The city," stated the Board of Health, "should not be led into transacting a business of this character." But to be prepared for emergencies, the laboratory continued to produce a regular supply of diphtheria antitoxin, and when emergencies did not materialize, it sold off the serum, which would otherwise have gone to waste. So in April 1902, over a thousand physicians and druggists signed a petition urging the mayor to root out this continued "commercialism" in the health department. Later that year the department announced it would cease all outside sale of antitoxin, though it would continue to distribute it free to physicians for treatment of the poor.

Troubles had also developed in the department's earlier efforts to control tuberculosis. Following Koch's isolation of the tubercle bacillus, a departmental report had concluded in 1889 that tuberculosis, then the leading cause of death, was communicable and preventable. Control, the department decided, would require the identification and supervision of its victims to ensure what was then thought to be proper sanitary care, including the disinfection of living quarters and the careful disposal of sputum. During the winter of 1893–94, the health department required dispensaries and other public institutions to report to it the names of all patients with tuberculosis. Physicians were only requested to do the same. To induce their voluntary cooperation, free laboratory tests for tuberculosis were offered. But when that failed, the department took the then unprecedented step of making tuberculosis notification by private doctors mandatory. There was ordinarily no interference with patients under the care of private practitioners, and other consumptives were generally only visited by medical inspectors, who left circulars and gave advice about preventing the spread of infection. But fear of tuberculosis was widespread, and many people were anxious about any official report of its presence in their family; some life insurance policies were void if tuberculosis was the cause of death. Objecting that tuberculosis was not contagious, practitioners opposed compulsory reporting as an invasion of their relationships with patients and of patients' rights to confidentiality. The president of the New York County Medical Society told its membership in 1897 that by requiring notification and offering free treatment, the health department was "usurping the duties, rights and privileges of the medical profession."[13] Nonetheless, over the next decade, the New York department achieved a relatively high level of tuberculosis notification, though in other cities the results were much less encouraging.[14]

The boundaries of government health programs were evident nowhere more clearly than in the development of school health services. Like other public health programs, health services for school children

shifted from environmental to individual concerns in the late nineteenth century and then ran into barriers imposed by private practitioners. In the mid-1800s, the first efforts in the schools sought to improve ventilation and heating and to eliminate overcrowding. The one
medical service occasionally provided was smallpox vaccination. In the
1890s the development of bacteriology began to have its impact, and
school health programs became increasingly medical in their approach.
Again, the chief objective was to control communicable disease. In 1894
Boston became the first city to employ school medical inspectors to
identify and send home the contagiously ill. In New York the next year,
the health department appointed a chief medical inspector and 150
part-time inspectors to make daily examinations of school children who
were thought by their teachers to be sick. "Acutely conscious of the del-
icate sensibilities of the medical profession," writes John Duffy, "the
Health Department stressed that the school inspectors were to give no
professional treatment. Their duties were to examine and to exclude
from school those children with communicable diseases. If treatment
were necessary, the care was to be provided by family physicians, hospitals or dispensaries."[15]

From this beginning, school health programs branched out into testing for eye problems and other physical impairments that might interfere with learning. But because the school doctors had little contact
with parents, and the families had little money, treatment often did not
follow the diagnosis of medical problems. In 1902, again in New York,
the city first introduced nurses into the schools, not only to find and
refer cases to physicians but also to speak with parents, treat minor conditions, teach self-care, and do follow-up work. That same year the department estimated that 18 percent of the city's school children were
suffering from trachoma and established an eye clinic in one of the city's
public hospitals to offer treatment. In a number of cities, over the protests of physicians, school health programs also moved from examination to treatment for at least minor problems. Some business was diverted from private practitioners, but as public health officials liked to
point out, the doctors also gained clients from the schools' diagnostic
tests and referrals. School health services lost some of their medical emphasis, however, as they were transferred from local boards of health
to boards of education, where by 1911 three of every four cities vested
control.

Gradually, the programs became locked into their original mission
of finding defects and preventing communicable diseases. Year after
year, inspectors and nurses would examine children, find poor hearing
or dental problems, and give the children notes to their parents saying

they should see a doctor or a dentist. When they were examined the next year, the health problems would still be there. "If only we could take some of the money we use for examining and reexamining children and pay to have the most important kinds of work done, we would be able actually to accomplish something," a school health administrator told a public health convention.[16] But there would be no integration of school health programs with health services, just as there was no integration of other public health activities. Private interests created a barrier to any unified organization.

FROM REFORM TO THE CHECKUP

The Modernization of Dirt and the New Public Health

The economic boundaries of public health were determined partly by constraints of cost—not simply the direct cost of public health programs to taxpayers, but the indirect cost of such measures to business and to society at large. In the first half of the nineteenth century, some authorities attributed epidemics to contagion and recommended quarantines—an economically damaging measure because of the disruption of commerce. Others ascribed epidemics to miasmas and advised general cleanups of the environment. The environmental approach may have been favored by commercial interests because it was less disruptive than the closing of markets. But wholesale cleanups and quarantines were both costly responses to disease. The advent of bacteriology not only increased the effectiveness of public health efforts; it also reduced their cost to society by doing away with indiscriminate interventions. The shift to more specific measures, such as regulation of the water or milk supply, provided the basis for an accommodation between public health and business interests. The more narrow focus of bacteriology also provided a rationale for public health officials to disengage themselves from commitments to moral and social reform.

A central element in this accommodation between health and commerce was a new conception of dirt. Ideas about dirt have serious political implications, as will be evident from a moment's reflection on today's struggles over toxic chemicals, radioactive waste, and other environmental pollutants. A broad conception of dirt may imply a need for a correspondingly large investment in cleaning things up. A more narrow conception may be much cheaper. At the turn of the century,

Charles V. Chapin—health commissioner of Providence, Rhode Island, and a leading figure in the field—pointed out that early public health legislation, influenced by the "filth theory" of disease, made no "distinction between dangerous dirt and dirt not dangerous, and warfare was waged against everything decaying and everything which smelled bad." The old sanitarians, Chapin argued, had been preoccupied with vague miasmas like "sewer gas" and wasted effort in diffuse measures. General cleanups did not necessarily remove all human fecal matter from the water supply.[17] Even the advent of the "germ theory" did not initially bring a precise understanding of how infection was transmitted. Mistakenly seeing danger in foul air and contaminated physical objects, public health authorities thought it necessary to isolate contagious disease hospitals and to fumigate all objects with which the sick came into contact. As scientists learned that disease-causing bacteria do not travel long distances by air, they became more skeptical of the value of such measures as fumigation. In 1906 Chapin attacked fumigation as a fetish, and in the next decade, other cities followed the example of Providence in ending the practice.

The new outlook brought with it a radically reduced view of the requirements of public health. Convinced that dirt per se did not cause infectious disease, Chapin dismissed general measures for cleanliness. "It will make no demonstrable difference in a city's mortality," he wrote in 1902, "whether its streets are clean or not, whether its garbage is removed promptly or allowed to accumulate, or whether it has a plumbing law." Once a community learned to dispose of its excreta, Chapin believed, environmental sanitation was not a public health issue. "I fail to see how poor housing in itself produces much disease," he said, explaining why he thought housing was not a public health matter.[18] In a short, popular book *How to Avoid Infection*, published in 1917, he wrote that it was "more important to remove adenoids from the child than it is to remove ashes from the back yard." Personal hygiene could replace public health activities. "Wash the hands well before eating and always after the use of the toilet. Teach this to children by precept and especially by example. Modern sanitary science enables the individual to protect himself even if his health department is inefficient." Personal hygiene was cheaper too. "The introduction, or even the purification, of a municipal water supply may require millions. . . . To wash the hands before eating and after the toilet costs nothing."[19]

Chapin's viewpoint was extreme, but it reflected a widespread shift in orientation that contemporaries referred to as the "new public health." C.-E. A. Winslow regarded it as the third phase of public health in its modern development. According to Winslow, the first phase, roughly from 1840 to 1890, had been a period of "empirical environmental sanitation"; the second, from 1890 to 1910, had witnessed the first applications of bacteriology and emphasized isolation and disinfection. The "new public health," Winslow said, began about 1910 and had two defining characteristics—an emphasis on education in personal hygiene and "the use of the physician as a real force in prevention" by organizing medical examination of the entire population. These characteristics, he argued, were evident in a series of new campaigns aimed at controlling tuberculosis and venereal disease, improving the health of infants and children, and dealing with other health problems.[20]

Although authorities such as Chapin presented the new public health as a response to the bacteriological findings, it had another function. Narrowing the objectives of public health made it more politically acceptable. As in other fields, the growth of professionalism saw a movement away from the broad advocacy of social reform toward more narrow judgments that could be defended as the exercise of neutral authority.

The emphasis on personal hygiene and medical examinations was not, in fact, always a logical response to bacteriological discoveries. The campaign against tuberculosis provides a case in point. The use of the tuberculin test, introduced around 1890 and refined in 1907, disclosed that latent tuberculosis infection was widespread in the population. The discovery of large numbers of people who were infected without being ill indicated that in combatting the disease, strengthening resistance—for example, by improving nutrition, housing, and working conditions—might be as valuable as preventing infection.

So, in the case of tuberculosis, bacteriological findings might logically have led to an interest in social reforms of the type Chapin and others in public health were repudiating as irrelevant to their professional tasks. But instead, the antituberculosis movement of the early 1900s sought primarily to change individual health habits, especially in children. One major effort, for example, grew out of the Christmas Seal campaign, a fund-raising effort of antituberculosis groups that enjoyed wide support after it was initiated in late 1907. The director of the campaign had the idea of inviting all children to enlist as "modern health crusaders." They would advance up a scale of honor as they performed "hygienic chores," such as brushing their teeth. By 1919 more than three million school children around the country were enrolled.[21]

As part of the emphasis on hygiene and medical examinations, the new public health movement stimulated the formation of a multitude of new clinics. Tuberculosis clinics, the vanguard among them, rose from only twenty in 1905, when the National Association for the Study and Prevention of Tuberculosis was organized, to more than five hundred in 1915. By 1915 there were at least 538 baby clinics in America, five times more than in 1910 when the National Association for the Study and Prevention of Infant Mortality was formed.[22] Though voluntary agencies operated some clinics, city health departments ran most of them. While the old-style dispensary had mainly dispensed prescriptions, the new clinics were primarily concerned with medical diagnosis and health education. The shift from the term "dispensary" to "clinic" was not merely linguistic. It reflected the increased use of diagnostic techniques and a reorientation from the mere giving of drugs to the more complex task of promoting changes in child care, diet, and living patterns. These were, of course, as much matters of culture and values as they were of scientific information, and where science left off and middle-class American standards of virtue took over it is impossible to say; but there can be little question that the new hygienic practices had value in preventing disease and preserving health, and it would be a mistake to dismiss the clinics merely as agents of social control.*

Perhaps nothing better illustrates the movement of public health from the environment to the individual than the growing emphasis on individual health examinations. I have already mentioned the inspection of school children beginning in the 1890s. The infant hygiene movement also stressed the importance of mothers seeking out the guidance of physicians in the preventive care of their babies. Pediatrics became the model of a medical specialty whose chief concerns were preventive. The campaigns against tuberculosis and venereal disease were influential in establishing the need for health examinations; both used relatively simple tests for identifying the presence of disease. Americans

---

*Some recent historians criticize the public health campaigns on this basis, but they use the concept of social control very loosely. For example, in an essay on three public health movements in the Progressive era, John Burnham writes, "Repeatedly, the leaders of American medicine sought to impose [their] values upon others, that is, to exercise social control."[23] Under this definition, any social movement, from a revival to a revolution, could be described as "social control." This indiscriminate use of the term deprives it of any precise meaning.

Social control properly refers to actions or mechanisms that tend to suppress deviations from the dominant rules in society. Though medicine and public health often contribute to social control, that is not all they do. The reduction of medicine to a form of social control neglects the inhibiting effects of disease on the human capacity for action of any kind. Insofar as public health and medicine reduce disease, they augment the power of individuals to realize their own objectives, not simply to fulfill socially prescribed obligations. The recent anti-Progressive historians, including both Marxists and liberals, tend to reclassify as social control events like the conquest of disease that were once properly regarded as historic achievements of human freedom. They remember the public health nurse who instructed mothers in infant hygiene as a kind of surreptitious agent of the police, insinuating bourgeois ideals into the authentic culture of the working class. That the nurse may have taught mothers how to prevent their babies from dying, we are now supposed to pass over as secondary and irrelevant.

were increasingly bound to submit to examinations to qualify for or retain jobs. Life insurance companies played a major role in introducing
Americans to health examinations, and in 1914 the Life Extension Institute, an organization associated with the insurance industry, began offering checkups through panels of physicians around the country.

Health examinations helped to foster the belief that Americans
needed more medical care and health supervision, for they almost uniformly showed that very few people were healthy and normal. The results of the draft physicals during World War I were considered especially persuasive evidence. Of 3,760,000 men examined, about 550,000
were rejected as unfit; and of the 2.7 million called into service, about
47 percent were said to have physical impairments. Among ten thousand workmen examined in one study, not one was reported in perfect
health. Ten percent had slight impairments; the other 90 percent were
in varying states of disrepair: 41 percent had moderate defects requiring
advice or minor treatment; 35 percent had moderate defects requiring
medical supervision; 9 percent had advanced physical impairments requiring systematic treatment; and 5 percent needed immediate medical attention. Among five thousand citizens of Framingham, Massachusetts, examined as part of a Metropolitan Life Insurance demonstration
project to control TB, 77 percent were recorded as ill with some disease. Two thirds of defects discovered were allegedly preventable. The
physicians' examinations found twelve times as much illness as a house-
to-house survey of self-reported sickness.[24]

The insurance companies and Life Extension Institute claimed substantial reductions in mortality among those who had preventive examinations, and in the 1920s the promotion of health examinations became
a major objective of public health organizations. The initiative came
primarily from lay enthusiasts, but the physicians took up the cause, too.
In 1922 the AMA endorsed the idea of examinations of those "supposedly in health." The National Health Council, which included representatives from the leading voluntary health organizations as well as
government public health officials, called for a three-day period when
Americans would go to their doctors for examinations. After the AMA
indicated that the nation's physicians would be hard pressed to handle
the three-day flood, the Council launched a campaign with the slogan,
"Have a Health Examination on Your Birthday."[25]

The public health sponsorship of preventive medical examinations
was, in effect, unpaid advertising for the medical profession. In Ohio
in 1922, the state board of health conducted diagnostic chest clinics in
twenty-two counties, examining about 1,600 people. Of these, 721 were
found either positively or potentially ill, and were referred to private

physicians. "Not less than 90 percent of these 721 persons are undergoing treatment," reported the board's director. Moreover, physicians in those counties reported an increased demand from relatives, friends, and neighbors. "The demand is for complete physical examinations, in numbers exceeding anything ever before known in those communities."[26]

While diagnostic and educational services were expanded under public health auspices, treatment typically was left to private physicians. However, the line between the two fields was often difficult to draw. Did a series of diagnostic tests, followed by advice about hygiene and diet, constitute health education or the practice of medicine? Physicians felt that, in certain respects, these programs extended the limits of public health too far and that some clinics smuggled in treatment under the guise of prevention. In Chicago, a venereal clinic organized in 1919 by some of the city's leading philanthropists provided treatment for $185 a year, compared with an average of $525 charged by private physicians. Even though the patients were overwhelmingly poor, the Chicago Medical Society denounced the clinic as unethical, accusing it of unfair competition, and expelled its staff physicians. When it expelled Dr. Louis Schmidt, a medical professor at Northwestern and president of the Illinois Social Hygiene League, for having accepted on the league's behalf $12,000 out of the clinic's surplus, the controversy became a national issue, symbolizing the AMA's struggle to resist public health intervention in medical care.[27]

The Prevention of Health Centers

Many public health officials were acutely aware of the limitations of their fragmented efforts. Some progressive critics argued for unified health centers in place of separate services for school children, programs for maternal and infant care, and clinics for venereal disease, tuberculosis, and other conditions. The health center movement began between 1910 and 1920, drew considerable attention through the thirties, and then faded, eventually to be revived in a quite different form in the 1960s. The centers that were built were primarily concerned with coordinating health department programs and local voluntary agencies within a particular neighborhood. In 1927 Michael Davis defined the health center as "an organization which provides, promotes, and coordinates medical services and related social services for a specified district." This was more wish than reality. Medical care was rarely incorporated, and the term "health center" was at the time applied very loosely to child welfare stations, settlement houses, hospital outpatient departments, and tuberculosis and venereal clinics. Consequently, statistics suggesting there were hundreds of such centers must be judged skeptically.[28]

The reigning conception of the health center as an auxiliary rather than an alternative to the private practitioner was evident even in the boldest proposals. In New York at the end of the First World War, Hermann Biggs, by then state health commissioner, suggested building a network of health centers as a means of meeting the needs of rural areas. A state survey had indicated that medical care in rural counties was deteriorating because of the steady decline in the availability of physicians. Biggs thought that if the state paid for half of the construction cost and a continuing share of the maintenance, counties that built health centers could attract physicians to rural practice. The problem was not that doctors in rural areas had trouble making a good living. "As a matter of fact," Biggs told a meeting of the New York County Medical Society in December 1920, "they do extremely well, they do far better relatively than a large number of the men in the cities. But a man who has been properly trained and had hospital service will not go willingly into the practice of medicine of twenty-five or thirty years ago.

"Just think for a moment what it would mean," he continued, "if you were cut off absolutely from all kinds of laboratory and X-ray service. If you were cut off from all association with your colleagues, from all assistance from specialists, and you were left to practice everything— every specialty in surgery, medicine, gynecology, obstetrics and everything else.

"Now that is exactly what the practice of medicine is in the rural districts of the State. I doubt if there is any one of us who would undertake this work. . . ."[29]

The health centers proposed by Biggs were an attempt to meet these deficiencies of rural practice. Consisting of a hospital, outpatient clinic, laboratory and center for public health work, they would offer private physicians and their patients X-rays, clinical consultations by salaried specialists, and bacteriological and chemical laboratory diagnostic tests. The plan, Biggs insisted, would "in no way supersede the local physician, but rather furnish him with facilities which he does not now have."[30]

Despite this conception of the centers as auxiliaries to private practice, opposition from the medical societies was vehement. "Too much power is given to the laity and too little to the medical profession . . . Too much power is given to the County Boards of Supervisors and Mayors of cities . . . Too much power is given to the State Department of

Health . . . Too little recognition and power is [*sic*] given to the medical profession," read the first four objections to the program in a physician's summary of arguments against it.[31]

When the bill came before the state legislature, it had the backing of public health, social welfare, labor, and farming groups, but was opposed by the medical profession. The doctors' opposition, according to C.-E.A. Winslow's account, proved fatal. In 1923, after twice being defeated, a law was finally passed authorizing state aid to counties for public health facilities, but no mention was made of health centers, and the funds were eventually used for standard public health functions.

There were other scattered efforts to build health centers, but profound and lasting changes were not made. Like school health services, health centers assumed a complementary relation to private practice; they diagnosed cases and sent them to physicians, aiding doctors in their business rather than competing with them.

The artificial separation of diagnosis from treatment, and more generally of preventive from curative medicine, was part of what later critics would describe as the "fragmentation" of the medical system. The defense of private interests set one of the limits to the rational organization of medical care in America. Wherever public health overreached the boundaries that the profession saw as defining its sphere, the doctors tried to push it back. Yet this was not just true of medicine. It was a cardinal principle in America that the state should not compete with private business. The physicians' view of the boundaries of public health was consistent with prevailing beliefs held by public officials regarding the boundaries of state action. One public health leader, describing his experiences in setting up county health departments in North Carolina, recalled that the county supervisors would first ask what the local medical society had to say. "You had to promise that you were going to do no curative medicine at all before you could set up a county health department." This promise, a critic observes, was "absurd" to make and "impossible" to fulfill since "in a rational attack on disease, the line between prevention and treatment must be crossed and recrossed many times."[32]

Yet the limitations on public health in the twentieth century were, in some ways, even more profound. The early public health reformers of the nineteenth century, for all their moralism, were concerned with social welfare in a broad sense. Their twentieth-century successors adopted a more narrow and technical view of their calling. As Barbara Rosenkrantz notes, the "dividing line" between the old and new ideologies of public health was "an explicit denial of responsibility for social reform." In Massachusetts in 1936, a commission made up primarily of physicians suggested that the state gradually withdraw even from preventive medicine, and looked ahead to a time when "the scope of public health [can] be limited to the regulation of the environment and the provision of technical aid to the physician."[33]

In retrospect, the turn of the century now seems to have been a golden age for public health, when its achievements followed one another in dizzying succession and its future possibilities seemed limitless. By the thirties, the expansionary era had come to an end, and the functions of public health were becoming more fixed and routine. The bacteriological revolution had played itself out in the organization of public services, and soon the introduction of antibiotics and other drugs would enable private physicians to reclaim some of their functions, like the treatment of venereal disease and tuberculosis. Yet it had been clear, long before, that public health in America was to be relegated to a secondary status: less prestigious than clinical medicine, less amply financed, and blocked from assuming the higher-level functions of coordination and direction that might have developed had it not been banished from medical care.

CHAPTER SIX

Escape from the Corporation 1900–1930

IN 1900, before physicians had successfully consolidated their authority, medicine was still a beleaguered profession. Or so many of its practitioners saw themselves—beleaguered by unscientific sectarians and quacks who preyed on the credulous sick; by druggists who plagiarized their prescriptions and gave free medical advice to customers; by too many of their own profession, turned out in profusion by medical schools; by hospitals that stole patients from them and denied them admitting privileges; and by public dispensaries and health departments that offered medical services to many people who doctors believed could afford to pay.

Over the next three decades, as these afflictions subsided, physicians became uneasy about various other organizations that potentially threatened their autonomy. Private practitioners wanted to keep their relations with patients unmediated by any corporation. They worried about companies that employed doctors to furnish medical care to their workers. Widespread adoption of this form of "contract practice," physicians feared, might engulf many of them in medical programs of poor quality, respected neither by labor nor management. In some areas, employers paid profit-making firms to provide medical services to their workers, and the firms in turn contracted with doctors to give treatment at low rates. These commercial intermediaries were especially distasteful to the medical profession. Some fraternal societies and employee associations paid contract doctors to provide cut-rate medical services to their members. And general practitioners were concerned, too, about the threat of competition from growing numbers of specialists and the rise of private clinics that were often controlled by a few powerful surgeons or internists.

Reformers, however, viewed these organized health services, particularly the private multispecialty clinics, as harbingers of a new order in medical care. The virtues of "cooperative teamwork" and "group medicine," they believed, would soon become apparent to all. Individualism in medical care had had its day, and now the development of technology and specialization would require the same coordinated organization in medicine that was emerging throughout the society.

These expectations were hardly unreasonable, but they proved to be wrong. As occasionally happens, the inevitable did not take place, at least not on schedule: The solo practitioner did not rapidly become extinct. Instead of expanding, organized health services were relegated to the sidelines of the medical system. And therein lies a puzzle: Why did such plausible judgments about the advantages of organization and the demands of technology and specialization prove incorrect?

The aborted development of organized alternatives to the solo practice of medicine and the individual, fee-for-service purchase of medical services also poses some larger questions about the relationship of medical care to the state and the capitalist economy. Government and the modern corporation offer two alternatives for coordinated organization; conceivably, either might have become the basis for an integrated system. In the previous chapter, I described how public health came to exclude therapeutic services. But why did doctors escape from the corporation? How do we explain the distinctive economic organization of American medicine as it emerged in the twentieth century?

PROFESSIONAL RESISTANCE TO CORPORATE CONTROL

Company Doctors and Medical Companies

The dislike of physicians for "socialized medicine" is well known, but their distaste for corporate capitalism in medical practice was equally strong. They had no more desire to be dominated by private corporations than by agencies of government, and consequently resisted the two forms in which business corporations threatened to move into medical services—the provision of treatment for their own employees through "company doctors" and the marketing of services to the public.

Medical services for workers were quite limited in the nineteenth century. The first to appoint company doctors were railroad and mining companies; one railroad began to employ physicians in 1860, but such arrangements became more common after the Civil War. In the 1880s, as accident rates rose in industry, steel makers and other manufacturers adopted the practice too. In this early period, the role of the company doctor was confined mainly to the surgical repair of victims of industrial accidents. Industrial medicine primarily involved the treatment of occupational injuries, not occupational diseases.[1]

The evolution of industrial medicine then followed a path that reflected developments in both medicine and industrial relations. In the early 1900s, while the surgical treatment of accidents remained paramount, industrial doctors began to conduct periodic as well as preemployment health examinations and became more concerned with the health supervision of workers. With the adoption of state workmen's compensation laws around 1910, industrial medicine also became increasingly involved in preventive medical engineering of the workplace. The rise of industrial hygiene and medical engineering were part of the same current that produced the theories of scientific management of Frederick Taylor. Both stressed the use of professional expertise in the analysis and design of the production process. Still later, in the 1930s and 1940s, as management became more preoccupied with problems of human relations and personnel motivation, industrial doctors devoted increasing attention to alcoholism and mental illness.

Employers had a practical interest in using medical services for recruiting and selecting workers, maintaining their capacity and motivation to work, keeping down liability and insurance costs, and gaining good will from their employees and the public. But they did not want to pay for medical services or the hidden costs of disease that their workers or the community would otherwise bear. The response of employers to these competing interests changed significantly between 1890 and 1920 as medicine became more effective, political protest and reform demanded a response to high rates of industrial injury, and employers themselves came to share the popular belief in the usefulness of medical knowledge. As of the 1890s, medical facilities at a plant might typically consist of a few kits in the hands of foremen. By the 1920s, organized medical departments with full-time physicians were common in the larger companies.[2] Even then, however, employers spent relatively little on medical care, and the little they spent went mainly for health examinations and plant engineering. But there was a "deviant" group of industries and firms that became extensively involved in financing and sometimes managing medical services. Before considering why most companies avoided responsibility for medical care, it will be useful to examine these exceptions.

The railroads were the leading industry to develop extensive employee medical programs. By the turn of the century, there were more than one million railroad workers; in the year ending June 30, 1900, the Interstate Commerce Commission reported that one out of every 28 employees was injured and one out of every 399 was killed on the job. To treat the huge toll in injuries—some to passengers and pedestrians as well as workers—there were more than six thousand railway surgeons.[3] Railway surgery was a specialty with its own journals and national associations. In their early days, railroad lines retained private practitioners along their routes to treat accident cases. However, as they moved into the unsettled areas of the West, they found it necessary to set up organized services under full-time chief surgeons. In the 1880s, the railroads established claims departments and relief associations to pay for medical expenses and provide some minimal support to disabled workers. The employment of surgeons and the establishment of relief funds were motivated not only by the special hazards of railroad work, but also by the interest of companies in protecting themselves from lawsuits. The function of the railway surgeon was to make a record of the injury as well as to treat it, and the surgeon often represented the company as an expert witness in damage suits. In several states, courts ruled that a worker's agreement not to sue a company for an injury was unenforceable, except when the worker accepted relief from a fund. Eight funds terminated all benefits if an employee attempted to sue.[4]

For the mining and lumber industries, as well as for the railroads, special geographical conditions were the principal reason for extensive company involvement in medical care. In the isolated areas where mining and lumbering companies conducted operations, physicians were generally unavailable. To induce doctors to move to these poor and sparsely settled regions, the companies had to guarantee them a salary, usually out of mandatory deductions from workers' wages.[5] As one might expect, company medical programs were much less common in urban areas.

Employee medical programs were also started in some companies as part of a more general movement in American business known as "welfare capitalism." To build up their workers' loyalty and "Americanism," employers provided a broad range of welfare services, including schools, housing, and social and religious programs, and even token representation in decision-making. The advocates of corporate paternalism wanted not only to instill the proper attitudes in workers, but also to spin an elaborate web of affiliations binding them to their companies. Unions might thereby be prevented from gaining a foothold.[6] Medical care functioned as an element in this strategy of control.

These various considerations—legal liability, geographical isolation, paternalism—influenced the extent and distribution of industrial contract practice. By the first decades of the twentieth century, company medical services could be found in the mining and lumbering camps of the Pacific states, the mining industry of the Rocky Mountains, and the coal fields of the Midwest and Appalachia as well as the mill towns of the Carolinas and Georgia and the nation's railroad industry. In 1930 these programs covered an estimated 540,000 workers in mining and lumbering and approximately 530,000 railway employees, plus a large though undetermined number of dependents.[7]

Before 1900 the industrial surgeon's home or office often served as an infirmary. But around the turn of the century, many of the railroads and other companies built their own hospitals and clinics. Generally only the larger firms owned and operated their own facilities; most arranged for treatment through independent physicians and hospitals for a flat rate per worker per month. The form of organization also seems to have depended on the degree of isolation from preexisting medical resources (the less developed the area, the greater the company's need to set up its own system) and legal considerations (under workmen's compensation laws in some states, firms could minimize medical costs and compensation awards by hiring physicians directly instead of paying for them through a state fund). But whether providing services in its own facilities or through independent physicians, the company usually controlled the choice of the doctor.

As a result, the system of payroll deductions for company doctors was frequently unpopular among workers, many of whom would have preferred to go to a practitioner of their own choosing. In cases of industrial injury, where medical evaluations determined compensation awards, they naturally distrusted doctors paid by the company. Unions continually pressed for the substitution of cash benefits for company medicine. The American Federation of Labor opposed as "paternalistic" all forms of compulsory medical care through employers.[8]

Though medical societies recognized the necessity of contract practice in remote areas, they regarded it elsewhere as a form of exploitation because it enabled companies to get doctors to bid against each other and drive down the price of their labor. In 1908 the physician who had been company doctor at Sears, Roebuck resigned because the Chicago Medical Society had excluded him from membership on the grounds that his services to employees' families at reduced rates constituted an unethical invasion of private practice. His successor at Sears insisted that the company drop services and suggested that its medical program instead concentrate on periodic examinations and health supervision. Doctors who worked for companies were generally regarded with suspicion by the profession. "For a surgeon or physician to accept a position with a manufacturing company was to earn the contempt of his colleagues," wrote Alice Hamilton, a physician and toxicologist who played a prominent role in exposing dangerous working conditions in the early decades of the century.[9]

The opposition of the medical profession to contract practice contributed to the reluctance of employers to expand medical services. Outside of the mining, lumber, railway, and textile industries, workers generally received limited medical care. A study of ninety plants in New England in 1921 found that in the "great majority," medical service was confined to treatment to keep the employee on the job. "If too ill to continue at his job he was sent home and advised to call his physician."[10] In 1926 a national survey of 407 plants, nearly all with more than 300 employees, reported that three fourths provided free medical services of some kind. Ten years earlier, a similar survey of 375 plants had found that 110 had no more than first-aid equipment; but by 1926 only 34 provided such limited services, while two thirds had facilities staffed by doctors. Still, in most industrial medical programs, the main functions were to treat work injuries, examine job applicants, supervise company sanitary conditions, and encourage hygienic practices. Workers who were seriously ill were generally referred to private practitioners or to a hospital.[11] Industrial medicine of this type proved to be acceptable to the medical profession, though there continued to be tensions between the AMA and industrial physicians.[12]

The limited development of company medicine is inseparable from the broader pattern of limited corporate involvement in the welfare of American workers. Corporate paternalism probably reached its height during the 1920s, but during the Depression it went into a steep decline. When businesses cut back, employee welfare programs were among the first things to go. With Social Security, the New Deal shifted the primary locus of responsibility for social welfare to the federal government. Also, the enactment of legal protections for collective bargaining and the accommodation of unions in heavy industry meant the abandonment of company-controlled services as a strategy of work incentives and discipline.[13]

The next step in providing medical care to workers would come in the 1940s through collective bargaining and group health insurance. Unlike company medicine, health insurance would enable workers to go to physicians and hospitals of their own choice and freed the medical profession from the threat of direct control by the large corporations. Like the constricted boundaries of public health, limited corporate involvement in health care protected professional sovereignty. Industrial medicine, like school health services and health centers, kept out of the domain of private medical practice.

The other form of business involvement in medical care, the sale of services to the public, was known as the "corporate practice" of medicine, and it developed on an even more limited scale. A series of legal decisions shortly after the turn of the century effectively precluded the emergence of profit-making medical care corporations in most jurisdictions. Between 1905 and 1917, courts in several states ruled that corporations could not engage in the commercial practice of medicine, even if they employed licensed physicians, on the grounds that a corporation could not be licensed to practice and that commercialism in medicine violated "sound public policy." These decisions were not models of rigorous legal reasoning. They were not applied to the employment of company doctors nor to for-profit hospitals, where the logic of the argument should have carried them.[14] Yet no one made much of a fuss. Respectable opinion did not favor "commercialism" in medicine.

The few exceptions to this pattern suggest that even if the courts had allowed profit-oriented firms, the growing economic power of the medical profession would have limited their development. In the states of Washington and Oregon, peculiarities in the workmen's compensation laws encouraged employers in the timber and mining industries to contract out medical services for their workers to for-profit "hospital associations." These companies—only some of which actually owned hospitals—provided medical and hospital care for a fixed sum per worker. Though started by doctors, they later fell under lay control. At first, the associations used their own physicians, but in time they subcontracted work to doctors in private practice, whom they paid on a fee-for-service basis. They also expanded from their original base in lumbering, mining, and railways to include other subscribers. In 1917 Oregon passed a Hospital Association Act that permitted corporations to provide medical and other related services without a medical license.[15]

These hospital associations, unlike later commercial health insurers, dealt directly with physicians and exercised some control over them. They required second opinions before authorizing major surgery and reviewed the length of hospital stays. They restricted medical fees, refusing to pay prices they deemed excessive. In short, they acted as a countervailing power in the medical market and limited the doctors' professional autonomy. The medical profession, used to dealing with relatively powerless individual consumers, was unhappy about these controls, but doctors continued to do business with the hospital associations because they guaranteed payment for low-income patients.

In 1932 the largest county medical society in Oregon established its own plan to compete with the commercial hospital associations, but when this initial effort proved unsuccessful it began to censure and expel doctors connected with the profit-making firms. In 1936 the Council of the Oregon State Medical Society, following AMA policy, ruled that it was unprofessional for a doctor to be employed by a hospital association that made "a direct profit from the fees." Nonetheless, these measures were unsuccessful in drawing away physicians who depended upon the associations for guarantee of payment, so in the 1940s the medical society changed its strategy. In place of its county plans, it set up a statewide program, Oregon Physicians Service, that offered prepaid services without regulating medical decision making. Thereafter, doctors refused to deal directly with the commercial hospital associations, forcing patients to pay medical bills and apply to the companies for reimbursement. Consequently, the hospital associations could control their costs only by withholding compensation from patients, thereby antagonizing subscribers and losing business to Oregon Physicians Service. In addition, by withholding medical records, the doctors were able to prevent the hospital associations from effectively restricting unnecessary procedures. And when the associations asked the courts to rule that the physicians' actions constituted restraint of trade, the courts supported the doctors. Confronted by a declining share of the market, the hospital associations abandoned their cost-control procedures and began to act like insurers rather than providers of medical service. Although they survived, they were not able to maintain their original function in the face of a professional boycott.

Other factors besides professional opposition probably also would have impeded profit-making medical care companies even if the courts had allowed them. Once blocked from regulating medical decisions, they would not easily have found other ways to cut costs and achieve any price advantage over solo practitioners. As long as physicians have access to community hospitals, there appear to be only limited economies of scale in medical care, in contrast to other industries where large-scale enterprises have replaced independent craftsmen. In addition, medical licensing laws would have prevented profit-oriented firms from reorganizing the production process and substituting lower-paid paramedical workers for physicians. At the same time, corporate organization sacrifices some of the economic advantages of self-employment. The self-employed often impose on themselves hours and working conditions that would be considered oppressive if imposed by anyone else. The individual entrepreneur, as John Kenneth Galbraith remarks, is "almost wholly free, as the organization is not, to exploit his labor force since his labor force consists of himself."[16] Physicians, like other small businessmen, have been prone to this "self-exploitation," and it seems improbable that, as professional workers, they could have been exploited as successfully by corporations as they were by themselves.

Consumers' Clubs

The medieval guilds, like modern corporations, provided social benefits as well as regulating production. Though the guilds died out, fraternal orders, mutual benefit societies, employee associations, and unions took up many of their beneficiary functions. In nineteenth-century America, fraternal orders and benefit societies became extensively involved in providing life insurance and aiding the sick and disabled; by the early 1900s, some eight million Americans belonged to fraternal orders, which, consequently, affected an estimated 25 to 30 percent of American families.[17] Some of these societies bordered quite closely on life insurance companies; others were significant as settings where men developed friendships outside of both the family and the workplace. The membership of many fraternal orders cut across social classes; workers and their bosses sometimes belonged to the same order and at times the same local lodge.[18]

Doctors came into contact with lodges for two reasons. They often conducted examinations required for the life insurance that the fraternal societies offered; and they began, particularly in the 1890s and after, to accept contracts to care for the lodge membership. The societies paid physicians at what the doctors regarded to be unconscionably low rates, typically between $1 and $2 per member per year. Members could sometimes get medical coverage for dependents for an additional dollar or two. From a lodge with three or four hundred members, a physician could wring out a meager livelihood. The more successful doctors were generally unwilling to take such work. But between the 1890s and First World War, many physicians often still needed lodge contracts, and some practitioners were so anxious to build up a clientele that they themselves organized private "clubs" to attract patients at bargain rates.[19]

Lodge practice was especially common in immigrant communities. A 1914 survey in New York City found "literally thousands of petty health insurance funds," mostly branches of larger fraternal organizations. While most other insurance plans typically paid only cash benefits in cases of sickness, these fraternal organizations furnished both income and medical care.[20] The Lower East Side of New York City was teeming with small benefit societies providing prepaid medical care for Jews who came from the same town or region in Eastern Europe. According to a 1909 survey by a Rhode Island doctor, George S. Mathews, one third of the Jews in Providence had contract doctors, and in some industrial areas, the proportion was as high as 50 percent. "In the rural districts and in the small towns the lodge doctor is almost unknown. Some sections of every city in the state are free from it. In other sections it is almost as rampant as it is in the East Side of New York City."[21] In Buffalo, New York, a local medical committee estimated in 1911 that lodge practice covered 150,000 people. Fraternal orders were also reported to be providing medical care in Pennsylvania, Michigan, Illinois, and California.[22] According to a Pennsylvania doctor, in seeking out new members, the orders "ever keep to the forefront the fact that they furnish free medical services."[23]

In Providence, Mathews found three types of contract practice: private clubs organized by doctors; lodge and fraternal organizations; and work and shop organizations. In one factory, there were two clubs organized by the workers—one with 700, the other with 400 members. The larger club paid a doctor $2.25 per member per year. Every day the doctor called at the factory to take down names from a slate on which workers had indicated they wanted to see him; this doctor had fifteen to thirty-five office calls a day, plus two or three house calls.[24]

Doctors who favored contract practice, Mathews reported, argued that "there is nothing unethical in it . . . the remuneration is nearly as good as that received in regular practice among the lower classes . . . this same poor man uninsured would contract a medical bill never paid, or else become a free hospital patient . . .the hospital and dispensary are much greater abuses than the lodge doctor . . ." On the other hand, most doctors opposed lodge practice as unethical and unfair to the profession. They cited incidents such as the following:

> [T]wo members in good standing in the State Medical Society openly in lodge meeting underbid one the other [*sic*]. One volunteered his services at $2 a head. The other dropped his price to $1.75. The first bidder then acceded to this price with medicines furnished. This occasioned a drop in bidder No. 2 in his price to include medicine and minor surgery. To the vast credit of the lodge neither bid was accepted but a non-bidder was given the job at $2.[25]

The AMA could see "no economic excuse or justification" for lodge practice, objecting to the unlimited service for limited pay and the "ruinous competition" it "invariably" introduced.[26] Many county medical societies refused membership to any doctor who contracted with a lodge. From Norristown, Pennsylvania, a doctor reported that the county medical society had called upon the seven doctors performing contract work for two fraternal orders to give it up; though three acceded, the other four refused and were expelled from the society.[27]

Despite professional opposition, young doctors just out of training were often obliged to take such work as a way of breaking into practice. Samuel Silverberg, a retired New York doctor who worked for a Jewish benefit society in the early 1900s, recalled that although the society paid him only $2 a year for a single member and $3 or $4 for a family, "I took the job because in that way I was sure of being able to pay the rent for my office. On my own I took in very little. . . .

"The society member would recommend the doctor to his friends, and in that way you could build up a practice. But it was hard, lots of running up and down tenement stairs. When I moved my office to the Grand Concourse, I gave up the society."[28]

"To abolish this mode of contract practice," a doctor told the Physicians' Protective League of New York in 1913, "is at present impossible. First because it is too well established, and secondly because we have as yet nothing better to offer to the young man who is in need of earning a sufficient amount to cover his expenses."[29] But over the next decades the declining supply of physicians reduced the availability of cheap professional labor and remedied the problem of lodge practice as it did that of the free dispensary. Doctors could not be found to work on the old terms, and the fraternal groups did not have the resources for more expensive, fee-for-service plans.

A few voluntary associations built relatively enduring medical programs and facilities. In San Francisco, as early as 1852, La Société Française de Bienfaisance Mutuelle constructed a hospital for its members, as did a German Benevolent Society in the city three years later. A century later they were still operating. But these instances—and there were others across the country—were more the exception than the rule. Neither fraternal nor employee groups became centrally involved in providing medical care in the United States. Nationally, there were 179 fraternal associations with 7.7 million "benefit" members in 1914, but only about 1 percent of the $97 million they paid out in benefits that year went for medical care. A survey of employee mutual aid associations in 1916 showed that only 17 percent regularly employed a physician. Another survey in 1930 by the National Bureau of Economic Research concluded that the number of people who obtained medical care through mutual aid associations and trade union funds was negligible.[30]

The medical care provided by the benefit societies had only a mixed reputation. Dr. Silverberg recalled, "Some doctors were devoted, many not. Some patients took advantage of the system and it wasn't always very pleasant. Most society members treated their doctor with respect, but some said, 'A society doctor? What can he know?' For more serious illnesses, they'd go to another doctor."[31] In national fraternal organizations that provided medical benefits, the branches with wealthier members tended not to employ lodge doctors. They had their own private physicians. In Norristown, about half the lodge members were reported to pay for their own private doctor, "preferring to have physicians of their own choice, as they think they get better service."[32] Originally, industrial and lodge practice—the earliest forms of prepayment—were seen as appropriate and necessary only for the working class. Collective organization had not yet been successfully projected as an ideal for medical care; it was, at first, only an expedient.

The Origins and Limits of Private Group Practice

Private group practices—also called "private group clinics" or "group medicine"—represented another form in which corporate organization entered medical care. Unless combined with contract practice for companies or lodges, private clinics did not necessarily involve any change in the mode of payment. Nor did they reflect any reduced economic power of physicians in relation to their clients. But group practice changed the relations of physicians to each other. Unlike lodge practice, it gathered physicians into a single organization, often with business managers and technical assistants, in a new and more elaborate division of labor. Typically, some doctors brought capital as well as labor to the enterprise and became its owners, while other doctors were their employees. And so group practice, though under the control of members of the profession, introduced a type of hierarchical, profit-making organization into medical practice.

The point of origin for group practice in America was the Mayo Clinic. Though in many ways unique, it was the prototype for other private clinics, and its development discloses some of the underlying forces that brought about the earliest groups. In the 1880s William and Charles Mayo joined their father in building up a large and flourishing general practice in Rochester, Minnesota, a small town in the cornfields ninety miles south of Minneapolis. Like their father, the two brothers increasingly specialized in surgery, adopting the newest techniques and creatively extending them in new operations. In addition to other work, William Mayo became a district surgeon for the Chicago and Northwestern Railroad, which played an important part in widening the radius of their practice. Their reputation for skill, invention, and exceedingly low mortality rates attracted both patients and professional respect. By the 1890s, when their father retired, they were doing hundreds of operations a year; by the turn of the century, about three thousand. Forced to choose between limiting their practice or bringing in new partners, they decided to expand partly because they wanted to be able to travel to the East and to Europe to keep up with new scientific developments. In 1892 they invited a respected, fifty-year-old neighboring practitioner to join them, and over the next ten years they added several younger doctors who were adept in new diagnostic techniques, such as blood tests, X-rays, and bacteriological examinations. As Helen Clapesattle explains in her history of the clinic, until the appointment of a young assistant surgeon in 1903, the Mayos chose "partners and assistants who could relieve them of the nonsurgical phases of the practice, while they kept the operating entirely in their own hands." The specialization in diagnostic techniques reflected both the tremendous scientific advances in diagnosis and the distinctive needs of the enterprise. "The primary function of the diagnosticians," writes Clapesattle, "was to pick from the procession of patients passing before them those whom the Mayo brothers as surgeons could benefit."[33] In 1904 the Mayos hired Dr. Louis B. Wilson, previously assistant director of the bacteriology laboratories at the Minnesota State Board of Health. The following year, Wilson worked out a method for staining fresh tissues that permitted him to do an analysis quickly enough to report to the Mayos while an operation was in progress. This was one of the key breakthroughs in the emergence of clinical pathology—that is, the use of pathology in medical practice rather than strictly for teaching and research.

Diagnostic work and research gradually became as important as surgery. By 1914, when the clinic opened its own building, there were seventeen doctors on the Mayos' permanent diagnostic staff as well as eleven clinical assistants, and in the 1920s, with the growing emphasis on preventive health examinations, the diagnostic services at the Mayo Clinic reached parity with surgery. The clinic also developed into a center of graduate medical education, augmenting its influence in the profession. In 1897 the Mayos began to bring in interns. Many practicing doctors also came to observe the Mayos at work, and they independently organized a Surgeons' Club to conduct what today would be described as courses in continuing education. In 1915, having accumulated a large fortune, the Mayos gave $1.5 million to endow the Mayo Foundation for Medical Education and Research, which later became affiliated with the University of Minnesota as a graduate medical school.

Originally, the Mayos' practice was strictly proprietary. They retained control even after other doctors joined them. Those taken into the partnership participated only in the income, not the ownership. However, in two stages beginning in 1919, the Mayos gave up ownership and converted the clinic into a nonprofit organization. In 1923 all former partners, including the Mayos, became salaried staff. Nonetheless, the Mayos still retained control; only as they withdrew from practice in the following decade did power pass to committees of physicians on the permanent staff. By 1929 the Mayo Clinic had become a huge organization: 386 physicians and dentists (211 permanent staff, 175 fellows) and 895 laboratory technicians, nurses, and other workers. The clinic had 288 examining rooms, 21 laboratories, and was housed in a fifteen-story building.[34]

From Rochester, the admirers of the Mayo Clinic spread out across the country. A young doctor who worked as an assistant at the clinic from 1906 to 1909, Donald Guthrie, founded the Guthrie Clinic in Sayre, Pennsylvania, in 1910. In the summer of 1908, a general practitioner from Topeka, Kansas, Charles F. Menninger, returned home from the Mayo Clinic. Sitting at the family dining table with his three boys—Karl, Edwin, and Will—he is said to have declared, "I have been to the Mayos and I have seen a great thing. You boys are going to be doctors and we are going to have a clinic like that right here in Topeka."[35] During World War I, the experience of the medical corps impressed many young doctors with the value of coordinated medical groups, and in the years immediately afterward many new groups were formed.

Data on the growth of group practice are unfortunately incomplete because the earliest surveys were conducted around 1930. An AMA survey conducted in 1932 found that, of existing groups, eighteen had been founded prior to 1912; in that year another nine were established. The period from 1914 to 1920 saw a high rate of growth, with a peak from 1918 to 1920. As of 1932 the AMA found about 300 group practices with a median size of between five and six physicians.[36] In another survey published in 1932, C. Rufus Rorem estimated that there were about 150 private group clinics in the United States, involving about 1,500 to 2,000 physicians. On the basis of a study of fifty-five of these clinics, Rorem put the median number of doctors in such groups at eleven.[37] This discrepancy is probably explained by differences in definition and methodology.*

The two surveys agreed on the predominance of the clinics in the Middle and Far West and their concentration in small cities. These geographical patterns are important clues to the forces that produced the group clinics. The AMA survey found half of the groups in cities with less than 25,000 people and two thirds in cities of under 50,000. On the other hand, only 4 percent of the groups were located in cities with a population of over half a million. Clinics in the East were rare.[38]

These findings contradict the usual expectation that complex organizations develop first and most rapidly in urban areas. But this may have been a case of the advantages of backwardness. The late Russell Lee, who founded the Palo Alto Clinic in Palo Alto, California, suggested to me in 1975 that the clinics grew up in the West because they met the demand there for specialized services, mainly surgery and diagnostic examinations. In the East, such services were provided by the established voluntary hospitals and their affiliated physicians. The absence of large and venerable voluntary hospitals in the West, particularly in small cities, created an opportunity in the early 1900s for the development of proprietary clinics.[39] Similarly, the 1933 AMA study pointed out that in large cities with ample hospitals and laboratory services, doctors did not have the same motive for forming groups; the available hospital and outpatient facilities provided medical care "for many who, in a smaller place, would patronize a group."[40]

The doctors originally involved in the clinics did not found them for ideological reasons. They did not, as Rorem observed, "regard group practice as an experiment in social reform."[41] The Mayos expanded without any initial design. Though they were often called the "fathers" of group medicine, William Mayo once remarked "if we were we did

*Rorem defined group clinics as groups of physicians, representing two or more specialties, who engaged in "cooperative and contiguous" practice, shared responsibility for patients, pooled their income, and employed a business manager. The AMA, however, rejected many of these qualifications in its definition, which included groups that did not pool income and represented only a single specialty. Rorem located clinics through the association of clinic managers, which probably led him to overlook many clinics too small to have a manager. The AMA located clinics through its network of county medical societies and consequently seems to have picked up many smaller ones.

not know it." Yet by 1910 he was saying that medical care had become a "cooperative science" and "individualism in medicine" could no longer continue.[42] In 1915, the reformer Michael Davis visited the Mayo Clinic; like Menninger, he saw the future, and it worked. Soon afterward he wrote of group practice as a remedy for the disappearance of the family doctor. It used to be that the family physician interpreted the specialists' advice; no longer was this so, even though the majority of doctors were still general practitioners. Families were calling on many specialists directly, and the result was inefficiency and lack of coordination. "Modern industry is the result of specialization, based upon progress in pure and applied science, *plus* organization," Davis wrote. "In modern medicine we have developed specialization . . . but in private practice we have not developed organization."[43]

Many doctors, however, were hostile to group practice, In communities where doctors had formed group practices, the solo practitioners tended to be "definitely antagonistic, even belligerent," Rorem reported.[44] They often complained that the groups cut fees below prevailing rates. Even the Mayos were bitterly criticized by colleagues in Minnesota who accused them of underselling and publicity seeking. The AMA never condemned group practice outright, but it worried about its impact and rarely missed an opportunity to point out its disadvantages. In an editorial in 1921, the association's *Journal* noted, "The development of modern medicine, and especially of scientific laboratory diagnosis, may make necessary some such cooperative plan as these groups are intended to provide. But what of the outcome of this new development? What of the physicians outside the group? Some evidently are seeing the advantages and are forming other groups—perhaps in some instances forced to do so in self-defense!" And then it asked the question that the rise of group practice inevitably posed to general practitioners, "Does it mean that the family physician is being replaced by a corporation?"[45]

Although they were profit-making organizations, group practices were not all legally organized as corporations. Many had created a dual organizational structure: a clinic organization comprising the medical practitioners and a property corporation that owned the plant and equipment. The clinic then leased the facilities from the property corporation. This split made possible a division of earnings that reflected the partners' varying contributions of labor and capital to the venture. The clinic itself might be organized as a sole proprietorship, a partnership, or a corporation.[46]

Legal arrangements aside, the early clinics had a definite class structure. Many of them began when a successful surgeon or internist built up an organization around his practice; these were called "one-man groups." In other cases, doctors who referred patients to each other and perhaps shared contiguous offices formalized their relations and began to add doctors to take care of additional work.[47] But though clinics varied in the distribution of power, the physicians in groups generally fell into two classes: owners, who shared in the partnership or stock, and employees, who received a wage. Rorem found the median age of the owning physicians to be forty-six, while the employed doctors' median age was thirty-four. Surgeons and internists predominated among the owners; pathologists, radiologists, and dentists were rarely among them.[48] In 1923 in an unusually graphic analysis of the workings of private clinics, Rexwald Brown, a doctor in group practice in Santa Barbara, California, described the older men as typically successful practitioners with many patients who had "passed through the weary years of small financial returns" and looked forward "to a lightening of their loads, a better service to their patients, opportunity for needed study and something of relaxation." Tensions with the younger staff were common, as Brown explained with evident bias:

> The younger men enter the group with little or none of the realities of general practice as a background. Many of them have been trained in hospitals devoted to special phases of disease. . . . Too much perhaps they expect the world to recognize them as having arrived in achievement. They know not the struggles, trials and hardships of building up a practice, and the slow yearly increase of income . . . .
>
> Thus, the stage is set for the attitudes of mind which become apparent as the group practice grows in volume. The younger physicians, be it understood, are on salary, and the group at its beginning has no material assets other than the equipment furnished by the older physicians. The real assets . . . are intangible . . . the practices of the older men, their years of contact with patients, their successes, reputations . . ..
>
> It is not long before the young specialist becomes cognizant that he is making good. His patients are numerous, and as he is well trained and skilful, his results win admirers. . . . He feels his compensation is not commensurate with his attainments and value to the group. He becomes restless, rather critical of the older men, who are finding time for medical conventions and vacations, and who are insisting on the younger men answering night calls and handling other exacting but essential routine matters of practice. He labors under the thought that he is being exploited. . . .

The young doctor's sense that he was exploited made it difficult for the clinic to continue in its old form. For as Brown explained, it would be unwise for the older doctors simply to fire the unhappy young man, since he had become "an integral part in the success of the group." The remedy, he suggested, was to give the younger man a share in the partnership, while creating an executive committee of senior partners to maintain some central control; he also recommended creating a departmental structure, in which each department would be assessed its share of the overhead and then allowed to keep the collections for its services.[49]

Such changes effectively recognized that the employed physician could not be indefinitely kept in the position of a wage earner. The difficulty of maintaining hierarchical control over the employed physicians tended to weaken the power of capital over labor in group practice. Groups sometimes broke up over these economic conflicts. In a speech to a conference of clinic managers after his report appeared, Rorem cited as a reason for their low growth internal differences among doctors about their relative economic value to the group.[50] The AMA noted in its study of medical groups that there was "powerful resistance" to industrializing medical practice. "The physician, unlike the industrial worker, always has the alternative of individual practice, should he prefer it to any form of association in his work."[51] And he often did.

After the spurt in growth following World War I, the spread of group practice seems to have slowed down. The rapid growth after the war may have been due to the lag in development of laboratory and hospital facilities in middle-sized cities after the need for those services had already been recognized. Later in the twenties, hospitals and laboratories expanded to meet the demand. "A much larger percentage of individual physicians can now obtain access to these without the necessity of forming a group," the 1933 AMA analysis of group practice claimed. "A perhaps excessive development of specialization has also made available a wide choice of specialists for consultation in most cities. These developments reduce the incentive to form groups in order to obtain access to equipment and consultations."[52] The private clinics fulfilled the expectations that specialization and technology would lead to the rise of complex organizations in medical practice, but they found only a limited niche in the twentieth century's first decades.

CAPITALISM AND THE DOCTORS

Why No Corporate Enterprise in Medical Care?

Doctors opposed corporate enterprise in medical practice not only because they wanted to preserve their autonomy, but also because they wanted to prevent the emergence of any intermediary or third party that might keep for itself the profits potentially available in the practice of medicine. It was "unprofessional," the AMA stated in a section of its code of ethics adopted in 1934, for a physician to permit "a direct profit" to be made from his work. The making of a profit from medical work "is beneath the dignity of professional practice, is unfair competition with the profession at large, is harmful alike to the profession of medicine and the welfare of the people, and is against sound public policy."[53] Not that the AMA believed it was wrong for doctors to make a profit from their work. Nor did it reprimand the physician owners of medical groups for making a profit off of the work of other doctors. The AMA opposed any one else, such as an investor, making a return from physicians' labor. The AMA was saying, in short, that there must be no capital formation in medical care (other than what doctors accumulated), that the full return on physicians' labor had to go to physicians, and consequently, by implication, that if medicine required any capital that doctors themselves could not provide, it would have to be contributed gratis by the community, instead of by investors looking for a profit. In other words, physicians must be allowed to earn whatever income the capital contributed by the community might yield to them.

Physicians did not want to be subjected to the kind of hierarchical controls that typically prevail in industrial capitalism. One function of the hierarchical organization of work in the capitalist enterprise is to make possible a much higher rate of capital accumulation than would otherwise occur. As the economist Stephen Marglin argues, "By mediating between producer and consumer, the capitalist organization sets aside much more for expanding and improving plant and equipment than individuals would if they could control the pace of capital accumulation."[54] Once the organization successfully inserts itself between the producer and the market—whether by virtue of superior efficiency through the division of labor, as Adam Smith argued, or by exacting greater effort and discipline from workers and substituting cheaper unskilled labor, as Marxists contend—the individual producer becomes dependent on the enterprise to secure work and a livelihood. The AMA was wary that a similar process might take place in medical care. "Not a small part of the business acumen of present society," stated its Bureau of Medical Economics, "is expended in seeking an opportunity to intervene in business relations between buyers and sellers in order to abstract a profit from the interflow of commodities and cash. Sometimes an actual service is performed by facilitating action and providing information to one or both parties." But in its most undesirable form, "such intrusion and tribute extortion has come to be known as 'racketeering.'" Anxious to avoid this sort of "intrusion" into medical care, the AMA cited the slogan of some French physicians—"no third party"—as a worthy example and declared, "Where physicians become employees and permit their services to be peddled as commodities, the medical services usually deteriorate, and the public which purchases such services is injured."[55]

The doctors objected not only to private enterprise but to any middleman coming between them and their patients, whether that third party was a company, a fraternal lodge or union, or any other organization. In 1911, one Pennsylvania doctor remarked of lodge practice that "the physician is being exploited for the benefit of the middleman; his services are purchased at wholesale and sold at retail."[56] The AMA objected also to nonprofit institutions deriving a profit from medical service, even though the profit might be used for "other 'philanthropic' purposes to the glory of the institution and its administrators."[57]

Since other groups also wanted to avoid hierarchical subordination and the extraction of a profit from their labor, the question may be asked: Why did doctors succeed? The answer, I believe, lies in the inability of corporate enterprise to insert itself successfully between producer and consumer in medical care under the economic conditions that prevailed in the early twentieth century. The physician had a resource that the ordinary worker lacked. Patients develop a personal relation with their physicians even when medical care takes place in a hospital or clinic. In this respect, hospitals and clinics are fundamentally unlike factories. The doctor's cultural authority and strategic position in the production of medical care create a distinctive base of power.* If, as often happened in group practice, the doctor threatened to leave, he might take his patients with him. This was the problem the group practices faced in dealing with their discontented young physicians. The older doctors might have brought capital to the enterprise in the beginning, but the younger doctors accumulated a kind of capital in the process of serving patients. They acquired reputations, devoted patients, and skill and experience. To substitute another physician, even if he were equally competent, might not succeed in holding the first physician's patients. (Though the group practice might have rotated patients among employed doctors to prevent the formation of individual loyalties, the failure to provide a personal doctor could have limited their competitive appeal.) The younger physicians generally had to be given a share in the partnership because they had the alternative of individual practice and, by virtue of their relations with patients, had acquired some of the group's capital.

*On the concepts of cultural authority and strategic position, see the Introduction.

A key consideration here is that the costs of going into individual practice were not inordinately high. Solo practice would have been much less attractive if physicians had no access to community hospitals.

The hospital itself also did not stand between the doctors and the market. On the contrary, the doctors came to stand between the hospital and its market. This was the source of doctors' control of hospitals, as hospitals increasingly depended on payment by patients rather than on bequests and donations. As I indicated in Chapter 4, the hospitals needed the doctors to keep their beds occupied. In this context, as in group practice, the physicians' authority with patients and their strategic position in the system represented a resource that gave them power over institutions.

By the 1920s, corporate organization was generally confined to the pharmaceuticals, hospital equipment, and other industries on the periphery of medical care. Wherever physicians were directly involved—in medical practice, hospital care, and medical education—corporate enterprise was limited. This had not always been so. Profit-making medical schools and hospitals were quite common in 1900, yet both were soon in decline. My argument here is that the profession's success in establishing its sovereignty in medical care depended on the banishment of profit-making businesses from medical education and hospitals as well as from medical practice itself.

Proprietary schools did not threaten to dominate physicians, but they could not attract the capital investment that a full-scale scientific education required. I have already discussed how medical schools, once virtually all proprietary, became nonprofit. Longer and more expensive scientific and clinical training, first adopted at a few universities and then required of other schools by licensing laws, made medical education unprofitable. The proprietary schools could not raise tuition high enough to make a profit because students would not have been willing to pay that much; a medical career then would not have returned so large an investment. Subsidies were inescapable, but proprietary schools found it impossible to obtain them. "So long as medical schools are conducted as private ventures for the benefit of a few physicians and surgeons who have united to form a corporation or a faculty, the community ought not to endow them," President Eliot of Harvard wrote. Only after eliminating the "fee system" was Harvard Medical School able to attract substantial endowments.[58] This was true elsewhere. In the 1890s, Jefferson Medical College in Philadelphia tried to raise money for a building fund, but had no success because of public awareness that the faculty took a profit. In 1894 William Potter, one of Philadelphia's wealthiest businessmen, was added to the board of trustees, and he at once insisted that Jefferson reorganize as a nonprofit corporation, which it did the following year. As a result, Jefferson was able to attract contributions and emerged as one of the few old medical colleges to survive independently of a university, though only by dropping its profit-making status.[59]

The transition to nonprofit organization in medical schools was the outcome of a long struggle over the licensing laws between medical societies and commercial schools. The proprietary schools had resisted the imposition of heavy licensing requirements, but they lost out as the medical profession grew in political strength and cultural authority. The reasons for their decline are bound up in the reasons for the rise of the profession—the growing ability of physicians to assert their collective interests over the more parochial interests of the physicians who profited from the commercial colleges.

In some ways, the hospital presents a striking contrast to the medical school. In the nineteenth century, while medical education was profitable and conducted as a commercial enterprise, hospital care was unprofitable and conducted as a charity. Around the turn of the century, medical education became unprofitable, while hospital care turned profitable. But in the end, the hospitals remained largely nonprofit too.

Although many proprietary hospitals were established around 1900, they were generally small and never accounted for a large proportion of total hospital capacity. In 1910, according to one estimate, proprietary hospitals represented 56 percent of the total number of hospitals, but they declined to 36 percent by 1928, 27 percent ten years later, and a mere 18 percent by 1946. In hospital beds, they accounted for only 6 percent of the total in 1934 and just 2.8 percent a decade later.[60]

Profit-making hospitals were generally converted to nonprofit corporations by the physicians who owned them. Originally, proprietary hospitals were a means of defending professional autonomy; many were founded in response to closed-staff organization at other institutions. The AMA reported in 1929 that doctors who ran hospitals for profit found the hospital itself "a losing proposition"; the advantage for the doctor was that the hospital "enables him to take care of a larger number of patients in a given time."[61] Physicians' interest in maintaining proprietary hospitals waned, however, as community hospitals opened their staffs to wider membership and doctors found they were able to have the public provide the capital for hospitals and maximize their incomes through their professional fees.

Various other considerations also persuaded doctors to yield title to most of the hospitals. Professional authority is, in some respects, a functional equivalent of property ownership. It gives physicians substantial control over the operation of hospitals and other medical institutions without encumbering them with the risks of investment. In addition, the charitable origins of the hospital left voluntary institutions with a variety of legal privileges, such as exemptions from taxes and charitable immunity from malpractice liability. These privileges put the profit-making hospital at a competitive disadvantage.

Some doctors—the proprietors of commercial medical schools, hospitals, and clinics—might have gained by profit-making organization. But the profession as a whole would have lost some of its independence and its control over the market. Corporate capitalism was kept out of medicine partly because of the support that courts, legislatures, unions, and the public gave to the ideal of a free profession; partly because of the absence of any decisive competitive advantage of corporate organization in medical practice at this stage of development (prior to the rise of third-party health insurance); and partly because of the economic power over organizations possessed by doctors as a result of their direct relation to patients. But the exclusion of the corporation from medical care, like the exclusion of the state, helped maintain the collective autonomy of the profession and reflected its general success in asserting its collective interests over the interests of individual physicians.

Professionalism and the Division of Labor

The primacy of the profession, particularly its success in resisting corporate domination, contributed to the development of a distinctive division of labor in medical care. In industry, despite the resistance of artisans, the dictates of the market broke up the work of skilled craftsmen into low-skill—and consequently cheaper—labor. In medicine, physicians maintained the integrity of their craft and control of the division of labor. While medicine itself became highly specialized, the division of labor among physicians was negotiated by doctors themselves instead of being hierarchically imposed upon them by owners, managers, or engineers. And professional interests and ideals decisively influenced the increasingly complex division of labor between physicians and the occupations that emerged with the growth of modern hospitals, clinics, and laboratories.

Doctors did not simply want to maintain a "monopoly of competence." They wanted to be able to use hospitals and laboratories without being their employees, and consequently, they needed technical assistants who would be sufficiently competent to carry on in their absence and yet not threaten their authority. The solution to this problem—how to maintain autonomy, yet not lose control—had three elements: first, the use of doctors in training (interns and residents) in the operation of hospitals; second, the encouragement of a kind of responsible professionalism among the higher ranks of subordinate health workers; and third, the employment in these auxiliary roles of women who, though professionally trained, would not challenge the authority or economic position of the doctor.

The growth of technology and organization raised a new and difficult question in medicine: Who would control and make money from the new kinds of work that were created? In deterring profit-making enterprises, the physicians removed the danger that the organization and profits of medical work would be controlled by managers and investors. But in the new division of medical labor, there were uncertainties about the boundaries of competence and authority of emerging technical and professional occupations. Doctors who specialized in technologically advanced fields, such as clinical pathology and radiology, wanted to maintain their primacy over the new occupations as well as their autonomy from hospitals. Although specialized training might be required to perform laboratory tests, X-rays, and anesthesia, it was not clear, as Rosemary Stevens points out, that the specialists had to be physicians. Nurses became strongly established as anesthetists before the 1920s, and nonphysicians were sometimes originally in charge of X-ray units. In the early stages of development, there were too few doctors trained in these fields to meet the demand. But in these and other areas, physicians ultimately prevailed and other medical personnel became their subordinates. Moreover, by the late 1930s, the hospital-based specialties were also successfully demanding that hospitals pay them by fee instead of salary. The radiologists and hospitals reached an understanding in 1937; the anesthesiologists the following year.[62]

The development of clinical laboratories offers a particularly graphic illustration of professional control of the division of labor. As late as 1890, most laboratory procedures used in medical care were performed by a doctor with a microscope and slides working in his home or office. Over the next decade, the number of tests and complexity of equipment began to increase significantly. Laboratories became complex organizations, operated by health departments, hospitals, and independent companies. The tests themselves, it became apparent, could be performed by specialists who were not physicians. But could these new specialists also interpret the tests to patients? And could they manage laboratories?[63]

The laboratory industry was divided primarily between hospital and commercial laboratories. As of 1923, according to an AMA survey, about 48 percent of hospitals had laboratories. Commercial laboratories, often operated by businessmen or chemists rather than doctors, were fewer in number; a survey in 1925 indicated that they represented about 14 percent of the total number of laboratories. Despite possible economies of scale, these outside laboratories continued to perform a small share of the tests over the next several decades. As William White has shown, the hospital standardization program of the American College of Surgeons played a critical part in ensuring that laboratories developed mainly in hospitals under the control of pathologists. The college's standards for certification required hospitals to have a laboratory and to place a physician, preferably a pathologist, in charge. Contracts with outside laboratories were not considered satisfactory. By giving the pathologists a monopoly on laboratory tests in the hospital, the surgeons evidently intended to subsidize less profitable procedures pathologists performed, such as autopsies. Originally a small franchise, hospital laboratories became extremely lucrative for the pathologists as tests increased.

The pathologists' control of the laboratory business naturally gave them power over other laboratory workers. In 1929 the recently formed American Society of Clinical Pathologists, made up exclusively of physicians, began operating a system for certifying laboratory personnel. Their program required medical technologists, the higher of the two grades it certified, to have two years of college and a year's working experience and to pass a written examination; they also had to be personally recommended by a physician. Six years later, the educational standard was raised to a college degree. The code of ethics stipulated that registered technicians and technologists "shall agree to work at all times under the supervision of a qualified physician and shall under no circumstances, on their own initiative, render written or oral diagnoses except in so far as it is self-evident in the report, or advise physicians and others in the treatment of disease, or operate a laboratory independently without the supervision of a qualified physician or clinical pathologist."[64] Since pathologists controlled the labor market for technicians, laboratory workers had a strong incentive to meet the requirements for certification. The pathologists opposed any government licensing of technologists, which would have reduced their flexibility in the use of personnel.

Thus professionalism did not mean the same thing for these paramedical workers as it did for physicians. Professionalism in this instance was not primarily an effort to monopolize a sphere of competence; subordinate professional institutions were developed under the aegis of physicians. The pathologists encouraged the development of a responsible professionalism among technologists to upgrade the quality of their work force and to free themselves from supervisory responsibilities.

Craft guilds in the sixteenth century, George Unwin writes, were "engaged in a constant struggle as to which of them should secure the economic advantage of standing between the rest and the market."[65] Twentieth-century American physicians were engaged in a similar struggle with other health care occupations such as laboratory technicians. Not only did the medical profession succeed in preventing corporations from standing between its members and the market; doctors themselves were able to occupy this strategic position, preventing those like laboratory technologists from assuming a competitive entrepreneurial role. The conflicts between obstetricians and midwives involved similar issues: The traditional midwife was a competitor; her successor, the nurse-midwife, was not. Of course, not all groups were so restricted; dentists and optometrists remained independent practitioners. And osteopaths and chiropractors also had unmediated access to the market, but they were often limited in their access to hospitals and right to prescribe drugs. Only physicians had access simultaneously to the market and to the full technological resources of the medical system.

Within medicine itself, the division of labor between specialists and general practitioners was also a point of conflict. When specialists claimed that various techniques and procedures required their skills, general practitioners often found themselves damned in the same breath as nonphysicians. The obstetricians who argued that midwives were inadequately prepared to handle deliveries frequently said the same of GPs.[66] Hence two different conflicts were often taking place on the same terrain. The specialists sought to achieve ascendancy over the nonphysician specialists in their areas—obstetricians over midwives, ophthalmologists over optometrists, anesthesiologists over nurse anesthetists, and so on. And they also sought to impress upon the general practitioner the limit of his abilities.

The outcome of these two conflicts, as of 1930, was very different. The nonphysician specialists were subordinated to the doctors' authority, usually permitted neither to practice independently of the doctor nor to interpret the results of tests or X-rays directly to patients. Nurses and technicians had no chance of working their way into positions as physicians. On the other hand, the general practitioners resisted any attempt to grant specialists exclusive privileges over some kinds of medical work, or to limit their opportunities for specialty training and career development.

Before the 1930s, there were no limits on the entry of general practitioners into specialty practice. The routes to specialization were numerous; there was no single path that could be easily monitored. Many physicians first went into general practice, developed an interest in a field and gradually restricted the cases they accepted. Others took internships emphasizing a specialty; still others learned special techniques as junior attending physicians. Some received training while serving as assistants to established practitioners. And some took short postgraduate courses in New York, Chicago, or other cities in America or Europe. There were thirteen independent, mostly proprietary postgraduate schools in 1910, according to Flexner, and by 1914 five were operated by universities. At this time, only a few doctors received their specialty training during residencies following their internships.[67]

Soon after the Flexner report came out, the lack of any standards or regulation in the practice of the specialties became identified as a problem by leaders in medical education and the specialties. A committee appointed by the AMA Council on Medical Education in 1913 recommended that the AMA regulate postgraduate schools and drive out commercialism in graduate as in undergraduate education. In 1915 it proposed a standard of two years of graduate training in addition to the internship. World War I accentuated the sense that specialty practice needed standards. In its examinations of physicians who claimed to practice a specialty, the military found many unqualified. Of the ophthalmologists, for example, 51 percent were rejected. After the war, the AMA council announced it would concentrate on reform of graduate training, but as Stevens points out, it had to move cautiously because of the influence of general practitioners in the AMA who wanted access to hospitals and opportunities for specialty training.[68] The system of certification by specialty boards, therefore, grew up outside the AMA and only developed on a general basis in the 1930s. And, even then, the specialty boards had no power to prevent uncertified doctors from practicing as specialists, or to compel hospitals to employ the boards' certification as a requirement for admitting privileges.

And so, even after some order was introduced into specialty training and certification, American medicine did not develop the kind of two-tiered system that emerged in England, where the specialists (consultants) acquired a monopoly on hospital positions. On the other hand, general practitioners in America were not guaranteed the role of GPs in England, where patients could consult a specialist only by referral from a general practitioner. Since patients went directly to specialists in America, the general practitioner did not stand between the specialist and the market. And, in the long run, this failure to gain a secure mediating role contributed to the breakdown of general practice.

The influence of professional sovereignty on the division of labor in American medicine created fluid boundaries within the profession, but sharp boundaries around it. Among physicians, the division of labor was only loosely regulated, but between physicians and other occupations, it was hierarchical and rigid. The possibilities of moving from nurse or technologist to physician were negligible; experience at one level did not count toward qualification at the next. Moreover, the subordinate occupations, such as nursing and laboratory work, became more hierarchically stratified than did medicine. The medical profession resisted any division into two classes; the nurses divided themselves into three (registered nurses, licensed practical nurses, and nurses' aides).

Had medical care become a corporate enterprise, the medical care firm (even if run by doctors) would have had an incentive to seek greater flexibility in its use of personnel. It might have tried to substitute the cheaper labor of ancillary workers for physicians in many areas that physicians insisted on retaining. It is not clear, for example, that obstetricians would always have been used in normal deliveries, or that pediatricians would have been the logical choice to take care of well babies. The firm might also have subjected its doctors to more hierarchical control: The physician with limited graduate training might not have been free, for example, to do whatever procedures he considered himself competent to perform. As in other industries, the management of the enterprise might have sought to take away from the workers control over the division of labor, which physicians retained through the system of professional sovereignty.

The Economic Structure of American Medicine

It may help, in bringing together the threads of the preceding analysis, to contrast it with two other explanations of the political economy of American medicine.

In perhaps the single most influential neoclassical treatment, Kenneth Arrow argues that the distinctive structural characteristics of medical care can be explained as adaptations to "uncertainty in the incidence of disease and in the efficacy of treatment." By special structural characteristics, Arrow means those that depart from the standard model of a competitive market: the ethical restrictions on physicians' behavior, such as the bar against advertising and overt price competition and the expectation that advice given by a doctor will be divorced from self-interest; licensing restrictions and the high, heavily subsidized cost of medical education; and special pricing practices—the sliding scale and the insistence of physicians on fee-for-service as against pre-payment.

Arrow suggests that these various structural features are attempts to compensate for imperfections in the medical market. His point of departure is the concept of "market failure"; as he puts it: "[W]hen the market fails to achieve an optimal state, society will, to some extent at least, recognize the gap, and nonmarket social institutions will arise to bridge it." The medical care market fails to perform efficiently because patients cannot assess the value of treatment, nor obtain insurance that would compensate them for any imperfect outcome. "The value of information is frequently not known in any meaningful sense to the buyer; if, indeed, he knew enough to measure the value of information, he would know the information itself." Patients are utterly dependent on physicians in ways that buyers are not normally dependent on sellers. Consequently, according to Arrow, other safeguards, such as ethical restrictions on physicians' behavior and licensing restrictions on entry into the market, arise to protect patients.[69]

Unfortunately, Arrow leaves unexplained the connection between the prevalence of uncertainty and the insistence of physicians on fee-for-service payment. Prepayment is itself an adaptation to uncertainty in the incidence of disease and the costs of treatment; if anything, the profession's opposition to contract practice (and later to health insurance, medical cooperatives, and other prepaid health plans) increased the burden of uncertainty that patients had to bear.

This missing link in Arrow's argument is related to more fundamental difficulties. Uncertainty in medical care is partly a product of the way the market is organized. If the purchaser of medical services were the state or some collective agency, such as a fraternal society, it could employ knowledgeable agents to choose among physicians and medical facilities. Uncertainty has also been enhanced by the medical profession—in fact, by some of the features Arrow discusses, such as codes of professional ethics that require doctors called in on consultations to withhold from patients information that would discredit a colleague. Of course, most uncertainty is not artificially manufactured. Uncertainty reflects more general cultural beliefs. Democratic thought in the early 1800s held that all that was useful in medicine was within the reach of ordinary men. As I've argued earlier, the advance of science and decline of confidence in common sense between the Jacksonian and Progressive eras helped restore a belief in the legitimate complexity of medicine. An increased sense of uncertainty (as was evident in the Supreme Court decision in Dent v. West Virginia) favored the reinstitution of licensing at the end of the nineteenth century.

But while the growth of uncertainty may explain why there were departures from the competitive market, it cannot explain the form the departures took. Other institutional arrangements, besides the restrictive practices adopted by the profession or enacted at its behest, would also have been adaptations to uncertainty, but they met resistance and were defeated. The particular alternative to the competitive market that developed in America cannot be derived from a purely abstract analysis; it requires an analysis that is both structural and historical. The structural features Arrow discusses have a history. He writes that when the market fails, "society" will make adjustments. This is too abstract. It is as if some inner dynamic were pushing the world toward Pareto optimality. One has to ask: For whom did the market fail, and how did "society" make these adjustments? The competitive market was failing no one more than the medical profession, and it was the profession that organized to change it—that barred advertising and price competition, lobbied for licensing laws, engaged in price discrimination, and fought against prepaid health plans.

Yet there is a still deeper problem. Arrow looks at the structure of the medical market as a rational adaptation to certain inherent characteristics of medical care; he attempts to explain the particulars of the system at a given moment in history in terms of universal features of medicine. There is the presumption that what is real is rational or, as the economists say, "optimal." (The sociological version of this fallacy is that what is structural must be functional.) The result is not so much to explain as to explain away the particular institutional structure medical care has assumed in the United States.

Recent Marxist interpretations maintain that the interests of corporate capitalism brought about the rise of scientific medicine. One account, E. Richard Brown's *Rockefeller Medicine Men*, argues that capitalists personally exercised control over the development of medicine through the foundations they established. In Brown's view, scientific medicine was consonant with the capitalist view of the world, while the more holistic orientations of homeopathy and herbal medicine were not. Scientific medicine, he writes, was "a tool developed by members of the medical profession and the corporate class to serve their perceived needs." The Rockefeller philanthropies favored scientific medicine because it helped "legitimize" the inequalities of capitalism by diverting attention from the social causes of disease; capitalists also had an interest in maintaining the health of their workers.[70]

One must, I suppose, have a deep appreciation of the fragility of capitalism to imagine that it might have been threatened by the persistence of homeopathy. Some of the most enthusiastic believers in scientific medicine, one needs to recall, were socialists, who were outraged by the failure to extend its benefits to the working class. No doubt the Rockefellers sought to gain public credit and good will by supporting research approved by medical authorities. But this no more proves that scientific medicine peculiarly benefited their interests than bequests to churches by the rich prove that Christianity peculiarly benefits millionaires. The legitimacy of capitalism rested on more ample foundations than the alleged ideological functions of medicine in focusing attention on bacteria rather than class interests. Compared to the beliefs in economic opportunity and religious and political freedom, medicine played an insignificant role in sustaining democratic capitalism in America.

Marxists frequently claim that capitalism encouraged an emphasis on medical care rather than public health and prevention. In support of this point, Brown cites Rockefeller investments in medical research, the uses of medical care in industry, and the alleged support of liberal capitalists for compulsory health insurance. This argument cannot survive close inspection. During the Progressive era, to the extent that corporations were concerned about health, they were interested mainly in preventive engineering and industrial hygiene rather than medical care; employers did not wish to assume the costs of medical treatment nor to offend private physicians by trespassing on their terrain. Almost all employers were opposed to compulsory health insurance; the organizations that Brown mentions as supporting such proposals actually led the opposition.[71] Much of the Rockefeller work did involve public health, and Brown himself writes that Frederick Gates, who managed the Rockefeller philanthropies, "insisted from the beginning of his career to its end that 'the fundamental aim of medical science ought to be not primarily the cure but primarily the prevention of disease.'"[72]

It is difficult to see why capitalism, as a system, would have benefited by favoring medical care over public health. Sanitary services were relatively inexpensive and undoubtedly a better investment than the services of physicians. To be sure, many companies resisted public health measures that would have increased their production costs or limited their markets. On the other hand, for equally self-interested reasons, life insurance companies actively stimulated public health measures. The expansion of trade, increasing coordination of economic activities, and complex needs of large businesses all created a demand for public health that industrial capitalism needed to satisfy. Moreover, reform movements, including the labor movement, were not simply spectators to developments cleverly engineered by capitalist foundations. The conflicting interests among businesses and between business and the public had to be resolved by government. Employers were not always united, and they did not win every battle; they did not need to.

There is no doubt that capitalism encourages an attitude of rational calculation that affects public health and health care as it does every other realm of life. The conservative economist Joseph Schumpeter observed that "although the modern hospital is not as a rule operated for profit, it is nonetheless the product of capitalism not only . . . because the capitalist process supplies the means and the will, but much more fundamentally because capitalist rationality supplied the habits of mind that evolved the methods used in these hospitals."[73] From William Petty to contemporary cost-benefit analysis, there have been attempts to apply the logic of rational calculation to medical care and public health. It is not possible to say that this inevitably favors medical rather than public health measures; quite often such calculations are used to prove the opposite. Reformers have often used such calculations to show that public health measures are rational social investments. The issue is not the use of equations but what goes into them.

The Marxists and, curiously enough, some right-wing advocates of the free market, have emphasized—excessively, in my view—the monopolization of medical practice by regular physicians. The repression of competing systems of medicine was only a minor and relatively unsuccessful means of advancing the interests of the profession. Though the regular physicians tried to suppress the homeopaths and botanics, the dissidents had to be brought in as partners in the licensing movement of the late nineteenth century. They disappeared only after they were licensed. Even the new forms of practice that emerged at the turn of the century won legal authority. The osteopaths and chiropractors were able to secure separate licensing statutes, and the Christian Scientists received protection as a religious denomination. The triumph of the regular profession depended on belief rather than force, on its growing cultural authority rather than sheer power, on the success of its claims to competence and understanding rather than the strong arm of the police. To see the rise of the profession as coercive is to underestimate how deeply its authority penetrated the beliefs of ordinary people and how firmly it had seized the imagination even of its rivals.

Yet changes in the distribution of power did play a major part in the social transformation of American medicine, and here we have the first of five major structural changes delineated in the preceding pages. This was the emergence of an informal control system in medical practice resulting from the growth of specialization and hospitals. The need for referrals and hospital privileges brought about a shift from dependence on clients to dependence on colleagues and promoted a change in the profession from a competitive to a corporate orientation. It gave impetus to strong professional organization and enabled physicians to assert their long-run collective interests over their short-run individual interests. It encouraged former rivals to put aside their differences and work together in behalf of licensing laws and other common political objectives. As professional bickering died down, the authority of the profession rose. The profession's mastery of itself was the precondition for its mastery of public sentiment.

Stronger collective organization and authority brought about the second major structural change, the control of labor markets in medical care. Licensing, of course, restricted the supply of doctors. The main function of medical licensing was not so much to exclude rival practitioners as to cut down on the number of regular physicians by making medical education unprofitable. For it was the licensing boards—and not primarily the Flexner report, as another familiar reading of history has it—that tightened the noose on commercial medical schools. Fewer graduates not only meant fewer practitioners competing with one another, but also cut off the supply of cheap professional labor for free dispensaries and contract practice. It gave physicians more control over the terms of their relationships with patients. And through certification programs and the encouragement of responsible professionalism among their subordinates, doctors secured the advantage of standing between other technical personnel and the market.

Third, the profession secured a special dispensation from the burdens of hierarchy of the capitalist enterprise. No "commercialism" in medicine was tolerated, and much of the capital investment required for medical practice was socialized. The reform of medical schools brought large subsidies into the formation of physicians' human capital, on which they received the return. The opening of community hospitals to private practitioners meant they were able to use the capital invested in hospital facilities by the public, at no charge and without any restriction on their fees. (Doctors originally paid for the use of hospitals by giving free care on the wards, but free service declined while the capital invested in hospitals and the value of hospital appointments increased.) Health departments, beginning with free laboratory diagnosis for diphtheria, provided physicians various technical services whose costs they also did not have to bear. Health centers and school health programs, by performing diagnostic work and making referrals to private practitioners, found new disease in need of treatment and thereby stimulated the demand for medical services. Privately endowed and later publicly supported medical research socialized the costs of technical innovation.

The elimination of countervailing power in medical care was a fourth element in the structural development of professional sovereignty. The state, corporations, and voluntary associations (such as fraternal societies) might have exercised countervailing power, but all were kept out of medical care, or on its margins. Their exclusion meant no organized buyers offset the market power of physicians. Doctors could then set prices according to what clients could pay. The absence of countervailing power was also a key to the political influence of the profession. As I noted in Chapter Three, those occupations that obtained licensing protection in the late nineteenth century had the advantage of not facing any organized buyers or employers who might have had an interest in preventing licensure from being imposed. Preserving that advantage gave physicians a clear field on many political issues strategically related to medical care.

The fifth development was the establishment of specific spheres of professional authority. Medical care came to be characterized by a series of internal boundaries demarcating the profession's domain. The vigilantly guarded border between public health and curative medical services was one example. In the hospital there was a split between two lines of authority, one professional, the other administrative. In the drug market there developed a division between ethical and over-the-counter drugs, the former available only by the authorization of a physician. The general absence of integrated organization and higher-level management in the medical system had the function of preserving the sovereign position of the profession. The various attempts to rationalize the organization of hospitals or of medical practice and public health foundered on the resistance of private interests. No program, policy, or plan was acceptable, even worth considering, unless it respected the professional sovereignty of physicians.

This pattern of structural accommodation to the interests of the profession was what confounded the early predictions that solo practice would be superseded because it was inefficient. With access to hospitals, physicians acquired the technological resources necessary for the practice of modern medicine without becoming part of an organization. Other institutions, such as health departments, performed diagnostic functions for them. These complementary relations allowed physicians to escape the pressures that might have forced them to accept organizational controls. Private medicine was sustained by the willingness of public institutions to assume part of its cost.

This was no devious trick of the profession. It was a political decision made in the hope of preserving the personal relations between doctor and patient. Now, it may be said that many Americans had no such relations with physicians—quite so, and they had little influence in the decisions. But, perhaps more important, what Americans saw of bureaucratic organization in medical care—the public dispensary, the company clinic—was not encouraging.

By the 1920s, the medical profession had successfully resolved the most difficult problems confronting it as late as 1900. It had put aside long-standing sectarian quarrels and won stronger licensing laws; turned hospitals, drug manufacturers, and public health from threats to its position into bulwarks of support; and checked the entry into health services of corporations and mutual societies. It had succeeded in controlling the development of technology, organizational forms, and the division of labor. In short, it had helped shape the medical system so that its structure supported professional sovereignty instead of undermining it.

Over the next few decades, the advent of antibiotics and other advances gave physicians increased mastery of disease and confirmed confidence in their judgment and skill. The chief threat to the sovereignty of the profession was the result of this success. So valuable did medical care appear that to withhold it seemed deeply unjust. Yet as the felt need for medical care rose, so did its cost, beyond what many families could afford. Some agency to spread the cost was unavoidable. It would have to be a third party, and yet this was exactly what physicians feared. The struggle of the profession to maintain its autonomy then became a campaign of resistance not only to programs of reform but also to the very expectations and hopes that the progress of medicine was constantly arousing. To continue to escape the corporation and the state meant preserving a system that was at war with itself.

BOOK TWO

THE STRUGGLE FOR MEDICAL CARE

Doctors, the State, and the Coming of the Corporation

CHAPTER ONE

The Mirage
of Reform

WHOEVER provides medical care or pays the costs of illness stands to gain the gratitude and good will of the sick and their families. The prospect of these good-will returns to investment in health care creates a powerful motive for governments and other institutions to intervene in the economics of medicine. Political leaders since Bismarck seeking to strengthen the state or to advance their own or their party's interests have used insurance against the costs of sickness as a means of turning benevolence to power. Similarly, employers often furnish medical care to recruit new workers and instill loyalty to the firm. Unions and fraternal societies have used the same means to strengthen solidarity. On more narrowly commercial grounds, insurance companies also gain advantage from serving as middlemen. To be the intermediary in the costs of sickness is a strategic role that confers social and political as well as strictly economic gains.

From the viewpoint of physicians, all such intermediaries, whether governmental or private, represent an intrusion and potential danger. Prior to the rise of third parties, doctors stood in direct relation to their patients as healers and benefactors. According to traditional ideals, which are not entirely fictitious, doctors gave care according to the needs of the sick and regulated fees according to the patients' ability to pay, which was, in effect, the doctors' ability to charge. This system did not always provide economic security for the physician, much less for the patient, but it meant that doctors did not face any larger and more powerful organization that could dictate their income and conditions of practice. And many physicians valued this freedom from hierarchical control more than the stable income that an organized system of payment or health insurance might have arguably provided.

The changing organization of economic life upset these simple arrangements. The demand for health insurance originated in the breakdown of a household economy, as families came to depend on the labor of their chief wage earner for income and on the services of doctors and hospitals for medical treatment. In individual households, sickness now interrupted the flow of income as well as the normal routine of domestic life, and it imposed unforeseen expenses for medical care. These were not merely private problems. In the economy as a whole, illness had an indirect cost in diminished production as well as a direct cost in medical expenditures. The politics of health insurance revolve around these four sorts of cost: (1) individual losses of income; (2) individual medical costs; (3) the indirect costs of illness to society; and (4) the social costs of medical care. In the last century, these have given rise successively to different interests in reform. Initially, insurance advocates emphasized the importance of spreading the risks of lost income to working-class families and reducing the loss of productive efficiency to society. After the 1920s, the rising individual risks of high medical costs created difficulties even for middle-class families and generated a new basis of interest in health insurance. And, most recently, reform has been preoccupied by the burden that rising medical costs impose on the society as a whole.

In America health insurance first became a political issue on the eve of the First World War, after nearly all the major European countries had adopted some sort of program. The rapid progress that workmen's compensation laws made in the United States between 1910 and 1913 encouraged reformers to believe that if Americans could be persuaded to adopt compulsory insurance against industrial accidents, they could also be persuaded to adopt compulsory insurance against sickness, which caused poverty and distress among many more families. The enactment of health insurance legislation in other Western capitalist countries suggested there was no fundamental reason that America could not do the same. Reformers believed as well that health insurance would not only benefit American workers; it would yield handsome returns for employers by creating a healthier and more productive labor force. So when they launched a national effort to enact compulsory health insurance, they anticipated broad support and believed it would, most likely, be the "next great step in social legislation." As would happen repeatedly in the next several decades, advocates of reform had the impression that victory was close at hand, only to see it vanish like a mirage.

This chapter explores why a government health insurance program eluded reformers—why there is, to this day, no national health insurance in America. The next chapter examines the system of financing and organization that appeared in its place.

A COMPARATIVE PERSPECTIVE

The Origins of Social Insurance

Financial protection against the costs of sickness, long a concern of voluntary associations, became a concern of politics in the late nineteenth century. In 1883 Germany established the first national system of compulsory sickness insurance. Organized through independent sickness funds, the program originally applied only to wage earners in some industries and trades. Besides medical attendance, it provided a cash benefit to make up for lost wages during sickness. Similar systems were set up in Austria in 1888 and in Hungary in 1891. Then in a second wave of reform, Norway adopted compulsory sickness insurance in 1909, Serbia in 1910, Britain in 1911, Russia in 1912, and the Netherlands in 1913.

Other European countries subsidized the mutual benefit societies that workers formed among themselves. France and Italy, which required sickness insurance only in a few industries such as railroads and shipping, gave relatively small subsidies, though the French expanded their program in 1910. On the other hand, Sweden, beginning in 1891, Denmark in 1892, and Switzerland in 1912 gave extensive state aid to voluntary funds and provided other strong incentives for membership. By 1907 the proportion of the population covered by sickness insurance in Denmark actually exceeded the proportion in Germany (27 compared with 21 percent).[1]

But in the United States during this period, the government took no action to subsidize voluntary funds nor to make sickness insurance compulsory. In the years between the adoption of compulsory insurance by Germany in 1883 and by England in 1911, the issue was hardly discussed in America. This long neglect and indifference require some explanation: Why did the Europeans adopt health insurance while Americans ignored it?

The European countries that instituted compulsory sickness insurance did so as part of a general program of social insurance against the chief risks that interrupted continuity of income: industrial accidents, sickness and disability, old age, and unemployment. We associate health insurance with the financing of medical care, but its original function was primarily income stabilization. Many early voluntary funds and some governmental programs included only a sickness benefit, or "sick pay," to compensate for lost wages; paying for medical care came later, or was distinctly secondary. The governmental programs were not universal because they were originally conceived as a means of maintaining the incomes, productive effort, and political allegiance of the working class. Participation was limited to wage earners below a given income and usually did not include their dependents, agricultural workers, the self-employed, or the middle and upper classes. These groups were considered either too difficult to cover (because of high administrative costs) or not in need of income protection.

Social insurance represented a new stage in the management of destitution in capitalist societies. From the rise of national economies to the emergence of industrial capitalism—that is, between the sixteenth and late eighteenth/early nineteenth centuries—the poor received assistance in their own parishes. Industrialization, however, generated growing complaints about the effects of local poor relief on the free circulation of labor and incentives for work. In what Gaston Rimlinger calls the "liberal break" with paternalism, governments abolished the traditional system of poor relief, restricted public assistance to almshouses where it would be available only under the most demeaning conditions, and forced the able-bodied poor to work or to emigrate. While the older forms of social protection survived in the mutual societies of artisans and skilled workers, liberalism reduced the government's role as the guardian of welfare.[2]

The advent of social insurance at the end of the nineteenth century signified a return to social protection. Social insurance departed from the earlier paternalism, however, by providing a right to benefits instead of charity. In this sense, it constituted an extension to social welfare of liberal principles of civil and political rights. On the other hand, social insurance departed from liberalism by expanding the role of the state and demanding compulsory contributions. Consequently, it represented an extension of obligations as well as freedom.[3] In this regard, it was no different from many other modern reforms. The right to a primary education, for example, typically entails an obligation to attend school, at least until some minimum age. The right to benefits under sickness insurance, while not requiring the sick to see a physician, typically has limited the insured to use of licensed practitioners and hence has extended social control of medical practice. Social insurance, moreover, required contributions from employers as well as workers. Hence, it represented an intrusion by the state into the prerogatives of businessmen in setting wages. Where liberalism had its greatest hold and where private interests were strong relative to the state, social insurance made the slowest headway. So, contrary to the modern view of the welfare state as a "liberal" reform (in the current American sense), social insurance was generally introduced first in authoritarian and paternalistic regimes, like Germany, and only later in the more liberal and democratic societies, like England, France, and the United States.[4] Partly because Germany industrialized later and faster, its traditional forms of social protection had partly survived when it faced the challenge of socialism. Perhaps as a result, it made a more direct transition to the social protection of the welfare state.

Political discontent precipitated the introduction of social insurance in both Germany and England. The German monarchy in the 1880s faced a growing challenge from the German Social Democratic Party. In 1875 the Socialists had been strengthened by a coalition between the followers of Marx and Lassalle. After outlawing the Social Democratic Party, Bismarck was still convinced that repression was insufficient and sought a "welfare monarchy" to assure workers' loyalty.[5]

In England labor unrest also preceded the introduction of social insurance in the early 1900s, but the political conditions were somewhat different. England was a parliamentary democracy in which the Liberals were attempting to hold on to their working-class support by championing social reform. In Germany, Bismarck introduced social rights to avoid granting wider political rights; in Britain, Lloyd George sought social rights within the context of existing rights to political participation. But both were basically defensive efforts to stabilize the political order by integrating the workers into an expanded welfare system. The proponents of social insurance also expected that it would increase industrial productivity and military power by diminishing class antagonism and creating a healthier labor force and army. As Lloyd George later put it in a memorable phrase, "You can not maintain an A-1 empire with a C-3 population."[6]

Germany and England may also have been predisposed toward social insurance programs by strong preexisting mutual benefit funds, which were notably active in providing sickness benefits. In Germany, various guilds, trades, industries, and mutual societies operated *Krankenkassen* ("sickness funds"). In England, even before 1911, nearly half the adult males—generally the conservative artisans and respectable, self-supporting workers rather than the very poor—belonged to friendly societies, which were powerful national organizations; voluntary sickness insurance covered about 13 percent of the population.[7] Although these preexisting funds represented obstacles to state control of social insurance, they also reflected a widespread awareness among workers of the value of insuring against the costs of sickness.

Why America Lagged

In the United States, the political conditions and preexisting institutions were altogether different. America was the country where classical liberalism had most thoroughly shaped the relations between state and society. As of 1900, American government was highly decentralized, engaged in little direct regulation of the economy or social welfare, and had a small and unprofessional civil service. Strengthening government became one of the central concerns of Progressive reform at the turn of the century, but its impact was limited. At the national level, government had little to do with social welfare, and in health its activities were minor. Congress had set up a system of compulsory hospital insurance for merchant seamen as far back as 1798 (following European precedents), but this was an altogether exceptional measure to deal with a group that was commercially and epidemiologically strategic because of its role in foreign commerce. Congress approved aid to mental hospitals in 1854, only to see the bill vetoed by President Pierce. It created a National Board of Health in 1879 but abolished it in 1883. In two stages in 1902 and 1912, it expanded the Marine Hospital Service into the U.S. Public Health Service but gave it few functions and little authority. The federal government continued to leave such matters to state and local government, and the general rule at those levels was to leave as much to private and voluntary action as possible. Although general hospitals in Europe became primarily governmental and tax supported, in America they remained mainly private. A system of government that followed such principles was not likely to be an early convert to compulsory health insurance.

Nor was there a challenge to political stability in America comparable to the challenge in Europe. In the 1890s, America experienced depression and unrest, but much of the unrest was agrarian and populist, and social insurance would not have responded to farmers' concerns. Socialism emerged as a political force only after the turn of the century, and even then the Socialist Party was nowhere near the political threat its counterparts were in Europe. At its height, in the elections of 1912 and 1916, the party attracted only 6 percent of the vote; this was, as it happens, precisely the time the health insurance campaign began. After a shaky start, American unions had begun to grow—membership, less than half a million in 1897, was up to 2 million by 1910 and 5 million by 1920—but this growth occurred under a conservative labor leadership suspicious of political reformers. The breach between the conservative trade unions and the Socialist Party prevented the emergence of powerful working-class support for social insurance.

Finally, voluntary sickness funds were less developed in the United States than in Europe, reflecting less interest in health insurance and less familiarity with it. At the turn of the century, European immigrants established numerous small benevolent societies in American cities offering sickness benefits to their members, but the more established fraternal orders, composed of older ethnic stock, mainly provided life insurance. Some local lodges of national orders gave assistance in sickness, but it was more fragmentary than in Europe.[8] Similarly, when unions provided sickness benefits, the locals generally did so, not the national organizations.

American unions oscillated in their attitude toward benefit programs. The first trade unions in the early nineteenth century had been as concerned with mutual aid as with jobs and wages. By the Civil War, however, they turned more toward bargaining with employers and discouraged benefits, since high dues might deter workers from membership. But after the war they began to adopt the theory that benefits promoted membership. In 1877 the Granite Cutters adopted the first national sick benefit plan. Still, unions had to weigh the gains in solidarity from benefits against the deterrent effects of high dues, and this limited their capacity to provide protection against the costs of sickness.[9]

Commercial health insurance was as yet little developed. Around 1850 several health insurance companies were established, but they quickly went bankrupt. However, a related form of insurance, protection against losses from accidental injury and death, did gain a firm footing in the second half of the nineteenth century. Beginning about 1896, firms engaged in this business started offering insurance against specific diseases and gradually broadened their policies to cover all disability from sickness or accident. Such policies were expensive because of administrative costs and were carried mainly by the middle class. There was also a small amount of health and accident insurance sold to workers, but because of overhead and profits, only about 30 to 35 percent of premium income was returned in benefits to subscribers. Frauds were common, and the larger, more respectable firms stayed away from the business.[10] John F. Dryden, who briefly experimented with sickness benefits when he founded the Prudential Insurance Company in 1875, commented in 1909 that conservative business practice dictated that an industrial insurance company had to limit itself to benefits payable at death. "[T]he assurance of a stipulated sum during sickness," he wrote, "can only safely be transacted, and then only in a limited way, by fraternal organizations having a perfect knowledge of and complete supervision over the individual members."[11] But while fraternal groups could remedy some difficulties that insurance companies encountered, they had problems of their own. Often they were improperly managed and too small to be actuarially sound; as their membership aged, their reserves frequently proved insufficient.

Because most sickness benefits were provided by small immigrant benefit societies and local chapters of fraternal orders and unions, early researchers found it hard to assemble accurate statistics regarding sickness insurance. But it seems likely that such insurance was less extensive in America than in England and Germany before governmental programs were introduced in those countries. In Illinois, Ohio, and California, where state commissions studied the problem around 1918, the proportion of industrial workers enjoying some form of sickness benefit— usually very minimal—was estimated at one third. The percentage would have been much lower if computed over the entire population. In the country as a whole, only a small fraction of the population can have had any protection against loss of earnings, and even fewer received any medical care or coverage of medical expenses through insurance.[12]

Yet American workers did spend a great deal of money for insurance to protect themselves against one related hazard. In the early twentieth century, commercial insurance companies enjoyed enormous success selling "industrial" life insurance policies to working-class families. The lump-sum payments provided by these policies generally paid for funerals and the expenses of a final illness. This business was the backbone of two companies, Metropolitan Life and Prudential, that had risen to the top of the insurance industry by collecting 10, 15, and 25 cents a week from millions of American working-class households. But because the premiums were paid on a weekly basis and lapses were frequent, these policies had to be marketed by an army of insurance agents, who visited their clients as soon after payday as possible. The administrative costs of industrial insurance were staggering; subscribers received in benefits only about 40 percent of what they paid in premiums. The rest went to the agents and the companies. Yet the fear of a pauper burial was so great that Americans bought $183 million of such insurance in 1911—about as much as Germany spent on its entire social insurance system.[13]

GRAND ILLUSIONS, 1915–1920

The Democratization of Efficiency

In America, reformers outside government, rather than political leaders, took the initiative in advocating health insurance. The idea did not enter political debate under antisocialist sponsorship, as it often did in Europe. Indeed, the Socialists in 1904 were the first American political party to endorse health insurance. At the center of the movement, however, was the American Association for Labor Legislation (AALL), founded in 1906, a group of "social progressives" who sought to reform capitalism rather than abolish it. The association's membership was small and primarily academic, and it included such notable figures as the Progressive economists John R. Commons and Richard Ely of the University of Wisconsin and Henry R. Seager of Columbia. The AALL's chief initial concern was occupational disease, and its first major success came in the campaign against "phossy jaw," a disease common among workers in match factories that could be prevented by eliminating phosphorous from the production process. The association was prominent in the drive for workmen's compensation. It sought the prohibition of child labor and also supported unemployment relief through public works, state employment agencies, and unemployment insurance. Officially, it took no position on unions, but many of its members supported unions and the association originally included several prominent labor leaders.[14]

The AALL's campaign for health insurance had the misfortune of getting under way just as Progressivism began to recede. As a political force, Progressivism reached its peak in the election of 1912, when the Progressives bolted from the Republican Party and nominated former President Theodore Roosevelt as their candidate. Much like Lloyd George and Winston Churchill, Roosevelt supported social insurance, including health insurance, in the belief that no country could be strong whose people were sick and poor. But his defeat in 1912 by Woodrow Wilson postponed for another two decades the kind of leadership that might have involved the national government more extensively in the management of social welfare. In America compulsory health insurance would not have the kind of national political sponsor it enjoyed in Germany and England.

In the December after the 1912 election, the AALL voted to create a committee on social insurance, and in June 1913 it organized the first national conference on the subject. Despite its broad mandate, the committee decided to concentrate on health insurance, and the following summer it drew up a model bill, the first draft of which was published in 1915.

The AALL's bill followed European precedent in limiting participation to the working class, though it gave medical coverage not just to workers but also to their dependents. Its program applied to all manual workers and to others earning less that $1,200 a year, except for domestic and casual employees. Benefits were of four kinds: (1) medical aid, including all physicians', nurses', and hospital services; (2) sick pay (at two thirds of wages for up to twenty-six weeks; at one third of wages during hospitalization); (3) maternity benefits for the wives of insured men as well as insured women; and (4) a death benefit of $50 to pay for funeral expenses. The costs, estimated at 4 percent of wages, were to be divided among employers and workers, each to pay two fifths, and the state, which would contribute the fifth remaining. The employers' share increased for the lowest-income workers. A worker earning $600 a year, the AALL estimated, would pay 80 cents out of a monthly premium of $2.[15]

The reformers formulated the case for health insurance in terms of two objectives. They argued it would relieve poverty caused by sickness by distributing the uneven wage losses and medical costs that individual families experienced. And, second, they maintained it would reduce the total costs of illness and insurance to society by providing effective medical care, creating monetary incentives for disease prevention, and eliminating wasteful expenditures on industrial insurance. This mixture of concerns was typical of the social Progressives. On the one hand, in emphasizing the relief of poverty, they made an appeal to moral compassion; on the other, in emphasizing prevention and increased national efficiency, they made an appeal to economic rationality.[16] Combining social meliorism with the ideal of efficiency fitted perfectly into Progressive ideology. It also reflected the political conditions of a democratic capitalist society, which made it incumbent upon reformers to gain the support of both the public and powerful business interests. Progressive health insurance was shaped by these political realities as well as by the economics of sickness and health care of the time.

Relieving poverty caused by sickness, as the reformers saw it, involved both compensating lost earnings and paying medical costs. The Progressives considered these equally important. Data from the period suggest that for individual workers wage losses were two to four times greater than health care costs, but for families as a whole, total losses of income and medical costs were roughly the same because of the additional health care expenses of dependents.[17] A study of 4,474 workers in a Chicago neighborhood showed that in the course of a year about one in four was sick for a week or longer and, from such sicknesses, lost an average of $119 or 13.7 percent of annual wages. The proportion of families that could not "make ends meet" increased to 16.6 percent among those with serious illness, compared to 4.7 percent among those without.[18] Advocates of health insurance also cited data from charities indicating that sickness was the leading immediate cause of poverty; a conservative estimate by the Illinois commission found it to be the chief factor in a quarter to a third of the charity cases in the state.[19]

I. M. Rubinow, a leading authority on social insurance who was both a physician and an actuary as well as a Socialist, saw health insurance as the means to cut the "vicious circle" of disease and poverty. It would prevent the families of the sick from becoming destitute and thereby prevent further sickness. Such a program had to be compulsory, Rubinow argued, to make it universal (that is, among low-income wage earners) and to secure contributions from employers and the public, who shared responsibility for the conditions that caused sickness. American workers, he wrote, "must learn to see that they have a right to force at least part of the cost and waste of sickness back upon the industry and society at large, and they can do it only when they demand that the state use its power and authority to help them, indirectly at least, with as much vigor as it has come to the assistance of the business interests . . . ."[20]

Yet, in advocating health insurance, most Progressive reformers spoke of stabilizing rather than redistributing incomes, and on behalf of a public interest in preventing poverty and disease rather than a special grievance of labor. Though their program had redistributive implications, they generally appealed for support on the grounds that all interests, including those of business, favored insurance.

This orientation was abundantly evident in the second half of the social Progressives' case for health insurance. As the AALL put it, health insurance had as one of its aims the "conservation of human resources," seen as analogous to the conservation of natural resources. Irving Fisher, then one of the country's most eminent economists, argued in a pres-

idential address to the AALL in 1916 that health insurance would have
its greatest value in stimulating preventive measures and hence was
needed not just "to tide workers over the grave emergencies incident
to illness," but also "to reduce illness itself, lengthen life, abate poverty,
improve working power, raise the wage level, and diminish the causes
of industrial discontent."[21] B. S. Warren and Edgar Sydenstricker of the
U.S. Public Health Service maintained that because a compulsory insurance scheme would require financial contributions from industry,
workers, and the community, it would encourage them to support public health measures in order to prevent disease and save money.[22]

In addition, compulsory health insurance, by including a funeral benefit, would eliminate the huge cost of marketing industrial insurance
policies, not to mention the profits. Hence, reformers claimed they
could finance much of the cost of health insurance out of the money
wasted on industrial insurance policies. Warren and Sydenstricker cited
a 1901 Bureau of Labor study showing that 65.8 percent of 2,567 families
had expenditures for industrial insurance averaging $29.55 per family,
while 76.7 percent had expenditures for sickness and death averaging
$26.78 per family.[23] In effect, instead of paying insurance agents to visit
them weekly to make collections, wage-earning families could pay for
doctors and nurses to visit them when they were sick. So the inclusion
of funeral benefits was not an idiosyncratic choice of Progressive reformers; it was part of their general program for increased social efficiency.

The arguments for health insurance reflected a great confidence
among Progressive reformers in the capacity of public health and medical care to prevent and cure disease. The achievements of medicine,
Rubinow said in a defense of health insurance, exceeded the wildest
dreams of a half century earlier. "If there was a rational basis for a certain medical nihilism so popular then, it has vanished long ago. No reasonable being will doubt the tremendous efficiency of competent medical aid."[24] The democratic view, instead of demanding that every man
be his own physician, now insisted that the services of physicians be
available to all. After reviewing the evidence that from a quarter to two
fifths of the sick were not receiving any medical care, a commission in
Ohio observed that all facts pointed to the need for a "democratization
of medical service," which meant wider distribution, not lay control.[25]

As ardent believers in the value of medical care and the legitimate basis
of professional authority, Progressive reformers had no basic quarrel
with physicians. Consequently, the AALL in 1914 sought to involve the
leaders of the medical profession in formulating the model health insurance bill. Anticipating some resistance by private practitioners, they

tried to be flexible about provisions that would affect doctors. To their pleasant surprise, they found that prominent physicians not only were sympathetic but wanted actively to help in securing legislation.[26] Among these cooperative physicians were some of the leaders of the AMA, including George H. Simmons, the editor of its *Journal*, and Frederick R. Green, secretary of its newly created Council on Health and Public Instruction, who wrote to the AALL's secretary, John Andrews, "Your plans are so entirely in line with our own that I want to be of every possible assistance."[27] He proposed setting up a three-man committee to work with the AALL. In February 1916, the AMA board approved the committee, and the Socialist I. M. Rubinow was hired as its executive secretary. The committee was located in the same building in New York City as the AALL, and its chairman, Alexander Lambert, Theodore Roosevelt's personal physician, was the AALL's medical advisor. At this point, the AMA and the AALL formed a united front on behalf of health insurance.

Yet there were points of tension between the reformers and the physicians, especially where the Progressive search for efficiency conflicted with the doctors' defense of their income and autonomy. Some reformers saw health insurance as an opportunity to subordinate medical practice to public health, to encourage the growth of group practice, and to change the method of payment from fee-for-service to salary or capitation (that is, per patient per year). These changes the doctors would not accept.

The relation of health insurance to public health was one issue on which the AALL was prepared to give way to the doctors. Public health officers, arguing that preventive medicine ought to be the overriding concern, wanted to make health departments the administrative agencies for health insurance. But Lambert, speaking for both the AALL and the AMA at a conference in 1916, noted that the physicians would be unwilling to submit to "absolute control" by public health authorities, and the doctors' preferences had to be respected.[28]

Other reformers like Rubinow wanted to use health insurance to promote a shift from individual general practice to specialized group practice under governmental control. The initially positive response of AMA leaders in 1915 encouraged Michael M. Davis, Jr., then director of the Boston Dispensary, to hope that America might be able to "improve on" Britain and Germany in the organization of services. In a letter to the AALL's John Andrews, Davis wrote that they ought to be careful not to tie health insurance "to a system of individualized private practice without creating a definite opening for . . . cooperative medical work in diagnosis and treatment." Davis added that he had "a good many ideas on organization" since visiting the Mayo Clinic.[29] But most physicians were unlikely to be enthusiastic about such ideas, which threatened to subordinate them in a bureaucratic hierarchy, and the most the AALL could do was to include a provision allowing local insurance committees to contract with group practices as well as with individual doctors.

Undoubtedly, the most serious point of tension was the method of paying physicians under health insurance. Reformers were reluctant to adopt any method that would cause serious financial problems for the insurance system, and European experience had clearly indicated that paying doctors for each service they performed was more likely to cause budgetary problems than if they were paid per capita, that is, according to the number of patients who signed up on their list for the year. Consequently, reformers recommended that doctors be paid on a capitation basis rather than by visit. Physicians, however, strongly objected to any form of contract practice as a result of their experience with fraternal lodges and industrial firms that forced them to bid against each other for group business. Trying to mediate the conflict, Lambert proposed paying doctors by visit out of a budget for physicians' services determined by the number of people insured in a local area.[30]

The AMA's initial cooperation with the AALL did not necessarily reflect any widespread enthusiasm among its membership. Two state medical societies, Wisconsin and Pennsylvania, had quickly endorsed the principle of compulsory health insurance, but others were apathetic. A survey of secretaries of state medical societies in late 1916 showed that the vast majority had not yet discussed health insurance.[31] At the AALL's annual meeting in late 1916, several physicians commented that the great majority of practitioners were probably opposed to health insurance, but expressed confidence that this was primarily because of ignorance. No doctor who had given it careful study was against it, commented Frederick Green of the AMA, but it would not be long before Green himself denied he had ever favored the measure.[32]

Although the Progressive Party broke up in the 1916 election after endorsing the Republican nominee, reformers could take some satisfaction in the early response that year to the proposal for health insurance. The Commission on Industrial Relations, created by President Wilson in the wake of labor violence, recommended health insurance in its final report. The labor committee of the U.S. House of Representatives held hearings on a resolution introduced by its sole Socialist member to create a national social insurance commission. Though the proposal failed to gain approval, several states established investigative commissions. Organizations of public health officers and nurses endorsed the measure. In short, health insurance seemed to be gaining support and moving toward public approval.

Labor and Capital Versus Reform

Yet there were also signs of trouble. To the chagrin of reformers, the American Federation of Labor (though not all its member unions or state federations) opposed the program. Samuel Gompers, president of the AF of L, repeatedly denounced compulsory health insurance as an unnecessary, paternalistic reform that would create a system of state supervision of the people's health. In an acrimonious debate with Rubinow at the 1916 congressional hearings on a national commission, Gompers assailed the Socialist's belief that government had to be called in to ensure workers' welfare and gave a ringing defense of the success of trade unions in raising workers' standard of living.[33]

This view was characteristic of Gompers and the AF of L, which at that time opposed legislation to establish a minimum wage, unemployment insurance, old-age pensions, or even an eight-hour day. Gompers insisted that workers could rely only on their own economic power, not the state, to obtain higher wages and benefits. He worried that a government insurance system would weaken unions by usurping their role in providing social benefits.[34]

Gompers' central concern was maintaining the strength of the unions. As Selig Perlman writes in his classic *Theory of the Labor Movement*, the "overshadowing problem" of American unions was "staying organized" because of the "lack of class cohesiveness in American labor."[35] All previous attempts in the United States to build unions had been wrecked during economic depressions. Early in his career, Gompers wrote that the most intelligent workers would remain members of a union in times of adversity, but the others, who had "no inclination or ability or time" to see its advantages, should find their interests made "so inseparable from the union as to make it a direct and decided loss to them to sever their connection. . . . I know of no better means than to make our unions beneficial and benevolent as well as protective."[36] As a young leader of the cigarmakers in New York, he had proposed in 1879 that the union provide sickness and death benefits. The measure was adopted, and in one year his local increased its membership from 300 to 3,000. "Gompers," writes a biographer, "believed that the phenomenal increase in the membership of Local 144 was due to the introduction of those benefits."[37] Explaining the AF of L's rejection in 1902 of a proposal for federal old-age pensions, Gompers wrote that "the unions desired to develop their own system of protection against all the vicissitudes of life as a means of gaining recruits. Social security would deprive them of that function."[38]

But, in fact, American trade unions had not much developed their own systems of welfare protection. They were increasingly gaining a stable membership, not by offering welfare benefits, but by controlling job opportunities. Gompers' views were based on the expectation that benefits would prove useful rather than any extensive use of them. Although his views prevailed in the national organization, other AF of L leaders, including Vice President William Green, saw less of a threat to labor solidarity from a governmental program and favored health insurance. Ten of the largest state federations within the AF of L, including California, New York, Massachusetts, Pennsylvania, and Wisconsin, supported health insurance proposals in their states. Only in New York, however, was organized labor a leading force in the campaign.[39]

Employers generally saw compulsory health insurance as contrary to their interests, despite some early business reaction that was tentatively sympathetic. A committee of the National Association of Manufacturers (NAM), a hard-line antiunion organization, reported in 1916 that voluntary insurance would be the "higher and better method," but it recognized that compulsory insurance might be necessary and, if so, all occupations ought to be included. This report was only accepted, not adopted, by the NAM, and like other business groups it soon joined the opposition to compulsory health insurance.[40]

Spokesmen for American business typically rejected the argument that health insurance would add to productive efficiency. The National Industrial Conference Board, a research organization established by major industrial trade associations, agreed that sickness was a serious handicap to the "social well-being and productive efficiency of the nation," but argued that direct investment in public health would have a higher return than cash benefits for the sick. Compulsory health insurance would not "materially reduce the amount of sickness"; the incentives for prevention would not work because the responsibility for most sickness could not be fixed. Indeed, days lost from work might increase because sick pay encouraged malingering; the conference board cited statistics indicating that days lost from work on account of sickness had increased in Germany after insurance was enacted. Nor would health insurance greatly reduce poverty. The figures suggesting sickness caused poverty ignored other causes. Also, many of those seeking charity would not have had health insurance because they were casual workers, self-employed, or unemployed. The large sums spent on health insurance, therefore, would benefit only part of the population;

in New York, the board calculated, the insurance bill would cover only one third of the population.[41]

Even the most liberal elements of business, represented in the National Civic Federation (NCF), generally opposed compulsory health insurance. The civic federation, founded in 1901 by journalist Ralph Easley to bring together the leaders of capital, labor, and the public in the interest of social harmony, included the more moderate big businessmen who were willing to recognize organized labor as a legitimate partner in American capitalism, at least outside of their own factories.[42] The NCF had been an ally of the American Association for Labor Legislation in the campaign for workmen's compensation, and it had some overlapping members, including Gompers, who served as a vice president of both groups. But even though the two organizations sought peaceful labor reform within the framework of capitalism, they grew increasingly estranged as the health insurance conflict unfolded. The AALL was composed mainly of academic reformers who saw themselves as pursuing the interests of the public rather than those of any class, while the civic federation sought a mutual accommodation between the interests of organized labor and those of big business. The social Progressives in the AALL were inclined to rely upon the judgment of professionals and the power of government, whereas organized labor and big business favored private bargaining outside the purview of the state. Gompers resigned from the AALL in 1915 in part over the association's frequent call for impartial experts and high-minded commissions to resolve social problems. Such experts Gompers distrusted as a distinct class with interests of their own. On the other hand, he remained in the National Civic Federation despite repeated attacks by left-wing labor leaders for collaborating with big business. The leaders of the AF of L, unlike many of the Progressives, accepted big business as inevitable and viewed unions as the necessary counterweight to protect the interests of workers. As has often been pointed out, American labor leaders resembled American businessmen in priding themselves on being practical, cynical about politics, and distrustful of intellectuals and their abstract schemes.[43] Furthermore, in regard to social insurance, neither unions nor big business at that time wanted any competition from government in social welfare programs that could potentially increase workers' loyalty to either of them.[44] Thus health insurance, rather than pitting labor unions against capital, pitted both of them against the reformers.

In 1914 the civic federation sent a committee to England to study recent social insurance legislation, and two years later it set up a social insurance department. At first, the federation criticized specific provi-

sions of American insurance proposals. By 1917, however, it was spear-
heading the opposition, charging that health insurance was a failure in
Europe that impractical reformers wanted to foist upon workers in the
United States even though labor—witness Gompers and the AF of
L—had no desire for it.[45]

One segment of business, well represented in the civic federation,
played a particularly active role in fighting compulsory health insurance—the insurance industry. Other commercial interests in health
care, such as pharmaceutical companies, assailed health insurance, but
none so relentlessly as the insurance firms. Where reformers mounted
campaigns for health insurance, the insurance industry aroused the opposition. Particularly active were representatives of the two firms, Prudential and Metropolitan Life, whose industrial life insurance business
was directly threatened by the reformers' inclusion of a funeral benefit.
As of 1915 Prudential held 38 percent and Metropolitan 34 percent of
industrial business.[46] Nor were their interests alone at stake; both firms
were closely linked through their investments and boards of directors
with other large corporations. The reformers, in their innocent enthusiasm for efficiency, were threatening to eliminate an important source
of profit for the insurance industry and of investment capital for American business. As a result, they unwittingly brought down upon themselves the concerted opposition of big business. The chief spokesman
for the insurance industry was Frederick L. Hoffman, a respected actuary who was vice president of Prudential and a member of the AALL
until 1917, when he resigned over the health insurance issue and became the reformers' most indefatigable critic. Nearly all the propaganda against compulsory health insurance, John R. Commons later
suggested, could be traced back to Hoffman, and this was only a slight
exaggeration.[47] Another insurance company vice president, Lee K.
Frankel of Metropolitan, chaired the National Civic Federation's social
insurance committee and prepared its response to health insurance.[48]
Yet a third key critic was P. Tecumseh Sherman, a lawyer for insurance
interests also active in the civic federation. These ties helped solidify
the opposition of insurance companies and employers to health insurance. On the other hand, the unions were divided among themselves
and at odds with the political organizations advocating reform.

Defeat Comes to the Progressives

In 1917 two developments changed the entire complexion of the
health insurance debate. The first was growing opposition from physicians. Though the AMA House of Delegates in June 1917 approved a
final report from its social insurance committee favoring health insur-

ance, this action did not reflect sentiment in state medical societies. In New York, the state council of the medical society had endorsed the model health insurance bill in December 1916, but meetings in county societies in January and February saw a groundswell of opposition. In March the state council met again and withdrew its earlier approval. The source of this opposition, according to Ronald L. Numbers, was "almost entirely economic in nature."[49] When legislative hearings were held in March, the doctors who testified were nearly all opposed to health insurance. In Illinois a committee of the state society reported in May that an insurance bill it had been prepared to fight in the legislature had never materialized: "We feel that the active opposition of the medical profession prevented its introduction."[50]

The second key development of 1917, the entry of America into the war in April, proved a major turning point in the insurance movement. Many physicians went into the service; the AMA closed down its committee on social insurance and I. M. Rubinow took another job. In Massachusetts, debate was suspended on a bill that had the support of prominent Boston physicians and progressive social and political leaders. Anti-German feeling rose to a fever, the government's propaganda bureau commissioned articles denouncing German social insurance, and opponents of health insurance now assailed it as a Prussian menace inconsistent with American values.[51]

The one public referendum on health insurance took place in this climate of wartime hysteria. In early 1917 the California social insurance commission recommended health insurance, and as a first and necessary step it proposed an enabling amendment to the state constitution. Some leaders of the state medical society favored the plan and kept the society neutral, but a large group of doctors formed an independent League for the Conservation of Public Health to oppose the measure. "What is Compulsory Social Health Insurance?" asked one of the league's pamphlets. "It is a dangerous device, invented in Germany, announced by the German Emperor from the throne the same year he started plotting and preparing to conquer the world." To doctors the league wrote that the state commission was "wholesaling medical services at bargain counter prices" and that two thirds of the population would be divided up among panel doctors "whose compensation would be fixed, and whose services would be supervised by political appointees."[52] Also prominent in the opposition were Christian Scientists, who operated through an agency financed by the insurance industry. In November 1918 the health insurance referendum went down to a thunderous defeat—358,324 to 133,858.[53]

Another promising effort failed in New York, where the State Federation of Labor and the AALL jointly sponsored a health insurance bill with the support of Governor Alfred E. Smith and a coalition of Democrats and Progressive Republicans. In 1919 the Senate passed the bill by a vote of thirty to twenty, but it died in the House, which was dominated by conservatives. In Ohio that year the insurance commission reported in favor of compulsory health insurance, but no action was taken; in Pennsylvania, the health insurance commission made no recommendation; and in Illinois, where the state commission had conducted the most thorough investigation, it voted seven to two against any health insurance proposal.[54]

The war, though only eighteen months long for Americans, proved to be the graveyard of an already faltering Progressive movement. It diverted attention from social reform, channeled the enthusiasm for doing good into a crusade abroad, and divided the old nationalist Progressives like Roosevelt from the more pacifist and isolationist elements of the movement. In the red scare immediately after the war, when the government attempted to root out the last vestiges of radicalism, opponents of compulsory health insurance associated it with Bolshevism and buried it in an avalanche of anticommunist rhetoric. Then, along with most other Progressive causes, health insurance vanished in the complacency of the 1920s.

Why did Progressive proposals for health insurance fail? Clearly the war cannot provide the whole explanation. The opposition was growing even beforehand. The early optimism may have been an illusion caused partly by the time it took opponents to organize a concerted response. Reformers themselves, conceding their own political naiveté, later looked back on their defeat as the work of special interests, mainly the doctors and the insurance companies. Writing in 1931, Rubinow recalled that reformers had been "intoxicated" by their success with workmen's compensation and failed to appreciate the opposition that employers, insurers, and others would raise. "Nothing can be more damaging in a military campaign than the failure to appreciate the strength of the enemy," Rubinow wrote, "except it be the failure to recognize the allies the enemy might acquire." Workmen's compensation had proved to be more expensive than reformers had anticipated, and health insurance would have cost employers, Rubinow admitted, "many times as much."* Businessmen could see on which side of the balance sheet such costs would go; they could not see the gains, which were indirect. The

---

*The AALL had estimated the cost of its program, including sick pay, medical aid, and maternity and funeral benefits at only 4 percent of wages, but in its Chicago survey, the Illinois commission found it would cost 7.5 percent of payroll just to cover lost wages and medical care.[55]

insurance companies "suddenly realized the tremendous possibilities of the field for themselves"; the inclusion of the funeral benefit was "a grave, tactical error because of the implied threat to the gigantic structure of industrial life insurance." The doctors got "panicky." Minor but vocal groups, such as Christian Scientists, entered the opposition out of fear that a government program would limit religious and medical freedom. "All these fears, some justified, some exaggerated, and some altogether fanciful, produced such a confusion of group conflicts that only a clear recognition of the need by the millions of American workmen might have overcome it, and that clear recognition was lacking."[56]

But the view that interest groups killed health insurance—true enough as a description of what happened—neglects the prior question of why these and other groups interpreted their interests as they did. Some historians treat these interests as if they were self-evident.[57] But the three main opponents—the medical profession, labor, and business—all had conflicting and ambiguous interests that made them initially uncertain and divided about what position they ought to take. That the AMA could have initially approved health insurance, while the AF of L opposed it, suggests how complex the identification of group interests may be. Some doctors believed health insurance would increase their incomes, and some labor leaders believed it would inhibit working-class organization. While these interpretations of their groups' interests were ultimately rejected, they were not self-evidently mistaken. Moreover, in European countries the interest groups analogous to the opponents in America often turned out to benefit materially from government health insurance programs. For example, the insurance industry in England ended up profiting from a health insurance system that permitted private firms to play a major role in carrying cash benefits.[58] Employers benefited from the greater political stability and diminished labor turnover that health insurance helped bring about. It is not difficult to imagine how American state legislators might have passed a health insurance program that would have enriched both insurance companies and doctors and, in the long run, strengthened the economic system. So it is not at all clear why doctors, insurance companies, and employers interpreted their interests as requiring the defeat of health insurance, when by its modification they might have satisfied those same interests.

Ideology, historical experience, and the overall political context played a key role in shaping how groups identified and expressed their interests. These factors are readily apparent if we compare the failure of health insurance in America with its earlier successes in Europe.

In neither Germany nor even Britain was the idea of compulsory health insurance fundamentally contested when it was originally proposed. The opposition did not suggest, as in America, that health insurance would subvert individual initiative and self-reliance. Many of the same groups as in America criticized the plans, but they concentrated on amending provisions that threatened to alter established relations of power. In Germany, the opposition, including conservatives and businessmen as well as socialists, resisted Bismarck's efforts to use social insurance to enhance the power of the state; and in its final form, health insurance was operated by decentralized sickness funds, rather than the imperial insurance office.[59]

The establishment of compulsory insurance in Britain also required compromise with private interests. The insurance companies and the doctors objected to the privileged role that Lloyd George's original plan gave the friendly societies. The insurance firms were worried that the friendly societies would gain an edge in selling life insurance, and the doctors had long chafed under the power the friendly societies exercised in the provision of medical service. So, splitting the program in two, Lloyd George satisfied the objections of the insurance companies by allowing them to carry cash benefits, and he met the objections of the doctors by placing control of medical benefits in the public sector under local committees on which the physicians were given representation. Thus the shift of medical care into the public sector in Britain arose partly because of the doctors' desire to liberate themselves from a form of client control. Dealing with educated civil servants may have been more palatable than dealing with the working-class officers of friendly societies. Moreover, as an incentive for cooperation, Lloyd George gave the doctors a large boost in income by increasing their rates of compensation. Even so, the British Medical Association, out of touch with its membership, called a last minute strike against the government. But the revolt fizzled as long-impoverished general practitioners found they could increase their incomes an average of 50 percent by signing up on panels to care for the insured.[60]

American doctors faced no dominating purchaser, like the friendly societies, from whom a government program might offer escape. The doctors' experience with contract practice and workmen's compensation was sufficient, however, to persuade them that any financial intermediary would like nothing better than to pay them as little as possible. So their own past strongly biased them against any extension of organized financing. "My own experience in speaking to physicians," wrote the chairman of the California commission in a private letter in 1918, "is that the only questions they ask are questions of detail . . . how much money they would get, whether they would have to get up nights at the demand of whoever called them . . ."[61] Progressive proposals, furthermore, caught the physicians in transition to more secure economic status; during the war, their incomes rose significantly.[62] Any positive economic incentive they might have had for favoring health insurance was diminishing.

The structure of government and the demands of politics, however, were of overriding importance in shaping the strategy of the opposition. In America, there was no comparable unification of political authority to compare with the power of Lloyd George or Bismarck. Even if an American president had wanted health insurance, he would not have had the leverage to force the opposition to compromise. Only a more serious threat to political stability in America could have so changed the terms of debate as to force interest groups to work within the framework of reform instead of against it. In the absence of such a threat, employers saw the immediate costs but not the distant and less certain gains, and their opposition, particularly through the National Civic Federation, was probably decisive. Workmen's compensation had won approval only after employers had found the liability system too erratic and unpredictable in its costs to serve their interests.[63] Had there been more of a socialist challenge, employers might have revised their views of the possible benefits of other social insurance programs, including health insurance. The physicians would have understood that some reform was unavoidable and worked to secure as favorable a plan as they could. Indeed, this was their initial reaction, but the more uncertain the passage of health insurance became, the more categorical became their opposition. Defeating health insurance in toto by opening up the ideological issues left uncontested in England and Germany was a safer strategy for the opponents than working within the framework of reform in the hope of turning it to their advantage.

EVOLUTION IN DEFEAT, 1920–1932

While the movement for compulsory health insurance slept through the 1920s, major changes were taking place in the economics of medical care as well as in American society and politics. So when the movement reawakened in the next decade, the reformers became engaged in a new and different struggle. The lessons of controversy and defeat, the

growing costs of medical care, and the now formidable political influence and cultural authority of the medical profession brought about a
subtle shift in the objectives of health insurance and the strategy of its
advocates.

Though the broad objective of health insurance continued to be relieving the economic problems of sickness, the focus of reform shifted
from stabilizing income and increasing efficiency to financing and expanding access to medical care. By the thirties, most of the leading figures in the movement regarded medical costs as a more serious problem than the wage loss of sickness. The reformers still favored cash
benefits in sickness, but relegated them to subordinate importance and
suggested their administration be entirely separate from coverage of
medical expenses. In another change that narrowed the focus to medical care, they dropped the funeral benefit as politically impractical. The
pursuit of social efficiency was now tempered by a greater willingness
to accommodate likely interest-group opposition. By this time, reformers also did not rest their case on the dubious claim that by providing
incentives for public health, health insurance would reduce the net
costs of illness to society and actually increase profits and wages. They
were now more prepared to grant that under an insurance program
the social costs of medical care would be unlikely to diminish. Instead,
they justified health insurance on the grounds that it would make more
predictable and manageable the uncertain and sometimes devastating
costs of medical care to individuals. It would also, they said, give Americans the means to provide for their "unmet medical needs." Furthermore, whereas the Progressives had limited health insurance to wage
earners and their families, reformers now extended the proposal to the
middle class as well. These changes, especially the last, signified a basic
departure from the traditional European conception of health insurance as a form of income maintenance and stimulus to productivity for
the industrial working class. And in Europe, too, health insurance, beginning as a program for wage earners, was gradually becoming a system of financing medical care for the entire population.

The shift in concern among American reformers from the wage loss
of sickness to medical expenses reflected an objective change in the
ratio of the two costs, particularly for the middle class. Estimates at the
end of the 1920s now showed that medical costs were 20 percent higher
than lost earnings due to sickness for families with incomes under $1,200
a year and nearly 85 percent higher for families with incomes between
$1,200 and $2,500. The relatively higher cost of medical care, wrote the
medical economist I. S. Falk, was "a new condition, different from what

prevailed in other times and in other countries" when they instituted health insurance programs.[64] Writing in 1937, Michael Davis commented, "The development of health insurance has shown a steady but slow change from the economic to the medical emphasis." According to Davis, not only was medical care now a bigger item in family medical budgets than wage losses, but coverage of medical expenses was more important than income protection because medicine had become so effective in relieving suffering and promoting health.[65]

The increasing attention to medical costs preceded the Depression and the revival of the health insurance movement. In 1934 Davis noted the "paradox" that concern about medical costs had emerged during the prosperous twenties and "that most published complaints regarding the cost arose from the middle class."[66] This new development is the key to explaining the new direction of the health insurance movement.

The rise in medical costs had its origins before the conflict over Progressive health insurance plans, but not until the twenties did the middle class feel the impact and reformers appreciate the change. The increase came in the costs of both physicians' services and hospital care. The cost of physicians' services rose because of both improved quality (as a result of scientific advance and greater investment in required education) and increasing monopoly power (as a result of licensing restrictions and other practices that by the 1920s were giving doctors significantly higher returns than their investment in education would have justified).[67]

The rise in hospital costs had its origins in the complete transformation of hospital care at the turn of the century, but hospital charges to patients were still relatively low when the Progressive era insurance plans were formulated. Among 211 families surveyed in 1918 in Columbus, Ohio, by the U.S. Bureau of Labor Statistics, hospital costs averaged only 7.6 percent of a total medical bill averaging $48.41 (of which about half went to physicians).[68] Consequently, the Progressives gave little attention to hospital costs or the problems of hospital reimbursement. By 1929, according to a much larger national study, hospital charges (not including doctors' and private nurses' hospital bills, were 13 percent of a total family medical bill averaging $108.[69] In 1934 Davis estimated hospital charges plus physicians' bills for in-hospital services at 40 percent of total family medical expenditures.[70] Some of the increase over the levels in 1918 may be laid to an increased volume of hospital services and higher unit costs, and some to the increased tendency of hospitals to impose charges for services that previously were given below cost or as charity.

But increasing average costs do not tell the whole story. The key new development was the increasing *variation* in costs, as a result of the infrequent but exceptionally large expense of hospitalized illness. These high bills for hospitalized illnesses were precisely what hit the middle class in the twenties and changed the political complexion of the health insurance issue. As of 1929 only one person in seventeen was hospitalized in the course of a year, but illnesses that required hospitalization accounted for 50 percent of all charges for medical care. In urban families with incomes of between $2,000 and $3,000 a year, medical charges averaged $261 if there was any hospitalized illness, but only $67 if there was none.[71] A small but significant number of families were now faced with bills that amounted to a third or half their annual income. As Davis wrote, "In former years when the range of sickness costs was lower, and few illnesses caused high expenditures, families with middle-class income felt financial pinch due to sickness much less frequently than today. Now people who are economically secure . . . against all ordinary demands, are not secure against the costs of sickness. Thus, the economic problems of medical care now implicate not merely wage-earners but the whole population." As a result, Americans needed a "new approach" to health insurance "because the costs of medical care now involve larger sums of money and affect more people than does wage-loss due to sickness."[72]

The decade of the twenties saw another development, long in the making, come to maturity and change the context of the health insurance debate: the consolidation of professional power. During and after the First World War, as I noted earlier, physicians' incomes grew sharply; and their prestige, aided by the successes of medical science, became securely established in American culture. The twenties were a decade when legislators, district attorneys, AMA publicists, and public health officials took up the war against "quackery" as a great cause of enlightened government and exposed and prosecuted "cultists" and operators of diploma mills.

The growing influence of the medical profession was evident in the fate of one of the few government programs enacted over the AMA's protests. In 1921 women reformers, taking advantage of the new power of the female franchise, persuaded Congress to pass the Shepherd-Towner Act, which provided matching funds to the states for prenatal and child health centers. These centers, staffed mainly by public health nurses and women physicians, sought to reduce rates of maternal and infant mortality by giving pregnant women advice on personal hygiene and infant care. As the historian Sheila Rothman writes, "Advances in health care were to come not from the construction of hospitals, medical research, or the training of medical specialists—or even from new cures for disease. Rather, educated women were to instill in other women a broad knowledge of the rules of bodily hygiene and in this way prevent the onset of disease." But private physicians began to take an increased interest in these functions, and in 1927 the AMA was able to persuade Congress to discontinue the program.[73]

A third development affecting medical care also became clearer in the 1920s, though it, too, had been in progress for more than two decades. This was the gradual depletion of physicians in rural areas as a result of migration to cities and the diminishing output of medical schools. As the importance of hospitals to medical care became more widely recognized, the inadequacy of rural facilities also drew increasing criticism.*

The growing concern in the twenties about the costs and distribution of medical care prompted the formation of a privately funded commission that represents one of the key landmarks in the development of medical policy. Significantly, the group called itself the Committee on the Costs of Medical Care. (In the Progressive era, it would have been the Committee on the Costs of Illness.) An independent body, the CCMC was created by some fifteen economists, physicians, and public health specialists, who met in April 1926 at a conference on medical economics in Washington, D.C. They designated a smaller committee, including Michael Davis, law professor Walton Hamilton, and public health professor C-E. A. Winslow, to formulate a plan of studies. A year later, the group—soon to number almost fifty and to include prominent members of the professions and representatives of major interest groups—agreed to seek financial support from foundations for a five-year program of research. The committee chose as its chairman Ray Lyman Wilbur, a physician who was president of Stanford University and Hoover's secretary of the interior. A prominent figure in the Republican Party as well as a past president of the AMA, Wilbur was ideally suited to make the committee respectable and newsworthy and to buffer it against criticism of possibly "socialistic" tendencies. He was also instrumental in raising over $1 million from eight foundations.

Many of those who founded and served on the committee, worked on its staff, or helped finance its research supported compulsory health insurance. Wilbur himself, though not prominent in the movement, had spoken in favor of the California health insurance referendum in 1918. But what turned out to be more central to the committee's viewpoint was a belief that medical care needed better organization. A pre-

*On these developments in the 1920s, see Book One, especially Chapter 3.

view of its perspective came from Harry H. Moore, who left the Public
Health Service to become the committee's staff director. In *American
Medicine and the People's Health*, published in 1927, Moore argued that
despite the progress medicine had made, its services were maldistributed and badly organized. There was no coordination beyond the
walls of any particular hospital or clinic. "[W]hat exists is not so much
a system as a lack of system," Moore wrote, in a line that would be ech-
oed by liberal reformers for the next half century.[74]

Sensitive to the risk of arousing opposition, the founders of the committee chose to concentrate on factual research and to "engage collaboration in quarters which would otherwise be closed to them," as one
private observer wrote in 1927.[75] So anxious were they to gain the confidence of the medical profession that the organizers of the CCMC included among their members seventeen physicians in private practice,
plus the AMA's secretary, Olin West. In conducting research, they enjoyed the cooperation of the AMA, the Metropolitan Life Insurance
Company, and other private organizations.

During its five years, the committee published some twenty-seven
research reports providing the most detailed information yet assembled
on medical care in America. It gave the first reliable estimates of national health expenditures (about $3.66 billion a year in 1929, or about
4 percent of national income, which worked out to approximately $30
per capita) and the first reliable breakdown of the "medical dollar" (29.8
cents to private physicians, 23.4 cents to hospitals, 18.2 cents to medicines, 12.2 cents to dentists, 5.5 cents to nurses, 3.4 cents to "cultists,"
3.3 cents to public health, 4.2 cents miscellaneous). From a survey of
nine thousand white families, the committee's staff determined that
while 13.8 percent of people in families with incomes over $10,000 a year
received no medical care in the course of a year, the comparable figure
for families with incomes under $1,200 was 46.6 percent. The commit-
tee also showed how unequally costs were distributed: The 3.5 percent
of families with the largest medical bills paid one third of the cost of
medical care in the country.[76] And in studies of different organizations
(private group clinics, industrial medical programs, moderate-rate hospital plans) and of different communities around the country, the
CCMC provided case studies of alternatives and experiments then in
progress.

Yet in the committee's militantly objective research, admirable as it
undoubtedly was, there were biases—unacknowledged and perhaps
unconscious. These were particularly evident in the committee's treatment of two subjects: the need for medical care and the problem of
power.

The committee estimated the need for medical care on the basis of data on the incidence of disease and a panel of physicians' judgments of the appropriate forms of treatment. From higher rates of disease the committee inferred greater need for medical care, not considering the possibility that a high incidence of illness might indicate even greater needs for changes in nutrition, improved hygiene, better housing, or more healthy working conditions.[77] In determining the need for medical care by asking doctors what levels of treatment were appropriate, the committee took the perspective of the individual practitioner as the basis for the social allocation of resources, even though other responses besides medical care might have reduced the level of illness more effectively and at lower cost. The committee assumed that doctors could set purely "technical" standards for medical care, independently of any economic analysis, as if achieving those standards in medical care would not cost money that might be spent to promote health in other ways.

"The real need for medical care is a medical, not an economic, concept," wrote Roger I. Lee and Lewis and Barbara Jones in their influential report for the CCMC on the determination of medical needs. "It can be defined only in terms of the physical conditions of the people and the capacities of the science and art of medicine to deal with them. Thus, it is not always a conscious need, still less an active desire backed by willingness to pay. The ordinary layman lacks the knowledge to define his own medical needs and can rely only on the expert opinion of medical practitioners and public health authorities."[78]

And as if to emphasize that their understanding of the needs of society was defined by the cultural authority of medicine, the authors proceeded to say that such a technical definition of the need for medical care was valid only in a society like America which believed in "the efficacy of scientific medicine" in promoting health. "Against an entirely different social background, as for example in modern India, need would represent merely the expression of a narrow professional opinion and would bear no relation to the 'needs' of society." In America the need for medical care could properly be defined by physicians because Americans "value health and have accepted the science and art of medicine as the proper instrument for its advancement."[79]

The committee's approach, not surprisingly, produced exceedingly high estimates of the needs for different types of medical services. Indeed, basing its judgment on the "reasonable standards" of its medical experts, the committee found that nobody was getting enough medicine: "[E]ven among the highest income group," the CCMC said in its final report, "insufficient care is the rule."[80] Ignorance as well as poverty prevented people from receiving as much professional attention as they should. "The amount of care which people need is far greater than that which they are aware of needing, and greater than that for which they are able to pay under present conditions."[81]

Since everyone needed more medical care, the proportion of national resources going to medicine would have to be increased. This was one of the central messages of the CCMC, and it was seen as a general principle: As national wealth increased in the future, greater rewards would come if income were spent on services, including medical care, rather than on commodities. Indeed, instead of health insurance merely being a means of covering existing costs, as the Progressives had seen it, the CCMC now spoke of insurance as a way of budgeting larger expenditures. Introducing the final staff report, Wilbur wrote, "More money must be spent for medical care; and this is practicable if the expenditures can be budgeted and can be made through fixed periodic payments—even as people are enabled to spend more for other commodities by installment than by outright purchase."[82] This was the new expansionary function of health insurance—not to maintain incomes, but to expand the use of medical care.

The implications of this growing expenditure on medical care for the power of those who controlled it, the committee did not explore. Like many other studies presented as objective research, the CCMC report was innocent of any critical reflection on the problems of power. Its positive evaluations of industrial medical services in cotton-mill towns and elsewhere never mentioned the role that such welfare programs played in consolidating the employers' control over their workers. In recommending the establishment of community medical centers, the CCMC final report suggested that the method of administrative control, whether similar to self-perpetuating hospital boards or to popularly elected school boards, was "relatively immaterial, so long as the members are interested, competent, devoted to the general good, and free from political interference."[83] The writers of the report also had a deep abhorrence of any competition among medical plans. Though they approved of prepaid group practice plans, they noted as one serious disadvantage the "increased opportunity for clinics to engage in competition as to price," which the committee thought "disastrous to professional standards and therefore to the welfare of patients."[84] Nowhere in the report was there any mention of the risk that the medical profession might exercise monopoly power.

Given such assumptions, the committee's conclusions should not be a surprise, though they do not fit neatly into the categories of political analysis. The members of the committee were not simply (to use Robert Alford's terms) "corporate rationalists," "professional monopolizers," or "equal health advocates." The CCMC report exhibits elements of each such tendency: It favored reducing economic barriers to medical care, turning over power to professionals, and rationally organizing medical care on a bureaucratic model.

The final report of the committee, endorsed by thirty-five of its members, called for the promotion of group practice and group payment for medical care. But though it endorsed group payment, the report opposed compulsory health insurance. A compulsory program, the majority said, would require an "unprecedented" subsidy from government, employers, or both to reach American standards of medical care. Voluntary plans were desirable as a first step, and it would be better to develop strong group practice organizations "before insurance becomes compulsory" since an insurance system, if established immediately, would tend to freeze individual practice in place. In a somewhat vague explanation of financing, the majority proposed that local governments contribute a share of the costs of group payment plans for low-income individuals "on a per capita or lump sum basis, assisted where necessary by the state or Federal government."[85] Eight signers of the majority report dissented on this issue alone, arguing that voluntary insurance would later block a compulsory plan and would never cover the poor "who most need its protection." Two other Progressives, Hamilton and Sydenstricker, dissented from the entire report.[86]

But the sharpest dissent came from eight of the private practitioners on the committee, plus a representative of the Catholic hospitals, who denounced the majority's recommendations on group practice as the "technique of big business . . . mass production." Such a plan would establish a "medical hierarchy" to dictate who might practice in any community. The doctors' own recommendations—that "government competition in the practice of medicine be discontinued"; that "government care of the indigent be expanded with the ultimate object of relieving the medical profession of this burden"; and that the general practitioner be restored to "the central place in medical practice"—were based, they said, upon the conviction that the medical profession was the "essential element" in medical care and that its influence should be "upheld and strengthened." Not only did they reject compulsory health insurance; they denounced voluntary insurance as well, which they said in other countries had "proved to be only a longer or shorter bridge to a compulsory system." They favored the use of insurance methods "only when they can be kept under professional control and destructive competition eliminated."[87]

Upon the release of the CCMC reports in late November 1932, an editorial in the AMA's *Journal*, endorsing the minority view, described the majority's proposals as an "incitement to revolution."[88] Not only the AMA treated the majority report as a radical document: *The New York Times* headlined its front-page story "Socialized Medicine Is Urged in Survey," and then quoted Wilbur as saying that medicine was on its way to some form of community organization and that the majority report was meant to keep the medical profession in control of such movements.[89] Politically, the CCMC utterly failed in its attempt to generate a new consensus for reform. The various dissenting opinions from both left and right gave an impression of discord and distracted attention from the wide area of agreement between the majority and minority views. The AMA's extreme reaction to the majority report confirmed the suspicions of many that it was risky even to advocate voluntary health insurance. Coming just as Franklin D. Roosevelt took office, the controversy over the CCMC helped persuade the new administration that health insurance was an issue to be avoided.

THE NEW DEAL AND HEALTH INSURANCE, 1932-1943

The Making of Social Security

The Depression might appear to have finally created the right conditions for passing compulsory health insurance. It revived the dormant social insurance movement as well as more radical currents in American politics. It saw not only the spread of unions, but the abandonment by the AF of L of its long-standing opposition to social insurance programs. And it brought to power a Democratic administration more willing than any previous to involve the federal government in the management of economic and social welfare.

But the Depression also revised the priorities of social reform. In the Progressive era, health insurance had been the top item after workmen's compensation on the agenda of social insurance advocates. Other Western countries generally moved on to health insurance as a natural outgrowth of insurance against industrial accidents. Old-age pensions typically came third, and unemployment insurance last.[90] But in America, with millions out of work in the thirties, unemployment insurance became the leading priority. Old-age benefits were second as a result of the movement of older Americans that had spontaneously gathered behind a retired physician, Francis Townsend, a sort of intuitive Keynesian, who proposed that the Depression be cured by giving every

American over sixty-five a monthly pension of $200 on two conditions: that they retire from work and immediately spend the money. Though it was a fantastic and implausible scheme—if carried out, it would have turned over half the national income to 8 percent of the population[91] —Townsend clubs had sprung up all over the country. Many congressmen had been obliged to pledge themselves to work for its enactment and saw Social Security as an acceptable way to escape from a commitment they had no intention of fulfilling.

Even before Roosevelt took office, there was a steady movement toward Social Security. Two states passed old-age pension laws in 1929, two more in 1930, five in 1931. As governor of New York, Roosevelt endorsed unemployment insurance in 1930; Wisconsin became the first state to adopt such a measure early in 1932. Although old-age pension and unemployment insurance bills were introduced into Congress soon after his election, Roosevelt refused to give them his strong support, waiting to prepare a program of his own. Then on June 8, 1934, he seized the initiative and announced that he would appoint a Committee on Economic Security to study the issue comprehensively and report with a program to Congress the following January. The committee was to consist of four members of the Cabinet and the federal relief administrator; it would be chaired by Secretary of Labor Frances Perkins.

Though Roosevelt indicated in his June message that he was especially interested in old-age and unemployment measures, the committee included medical care and health insurance in its research. Its subcommittee on medical care was chaired by Walton Hamilton and its technical study was directed by Edgar Sydenstricker, the two liberal dissenters from the CCMC majority report.

From the outset the prevailing sentiment on the Committee on Economic Security was that health insurance would have to wait. Edwin Witte, the staff director, recorded in a confidential memo in 1936 his "original belief" that medical society opposition precluded any action on health insurance. This view was shared by Secretary Perkins. Harry Hopkins, the relief administrator, was "more interested in health insurance than in any other phase of social insurance, but also realized that this subject would have to be handled very gingerly."[92]

Nor was this sentiment confined to members of the committee. In an article published in October of 1934, Abraham Epstein, the founder of the American Association for Social Security and a leading figure in the movement, advised the administration to be politically realistic and specifically to go slow on health insurance because of the opposition it would arouse—this from someone who later would become severely critical of the conservatism of the Social Security bill.[93]

Even the naming of Sydenstricker to direct the committee's research on health insurance caused an uproar in the medical profession. Witte recalled that "telegraphic protests poured in upon the President." An editorial in the AMA's *Journal* said Roosevelt would try to ram health insurance through Congress. But the protests stopped abruptly after the first meeting of an advisory committee on medical care that included the presidents of the AMA, the American College of Surgeons, and the American College of Physicians. This sudden quiet, which proved no more than a momentary truce, created the impression that the AMA might be willing to accept health insurance in some form. Sydenstricker had been arguing within the committee that at least part of the profession could be won over. His view gained force in the fall of 1934 when the American College of Surgeons endorsed compulsory health insurance. But once again reformers were seeing a mirage. At a National Conference on Economic Security in November, two prominent physicians who had been expected to favor health insurance, or at least not to oppose it, denounced the measure. At that point, Witte and Perkins returned to their original view that immediate action on health insurance would be politically unwise. On November 15, Secretary Perkins told the AMA that the committee's study of medical care would require additional time, which meant that no recommendations on health insurance would be presented to the president in January. The delay signaled a weakness that the AMA was able to exploit.[94]

Some members of the Committee on Economic Security and its staff thought that Congress would act quickly on unemployment and old-age programs and that health insurance could be introduced later in the same session. This expectation proved to be mistaken. Even a discussion of general principles for health insurance in the committee's January report aroused a storm of protest from the AMA. These principles included assurances that private medical practice would continue; that the medical profession would control professional personnel and procedures; and that doctors would be free to choose their patients, the method of reimbursement, and whether to participate in insurance practice. Without definitively recommending a plan, the committee listed as goals the provision of adequate medical services, the budgeting of wage losses and medical costs, "reasonably adequate remuneration" to practitioners, and new incentives for improved medical care. The system the committee envisioned was to be state administered, and state participation would be optional. The role of the federal government was to provide subsidies and set minimum standards for states that adopted a health insurance program. As the reformers now generally agreed, cash benefits in sickness would be separate, probably linked with unemployment insurance.[95]

The Social Security bill itself included only one glancing reference to health insurance as a subject the new Social Security Board might study. Nonetheless, the declaration of principles in the committee report was widely reported in the medical press as if it were a legislative proposal. Alarmed by what might follow, the AMA called a special meeting of its House of Delegates in February 1935—only the second in its history—where it once again denounced compulsory health insurance and any lay control of medical benefits in relief agencies. But in what appeared to be a small concession to moderates, the association accepted voluntary insurance plans for medical service, so long as the plans were under the control of county medical societies and followed AMA guidelines.[96]

Though sentiment in favor of health insurance was still strong among members of the Committee on Economic Security, Witte was convinced that any health insurance amendment would "spell defeat for the entire bill." The president shared this judgment, and informed Secretary Perkins to file a report on health insurance, reserving for himself any decision about how to proceed. The committee's report, transmitted in June 1935, supported a program that would have been optional for the states, but compulsory for residents of those states where it was adopted. But in a separate letter, recognizing how "controversial" the subject was, Secretary Perkins advised the report not be made public until the Social Security bill was safely passed. Roosevelt never released the report. This secrecy in itself testifies to the administration's wariness, since the committee proposed giving only "small financial aid" to the states and did not suggest any legislative action until further study by the Social Security Board.[97]

The omission of health insurance from the Social Security Act was by no means the act's only conservative feature. It relied on a regressive tax and gave no coverage to some of the very poor, such as farm laborers and domestics. The standards for unemployment insurance were weak. Requirements that state pensions for the aged had to assure a "reasonable subsistence compatible with decency and health" were struck out, according to the economist and later Senator Paul Douglas, because of objections by Southern political leaders that the federal government might use such phrases to force their states to pay higher pensions to blacks than they thought desirable.[98] Though the Social Security bill finally passed both houses by a wide margin, it had a hard time in the Senate Finance Committee, where it was approved by only a few votes.

While omitting health insurance, the act extended the government's role in public health in several provisions unrelated to social insurance. It gave the states funds on a matching basis for maternal and infant care, rehabilitation of crippled children, general public health work, and aid for dependent children under age sixteen. This last provision was to have unanticipated implications for medical care.

The Depression, Welfare Medicine, and the Doctors

Increased state and federal financing of medical services for the poor originated inadvertently and inconspicuously during the Depression. It was a hidden consequence of the failure to develop a health insurance system that would have covered the middle class and the poor alike.

The fall in personal incomes after 1929 severely curtailed the use of medical services by the poor. In ten working-class communities studied between 1929 and 1933, the proportion of families with incomes under $150 per capita had increased from 10 to 43 percent. Families whose incomes had dropped from over $425 in 1929 to less that $150 per capita in 1933 called upon physicians only half as often as did families whose incomes remained above $425 per capita throughout the entire period.[99] A 1938 Gallup poll, asking whether people had put off seeing a doctor because of the cost, found that 68 percent of lower-income respondents had done so, compared with 24 percent in the upper-income brackets.[100]

Less use of medical services and reduced ability to pay meant lower incomes for physicians. According to one study, the average net income of doctors in California fell from approximately $6,700 in 1929 to $3,600 in 1933. Nationally, according to Kuznets and Friedman, private practitioners had lost 47 percent of their 1929 incomes by 1933. A 1933 government survey compared the ratio of bills unpaid six months or more to the total number of accounts receivable for the same period for different types of creditors. The delinquency percentage for department stores was 8.9 percent; for grocery stores, 24.7 percent; for landlords, 45.1 percent; for dentists, 55.6 percent; and for physicians, 66.6 percent.[101] Not only were patients seeing doctors less often; they were paying their doctors' bills last.

Hospitals were in similar trouble. Beds were empty as utilization fell, bills were unpaid, and contributions to hospital fund-raising efforts tumbled.

So private physicians and private charities simply could no longer afford to meet the demand for free services. For the first time, they asked welfare departments to pay for the treatment of people on relief. Before the Depression, medical care had been a minor function of welfare agencies, but now it grew in significance. Beginning about 1930, medical care became recognized in many localities as an "essential relief need." Many cities and a few states gave beneficiaries a right to needed service at public expense; increasingly, welfare agencies provided supplemental payments to help defray medical costs. As federal and state relief funds became available, local hospitals and social agencies began to charge welfare departments for services previously rendered free, so the cities could get reimbursed and shift costs to the state or federal government. This system of welfare payment for medical care was seen as a temporary expedient, but it continued after the Depression ended.[102]

Yet another federal program helped pay for medical care in the farming areas of the country. In 1935 the Resettlement Administration began to set up and subsidize cooperative medical prepayment plans among the poor farmers it was assisting. The agency had found that many of its clients defaulted on loans when they fell sick. Under these programs, which in 1937 were taken over by the Farm Security Administration (FSA), the local medical society typically agreed to accept a limit on the total fees they would receive. In effect, this was government-sponsored health insurance. Barely noticed in political debate, the plans covered a quarter of the population of the Dakotas.[103]

These new developments disturbed the AMA. Never before, warned its Judicial Council in 1934, had government so invaded private medical practice as through federal emergency relief. The willingness of physicians to accept government payments "must be considered as a temporary expedient only, due to the unparalleled stress of the times, and must be discontinued as rapidly as the stress on the profession is relieved." Some state and county societies had recommended to their members that they provide services to all in need and refuse to accept compensation from the government. The AMA Judicial Council agreed: "One of the strongest holds of the profession on public approbation and support has been the age-old professional ideal of medical service to all, whether able to pay or not. . . . The abandonment of that ideal and the adoption of a principle of service only when paid for would be the greatest step toward socialized medicine and shortly state medicine which the medical profession could take."[104] Like men ashore urging self-reliance on their drowning companions, the wealthy doctors in the AMA were asking their poorer colleagues to hold the line against health insurance.

The Depression posed a severe test for the AMA. It was no easy matter to maintain a common front against government intervention when physicians themselves were in economic difficulty. Many doctors whose waiting rooms were empty and whose bills were unpaid were now more willing to consider some form of health insurance. In Michigan a liberal faction sympathetic to compulsory insurance gained power in the state medical society in 1932, only to face a campaign by the AMA aimed at restoring conservative control. In March 1935 the California Medical Association endorsed compulsory health insurance in a vote reported to express the views of the "little men" in the profession who knew what costs meant to patients as well as to themselves.[105] And as we have already seen (Book One, Chapter 6), in Washington and Oregon—two states where many doctors had long been out of compliance with AMA rules against contract practice—the county medical societies tried during the Depression to drive out profit-making medical corporations by setting up a health insurance program of their own.[106]

Health insurance promised to stimulate use of physicians' services and help patients pay their bills. The AMA's response to the economic crisis, however, emphasized restricting the supply of doctors rather than amplifying the demand for their services. In 1934 Walter Bierring, the incoming president of the association, recommended eliminating half the medical schools in the country.[107] That same year the AMA's Council of Medical Education warned medical schools against admitting too many students, and enrollments thereafter declined. (Each of the five years prior to 1934 had shown an increase in applicants accepted by medical schools; each of the next six years showed a drop.) In the same period, medical licensing boards adopted more rigorous standards for foreign physicians, then arriving in growing numbers in flight from the Nazis. The proportion of foreign doctors failing the examinations increased from 5.7 percent in 1930 to 20.7 percent ten years later.[108]

In effect, the reformers and the AMA were engaged in a struggle for the political loyalties of physicians. Hoping to pry loose at least part of the profession, reformers often emphasized, as a virtue of health insurance, its value to physicians in shoring up their incomes. The appeal did not succeed. None of the movements toward health insurance within the profession proved long lasting. The Michigan medical society was back in conservative hands by 1935. The American College of Surgeons quickly rescinded its endorsement of compulsory insurance after the death of its founder, Franklin Martin, who had used his prestige on behalf of the measure. The proposal endorsed by the California state association would have restricted eligibility for health insurance and vested all control in the medical profession. These conditions so aroused the opposition of reformers that they destroyed any chance of legislative approval.[109] The insurance plans adopted by doctors in Washington and Oregon, though providing service at fixed rates, were aimed at eliminating lay-controlled competition. Therefore, even these moves toward health insurance were fundamentally in line with the AMA's objectives.

In the mid-thirties, the AMA began to adjust its position on health insurance, at least in its official pronouncements. Instead of opposing all insurance whether voluntary or compulsory, it began to define the terms on which voluntary programs might be acceptable. These terms, as we shall see in more detail in the next chapter, insisted that there be no direct intervention in the doctor's business by any financial intermediary. The AMA would countenance group hospital insurance plans only if limited to paying hospital bills, and it would allow voluntary insurance for medical service only if controlled by county medical societies. Yet while accepting such plans in principle, the AMA did nothing to encourage their development.

Despite pressures, the AMA held its membership, and it held its ground. Though between 1930 and 1935 the proportion of doctors belonging to the association fell from 65.1 to 60.8 percent, five years later membership reached 66.8 percent, higher than ever before.[110] The ties that bound physicians to the AMA, as I indicated earlier, were based on career imperatives as well as a shared professional culture. Membership in the local medical society, which required membership in the national organization, was the key to hospital privileges and patient referrals as well as malpractice liability protection. The inner fraternity who typically controlled the local society discouraged wayward tendencies. The AMA was a democratic organization, but in the 1920s and 1930s, as Oliver Garceau showed in a careful study of its internal political life, the association was dominated by an "active minority" composed primarily of urban specialists. These physicians ran its governing councils and were disproportionately represented among the long-term members of its House of Delegates. They had little use for dissent. Votes in AMA meetings and elections were typically unanimous; dissenting opinions were seldom recorded in its proceedings and almost never given any space in its journal. "The basic attitude of the active minority," wrote Garceau, "appears to be that the differences of opinion are dirty linen. Quite understandably they wish to keep dirty linen from public inspection."[111]

How well this active minority represented professional opinion is unclear. A 1938 Gallup poll was widely reported as showing that seven out of ten doctors actually favored compulsory health insurance, but the survey had asked only about voluntary insurance, and the significance of the finding is uncertain because the question asked was so vague.[112]

Undoubtedly, more doctors disagreed with the AMA's policies than its leadership acknowledged, but fewer than the reformers hoped for. Most physicians were politically inactive and seemed content to let a small group of financially successful specialists set policy for the profession.

Aside from the few doctors who belonged to the socialist American League for Public Medicine, the only significant organized dissent from AMA policies emerged in 1936–37 among a group of liberal academic physicians calling themselves the Committee of Physicians for the Improvement of Medicine. In a short statement of "Principles and Proposals" signed by over 400 doctors by the fall of 1937, the group recognized that health was a "direct concern of the government" and called for the formulation of a national health policy. They urged that public funds be used to finance medical education and research; laboratory, diagnostic, and consultative services in hospitals; preventive and public health work; and medical care for the "medically indigent." By no means a radical organization, the committee did not declare in favor of compulsory health insurance, though some who signed the committee's statement supported it. The distinguishing feature of the group's position was its emphasis on education, research, group practice, and hospitals in contrast to the AMA's celebration of the individual practitioner.[113] In 1938 John Peters, the committee's secretary and Ely Professor of Medicine at Yale, author of over 200 scientific articles, told the American College of Surgeons that the practitioner had fallen "almost completely into the derivative position of distributor or dispenser" of medical care. Educational and research institutions had taken over the "productive services" of medicine, and no program for improving medical care that considered "only the distributors to the neglect of these productive services" could be satisfactory. "It is a little tiresome," Peters went on, "to hear from our professional publicists of medicine that only practitioners have any comprehension of the problems of medical care . . . . They exploit scientific services to which they have contributed nothing."[114]

Though it had little political influence at the time, the Committee of Physicians foreshadowed the emphasis on medical research and hospital care that was to pervade government policy after 1945. Some reformers, however, misread the patrician liberalism of academic physicians as a sign of a deep rift in the profession that might aid their cause. The AMA itself seems to have overreacted. Before the initial statement of the Commitee of Physicians was released, the AMA's *Journal* denounced the group, insinuating that they had obtained signatures by devious and deceptive means.[115] Yet while some of the dissidents used acerbic language to describe the profession's leadership, the committee never split off from the AMA, nor did it presage widespread professional acceptance of government-sponsored health insurance. It did, however, shatter the image of a unanimous profession that the AMA was trying to project. In that respect, the Committee of Physicians contributed to the pressure that led the AMA in 1938 to make its biggest concessions to reform, as it sought anxiously to stop what now seemed like the most serious movement yet toward compulsory health insurance.

A Second Wind

The new push for health insurance in the late thirties developed within the Roosevelt administration, though it never received the president's full backing. In 1935 an Interdepartmental Committee to Coordinate Health and Welfare Activities, consisting of assistant Cabinet secretaries, had been set up to oversee the various federal social programs that had grown up helter skelter in different agencies. The Public Health Service was then located in the Treasury Department; the Social Security Board was an independent agency; and the Children's Bureau, which dealt with maternal as well as child health, was to be found, perhaps appropriately, in the Department of Labor. Chaired by Josephine Roche, assistant secretary of the Treasury, the Interdepartmental Committee first concentrated on coordinating programs and then turned to a study of the nation's health needs. In March 1937 it established a Technical Committee on Medical Care, which several months later it authorized to formulate a national health program. Following the CCMC and the Committee on Economic Security, this was now the third group in ten years to take on the task. I. S. Falk, who had been on the staff of the two previous committees, represented the Social Security Board in this new effort and was the chief spokesman within it for health insurance. The Public Health Service had three representatives; the fifth member and chairman was the assistant chief of the Children's Bureau, Martha Eliot.

These agency affiliations are important to keep in mind because of a new element in the politics of health insurance: internal conflict among government bureaucracies over the priority of health insurance versus other programs. At the inception of the committee's work, Dr. Eliot suggested that instead of all working together, they work separately on the sections of the program that would affect their particular agencies—an indication of the narrowing allegiances that would characterize health politics for many years to come.[116]

The Technical Committee's final report resembled the recommendations made by the Committee on Economic Security three years earlier. Like the earlier committee, it favored subsidies to the states to operate health programs instead of a national insurance system. It proposed (1) expanded public health and maternal and child health services under the Social Security Act; (2) expansion of hospital facilities through federal aid to the states for construction and three years of operating support; (3) increased aid for medical care for those on relief and others who had no funds for health care; (4) consideration of a general medical care program supported by taxes, insurance, or both; and (5) federal action toward a program of compensation for wage losses due to temporary or permanent disability. These recommendations were not entirely consistent—if the fourth were fully carried out, the third would not be necessary—and the committee recognized that they could not all be put into effect immediately. The first two were deemed most important. The report withheld as complete support for health insurance as it gave to other measures.[117]

The president decided to make public the part of the committee's report that described the nation's health needs and to call a conference in Washington, D.C., on the national health program. This conference, which convened in July 1938, represented an important moment for reformers in their drive for public attention. The conference brought to Washington over 150 representatives of labor, farmers, and the health professions—though not, as AMA Secretary Morris Fishbein told the hosts, American business—in what the AMA construed to be an effort to orchestrate support for a predetermined agenda. And though the delegates were concerned most about the programs that directly affected them, they strongly supported the Technical Committee's view of the nation's health needs and its entire program.

So concerned was the AMA about the public response to the National Health Conference that the following Sunday its representatives met with the Interdepartmental Committee to offer a deal. They would support all the other recommendations if the committee would agree to drop compulsory health insurance. The committee declined this offer.[118] The AMA then called another emergency session of its House of Delegates, which for the first time approved protection of loss of income during illness as well as cash indemnity insurance, so long as it met the approval of county and state medical societies. It also endorsed the expansion of public health services and even recognized that federal aid might be required for the care of the medically indigent, though these efforts had to remain under local authority.[119] The aim of this new and more receptive stance was plainly to isolate compulsory insurance from other issues and thus to bring about its defeat. The AMA then succeeded in gaining support for its new position from other organizations, including the American Public Health Association. The APHA, reflecting differences of opinion about the legitimate boundaries of public health, was divided between those who believed public health required a concern for medical care and those who believed that public health came first and medical care was best left to clinicians.[120]

The AMA could not have known that events unrelated to medical care were about to make its conciliatory stance politically unnecessary. Initially, Roosevelt's reaction to the National Health Conference was so enthusiastic, according to Arthur Altmeyer, chairman of the Social Security Board, that the president wanted to make the national health program an issue in the 1938 election. Then he changed his mind and said maybe it would be better to wait until the 1940 presidential election.[121] Yet Roosevelt never made it an issue in either. The 1938 elections brought a major conservative resurgence. From that year on, conservative Dixiecrats and Republicans formed a congressional alliance that made any further innovations in social policy extremely difficult. Almost all major New Deal legislation dates from before 1938. Thereafter, the administration lost influence with Congress and turned its attention to foreign affairs. Shortly after the 1938 election, Roosevelt sent the national health program to Congress with a message recommending it for "careful study" but no immediate legislative action.[122]

However, in February 1939 Senator Robert F. Wagner of New York, a prominent liberal and administration ally, introduced a bill incorporating the report's recommendations. Wagner emphasized the extent of agreement between his proposal and the AMA's recent position. The only difference, he said, was health insurance, which his bill left as an option to the states.[123] But in spite of its earlier concessions, the AMA now testified against the legislation in toto. Although the Wagner bill, hardly a radical measure, was reported to face only minor opposition in the Senate, the president indicated late in 1939 that he only wanted aid for hospital construction. Whether concern about the cost or election-year implications were uppermost in his mind is unclear. In January 1940 Roosevelt sent a message recommending a modest program to construct hospitals in needy areas, but even this bill, though passed by the Senate, died in the House.[124]

So petered out the movement for compulsory health insurance after the National Health Conference. Just as the AALL's campaign ran into the declining fortunes of Progressivism and then World War I, so the campaign of the thirties ran into the declining fortunes of the New Deal and then World War II. However, more was at work in this new defeat than bad timing. Roosevelt's unwillingness to press for health insurance was basically consistent with the pattern of his administration. The New Deal responded to organized pressures. "Roosevelt's predilection for balanced government," the historian William Leuchtenberg writes, "often meant that the privileges granted by the New Deal were in precise proportion to the strength of pressure groups which demanded them. . . . causes which were not sustained by powerful interest groups frequently made little headway."[125] In the passage of Social Security, the Townsend movement and riots of the unemployed gave old-age pensions and unemployment insurance priority. No similar pressure existed for health insurance—but there was much pressure against it.

One study of the omission of health insurance from the New Deal argues that the fundamental obstacle to its passage was that Americans were not yet ready to abandon traditional ideals of individualism and adopt the new concept of freedom that health insurance embodied.[126] There are two chief difficulties with this interpretation. The first is that the individualistic values of Americans were an obstacle to all major social insurance programs. Yet by the end of the New Deal, the United States had adopted compulsory unemployment insurance and old-age pensions as well as workmen's compensation. Health insurance was the exception, but it demanded no greater a departure from individualism than did the other programs.

The second difficulty is factual. Public opinion polls suggest that Americans were ready in the Depression and after to abandon individual responsibility for the costs of sickness. Beginning in 1936, national polls asked a series of questions about health insurance. The data from these surveys present a complex, though consistent picture.[127]

When Americans were asked whether government ought to help people pay for the medical care they need—a direct test of their belief in self-reliance—the answer was overwhelmingly yes: Three of every four people approved of such help in polls taken in 1936, 1937, 1938, and 1942. Beginning in 1943, the polls also asked whether people thought it was a "good idea" if Social Security also paid for doctors' and hospital care that Americans might need in the future. This, too, a majority approved: 58 percent in 1943 and 68 percent in 1944 and 1945.

Yet another question, however, introduced the consideration of higher Social Security taxes to pay for health insurance. When the issue was presented this way, support fell to 44 percent in 1943 and 51 percent in 1945. In still another variation, respondents were asked to choose between "a plan set up by the government which would require every person to take part" and "a plan set up by the medical profession which would include only those persons who were interested." The private plan gained a slight edge among respondents in 1944 and 1945 when higher taxes were also mentioned in connection with the government program, while in another poll, which omitted reference to taxes, a majority supported national health insurance. Finally, yet another type of survey question asked for open-ended responses about what "could" or "should" be done about making it easier to pay medical bills. In two such surveys only about 13 percent spontaneously came up with national health insurance.

These different survey results allowed both advocates and opponents of national health insurance to claim majority support, so in 1945 the Opinion Research Corporation made a careful attempt to find out more exactly what people thought. It asked people three questions in succession: first, whether they thought it was a good idea if Social Security paid for medical care that people might need in the future; second, whether it was a good idea if some "pay-in-advance plan for doctor and hospital care were offered by insurance companies through employers all over the country"; and third, whether it would matter much which plan was offered, and if so, which would be better? The answers were revealing: 68 percent thought extending Social Security was a good idea; 70 percent approved of private plans; and, in answer to the final question, 35 percent chose Social Security, 31 percent the private option, 17 percent said it wouldn't matter, and another 17 percent gave "qualified" answers or no opinion.

These polls suggest that while a majority would have accepted and approved national health insurance, only about a third of the population clearly preferred it to a private system. Public approval existed, but strong sentiment in favor did not. However, there was no clear preference for private plans, and so public opinion does not account, in any simple fashion, for the outcome of the conflict.

In a revealing remark to a key Senate committee chairman in 1943, Roosevelt said, speaking of health insurance, "We can't go up against the State Medical Societies; we just can't do it."[128] Whether or not the president could have successfully challenged the AMA is an impossible question to answer. Altmeyer, who was intimately involved in the decisions, believed the president's judgment was right in 1935 but wrong in 1938. He later wrote that after the National Health Conference the administration could have secured favorable congressional action "if the President had actively supported" Wagner's bill.[129] At that moment, the obstacles to health insurance may have been more political than structural—that is, more a matter of a political judgment than of the kind of overwhelming opposition that blocked reform during the Progressive era. But hindsight, of course, is cheap, and reformers may also see mirages in the past.

SYMBOLIC POLITICS, 1943–1950

Socialized Medicine and the Cold War

Compulsory health insurance had stood on the periphery of national politics throughout the New Deal—omitted from Social Security, never fully backed by the president, subordinated to other programs even by many reformers. In the 1940s the issue finally moved into the center arena of national politics and received the unreserved support of an American president. But the opposition also acquired new strength. For now compulsory health insurance became entangled in the cold war, and its opponents were able to make "socialized medicine" a symbolic issue in the growing crusade against communist influence in America.

The shift to the national arena was written into health legislation in the forties. Even as late as the Wagner bill of 1939, reformers were still proposing health insurance as a state option. But by the early forties, as it became clear the Supreme Court would accept a national program, the advocates of reform felt less constrained by possible states' rights objections. They finally proposed that health insurance be operated as part of Social Security. They also dropped most limitations on coverage: National health insurance was to be universal and comprehensive. These principles were incorporated into a bill first introduced in 1943 by Senator Wagner, Senator James Murray of Montana, and Representative John Dingell of Michigan.[130] The Wagner-Murray-Dingell bill also called for other changes in Social Security that were meant to bring about a system of "cradle-to-grave" social insurance comparable to the Beveridge plan then being discussed in Great Britain.

As is often the case, a new generation of reform saw a turnover in organizational leadership. After the deaths of John Andrews, who had directed the American Association for Labor Legislation, and Abraham Epstein, who had founded the American Association for Social Security, the two main organizations concerned with health insurance had disappeared. In February 1944 representatives of organized labor, progressive farmers, and liberal physicians met in the office of Senator Wagner to set up a new group called the Social Security Charter Committee. Two years later, under Michael Davis, this became the Committee for the Nation's Health.[131]

Toward the end of his life, Roosevelt had indicated that he would finally press for health insurance once the war was over. In 1944 he asked Congress to affirm an "economic bill of rights," including a right to adequate medical care. Shortly after becoming president, Truman re-

peated the request and in November 1945, three months after the end
of the war, he called upon Congress to pass a national program to assure
the right to adequate medical care and protection from the "economic
fears" of sickness.[132]

Truman's plan closely resembled the national health program of 1938,
but there was a difference in emphasis. The president was now strongly
committed to health insurance, and he was more forthright in advocating expanded investment in the medical system. Reversing the order
of the 1938 program, Truman's first recommendation called for expansion of hospitals and the second for increased support of public health
and maternal and child health services. Truman's third recommendation, federal aid to medical research and education, had not been part
of the earlier program. Most significant, whereas the 1938 program had
a separate proposal for medical care for the needy, Truman proposed
a single health insurance system that would include all classes of the
society, even those like professionals, agricultural workers, and domestics not covered by Social Security. Public agencies would pay the insurance premiums of those too poor to pay for themselves. The president
readily admitted that this extension of services would cost more money.
Medical services "absorb only about 4 percent of the national income,"
Truman stated. "We can afford to spend more for health."[133]

Truman was emphatic, however, that this program was not "socialized medicine." Under his plan, he stated, "our people would continue
to get medical and hospital services just as they do now."[134] Altmeyer,
as chairman of the Social Security Board, said that doctors and hospitals
would be permitted to choose "the method of remuneration they desire" and that doctors had the right to expect higher average earnings
than they had received before.[135]

Thus the Truman program was expansionary in several senses: It
aimed to expand access to medical care by augmenting the nation's
medical resources and reducing financial barriers to their use, and it
promised doctors higher incomes and no organizational reform. Since
voluntary hospital insurance was now rapidly developing among the
middle class, the comprehensive and universal features of the program
became central to its identity. Unlike the Progressives, who had proposed a plan only for the working class and who sought economies in
medical organization and greater efficiency for society, liberals after the
New Deal were both more egalitarian on distributive issues and less
radical on organizational ones.

The accommodating attitude toward physicians in the plan did not
win the Truman program any support from that quarter. Immediately
after the president's message, the National Physicians Committee, a

professional lobby set up in 1938 to receive contributions mainly from the drug industry, sent out an emergency bulletin calling upon doctors to resist the program. The AMA said in an editorial that Truman's health insurance plan would make doctors "slaves." In December the AMA House of Delegates offered as an alternative the extension of voluntary insurance and expanded public services for the indigent.[136]

Public reaction to Truman's plan was initially sympathetic. Among those who had heard of the proposal, 58 percent approved in national polls taken in November 1945.[137] However, more complex surveys in California and New York disclosed several points of weakness in public support for compulsory health insurance. A survey conducted for the California Medical Association in 1943 found that while a "socialized government controlled medical plan" was approved 50 to 34 percent, support for a government program fell to about one quarter when it was compared with voluntary insurance.[138] Another survey, conducted in January 1946 in New York for a legislative commission, found that the comprehensive program liberals were advocating had less support than a more modest plan.* This division in sentiment between the core supporters of health insurance and the public represented a hidden but serious political problem: What the supporters wanted most, the public was least willing to approve. Finally, all surveys indicated that support for compulsory insurance varied inversely with social class. The AMA had as its allies those who ran community organizations, the media of opinion, the large corporations.[140]

The medical profession's struggle to turn around public opinion began in California, where the liberal Republican Governor Earl Warren proposed a health insurance plan much like the one the California Medical Association had favored ten years earlier. The doctors now hired a public relations firm, Whitaker and Baxter, to combat the proposal. Explaining that "you can't beat something with nothing," the firm urged the doctors to publicize their support for voluntary insurance. It then secured endorsements from private groups and businesses and had doctors and their friends visit public officials and the heads of community organizations. During this campaign the number of papers

---

*The New York survey tested public reaction to four alternative proposals, each presented with estimated monthly costs. A compulsory insurance program covering all services for children, plus laboratory tests and visiting nurses for others, would have been approved 64 to 25 percent in a state referendum. A plan to cover hospital expenses for everyone would have been adopted 55 to 31 percent. The third alternative—covering the services in the first two plans, plus all surgical and maternity bills—would have passed more narrowly, 47 to 37 percent. But the most comprehensive plan, including all doctors' bills in addition to the services in the first three proposals, would have been defeated 38 to 47 percent. Yet among the respondents who supported any plan, this last alternative was preferred.[139]

in the state opposing the Warren plan increased from about 100 to 432. In an article in the AMA's *Journal*, the secretary of the California Medical Association explained that newspaper executives had at first been unsympathetic because doctors did not advertise. "We now have an answer to that," he continued, explaining that the association had begun advertising at the rate of $100,000 a year. "We have found the response from editors, in publicity, has been beyond anything we expected when we started the campaign."[141] The Warren plan was defeated.

In Congress, the reception of Truman's proposal was mixed. The chairman of the House committee was an antiunion conservative who refused even to hold any hearings, and in the Senate, hearings yielded more controversy than support. In his introductory remarks the first day, Senator Murray, the committee chairman, asked that the health bill not be described as socialistic or communistic. Interrupting, Senator Robert Taft of Ohio, the senior Republican, declared, "I consider it socialism. It is to my mind the most socialistic measure this Congress has ever had before it." Taft suggested that compulsory health insurance, like the full employment act, came right out of the Soviet constitution. When Murray refused to allow him to continue, Taft walked out, announcing that Republicans would boycott the hearings.[142]

While not as vehement as the AMA, most other health care interests opposed the Truman plan. The American Hospital Association favored government subsidies for private insurance. Support for voluntary insurance was also the position of such groups as the American Bar Association, the Chamber of Commerce, and the National Grange as well as most of the nation's press.

Even the agencies of the federal government did not all wholeheartedly back the president's plan. The Children's Bureau was more interested in expanding an insurance program for wives and dependents of servicemen that had been started during the war. The bureau was wary of jeopardizing the future of this program by associating it with the more controversial national health bill. The medical director of the Veterans Administration opposed the Truman plan, and the chief of the Public Health Service was "decidedly cool."[143]

In 1946 Truman himself gave the proposal only occasional publicity. Even though in the spring of that year he expressed some hope that the bill would pass, its chances were nil. In August, the president signed into law the Hospital Survey and Construction Act, which carried out the first recommendation in his plan. But this part had the approval of the AMA; its approval was no sign the rest would be carried out.*

---

*On the hospital construction program, see Book Two, Chapter 3.

Although the supporters of the president's program said they would try again after the next election, the Republicans took control of Congress in 1946 and had no interest in enacting national health insurance. Senator Taft, who now replaced Murray as chairman of the Committee on Labor and Public Welfare, had his own plan for the nation's health: a system of welfare medicine for the poor financed by federal aid and administered by the participating states. Liberals objected that the program segregated the poor from other Americans, subjected them to a humiliating means test, and provided charity rather than the right to service which they would have under health insurance. Taft responded that his plan left most Americans to pay for medical care as they paid for other commodities. Only the poor, he argued, should be subject to "compulsory" medicine and they should "have to take it the way the State says to take it."[144] Taft, however, made no serious effort to pass his measure and may have proposed it only to gain AMA support in his bid for the presidency.

The Republicans now charged that national health insurance was part of a larger socialist scheme. In May 1947 Senator Homer Ferguson accused the administration of illicitly spending millions "in behalf of a nationwide program of socialized medicine." A House subcommittee investigating government propaganda for health insurance concluded that "known Communists and fellow travelers within Federal agencies are at work diligently with Federal funds in furtherance of the Moscow party line." The charge centered on one employee on I. S. Falk's staff who had written a positive account of socialized medicine in New Zealand. The Federal Security Administrator immediately called off a trip by the suspect employee and ordered an FBI investigation, which later cleared him of any communist affiliations.[145]

If the Republicans used health insurance as a symbolic issue for political purposes, so did Truman. The president and his aides focused more attention on the national health bill as the 1948 election approached. FSA Administrator Oscar Ewing convened yet another conference to define the nation's health needs. Though this National Health Assembly only endorsed voluntary insurance, Ewing transmitted a final report to the president reaffirming the need for his original program.[146] In his campaign, Truman cited national health insurance as an example of the Republican "do-nothing" Congress that had obstructed his best efforts to secure liberal programs. Fighting to keep votes from the left-wing Progressive candidate Henry Wallace, Truman continually hammered at the issue, promising national health insurance if the Democrats were returned to power.

After Truman's surprise victory, the AMA thought armageddon had come. It assessed each of its members an additional $25 just to resist health insurance and hired Whitaker and Baxter to mount a public relations campaign that cost $1.5 million in 1949, at that time the most expensive lobbying effort in American history. As in California, Whitaker and Baxter used pamphlets, the press, public speakers, and private contacts to stress that voluntarism was the American way and to persuade private organizations—1,829 of them, according to its count—to endorse the AMA position. "Would socialized medicine lead to socialization of other phases of American life?" asked one pamphlet, and it answered, "Lenin thought so. He declared: 'Socialized medicine is the keystone to the arch of the Socialist State.' "[147] (The Library of Congress could not locate this quotation in Lenin's writings.) So successful was the campaign in linking health insurance with socialism that even people who supported Truman's plan identified it as "socialized medicine," despite the administration's insistence it was not. Support in public opinion polls, among those who had heard of Truman's plan, dropped from 58 to 36 percent by 1949; three quarters of those who had heard of the plan knew of the AMA's opposition.[148] As anticommunist sentiment rose in the late forties, national health insurance became vanishingly improbable.

Yet compromises were available that might have faced less opposition. In November 1947 the financier Bernard Baruch recommended a national system of voluntary health insurance for high-income Americans and compulsory insurance under Social Security for low-income people, an arrangement common in many Western countries and similar to the original Progressive era proposals. Because of possible business support for Baruch's plan and the likely approval of some Southern Democrats, Michael Davis urged it be given consideration. The AF of L was willing, if necessary, to exempt families with incomes over $5,000 a year as well as farmers. This compromise, however, was doomed as Truman's breach with Southern Democrats over civil rights widened.[149]

A second compromise, sponsored by several Republicans in Congress, including Senator Jacob Javits of New York and Representative Richard Nixon of California, called for a locally controlled, government-subsidized, private nonprofit insurance system, with premiums scaled to subscribers' incomes. Unlike other Republican proposals, this one had no means test. Altmeyer later wrote that the Democrats made a serious mistake in not seeking a compromise of this sort.[150] Another proposal for subsidizing the purchase of private insurance by the poor, sponsored by Representative Lister Hill and Senator George Aiken, had considerable support, but neither the AMA nor liberals were interested.

The deadlock over health insurance stands in contrast to the expansion of Social Security in other areas during the postwar period. Amendments passed in 1950 broadened coverage under old-age and survivors' insurance to include an additional 10 million Americans and raised payments by an average of 80 percent. The opposition of the AMA and the Chamber of Commerce, however, still blocked the addition of coverage for those permanently and totally disabled before age sixty-five. The AMA denounced disability insurance as "another step toward wholesale nationalization of medical care and the socialization of the practice of medicine."[151] Yet in an obscure provision, the 1950 amendments provided matching funds to the states for payments to doctors and hospitals for medical services to welfare recipients. These "vendor payments," as they were called, increased the federal subsidies for welfare medicine that had been growing quietly since the Depression.

The passage of these amendments, with no provision for health or disability insurance, confirmed the pattern of government intervention since 1935. Instead of a single health insurance system for the entire population, America would have a system of private insurance for those who could afford it and public welfare services for the poor. The year 1950 also saw the attention of the Truman administration turn to Korea and the decline of any serious effort to pass national health insurance. Discouraged by yet another defeat, the advocates of health insurance now turned toward a more modest program they hoped the country would adopt—hospital insurance for the aged.

As the movement for national health insurance stalled, the coalition supporting it began to break up. A faction within the Committee for the Nation's Health, led by Albert and Mary Lasker, two wealthy donors, urged that the committee shift attention from health insurance to federal aid for medical education and research. Michael Davis resisted this change, and when organized labor supported Davis, the Laskers and the Rosenwald family withdrew their financial support. Although the Democratic Party and organized labor made up the deficit for a few years, the committee finally went out of business in 1956. So closed yet another effort at reform.

Three Times Denied

Why had reform failed yet one more time?

The burial of national health insurance during the cold war was only the culmination of a long process of treating it in symbolic terms. America is frequently described as a less ideological society than Europe, more given to interest-group than ideological politics. The AMA's battle against health insurance is often cited as a premier case of interest-group political influence. But throughout the debate over health insurance in the United States, the conflict was intensely ideological, much more so than in Europe. The interest groups opposed to health insurance repeatedly found it useful to cast the issue in ideological terms. By accusing the supporters of health insurance of being the agents first of German statism and then of Soviet communism, they meant to inject a meaning into health insurance that the reformers deeply resented. The reformers' efforts to detoxify the conflict were to no avail. And their attempt to present national health insurance as a technical matter of meeting the "health needs" of the society had its ideological bias, too.

Each side in the controversy sought to prevail by linking its case to some deeply rooted aspect of American belief (liberty for the opponents, and efficiency and fairness for the supporters). The opponents did not win because their views were more truly rooted in American culture than those of the supporters. Each side had a plausible case in playing up the American values that favored its cause. So the values themselves do not provide an explanation for the outcome.

Public opinion, as I indicated earlier, was highly malleable. It was generally in favor of health insurance but uncertain as to what kind. The opponents were able to take advantage of this uncertainty to nullify whatever advantage the reformers originally held in public support. Then, like many other highly organized lobbies, they were able to marshall political influence to prevent any action from being taken against their interests.

Between the two sides in the conflict, there was a gross imbalance in resources—partly material, partly social, partly symbolic. And these imbalances reinforced one another: The edge that the opposition enjoyed in its social bases of support could be translated into material advantages and means of influence.

The gap in material resources was overwhelming. While the reformers struggled along on shoestring budgets, the opponents had access to considerable wealth. The annual budget of the Committee for the Nation's Health was about $50,000; in 1950 it spent only $36,000. That same year, the AMA spent $2.25 million in its "national educational campaign" against national health insurance. More than $1 million was spent in two weeks in October alone, just before the 1950 congressional elections. During that period, the AMA also offered businessmen the opportunity to join in sponsoring advertisements denouncing compulsory health insurance. Companies paid over $2 million for this privilege. In those two weeks, as Monty Poen describes it, "every bona fide weekly and daily newspaper in the United States (10,033 in all) carried a five-column-wide, fourteen-inch-deep ad from the AMA or from one of its business allies decrying the enemies of free enterprise, while 1600 radio stations broadcast spot announcements and 35 magazines carried similar advertisements."[152]

But this material advantage, as the participation of business in the AMA's campaign suggests, was itself only a reflection of the ample social foundations of the opposition's strength. Beginning with the National Civic Federation and the insurance industry during the Progressive era, the most powerful economic interests in the society had opposed health insurance. Both economic and ideological considerations brought the AMA its business support. Many employers did not want the additional cost of health insurance, which constituted a de facto increase in the minimum wage, while others stood to gain from providing health benefits on their own. And, more generally, they shared a desire to draw the line against socialism. The AMA also benefited from alliances with the specific industries that profited from a private market in medical care. Organized medicine received large contributions from pharmaceutical firms to fight health insurance, in addition to the revenues from pharmaceutical advertising in AMA journals. The doctors received this support in part because of the strategic location they held in the marketing of drugs; their gatekeeping function allowed them to collect a toll for use in political agitation. Physicians were also able to draw upon the elaborate network of contacts that medical practice yields. Congressmen and state legislators, newspaper editors, and other community leaders frequently found their personal physicians paying them a visit to talk about health insurance. Many doctors' offices became outposts in a political struggle, dispensing literature, cartoons, and other propaganda against "socialized medicine."

The changing ideological temper of the postwar period was itself a resource for the opponents of health insurance. The forties witnessed a growing confidence in American capitalism as anxiety about a relapse into Depression abated. In 1942 a Roper poll for *Fortune* had found that only 40 percent of Americans definitely opposed socialism, while 25 percent were in favor of it and 35 percent said they had an open mind. By 1949 a Gallup poll found that only 5 percent of the public wanted to move more in the direction of socialism, while 61 percent wanted to move more in the opposite direction.[153] This cold war ideological shift was not decisive. Otherwise one would not have expected the liberalization of Social Security in 1950. The rejection of health insurance stands out as an exception to the postwar pattern of rising social welfare expenditures in the United States and other advanced Western societies. In most of Western Europe, governments that were no less anticommunist than the United States took part in the steady expansion of health insurance to all sectors of the society. Only in America was growing anticommunism channeled into opposition to health insurance.

In the face of all these considerations—material, social, symbolic—the potential supporters of national health insurance sought other remedies to their problems. The middle class continued to buy private insurance, and the unions began to look to collective bargaining for health benefits.

Another large group, American veterans, received extensive medical care in the hospitals and clinics of the Veterans Administration (VA), which were greatly expanded and modernized after the Second World War. Veterans were entitled not just to treatment for war-related injuries, but to all medical care to the extent the VA had room for them. A rule requiring them to vouch that the services were otherwise beyond their means was not seriously enforced. So this large group of working-class, predominantly white males was able to receive government-financed health services, which when advocated for other Americans were denounced as likely to undermine self-reliance. The AMA opposed the extension of the veterans' program to nonservice-connected illness, but the veterans were one lobby even the medical profession could not overcome.

So instead of the universal system that Truman had proposed, American society provided insurance against medical expenses primarily to the well off and the well organized. The people who lost out were those without membership in groups, like the veterans and unions, that had political influence or economic power. The poor, for whom health insurance was originally conceived, were precisely the ones who did not receive its protection.

The political failure of universalism also had its reflection in the fragmentation of public policy. Each government agency—the Children's Bureau, the Public Health Service—pursued its own agenda. The hospitals sought relief through aid for construction, and the medical schools through aid for research. The culmination of this piecemeal approach was categorical legislation on behalf of constituencies organized around specific diseases, such as cancer and heart disease. The opposition to compulsory insurance did not prevent a steady growth in state intervention in medical care. Government financing increased, but it was channeled into avenues that did not, at least immediately, threaten professional sovereignty.

CHAPTER TWO

The Triumph of

Accommodation

THE DEFEAT of national health insurance meant that health insurance in America would be predominantly private, but it left open what form a private system would take. Private health plans began to grow significantly during the thirties. Out of a great variety of early institutional forms, a few organizations took off into sustained growth in the forties and by mid-century settled into a relatively stable pattern. The problem now is to explain the structure and consequences of this system.

I noted at the beginning of the previous chapter that employers, unions, and insurance companies all stand to derive some advantage of good will, power, or profit from serving as a financial intermediary in health care. But once they become involved, they need to control their financial liability—a nettlesome problem because the physician's authority and the uncertainties of medical care make it hard for third parties to exercise effective control. Insurance ordinarily requires that any hazard insured against and the losses arising from it be unambiguous when they occur and beyond the control of the insured. Otherwise, the insurers cannot estimate their probable costs and the insurance itself may increase the losses—a problem known in the theory of insurance as "moral hazard." The difficulty in controlling costs in health insurance arises because sickness is not always a well-defined condition and many of the costs of treatment are within the control of the insured. The costs are also partly within the control of the physician and hospital, which may profit from additional services and raise prices as the patient's ability to pay increases. So, particularly in a society where the government does not directly finance and operate the hospitals, health insurance involves a severe problem of moral hazard. Various types of private health plans offer different responses to this problem. Some of these responses accommodate the interests of private physicians and hospitals more generously than do others, and in the differences among them lies the key to understanding why some forms of organization have prevailed over the alternatives.

The strategies that private health plans use to limit their financial risks depend on the type of benefits they provide and how the plans are controlled. Indeed, from these two variables alone, nearly all of their other characteristics can be derived. Medical benefits—leaving aside sickness and disability benefits that make up for lost earnings—can be of three general kinds:

1. Indemnity benefits, which reimburse the subscriber for medical expenses, though usually not the entire bill
2. Service benefits, which guarantee payment for services directly to the physician or hospital, often covering the subscriber's bill in full
3. Direct services, that is, the provision of health services to the subscriber by the organization receiving prepayment

Since these benefits require different kinds of transactions, they also vary in the sort of involvement they create between the third party and the providers of medical care. Each of them leads to different strategies for controlling risk.[1] And each has different organizational and political implications.

Under an indemnity plan, the subscriber incurs a medical expense and then submits a claim. Indemnity benefits typically create the least involvement between third party and provider because the third party conducts all financial transactions with the patient. Consequently, the physician and hospital need have no direct relation to the indemnity plan, and the indemnity plan has no responsibility for the quality of services the subscriber receives. Indemnity plans—generally the business of insurance companies—usually try to control their potential liabilities by excluding discretionary expenses, setting fixed limits on reimbursement for specific services and overall costs, and/or stipulating that the subscriber pay an initial deductible and ongoing share of the cost, in the expectation that this incentive will prevent or at least reduce over-use of services. Thus the indemnity plan seeks to limit costs by con-straining the consumer rather than the provider.

Under a service-benefit plan, the subscriber receives care from a phy-sician or hospital, which then, if it participates in the plan, claims reim-bursement directly from the third party. (If the provider does not partic-ipate, the subscriber may be entitled to an indemnity.) Service benefits typically create more involvement than indemnities between third par-ties and providers since the third party now pays the provider directly, which may force them to enter into periodic negotiations. The plan de-pends for its survival on the providers' willingness to accept its payments and limit the use of services. Hence, it may try to control its risks either by negotiating a service contract or fee schedule and maintaining a close relation with providers, or by monitoring their charges and behavior and excluding from participation those who abuse the plan. The second strat-egy obviously threatens the autonomy of providers, and so the control of a service-benefit plan is of vital importance to them. Though there are a few notable exceptions, most service-benefit plans have accordingly been organized by doctors and hospitals themselves through nonprofit organizations they at least initially controlled.

Direct services call for an even higher level of involvement between plan and provider: The doctors and often the hospitals are integrated into the same organization that enrolls subscribers. The plan may now try to control its financial risks through the full panoply of budgetary and organizational techniques, including regulating the facilities and equipment available to physicians and carefully screening and channel-ing patients. And since this organization is now directly responsible for the quality of services as well as their cost, it is doubly interested in in-fluencing the behavior of doctors and other providers.

Historically, plans offering these different sorts of benefits have also had different theories about what they were doing. The difference is partly expressed by the two terms traditionally used to describe what the plans provide: "insurance" and "prepayment." (I say "traditionally" because the distinction has become less sharp since the 1930s and 1940s.) On the one hand, the insurance approach aims to protect subscribers against losses that are infrequent and financially consequential. Accord-ing to insurers, expenses that are regular or small should be dealt with in a normal budget, so as not to add the administrative cost of insurance. In addition, the insurers' difficulties in preventing abuse (that is, moral hazard) have made them reluctant to cover routine medical expenses. At the other extreme, the direct-service plans see themselves as providing prepayment for comprehensive health care, including primary and preventive service. Unlike indemnity plans, they have been disinclined to make patients share in the cost at the point of treatment so as not to discourage use of preventive care in the early stages of illness. The service-benefit plans stand between the two other types: While not as comprehensive as direct-service prepayment, they at least originally claimed to cover the cost of services in full. Organizationally, they have been more like insurance firms; ideologically, more like prepayment plans.

The variations in third-party involvement with providers explain these differences in coverage. Since the direct-service plans have the most control over providers, they have less need of cost-sharing as a means of controlling their own financial risk. They are also better suited to include primary and preventive health services, which are otherwise difficult to monitor. Because the service-benefit plans may negotiate fee schedules or contracts with providers, they can partially limit their risk through these avenues. However, since the indemnity plans have neither authority over providers nor contracts with them, they need some other means to limit their liabilities—traditionally limits on the range and depth of coverage.

The variations in third-party involvement also affect the range of choice available to the patient. While the indemnity plans, having no relation with providers, typically allow subscribers free choice of any licensed practitioner or facility, direct-service plans have their own physicians and sometimes their own hospitals. The "open panel" of the indemnity plan goes with its low reliance on regulating the physician and hospital in controlling its risks, while the "closed panel" of the direct-service plan is the concomitant of its high reliance on organizing and controlling services. Once again, the service-benefit plans come somewhere in between: Most plans, controlled by providers, generally allow subscribers to use all doctors and hospitals *willing* to participate, while a few lay-controlled plans allow subscribers to choose among those *approved* to participate.

These characteristic tendencies have led plans to be associated with specific ideological views. The indemnity plans march under the banner of free choice of physician and hospital, while the direct-service plans claim an emphasis on preventive and comprehensive care, a high standard of quality, and low economic barriers to regular medical service. The service-benefit plans tout the advantages of both free choice and prepayment.

Conceivably, indemnity, service, and direct-service plans could each have been set up and controlled by investors, providers (that is, doctors or hospitals), nonprofit community boards, or consumer organizations. And, in fact, examples of nearly every possible arrangement have existed at one time or another. Indemnity plans, for example, have been organized by physicians, by groups of consumers (for example, unions), and by commercial insurance companies. Service-benefit plans were originally organized on the West Coast as investor-owned enterprises, later by physicians and hospitals, and in a few cases by unions and consumer boards. The direct-service plans have had the most diverse patterns of control: Some have been owned by investors, some by physicians or hospitals, some by nonprofit community organizations, some by consumer cooperatives. But out of the many possible combinations, three forms prevailed by mid-century: provider-controlled, predominantly service-benefit plans (Blue Cross), provider-controlled plans that mixed service and indemnity benefits in varying proportions (Blue Shield), and commercial indemnity plans. The emergence of these forms came only after a process of institutional selection in which the other alternatives were eliminated or greatly restricted in their development.

Before the 1930s, the only extensive private health plans offered direct services, usually to employees in an industry. Private health insurance had hardly developed because of what appeared to be unavoidably high expenses. The key obstacles were the difficulty in monitoring abuse, the high acquisition and collection costs because of the commissions paid to insurance agents, and the likelihood of "adverse selection" (that is, the purchase of insurance by those most likely to become sick). One partial solution to these problems lay in group enrollment. By selling insurance via employers to large groups of workers, an insurer could restrict its policies to a predominantly healthy population. Getting employers to deduct the premium from payrolls could also greatly reduce the collection costs. In 1914 the Metropolitan Life Insurance Company introduced a disability insurance plan of this sort to cover its own home office employees. In 1919 the Illinois Insurance Commission noted the potential for group health insurance, but commented that unions were opposed because they believed it to be aimed at tying men to their jobs, weakening the union, and sorting out bad physical risks. The insurance companies were still treating it as "experimental" because of fear of "simulation and malingering." In the twenties, group disability insurance became more common; the major advance came in 1928 when General Motors signed a contract with Metropolitan to cover 180,000 workers.[2] These policies were still mainly concerned with income protection rather than payment of medical expenses. A study in 1930 concluded that benefits paid out for medical expenses amounted to only about 10 percent of benefits paid under health insurance. Some policies emphasizing medical expenses were available, but they were "in no sense important in insurance, very few being issued."[3]

However, a new element in health insurance had developed quietly during the 1920s: the rising costs of hospital care and the new salience of such costs for middle-class families. This development had opened up a new market for health insurance, just as it had changed the politics of health insurance. It lay waiting for some organization to master the problems of adverse selection, acquisition costs, and provider acceptance when the Depression struck in 1929.

THE BIRTH OF THE BLUES, 1929–1945

The Emergence of Blue Cross

In 1932 the Committee on the Costs of Medical Care reviewed some twenty-five different plans and experiments in medical care and health insurance then in progress. Inconspicuous among these (number 19 to be exact) was insurance for hospital care, which the CCMC dismissed as failing to encourage preventive services or group practice and too limited even to cover most high-cost illness.[4] The authors of the report, like others at the time, had no idea that "group hospitalization" would shortly become the gateway to health insurance in America.

The conventional account of the history of Blue Cross puts its origins in Dallas in late 1929, when the Baylor University Hospital agreed to provide 1,500 school teachers up to twenty-one days of hospital care a year for $6 per person. Soon Baylor extended the arrangement to other groups including several thousand people. Several other community hospitals in Dallas adopted similar plans. Dallas' Methodist Hospital used a private solicitation company, grandly called the National Hospitalization System, which charged $9 a year, retaining one third for expenses and profits.[5] These early arrangements were all direct-service plans, set up by individual hospitals in competition with each other.

As these plans emerged, the Depression began to expose the financial insecurity of the nation's voluntary hospitals and encourage them to turn to insurance for a solution. In just one year after the crash, average hospital receipts per person fell from $236.12 to $59.26, and average hospital deficits rose from 15.2 to 20.6 percent of disbursements.[6] In 1931, according to AMA data, only 62 percent of the beds in voluntary hospitals were occupied on an average day, compared to 89 percent in government hospitals.[7] In late 1932 the president of the American Hospital Association said in a letter to its members that the AHA "would be unmindful of the members' interests if it did not recognize the possible breakdown of the voluntary hospital system in America . . . ."[8] And in a book published that year called *The Crisis in Hospital Finance*, Michael Davis and C. Rufus Rorem warned that hospitals could not continue to rely on patients to pay all their bills when they were hospitalized; the costs had to be budgeted in advance through insurance. "The life of voluntary hospitals is threatened because of the instability and unevenness of this main source of income," they wrote, referring to payments by patients.[9]

Single-hospital plans, like those developing in Dallas, might well have brought more instability to the hospital industry because of the competition they would have promoted. But another response was already developing. In July 1932 the community hospitals of Sacramento jointly offered hospital service contracts to employed persons, and in January of the following year, hospitals in Essex County, New Jersey, authorized a similar joint plan. In February the AHA approved hospital insurance as "a practicable solution" to the problem of distributing the costs of hospital care, and that spring its Council on Community Relations and Administrative Practice adopted some guiding principles. The plans were to be nonprofit, to emphasize the public welfare, and to limit themselves to dignified promotion. They were only to cover hospital charges, thereby not infringing on the domain of private practitioners. And, most important, they were to provide "free choice" of physician and hospital, a requirement that ruled out the single-hospital plan.[10]

City-wide plans were organized in St. Paul that July, and the next year in Washington and Cleveland.

Unlike insurance companies, these plans were organized with hardly any starting capital. The Cleveland plan, for example, was launched with only $7,000 from a local welfare organization. This was possible because of "hospital underwriting." Instead of backing the promise of service with financial reserves, the plan had its member hospitals agree to provide service regardless of the remuneration they would receive. The hospitals' guarantee of benefits took the place of the capital funds that the plans would have otherwise needed to protect subscribers' interests.[11] "The drive and enthusiasm for the Blue Cross idea," writes Odin Anderson, "originated with the early pioneers, not the hospitals."[12] But it was the hospitals that provided the underwriting: Other proposals, as we shall see, also had supporters with a lot of idealistic enthusiasm, but no resources—and that made the difference.

The first few plans had been regarded as nothing more than the sale of hospital services on a prepaid basis and, therefore, within the voluntary hospitals' legal powers. In New York, however, the state superintendent of insurance ruled that a hospital-service plan would be insurance and hence subject to all insurance regulations, including requirements for reserves. So hospital and medical leaders pressed for a special enabling act, which became law in New York in May 1934, exempting such plans from the reserve requirement. At the same time it provided that the insurance department regularly review the plan's rates and financial condition. The law also required that a majority of the directors of the plan be administrators or trustees of the hospitals that contracted to provide service. The hospitals were able to gain this authority since they were underwriting the plans. And in several plans that ran into trouble over the next decade, including New York's, the hospitals were obliged temporarily to accept reduced payments. This guarantee faded in importance, however, as the plans developed their own reserves, which were, in effect, contributed by subscribers.[13] But the original hospital underwriting provided a basis of legal support for long-term control of Blue Cross by the voluntary hospitals.

The question of hospital control would not have been so important, except for the drift from competitive, single-hospital to community-wide plans that effectively became monopolies in hospital prepayment. Rorem, who became the AHA's chief expert on group hospitalization, ruefully recalled in 1944 that the early single-hospital plans had resulted in "competition among the hospitals, and interference with the subscribers' freedom of choice and the physicians' prerogatives in the care of private patients."[14] It is unclear, however, why subscribers would have had less choice if they could choose from a variety of plans offered by hospitals in their community. The AHA did not encourage community-wide plans in addition to single-hospital plans, but instead of them. In this respect it denied consumers the choice of contracting with a single-hospital plan and possibly securing a more favorable price.[15]

Whether because they were less attractive to consumers or because they were actively discouraged by the AHA and local hospital councils, the single-hospital plans grew more slowly than the community-wide ones. In July 1937 Rorem could report that while the single hospital plans had 125,000 subscribers, about as many as a year before, the "free-choice" plans had grown from 200,000 to 800,000. The New York plan alone had 350,000 subscribers.[16]

The AHA now took an active role in promoting group hospitalization. In 1937 it requested a grant from the Julius Rosenwald Fund to set up a Committee on Hospital Service (later called the Hospital Service Plan

Commission) to aid community efforts. Rorem became executive director. The following year this committee adopted a revised set of principles for Blue Cross plans, specifying that there be no competition
among them. Each was to have its own defined territory. The AHA now
also stipulated that plans be supervised by the states through insurance
or other departments, that they provide reserves of service rather than
cash, and that they offer service benefits rather than indemnities.[17]

By 1939 twenty-five states had passed special enabling acts for hospital service plans. Like the original New York law, these typically provided that a majority of the directors would represent hospitals, gave
the insurance commissioners the power to review rates and financial
operations, and declared the plans charitable and exempt from taxes.
(In several other states, Blue Cross plans were allowed to operate under
general incorporation statutes, which have no requirements for reserves.)

Blue Cross had been started against the advice of professionals in the
insurance industry. Actuaries did not believe adequate statistics were
available to predict losses with confidence. Moreover, service benefits
violated the concept of limited liability and the rule that insurance
should never increase the hazard. "Insurance theory," writes Duncan
MacIntyre, "says that the hazard insured against should be definite and
measurable. In some respects service contracts were like blank checks
for subscribers, physicians, and hospitals; they were open-ended and
did not limit the plans' dollar liabilities." Their "first-day, first-dollar"
coverage would encourage hospitalization. Initially, one insurance expert later recalled, "a group of insurance men . . . told Mr. C. Rufus
Rorem that the [hospitals' financial problems] could not be solved by
insurance." But when Blue Cross defied their expectations, the companies were, as C. A. Kulp describes it, "half-dragged, half-lured" into the
field. In 1934 commercial carriers began offering indemnity coverage
against hospital expenses on a group basis. Four years later they extended group coverage to surgical bills.[18]

Since it enjoyed tax exemptions and privileged relations with hospitals, Blue Cross held an early advantage over its commercial competitors. However, the insurance companies had larger financial resources
and long-established relations with employers. By 1940 the insurance
companies had about 3.7 million subscribers, while the thirty-nine Blue
Cross plans in operation had a total enrollment of more than 6 million.[19]

Holding the Line

The AMA looked guardedly upon these developments in hospital insurance, anxious to prevent any invasion of its territory. "If hospitals
are permitted to include medical services in their contracts for medical
care," the association warned in 1935, "the avenue is opened and the
precedent set for the practice of medicine by hospitals."[20] Though the
AMA endorsed voluntary hospital insurance in principle in its response
to the national health program of 1938, it warned again that "these plans
should confine themselves to provision of hospital facilities and should
not include any type of medical care."[21] The physicians objected, for
example, that radiology and anaesthesia were medical rather than hospital services and so ought not to come within hospital prepayment
plans.

Yet while quarreling over their exact boundaries, hospitals and doctors basically succeeded in accommodating each others' interests by
splitting off hospital from medical insurance. Doctors undoubtedly benefited from this new development. Davis and Rorem pointed out in 1932
that among uninsured hospital patients, the doctor was the "residual
creditor." In a small study they conducted, patients paid a lower proportion of doctors' than hospitals' bills for hospitalized illness.[22] But once
insurance paid the hospital bills, patients were more likely to be able
to pay their physician. A 1936 survey of local doctors' response to the
Baylor Hospital plan found overwhelming approval: Nearly half said
the plan made it easier to collect professional bills.[23]

But physicians were still wary of applying the same principles to medical care. Many doctors, like those who wrote the CCMC minority report, suspected that voluntary health plans would only be a bridge to
compulsory insurance and that any financial intermediary would ultimately impose controls on their incomes. In June 1934, just before the
battle over Social Security began, the AMA spelled out the conditions
it required of private health plans in ten principles for medical service.[24]

These ten principles, a kind of codification of professional ideology,
expressed plainly and without reserve or qualification the doctors' sense
of their own prerogatives. "All features of medical service in any
method of medical practice should be under the control of the medical
profession," ran the first principle. The fifth described all the institutions involved in medical care as "but expansions of the equipment of
the physician" and added, "The medical profession alone can determine the adequacy and character of such institutions." According to

the tenth principle, "There should be no restrictions of treatment not formulated and enforced by the organized medical profession," which in other words meant the AMA should formulate and enforce whatever restrictions on treatment there might be.

The second, third, and fourth principles defined acceptable relations between doctors and patients. Stated the second: "No third party must be permitted to come between the patient and his physician in any medical relation." Rule 3 insisted that patients had to have "absolute freedom to choose a duly qualified doctor of medicine . . . from among all those qualified to practice and who are willing to give service." The fourth principle maintained that "a permanent, confidential relation between the patient and a 'family physician' must be the fundamental, dominating feature of any system."

The reformers of the thirties did not disagree with these principles, including the prerogatives of the profession. The controversy centered on their economic implications. The doctors took professional authority, patient confidentiality, and free choice to require a specific set of economic relations, and these were spelled out in principles 6 through 9. "However the cost of medical service may be distributed," ran principle 6, "the immediate cost should be borne by the patient if able to pay at the time the service is rendered."[25] This was the basic point of contention, for it meant that except for the poor, no form of health insurance was acceptable that paid doctors' bills as opposed to indemnifying patients. Indemnity plans might be allowable; service-benefit and direct-service plans were definitely not. In other words, doctors would not accept any system of payment that confronted them with an organized payor. Principle 7—"Medical service must have no connection with any cash benefits"—was now generally accepted by reformers. Eight was more disputed: "Any form of medical service should include within its scope all qualified physicians of the locality covered by its operation who wish to give service under the conditions established." Seemingly innocuous, this requirement would prevent a group of doctors from offering care to patients at any lower price than their colleagues. In the name of free choice, it effectively eliminated the possibility of competition and the right of patients to choose among competing physician groups. Finally, the ninth principle called for limiting relief programs to those below the "comfort level" of income.

In short, the AMA insisted that all health insurance plans accept the private physicians' monopoly control of the medical market and complete authority over all aspects of medical institutions.

Despite these demands, however, many forms of medical service then in operation did not comply with the AMA guidelines. Nearly all of these plans grew, in one way or another, out of industrial organizations. I earlier described the origins of industrial medical services in the mining, lumber, and railroad industries.* Even though the original circumstances that prompted these arrangements had sometimes disappeared, many of the plans had grown and been adopted by firms in other industries. As of the early 1930s, a survey showed that about 400 businesses had "more or less complete" medical care for their employees. About two million workers in America received health care this way.[26]

I also earlier mentioned the private companies in Washington and Oregon, which contracted with employers originally to care for compensable injuries but later extended their services to include care of ordinary sickness. These "hospital associations" had led physicians in those states to form their own prepayment plans, which provided comprehensive service benefits. In Washington, the state medical society in 1933 established a bureau to coordinate the county plans.[27]

There were also numerous prepaid contracts between employee associations and physician groups. In 1929, the same year the Baylor plan was initiated, employees of the Los Angeles Department of Water and Power arranged with two physicians, Donald Ross and H. Clifford Loos, to provide comprehensive services for about 2,000 workers and their families. The plan was unusual in that it provided for hospital as well as medical care. Soon other employee groups, mostly from governmental agencies, joined the program, and by 1935 the Ross-Loos Clinic had enrolled more than 12,000 workers and 25,000 dependents. Each subscriber paid $2 a month, plus some additional fees (hospitalization for dependents was not originally included). As of 1934, subscribers paid an average of $2.69 a month, less than half the cost incurred by similar urban families according to a California state survey that year.[28]

Nearby, beginning in 1933, a young surgeon named Sidney Garfield and several associates were providing medical care on a prepaid basis for some 5,000 workers who were building an aqueduct across the desert to Los Angeles. The workmen's compensation insurance companies paid Garfield a percentage of their premium income to take care of accident cases; the men contributed 5 cents out of their wages for other medical services. Five years later Garfield began providing similar services for men working at the Grand Coulee Dam for Henry J. Kaiser.[29]

And there were other such arrangements. In Dallas, a mutual benefit association of about 800 street railway workers contracted with a pri-

*See Book One, Chapter 6.

vate clinic for medical services. The workers each paid 85 cents a
month, while the company contributed $100 monthly. Streetcar work-
ers in Houston and Fort Worth worked out similar prepayment
plans.[30]

In one sense, these were simply extensions of traditional industrial
and employee medical services. Interviewed at age eighty in 1973, Dr.
Ross of the Ross-Loos Clinic, which was still operating (with over 120,000
subscribers), recalled that "no one really thought of what we were doing
as 'prepayment' in those days."[31] But in combining the prepaid employee medical contract with the independent physician group and
comprehensive care, they were actually making a more significant
change in the structure of medical services than they understood. A few
such physician-controlled, prepaid group practice plans had developed
in mining communities in the Mesabi Iron Range at the turn of the century. Some other prepaid clinics grew up along with the lumber industry in the Northwest.[32] But this type of organization would become
widespread only decades later.

The first self-consciously radical attempt to reorganize medical care
on a prepaid, comprehensive basis came out of the cooperative movement. In 1929—the year that the Baylor and Ross-Loos plans were organized—the first "medical cooperative" in America was formed in rural
Oklahoma. During the thirties and forties a number of others appeared
across the country. The medical cooperatives, as the leader of the movement explained, emphasized four principles: group practice, prepayment, preventive medicine, and—uniquely—consumer participation.[33]
The medical profession was unremittingly hostile, and by the end of
the decade succeeded in convincing most states to pass restrictive laws
that effectively barred consumer-controlled plans from operating.

The modern cooperative movement, which dates from nineteenth-
century England, has occupied a position between the great ideological
camps of the modern world. Although cooperatives express some of the
fundamental concerns of socialism for equality and collective action in
economic life, they make no direct challenge to the capitalist order. In
fact, many of their strongest supporters in America have seen them as
yet another form of free enterprise, able to compete with business on
its own terms. Similarly, some advocates of medical cooperatives argued that they were an alternative to "state medicine" and could compete with private physicians, if only given a fair chance on the free
market.

In the United States, cooperatives have been predominantly a legacy
of rural Populism, a movement with the same ambivalent relation to
capitalism. Despite many attempts in the nineteenth century, urban

craftsmen and workers failed to build their own producers' cooperatives. Farmers were more successful in creating cooperatives for marketing and other purposes. So it was no accident that a small farming community, rather than a big city, proved to be the setting for the first medical cooperative.

The cooperative health plan established in 1929 at Elk City, Oklahoma—a town of six thousand in the western part of the state—was the creation of a local physician, Michael Shadid, who had been in practice twenty-two years, seventeen of them in the same county. Shadid was a prosperous, middle-aged doctor, who as a young man had emigrated to America from what later became Lebanon. In his autobiography, he recalls a day in 1928 when he drew up a balance sheet "not primarily a financial one, but of my life as a whole." Out of this mid-life crisis came an urge to act on the socialist ideals of his youth, and from the various farm cooperatives in Elk City he took the idea of putting medical care on a new and more democratic foundation.[34]

Shadid first approached his colleagues with a plan for a medical cooperative embracing all the local physicians. He thought that if they enrolled six thousand families from the vicinity at $50 per year, they could provide medical and surgical care, protect their patients against sudden medical expenses, and with a sum of $300,000 pay twelve general practitioners and eight specialists, more than the area then had. When his colleagues proved unsympathetic, he turned to "some of the more progressive farmers," enlisting their help and obtaining membership subscriptions from them. However, once the project took form and work began on a hospital, the other physicians published a manifesto declaring the plan, as one might expect, "unethical." Had it not been for the populist Oklahoma Farmers' Union, which helped Shadid obtain a loan from an insurance company to complete the hospital, the cooperative would have failed at once.

The local medical profession then entered into a long campaign of sabotage. It tried repeatedly to deprive Shadid of his license, and it would have succeeded except for the intercession of the Farmers' Union with the governor and state legislature. The county medical society, wary of giving Shadid grounds for litigation by expelling him directly, dissolved and then reorganized eighteen months later without him, depriving him of malpractice insurance. Shadid's efforts to recruit other physicians were also undermined. The first doctor who joined left for fear of losing his license. Medical school graduates who had been approached by Shadid were informed by the local medical society that the plan was "in disrepute." Shadid found it difficult to employ qualified physicians and was saddled with incompetents. In its attack the profession used its licensing authority and network of collegial controls, while Shadid called on political allies for his defense. With timely outside support, his program was able to survive and serve as an example to a few other towns in Oklahoma and Texas where cooperative hospital associations were organized.[35]

The federal government also stimulated the development of rural health cooperatives. "Possibly as many as one fourth" of the prepayment plans set up by the Farm Security Administration in the thirties and early forties—at their height enrolling more than 600,000 low-income people—were governed by formal associations with elected boards of directors.[36]

Cooperatives appealed to many who approved government health insurance, but not all who supported one program supported the other. For example, the Congress of Industrial Organizations (CIO), at its first convention in 1938, said while health cooperatives accustomed people to distributing the costs of medical care, they were "no substitute for a national health program."[37] Shadid, on the other hand, advocated cooperative medicine as "the only successful alternative to compulsory health insurance."[38] While most progressives supported extensive government intervention, he asked government only to subsidize the poor to enable them to enroll in programs that would be otherwise autonomous and participatory.

Radical though he was, Shadid had no intention of doing away with medical authority, but he defined its jurisdiction more narrowly than did the AMA. Consumers would have control over the "business" matters of medical care, "and for this doctors should be grateful, for it leaves them free to devote themselves to their professional work." Shadid wrote, "Many doctors fear state medicine, but cooperative medicine is not state medicine. Under state medicine the state—that is, the politicians—will run the show. But under cooperative medicine, the doctor remains in control of the professional end of the work. . . . [Doctors] will deal with the board of trustees, not as individuals, but as a group for self-protection. They will have something to say about their compensation, their hours of work, their vacations, and possible bonuses."[39]

Of course, "something to say" was not exactly what the AMA had in mind. Even when direct-service prepaid plans were controlled by physicians, the AMA disapproved of them as a form of "unethical" contract practice. The founders of the Ross-Loos clinic and of prepaid plans in Milwaukee and Chicago were expelled by their local medical societies. Fee-for-service practitioners particularly resented the loss of thousands of patients because of the Depression.[40] If these physician-controlled plans were unacceptable to the AMA because they created "unfair" competition, the medical cooperatives were doubly anathema because they subjected doctors' incomes and working conditions to direct control by their clients.

The whole question of "cooperative medicine" finally came to a head when the AMA was indicted on charges of violating the Sherman Antitrust Act in its efforts to suppress the Group Health Association (GHA) of Washington, D.C. GHA was organized in 1937 as a nonprofit cooperative by employees of the Federal Home Loan Bank. The plan was to provide medical and hospital care through salaried physicians to subscribers, who were, at the outset, all federal employees, 80 percent earning less than $2,000 a year. Control of the program rested in a board elected by the membership.[41]

Even before the cooperative began service, the AMA called on legal authorities to take action against what it regarded as a form of "unlicensed, unregulated health insurance and the corporate practice of medicine." Unable to prevail on government, it undertook a full-scale campaign to put GHA out of business. As an appellate court later found, the AMA and local medical society threatened reprisals against any doctors who worked for the plan, prevented them from obtaining consultations and referrals, and succeeded in persuading every hospital in the District of Columbia to deny them admitting privileges, thereby cutting off members of the cooperative from hospital care.[42]

In December 1938 the Justice Department, in a move directed by Assistant Attorney General Thurman Arnold, secured an indictment against the national and local medical organizations and their officers for conspiracy in restraint of trade to destroy the Group Health Association. The AMA did not contest the salient facts in the case. When the indictment was handed down, Morris Fishbein, speaking for the AMA, pledged a legal effort to "establish the *ultimate right* of organized medicine to use its discipline to oppose types of contract practice damaging to the health of the public."[43] The AMA's legal defense argued that medicine was a profession, not a trade, and that the antitrust laws consequently did not apply to it. This view was accepted by a lower-level federal court but thrown out by the Court of Appeals. In 1943 the Supreme Court upheld the conviction of the AMA on antitrust violations, but by then it was little more than a moral victory for the supporters of the cooperatives.[44]

For despite the Court's verdict, the organized profession was able to block other cooperative and prepaid group practice plans from developing. The likely reprisals against a physician who joined a prepaid group were well known. Some state courts interpreted the rule against the "corporate practice" of medicine to preclude medical cooperatives as well as profit-making medical corporations. And, beginning in 1939, medical societies successfully lobbied for state intervention to assure professional control of prepayment plans. Within the next decade twenty-six states passed laws effectively barring consumer-run medical service plans. In these states, either the incorporators of a medical service plan had to be doctors, or a majority of directors had to be doctors, or (in sixteen of the states) the plan had to be approved by the state medical society. Seventeen of the states required all plans to allow free choice of physician.[45] Free choice ruled out the direct-service programs, such as prepaid group practice plans. It also prevented a service-benefit plan from including only those doctors and hospitals that might agree to charge a lower price or give better service. And since free choice was actuarially feasible in a service-benefit plan only if the doctors accepted a definite fee schedule, and since only the medical society could provide such a fee schedule, the requirement for free choice conferred a monopoly in medical-service plans on the profession.

The Physicians' Shield

The state laws banning lay-sponsored prepayment authorized service-benefit plans controlled by physicians. (Another fourteen states authorized physician-controlled plans without barring lay-sponsored programs.) But before 1939 the AMA and its constituent societies, except in Washington and Oregon, had actually never approved any kind of service plan even under professional control. The ten principles it adopted in 1934 had ruled out any service benefits. In 1938 the AMA House of Delegates added a statement that "in any plan or arrangement for provision of medical services the benefits shall be paid in cash directly to the individual member. Thus, the direct control of medical services may be avoided. Cash benefits only will not disturb or alter the relations of patients, physicians and hospitals."[46] But many state societies began to differ on this point, and in 1942 the association modified its stance, approving service benefits in a plan "sponsored by a constituent state medical society."[47] A plan that paid doctors directly was all right if the doctors ran the plan. In 1943 the AMA created a commission to coordinate medical-service plans under medical society control. Yet despite this formal approval, there continued to be much tension between the AMA hierarchy and the physicians who established what later became known as Blue Shield plans. One early Blue Shield leader later recalled, "The AMA hierarchy was unalterably opposed to Blue Cross and Blue Shield."[48]

Yet the majority of doctors accepted service benefits under medical society control as a preferable alternative to compulsory insurance and lay-controlled voluntary prepayment. One of the first statewide plans sponsored by a medical society appeared, logically enough, in California, where a government program seemed a serious possibility. The California Medical Association, after its brief flirtation with compulsory insurance in 1935, had begun considering sponsoring its own voluntary alternative. In 1939, under the leadership of Ray Lyman Wilbur, it introduced California Physicians Service, which originally offered coverage for home and office visits as well as doctors' services in the hospital. The governor of California was then advocating compulsory insurance for all workers with incomes under $3,000 a year, and so the CMA set $3,000 as the income-limit for family participation in its voluntary plan. (In 1939, more than 90 percent of Californians had incomes low enough to qualify.) That same year, the medical society in Michigan also organized a prepayment plan.[49]

In the next few years similar plans were started in New York, Pennsylvania, and other states. Their development was stimulated not only by physicians' interest in forestalling alternatives, but also by the concern of Blue Cross to hold off the commercial insurers now entering the market. While Blue Cross was barred from providing coverage of physicians' bills, the indemnity insurers were not, and so Blue Cross plans in some states took an active role in assisting at the birth of their younger sibling, Blue Shield.

The early Blue Shield plans in California and Michigan were beset by difficulties. They had no mechanisms for controlling utilization and proved unable to maintain expected levels of payment. Rather than use a fee schedule, California Physicians Service set up a "unit value" system that assigned relative values to different physicians' services in units that ideally were supposed to be worth $2.50. Doctors agreed to accept whatever payment levels the plan could afford. Because of the failure to control utilization, the units were worth just $1.30 after the first accounting period and fell to $1.10 by December 1940. After CPS excluded subscribers' first two visits from coverage and raised rates for women, payments to physicians began improving and by 1944 reached $2.25 a unit of service. But many physicians were still unhappy. Twenty-one doctors in Alameda county protested that CPS was just like socialized medicine because "an *agency* controls both cost to patient and fee to doctor."[50] These physicians sought help from northern California Blue Cross, which began offering medical and surgical coverage on an indemnity basis. CPS reacted by adding service coverage for hospital care, and so the two "Blue" plans in California found themselves in open competition with each other.

However, this was an unusual breakdown in relations. In most states, the Blue plans cooperated, often sharing administrative facilities. Blue Shield was clearly the junior partner: More than half its plans were administered by Blue Cross and had no staff of their own; only their policy-making bodies were separate. Organizationally, Blue Cross plans had a headstart of about seven to ten years, and they grew more rapidly mainly because early buyers of health insurance gave hospital coverage priority. By the end of 1945, Blue Cross had more than 19 million subscribers nationally, while Blue Shield had only about 2 million.[51]

The Blue plans also had significant differences in policy. Blue Cross was somewhat closer to the prepayment approach, Blue Shield to insurance. While all the hospital plans offered service benefits, some of the medical plans gave only cash indemnities, often limited to bills for doctors' services in hospital. The Blue Shield plans that offered service benefits restricted them to low-income subscribers. This contrast between the Blues originated from the greater use of price discrimination (that is, the sliding scale) among physicians. Many doctors disliked service benefits because they received the same fees for patients of different incomes. Accustomed to sliding their fees upward for wealthier patients, they felt service benefits caused them a net loss in earnings.[52] They were willing to provide service benefits for low-income subscribers mainly as a defensive compromise to ward off government insurance. And while assured of direct payment for low-income patients, they could still charge their wealthier clients more. Some doctors, moreover, chose not to participate in Blue Shield; only the participating physician agreed to accept the plan's fees as full payment. (Subscribers entitled to receive service benefits received only an indemnity when consulting a nonparticipating practitioner.) So Blue Shield permitted private physicians to maximize their incomes in whatever way they preferred.

Ideologically, the Blues reflected the political differences between the voluntary hospitals and the medical profession. Blue Cross plans maintained they served the entire community and presented themselves as progressive organizations. Some of the early founders of Blue Cross were not actively hostile to proposals for compulsory health insurance. Blue Shield, on the other hand, was clearly aimed at preventing a government program from being adopted. While Blue Cross maintained that it was a community-sponsored effort and democratically controlled, the Blue Shield plans had no such pretense. The medical profession maintained it had a right to a controlling voice.

The Blue Cross plans, nonetheless, were also provider-controlled. In twenty-one of twenty-eight plans surveyed by Louis Reed in 1948, hos-

pital representatives constituted a majority of the directors—in ten of
these, such majorities were required by law. Moreover, while member
hospitals chose hospital representatives and medical societies often
chose medical representatives on Blue Cross boards, the so-called "public representatives" were typically chosen by the board members whom
the doctors and hospitals had elected. Most of the public representatives, according to Reed, were "heads of large concerns, lawyers, bankers"; there was "far more representation of business or employers than
of labor or farm groups."[53]

So despite their ideological differences, Blue Cross and Blue Shield
were substantially the same. Just as the AHA opposed single-hospital
plans, so the AMA opposed prepaid group practice plans, even when
controlled by physicians. In both cases, the direct-service alternatives
would generate competition and prevent the exercise of monopoly
power. The organizations set up by the hospitals and doctors could
achieve a monopoly in service-benefit policies because no other firm
could obligate itself to pay for services without an agreement with providers about their price. The hospitals refused to make such agreements
with plans other than Blue Cross, and the doctors generally boycotted
any plan not controlled by the profession that sought to make them
abide by a fee schedule. The dependence of service-benefit plans on
the cooperation of doctors and hospitals explains why they have generally been organized and controlled by providers rather than by investors or consumers. The boycotts by providers of single-hospital plans,
prepaid group practices, and especially medical cooperatives help explain the scarcity of those direct-service alternatives. The only serious
competition available was commercial insurance on an indemnity basis,
which imposed no controls on doctors and hospitals whatsoever. As
we've seen, the AMA actually preferred indemnity insurers even to the
profession's own Blue Shield plans. So, as of 1945, the structure of private health plans, it seems fair to say, was basically an accommodation
to provider interests. While there was competition for subscribers, it
remained within the constraints the providers set.

At the same time, the private insurance system was also an accommodation to the interests of the middle class. Lower-income families were
greatly underrepresented among early subscribers to Blue Cross, as surveys in Michigan, California, and New York showed.[54] Moreover, Blue
Cross was a much better deal for middle-income than for low-income
subscribers. Indeed, that was the reason so few low-income families enrolled. Instead of the old sliding scale, Blue Cross charged the same premium for all income levels. In 1946 a New York state commission asked
what proportion of their income different kinds of families would have

to pay to receive the same level of medical service as families with in-comes of $5,000 or more. First, it assumed that families would continue to pay for services according to the sliding fees currently charged them. In that event, families earning under $1,000 a year would have to spend 7.5 percent of their income to get "full" service instead of the 4.1 per-cent they currently spent on medical care. Families earning $5,000 or more would continue to spend 2 percent of their annual income.

The commission then assumed that the families would receive full service on an insurance basis, with the same premium being charged without regard to income. In that event, families earning less than $1,000 would have to spend 15.7 percent of their income for coverage, while families with $5,000 or more income would have to spend only 1 percent of theirs. In general, insurance began reducing the proportion spent on health care once incomes passed $2,500. As the commission wrote, "Insurance presents a distinct financial advantage to those earn-ing more than $2,500 per year, since they can obtain adequate care at less than the average cost which they are accustomed to pay. For the lower-income groups, the percentage of family income required is so great as to be prohibitive."[55]

In his history of health insurance during the New Deal, Hirshfield notes that some of the plans that began during the period survived, while others did not. "How and why did this selective process work?" he asks. The answer, he says, lies in "the operation of a free and compet-itive American society."[56] This is a more rosy view than the facts permit in light of the anticompetitive efforts of the medical societies and hospi-tals to suppress alternatives and their use of state intervention to fur-ther their objectives. It is also oblivious to the economic impact on rich and poor of different forms of organization. The process of organiza-tional selection was not exactly an open and fair contest; the dominant institutional, professional, and class interests biased the outcome in their own favor.

THE RISE OF PRIVATE SOCIAL SECURITY, 1945–1959

Enter the Unions

After the Second World War, the provider-organized health plans lost some of their dominance. Unions gained bargaining leverage on be-half of their members. Several independent, lay-controlled direct-service plans gained a stable, though still peripheral position in the health care system. And the commercial insurance companies took more than half of the market away from Blue Cross. All these developments were related to the rise of a system of private social security.

Even before the war, health insurance had begun to emerge as a benefit received via employment. The use of employee groups in marketing and administration removed two long-standing obstacles to private insurance. It diminished the likelihood that only the more sickly would buy insurance, and it reduced the huge administrative expenses of individually sold policies. In this respect, it was a functional substitute for social insurance, which is built on employment relations for much the same reasons. However, as a fringe benefit, varying from one firm to another, private insurance permits the employer to enjoy some credit that would otherwise go to the government. A more or less fortuitous development during the war stimulated the interest of employers in using group health plans to improve loyalty and recruitment. In 1942 the War Labor Board decided that fringe benefits up to 5 percent of wages would not be considered inflationary, and so employers, finding labor scarce during the war, increased employee benefits to attract and keep their workers. Total enrollment in group hospital plans grew from less than 7 to about 26 million subscribers (with Blue Cross holding three quarters of the market). Yet this was still only a fifth of the population, most of whom were as yet unprotected against any medical expenses other than hospital bills.[57] The great expansion of employee health plans came after the war, and it took on new implications when in the late forties labor unions gained the right to bargain collectively for health benefits.

Collective bargaining and Social Security were the two great institutional legacies of the New Deal in social policy. The National Labor Relations Act (known as the Wagner Act), which was passed the same year as Social Security, limited the tactics employers could use in resisting unions, set up procedures for elections, and required management to bargain with unions that won the right to represent their workers. What Social Security failed to achieve in industrial welfare, the Wagner Act provided an alternative means of pursuing. So in the 1940s, when Congress again declined to add health insurance to Social Security, workers sought protection against the costs of illness through what John R. Commons once called the "private legislation" of collective bargaining.

This new setting for decision making about medical care profoundly affected its financial and organizational structure in the postwar period. Consumers previously had little organized influence in medical care, but once unions began bargaining collectively with management over health care, it was a short step for them to bargain collectively with doctors, Blue Cross, commercial insurance companies, and direct-service medical plans. For the first time, unions became a significant influence not just on the services received by their own members, but on the medical care system as a whole.

The relations of employers and workers had previously influenced health care, but in a different way. Employers and unions had both tried to use medical care to strengthen their hand in the battle for workers' allegiances. The antagonism between them had produced two separate "traditions," as Raymond Munts calls them: a management tradition of company-run medical services, strong in the mining, lumber, and textile industries; and a union tradition of labor-run clinics and insurance programs, strong only in the garment industry. Until the late forties, companies and unions had rarely cooperated in financing and administering medical care.[58]

Most of the employee benefit plans that companies expanded during World War II were management controlled. As of 1946 only about 600,000 workers, according to a Bureau of Labor Statistics survey, were covered by health plans negotiated by unions. Even in unionized industries, the unions had not been able to force management to bargain over welfare benefits. The Wagner Act required that management bargain over "wages and conditions of employment," but it left unclear whether conditions of employment included such benefits as health care. The major industrial corporations, not wishing to lose a source of company loyalty, were firmly opposed to bargaining over health and welfare. The unions resented this claim of "management prerogative." One reason they so strongly supported national health insurance was that even when they could get insurance protection, they had no role in negotiating it. The conflict was less over what share of the costs employers and workers would bear than over who would control and shape the benefits.

Nevertheless, until after the war the major industrial unions had other priorities. Preoccupied with organizing, recognition, and survival, they gave relatively little attention to welfare programs. But in 1946 the CIO declared a high priority for welfare programs, including health insurance, and by 1948 some ten unions had negotiated health and welfare plans, even though management was not legally required to bargain over those benefits.[59]

The unions' struggle for influence in welfare programs was one of their few political successes during the postwar period. Strikes during and immediately after the war antagonized much of the middle-class public, and in the backlash against the unions, employers took the opportunity to get back some of the control they had lost. Rewriting labor relations law in 1947, the Republican Eightieth Congress came close to specifically excluding benefit programs from collective bargaining. But Senator Taft, concerned that such a provision might jeopardize passage of the Taft-Hartley Act, restored Wagner's ambiguous phrase "wages and conditions of employment" in defining items subject to bargaining. Soon after, the Supreme Court ruled in the Inland Steel case that benefit plans did, indeed, come within "conditions of employment."[60] The unions had won the right to a say in health care.

This decision coincided with increasing doubts among labor leaders that Truman's national health insurance plan would be enacted and with the national campaign launched by the AMA to show that voluntary health insurance was the "American way." For the first time, the AMA was actually promoting health insurance. These were also years of increasing prosperity: Real wages in manufacturing, not including fringe benefits, jumped 31 percent in the decade after 1945.[61]

In the next few years after the Inland Steel decision, most of the major industrial unions concluded agreements for greatly expanded health benefits. Between 1948 and 1950 the number of workers covered by negotiated health plans jumped from 2.7 to more than 7 million. By the end of 1954, 12 million workers and 17 million dependents were enrolled in collectively bargained health plans. Unions were now negotiating the purchase of a fourth of the health insurance in America.[62] Management prerogative had given way to bargaining and joint control—a change that reflected the general shift in American labor relations from conflict to accommodation.

The collective bargaining agreements expanded the scope of coverage as well as employers' contributions. Coverage of medical expenses began to catch up with insurance against hospital bills. By the end of 1954, over 60 percent of the population had some type of hospital insurance, 50 percent some type of surgical insurance, and 25 percent medical insurance (though often only for in-hospital services).[63] As of 1945, according to an insurance industry study, employers probably paid only about 10 percent of the net cost of hospital and medical expenses. But by 1950 collective bargaining agreements were requiring them to pay about 37 percent of the net cost for workers and about 20 percent for dependents.[64]

Unions and management often differed about which of the two major forms of protection to provide. Many unions preferred Blue Cross because it guaranteed full payment for services, whereas the commercial companies' indemnities might leave their members with out-of-pocket expenses. Blue Cross was also more willing to expand the range of its benefits. But from management's point of view, the commercial insurers' were often more flexible because of the variety of cost-sharing provisions they were willing to provide. Also, as an industry study pointed out, insurance carriers permitted each firm to "acquire its own [health] plan, known by its own name" whereas Blue Cross kept to itself the credit for paying bills.[65]

The growth of negotiated plans forced both the Blues and the commercial companies to adapt. Cautious in their early years, they now began to liberalize their policies. Both service and indemnity plans began to cover longer hospital stays. Blue Cross had to offer a greater variety of policies to meet the flexibility of the commercial insurers; Blue Shield plans had to raise their income ceilings. The commercial insurers grudgingly became more involved in prepaying routine expenses in ways that violated the traditional theory of insurance. Blue Cross, since its organization and policies varied from one state to another, had to develop greater national coordination before it could offer coverage to the employees of companies that operated nationwide.

Structural differences among industries mediated the impact of collective bargaining on health care. The major division, generally speaking, occurred between the more highly concentrated industries with relatively few employers, and the more competitive, multi-employer industries. In the more concentrated industrial sector, unions negotiated nationally with the management of each firm, while in the competitive sector negotiations were local and often involved employer associations. The larger employers usually developed their own benefit plans, retaining control over the choice of an insurance carrier and taking care of many of the administrative details in processing forms. (Sometimes, the insurer sent its indemnity check to the employer, who in passing it on could use it "as an opportunity to impress the employee with the company's interest in his welfare."[66]) In the multi-employer industries, on the other hand, where workers frequently changed employers, the health plans were established across the industry rather than for the firm and administered by trustees chosen by both labor and management under provisions of the Taft-Hartley Act. These jointly run, Taft-Hartley funds became key intermediaries in financing health care for workers in the construction, coal-mining, and service industries.

In negotiating with large companies, unions generally bargained for a package of insurance benefits as well as for an employer contribution. (On the other hand, in bargaining with smaller employers, they typically could negotiate only a specific money amount.) The result was to give larger employers more of an interest in controlling the costs of health care, since they became committed to pay for a level of benefits, however much it cost. In the next few decades, as the benefit packages expanded, this interest was to become one of the most powerful new elements in the politics of American health care.

The effects of collective bargaining on health care were also influenced by the ideological differences among unions. Progressive unions, like the United Auto Workers (UAW), were more disposed to favor the prepayment approach, while the dominant business unions were at least initially comfortable with indemnity coverage. While the business unions regarded health insurance as one of many benefits, the reformist unions often saw their role in negotiating health plans as an opportunity to improve community health services. They wanted service-benefit or direct-service programs that offered comprehensive care and consumer participation. Though such unions were few, they played a major role in promoting the development of prepaid group practice plans in the postwar era.[67]

A Struggle for Control

Yet the union that took the lead in expanding health and welfare benefits—the United Mine Workers of America (UMWA), led by John L. Lewis—was a special case. Company-run medical services in mining communities formed part of an elaborate and deeply resented web of class domination. Among the miners the struggle for improved health care necessarily involved a struggle for control. So in the late forties, the UMWA seized an historic opportunity not just to secure more medical benefits, but to take control of medical care away from the coal operators. Though no other large union achieved as much direct control over medical care, the origins of the mine workers' medical program underline the significance of class conflict and accommodation in shaping the structure of health services.[68]

Coal mining had long been a volatile and competitive industry, subject to periodic swings of demand and to violent strife between mine operators and workers. A long period of depression beginning in the twenties had ended roughly about 1937, but competition and often violent strikes continued to disrupt the industry. Soon oil and gas would take away coal's primary markets, and the operators would come under severe pressure to cut prices and improve productivity to stay competitive. In this process, the mine workers' union was to play a crucial and unexpected role.

Class conflicts are not necessarily a zero-sum game: It depends on how they are organized and pursued. Unionization, much evidence shows, has actually improved the economic performance of many industries and firms.[69] The chief gain that employers generally derive from unionization is increased stability. Collective bargaining agreements bring greater control of wildcat strikes, less turnover of workers, more "management by policy" than by ad hoc decision making. Higher wages often increase productivity by providing an incentive for greater mechanization and eliminating the less efficient companies that cannot afford to mechanize or pay union wages. Since unionization may result in greater concentration of ownership and control, the leading firms may be willing to strike up an alliance with the unions to drive out less efficient, nonunion competitors: Both can then share in the higher profits that increased productivity and reduced competition afford. It was by making an alliance of this kind in the late 1940s that John L. Lewis secured an unprecedented agreement from the mining companies that gave the mine workers' union control of company-financed medical care.

As early as 1941 the UMWA had sought influence in selecting doctors and controlling medical facilities, but as in other unions, the issue did not become a priority until after the war. In 1946 Lewis accused the mining companies of extorting $60 million a year for "pseudo-hypothetical and substandard medical service, hospitalization and insurance." Instead of a wage increase, he demanded that operators contribute a royalty of 5 cents on every ton of coal produced to finance a welfare fund to be operated by the UMWA. When the mine owners refused, workers went out on strike April 1, 1946.[70]

This was the first of three strikes over the next four years that resulted in the transformation of the coal industry. Seven weeks after the first walkout began in 1946, Truman seized the mines to prevent a national economic crisis. Playing government off against the owners, Lewis reached an agreement with the federal administrator that provided for enforcement of a safety code, an impartial report on public health and health care among the miners, and two separate welfare funds, one mainly for pensions and the other for medical and hospital care. Lewis won complete union control over the medical fund. Obstruction by government and mineowners, however, prevented the agreement from being quickly carried out. The strike was also one factor in arousing the anti-union backlash that led to passage of the Taft-Hartley Act the next year, which specifically forbade union-controlled welfare funds to which employers contributed. But the survey of miners' health released in 1947 by the Department of the Interior revealed conditions so appalling that public sympathy finally brought about activation of the funds. When the government returned the mines in the summer of 1947, the owners agreed to pay a 10-cent-a-ton royalty and to merge the funds under a Taft-Hartley, tripartite board (one member selected by the union, one by management, and one neutral trustee).

In March 1948, however, the miners struck again after negotiations broke down, partly over the UMWA's demand for $100 a month pensions. The settlement raised royalty payments to 20 cents a ton—still inadequate to finance the benefits the UMWA was trying to guarantee. And, once again in 1949, the industry was in crisis, when the coal operators turned to fierce price cutting as coal lost its markets to oil and natural gas. Announcing that if the companies could not control overproduction the union would, Lewis unilaterally declared a three-day work week. Southern coal operators then withheld royalty payments to the health and welfare fund, and the miners went out on strike again.

But this time, under threat of another presidential seizure of the mines, Lewis struck a deal with the large operators that kept the peace in the coal industry, without interruption of strikes, for the next twenty years. The union guaranteed that it would not resist massive mechanization that would throw thousands of miners out of their jobs. The owners agreed to a wage increase, higher royalty payments to finance the retirement and health programs, and the appointment of Josephine Roche as the third, "neutral" trustee. Roche, already the fund's director, was a close friend of Lewis; her appointment as neutral trustee gave the union effective control. So, although the miners' fund formally complied with Taft-Hartley requirements, it was a union program.

The fund brought about a dramatic change in miners' health and medical care. The 1947 Interior Department report had found minimal public health and sanitary facilities in mining areas, inordinately high rates of infant mortality, and a system of medical care in which coal operators chose physicians on the basis of personal friendships and "financial tie-ups" rather than professional ability. The prepayment plans to which miners were forced to contribute were grossly inadequate. Company doctors, moreover, submitted workmen's compensation claims in only 21 percent of industrial injuries, whereas noncompany physicians submitted claims in 89 percent of such cases they treated.[71] By limiting medical care to company doctors, coal operators could deny workers verification for compensation claims as well as knowledge of industrial diseases.

The report estimated there were about fifty thousand miners disabled by mine-related injuries who needed rehabilitation. These disabled miners were the UMWA's first priority when the fund began operating in 1948. Thousands were sent off to rehabilitation centers in New York and California to be helped to resume more normal lives.

Then in early 1949, the fund began a general medical care program, initially offering comprehensive coverage, from dental care to hospitalization, and relying on the practitioners and facilities available in mining areas. The UMWA soon discovered that this was both too much and too little: too much because of the huge backlog of unmet need and the expense of unregulated fee-for-service financing; and too little because mining areas often did not have adequate facilities and competent physicians. The medical program was temporarily suspended (except for those already hospitalized) during the miners' third postwar strike. Major changes were made thereafter. The fund no longer covered home and office visits, drugs, mental hospitalization, and routine dental and eye care. Any tonsillectomies or adenoidectomies (two common sources of abuse) required prior authorization to be reimbursed. Furthermore, any doctor or hospital with which the fund had not made arrangements had to get permission before hospitalizing or performing surgery on a beneficiary. As a result, the fund could refuse payment to private doctors whom its staff physicians judged to be incompetent or excessive in their charges.

In the early 1950s, the fund also began paying doctors on a retainer basis (physicians were sensitive about the word "salary") because of continuing problems with unnecessary services, particularly hospitalization, under fee-for-service payment. Originally, the fund paid retainers to individual practitioners, but it soon began to set up multispecialty group practice plans. Open to the community on a fee-for-service basis, these clinics served miners without direct charge; their budgets were supported by the fund in proportion to the share of total services used by its beneficiaries. The fund and the community also participated in governing the clinics. A clinic's medical group could hire and fire physicians, but the community board and regional office of the miners' fund could veto any hiring decision and terminate a doctor's service on notice. The programs also promoted a different consciousness among physicians. Some now saw themselves as "union doctors," whose job was to serve the miners and their families rather than the companies.[72] Finally, in the 1950s, the miners' fund also established a string of ten hospitals in coal-mining areas.

From a structural perspective, the miners' fund began as an open-panel, service-benefit program. But this model soon proved unstable. In the late fifties, the fund moved to restrict and regulate more closely the private practitioners who continued to treat its beneficiaries. These efforts brought loud protests from medical societies. Doctors who worked for the miners were expelled or denied admission by some county associations. But by the end of the decade, all physicians and hospitals had to be on an approved list to be paid by the fund. The fund's own doctors reviewed decisions by private practitioners about referrals, hospitalization, surgery, and length of hospital stay. Doctors who violated acceptable standards lost their approval. The miners' fund was able to impose these controls—in effect, its own accrediting system— because as a self-insured fund, it paid providers directly, not via an organization like Blue Cross or Blue Shield that the providers themselves controlled. By developing group practice plans and hospitals, the union further increased its leverage with providers. The programs it organized, as well as the sanctions it gained over private physicians, radically transformed the miners from a group that was virtually powerless in health care into a major force in controlling the cost and quality of medical services in coal-mining regions.

Other unions also had a "medical education" in the fifties, as they learned the hazards and limitations of health insurance and fee-for-service payment. Union leaders began to attribute rapidly rising costs to the excess hospitalization that third-party insurance encouraged. Many union members were also annoyed that indemnity benefits often did not cover their full medical bills. It seemed that doctors, who were accustomed to setting fees according to their patients' ability to pay, were raising charges now that their insured patients could afford to pay more. "In a local in Butler, Pennsylvania," reported an official of the United Rubber Workers, "we started out with an insurance program that provided fifty dollars for the maternity fee. We had found that for a number of years the maternity fee in that community was $50.

"Strange as it may seem, in less than a year we found that the standard charge for maternity in Butler went to $75. Then we came in with the surgical schedule we now have which provides $75 for normal delivery. We now find that the normal delivery charge in Butler is $125." Bargaining for higher medical benefits seemed to benefit the medical profession more than the union's own members.[73]

The search for a remedy led in several directions. One was to shop for the best bargain among competing insurance companies. A second alternative was to monitor the cost and quality of medical service, but this was a strategy open only to a union like the UMWA that directly controlled payments to doctors and hospitals. A third alternative was to try to get physicians to accept a fee schedule. However, they were generally unwilling to do so, except when faced by a fourth possibility: the establishment of a labor health center offering prepaid medical care, or the enrollment of a union's members in a prepaid group practice plan developed by some other organization.

Most health centers set up by unions were diagnostic clinics that did not much threaten private practitioners. Unions were reluctant to go further because of medical society opposition. "There would be many occasions when medical care would be needed, maybe urgently needed, for acute illness," explained one doctor who worked for a labor health center. "Local physicians would be reluctant to respond . . . if our activities encroached upon their sovereignty."[74] However, in the postwar period a few programs—the Labor Health Institute in St. Louis being the most notable example—developed into full-scale group practice prepayment plans. Some physicians worried that organized labor might use its purchasing power to opt out of the prevailing system entirely. When unions in San Francisco were considering building their own prepaid health center, the medical society quickly condemned the idea.[75] But the threat never materialized in San Francisco or most other cities. The unions did not have the resources to carry it off. Since they were organized along occupational or industrial lines, they were not especially strong at the community level, where health services needed to be built. Nonetheless, the unions were vital in providing large numbers of subscribers for some of the new prepaid group practice programs that began in the postwar period. Indeed, the rise of group practice plans, particularly on the West Coast, might never have happened without them.

The Growth of Prepaid Group Practice

Though overshadowed by the huge expansion of the Blues and commercial insurance, direct-service prepayment plans finally gained a stable and independent position in the decade after 1945. They also began to develop into a new kind of corporate medical organization.

The early direct-service plans had been organized mainly as appendages to industry, but in the postwar period employee health benefits took the form of group health insurance rather than medical services.* Some of the old industrial plans, such as those for railroad workers, now began to decline. The railroad brotherhoods regarded the company hospitals as vestiges of paternalism and negotiated for cash benefits that would allow workers to use community facilities. The only major postwar initiative in prepayment based in an industry was the mine workers' program, an exception in this respect as in others.

Physician-sponsored plans and cooperatives also did not greatly expand. As of 1946, some 56 of 368 medical groups with three or more

*See Book One, Chapter 6, on the limited development of industrial medical care.

doctors offered prepayment plans of some kind, but these plans generally represented only part of their practice.[76] The doctors were not eager to see them expand.

The cooperative movement also did not flourish and multiply in the postwar period. The FSA plans, which had declined during the last years of the war, were finally terminated in 1947.[77] In the late forties, over a hundred small rural health cooperatives were founded. Nearly all of these were in the Southwest, fifty in Texas alone. But, opposed by doctors and short of resources, few of them survived for as much as a decade.[78] Such small cooperatives were not actuarially sound. They might perhaps have been saved by an extended, federated form of organization that would have allowed them to gain stability from larger scale, but this they never achieved. So although they originated as a rural movement, the medical cooperatives, such as they were, survived primarily in the cities.

The most important new cooperative was organized in Seattle at the end of the war by members of the Grange, the Aero-Mechanics Union, and local supply and food cooperatives. The capital for the project was raised from 400 families who as charter members contributed $100 apiece. By a stroke of fortune, a prepaid clinic in Seattle previously operated on a proprietary basis had just been sold to its physicians because of an expected decline in the city's economy after the war. The cooperative was able to buy the clinic, in the process acquiring its own sixty-bed hospital as well as some of the practice the doctors had built up. These assets provided a foundation for growth and protection against the efforts of local physicians to sink the plan. "In the face of firm opposition by the King County Medical Society which kept our physicians out of the Society, out of the Hospitals, and out of post-graduate training courses, our staff would most certainly have had no hospital in which to place members of the Cooperative," one of the original doctors later recalled. Unlike many other cooperatives, the Group Health Cooperative of Puget Sound early became committed to a policy of expansion, financed by the sale of bonds to its own members. Without government assistance, it grew steadily into the largest and most successful cooperative plan in the country. Three decades after it was established, its membership was well over 200,000, about a fifth of the Seattle area population.[79]

Another new postwar plan on the West Coast developed out of the medical services Henry J. Kaiser arranged for his employees. Kaiser had been impressed by the program Dr. Sidney Garfield had set up for his workers at the Grand Coulee Dam in 1938. During World War II, the industrialist decided to carry over the same practice of providing comprehensive health services to workers in his shipyards and steel mills on the West Coast, even though they were in closer proximity to urban medical resources. Unlike the earlier medical plans in remote areas, this new program threatened to compete with private practitioners, but because of the war, local hospitals and physicians were considerably overburdened and offered little opposition. In 1942 Kaiser set up two Permanente Foundations to run the medical programs—one for the Vancouver-Portland region, the other for his workers in Richmond (near Oakland) and Fontana, California. At their zenith, these programs covered about 200,000 people, but as the war ended, the work force declined precipitously. The plans had almost closed when in late 1945 the decision was made to open them to the public. With an almost missionary zeal, Henry Kaiser believed he could reorganize medical care on a self-sufficient basis, independent of government, to provide millions of Americans with prepaid and comprehensive services at prices they could afford. Ten years after the war, the Kaiser-Permanente health plan had a growing network of hospitals and clinics and a half million people enrolled.[80]

The impetus for another new prepayment plan came from New York Mayor Fiorello La Guardia. The Municipal Credit Union had found that the major source of financial distress among city employees was indebtedness caused by illness. In 1943 La Guardia appointed a committee to plan a prepayment program. This group, however, was hopelessly divided. The representatives of the medical profession insisted on a fee-for-service indemnity plan, while others wanted compulsory health insurance. A third faction supported prepaid group practice. The mayor agreed with the third group, dissolved the committee, and appointed a new one to make plans. In 1946 the new committee secured the necessary legal authorization, received start-up loans from foundations (later repaid), and organized medical group practices—twenty-two of them, including over 400 doctors, by March 1, 1947, when the plan began operation. Because of state law, however, the Health Insurance Plan (HIP) of New York was able only to provide medical services. Subscribers had to take out a separate contract with Blue Cross for hospital care. Employees who chose the joint HIP-Blue Cross coverage paid half the premium, the city the other half. By the mid-fifties, HIP's enrollment was also pushing a half million.[81]

The appeal of these prepayment plans originally had little to do with any price advantage in their premiums. Indeed, their premiums were usually more expensive than insurance. However, their coverage was also more comprehensive. When compared with indemnity or service-benefit plans, they had relatively few exclusions, limits, or copayments.

This "certainty of coverage" became especially important to the unions as they grew irritated with insurance benefits that not only left their members at risk for many medical expenses, but also seemed to stimulate higher prices by fee-for-service providers. The prepaid group practice plans, moreover, offered service of apparently high quality, partly because of the advantages of group practice, such as easier consultation among specialists, as well as the greater emphasis on preventive care.

Yet several factors inhibited enrollment even by some who were interested in joining. Unions that were bound by national bargaining agreements at first had difficulty working out local options to enroll in Kaiser or other prepaid groups. Also, many employers were wary of participating in any medical plan that the AMA disapproved. And, third, typically not all workers in a firm wanted to receive medical care from a group practice plan, and initially employers offered only one type of coverage.

This latter difficulty brought about a key change in Kaiser's enrollment policy. Like other health plans, it originally expanded by signing up entire employee groups via their representatives. But in 1948, at first by necessity, Kaiser participated as one of several options in a plan offered to city employees of San Francisco. The other alternatives were a service-benefit program, including all private physicians willing to participate, and two small group practice plans. This multiple-choice arrangement grew out of a crisis prompted by a massive boycott by the medical profession of the service-benefit option, originally established in 1938 as a compulsory insurance program for city employees—one of the few independent, service-benefit plans run by consumers. At its inception, over a thousand of San Francisco's 1,250 physicians had signed up to participate, which meant charging no more than the plan's fee schedule allowed. But by 1948 they were dissatisfied with the fees, worried that their participation indicated approval of compulsory insurance, and angry over a requirement that they consult the plan's director before hospitalizing a beneficiary. All but ninety doctors resigned and thereafter refused to accept the plan's fees as payment in full. While the plan could still provide indemnity benefits to its members, the boycott threatened to destroy the far greater protection that service benefits afford. It was at this point that Kaiser and the other group practice plans were brought in as additional options.[82]

"Dual choice"—so-called because employees were usually offered just two options—soon became standard practice for groups that enrolled in Kaiser. Kaiser's management initially liked the arrangement because it helped gain access to employee groups not all of whose members would find it convenient or desirable to join a group practice plan.

It also helped dispel charges by the AMA that closed-panel programs denied free choice of physician. Kaiser discovered other advantages, too. Dual choice provided a periodic outlet for patients who were dissatisfied, and it limited the bargaining power of union negotiators, since the union's members now decided individually rather than as a group whether to continue to enroll. So by 1954, Kaiser adopted the policy that any employee group for whom it provided service also had to provide its members choice of an open-panel insurer. Dual choice gradually spread from the San Francisco area to other parts of the country, though in the 1950s it continued to be an unusual practice among employers even in California.[83]

The growth of Kaiser and HIP aroused deep anxiety among private practitioners in California and New York because these new direct-service prepayment plans, unlike the old industrial medical services, were attracting middle-income patients who were the profession's bread and butter. Doctors in one California community after another went into a panic when the "closed-panel colossus" (as one medical magazine called Kaiser) moved into their area.[84] The usual methods of fighting prepayment did not work. The medical societies could not block Kaiser's access to hospital facilities because Kaiser built its own hospitals. Legal actions proved useless. The courts in the Pacific States upheld lay-controlled prepayment plans. In 1951 the Supreme Court of Washington State ordered the King County Medical Society to stop boycotting Group Health Cooperative.[85] So the standard response of physicians in a community was to organize a more generous service-benefit plan than Blue Shield offered in order to compete more effectively with Kaiser. After Kaiser had signed up several large employee groups in San Pedro, just outside of Los Angeles, the doctors in the community organized an "all-out" service-benefit plan that cut fees and left no extra charges for any service covered. Notwithstanding professional rules against advertising, the medical society ran large notices in the newspapers and on highway billboards to publicize their new program.[86] In Pittsburgh, California, the doctors, their wives, and members of the local hospital auxiliary handed out literature to workers in the parking lot of a steel factory as shifts changed on the day in 1953 when the workers voted on whether to enroll in Kaiser or a new "Doctors' Plan." A sound truck exhorted workers to "Retain your family doctor," and warned, "Don't be a captive patient." At one point, as Joseph Garbarino describes the campaign, the doctors thought they might be forced to leave the parking lot and made plans to drop leaflets from an airplane. But despite all efforts, the workers voted 2,182 to 440 in favor of Kaiser.[87]

One of the most elaborate and successful responses came in San Joaquin County, south of Sacramento, where in 1954 the local physicians assumed the risk for a service-benefit plan that offered benefits as comprehensive as Kaiser's. Like the old FSA arrangements, the doctors agreed to accept reduced fees if the plan's revenues were inadequate and to police their own membership to prevent abuse. This was the germ of what later came to be called "independent practice associations," plans that charge consumers a flat rate per year for service but pay private physicians by fee-for-service.

The response of the medical profession to Kaiser was entirely in keeping with the long-term pattern of defensive prepayment adopted ever since physicians in Washington and Oregon set up their own plans to fight commercial prepayment organizations. Blue Shield had begun as a defensive program and evolved toward less generous benefits as the threat of compulsory insurance eased. Where a new threat emerged, such as Kaiser in California, the medical societies came forward with more comprehensive benefits and a greater willingness to control prices and curb abuses by their members. Like other monopolies, the profession adjusted its policies when faced by the prospect of competition.

Yet these price-cutting and public relations efforts by physicians failed to prevent Kaiser's growth. Nor did boycotts lay low Group Health Cooperative or HIP. Unlike lay-sponsored service-benefit programs, prepaid group practice plans, particularly if they have their own hospitals, are relatively insulated from the pressures of private physicians. Service benefits require the cooperation of private practitioners, who hold the power to turn service benefits into indemnities if they call a boycott. This was what happened to the city employees' service-benefit plan in San Francisco and the earlier commercial plans in Washington and Oregon. Only the United Mine Workers was able to run a successful service-benefit program independent of the medical profession. With 1 million beneficiaries, the mine workers' fund had sufficient market power, particularly in small mining communities, to secure cooperation from doctors. Even so, the fund had to sponsor its own medical group practices. In general, the more self-contained a lay-controlled prepayment plan, the less it depends on private practitioners and the better its chances of survival in a hostile environment. This is why in America consumer-controlled programs have also tended to be group practice plans.

In addition, direct-service, group practice plans have broader, more effective, and less intrusive means of influencing physicians than do service-benefit plans. Under service benefits, a plan can control its costs only by regulating physician decisions at a distance. The San Francisco program was plunged into crisis when it tried to limit professional sovereignty (that is, to review doctors' decisions about hospitalization). The group practice plans, on the other hand, can create an environment of constraints, such as a fixed supply of hospital beds, which are then taken as given in day-to-day medical decision making. The plans can also provide incentives to encourage the physicians to identify with the organization's needs and participate in keeping down its costs. Kaiser and other prepaid plans have had relatively low rates of hospitalization, in part because they have had no incentive to hospitalize, but also because they can influence their staff without compromising the physicians' sense of their own authority and autonomy.

The prepayment plans varied in the ways they incorporated physicians into their organization. At Group Health Cooperative, the doctors were employees. At HIP, in contrast, the physicians were organized in independent medical group practices, which owned their own facilities and had fee-for-service as well as prepaid patients. (This arrangement gave rise to continual complaints that HIP's subscribers were being given short shrift.) At Kaiser, the physicians were originally organized during the Second World War as a proprietary group, Sidney Garfield & Associates. After the war, as part of the general reorganization of the plan as a nonprofit trust, the doctors in different regions reorganized into partnerships. As in HIP, the medical groups contracted with the health plan to care for patients. But Kaiser's doctors could not see their own private patients and did not have title to the facilities. So though they enjoyed some collective autonomy in judging each others' performance and determining salaries and promotions, they were not as independent in their command over resources as were HIP's physicians.

These three plans stood for radically different theories of organizational government. Group Health Cooperative was owned by its membership, who voted on a one-member, one-vote basis to elect trustees and to make major policy decisions. The cooperative sought active participation by conducting referenda by mail and periodic assemblies.[88] Kaiser, on the other hand, declined to give its subscribers any role in governing the plan. Power resided in two corporations controlled by the Kaiser family and its company executives. HIP, yet a third type, was governed by a self-perpetuating board that included liberal representatives of business, labor, the medical profession, and government. Cooperative democracy, corporate capitalism, interest-group pluralism—any of these was possible within the relatively self-contained structure of prepaid group practice.

Lay control, in whatever form, was long unacceptable to the AMA.

But because of a long string of legal defeats, the association gradually became reconciled to vigilant coexistence with prepaid group practice. In 1955 the AMA appointed a special commission on medical plans, headed by Dr. Leonard Larson, chairman of its board of trustees. Its final report, released in 1959, still condemned programs that "purport to provide medical care." Financing, it maintained, was "the only proper function of a medical care program." But the committee also found no evidence of any lay interference in medical decisions in Kaiser or other prepaid plans, and it indicated that free choice of medical plan was an acceptable substitute for free choice of physician.[89] Though within weeks the AMA House of Delegates again affirmed the need for free choice of physician in any health plan, the Larson report ended official sponsorship of reprisals against prepaid group practice.

Besides the risk of antitrust prosecution, one reason the AMA was willing to accept a truce with lay-controlled prepayment plans was that they represented only a limited threat in the 1950s. Despite their success in a few areas, such plans were small by comparison with commercial insurance, Blue Cross, and Blue Shield. The need to avoid dependence on private practitioners meant that they had to establish their own facilities. As a result, they were extremely costly to start. Without any government aid, capital for such ventures was scarce. So for the time being, prepaid health plans were no more than a peripheral development.

The Commercial Edge

After the war, commercial indemnity insurance enjoyed the most rapid expansion of any form of health coverage. By the early 1950s, not only did commercial insurers have more subscribers than Blue Cross and Blue Shield, but they were also forcing the Blues to do business on their terms. And, paradoxically, by that very process, they were pushing the system ultimately toward some form of government intervention, as voluntary health insurance became increasingly incapable of providing protection to high-risk groups like the aged.

But this contradiction was barely evident during the period of rapid growth after the war. Between 1945 and 1949 commercial group hospital insurance policies jumped from 7.8 to 17.7 million; individual coverage climbed to 14.7 million. Minus duplication, the total number of people covered solely by commercial insurers in 1949 was estimated at 28 million, compared to over 31 million enrolled in Blue Cross. (Independent plans covered about 4 million people for hospital care.) Commercial insurers were then far ahead of Blue Shield in coverage of surgical bills (22.7 versus 12 million people), and two years later, they pulled ahead of Blue Cross in hospital coverage as well. As of 1953 commercial carriers provided hospital insurance to 29 percent of Americans, Blue Cross to 27 percent, and independent plans to 7 percent.[90]

As commercial health insurance expanded, the character of the industry changed. Before the 1940s there had been a relatively small number of firms, mainly casualty insurers and specialized health and accident companies, which sold policies primarily to individuals. Between 1942 and 1949 the number of firms offering insurance against hospital expenses increased from 28 to 101. Commercial insurers continued to sell more individual policies than the Blues, but as employee benefit plans expanded, their business tilted toward group insurance. That meant a shift in industry leadership from the casualty to the life insurance companies, such as Metropolitan and Prudential, which dominated the group market.[91] The campaign that they had waged thirty years earlier against a government program was finally paying off.

The difference between the insurance companies and the Blues involved more than a contrast between for-profit and nonprofit enterprise. Indeed, whether any clear distinction can be drawn on that basis is doubtful. On the one hand, some of the leading insurance firms, such as Metropolitan, were mutual companies nominally owned by their policy-holders; all "surpluses" were supposedly returned to them. (In fact, the mutual form guaranteed that a self-perpetuating board of directors would have control of the companies' huge financial assets.) On the other hand, the allegedly nonprofit medical society plans were clearly aimed at increasing the income of the physicians who controlled them. Only the law said they were not for profit. As in the case of hospitals, providers preferred the nonprofit form of organization because of the advantages of tax exemption and the desire to avoid any alienation of control or the extraction of any profit from their services. Probably for the same reason, the provider-controlled Blue plans were more successful in holding down the proportion of income retained for administration, commissions, and "surplus." Of every dollar of premium income on health insurance, Blue Cross retained about 6 cents, Blue Shield about 10 cents, and commercial insurers 21 cents.[92] (However, the higher retention rate for the latter was due partly to a greater proportion of individual policies.) The Blues cited the fact that they distributed more of their income in benefits as evidence of their community orientation. But since they mainly provided service benefits (payments to providers), the pattern is sufficiently explained by the interests of their principals.

Despite their lower overhead, the Blue plans had several decided disadvantages in competing with commercial insurers. While the commercial carriers could provide employers one-stop service for a variety of types of insurance, the Blues were restricted by their enabling laws to provision of health insurance only. The Blue plans were also locally controlled and loosely coordinated, which impeded their ability to offer national coverage. And many employers preferred indemnity plans because they were more flexible in the range of benefits and costs; also, indemnity plans could be organized to give the employer a direct administrative role and hence the opportunity to enjoy the gains in good will from making payments to workers at times of adversity. But probably the most important attraction to employers was that the insurance companies were willing to give them a lower price on healthy, low-risk workers.

This was called "experience rating," and it stood in sharp contrast to the way in which social insurance systems and even Blue Cross distributed the costs of health care. Under government programs of health insurance, premiums may be progressively scaled by income. Under Blue Cross, subscribers generally paid the same "community" rate, at least for group policies. (Individual policies cost more.) But under commercial insurance, every employee group was charged according to its "experience." A young, relatively healthy group received a reduced rate because the costs it experienced were low. By the same token, an older, relatively unhealthy group had to pay more because its costs were likely to be high.

Each of these practices was justified by a different theory of equity, and each was linked to specific social conditions. Social insurance redistributes costs from high- to low-risk groups, but such redistribution is possible only when the state legally requires contributions. Otherwise, the low-risk groups will not participate. Any voluntary health plan has a limited capacity to redistribute costs because it cannot compel low-risk groups to accept higher rates than their level of risk demands. If it "overcharges" them, they may be offered a cheaper rate by a competitor or simply decide to self-insure (that is, to set aside money in their own insurance fund). When the Blue plans began, they were relatively free from competition and were able to adopt uniform rates as part of their effort to make voluntary insurance available to the whole population and to forestall a compulsory program. Though hardly progressive, community rates keep down costs for high-risk groups. But in the prevailing norms of commercial insurance, equity consists in charging every group according to its risk. In this view, a community rate that charges everyone the same is inequitable because it costs healthy people too much—that is, more than they would have to pay for insurance in a competitive market.[93] Equity here is indistinguishable from the logic of competition.

Experience rating allowed the commercial insurers to undersell the Blues in competing for low-risk employee groups. Although many unions as well as employers heeded the commercial carriers' appeal to get the most out of their "welfare dollar," other unions, like the auto and steel workers, were faithful to Blue Cross because of their commitment to service benefits. Many Blue Cross leaders were reluctant to accept experience rating because it seemed to contradict their ideals and undermine their claim on subscriber loyalty. Though some plans had experience rated a few large employee groups as early as 1940, the practice became a subject of controversy when many more adopted it in the fifties. In 1952, when only 4 percent of Blue Cross enrollment was experience rated, the directors of plans in four Midwestern industrial states introduced a resolution at an annual Blue Cross conference condemning the practice as "contrary to the community service ideal" and likely to "destroy the voluntary, non-profit prepayment plans throughout the United States." A study conducted in response to the resolution urged Blue Cross plans "to make an honest effort to withstand the pressures" for experience rating.[94]

But the logic of competition played itself out almost inexorably. As the commercial insurers began to pick off the low-risk employee groups, they threatened to leave the high-cost population to the Blues. Had this process continued indefinitely, Blue Cross and Blue Shield would have been forced to raise their rates so high that even average-risk groups would have found it cheaper to buy commercial insurance. Eventually, the Blue plans would have become "dumping grounds" for the aged and the poor. This, however, was a function they preferred to leave to the government, and so, despite their reluctance, they, too, moved toward experience rating. By the end of the fifties, a majority of the plans were experience rating at least some employee groups— and as a spokesman for California Physicians Service pointed out, "Once you experience rate the good groups, you have to experience rate the bad groups too."[95]

The commitment of Blue Cross to service benefits also began to erode. As the costs of medical care and health insurance increased, the plans sought ways to keep down their premiums. One way was to raise the share of the costs borne directly by the consumer. Between 1945 and 1953, the proportion of Blue Cross enrollees with service benefits fell from 96 to 76 percent.[96]

So the competition between commercial insurers and the Blues produced a tendency toward convergence. Ironically, though Blue Cross had developed a form of insurance that insurance companies themselves were not originally willing to offer, its success invited imitators and unleashed forces that undermined the principles on which it began. But this, in a sense, was true of the entire health insurance system: While growing rapidly, it was unleashing forces that would eventually help bring about the government intervention its leadership hoped to avoid.

THE ACCOMMODATION OF INSURANCE

America had taken a different road to health insurance from the one taken by European societies, and it arrived at a different destination. The original European model began with the industrial working class and emphasized income maintenance; from that base, it expanded in both its coverage of the population and its range of benefits. The original Progressive proposals for compulsory health insurance had shared much of this orientation, except that the American Progressives had a distinctive interest in reorganizing medical care on more efficient and rational lines. The defeat of that early conception meant there was no prior institutional structure for health insurance when the middle class encountered its problems of paying for hospital costs during the 1920s and when the hospitals encountered problems meeting their expenses during the Depression. So instead of an insurance system founded originally to relieve the economic problems of workers, America developed an insurance system originally concerned with improving the access of middle-class patients to hospitals and of hospitals to middle-class patients. The Progressive interest in group practice, capitation payment, and incentives for prevention was rejected, and an insurance system developed under the control of the hospitals and doctors that sought to buttress the existing forms of organization. This was the basis for the accommodation of private insurance.

Commercial insurance companies entered the field almost by the back door. Their initial business in the field involved disability insurance for the middle class. Indemnity coverage for hospital expenses, as one insurance expert puts it, "began as a frill on the accident form."[97] Only after Blue Cross had demonstrated its feasibility did the commercial carriers become significantly involved. Indemnity plans, like the provider-controlled service-benefit plans, offered no threat of control to private practitioners. Indeed, the AMA actually preferred commercial indemnity plans to Blue Shield because cash benefits meant no interference in the individual doctor's right to set his own fees.

The system then evolved through a process of restricted competition. The competition between the Blues and the commercial plans resulted in a broader range of benefits, but it also forced the Blues to adopt experience rating. The competition that might have come from direct-service plans was a factor only in a few areas of the country, such as California. Through boycotts and other techniques, the medical profession inhibited the industry from developing in the direction of comprehensive, direct-service plans, or consumer-controlled service-benefit plans. The only way a lay-controlled program could protect itself from provider boycotts was to insulate itself through the self-contained structure of prepaid group practice, but because of the start-up costs this entailed, the lack of any government assistance, and the legal barriers in more than half the states (in contrast to the favorable enabling laws given to Blue Cross and Blue Shield), the plans could not escape from a marginal position.

Just as European health insurance reflected the earlier sickness funds and friendly societies, so American private insurance was "piggy-backed" on preexisting organizations. In the United States these were the voluntary hospitals, the medical profession, and the life insurance industry. Some of the regional differences in development show this piggy-back pattern. Blue Cross plans held an edge in the older sections of the country, the Northeast and North Central States, where voluntary hospitals were strongest. On the other hand, where hospitals were primarily proprietary and governmental, commercial insurance did better.[98] Independent plans, such as Kaiser, made the most progress in the West, benefiting from an earlier tradition of comprehensive industrial medical care in isolated communities.

Although physicians were not solely responsible for this system of health insurance, they greatly benefited from it. By deflecting insurance first into the private sector and then away from direct services and lay control, the profession was able to turn the third-party insurer from a potential threat into a source of greatly increased income. The evolution of hospitals had followed the same pattern. Initially, the rise of hospitals threatened to take income away from the general practitioners who were cut off from hospital privileges. But because of the hospitals' financial need to keep their beds filled, they opened up access to physicians on generous terms and became dependent on the physicians' good will. Similarly, government health insurance and lay-controlled prepayment threatened to limit physicians' incomes by restricting fees or the number of patients a doctor could serve. But through the use of political influence and economic power, in conjunction with insurance companies and other powerful interests, doctors were able to avoid the dangers of hierarchical control and competition. The insurance system accommodated their interests, and on those terms they accommodated health insurance.

The rise of private insurance added to the market power of the profession. Although licensing laws were the original means of restricting entry into medical practice, eligibility for reimbursement now became the chief obstacle for any competing group of practitioners. Even if midwives or chiropractors could circumvent licensing laws, they usually could not get reimbursement from Blue Shield, nor could their patients get reimbursed under indemnity plans. The insurance companies used the doctors as gatekeepers to benefits. In this respect, the insurance companies' interest in controlling costs strengthened the profession's authority.

Channeling health insurance through employment helped satisfy many interests simultaneously. As a fringe benefit, health insurance benefited the employer as well as the worker, solved problems in the marketing of private insurance, gave the providers protection against a government program, and offered the unions an alternative to national health insurance and a means of demonstrating concern for their members. Yet while serving these powerful interests, the fringe-benefit system clearly did not serve the interests of those who were retired, out of work, self-employed, or obliged to take a low-paying job without fringes. Those who had to buy insurance individually had to pay more for the same coverage than those who received it as a fringe benefit. While Blue Cross retained about 7 percent of income for administrative expenses in group insurance during the 1950s, it retained 22 percent on individual policies. And this was much better than the commercial insurers, which retained 50 percent on individual policies[99]—about as much as they had for industrial life insurance. And, of course, because the companies competed partly by seeking the best risks, they avoided many of the chronically ill and the poor altogether. The health insurance system was set up in a highly regressive fashion: first, because it was based on employment; second, because of the practices of community and experience rating; and third, because of the favorable tax treatment of private insurance. (The Internal Revenue Code of 1954 confirmed that employers' contributions to health benefit plans were tax exempt; indirectly, this exemption constituted a massive subsidy to people who had private insurance policies.) In leaving out millions of Americans, the insurance system actually worsened their position because of the inflationary effect that insurance had on the cost of medical care. Private social security was not a neutral force on those left out; it hurt them, and much government intervention was required just to redress the inequities it created.

The distribution of health insurance was a direct outcome of the sort of private system that developed in America. By mid-1958 nearly two thirds of the population had some coverage for hospital costs, the most common type of insurance. A family's chances for insurance depended on its income and the employment situation of its main earner. If a family's income were among the highest rather than the lowest third of the population, it was twice as likely to have some insurance (about 80 versus 40 percent). When the main earner was fully employed, the probability of having some insurance was 78 percent. When the main earner had only a temporary job, the probability was only 36 percent; if retired, 43 percent; if a housewife, just 32 percent; if disabled, only 29 percent. Where the main earner was employed in manufacturing, the chance of having insurance was 91 percent; where employed in construction, 65 percent; and where in agriculture, forestry, or fishing, only 41 percent. If the family lived in a metropolitan area, its chances of having insurance were 75 percent; if they lived in a farm area, 44 percent. Two thirds of those who lived in the Northeast, the Midwest, or the West had some insurance, but only about half of those who lived in the South.[100]

Yet whatever its distributive inequities, the private insurance system provided enough protection for the groups that held influence in America to prevent any great agitation for national health insurance in the 1950s. Oddly enough, although labor favored a compulsory system, its success in pursuing health benefits through collective bargaining had undermined the movement for a government program. The use of collective bargaining had created, in Garbarino's phrase, "a semicompulsory substitute for compulsory health insurance." The union shop, which in the early fifties made union membership mandatory for over two thirds of the production work force, enabled the unions to establish a "private fiscal system" able to levy a "tax" for health insurance.[101] The government supported this private tax system by making employers' contributions into it exempt from the government's own taxes. Private, voluntary insurance was neither strictly voluntary, nor strictly private, but its compulsory and public features were hardly noticed.

This new system of financing increased the share of national income going to health care and stabilized the financing of the whole industry. Prior to insurance, doctors and hospitals had to wait for months or years to be paid for their services. Money for health care came last in a family's budget, after food, rent, and other necessities had been covered. Now, most of the money for medical care was taken out of employees' paychecks before they received them. The result was that Americans did not much reduce spending for medical care during recessions. So even though government insurance was defeated, health care succeeded, as an industry, in winning a guaranteed income. In the prosperity of the postwar years, this income grew very large indeed.

CHAPTER THREE

The Liberal Years

THE POSTWAR decades of economic expansion saw a dramatic growth in the scale of American medicine. From modest prewar beginnings the United States built up an immense medical research establishment. It enlarged and equipped the most scientifically advanced hospitals in the world and created an entirely new network of community mental health centers. Between 1950 and 1970, the medical work force increased from 1.2 to 3.9 million people. National health care expenditures grew from $12.7 billion to $71.6 billion (up from 4.5 to 7.3 percent of the GNP), and medical care became one of the nation's largest industries.[1] But the growth in scale, made possible by prosperity and the rise of private health plans, was only the most visible expression of American devotion to medicine in the pursuit of health.

Americans now gave science unprecedented recognition as a national asset. During World War II the research effort that produced radar, the atom bomb, and penicillin persuaded even the skeptical that support of science was vital to national security. At the war's end, an advisory board on medical research reported, "Penicillin and the sulfonamides, the insecticide DDT, better vaccines, and improved hygienic measures have all but conquered yellow fever, dysentery, typhus, tetanus, pneumonia, meningitis. Malaria has been controlled. Disability from venereal disease has been radically reduced by new methods of treatment. Dramatic progress in surgery has been aided by the increased availability of blood and plasma for transfusions." Compared to World War I, the death rate from disease in the Army had fallen from 14.1 to .6 per 1,000 soldiers.[2]

Postwar recognition of a national interest in science and medicine also stemmed from America's new role of international leadership. The United States emerged from the Second World War as the major economic and military power in the world. European economies were devastated while American industrial production and national income more than doubled during the war. In 1947 the United States produced more than half the world's manufactured goods, 62 percent of its oil, and 80 percent of its automobiles.[3] It was also producing a larger share of the world's science than ever before (with the help, to be sure, of European scientists who had fled from the Nazis). Spokesmen for American science pointed out that it would be neither wise nor possible for the United States to depend any longer on European, much less German, scientific achievement. And in the cold war, science assumed a symbolic as well as a practical function in maintaining America's position as "leader of the free world."

At home the advance of science and medicine, like economic growth, offered the prospect of improved well-being without requiring any profound reorganization of society. Liberal opinion held that America had transcended the need for drastic political reform by incorporating progressive change into its free institutions. Medical science epitomized the postwar vision of progress without conflict. All could agree about the value of medical progress, and all could benefit from it (that is, if they could afford the cost, as the advocates of national health insurance would add). On the page that *Time* magazine devoted each week to medicine, Americans could read about the latest "wonder drugs" and other miracles of modern medicine. Here was evidence that life was getting better. Here was proof that this was already, as Henry R. Luce called it, "the American century." The routine of innovation was one of the fruits of what Luce's editors at *Fortune* wryly referred to as capitalism's "permanent revolution."

Prosperity gave Americans the opportunity to worry about their health, and it also changed the health problems they worried about. From the beginning of the twentieth century, the chief sources of mortality had been shifting from infectious to chronic disease. The Depression and the war, however, had diverted attention to more urgent needs than chronic illness. Now facing the medical problems of peace, scientists and the public became more concerned about cancer, heart disease, and those conditions, such as obesity and neurosis, on which only an affluent society can afford to dwell. And at a time when the antibiotics were providing effective therapeutic means for treating infectious diseases, chronic illness reengaged medicine intimately in questions of social behavior and moral choice.

Liberal-minded people approved of a broad extension of medical authority into the regulation of social life. The consensus of the enlightened favored substituting therapeutic for punitive responses in the social management of delinquency, alcoholism, narcotics use, and sexual deviation. Psychiatry, previously concerned primarily with the care of the insane, had been institutionally marginal in America before World War II. Now it moved into the "mainstream" of American medicine and American society and enormously expanded its claims and its clientele. Whereas formerly its province was mental illness, now it became mental health. In the postwar years, the advocacy of professional intervention to advance mental health took on an evangelistic fervor. Here politics and professionalism were at work together. With the collapse of the left as an ideological force, social reformers increasingly appropriated the language of clinical medicine. Psychiatrists were at the vanguard of this movement to redefine social problems in medical terms. Therapeutic intervention so often failed, they argued, because it was too late; what was needed was "mass preventive psychiatry" in which medical judgment participated in all manner of activities from child rearing to international peace keeping.[4]

The conflict between liberals and the AMA over national health insurance should not obscure the deeper alliance between liberalism and medicine in the postwar decades. Both liberal and medical opinion supported a broad mandate for professional authority. Liberals and physicians did not differ in their enthusiasm for medicine, only about the form in which enthusiasm ought to be expressed. The movement toward incorporating medicine into the state had to find channels of expression acceptable to the organized profession. The use of psychiatry in social welfare and the courts did not offend any interest of private practitioners. Public support for medical research, hospital construction, and other forms of resource development also posed fewer problems for the AMA than did health insurance. These programs typically increased the capital resources of the system (scientific knowledge, physical infrastructure) without limiting physicians' income from it. Acceptable measures were forms of complementary rather than competitive investment.

In medicine, as in the broader society, the vision of growth without conflict broke down in the 1960s. The postwar expansion did not remedy the acknowledged deficiencies in the distribution of medical services. Aiding medical research and facilities construction, without providing for primary care, set off an unbalanced expansion that became increasingly costly and irrational. The first phase of postwar policy, favoring growth without redistribution, gave way by the mid-1960s to policies that tried to improve distribution yet without any fundamental reorganization of the system. Still later, in the 1970s, public policy, after pursuing growth and redistribution without reorganization, accepted the need for reorganization to *stop* growth.

The succession of objectives in medical policy—expansion, equity, cost containment—paralleled the more general succession of concerns in postwar social policy. The predominant issue in the late 1940s in housing, transportation, and other fields was the problem of inadequate supply. Home mortgage guarantees and the highway trust fund were of a piece with federal aid to hospital construction. Social policy sought to underwrite the expansion of infrastructure that made possible the new middle-class life in the suburbs. By the mid-1960s the federal government became increasingly concerned with the stubborn problems of those who were left behind, and policy shifted in many areas to explicitly redistributive objectives. And in the 1970s, with persistent stagflation, social policy became increasingly sensitive to cost. In this and the following chapter, my objective is to show how this evolution specifically affected medical care and the medical profession: how postwar public policy initially respected and then threatened to undermine the sovereignty of American medicine.

AID AND AUTONOMY, 1945-1960

Public Investment in Science

The Second World War, more than the New Deal, marked the beginning of the great expansion of the federal government's support of medicine. This was notably the case in both medical research and mental health.

American scientists before the war generally opposed any large-scale federal financing or coordination of research.* Between 1900 and 1940, the primary sources of financing for medical research were private. Pri-

---

*This was the position, for example, of the National Academy of Sciences. Created during the Civil War, the academy soon after became largely an honorific rather than an advisory body, as it was originally intended to be. The National Research Council, set up during World War I as the academy's operating arm, also quickly fell into disuse. Until World War II, the pattern of the federal government was to create central scientific organizations in war and ignore them in peace.[5]

vate foundations and universities were the principal sponsors and hosts
of basic research. The most richly endowed research center, the Rockefeller Institute for Medical Research, was established in New York in
1902 and by 1928 had received from John D. Rockefeller $65 million
in endowment funds. In that same period, wealthy donors set up several
other independent institutes, but most medical research was conducted
by scientists in universities, supported by endowment income, special
research funds, and foundation grants.[6]

The other major private sponsors of research were pharmaceutical
companies, which grew rapidly after the 1920s. Unlike the nonprofit patrons, they were interested primarily in applied research and hired scientists to work in their own laboratories. An estimate in 1945 put the
research expenditures of the drug companies at $40 million, compared
to $25 million for the foundations, universities, and research institutes.[7]
There were, in addition, several smaller sources of private financing:
voluntary health agencies, such as the National Tuberculosis Association, which initiated a research program in 1921; professional societies,
such as the AMA, which offered small research grants beginning in 1903;
the Metropolitan Life Insurance Company, which supported public
health research; and a few private group practices, such as the Mayo
Clinic, that set up research foundations.

By comparison with all private sources, the financial contribution of
the federal government was relatively small. In the early 1900s, the budget of the Rockefeller Institute alone was many times larger than federal expenditures for medical research. The one area of research for
which Congress generously appropriated money was agriculture. As
critics liked to point out, congressmen were prepared to spend more
money to figure out how to save hogs than how to save people. Had
human beings sold for as high a price as pork, the situation might have
been different. In its heyday, from the 1890s to the 1930s, the Department of Agriculture was the leading agency of the federal government
with scientific interests and the locus of much health-related scientific
work. It was altogether natural for Congress to assign Agriculture responsibility to enforce the 1906 food and drug law; under this authority,
its Bureau of Chemistry conducted toxicological and pharmacological
studies. Concern about pesticides containing lead and arsenic produced
early research on environmental toxins. Indirectly, agricultural research yielded some notable medical advances. Work in veterinary
medicine improved understanding of the transmission of disease, and
research in soil chemistry led to the discovery by René Dubos of the
early antibiotic gramicidin, to Selman Waksman's work on streptomy-
cin, and to the discovery of the other antibiotics that followed penicillin.[8]

Direct federal sponsorship of medical research originated in the role of the old Marine Hospital Service in the control of epidemics. In 1887 a young doctor, Joseph J. Kinyoun, set up a bacteriological laboratory in the Marine Hospital at Staten Island, New York. Four years later this Hygienic Laboratory was moved to Washington. It received authority to test and improve biological products in 1902 when Congress passed the Biologics Control Act to regulate vaccines and sera sold in interstate commerce. That same year, the Hygienic Laboratory added divisions in chemistry, pharmacology, and zoology, though its annual budget was still less than $50,000. In 1912 the service—by then called the U.S. Public Health Service—was authorized to study chronic as well as infectious diseases. Though working with limited funds, its medical officers made several important contributions, including a vaccine against Rocky Mountain spotted fever. In the 1920s, one of its physicians, Joseph Goldberger, showed that pellagra was not an infectious but a deficiency disease that could be prevented by proper diet. In 1930, reorganized under the Ransdell Act, the Hygienic Laboratory became the National Institute of Health (NIH), and in 1938 it moved to a large, privately donated estate in Bethesda, Maryland, which is still its home today.[9]

Until the 1930s, nearly all the medical research financed by the federal government was conducted in government laboratories. In 1937, however, Congress departed from this practice when it passed the first of a series of measures to promote cancer research and cancer control. The legislation set up a National Cancer Institute under NIH, but for the first time, Congress also authorized the Public Health Service to make grants to outside researchers. In addition, it created a program of training fellowships. These proved to be important institutional precedents, though the funds involved were still quite limited. As late as 1938, the research budget of the Public Health Service was only $2.8 million, compared to $26.3 million for the Department of Agriculture.[10]

The war gave medical research priority. In July 1941 President Roosevelt created an Office of Scientific Research and Development (OSRD) with two parallel committees on national defense and medical research. The Committee on Medical Research (CMR) undertook a comprehensive research program to deal with the medical problems of the war. The work, costing $15 million, involved 450 contracts with universities and another 150 with research institutes, hospitals, and other organizations. Altogether, some 5,500 scientists and technicians were employed in the enterprise. Since the Japanese had seized the sources of quinine in the Pacific, the United States required a substitute in the treatment of malaria. Researchers were able to develop and standardize a synthetic, atabrine, that proved even more effective than quinine. In a major breakthrough, scientists isolated the therapeutically useful derivatives of blood, such as gamma globulin. Interest in penicillin was initially stimulated by its possible use against staphyloccic infections. Though the therapeutic value of penicillin had been demonstrated in the 1930s, it could be produced only in minute quantities at great cost. The CMR contracted with the Bradley Polytechnic Institute in Peoria, Illinois, to improve the strains and media for producing penicillin. Soon it was being turned out in 15,000-gallon tanks, and by the war's end was available for civilian as well as military use.[11]

The development of penicillin was paradigmatic of wartime medical research. Most of the work took advantage of the tremendous backlog of scientific ideas awaiting application. It was carried out primarily in independent laboratories. Scientific decisions were left to panels of independent scientists, and there was little government control of scientific work after grants were awarded. This was the pattern even in OSRD's military research, and it was widely considered not merely a success, but a lesson for the future that was pregnant with political meaning.

Early in the twentieth century, American science and graduate education were deeply influenced by German models. Now Germany provided a model in reverse. The Nazis had purged the universities and laboratories and centralized control of research, and by politically tampering with science slowed its progress. The allied victories in scientific work seemed to testify for a political system that gave science as well as its citizens more autonomy. This experience strengthened the case of American scientists, universities, and the medical profession that the research sponsored by government ought to be performed under minimal control primarily in independent institutions, rather than in government laboratories as was generally the practice in Europe. Here was yet another point of structural choice, when American institutions moved toward greater private control and functional autonomy than has been the European pattern.

Even before the war was over, President Roosevelt in a public letter asked Vannevar Bush, head of OSRD, to recommend plans for postwar government aid to science, including what could be done to aid "the war of science against disease." Bush's report, *Science: The Endless Frontier,* insisted on the vital need to aid science and to preserve its autonomy. Basic research, Bush wrote, is "scientific capital"; "more and better scientific research is one essential to the achievement of our goal of full employment." Consequently, he favored federal money for scholarships and research. But science had to be kept free: free from the influence of pressure groups, free from the necessity of producing immediate practical results. The mechanism he proposed for achieving these objectives was an independent National Research Foundation whose trustees would be appointed by the President from nominees submitted by the National Academy of Sciences.[12] Though this idea had wide support, the exact arrangements were a sticking point. Some liberals in the Senate wanted more assurance that the public would receive a return on its investment; they favored greater public control and public ownership of discoveries made under federal grants. Some scientists were afraid of just such demands and worried that even Bush's proposal was leading them down the slippery slope into socialism. It took several years to resolve these issues, and the National Science Foundation (NSF) was not established until May 1950.

By that time, another agency, the Public Health Service, had gained the leading role in medical research. The service had gradually accumulated a wide, if desultory, array of functions that reflected the diverse repertoire of bit parts the federal government was called upon to play in medicine. Transferred from the Treasury Department to the Federal Security Agency in 1939, the Public Health Service operated medical services for merchant seamen, inmates of federal prisons, Coast Guardsmen, lepers at a hospital in Louisiana, and narcotics addicts at two hospitals in Texas and Kentucky. It conducted medical examinations of immigrants, federal employees, and longshoremen. It administered the public health grants to the states created by the Social Security Act of 1935 as well as special programs of state grants for the control of venereal disease and tuberculosis. It was responsible for administering the Biologics Control Act and the cancer program as well as its own intramural research in NIH. In 1944, in the process of consolidating the statutes governing the PHS, Congress authorized it to make grants for outside investigations in fields of medicine other than cancer research. At the time, little money was available for the purpose, but at the war's end, the CMR's projects still in progress were transferred to NIH. With this transfer, the NIH research budget grew from $180,000 in 1945 to $4 million in 1947.[13]

In the late forties, a new force began to be felt that greatly spurred the expansion of NIH. This was the emergence of a private, lay lobby for medical research. Its chief architects, Mary Lasker and Florence Mahoney, brought money and influence to a cause of ready-made appeal. Mrs. Mahoney's husband owned the Cox newspaper chain, and Mrs. Lasker and her husband, who had made a fortune in advertising, had recently taken a major role in reorganizing the American Society for the Control of Cancer. The Lasker group had led the organization, which they renamed the American Cancer Society, to introduce modern advertising techniques and to devote the proceeds to cancer research. Mass fund raising for medical research had already been turned into a high art by the National Foundation for Infantile Paralysis, created in 1937. The huge success of its March of Dimes and other voluntary fund-raising efforts for medical research in the late 1940s testified to the new status of research as a popular cause. Public opinion polls confirmed the breadth of this sentiment, and politicians were not insensible to the possibilities. Opponents of national health insurance could display their deep concern for health by voting generous appropriations for medical research. The Lasker lobby cultivated key figures in Congress, and the new Surgeon General appointed in 1946, Leonard Scheele, began to work closely with both groups in what became one of Washington's classic "triangles" of influence.[14]

This "noble conspiracy," also known as "Mary and her little lambs," believed that the doctors and research scientists were too accustomed to thinking small. Mary Lasker encouraged them to ask for more money from Congress than ever before, and lo and behold, Congress voted it. Like the voluntary health organizations, NIH discovered that the way to open wide the public's purse was to call attention to one disease at a time. This was called the "categorical" approach. In 1948, when Congress created a National Heart Institute, NIH became the National Institutes of Health. Five other categorical institutes followed. In 1950, the year the National Science Foundation was established, Congress authorized the Surgeon General to set up such research institutes as he saw fit. Medicine would not be incorporated into a single national program of scientific research, as Bush had advised. Just as the cancer, polio, and other voluntary groups went directly to the public rather than take part in United Way fund raising, so medical researchers went directly to Congress rather than via a unified science foundation to take advantage of the distinctive good will medicine enjoyed.

In 1950 the NIH budget grew to $46.3 million, of which about one third went to extramural grants. A new Clinical Center opened on its Bethesda campus in 1953. Since the beginning of the war, funds for medical research had grown at a staggering rate. Between 1941 and 1951, the federal budget for medical research rose from no more than $3 million to $76 million. Total national expenditures for medical research increased from an estimated $18 million to $181 million.[15]

To a remarkable degree, control over research was ceded to the scientific community. The approval of grant applications as well as basic policy issues rested with panels of nongovernmental scientists. The individual scientist, too, enjoyed autonomy within the constraints of professional competition. The officials in charge of the NIH Division of Research Grants wrote in 1951, "The investigator works on problems of his own choosing and is not obliged to adhere to a preconceived plan. He is free to publish as he sees fit and to change his research without clearance if he finds new and more promising leads. He has almost complete budget freedom as long as he uses the funds for research purposes and expends them in accordance with local institutional rules."[16] This grant of autonomy expressed, in a concrete way, the public trust in science and governmental acceptance of scientists' demand that they be left to follow their own rules.

Of the various divisions of NIH, none grew faster than the National Institute of Mental Health (NIMH), created in 1949 under legislation passed three years earlier. Like medical research, psychiatry had emerged from World War II with an enhanced public image. But whereas the achievements of medical research led to recognition, the recognition of psychiatry during the war was, quite likely, its greatest achievement.

The modern military, even more than other organizations, requires an elaborate system for selecting, classifying, ranking, and discharging people. In the twentieth century, as Morris Janowitz has pointed out, the means of control in the military have shifted from authoritarian and coercive techniques to more subtle, psychological manipulation.[17] This evolution follows a pattern broadly evident in society, but the acute needs for control in the military have made it a proving ground for the psychological professions. The First World War saw the introduction of psychological testing for the assignment of military personnel and the creation of a Division of Neurology and Psychiatry to screen recruits and treat all mentally disturbed servicemen. World War I, however, did not leave a lasting mark on military psychiatry.

In the Second World War, more than 1 million men were rejected from military service because of mental and neurological disorders, and another 850,000 soldiers were hospitalized as psychoneurotic cases during the war. Psychiatrists and others later presented both these statistics as measures of the America's great unmet need for psychiatric services. In 1940 the Army had only 25 medical officers assigned to psychiatry, but during the war it had to assign 2,400 more. Their chief, Dr. William Menninger, held the rank of brigadier general, the highest ever for a psychiatrist. According to Menninger, when the war began psychiatry had relatively little latitude for effective intervention. Psychiatric patients were frequently regarded as malingerers; if the men were obviously ill, the psychiatrist was told to diagnose and discharge them. During the war, however, the psychiatric services were given more authority, and they claimed unexpected success in the treatment of psychiatric patients. In the profession's view, the military experience encapsulated the more general shift in the twentieth century from a purely "descriptive" psychiatry, which classified the mentally ill without helping them, to a "dynamic" psychiatry that was of positive benefit.[18]

The arrival of European refugee psychiatrists also contributed to the growth of a more influential psychiatric profession. Although after Freud's visit to America in 1909 his ideas enjoyed a wider circulation in the United States than in much of Europe, private psychiatric practice continued to be rare. As late as 1930, nearly three quarters of the members of the American Psychiatric Association worked in state mental hospitals. Institutional psychiatry still had a predominantly organic orientation. The rural location of the state hospitals contributed to professional isolation. The 1930s and 1940s saw a shift in both professional views and professional practice, as more urban, psychoanalytically-oriented practitioners won a middle-class clientele and a wider popular and intellectual audience. In 1948 William Menninger could write, without undue exaggeration, that psychiatry "probably enjoys a wider popular interest at the present time than does any other field of medicine."[19]

Public attention was also drawn to psychiatry at the end of the war when a national scandal erupted in the press over conditions in state mental hospitals. The newspaper scandal is a periodic feature of the history of mental institutions, and it takes at least two forms. In the scandal of repression, normal or not-so-dangerous people are shown to have been railroaded into institutions. The scandal of the 1940s, however, was of a second type, the scandal of neglect. During the war, conscientious objectors had been sent to work as aides in mental institutions. Appalled at what they saw, they formed an organization to publicize conditions there. The story was picked up by newspapers and magazines and even became the subject of a best-selling novel *The Snakepit*. In one of the most widely read exposés, *The Shame of the States*, based on visits to two dozen institutions, the historian and journalist Albert Deutsch reported scenes rivaling the horrors of Nazi concentration camps: half-starved mental patients herded into filthy, barn-like wards and stripped of every vestige of human decency. Like others at the time, Deutsch believed that mental hospitals needed closer relations with medicine as well as more resources. In a typical expression of the growing progressive faith in psychiatry, Deutsch wrote, "It is because modern psychiatry is a stranger to so many mental hospital wards that many more patients don't return to their communities as cured."[20]

Aroused by the war experience and the state hospital scandal, Congress passed the National Mental Health Act in 1946. The Lasker lobby and psychiatrists in the Public Health Service originated the proposal and orchestrated congressional hearings and public support. (Since 1930 the Public Health Service had a small division of mental hygiene that ran the two federal narcotics hospitals and psychiatric services in federal prisons.) The new program was representative of the beliefs of the time. It provided funds for medical research and training programs, and it gave the states aid for mental health clinics and other special efforts. Research and training, however, became the priorities. Between 1948 and 1962, NIMH research grants rose from $374,000 to $42.6 million, training grants were up from $1.1 to $38.6 million, but state grants rose only from $1.7 to $6.6 million.[21] Under the broad mandate of mental health, the agency's research programs expanded to include such diverse problems as child development, juvenile delinquency, suicide prevention, alcoholism, and television violence. Its training programs sought to attract physicians by providing more generous stipends to residents in psychiatry than were available in other specialties. Moreover, the government required nothing in return, such as a commitment to work for some period in the state mental hospitals, whose shortages of psychiatrists had originally prompted the legislation. If young psychiatrists took advantage of the public purse and then practiced among the well-to-do, this choice had to be accepted. It was no business of public policy to influence it. This, too, reflected the premise that federal aid must not compromise professional autonomy.

One national experience in the 1950s seemed to confirm the value of waging concerted campaigns of medical research against specific diseases. I have already mentioned that the National Foundation for Infantile Paralysis was, by a wide margin, the single most popular medical cause in the postwar period. Polio was not the most prevalent disease at the time; its contribution to overall mortality rates was small. But it was deeply feared as the leading crippler of children. Its incidence had actually been growing throughout the twentieth century; in 1952 more children died of polio than of any other infectious disease. It was also more common among the middle and upper classes. Every year, promising that "research is winning the battle against polio," the March of Dimes would raise more money than any other health campaign. And in answer to the public's hopes, medical research—supported in this case by voluntary donations—produced an effective vaccine. Probably no event in American history testifies more graphically to public acceptance of scientific methods than the voluntary participation of millions of American families in the 1954 trials of the Salk vaccine. The methodological conscience of epidemiologists had demanded that these trials be double-blind: Neither doctors nor teachers, neither parents nor children, knew whether the children were receiving vaccine or placebo. And when on April 12, 1955, epidemiologists at the University of Michigan announced the results showing that the vaccine worked, pandemonium swept the country. "More than a scientific achievement, the vaccine was a folk victory," observes Richard Carter in his biography of Jonas Salk. "People observed moments of silence, rang bells, honked horns, blew factory whistles, fired salutes, kept their traffic lights red in brief periods of tribute, took the rest of the day off, closed their schools or convoked fervid assemblies therein, drank toasts, hugged children, attended church, smiled at strangers, forgave enemies."[22]

The magic of science and money had worked. And if polio could be prevented, Americans had reason to think that cancer and heart disease and mental illness could be stopped, too. Who knew how long human life might be extended? Medical research might offer passage to immortality. Between 1955 and 1960, unswerving congressional support pushed up the NIH budget from $81 million to $400 million.[23]

More money for research met no objections from the AMA. However, the story of aid to medical education was different, and it is worth recalling the contrast. In 1949 Congress was close to approving a five-year program of grants and scholarships for medical schools to increase the nation's supply of physicians. A bill had passed the Senate and was reported out of House committee when it hit a small snag. Yet it seemed likely to pass the next year. The House of Delegates of the AMA approved the measure in December 1949. However, two months later, concerned about setting dangerous precedents, the AMA board reversed its position, and the bill died in Congress. Despite wide support from other groups, aid to medical education was blocked throughout the 1950s.[24] Funding for medical research indirectly aided some expansion of medical enrollments but only barely enough to keep pace with population growth. The great increase in demand for medical care, with no corresponding increase in the supply of physicians, was to have repercussions for years.

The Tilt Toward the Hospital

As public officials formulated postwar science and medical policy in the mid-1940s, the postwar economy was never far from their minds. The first thought of those in the Roosevelt administration who initiated Vannevar Bush's report was that innovations generated by scientific research could create new businesses and new jobs. Interest in aiding hospital construction also arose in large part because of its potential for creating employment. Here was a public works program that conservatives would support as an alternative to national health insurance. The hospital industry itself was agitating for aid. Its needs for capital investment had been deferred during a decade and a half of depression and war. In addition, millions of returning veterans would need medical attention. So, almost without dissent, two hospital construction programs were adopted immediately after the war—one to expand the Veterans Administration hospitals, the other to aid the nation's community hospitals.

By World War II, the VA, with ninety-one institutions, was already operating the largest hospital system in the country. However, corruption, low pay for medical staff, and the isolated location of many rural facilities gave VA hospitals a dismal reputation. The new leaders of the agency after the war resolved to end its professional isolation as well as improve its physical plant. They decided to build new facilities in urban areas and, wherever possible, to establish close affiliations with medical schools. These affiliations involved the use of VA hospitals for clinical research and training in the health professions. Medical school committees received the right to vote on appointments to the VA medical staff. As a result, the revitalization of the VA, like the development of NIH, funneled new resources to the medical schools and expanded their role in running American hospitals.[25]

The tilt toward technology in postwar health policy was nowhere more evident than in the decision to provide construction funds for community hospitals through the 1946 Hospital Survey and Construction Act (known as the Hill-Burton program, after its Senate sponsors, Lister Hill and Harold H. Burton). Proposals for national health insurance and the earlier report of the Committee on the Costs of Medical Care favored financing comprehensive medical services. But the measures adopted in the late forties put the power of public finance behind hospitals alone.

Planning for postwar hospital construction, as for postwar scientific research, began before the war was over. In 1942 the American Hospital Association decided to organize a national commission to develop—or, perhaps more accurately, to develop support for—a national program for hospitals. At that time, the AHA was still a relatively weak organization, with an annual budget of about $100,000. Three private foundations—Kellogg, Commonwealth, and the National Foundation for Infantile Paralysis, none of which had supported the CCMC—agreed to help underwrite the commission. (The Rockefeller Foundation declined to participate on the grounds that a more comprehensive approach was needed.) The Public Health Service provided extensive staff support as if the commission were an official undertaking, and the AHA rounded up the usual array of college presidents, corporate executives, and professional dignitaries to serve as the commission's highly impartial membership.[26]

The Commission on Hospital Care, as might be expected, recommended a huge program of hospital construction: an additional 195,000 beds (an increase of 40 percent) at a capital investment of $1.8 billion. Annual operating costs would add $375 million a year to the nation's health care bill, but the benefits, said the commission, would "fully justify" the expenditure.[27] These benefits the commission evidently considered too obvious to establish. Still less did it weigh them against the potential benefits of alternative investments in health care or other fields.

The commission's final report appeared after Hill-Burton was passed. But its pilot survey of hospital needs in Michigan guided surveys in other states, and by the time Congress acted, forty-four states had surveys in progress. This preparation made possible rapid implementation of the program.

The law carefully limited political, especially federal, discretion. In addition to $3 million for state surveys and plans, it originally authorized $75 million a year for five years to aid hospital construction. But federal administrators had no say as to how much any state or individual hospital would receive. In redrafting the bill, Senator Taft introduced a formula for allocating money among the states based on their population and per capita income. The states in turn distributed funds to applicants. While the law set procedural guidelines for state distribution of the money, it specifically barred any federal regulation of hospital policy. The states were to estimate regional hospital needs; when an applicant from an area received a grant, the area would go to the bottom of the list and wait another turn. These arrangements were meant to minimize "politics"; the entire process was presented as a scientific exercise.[28]

The expansionary bias of the program was evident in the fate of the ceiling it set on hospital growth. The law limited aid to states with no more than 4.5 hospital beds per 1,000 people (a figure suggested by industry experts that was far above the levels in any state). This ceiling gradually became a target. In later congressional hearings, the program's directors would define the need for additional hospital beds by the gap between existing ratios and the 4.5 maximum. Other medical services, such as primary care, did not benefit from any such legislative standard. Furthermore, the standard for hospitals was impervious to changes in medical practice, such as the growing belief in early ambulation instead of extended bed rest after surgery.

Between 1947 and 1971, the $3.7 billion disbursed under the program contributed to 30 percent of all hospital projects and provided an average of about 10 percent of the annual cost of construction. The program also generated an estimated $9.1 billion for hospital construction in local and state matching funds. Hill-Burton was modified in 1954 to permit grants to long-term care and ambulatory care facilities, but as of 1971, more than three quarters of the money had gone to hospitals.[29]

Advocates of Hill-Burton originally argued that the program would help provide access to hospital care for families and communities that otherwise could not afford the cost. The formula for allocating funds among the states favored those with low per capita income. In this regard, the law was redistributive. Over the next two decades, the supply of hospital beds in low-income states rose to the levels in high-income states; careful analyses suggest Hill-Burton was responsible for this change.[30]

Within states, however, the funds went disproportionately to middle-income communities.[31] This pattern resulted in part from the law itself. Communities were initially required to raise two thirds of the construction cost on their own.[32] Sponsors also had to show that hospitals supported by federal grants would be financially viable. "Which are the communities among those needing hospitals, that cannot meet these requirements?" asked Senator Wagner during the original congressional debate. "Obviously, the poorest communities—the very ones that need help the most; these are the ones that will have to be turned down."[33] Liberals did secure a concession in the legislation requiring that hospitals receiving assistance make available "a reasonable volume of hospital services to persons unable to pay." But for the next twenty years, no regulations were issued specifying what a reasonable volume might be, and the provision went unenforced.[34]

Many hospitals in the South aided under the program refused to treat black people. The law itself prohibited discrimination by any assisted hospital, but said its conditions were met if separate but equal facilities were available in an area. The Supreme Court did not rule these provisions of Hill-Burton unconstitutional until 1963.

The original objectives of Hill-Burton included improved coordination of hospital development; this was the point of requiring state plans. Some saw the measure as a step in integrating regional health services. But the law required no continuing coordination among hospitals after grants were made. In the long run, the Hill-Burton program probably retarded integration in the industry, since it provided money that enabled many smaller and uneconomical hospitals to keep operating.

All four of the major postwar programs—medical research, mental health, the VA, and community hospital construction—showed a common pattern in respecting the sovereignty of the medical profession and local medical institutions. While the functions of government were expanded, the sphere of political discretion was deliberately restricted. In NIH the mechanism for restricting political control was the required approval of grants by panels of experts drawn from outside government. NIH, as Don Price has observed, was the only agency of the federal government whose full-time officers could not allocate money without the approval of part-time committees representing the beneficiaries![35] The mental health program was initially established under NIH and shared its orientation to research and training and its reliance on peer evaluation. Political control in the VA was restricted by granting the power to appoint physicians to the "dean's committees" of medical schools with which VA hospitals were affiliated. And in the Hill-Burton program a formula for grant allocation and statutory prohibition of federal intervention in hospital policy limited political discretion. In effect, by earmarking money for specific purposes and then outlawing federal interference, Congress and the professions joined in restricting any tendency toward administrative rationalization.

So, despite the growth of government aid to medicine, professional sovereignty was now buttressed by other kinds of claims against government control. In the Hill-Burton program, states' rights and community autonomy were invoked as the basis for limiting federal intervention. These claims have a constitutional heritage behind them. On the other hand, medical research, like all scientific research, demands autonomy as a necessary condition of free inquiry. As Edward Shils has written, the autonomy of science has its own distinct origins, independent of the liberal tradition.[36] The medical profession itself appealed for autonomy partly on the grounds of the privacy of the doctor-patient relationship. That was yet another basis for resisting government. These various elements were now combined to constitute a powerful case that public aid to medicine should not bring public control.

THE STRUCTURAL IMPACT OF POSTWAR POLICY

The New Structure of Opportunity

The new forms of national investment were meant to expand and strengthen medical research and hospitals. That they did. But they also changed the careers of thousands of physicians and in other, unexpected ways altered the postwar development of medical care.

The infusion of money into research and training programs created new opportunities in—and for—medical schools. During the 1940s, the average income of medical schools tripled from $500,000 to $1.5 million a year; by 1958–59 the average school's income was up to $3.7 million and ten years later to $15 million.[37] Medical schools became sprawling, complex organizations that now saw their missions as three-fold: research, education, and patient care (usually in that order). Full-time faculty increased 51 percent between 1940–41 and 1949–50, according to a study of thirty-two institutions. And during the next decade, full-time positions doubled nationally, increasing from 4,212 in 1950–51 to 11,319 by 1959–60.[38] Though some growth in positions was due to the establishment of new schools, older institutions expanded far beyond the expectations of their own administrators. In 1957, when the average department of (internal) medicine had a staff of fifteen, a survey of chairmen around the country disclosed that by 1970 they hoped the number might rise to thirty-two. Robert G. Petersdorf, who was chairman at the University of Washington, notes that his department was five times that large by 1970 and that this growth was typical.[39] And, not surprisingly, growth meant differentiation: The departments acquired new subspecialty divisions, which opened up new avenues for promotions.

This expansion radically changed academic medicine. In the 1920s and 1930s, promotions in medical schools were slow and uncertain. Vernon Lippard, a dean of Yale Medical School, notes that on each service, teaching hospitals then had two or three times as many interns as first-year residents, twice as many first as second-year residents, and so on until, after three to five years, one survivor emerged as chief resident. This man might then become an instructor and enter into another competition to become an assistant professor. Money for research was scarce and, as Lippard recalls, security was rarely achieved before age forty.[40]

The U.S. Congress changed all that. NIH research grants helped to build new research centers, especially in the West, and training grants provided the stipends for an enlarged corps of investigators. The growth of subspecialties broke down the old pyramidal pattern, since a larger number of residents could now rise to senior posts. As the demand for academic physicians rose, so did their income. And, like other academics in the postwar period, medical school professors also became more geographically mobile. One key consideration in attracting faculty became the provision of research space and clinical facilities. This increased the interest of medical schools in expanding their network of affiliated hospitals and acquiring land in local neighborhoods, tearing down residential buildings, and replacing them with institutes, clinics, and hospitals.

Inevitably, these developments had reverberations within and outside the medical schools.

The growth of full-time faculty in clinical as well as basic science departments meant the displacement of local physicians who had served as part-time instructors. Some private doctors also lost admitting privileges at hospitals that were affiliating with medical schools. To gain affiliation, the hospitals usually had to permit the medical schools either to initiate or approve staff appointments. The medical schools believed they required this authority to maintain the quality of graduate medical education. In their view, many older physicians, often general practitioners, were unacceptable as instructors. And when medical professors became chiefs of services in newly affiliated hospitals, the doctors who previously held those positions were also displaced.

Displacement brought resentment and recriminations. In a study in the early 1960s of relations between medical schools and private physicians in eight communities, Patricia Kendall found widespread anger and bitterness among the practitioners. "A lot of us," one practitioner remarked, "feel that the medical school would dominate all of our hospitals if it could." A medical school professor reported that "the practitioners have lost prestige and they feel it. Some of the doctors who were respected in the town are no longer in the same position of authority and respect that they were before we came here." The local doctors ("LMDs," as they are sometimes called) resented the loss of influence over medical school policy and of access to hospital beds. They did not like the emergence of a new group of doctors who received publicity for their research and were quoted in the newspapers and who, it seemed, were frequently brash and condescending. The medical professors, in turn, often thought the local practitioners were out of date. "The organized practitioners of medicine," one professor told Kendall, "are so God-damned reactionary that I feel leery about educating them."

"How reactionary?" she asked.

"In every way," he responded, "politically, socially, economically, and educationally."[41]

These tensions were softened by the general prosperity that both groups enjoyed. Between 1945 and 1969, while the consumer price index rose at an annual rate of 2.8 percent, physicians' fees rose 3.8 percent and their annual incomes at 5.9 percent a year. The average net profit from medical practice rose from just over $8,000 in 1945 to $32,000 in 1969.[42] The postwar economic expansion meant that private doctors had all the business they could handle. Conflict was also partly relieved by the new geography of urban medical care. While the medical schools remained in the cities, many of the private doctors followed their patients to the suburbs.

Inside the medical schools, the growth of research funds changed the relation between the science and clinical departments. "One generation back," a professor recalled, "surgeons here were very strong, both clinically and administratively, and could pretty much run the whole school." Now the budget of the department of experimental medicine was five times the budget of the surgery department. "The preclinicians," the professor continued, "have almost always had the idea that the clinicians are robber barons; now they feel that anyone really interested in clinical work bears watching, that he is an anachronism."[43]

The relations between science and clinical departments were also growing more distant because they were no longer functionally interlocked. For example, before the war, the science departments often performed diagnostic tests and other work for the clinical faculty. By the 1960s these ties had disappeared. "In the 1920s," writes Lippard, "the basic sciences were taught by individuals who, although often not physicians, had an interest in clinical medicine and made an effort to relate their instruction to clinical problems. As they were relieved of clinically related responsibilities they turned their attention to more fundamental issues." This shift was related to the movement of medical science toward the molecular level of analysis. As Lippard notes,

The anatomists lost interest in gross anatomy and became electron microscopists and cellular biologists; the biochemists turned from nutrition and intermediary metabolism to molecular structure and enzymology, and the physiologists from the function of mammalian organ systems to cells; the bacteriologists became microbiologists concerned with microbial physiology and genetics; and the pharmacologists turned from studying the effect of drugs on intact animals to chemistry and the effect of chemical agents at the cellular level.[44]

This divorce of the basic sciences from the more immediate concerns of clinical medicine created new tensions and problems in medical education. The tremendous growth in knowledge—and in faculty—led to increased competition for time in the medical curriculum. Many professors thought their fields were not getting enough attention. Many students felt they were being forced to learn more than they could absorb and that much of the curriculum was marginally relevant to their future professional work. The grueling first-year work in anatomy—medicine's "boot camp," as one doctor calls it—had long epitomized this ordeal. Criticism now also came from those who wanted to give psychiatry more of a place in medical school and to provide a more comprehensive education in the social and psychological problems that physicians confront in medical practice. But established claims to an already crowded schedule were difficult to dislodge.

"It's easier to move a cemetery than to change the curriculum," one dean was reported to exclaim.[45] In the nineteenth century, when medical schools were often accused of robbing corpses, the dean might have been presumed to be making the comparison from personal experience.

Change came easier in the last two years of undergraduate medical education, which students spent in clinical clerkships on hospital wards. The emphasis in clinical instruction changed as the mix of hospital patients shifted with the decline of infectious diseases. A major step in reorganizing the preclinical years occurred in 1952 when Western Reserve (now Case Western) adopted a new curriculum organized by body systems (cardiovascular, respiratory, renal, and so on) rather than by discipline. Many schools adopted this pattern or variations upon it. Some schools, notably Stanford, also permitted more electives. The postwar variations between progressive and conservative schools reintroduced a degree of heterogeneity in medical education that had been missing since it had assumed the rather rigid form often attributed (mistakenly) to Abraham Flexner.

Yet despite some variation in curriculum, one tendency was common virtually everywhere, and that was increasing specialization. In a study at Cornell in the 1950s, Patricia Kendall and Hanan C. Selvin found a dramatic change in students' plans while in medical school. The proportion planning to be general practitioners dropped from 60 to 16 percent between the first and fourth years. Students planning to be specialists jumped from 35 to 74 percent, and those going into teaching and research increased from 5 to 10 percent. "I can see why specialization is the rage today," one student wrote in his diary. "Medicine is so large now that a doctor doesn't feel confident unless he knows at least one field extremely well, rather than a little about all subjects." With this type of reaction in mind, Kendall and Selvin—and many others—

pointed to the growth of knowledge as the key factor leading medical students to become specialists.[46]

The difficulty with this view is that the distribution of opportunities does not always correspond to the inclinations of students. In other countries, the psychological distress of medical students facing the burden of modern science may be no less severe, but the positions available for specialty training and specialty practice are limited. In the legal profession in America, the burden of knowledge is staggering, but young lawyers need to be prepared to handle whatever cases they are assigned in the firms or bureaucracies that provide jobs. Early, formal specialization is discouraged. The rate of specialization in any field depends primarily on the opportunities and incentives generated by the market and the state. Throughout their education, students adjust their aspirations as they discover what awaits them outside. If it were the case that specialists earned less than general practitioners (or received a low return on their investment in advanced training), we might need a psychological explanation to understand what other rewards they would gain from entering a specialty. But this was not the case in postwar medicine. The economic rewards to specialization were considerable.

Three structural factors were especially important in producing the rising rate of specialization. First, the system for certifying medical specialists that had developed in the 1930s included no regulation of the size or distribution of the specialties. Second, beginning in the war, hospitals (and their associated physicians) had strong incentives to set up training programs for specialists—indeed, to create more openings for specialty training than there were American graduates to fill them. And, third, government subsidies, the high returns to specialty practice created by health insurance, and the lack of a corrective mechanism that would have reduced specialist incomes as their numbers increased gave physicians strong, continuing incentives to pursue the training opportunities hospitals created.

Since the 1930s, the organized medical specialties had acquired enough power to sensitize young doctors to the value of certification, but not enough power to become exclusive clubs. The development of certification began with the autonomous efforts of two early specialty groups. The ophthalmologists created the first examining board in 1916; the otolaryngologists the second in 1924. It is probably no accident that both fields keenly felt competition from non-M.D. specialists. The great expansion in examining boards occurred during the Depression of the 1930s and likewise partly represented a response to intensified competition. Like limits on entry into a profession, limits on entry into a specialty have the potential to create monopoly returns. In 1930, when the obstetricians and gynecologists established the third examining board, they excluded doctors who did not limit their practice 100 percent to women. As Rosemary Stevens points out, "By these measures, no general practitioner, however large the proportion of his practice devoted to obstetrics or gynecology and however thorough his training in these fields, might be admitted to examination or considered for a diploma." By 1940 five of the specialty boards required 100 percent limitation of practice.[47]

As independent groups began to carve up medicine into specialty divisions, leaders of the profession moved to establish some order. In 1933 representatives of the AMA Council on Medical Education and Hospitals, the AMA specialty sections, the four examining boards then in existence, and other medical groups agreed to form a coordinating body. This became the Advisory Board for Medical Specialties (since 1970 called the American Board of Medical Specialties). Together with the AMA, this board set general standards for the examining boards and settled jurisdictional disputes. At least three years of training after internship were required for certification in any specialty. Certified specialists had to be members of the AMA (a requirement dropped in 1939). Twelve fields were listed as appropriate for certification, and by 1937 all twelve examining boards had been established. (Eight others were added in later years.) In 1940 the first edition of the Directory of Medical Specialists was published. For the first time, an elite within the profession received formal recognition.[48]

Yet numbers were not controlled. While the specialty boards initially hoped to limit hospital privileges to physicians they certified, this objective had to be abjured because of uncertainty about whether the courts would block such a move on antitrust grounds. (This concern arose after the Supreme Court's decision in the Group Health case.) The general practitioners in the AMA also continued to stand in the way of any limits on specialty practice or opportunities for specialty training. So the relations between GPs and specialists remained loosely defined. Patients could still go directly to a specialist without the mediation of the GP, and the GP could call himself a specialist without the approval of an examining board.

Yet repeated experience signaled the growing value of certification. During World War II, the AMA and the specialty boards aided the military in identifying properly certified specialists, who promptly received higher rank. This experience, as Stevens notes, gave doctors a "healthy respect for the value of board certificates."[49] After the war, the VA also ruled that no doctor would be treated as a specialist without board certification. Aided by GI Bill education benefits, thousands of returning physicians decided to seek certification. When the VA ruled that hospitals could receive payment for graduate training of physicians, it encouraged hospitals to set up programs to take advantage of the subsidies.

This was by no means the only advantage hospitals derived from graduate training programs. Interns and residents provided hospitals with relatively inexpensive professional labor. The hospitals with ample house staff could do more thorough workups of patients and perform a variety of functions for busy private practitioners. Without house staff, hospitals could not easily secure coverage at nights and on weekends. The demand for house staff initially increased when doctors were called into the armed forces but continued to grow afterward. The number of residency positions shot up from 5,000 to over 12,000 between 1940 and 1947 and reached 25,000 by 1955.[50]

Students in medical school, like young doctors in the Army, could plainly observe how general practitioners were treated. The universities generally did not want GPs to admit patients at affiliated hospitals. As the medical schools replaced part-time instructors from private practice with full-time professors from research backgrounds, they were also substituting new models of professional competence.

The higher income enjoyed by specialists, compared to general practitioners, continued throughout the postwar period and cannot be explained by the added costs of advanced training. And the hospital-oriented specialties, such as surgery, consistently maintained an edge in income over the specialties whose work was primarily office-based, such as internal medicine. They held this edge in spite of working fewer hours a week.[51] Part of the explanation is probably that the hospital-oriented specialties had a higher proportion of cases covered by insurance. Specialty incomes vary directly with the percentage of work reimbursed by third parties.[52] Since insurance developed faster for hospital than for office services, it encouraged doctors to move into hospital-oriented fields. Furthermore, the expansion of house staff and other hospital employees in the postwar period made hospital-oriented doctors more productive. They could see more patients in less time as hospital employees took over such functions as postoperative care. Hospital costs increased, but physicians did not cut their fees, even though they were spending less time to produce their services. And that, too, helped raise their incomes.[53]

Before the war, the great majority of doctors in active practice—76.5 percent in 1940—reported themselves as general practitioners or part-time specialists. The percentage of doctors reporting themselves as full-time specialists jumped from 24 percent in 1940 to 37 percent by 1949.

By 1955 the proportion rose to 44 percent; five years later to 55 percent; and in 1966 to 69 percent. Most dramatic was the growth in surgical specialties from only 10 percent of the profession in 1931, to 26 percent in 1960, and over 30 percent by 1969.[54]

The New Structure of Power

When opportunities in a profession change, so does the profession. Before the war, most doctors went directly into practice after an internship of one year and then practiced independently. In 1930 only one physician in sixteen worked in a hospital full-time. Much medical care—four of every ten encounters between doctors and patients—still took place in a patient's home. As of 1935, half of all births attended by doctors were home births.

By the 1950s, most doctors served at least three years in a hospital residency after internship, and one doctor in six worked full-time in a hospital. Ninety-six percent of all births were hospital births, and only one in ten contacts with doctors occurred in patients' homes.[55]

The tremendous increase in physicians in teaching, research, government, and other institutional positions took place while the ratio of doctors to population was little changed. Between 1940 and 1957, institutionally employed physicians jumped from 12.8 to 26.5 percent of the profession. Doctors in private practice declined not only as a proportion of physicians, but also in relation to population, down from 108 to 91 per 100,000 people.[56]

The concentration of medical work in hospitals and doctors' offices, the growth in demand for personal health services, and the declining availability of private practitioners made it possible for doctors to increase their volume of practice dramatically. The average private physician in 1930 saw about fifty patients a week; by 1950 he saw more than one hundred.[57]

Some observers have suggested that hospitals replaced private practitioners as the most powerful force in the postwar medical system. This does not express their relation accurately. They were not involved in a zero-sum situation. Rather, the power of the medical system as a whole increased. Both doctors and hospitals shared in this expansion. While hospitals expanded, their very expansion increased their need to satisfy the doctors who could keep their beds filled. More beds provided doctors with more alternatives for hospitalizing their patients. In a 1968 study of a medical center (unidentified, but clearly Yale-New Haven), August Hollingshead and Raymond Duff record that the administration at one point proposed taxing the affiliated private doctors to support the house staff. Since the house staff performed services for which the practitioners often charged fees, this idea might not seem unreasonable. Of course, the ensuing uproar among the private physicians caused the proposal to be withdrawn. The hospital could not afford to antagonize them.[58]

The profit that doctors and hospitals derived from house staff was one of the driving forces of the postwar medical system. As demand for house staff grew, competition among hospitals intensified. Between 1940 and 1950 the proportion of approved house staff positions that hospitals were unable to fill rose from 10 to 30 percent. The house staff shortage, of course, resulted directly from the decision to expand hospitals without expanding medical school enrollments. By 1957 hospitals were looking for more than 12,000 interns annually, but American medical schools were graduating fewer than 7,000 students a year.[59]

The competition for available graduates led to improved stipends for house staff and a rationalized system of intern placement. But more significantly, it also led hospitals to look abroad to fill their openings. Congress and state legislatures cooperated by making it easier for foreign-trained doctors to enter and work in the United States. During the 1950s foreign medical graduates increased from 10 to 26 percent of all house staff.[60] Initially, these doctors came primarily from Europe, but in the 1960s a major influx began from Asia, mainly Korea, India, and the Philippines. Though ostensibly in America for graduate training in hospitals, the majority chose to remain permanently. Like other immigrants, they often took jobs that Americans did not want (for example, in state mental institutions). In effect, the peculiar slant of American health policy (expanding hospitals, but keeping down medical enrollments) was producing a new lower tier in the medical profession drawn from the Third World.

Intensified competition for American graduates also had the unanticipated consequence of enlarging the role of medical schools in the hospital system. Academic physicians had long favored consolidating graduate medical education under medical schools, but the private doctors who benefited from house staff in community hospitals were too influential in the AMA to permit that to happen. As of 1959, unaffiliated hospitals represented 73 percent of hospitals with approved residency programs; though on the average smaller than affiliated programs, the unaffiliated offered 42 percent of all residency positions. But they were at a serious disadvantage in attracting American interns and residents. To strengthen their position, more community hospitals sought medical school ties.[61]

As a result, the postwar decades saw a steady extension of the power of medical schools into the hospital systems of metropolitan areas. In New York City seven such networks radiated out from the city's medical schools, covering half the hospital beds in the city. Chicago had six such networks; Philadelphia five. These medical school empires, as their critics called them, now held a powerful position in medical affairs: They could grant or withhold teaching positions, hospital privileges, and the assorted capital equipment and labor that hospitals provide. As of the early 1970s, the proportion of general hospital beds in affiliated hospitals in the major metropolitan areas ranged from 32 percent in Detroit to 79 percent in Philadelphia. Nationally, the proportion of approved residencies in unaffiliated hospitals fell to less than 10 percent of all positions.[62]

At the hub of these empires was typically a cluster of institutions linked directly to the medical school in a university medical center. Columbia-Presbyterian in New York City is generally acknowledged to have been the first medical center of this kind. In 1910 Columbia University and Presbyterian Hospital reached an understanding on the principles of an affiliation; this was basically the kind of model already established at Johns Hopkins. But by the time the Medical Center actually opened in 1928 at a new site in upper Manhattan, it had grown to include ten separate institutions, including various hospitals, clinics, and schools that had previously been independent. As the center continued to grow, it integrated record keeping and other services. In the late 1940s it began adding a series of research institutes.[63] This became the general pattern. A medical center typically would have not only a medical and dental school but also schools in pharmacy, public health, nursing, and other paramedical occupations; research institutes for heart disease, mental illness, cancer, rehabilitation, and other fields; several general teaching hospitals, perhaps a women's hospital, a children's hospital, a psychiatric hospital, various clinics, doctors' office buildings, and so on. Universities became the umbrella organizations for America's regional medical centers, which instead of being organized around the immediate needs of patients, were oriented primarily toward research and training. Did this show a magnificent concern for the health of future generations? Alas, there may have been other motives. In any event, what was remarkable about this arrangement is how little remarked it was.

The rise of the medical centers introduced a significant bureaucratic element into professional experience. But accounts such as Duff and Hollingshead's indicate that power in medical centers resides not so much in the administration as in the "chairmen-chiefs." These are the professors who simultaneously serve as chairmen of the major medical school departments and chiefs of medicine, surgery, psychiatry, obstetrics-gynecology, and pediatrics in the teaching hospitals. They control the key policy-making boards in both institutions. Their judgments shape the careers of the house staff. They are the ones to whom interns and residents must turn for support when conflicts arise, and on whom they must depend for recommendations. "It is inconceivable," an administrator commented, "that the university would try to carry out a policy contrary to the wishes of the department chairmen of the Medical School and damned difficult for the hospital to carry out a policy contrary to the wishes of the chiefs."[64] This is almost a textbook definition of power.

As powerful as these medical school empires were, they did not embrace the entire system of medical care in America. Though they were increasing their share of the nation's hospital system, the hospitals affiliated with medical schools still represented only 25 percent of the community hospital beds in the country in 1972.[65] While the medical schools were dominant in the metropolis, theirs was only one of several spheres of medicine.

By the 1960s the medical profession had developed three more or less distinct sectors.[66] First of all, there were the doctors who worked in medical schools and hospitals, including the house staff and full-time faculty, whose priorities were research and training. This was a far more significant group than it had been before the war. The chief feature of their relations with patients was that they rarely had any long-term relations with them at all. Physicians in training or engaged in research do not require their patients' good will for future business. Their professional rewards depend on the opinion of colleagues. Those who make their careers in research operate in a "grants economy" whose key decision makers are professionals at other institutions. All these factors contribute to professional autonomy and, not coincidentally, to the powerlessness of patients and to their objectification as "clinical material."

The second group were the private, primarily office-based practitioners who in large numbers had moved to the suburbs. Though they had lost control of some medical institutions, they still had a privileged and dominant role in community hospitals. As a group, they were doing far better economically than ever before, since consumer demand and hospital resources had grown rapidly, while their own numbers had not. Theirs was a sellers' market. Still, they depended more on the good will of patients than did institutionally based physicians, and they also required the good will of their colleagues in private practice for referrals, staff privileges at local hospitals, and malpractice defense. These kinds of interdependence fostered professional solidarity, and indeed, these doctors were the organizational base of the AMA. However, many were beginning to identify more strongly with their specialty than with the profession as a whole, as was evident in the more rapid growth of membership in specialty societies and the relative increase in subscriptions to specialty journals over general medical publications.

And, finally, there were the doctors working in rural or inner-city areas or state institutions. Smallest in number, lowest in prestige, these were often older general practitioners or, increasingly, younger foreign medical graduates. They were the most professionally isolated of physicians, though some worked almost in the shadows of the great medical centers.

The contrast among physicians was only a reflection of contrasts in the medical care system. Gleaming palaces of modern science, replete with the most advanced specialty services, now stood next to neighborhoods that had been medically abandoned, that had no doctors for everyday needs, and where the most elementary public health and preventive care was frequently unavailable. In the 1960s many began to observe that abundance and scarcity in medicine were side by side. After World War II, medicine had been a metaphor for progress, but to many it was now becoming a symbol of the continuing inequities and irrationalities of American life.

REDISTRIBUTION WITHOUT REORGANIZATION, 1961–1969

The Liberal Opportunity

The triumph of the liberal agenda in the mid-1960s brought a new generation of programs and policies in health care. Like the generation of '46 (NIH, Hill-Burton), the new programs reflected the distinctive environment of their time. The postwar celebration of American achievement—that extended self-congratulation of a society which believed it had solved life's most serious problems, except what to do with one's spare time—had begun to die down at the end of the fifties. Recurring recessions, rising unemployment, and slow economic growth in the Eisenhower years led to talk that America had "lost its way." When John F. Kennedy campaigned for president, he spoke of "getting the country moving again." In its spirit and ambitions, the Kennedy administration continually challenged the settled complacency and resistance to change in Congress and the "permanent government." Yet for all its impatience, the Kennedy administration by no means had a radical program. As the journalist Godfrey Hodgson writes, Americans in the early 1960s wanted change, but they did not want to *be changed*.[67] This was very much the case with regard to medical care. Americans wanted medicine to bring them change (new advances, more services), but they were not yet prepared for the sake of health to make changes in their way of life or their institutions.

As the 1960s began, the themes of criticism and reform were conventional but expressed with greater vehemence. The movement for a contributory hospital insurance program for the aged, already called Medicare, was gathering force. Concern about a "doctor shortage" began to grow. A 1959 government report declared that if the current ratio of doctors to population were just to be maintained, the output of American medical schools would have to be increased from 7,400 to 11,000 graduates a year by 1975. But to satisfy higher demand for services per capita and growing requirements for doctors in research and teaching, the report concluded an even larger expansion of medical schools was needed.[68] Nurses were also said to be in short supply. The need for more "health manpower" became widely accepted, and in 1963 Congress adopted the first of a series of measures to aid and expand education in the health professions.

The emerging view among liberals in health policy was that federal policy overemphasized hospital construction, while ambulatory care was neglected. In January 1959 Milton Roemer and Max Shain completed an influential study which argued that the supply of hospital beds was "probably the most fundamental" of all factors determining their use under health insurance. The "simplest fact of hospital operation," they wrote, "is the magnetism of an empty bed when payment for its use is assured." As hospital beds were built, physicians admitted patients they would otherwise have treated at home. "A half century ago," they noted, "only the most desperately ill were hospitalized; cases of pneumonia, tonsillectomies, deliveries, heart attacks, fractures were treated at home or in the doctor's office. Today not only are these cases hospitalized, but so are cases of multiple-tooth extractions, psychoneurosis, epilepsy, diabetes for insulin stabilization, or any obscure condition for diagnosis. All this is made possible by an increase in the relative supply of beds, and reciprocally it creates pressures for continual expansion of the bed supply." They pointed to evidence that much being done in hospitals could be done as well elsewhere if adequate provision had been made for less expensive outpatient and nursing care.[69]

Criticism of the single-minded emphasis on hospital construction took the same course as contemporary criticism of the bricks-and-mortar approach of urban renewal. Indeed, the same words recurred in writing about urban affairs and medical policy: "community," "coordination," "comprehensive services." In both cases, critics attacked established policy for its fragmented approach and lack of understanding of broader "community needs."

The field of medicine where the "rediscovery of community" found an immediately welcome reception was mental health services. A movement away from mental hospitals had already begun in the mid-1950s. The national census of mental hospitals declined from a peak of 634,000 in 1954 to 579,000 by 1963.[70] The predominant, though contested, explanation for the drop is that the discovery and introduction of the major tranquilizers (e.g., Thorazine) was the decisive event. Patients who were previously hospitalized could now be safely treated, or at least more safely ignored, on an outpatient basis. Another interpretation points to the adoption by Congress in 1956 of amendments to Social Security that provided greater aid to states to support the aged in nursing homes. Mental hospitals had been filled with unwanted older people suffering only from a harmless senility. By transferring such patients from mental hospitals to nursing homes, the states could transfer part of the cost of upkeep to the federal government.[71] Probably both drugs and nursing homes had some effect on the decline of mental hospitalization. The shift also began to receive strong encouragement from advocates of "community psychiatry," who argued that the state hospitals reinforced disability and isolation, while local services and halfway houses could help return the mentally ill to normal roles in society.

The Kennedy administration took up the cause of "community care" and turned it into a major new federal program. In 1960 a national commission set up by Congress five years earlier to reexamine mental health services called for a major new commitment of federal funds; among its proposals was more money for community clinics, but it favored more hospital aid, too.[72] The Kennedy administration chose to emphasize community services alone, along with more money for research and training, in what the president in February 1963 called a "bold new approach" to the problems of the disturbed and retarded. With new "community based" mental health services, he told Congress, "reliance on the cold mercy of custodial isolation will be supplanted by the open warmth of community concern and capability."[73] Congress agreed that year to the proposal for construction funds for the new community programs, and two years later it added money for initial staffing grants.

In a variety of ways, this program presaged the later initiatives of the 1960s. It created a new kind of organization, the community mental health center, which was meant to overcome the rigidities of the traditional social service agencies. In contrast to Hill-Burton, it linked the federal government and local communities and reduced the role of the states. However, there was no permanent federal funding; the program was meant to be a demonstration project. Ultimately, other sources were supposed to sustain the effort, if evaluations showed it to be effective. In this respect, the government took up the practice of the big foundations in distributing "seed" money and demanded new services from the social sciences to determine whether anything sprouted that was worth cultivating. And, finally, there was a linguistic shift: The use of the term "centers" rather than "clinics" suggested they would go beyond traditional medical functions. Just as the substitution of the term "clinic" for "dispensary" at the turn of the century indicated a widening of institutional mandate for ambulatory services, so, too, did substituting "center" for "clinic."

The two major contributions of President Kennedy to domestic policy—and indirectly to medical care—both came after his death. One was the tax cut he initiated in the face of a budget deficit. Enacted in 1964, it propelled the economy into its fifth successive year of expansion and brought in higher revenues at lower rates, as his advisers predicted. After the sluggish Eisenhower years the Democrats' economic record was dazzling. The economy expanded by one fourth between 1961 and 1965; the annual rate of growth, after adjusting for prices, was 5.3 percent.[74] Thanks also to the Republicans' nomination of Barry Goldwater, Democrats harvested the votes in 1964, picking up thirty-two seats in the House to gain a margin not seen since the New Deal. For liberals, it was a rare moment of political opportunity.

The fruits of economic policy made possible, among other things, the second of Kennedy's initiatives. In the year before he died, evidently convinced that a rising tide would not lift all boats, the president had asked his advisers to begin developing an antipoverty program. A crusade against poverty appealed to Kennedy as a way to rally Americans in a positive cause. The civil rights movement was also increasingly emphatic about economic issues; the 1963 March on Washington demanded jobs as well as freedom. The summer of 1963 saw the start of the ghetto riots. Almost immediately after Kennedy's assassination, Lyndon Johnson took up the cause of economic opportunity, and on January 8, 1964, he stood before both houses of Congress to announce "unconditional war on poverty in America."

Although contemporary liberal analyses continually stressed the importance of bad health as a link in the "cycle of poverty," medical care was at the outset not a central part of the antipoverty program. In his

Great Society speech, Johnson's only specific references to medicine were to Medicare and more money for training health professionals. These were not aimed specifically at the poor. The initial priorities of the antipoverty program turned out to be community action and education. But, once under way, the antipoverty effort and other Great Society programs became deeply involved in medical care.

What forces shaped government intervention in the 1960s? In his study of the community action program, Daniel Moynihan argues that liberal academic reformers were chiefly influential as its originators.[75] This was also the case in regard to the neighborhood health centers that emerged shortly out of the community action effort. But these intellectual influences were relatively marginal in medical care, and they grew progressively weaker as programs were winnowed out. The system created in part by postwar public policy now imposed demands for support and continuity that obstructed efforts to move policy in a new direction.

Redistributive Reform and Its Impact

A few general forces were at work in initiating the profusion of medical programs that emerged in the 1960s. Ideologically, nearly all the programs were framed, in one way or another, as responses to the public concern for greater access to medical services. But different interests called for different strategies in meeting (and even conceiving) that objective.

The structural impact of postwar policy, as I have described it, had been to create an immense new system of medical schools, teaching hospitals, and other allied institutions that now, to some extent, counterbalanced the private practitioners. This system demanded to be fed. Its representatives saw an inescapable role for themselves in solving the problems of society. Self-interest and noble aspirations both dictated that they begin a new chapter in the history of social reform. The community hospitals, though tied to private physicians, had their own independent interests, represented by the AHA and Blue Cross. They, too, demanded support under any new program.

A second and distinct influence came from the older and broader constituencies outside medical care that continued to favor a compulsory and contributory health insurance system. The labor movement was the most significant of these groups. Liberal political leaders favored its cause. Their agenda still consisted primarily of the unfinished business of the New Deal. While they wanted an insurance system, they had no objection to the programs sought by medical institutions to build additional capacity. In fact, one seemed to require the other. Their chief conflict came with those who still wanted to restrict government aid to the poor on public assistance.

And, finally, there were the critics who took the view that something more radical needed to be done. The term "community medicine," ambiguous though it is, may stand for their viewpoint. They wanted "comprehensive" services that trespassed the conventional limits of medicine. They saw their primary mission among the poor, and they favored greater community participation in health services. Before the late sixties, this viewpoint had no constituency to speak of outside the small band of progressives in public health and academic medicine.

Medicare was initially the overriding political issue. In 1958 a congressman from Rhode Island, Aime Forand, introduced a new and extremely modest proposal covering only hospital costs for the aged on Social Security. Unsurprisingly, virtually the same political constellation appeared that had existed ten years earlier. As before, the AMA undertook a massive campaign to portray a government insurance plan as a threat to the doctor-patient relationship. But by concentrating on the problems of the aged, liberals began changing the terms of debate.

The turn toward the aged aroused support from a growing constituency that felt the problem of hospital costs with unusual keenness. In the course of a year, one in six of those over sixty-five entered a hospital and stayed, on the average, twice as long as someone under sixty-five. Hospital care doubled in price during the 1950s. The aged could be presumed both needy and deserving, and the contributory nature of Social Security gave the entire program legitimacy. In 1959 a new Senate subcommittee on aging held hearings around the country. "The old folks lined up by the dozen everyplace we went," one staff member later recalled. "And they didn't talk much about housing or recreational centers or part-time work. They talked about medical care." Within two years, congressmen were reporting more mail on the subject than on any other pending legislation. A news magazine reported that pressure for the bill was "assuming the proportions of a crusade." Opinion polls had shown support before, but in the entire history of the campaign for national health insurance, this was the first time that a groundswell of grassroots support forced the issue onto the national agenda.[76]

In 1960 Congress responded to the pressure for Medicare by passing a substitute measure introduced by two of the most powerful members of Congress, Senator Robert Kerr of Oklahoma and Representative Wilbur Mills, chairman of the House Ways and Means Committee. The Kerr-Mills program extended federal support for welfare medicine programs in the states. The benefits were subject to few limits, and the federal government would provide between 50 and 80 percent of the funds (higher percentages going to poorer states). But the beneficiaries would be limited to the aged poor, and so Kerr-Mills did not settle the issue. Liberals opposed any "means-tested" program on principle as a source of humiliation to the aged and as an inadequate response to their financial and medical needs. They also charged that the states would not move vigorously to take advantage of Kerr-Mills. Three years later, reports confirmed that prediction. Many states had not acted at all, and five large industrial states, with one third of the nation's population, were receiving 90 percent of the funds.[77]

Despite President Kennedy's support, Medicare was short of votes in Congress until the Democratic sweep in 1964. It then received the highest priority among Great Society programs. However, strategists for the bill, still smarting from past defeats by the AMA, were against expanding its provisions to include physicians' services or to cover any broader group than the aged. At a time of expansive reform, they continued to back a measure framed in the more conservative 1950s. Ironically, the AMA, which now introduced its own "Eldercare" plan for expanding voluntary insurance, stressed that its program would provide the aged broader benefits, including physicians' services. The senior Republican on the Ways and Means Committee also introduced a proposal for a voluntary insurance plan, subsidized out of government revenues, that would cover major medical risks and include doctors' services and drugs. The share paid by the aged would be scaled to their Social Security benefits.

These proposals called attention to the limited benefits and regressive financing of the administration's Medicare plan. An AMA-financed survey found that 72 percent of those questioned thought Medicare ought to cover doctors' bills as well. Concerned about likely public disappointment, Representative Mills decided to expand the legislation. In an ingenious move, he proposed combining the administration's and the Republican measures and then adding a third program to aid services for the poor. The result was what one observer described as a three-layered cake. The first layer was the Democratic plan for a compulsory hospital insurance program under Social Security. This became Part A of Medicare. The second layer was the revised Republican program of government-subsidized voluntary insurance to cover physicians' bills. This became Part B of Medicare. And the third layer, called Medicaid, expanded assistance to the states for medical care for the poor. President Johnson signed the programs into law July 30, 1965. Some physicians initially swore they would organize a boycott, but cooler heads prevailed in the AMA and, after it went into effect a year later, the profession not only accepted Medicare but discovered it was a bonanza. The story was different with Medicaid.

Though adopted together, Medicare and Medicaid reflected sharply different traditions. Medicare was buoyed by popular approval and acknowledged dignity of Social Security; Medicaid was burdened by the stigma of public assistance. While Medicare had uniform national standards for eligibility and benefits, Medicaid left the states to decide how extensive their programs would be. Medicare allowed physicians to charge above what the program would pay; Medicaid did not and participation among physicians was far more limited. The objective of Medicaid was to allow the poor to buy into the "mainstream" of medicine, but neither the federal government nor the states were willing to spend the money that would have been required.[78]

The same Congress that enacted Medicare adopted a host of other measures to expand health services. One of these, the Regional Medical Programs, is particularly revealing of the tilt toward the hospitals and medical schools that persisted in government policy even as it became more redistributive in its objectives. In 1964 a Presidential Commission on Heart Disease, Cancer, and Stroke (the Debakey Commission), which had been appointed at the behest of the Lasker lobby, recommended a massive commitment of federal funds to establish "a national network of regional centers, local diagnostic and treatment stations, and medical complexes designed to unite the worlds of scientific research, medical education, and medical care."[79] The report paid no attention to any environmental, nutritional, or other public health and preventive concerns. Like the report of the Hospital Commission of the 1940s, the Debakey Commission report was a classic of the kind of myopia that the medical establishment of the mid-twentieth century confused with visionary ideals. No one, as Elizabeth Drew later pointed out, ever asked whether other diseases, such as those affecting children, or diseases that could actually be cured, might be more worthy of federal effort. The commission's conclusions in favor of a medical assault on heart disease, cancer, and stroke were foreordained by the commission's name and its composition (the Lasker lobby, as one of its representatives said, had a "quorum"). The aim was to make medical services more available, but there was little thought as to whether such an investment might actually make any difference in health.[80]

The neighborhood health centers reflected yet another approach to improving access to health care. Though the original Office of Economic Opportunity (OEO) legislation included no specific provisions for medical care, local community action programs became involved in various health care projects. The program's directors decided, however, that instead of supporting more fragmented services, they would support the development of new institutions to provide comprehensive ambulatory care. Accordingly, they took up the initiative of two professors of community medicine at Tufts University, H. Jack Geiger and Count D. Gibson, Jr., to establish a model comprehensive health center in a housing project in Boston. The proposal was expanded to include a second center in rural Mississippi. By the summer of 1966, eight health centers were approved for funding as demonstration projects under OEO's authority for research and development. In 1967 Senator Edward M. Kennedy sponsored an amendment to authorize special funds for comprehensive health services, and over the next four years OEO helped to start about one hundred neighborhood health centers and other comprehensive service projects. HEW supported another fifty centers under the authority to support demonstration projects granted it in the Comprehensive Planning Legislation passed in 1966. In addition, older programs, such as Hill-Burton and community mental health centers, were modified to focus efforts on low-income communities.

The aim of the health centers program was to create a "one-stop" facility in low-income communities that could provide virtually all necessary ambulatory health service. The centers would try to employ as many local residents as possible and encourage community participation in running the organizations. Part of the objective was to develop indigenous competence and leadership. This concern reflected the general aim of the War on Poverty to "help the poor help themselves"—a fundamentally conservative idea that had radical implications in the context of modern professionalism. Initially, the centers did not observe the conventional boundaries of medicine. A good example comes from the early project started at Mound Bayou, Mississippi, where malnutrition proved to be one of the most serious health problems. As Jack Geiger describes it, when the health center began stocking and prescribing food for the malnourished, some officials objected that its pharmacy was only supposed to carry drugs for the treatment of disease. To which the staff responded, "The last time we looked in the book, the specific therapy for malnutrition was food." The center also became involved in starting farm cooperatives, public transportation, and other local projects.[81]

Like the mental health centers, the neighborhood health centers were started on the premise that as demonstration projects they had only temporary federal funding. Once again, a national program planted a new type of organization at the local level, outside existing bureaucracies. But these aspects of the program were also the source of its vulnerability. In the long run, the centers were supposed to derive their funds from other sources, such as third-party reimbursement. Medicaid, however, did not cover the broad range of services the centers provided. (As of 1975 Medicare and Medicaid generated only 10 to 20 percent of operating income for most centers.) Furthermore, in 1967 Congress restricted the centers to providing free services to low-income families; two years later, this restriction was interpreted as limiting paying patients at the centers to 20 percent of their total registrants. These provisions were adopted at the behest of private practitioners who did not want the health centers competing with them for good business (the old story of "dispensary abuse" again). But as Karen Davis and Cathy Schoen point out, "These restrictions guaranteed the almost total dependence of the neighborhood health center program on public funds."[82]

About half the medical schools in the country participated in developing or staffing health centers. Hospitals and health departments also took part as sponsors. But they frequently became embroiled in conflicts with community representatives, and as federal funds for developing centers became more scarce in the early 1970s, the interest of the medical establishment in the program cooled considerably.

In plans developed by HEW in 1967, the administration looked mainly to health centers rather than Medicaid as the main vehicle for providing medical care to poverty areas. Plans called for one thousand centers serving 25 million people by 1973. This program, of course, was never carried out. Little money was available for community medicine in the sense the health centers were demonstrating. While the Medicaid budget ballooned, the growth of the centers was stunted. Yet neighborhood health centers were not any less successful. In fact, studies suggest they had positive effects on the health of their communities and significantly reduced use of hospitals (savings that they did not capture).[83] But policy makers did not deliberately choose to push Medicaid over neighborhood health centers on the basis of any evaluation of relative cost effectiveness. Medicaid simply had the advantage of institutional compatibility. It covered what would otherwise have been bad debts for hospitals and raised no challenge to private interests in the medical sector. Although neighborhood health centers managed to survive (and even grow in the later seventies), they never became more than a marginal alternative.[84]

The programs of the 1960s represented a second stage in the extension of medical services in American society in the twentieth century. The first stage was the extension of services to the working class and the South in the period after the Second World War. The growth of health insurance as a fringe benefit of employment and the rise of real incomes in the 1940s and 1950s made it possible for working-class families to enjoy greater access to medical services than they had before the war. Similarly, the Hill-Burton program brought about the development of hospitals in the South and other areas of the country where previously arrested economic development had made medical resources relatively scarce. The studies of the Committee on the Costs of Medical Care, carried out between 1928 and 1931, showed that middle-income families then used health services at a rate that was closer to the low use by the poor than the high use by the rich. But by the 1950s the receipt of health services among people of moderate incomes was approaching the level of higher-income households. Now it was the poor, rather than the rich, who stood out as different from the rest of society. This shift may be described as a change from mass exclusion to minority exclusion from medical care. And it followed the general pattern in postwar America that John Kenneth Galbraith, Michael Harrington, and others have described as the shift from "mass poverty" to "minority poverty." The social programs of the 1960s were aimed at alleviating minority poverty; the health programs were aimed specifically at reducing the exclusion from medical care of the poor and the aged, who were marginal to the core sectors of the economy where health insurance was available as a fringe benefit.

There is little question that these efforts had an impact. The decade after 1965 witnessed a sharp increase in the use of medical services by the poor. In 1964 the nonpoor saw physicians about 20 percent more frequently than the poor; by 1975 the poor visited physicians 18 percent more often than the nonpoor. In 1964 whites saw physicians 42 percent more often than blacks; by 1973 whites still saw physicians more often, but only by 13 percent. In 1963 those with incomes under $2,000 a year had only half as many surgical procedures per 100 people as those with incomes of $7,500 or more, but by 1970 the rate for the low-income group was 40 percent higher.[85] Most of this increase was probably due to Medicare and Medicaid. Data from 1969, for example, show that for every level of health status, public assistance recipients eligible for Medicaid used medical services much more often than other poor people not eligible for Medicaid.[86]

However, another reason for increased use of medical care by the poor—virtually unnoticed in research in this area—was that the composition of the poverty population was changing. Between 1959 and 1969, according to the standard government data, the poverty population dropped from 22.4 to 12.8 percent of the American people. But as the poverty population diminished, it included an increasing proportion who were poor because the head of household could not work.[87] The reduction of poverty among working families seems to have left a higher proportion of chronically ill and disabled people among the poor relative to the rest of society.[88] The rising use of health services by low-income people may partly reflect this change in composition of the poverty population.

Various studies taking into account differences in health do show increased use of medical care relative to "need." These studies disagree as to whether the poor gained equal access to medical care in the 1970s when the redistributive programs reached their peak. But the balance of evidence suggests that significant differences remained even then in use relative to need and in the quality of services received by the poor.[89]

The continuing differences in the access of the poor to medical care reflected the limitations of the programs established in the 1960s. Even before the cutbacks of the Reagan administration, Medicare covered less than half of the health expenditures of the elderly, Medicaid covered only one third of the poor, and neighborhood health centers reached only an additional 5 percent.[90] Because of differences in eligibility requirements for Medicaid, the proportion of the poor able to receive benefits varied sharply among the states. Medicaid omitted from coverage most two-parent families and childless couples, widows, and other single persons under sixty-five years of age, families with fathers working at low-paying jobs, and medically needy families in the twenty-two states that did not provide such coverage.[91]

So by 1970 the structure of inequality had changed once again. Those without any financial protection in sickness, public or private, were households with part-time or recently unemployed workers and the working poor who earned too little to afford private insurance and too much to qualify for public assistance. Along with the many poor people excluded from Medicaid because they failed to fit into eligibility categories, these were the medically excluded even in the heyday of redistributive effort—those who wandered in what might be called the "Medicaid-private insurance corridor," the purgatory of categorical social welfare systems.

The Politics of Accommodation

Buried in the detail of the Medicare statutes and administrative regulations were a number of far-reaching decisions about the organization and financing of health care in America. I will mention only two of them because of their bearing on the present argument and later developments in health care.

In setting up Medicare, Congress and the administration were acutely concerned to gain the cooperation of the doctors and hospitals. Consequently, they established buffers between the providers of health care and the federal bureaucracy. Under Part A of Medicare, the law allowed groups of hospitals, extended care facilities, and home health agencies the option of nominating "fiscal intermediaries," instead of dealing directly with the Social Security Administration. These intermediaries were to provide reimbursements, consulting, and auditing services. The federal government was to pay the bills. As expected, the overwhelming majority of hospitals and other institutions nominated Blue Cross. Under Part B, the secretary of HEW was to choose private insurance agents called "carriers" to serve the same function in a geographical area. The majority of these carriers turned out to be Blue Shield plans. As a result, the administration of Medicare was lodged in the private insurance systems originally established to suit provider interests. And the federal government surrendered direct control of the program and its costs.

The second key decision involved the rules of payment for hospitals under Medicare. The legislation adopted the practice followed by Blue Cross of paying hospitals according to their costs rather than, for example, a schedule of negotiated rates. And in carrying out this provision, the administration agreed to rules for calculating costs that were extremely favorable to the hospital industry. The hospitals wanted Medicare to pay depreciation on hospital assets. Depreciation for a nonprofit institution is a peculiar idea; when a community donates capital to an institution, it does not necessarily agree to replace it. Yet the administration agreed not just to pay depreciation, but to pay it on an accelerated basis and to include Hill-Burton assets. Moreover, by providing capital through reimbursement, it would provide the most capital to the hospitals with the newest and most expensive facilities. And, unlike Hill-Burton, which originally required a planning procedure for setting priorities, the capital would flow without any governmental review of the relative needs of different areas. In a study of Medicare, Judith Feder notes that administration officials understood all these drawbacks of liberal reimbursement, but ignored them in making policy.

Why? Partly because senior SSA [Social Security Administration] and HEW officials accepted the consensus in the health field that hospital "improvement" was a good thing. . . .But even they would have been less generous if the hospitals had not pressed them. What made these officials . . . [give in] was their commitment to a "proper takeoff" for Medicare. Some observers have said that Medicare officials feared a hospital boycott if they did not give in. The officials themselves explain their position differently. Their feeling, according to a senior SSA official, was that the hospitals would have to go along . . . . "But there's a real difference in launching a program with the help of the hospitals as opposed to against them. To an administrator, that difference makes all the difference in the world."[92]

This was the politics of accommodation, and it affected every aspect of government policy.

The decision to provide capital reimbursement under Medicare involved millions of dollars annually in federal expenditures over and above the money still being spent through the Hill-Burton program. So, despite the widespread sense that federal policy ought to shift its emphasis to ambulatory care, the government was still putting big money behind hospital expansion. Medicare enormously strengthened the financial position of the hospital industry, enabling hospitals to accumulate and borrow capital on their own more easily. This greater financial independence undermined the simultaneous efforts to improve voluntary planning and coordination of medical facilities.

The emergence of health planning in the 1960s was part of the general attempt to provide "comprehensive" and "coordinated" services. In the United States, where planning has never been widely approved as a role for government, health planning was a limited exception. It had begun with voluntary hospital planning. The earliest efforts, such as the Hospital Planning Council of Greater New York, established in 1938, grew out of attempts to coordinate hospital philanthropy. These efforts to rationalize the hospital industry, often led by large employers, took place primarily in such cities as Rochester, Pittsburgh, and Detroit, where industrial leadership was highly concentrated. Between 1938 and 1962 only eight such local hospital planning agencies were established in the country. In 1962, however, the movement received a major boost when Hill-Burton funds became available for such activities on a fifty-fifty matching basis. By 1965 there were fifty areawide agencies. Then, in 1966, Congress adopted legislation for Comprehensive Health Planning, which authorized partial federal funding for planning agencies. But the whole effort was vitiated from the start by the refusal to give the agencies any control over the allocation of health care capital or the reimbursement system that determined the flow of revenues.[93]

The meager record of planning agencies was consistent with the deeper tendencies at work in federal policy. While government expanded its redistributive efforts, it continually sought to reassure pri-

vate interests that it would make no effort to control them. Like Hill-
Burton, Medicare included a specific provision that no part of the law
meant to authorize any changes in the organization of medical services.
And, indeed, initially there were none.[94]

To provide medical care or other services, the state can act via the
market or its own agencies. If it chooses to rely on the market, it has
the option of buying or subsidizing privately produced services through
direct appropriations or tax incentives. Alternatively, it can "produce"
and distribute medical services directly. The American pattern has
been to rely on the market. And, curiously, the programs of the 1960s
not only followed that pattern but strengthened it. As government financing expanded, the tendency was for the government production
of medical care to diminish. Outside of the armed services and various
other special categories, the few spheres of government production had
been veterans' and welfare medicine. When Medicare and Medicaid
made the indigent eligible for subsidized care in private institutions,
they undermined the rationale for municipal, veterans', and other government hospital services.

Some might argue that this preference for privately produced services reflects a typically capitalist bias, but other capitalist societies lean
more in the opposite direction in medical care. Britain and Sweden
have replaced systems of national health insurance with national health
services, thereby moving off the market into direct production and assuming greater control over the health system. The extent of variation
in medical services among capitalist countries suggests that there is no
simple correspondence between capitalism and medical care, at least
not in organizational and financial structure.[95]

The medical profession does not have the same basis of power as large
corporations. Private capital is not simply one of several interest groups
in society; the economy and hence the government's own tax revenues
depend on "business confidence." Hence business confidence generally
acts as a constraint on policy without businessmen ever having to lobby
on behalf of their interests as a class. If government threatens to undermine business confidence, it jeopardizes its own stability by bringing
about a reduction in investment and a general economic crisis, with rising unemployment and lower tax revenues. The medical profession
clearly does not have this degree of "structural power."[96] Government
can lose the confidence of doctors without grave economic repercussions. If threatened, doctors can try to withdraw their "human capital"—that is, to strike or even to emigrate. But these threats are much
harder to carry out than a shift of business investment. Opposition from
doctors is a potentially serious problem, but it is far from insuperable.

As the case of Medicare illustrates, the power of doctors and hospitals to withhold cooperation from a government program helped them to secure long-run advantages. The AMA may have lost its long campaign against government insurance at a rare moment of liberal political success. But the superior political organization of the AMA and the hospitals enabled them to shape what might be called the "interior" of reform. The AMA's dread predictions that Medicare would be a disaster made it especially important for the administration to demonstrate quickly to the public that services would be available when they wanted them. An administration more concerned with the budgetary consequences of concessions than with smooth take-off would not have yielded as much. The government and liberal reformers would pay a price for this choice later on. So would the doctors and the rest of the health care industry, for the concessions they won in public money would hurt them later in public confidence.

It was almost as if an internal dynamic were playing itself out in the postwar decades. In virtually the classic Marxian fashion, the expansion of the forces of production in health services—government subsidies, private insurance, technology, consumer demand—was breaking down the old social relations of production and preparing the way for more decisive change. As the institutional side of medicine expanded, the medical profession itself became more divided, especially between academic medicine and private practice. The cohesiveness of the profession, so vital to its past successes, was beginning, like so many other things in the 1960s, to come apart. New interests emerged inside medicine that began to overshadow the private practitioners. And as public dissatisfaction increased with rising costs, these new forces threatened to reduce the sovereignty that private doctors had long exercised over medical care.

CHAPTER FOUR

End of a Mandate

MEDICINE, like many other American institutions, suffered a stunning loss of confidence in the 1970s. Previously, two premises had guided government health policy: first, that Americans needed more medical care—more than the market alone would provide; and second, that medical professionals and private voluntary institutions were best equipped to decide how to organize those services. Until the 1970s the first of these premises had not yet undermined the second. Increased federal aid initially did not much enlarge the scope of public regulation. Practitioners, hospitals, researchers, and medical schools enjoyed a broad grant of authority to run their own affairs.

In the 1970s this mandate ran out. The economic and moral problems of medicine displaced scientific progress at the center of public attention. Enormous increases in cost seemed ever more certain; corresponding improvements in health ever more doubtful. The prevailing assumptions about the need to expand medical care were reversed: The need now was to curb its apparently insatiable appetite for resources. In a short time, American medicine seemed to pass from stubborn shortages to irrepressible excess, without ever having passed through happy sufficiency. Rising costs brought medical care under more critical scrutiny, and the federal government, as a major buyer of health services, intervened in unprecedented ways.

Slow economic growth and persistent inflation in the seventies undoubtedly lay behind the shift from a redistributive to a regulatory politics in health care, but the new constraints were not purely economic in origin. Even the response to rising costs cannot be entirely understood apart from a diminished faith in the efficacy of medicine and increased concern about its relation to other moral values. Many worried—and the courts often agreed—that doctors and hospitals might abuse their power, if patients' rights were not more clearly protected. The women's movement also challenged the authority and power of the profession. For the first time in a century, American physicians faced a serious challenge simultaneously to their political influence, their economic power, and their cultural authority.

And yet the 1970s did not yield a victory for medicine's progressive critics. One dose of inflation and disillusionment with medicine produced a movement for reform, but a second dose produced impasse and despair, and a third dose a movement against many of the changes adopted earlier. Like American politics more generally, the politics of health care passed through three phases in the 1970s:

1. A period of agitation and reform in the first half of the decade, when broader entitlements to social welfare and stricter regulation of industry gained ground in public opinion and law

2. A prolonged stalemate, beginning around 1975, when the preoccupation increasingly became coping with inflation, doubts arose about the value of medical care, and initiatives such as national health insurance were set aside

3. A growing reaction against liberalism and government, culminating in the election of President Reagan in 1980 and the reversal of many earlier redistributive and regulatory programs

Despite these shifts, the underlying tension remained throughout the 1970s—and continues today—between a medical care system geared toward expansion and a society and state requiring some means of control over medical expenditures. By 1980 health care expenditures reached $230 billion, up from $69 billion in 1970, a jump from 7.2 to 9.4 percent of GNP.[1] Growth of this kind cannot be indefinitely sustained regardless of the administration in Washington; other sectors of the economy cannot and will not support it. Yet controlling expansion means redrawing the "contract" between the medical profession and society, subjecting medical care to the discipline of politics or markets or reorganizing its basic institutional structure. This is what began to happen in the 1970s.

LOSING LEGITIMACY, 1970–1974

Discovery of a Crisis

The 1970s opened with ominous declarations of a "crisis" in health care. The wide use of the term "crisis" did not simply register an objective reality—it changed it. Crises make hard decisions seem unavoidable; they change the political agenda and create political opportunities. For years liberals had been trying to persuade Americans to recognize a health care crisis in order to open the way for reforms beyond Medicare. On assuming office, the Nixon administration confronted rapidly escalating costs in Medicare and Medicaid, and it, too, adopted the rhetoric of crisis. "We face a massive crisis in this area," President Nixon told a press conference in July 1969. "Unless action is taken within the next two or three years . . . we will have a breakdown in our medical system."[2] In January 1970 *Business Week* ran a cover story on the "$60 billion crisis" that compared medical care in America unfavorably to national health programs in Western Europe.[3] That same month, the editors of *Fortune*, in a special issue on medical care, declared that American medicine stood "on the brink of chaos." Their indictment was as stinging as any in the liberal press:

Much of U.S. medical care, particularly the everyday business of preventing and treating routine illnesses, is inferior in quality, wastefully dispensed, and inequitably financed. Medical manpower and facilities are so maldistributed that large segments of the population, especially the urban poor and those in rural areas, get virtually no care at all—even though their illnesses are most numerous and, in a medical sense, often easy to cure.

Whether poor or not, most Americans are badly served by the obsolete, overstrained medical system that has grown up around them helter-skelter. . . . the time has come for radical change.[4]

A survey of heads of families in 1970 found that three quarters agreed with the statement, "There is a crisis in health care in the United States."[5]

First and last, this was understood to be a crisis of money. In the phrase of the day, the costs of medical care were "skyrocketing." If allowed to continue, "runaway" inflation would "price medical care out of the reach of most Americans." No discussion of the health care crisis was complete without stories of the many families that were ruined financially by staggering medical bills. But in the early seventies, the list of medicine's inadequacies always went beyond its expense. As Karl

Yordy, an analyst at the Institute of Medicine said in 1973, "The cost question turned the spotlight on the other deficiencies of the system."[6] Even with all the additional public expenditures, the poor were still not receiving adequate medical care. Middle-class families were upset that they couldn't find a doctor evenings or weekends. As general practitioners became a rapidly dwindling species, many people were frustrated that they no longer seemed to have any access to medical care even in areas where doctors and hospitals were numerically abundant. And, for all the costs, the health of Americans did not seem to be as good as that of the people of most other industrialized countries. The articles announcing the health crisis typically pointed out that Americans— even excluding blacks—had higher infant mortality rates and lower life expectancy than most Europeans.

Most of these facts were hardly new, but the attention paid to them was unprecedented. For the moment, the liberal critics of medical care commanded the political debate. Their conceptions of the problem and their remedies now became common wisdom. American medicine, the consensus held, was overly specialized, overbuilt and overbedded, and insufficiently attentive to the needs of the poor in inner-city and rural areas. The system needed fewer hospitals, more "primary" care, incentives to get doctors into underserved communities, and better management and organization. And most of all, Americans required national health insurance—not a giveaway to the providers like Medicare, but a "rational," "coordinated" program that would include "tough cost controls."

After a hiatus of twenty years, national health insurance again began to receive attention in November 1968, when Walter Reuther, president of the United Auto Workers, issued a new call for its passage in a speech to the American Public Health Association. Reuther played the leading role in organizing a new Committee for National Health Insurance, and in January 1969 Senator Edward M. Kennedy, a member of the group, announced he would introduce legislation. Then in a remarkably short time, the idea received wide acceptance and the number of alternative plans proliferated. By 1970 the traditional opposition to national health insurance was so frail that the AMA, the hospitals, and the insurance industry were each sponsoring their own proposals.

Conservatives and liberals still had their disagreements about the scope of health insurance and the roles of the public and private sectors. But even some conservatives now acknowledged that reforms had only begun with Medicare and Medicaid, that federal programs were a hodgepodge, and that an overall program of national health insurance might be desirable. Since expanded entitlements to health care were likely, changes in the organization of health services would be a fiscal necessity.

In the early seventies, unlike later in the decade, the sense of crisis in health care was accompanied by considerable optimism about the possibilities for successful reform. The record of the Kaiser Health Foundation suggested it was possible to provide high quality prepaid health care at 20 to 40 percent lower cost than fee-for-service medicine. Advocates of the "health team" approach hoped that nurse practitioners, physicians' assistants, and other "physician extenders" could improve access and efficiency. High rates of surgery and hospitalization suggested that more careful peer review might significantly reduce expenses by discouraging unnecessary procedures. Extensive duplication of facilities and equipment suggested that effective health planning could yield notable benefits and savings.

For the first time since the Committee on the Costs of Medical Care, the economic and political leadership of American society seemed ready to bring about changes in the organization of medical care over the opposition of the providers. The doctors, hospitals, and insurance companies were now completely on the defensive, trying to hold back a tide of disaffection. So in a political sense, the medical system was very much in crisis, not because it was really about to break down, as the president and the business press suggested, but because it had lost their confidence. Medicine had overdrawn its credit. It had also aroused a variety of new social movements to much bolder opposition. Two processes were at work in producing this extraordinary loss of favor. I will call them *the contradictions of accommodation* and *the generalization of rights*.

The Contradictions of Accommodation

The concessions that the doctors and hospitals had secured in Medicare and other public programs denied the government any leverage to control costs. But once those costs began to escalate, government acquired an independent interest in reorganizing the system and the political influence of the providers began to erode. Employers paying rising insurance rates also increasingly began to distinguish their interests from those of the health care industry. The politics and institutions of accommodation, in other words, were their own undoing. Their contradictions were driving government and business to pronounce health care in crisis and to seek reform.

The cost problem took on a new meaning by 1970. Although medical costs were rising before 1965, they had been regarded mainly as a problem for individuals and families. Congress generally favored increasing total health expenditures in the belief that medical care was a prudent and popular social investment. After 1970, however, public officials began to regard the aggregate costs of health care as too high and to doubt that the investment was worth the return in health.

Two objective realities had changed. Medical costs had begun to rise much more sharply, and government's share of costs had increased. The rate of growth in the cost of medical services rose from 3.2 percent a year in the seven years before Medicare to 7.9 percent annually during the five years afterward. (Meanwhile, the inflation rate for all other services in the consumer price index increased from 2.0 to 5.8 percent annually.) National health expenditures, up from $142 to $198 per capita between 1960 and 1965, had risen to $336 per capita by 1970. Hospital costs had become especially troublesome. From 1950 to 1965 per capita expenditures on community hospitals rose 8 percent annually; after 1965 the rate of growth jumped to 14 percent a year.[7]

The impact on government was even more severe. Its share of national health expenditures jumped from 26 to 37 percent between 1965 and 1970. In that same period, the annual rate of increase in state and federal health expenditures was 20.8 percent. The $10.8 billion government had spent in 1965 became $27.8 billion by 1970.[8]

Many now doubted the need for these high expenditures. Health services research indicated that Americans had too much surgery and that perhaps one fifth of the patients in hospitals did not need to be there. News stories told of doctors and nursing home owners making small fortunes off government programs through inflated reimbursements or outright fraud.

Many attributed rising health care costs to Medicare and Medicaid, or to advances in science; but a more fundamental explanation lay in the basic incentives in the health care system, especially its financing arrangements, which Medicare and Medicaid had only reinforced. To be sure, advances in science and technology created new demands for investment. The advances during and after World War II had been in relatively inexpensive drugs; after 1960 they increasingly involved complex equipment and procedures. Hospital employees also had long been paid substandard wages; now they wanted to catch up to comparable workers. Doctors wanted more assistants to enable them to perform new tests and procedures. In hospitals—where most of the growth in costs came—the clamor for more resources was constant, relentless, and plausible. But the cause of rising costs was not so much the intensity of the clamor as the financial arrangements that allowed hospitals to yield to it. As Martin S. Feldstein put it, "increases in the components

of cost" were "primarily the result and not the cause of higher prices."
The tolerance of the market for higher prices allowed costs to increase.
Higher incomes and higher expectations were partly responsible for
that increased tolerance, but the key was the structure of financing.[9]

As third parties, both private insurers and government programs effectively insulate patients and providers from the true cost of treatment
decisions and so reduce the incentive to weigh costs carefully against
benefits. From 1960 to 1975 the share of health care expenditures paid
by third parties increased from 45 to 67 percent.[10] Like most private
plans, Medicare and Medicaid reimburse providers on a fee-for-service
basis. Since under fee-for-service, doctors and hospitals make more
money the more services they provide, they have an incentive to maximize the volume of services. Third-party, fee-for-service payment was
the central mechanism of medical inflation.

In addition, the reimbursement practices for hospitals and doctors
were peculiarly designed to encourage higher costs. As I have already
mentioned, Medicare and Medicaid, like Blue Cross, chose to reimburse
hospitals on the basis of their costs. Under such a system, any institution
that reduced its costs would reduce its income, possibly for years to
come, since the record of past costs affects future reimbursement levels.
On the other hand, the greater its costs, the higher its reimbursements.
Thus hospitals were encouraged to solve financing problems, not by
minimizing costs but by maximizing reimbursements. What was individually a solution for hospitals was, in aggregate, a problem for society.

Instead of establishing a fixed fee schedule, Medicare paid doctors according to their "customary" fees, assuming them to be the "prevailing" fees in the area or, failing precedent, to be "reasonable." Fees
began to soar when some young doctors, who had no record of charges,
billed at unprecedented levels and were paid. When their older colleagues saw what was possible, they, too, raised their fees, and soon
what was customary was higher than ever before. Blue Shield adopted
a similar system ("usual, customary, and reasonable" reimbursement),
and the result was rampant inflation in medical fees.[11]

This system continues today. Reimbursements reflect the prevailing
charges in a community and thus favor doctors who practice in high-
priced areas. Since reimbursement rates also depend on a physician's
record of past charges, the system gives doctors an incentive to keep
pushing their prices up to improve their profile. Medicare also permits
doctors to charge patients over and above what the government will
pay.

But probably most important, the prevailing relative fees paid physicians provide higher compensation for services performed in a hospital

than for identical services performed in an office. Doctors earn more, for example, for a follow-up hospital visit than for an office visit, even though the hospital visit costs the doctor far less to produce. In the mid-1970s, according to data assembled by Mark Blumberg, doctors earned 50 to 60 percent more per hour for hospital labor time. Third parties also pay more per minute of physician time for certain procedures and auxiliary services. Originally, these procedures were often complicated and time-consuming, but as Blumberg points out in his historical analysis of doctors' fees, prices have typically remained high even when the procedures have been simplified. As a result, some services, like cataract surgery, are financial "winners" because they pay much more than they cost to produce, while other services, like talking to a patient, are "losers" because they pay less than they cost. These relative prices also result in higher incomes for those specialties that do more procedures and practice more in hospitals.[12] A cardiac surgeon, writing in *The New England Journal of Medicine*, has estimated that members of his own specialty doing coronary bypass operations in 1979–80 were earning an average of $350,000 a year on that operation alone. And since they were doing many other operations, notes Dr. Benson Roe, "it is conservative to estimate that their average gross income exceeds $500,000." Originally, the surgeon took part in the entire procedure, from the diagnostic studies through all stages of the operation to post-operative care. Now the surgeon has been relieved of many of these responsibilities by assistants and technicians, whose services are all billed separately. "Under these circumstances," writes Dr. Roe, "one might expect the surgeon's fee to have dropped considerably, but it has not. On the contrary, fees for cardiac surgery have escalated at a rate that far exceeds the inflation factor."[13]

Distorted prices distort decisions about services, careers, and investments. In the system as a whole, the biases they create regularly produce overuse of hospital care, tests, and surgery and encourage more doctors to enter specialties like surgery than the society needs.

The dynamics of the system in everyday life are simple to follow. Patients want the best medical services available. Providers know that the more services they give and the more complex the services are, the more they earn and the more they are likely to please their clients. Besides, physicians are trained to practice medicine at the highest level of technical quality without regard to cost. Hospitals want to retain their patients, physicians, and community support by offering the maximum range of services and the most modern technology, often regardless of whether they are duplicating services offered by other institutions nearby. Though insurance companies would prefer to avoid the uncertainty that rising prices create, they have generally been able to pass along the costs to their subscribers, and their profits increase with the total volume of expenditures. No one in the system stands to lose from its expansion. Only the population over whom the insurance costs and taxes are spread has to pay, and it is too poorly organized to offer resistance.

The obvious defect is the absence of any effective restraint. Yet this is no accidental oversight. It is, as we have seen, the outcome of a long history of accommodation to private physicians, as well as to hospitals and insurance companies, which in their own internal organization had adjusted to the practitioners' interests. This institutional phalanx succeeded in blocking any form of control or any alternative form of organization that would have threatened their domination of the market.

Public dissatisfaction about access to medical care had much the same origins as excessive costs. Political accommodation of dominant private institutions in medical care allowed them to pursue their own internal priorities. No limits were placed on the number or variety of medical specialties, while specialists received higher insurance reimbursements than general practitioners. Almost every conceivable encouragement was given to hospitals to grow. Most insurance covered hospital care; doctors' services, if given in hospitals, were more likely to be covered and paid at a higher rate.

So just as the financing system promoted overexpansion in some areas, it produced an undersupply of services in others. The incentives that favored hospital care promoted the neglect of ambulatory and preventive health services; the incentives that favored specialization also caused primary care to be neglected. Paying doctors according to the fees prevailing in their areas encouraged doctors to settle in wealthy suburbs rather than in the rural or inner-city areas.

Paradoxically, public financing weakened the medical institutions in the public sector. Medicaid drained state and local government budgets for health care, allowed the eligible poor to go to voluntary hospitals, and left municipal and other public institutions with limited resources to care for the millions of people who remained uninsured.

The same reimbursement practices that encouraged community hospitals in wealthy areas to expand caused financial difficulties for hospitals in poor neighborhoods. The effect of cost-based reimbursement on the solvency of hospitals depends on the relative proportions of charity and privately insured patients. Medicare and Medicaid, both cost-based payers, do not consider charity care to other patients as a cost of service to their beneficiaries. (Blue Cross plans vary.) Hence hospitals have to recover the costs of charity from some other source, such as those patients who pay charges (usually people covered by commercial insurance who then receive indemnity benefits). Hospitals with few charity patients and many privately insured ones have little difficulty raising charges on the latter to make up their losses. But hospitals with many charity patients, few privately insured, and the remainder paid at cost can easily find themselves in deep trouble. These are typically hospitals that serve the poor.

The differences between cost-based payers and charge-based payers led to unexpected political effects. The commercial insurance companies worried that if the government tried to solve its fiscal problems simply by tightening up cost-based reimbursement, the hospitals might shift the costs to patients who pay charges, which would force up commercial insurers' rates and make them less competitive with Blue Cross. Hence the commercial insurance industry began to favor more comprehensive responses, such as community health planning or state regulation of hospital charges.[14]

Thus three powerful forces were now arraying themselves against the health care providers in a drive for greater state intervention—the insurance industry, the employers, and the government itself. In the seventies, these interests found themselves in a temporary alliance with long-time liberal critics of the health system and a variety of new social movements demanding reform.

The Generalization of Rights

Every society shapes the demands made against it. In the United States, the two-party system, the absence of a socialist tradition, and the distinctive role of the judiciary in interpreting the Constitution encourage the dissatisfied to organize in social movements outside the political parties and to present their demands as claims under the Bill of Rights. These tendencies were never more in evidence than during the 1970s.

The civil rights' struggle lost its momentum as a protest movement in the seventies, but it set the example for dozens of other movements of similar purpose. Instead of marching through the streets, they marched mainly through the courts. And instead of a single movement centered on blacks, the new movements advocated the rights of women, children, prisoners, students, tenants, gays, Chicanos, native Americans, and welfare clients. The catalogue of rights and of groups entitled to them was immensely expanded in both variety and detail. Medical care figured prominently in this generalization of rights, particularly as a concern of the women's movement and in the new movements specifically for patients' rights and for the rights of the handicapped, the mentally ill, the retarded, and the subjects of medical research.

Health care as a matter of right, not privilege: No other single idea so captures the spirit of the time. The law did not, in fact, recognize any general right to health care, and philosophers and lawyers questioned what a right to health care or to health itself might require. But despite such objections, the claim was for a time so widely acknowledged as almost to be uncontroversial. The entitlement programs had created a specific set of rights to medical care, but only for those who could establish eligibility. Some hospitals, having accepted federal funds under the Hill-Burton program, had obligated themselves to provide charity care—an obligation that attorneys for the poor sought to enforce in the courts in the early 1970s. Other legal claims were raised on behalf of patients committed to mental institutions. In a notable case in 1971, *Wyatt* v. *Stickney*, a federal court in Alabama ruled that patients in one of the state's mental hospitals had a right to psychiatric treatment as long as the state kept them confined.[15]

The new health rights movements were also concerned with rights *in* health care, such as the right to informed consent, the right to refuse treatment, the right to see one's own medical records, the right to participate in therapeutic decisions, and the right to due process in any proceeding for involuntary commitment to a mental institution. Claims of a right to health care demand equality between rich and poor, whereas rights in health care demand greater equality between professional and client. For every right, there are always correlative obligations. Recognition of a right to health care would obligate the state to guarantee provision of services. Recognized rights in health care, such as informed consent, obligate doctors and hospitals to share more information and authority with their patients. Thus the new health rights movement went beyond traditional demands for more medical care and challenged the distribution of power and expertise. These efforts, like the attempts to enlarge entitlements to services, met some success in the courts. Indeed, few other developments so well illustrate the decline of professional sovereignty in the 1970s as the increased tendency of the courts to view the doctor-patient relationship as a partnership in decision making rather than a doctors' monopoly. On the issue of informed consent, the courts took the view that doctors had an affirmative duty to present all material facts, including risks of treatment, to the patient. (A patient can sue a physician for malpractice if the doctor fails to disclose such risks and the patient suffers an injury.) Public authorities, beginning in the 1960s, also adopted new safeguards to assure the right of informed consent to the subjects of medical research.[16]

In 1972 the trustees of the American Hospital Association, following the lead of some local hospitals and health centers, adopted a Patient's Bill of Rights, which included rights to informed consent and to considerate and respectful care. Though well received by the press, the declaration prompted one critic, Dr. Willard Gaylin, to remark that it was an example of "the thief lecturing his victim on self-protection," since it only returned to patients some legal rights that hospitals had previously stolen from them.[17]

One of the AHA's more controversial provisions said patients had the right to refuse treatment "to the extent permitted by law." The controversy that ensued concerned the proper limits of medical intervention—whether, for example, doctors and hospitals were bound to honor the request of a dying patient no longer to be kept alive. Some worried that medicine might lose its commitment to sustain life if the commitment were qualified in any way; others argued that hospitals were keeping alive patients who no longer wanted to live. The controversy was symptomatic of a deeper problem. A French physician calls it "therapeutic relentlessness."[18] In its commitment to the preservation of life, medical care ironically has come to symbolize a prototypically modern form of torture, combining benevolence, indifference, and technical wizardry. Rather than engendering trust, technological medicine often raises anxieties about the ability of individuals to make choices for themselves.

Advocates of patients' rights made their case as much from these concerns as from concerns about the poor. In so doing, they raised radical questions about the prerogatives of the doctor's role. Implicit was a belief that the interests of doctors and patients frequently diverged, and hence that patients needed protection, especially in relation to medical research and the use of experimental techniques, such as psychosurgery. Some doctors did not appreciate this signal of distrust. "What I resent, and resent very deeply," said one surgeon in 1977, explaining why he objected to review boards supervising the selection of patients for psychosurgery, "is the idea that has been prevalent for the past seven years that patients have to be protected from physicians. This is a terrible, terrible thought to me. The best guardian that you can have of your welfare when you are ill with anything is your physician."[19]

This was precisely what many Americans had ceased to believe. Since the Progressive era, as David Rothman has written, reformers had assumed that professionals, including physicians, would act in the interests of the dependent; consequently, they were willing to give them wide discretion in institutions such as prisons and hospitals. By the 1970s, reformers had become intensely skeptical of professionals and the benevolent institutions they supervised.[20] From this distrust emerged a variety of legal safeguards aimed at limiting professional autonomy and power. A related movement also developed to "deinstitutionalize" the dependent and "demedicalize" critical life events, such as childbirth and dying. The interest in hospices and home births derived, at least in part, from a desire to escape professional dominance as well as the desensitizing environment of the hospital. In the view of its critics, the hospital had become a zone of medical domination, and the only escape was to remove the "patient" to a setting where medical authority would be secondary.

Perhaps nowhere was the distrust of professional domination more apparent than in the women's movement. Feminists claimed that as patients, as nurses, and in other roles in health care, they were denied the right to participate in medical decisions by paternalistic doctors who refused to share information or take their intelligence seriously. They objected that much of what passed for scientific knowledge was sexist prejudice and that male physicians had deliberately excluded women from competence by keeping them out of medical schools and suppressing alternative practitioners such as midwives.

The most direct consequence of the feminist movement for medicine was a sharp increase in the number of women entering the profession. As late as 1970, only about 9 percent of medical students were women; by the end of the decade, the proportion had passed 25 percent. But just as striking as the change in numbers was the change in consciousness. The older generation of women physicians had felt obliged to prove they could make it on the terms set by the dominant male physicians. The younger generation of women physicians demanded that male physicians change their attitudes and behavior and modify institutional practices to accommodate their needs as women.[21] Here the new consciousness of rights invaded the house of medicine and insisted on changes in the rules of professional behavior and practice.

The more radical elements of the women's movement argued that women had to take medicine "into their own hands." In 1969 members of the Chicago Women's Liberation Union organized an underground referral service for abortions. Several women then learned how to perform the procedure themselves, and by 1973, when the Supreme Court issued its decision legalizing abortion, they were doing abortions at the rate of fifty a week for far less than private abortionists charged. In the early seventies women's groups also began learning gynecological self-care and encouraging a revival of lay midwifery. Feminists argued that medical care needed to be demystified and women's lives demedicalized. They maintained that childbirth was not a disease and normal deliveries did not require hospitalization and the supervision of an obstetrician.[22]

The conflict over home birth proved to be one of the most bitter between the medical profession and the women's movement. While no state forbade home birth, the American College of Obstetricians and Gynecologists actively discouraged it as unconscionably risky. Doctors who participated in home births by offering backup in emergencies were threatened with loss of hospital privileges and even their medical licenses. Midwives in California were prosecuted for practicing medicine without a license.[23]

The developments in feminism were related to a broader revival of a therapeutic counterculture with political overtones. Folk, non-Western and entirely novel therapies gained not only a clientele but also surprising respectability, in part because they belonged to a broader cultural and political movement. Much of the new counterculture went under the rubric "holistic medicine" and presented itself as a humane alternative to an overly technical, disease-oriented, impersonal medical system. Just as nineteenth-century heroic medicine had given rise to therapeutic dissent, so did twentieth-century technological medicine. And just as nineteenth-century critics called for a democratization of medical knowledge ("every man his own doctor"), so did the new advocates of self-care.

Therapeutic dissent also had political associations on the right. The movement to legalize the alleged cancer-cure laetrile had links to conservative organizations opposed to federal intervention in private affairs. They, too, saw the content of medical practice as imbued with political meaning.

The left-wing advocates of health rights saw a common thread linking national health insurance, community participation on the boards of health centers and hospitals, and individual patients' rights to take part in their own treatment and to treat themselves. The issue was basically professional dominance, and their aim was to increase the power of consumers. This new consciousness about medicine shaped new intellectual developments. In medical ethics, medical sociology, and medical history, the dominant sympathies began to change. Much of the traditional work in these fields was written from the physicians' viewpoint, if not by doctors themselves. Increasingly, over the past decade, philosophers, lawyers, sociologists, historians, and feminists, newly interested in health care, have portrayed the medical profession as a dominating, monopolizing, self-interested force. Once a hero, the doctor has now become a villain, and the resentment of this new work by the profession and older scholars in these fields has been intense.

This intellectual shift reflects a deepening ambivalence about medicine in the entire society. While Americans express confidence in their own personal physicians, they are more hostile to doctors as a class. The desire to enter medicine as a career is undiminished, but there is great antagonism toward those who do. This ambivalence is evident in the patients' rights and women's movements, which simultaneously claimed rights of access to and rights of protection against medical authority.

The generalization of rights and the intensification of ambivalence toward medical authority contributed to the pressure for government intervention. Advocates for the mentally ill, the handicapped, and other patients sponsored new laws and pursued litigation that led to greater regulatory control. During the seventies, the mobilization of these groups also blocked any resolution of the cost problem simply by wholesale cutbacks in public expenditures. Growing acceptance of a right of equal access to medical care meant that cost control had to be built into the medical system. If health care was a right, structural reform was a necessity.

The Conservative Assimilation of Reform

In the early 1970s, American medicine seemed to be caught in a political vise between the concern of government and business about high costs and the demands of protest movements and liberals for equality and participation in medical care. Both sorts of critics agreed health care was in crisis, and both ascribed responsibility to the medical profession. "The doctors created the system. They run it. And they are the most formidable obstacle to its improvement," said one writer in *Fortune* in 1970.[24] This was a sentiment the advocates of health rights vigorously seconded.

Reform, both types of critics agreed, would require an extension of the boundaries of the political. An undersecretary of the Department of Health, Education and Welfare (HEW) in the Nixon administration, John G. Veneman, put the point succinctly at a news conference June 3, 1971: "In the past, decisions on health care delivery were largely professional ones. Now the decisions will be largely political."[25] This, too, was a belief the advocates of health rights shared.

From different directions, the efficiency-oriented and the rights-oriented critics had arrived at many of the same reform proposals. Liberals had long supported prepaid group practice, expanded use of a health team including nurse practitioners and physicians' assistants, auditing of professional performance, and health planning as ways to improve medical care. In the early seventies, conservatives began to appropriate many of these ideas as ways to cut costs. Liberals also thought there would be savings from reform but hoped to use the savings to make health insurance universal and comprehensive. Yet even without consensus about the ends of reform, there was agreement about many of the means.

In its early years, 1969 to 1971, the Nixon administration fought a rearguard action against the social programs of the Great Society, but the political climate was still predominantly liberal. Democrats controlled Congress by a wide margin, and the administration was typically in the position of responding to liberal initiatives. Nixon was not a doctrinaire conservative. Despite the impression created by deep cuts in Great Society programs, his administration actually presided over a shift in the federal budget from defense to social expenditures, a huge expansion of Social Security, a wave of environmental and health and safety legislation, and acceptance of population planning and other ideas that had long been considered too controversial for liberal administrations to carry out. The president's proposal of a guaranteed minimum income was particularly out of line with conventional Republican philosophy, as was his adoption of wage-price controls and his opening to China. Nixon accepted the gospel of macroeconomic management according to Keynes. Under constant siege from Vietnam through Watergate, struggling to gain the offensive, the president assimilated and recast liberal ideas. This is exactly what happened in medical care.

Indeed, health care policy in the 1970s is a paradigmatic case of the conservative assimilation of reform—and its subsequent repudiation by conservatives themselves.

In 1970 the liberal initiative in medical care was the Health Security plan introduced by Senator Edward Kennedy and Representative Martha W. Griffiths of Michigan. Health Security called for a comprehensive program of free medical care, replacing all public and private health plans in a single, federally operated health insurance system. Though it did not involve any nationalization of facilities nor require physicians to work on salary, it would have set a national budget, allocated funds to regions, provided incentives for prepaid group practice, and obliged private hospitals and physicians to operate within budget constraints. There were to be no copayments by consumers.[26]

In response to Kennedy's political challenge and the threat of rising costs, the Nixon administration in late 1969 began preparing a strategy of its own. In a memo to presidential assistant John Ehrlichman in December 1969, Lewis H. Butler, an HEW assistant secretary, wrote that "ultimately some kind of national health insurance should be enacted, but the immediate problem is to train more doctors and subprofessional people, and get away from hospital-dominated care into more efficient systems."[27] On February 5, 1970, Butler, Veneman, and a few other HEW officials met with Paul M. Ellwood, Jr., a Minneapolis physician who directed the American Rehabilitation Foundation. Ellwood had been trying for several years to get a hearing for his view that reform of the health system had to address its "structural incentives." In rehabilitation, as in other fields, fee-for-service payment penalized medical institutions that returned patients to health. The financing system, Ellwood argued, ought to reward health maintenance; prepayment for comprehensive care could achieve that end. So as an alternative to both fee-for-service and centralized governmental financing, Ellwood favored the development of comprehensive health care corporations, like the Kaiser plan. At the meeting in Washington, he first suggested calling them "health maintenance organizations" (later simply HMOs). The federal government could begin prepaying for services under Medicare and Medicaid and use its resources to stimulate development of prepaid plans. Butler was immediately sympathetic but did not want the type of organization to be narrowly prescribed by the federal government. The appeal of the "health maintenance strategy," as it soon was called, was that rather than requiring a new government bureaucracy and large public expenditures, it called for stimulating private initiative. A proposal prepared by Ellwood's associates the next month identified the choice in health policy as between a "health maintenance industry that is largely self-regulating" and "continued or increased federal intervention through regulation, investment and planning."[28] In those terms, HMOs made a lot of sense to Republicans.

The initial reception of the health maintenance strategy in the federal bureaucracy was less than enthusiastic, and among the president's aides it had to compete with a variety of other proposals. But the White House gave its approval in March 1970, and HEW Secretary Robert Finch announced that the administration would seek legislative authority for an HMO option under Medicare and Medicaid. After succeeding Finch as secretary in June, Elliot Richardson became the program's most committed advocate. Later that year he decided to press ahead with a program to start HMOs even before Congress approved any new legislation. The administration would use funds already available under other programs.

By late 1970 political pressures were calling for a public response to what the president had already described as a "massive crisis" in health care. Senator Kennedy had made health care his major interest in domestic policy and was touring the country to hold public hearings on the "health care crisis." Earlier, in September 1969, the National Governors' Conference overwhelmingly endorsed a proposal for national health insurance by New York Governor Nelson Rockefeller. In 1970 the Senate Finance Committee approved 13 to 2 an amendment to Social Security introduced by its chairman, Russell Long, to establish a national insurance program for "catastrophic" health care costs. The measure was deleted on the Senate floor, but with Long's sponsorship might well pass in the next Congress. Presidential advisers saw health care as a major issue in the next election. Searching for a strategy that could compete politically, the White House authorized Richardson to prepare a presidential health message for early the next year, which would offer an alternative national health insurance plan and call attention to HMOs as the centerpiece in the administration's approach. At the last minute, presidential counselor Donald Rumsfeld submitted a counterproposal to establish 800 neighborhood health centers, an idea that was rejected because it looked too much like a revival of the Great Society.

Instead, on February 18, 1971, President Nixon announced "a new national health strategy." HMOs were the major innovation proposed for medical care. The traditional system, Nixon said, "operates episodically" on an "illogical incentive" encouraging doctors and hospitals to benefit from illness rather than health. HMOs reversed that incentive. The president called on Congress to establish planning grants and loan guarantees for new HMOs. About half the $45 million requested for grants would be earmarked for medically underserved areas. In 1971, some thirty HMOs were in operation. The administration's goal was to help create 1,700 HMOs by 1976, enrolling 40 million people. By the decade's end, it hoped to see HMOs available to 90 percent of the population.[29]

HMOs were also adopted as part of state health policy by Governors Ronald Reagan and Nelson Rockefeller; the business press and the business-sponsored Committee for Economic Development sung the virtues of HMO. A remarkable change had taken place. Prepaid group practice was originally associated with the cooperative movement and dismissed as a utopian, slightly subversive idea. The conservative, cost-minded critics of medical care had now adopted it as a more efficient form of management. They had substituted a rhetoric of rationalization and competition for the older rhetoric of cooperation and mutual protection. The socialized medicine of one era had become the corporate reform of the next.

Changes in the substance of the idea also came with changes in its sponsorship. The Nixon and Reagan administrations welcomed profit-making corporations as part of the health maintenance industry. This was antithetical to the traditional advocates of prepaid group practice and made them wary of the administration's program. Furthermore, the term "health maintenance organization," introduced with premeditated ambiguity, referred not only to prepaid group practice, but also to comprehensive "medical care foundations." These were organizations, like the San Joaquin Medical Care Foundation, which receive prepayments from subscribers and then reimburse independent physicians and hospitals on a fee basis.* The foundations were typically established by doctors when threatened by competition from prepaid group practice; liberals saw them as attempts by the profession to preserve its monopoly control. However, by putting doctors collectively at risk for medical costs, the foundations—or "independent practice associations" (IPAs), as they are called today—do provide an incentive to control the use of resources. The foundations developed systematic peer review procedures for cutting unnecessary services and regulating the quality of care. The control may be more limited than in prepaid group practice since it is exercised at a distance. But because the foundations permit doctors to remain in their own private offices, they are more acceptable to the profession and organized with lower initial expense.

As Nixon recast the liberal idea of prepaid group practice, so he recast national health insurance. The proposal he announced in February 1971 would have required employers to provide a minimum package of health insurance benefits under a National Health Insurance Standards Act. It would also have set up a federally run Family Health Insurance Program to provide a less generous package of benefits for low-income families. At the same time, the administration called for cutbacks in Medicare to pay part of the added cost. Opponents were outraged. The mandated employer plans, they said, would provide a "windfall" to the private insurance industry. The government would provide a second-class standard of coverage for the poor and actually reduce coverage for the poor in some states. And the entire plan would still leave uninsured 20 to 40 million people who fell outside its two programs.

The least controversial part of Nixon's 1971 national health "strategy" was a call to increase the supply of physicians and change the method of subsidizing medical schools. The administration was much influenced by a report of the Carnegie Commission on Higher Education, which urged that more support to medical schools be given in the form of "capitation grants" (so many dollars per student) with bonuses for increased enrollment. In 1971 Congress introduced the capitation grants in a revised Health Manpower Act.[30]

---

*On the San Joaquin program, see Book Two, Chapter 2.

The AMA was not happy about these developments, especially the endorsement of HMOs, which it publicly regretted and privately tried to reverse. But it was now trying to improve its "negative" image. In 1971 for the first time in a half century, AMA membership fell to 50 percent of the profession as young doctors refused to join. Radical physicians had organized a competing organization, the Medical Committee for Human Rights, which then claimed 7,000 members.[31] Adopting a more liberal public stance, AMA leaders professed concern for the poor and called for a shift to family practice. The AMA's Medicredit national health plan provided tax credits for buying private insurance. Purely a subsidy, and a limited one at that, the plan had no cost controls whatsoever. "Organized medicine shouldn't concentrate only on the private interests of its members," said the AMA's president in 1970. "It should, and does, concern itself with such social issues as sex education, alcoholism, air pollution . . . ."[32] The AMA's president the next year, Walter Bornemeier, called on the organization to support neighborhood health centers where doctors could be paid by fee-for-service, salary, or capitation as they chose: "[I]f we bring comprehensive medical care back into the population centers, the neighborhoods, and have medical care available 24 hours a day, seven days a week, the people will tell Congress that the present system does not need to be restructured."[33]

Yet these concessions to public opinion alienated die-hard conservatives who argued that the AMA had sold out its membership. As government intervention increased over the next several years, so did these right-wing protests within the organization.

Impelled by rising costs, state governments led the way toward stiffer regulation of the health care industry. New York in 1964 had been the first state to regulate capital expenditures of hospitals and nursing homes, but few followed its example until soaring Medicaid expenditures at the end of the decade obliged state legislatures to take action. By the end of 1972, twenty states required medical institutions, usually both hospitals and nursing homes, to get state approval for construction projects and other large capital investments. Though the states vested authority for these "certification of need" programs in state boards and commissions, they often gave local planning councils an advisory role in the review process. In many states, this was the first time that planning and regulation had been related to each other.[34]

The interest of state legislatures was plainly cost control. However, the main inspiration for certificate-of-need came from the American Hospital Association and its state affiliates. The hospitals, anxious to avoid other forms of control, stood to benefit from the limits on competition that this sort of regulation would create. Opposed were profit-making hospitals and nursing homes and some state medical societies, which objected to anyone but doctors regulating medical services. However, state officials, labor, and business accepted the argument that capital regulation would be an effective means of cost control. According to the current wisdom, which had become known as Roemer's Law, hospital beds would be used to the extent they were available, and so regulating their availability was the most effective way to cut costs.

Besides regulating capital investment, a few states also enacted laws to review and regulate hospital rates. These programs varied in coverage: Some covered only the rates charged Medicaid beneficiaries, while other programs applied to all patients. New York began regulating hospital rates in 1971. Other states passed legislation in the next two years, but mandatory rate regulation did not get seriously underway until 1975-76. Once again, regulation was not introduced primarily by liberals; for example, the governors of New Jersey and Connecticut, two states to adopt mandatory controls, were conservative Republicans.[35]

The most drastic price regulation, also a Republican measure, came in August 1971, when President Nixon imposed a general wage-price freeze. When modified that December, the program singled medical care out for special treatment, limiting doctors' fees to annual increases of 2.5 percent and hospital charges to increases of 6 percent (about half the inflation rate in medical care preceding the freeze). And when price controls were lifted in January 1973, they were retained only for health care and for the food, oil, and construction industries. The decision to maintain controls on health care reflected concern about the structural flaws in the industry that were felt likely to generate raging inflation again. Once more, a specific interest of the state was involved: Health expenditures had risen from 4.4 percent of the federal budget in 1965 to 11.3 percent in 1973.[36]

In 1972 the federal government also became involved in regulating health care capital and medical practice. As part of amendments to Social Security, Congress gave HEW power to deny full Medicare reimbursement to hospitals and nursing homes for a capital investment that planning agencies did not approve.

In those same amendments, Congress created a new system for controlling services financed by Medicare and Medicaid. The original Medicare law had required hospitals to set up committees of their medical staffs to review whether services were actually necessary. But these "utilization review" committees, as they were called, had no formal criteria of evaluation, no power to deny payment, and no incentive to be effective. In October 1969 the Nixon administration proposed giving HEW authority to appoint "program review teams" of doctors, other health professionals, and consumers to deny payment for unnecessary Medicare services. The AMA responded that the bill gave HEW too much power and that such review ought to be a responsibility of physicians alone. The next year the AMA suggested as an alternative that HEW contract with state medical societies to carry out peer review. This suggestion was taken up by Senator Wallace Bennett, a conservative Utah Republican, who offered a modified version of the AMA's plan in August 1970.

Senator Bennett proposed that HEW contract with Professional Standard Review Organizations made up only of physicians, but that these PSROs not be state medical societies. Bennett's models for PSROs were medical care "foundations," which by 1970 were reviewing utilization under Medicaid programs in over twenty states. The foundations used computers to identify cases that deviated from statistical norms, such as hospital stays that were inordinately long. These cases were then investigated to determine whether the Medicaid program had been abused.[37] Impressed by evidence that the programs could control costs, Bennett wanted them installed throughout the country. The AMA objected to several features of his proposal, especially its provisions for national norms of health care, government ownership of records, and mandatory advance approval by PSROs for elective surgery. Nonetheless, the Senate passed the bill, though the legislation died for lack of time that year to resolve differences with the House, which had passed the administration's original proposal.

When peer review came up again in 1972, the AMA secured some important modifications. National norms were out; the federal government would not own the data; preadmission certification for elective surgery would no longer be mandatory; and a requirement was added that only physicians could participate in decisions. Although the original version of the bill included outpatient care, the final legislation limited the responsibilities of PSROs to institutional services.

Despite the AMA's role in initiating the idea, many of its leaders were outraged. An AMA leader called it the most dangerous government intrusion into medical practice in American history. On the other hand, liberals opposed PSROs because of the complete exclusion of consumers from representation in the program. It was a case of "the fox guarding the henhouse," said Ralph Nader's Health Research Group, which pointed out that on licensing boards and hospital review committees, the profession had been less than zealous in regulating its own members.[38]

Yet another form of federal regulation was introduced by legislation finally passed in December 1973 to aid HMOs. The law required busi-

nesses with more than twenty-five employees to offer at least one qualifying HMO as an alternative to conventional insurance in their health
benefit plan, if there were a qualifying HMO in the vicinity. The law
also provided grants and loans to develop new HMOs. To qualify, an
HMO had to offer, as basic services, not merely hospitalization, physicians' services, emergency care, and laboratory and diagnostic services,
but also mental health care (up to twenty visits), home health services,
family planning, and referral services for alcohol and drug abuse.
(There was an additional list of supplemental services that had to be
offered on an optional basis.) The act did not allow HMOs to offer lower-
priced contracts with more limited benefits to meet the purchasing
power of lower-income workers. At the same time, it offered no assistance to such groups to help them afford the high premiums. Another
set of provisions required HMOs to charge all subscribers the same
"community" rate and to allow open enrollment of individuals, regardless of health, for at least thirty days once a year. The same requirements were not imposed on the insurance companies with which the
HMOs had to compete. The original theory of the health maintenance
strategy was to encourage competition in order to avoid federal regulation. Instead, the 1973 law threatened to make HMOs the most heavily
regulated part of the entire health care industry and less competitive
with conventional health insurance than they had previously been.

The climax of this wave of regulatory legislation came in 1974 with
the passage of a new health planning law. The law originated when
some thirteen categorical grant programs were due to end June 30,
1973. These included the Hill-Burton hospital grants, the Regional Medical Program, and Comprehensive Health Planning. The administration
wanted to allow the programs to expire. After initially extending them
for a year, Congress accepted the need for consolidation and agreed
to terminate many of the programs in a compromise that yielded a new
planning law.

The consensus was that health planning had failed because the agencies had no power to enforce their decisions and were dominated by
providers, on whom they depended for half their income. The administration's alternative was to give the states funds to establish certificate-
of-need and rate-setting programs. Senator Kennedy, on the other
hand, wanted to vest authority in independent, local, consumer-
controlled boards that would be financed by and accountable to the federal government. These boards would be able not only to review new
projects, but also to close down hospital and nursing home beds they
decided were unnecessary. In the final legislation, the administration
and congressional liberals had to compromise not only with each other,

but also with the lobbyists for the doctors and hospitals, who blocked proposals to include rate setting, authority for planners to decertify health facilities, and any regulation of equipment in physicians' offices.[39]

The National Health Planning and Resource Development Act (93-641) established, as the foundation of a new planning system, some 200 Health Systems Agencies (HSAs), to be run by boards with consumer majorities representative of their areas. But the HSAs were not given any decision-making power; they were to draw up three-year Health System Plans, review proposals for new projects, and send recommendations to the states on certificates of need and to Washington on proposed uses of certain federal funds. All states were required to pass certificate-of-need legislation and to establish State Health Planning and Development Agencies (SHPDAs) and Statewide Health Coordinating Councils (SHCCs). The act also created ten regional Technical Assistance Centers and, at the federal level, a new Bureau of Health Planning and Development and a National Health Planning Advisory Council. Although the federal government would not directly operate the local HSAs, it would finance their activities, decide whether their contracts would be renewed, and establish guidelines for the health plans that the HSAs and the states would produce.

To advocates of a coordinated health system, this hierarchy of planning agencies looked like the framework for a future national health service. The law seemed to be a decisive rejection of the view that the market could correct itself and that the doctors and hospitals had the last word on how medical care ought to be organized.[40] The AMA saw the law the same way. Russell Roth, an AMA president, complained that doctors and administrators had been "pointedly relegated to a minor role" and spoke of the "general resentment in the professional community" that it wasn't entrusted with leadership of the effort. Of the consumers' role, Roth observed, "Passengers who insist on flying the airplane are called hijackers!"[41]

The PSRO and health planning laws specifically excluded physicians' office practices from regulation, but they threatened to limit doctors' discretion in institutions. Physicians would now have to be more concerned about deviations from conventional standards. With stronger planning authorities, they could no longer assume that their definitions of what hospital resources were necessary would prevail. The new forms of regulation also indirectly encouraged hospitals to regulate physicians. If PSROs denied payment for inappropriate care, the hospitals would lose reimbursement, even though a doctor authorized the treatment. As a committee of the AHA noted, "Hospitals thus are forced to

accept financial responsibility for the actions of physicians practicing
in them. Hospital boards of trustees must increasingly exercise the authority conveyed to them by law to supervise their medical staffs."[42]
Similarly, the increased tendency of the courts to hold hospitals liable
for the malpractice of their staff physicians also encouraged greater hospital regulation of medical practice. The once complete authority that
doctors exercised over medical practice in hospitals was now qualified.
At least in institutional practice, the costs and benefits of what doctors
did when treating their patients would now be a concern of the government.

The new health care planning and regulation of the 1970s departed
significantly from earlier programs. Earlier regulation—physician and
hospital licensing and hospital accreditation—had sought only to guarantee minimum standards of quality. Like the 1962 amendments to
federal drug regulation, the new health care regulation required that
a medical service be demonstrably beneficial. Postwar planning was
planning for expansion; now planning aimed at containment. Previously, regulation and planning had little connection with each other;
now they were formally linked. Moreover, federal and state programs
were interconnected, as the federal government tried to reinforce
state controls by mandating and subsidizing regulation of health care
capital.

The new planning and regulation resembled earlier efforts in the continued reliance of the federal government on independent, local quasi-
governmental agencies. (Doctors were given a right of first refusal in
constituting PSROs; while HSAs might be local government units, nine
out of ten were private nonprofit corporations.) But this choice of organizational form was less important than the decision of Congress to finance the programs without local contributions. Furthermore, instead
of ad hoc evaluation, both the planning and PSRO laws required the
development of explicit guidelines and standards. These were movements towards greater social control of medical care.

The growing health care regulation of the 1970s fits into neither of
the two most commonly held theories of regulation—that regulation
typically originates in the efforts of producers to use the state to exclude
competition, or that it is initiated by liberals unsympathetic to private
enterprise. The distinctive factor in this instance is that a large share
of medical costs had been socialized. Government, employers, and commercial insurers balked at both the rise in costs and the uncertainty that
inflation created for them. To be sure, the hospitals influenced the
movement toward certificate-of-need, and doctors were given complete control of PSROs. But the sum total of these regulatory efforts,

as the doctors and hospitals soon discovered, went far beyond what they wanted.

The entire debate over HMOs, PSROs, and health planning assumed that these agencies would be critical in controlling costs under national health insurance. During 1973 and 1974, the Nixon administration and Congress appeared to be making rapid progress toward a political compromise, and enactment of a program seemed imminent. After the 1972 election, the new secretary of HEW, Caspar Weinberger, had called for a review of Nixon's earlier health insurance plan. To the surprise of those who had nicknamed him "Cap the Knife" for his budget cuts, Weinberger decided to back a much enlarged insurance plan, as a preferable alternative to the multitude of categorical grant programs HEW was running. The new plan would have covered the entire population and provided far more comprehensive benefits than the administration had offered in 1971. Once again, it would have used private insurance companies to provide coverage for the employed, and established a separate government-run program for the rest of the population. But this time there were to be no differences in the minimum benefits between the two programs. Patients would pay 25 percent of medical bills, up to a maximum of $1,500 a year. Despite the opposition of almost all of Nixon's Cabinet, the president approved the plan. In a message to Congress February 6, 1974, he described national health insurance as "an idea whose time has come in America." Asked about the costs of the program, which were estimated to be about as high as Kennedy's, Weinberger replied at a press conference the next day, "I consider the total [cost] as not a very significant figure."[43] This was an unusual attitude for the secretary. Many in Congress were so mean-spirited as to suspect that President Nixon was trying to divert attention from the Watergate affair.

Meanwhile, Senator Kennedy joined with Representative Wilbur Mills to support a plan that would allow private insurers to act as fiscal intermediaries and thereby retain some self-respect, not to mention a profitable rate of return. Like the administration's bill, the Kennedy-Mills plan required copayments of 25 percent; no individual or family would have to pay more than $1,000 in any year. In June, Senator Kennedy announced, "A new spirit of compromise is in the air" and suggested a bill could reach the president's desk by the fall.[44]

The labor unions and liberal organizations, however, refused to accept any compromise and insisted on the original Health Security plan. Anticipating a liberal sweep after Watergate in the 1974 elections, the director of the Committee for National Health Insurance announced,

"We will resist action this year because we need a veto-proof Congress to get a bill past Nixon."[45] Also anticipating a more liberal Congress, the commercial health insurance companies tried to get a modified version of Senator Long's "catastrophic" insurance plan adopted. Ironically, the usual roles were reversed: Now the insurance companies were in a hurry to get a bill passed, while labor wanted to wait. Without labor's support, Kennedy's attempt at compromise had no chance. Even though opposition to national health insurance had "melted" away (as the economist Alice Rivlin put it), none of the proposals could command a majority.[46]

If the name on the administration's plan had not been Nixon and had the time not been the year of Watergate, the United States might have had national health insurance in 1974. But if it were not for Watergate, Nixon might never have endorsed a bill that nearly all his Cabinet considered reckless. Soon not only Nixon, but also Representative Mills ended his political career in scandal. This was the last moment in the 1970s when any such program had a serious chance of adoption. The conservative assimilation of reform had stopped just short of national health insurance.

HEALTH POLICY IN A BLOCKED SOCIETY, 1975–1980

An Obstructed Path

When the blizzard of regulation stopped, the federal government found itself snowed in. Between 1971 and 1974 Congress had passed a great deal of complicated legislation. The laws were especially detailed because of Democratic reluctance to trust the Nixon administration with much discretion. Some were so severely compromised in passage as to be nearly unworkable. And each provoked bureaucratic conflict and litigation that took years to resolve. Meanwhile, little was accomplished and the impression was conveyed that the reforms were a failure.

In 1974-75 a severe economic recession, accompanied by soaring inflation, arrested new initiatives to expand medical care and other social programs. Throughout the advanced capitalist societies, the first brush with the energy crisis and the ensuing economic slowdown brought about a backlash against the welfare state. In the United States, the recession was also a political watershed, marking the end of the postwar growth of social entitlements.

The rise in the inflation rate was particularly steep in health care. Price controls had been kept on the industry for over a year longer than on the rest of the economy when they were finally removed April 30, 1974. Since August 1971, increases in the price of medical services had been kept to an annual rate of 4.9 percent, while other services had risen 5.2 percent a year. Then, in the last eight months of 1974, the inflation rate in medical services hit an annual rate of 12.1 percent (compared to 9.5 percent for other services). In 1975 medical care continued to run about three points ahead of the economy's 6.8 percent inflation rate. Inflation in the health sector was having "serious repercussions throughout the economy," the President's Council on Wage and Price Stability warned in 1976.[47]

In the early 1970s, rising costs made public efforts to improve access to medical care seem all the more urgent; now they made such efforts seem all the more risky. Efficiency and redistribution had been coequal concerns in health care politics. Increasingly, the political preoccupation became cost containment alone.

The combined impact of recession and inflation hopelessly stalled the movement for national health insurance after 1974, despite the election of a heavily Democratic Congress. In his first message to Congress August 12, 1974, President Ford had asked for passage of national health insurance. But in his 1976 State of the Union Address, he withdrew the administration's plan, saying it would make inflation worse. Privately, economic advisors, such as Treasury Secretary William Simon, were arguing that national health insurance would be "an unmitigated disaster that could bankrupt the country."[48]

The seemingly inexorable rise in entitlement programs gave Congress pause about any further additions to government responsibility. By fiscal year 1977, Medicare and Medicaid outlays were double what they had been only three years earlier.[49] This spectacular growth left little money for discretionary health care programs, some of which were aimed at organizing medical care more efficiently. Rising costs had driven health policy in the early seventies. Now, as one HEW official remarked, they were driving and paralyzing policy at the same time.

In the federal health bureaucracy, while the entitlement programs ate up money, the formulation of regulatory policy ate up time. It took almost two years for HEW to issue proposed regulations for utilization review under the PSRO program. An obscure provision of the HMO law led to a protracted conflict between HEW and the Labor Department over collective bargaining rights; two years elapsed before HEW could release the dual-choice regulations that enabled HMOs to offer their services to employees receiving health insurance as a fringe benefit. The health planning guidelines were not published until September 1977, more than two and a half years after the bill had been signed into law. And, when published, they unleashed a storm of protest from rural areas that thought their hospitals might be in jeopardy.

In health reform, a little known law of nature seems to require that every move toward regulation be followed by an opposite move toward litigation. The American Association of Physicians, a right-wing faction in the AMA, sued the government over the constitutionality of PSROs. The AMA itself sued when the proposed utilization review regulations were issued. It sued again to block the health planning law from being carried out. The Association of American Medical Colleges sued over regulations imposed on medical schools. These lawsuits did not reverse the tide of regulation, but they slowed it down.

The alternative to regulation was supposed to be the competition stimulated by the rise of health maintenance organizations. But the HMO strategy had wilted before the immense structural and political barriers to innovation in the health industry. No upheaval of the sort the Nixon administration originally envisioned could have been accomplished except by undermining the autonomy and power of private practitioners. The doctors felt directly threatened, and the AMA mounted an aggressive campaign against the program, stalling passage of legislation in Congress and persuading the White House to cut back its plans. Several other developments slowed the program. Congressional committee chairmen were upset about Secretary Richardson's decision to carry on the program without authorization and requested in the spring of 1972 that further grants for HMO projects be halted. The departure of Richardson from HEW was a damaging blow; his successor, Caspar Weinberger, regarded HMOs as one of many demonstration programs. Instead of adopting the HMO idea as a long-run strategy, as the administration had at first suggested, Congress agreed to adopt it only as an experiment.

Experiments may be framed in ways that critically affect their success. So it was with the 1973 HMO Act. The original bills in Congress had followed one of two approaches. The first essentially called for high subsidies and high requirements for HMOs; the second for low subsidies and low requirements. Either of these probably would have been more workable than the final legislation, which called for low subsidies and high requirements. As originally passed, the act required qualifying HMOs to offer a broad range of minimum services, open enrollment, and community rating and to undertake complex and costly new administrative tasks. These requirements, as I've indicated, threatened to handicap HMOs in competition with conventional insurance. The open enrollment requirement threatened to prevent the plans from prudently controlling their own rate of growth.

The immediate impact of the law was damaging. The dual-choice provision, which should have given HMOs access to consumers, turned out to have the opposite effect in the short run. In the two years before HEW issued final regulations, employers held up making any arrangements with HMOs because of uncertainty about which plans would qualify under the statutes. The restrictive statutory definition of HMOs discouraged any revival of the HMO assistance program, which had been halted in mid-1972. Some money appropriated for the program had to be returned to the Treasury. Most important, the administration had lost interest in an initiative that aroused much political opposition and seemed to offer little immediate return.

HMOs take years to develop. They require major infusions of capital and trained, professional managers. Neither the capital nor the management skills were readily available. Even under the most salutary conditions, some enterprises in an emerging industry will fail. HMOs were no exception. Moreover, most hospitals and doctors had no particular interest in starting up HMOs or seeing them succeed. In some cases, they were outright hostile. In view of the contradictory requirements of federal legislation, the meager effort by HEW, the intrinsic risk in starting new business organizations, and the lack of motivation in the industry to initiate HMOs or to cooperate with them, the slow development of HMOs in the mid-1970s should hardly have been a surprise. Nonetheless, along with the slow progress of the regulatory and planning programs, the undelivered health system seemed one more piece of evidence that reform of the health care delivery system would not work.

The Generalization of Doubt

In the mid-1970s the criticism of medical care took a new turn. Instead of merely questioning whether hospitalization and surgery were excessive, critics began to ask whether medical care made any difference in the overall health of the society. The nineteenth-century doctrine of therapeutic nihilism—that existing drugs and therapies were useless—was revived in a new form. Now the net effectiveness of the medical system as a whole was called into question.[50]

The doubts that suddenly enveloped medical care reflected a broader current of skepticism about the value of the social services. The schools were as much the target as medical care. So were efforts to rehabilitate criminals. In each case, the criticism came from both the left and right. Radicals characteristically charged that the service—schooling, rehabilitation, medical care—was basically a form of social control. Conservatives objected to the growth of government. These criticisms were amplified by empirical studies questioning the long-run effects of schooling on economic status, of rehabilitation on ex-convicts, and of medical care on health. Economists argued that the growing social investments were simply not cost effective.

The attack on medical care originated with increasing criticism in the 1960s of psychiatry and mental hospitals. The work of Thomas Szasz and Erving Goffman and books and movies like *One Flew Over the Cuckoo's Nest* portrayed institutional psychiatry as an instrument of therapeutic oppression. Mental health programs, radicals said, channel social discontent into self-reproach and help label as "deviant" people who have "the right to be different." Social scientists conducted empirical studies casting doubt on the long-term effectiveness of psychotherapy. Psychoanalysis, sad to say, had trouble passing the test of cost-benefit analysis. Politically irrelevant in the sixties, cost-ineffective in the seventies, psychiatrists took it on the chin from all sides.

From psychiatry criticism spread to medicine at large. It had long been known that medical care, especially when compared with the environment or social behavior, has relatively modest effect on mortality rates. Nonetheless, the idea that Americans were getting a diminishing return from their increasing investment in medical care hit with the force of a thunderclap in the mid-1970s. It suddenly struck intellectuals and policy makers of diverse persuasions that this was the answer to those who constantly wished to expand access to medical care. "The marginal value of one—or one billion—dollars spent on medical care will be close to zero in improving health," wrote the neoconservative Aaron Wildavsky in a clever essay that gave the title *Doing Better and Feeling Worse* to an influential volume on health care sponsored by the Rockefeller Foundation. In that same volume, the foundation's president, John Knowles, called for greater emphasis on changing unhealthy individual behavior.[51] And in another emblematic book of the period, *Medical Nemesis*, the radical social critic Ivan Illich argued that medical care caused more disease than it cured and that people would be healthier if they liberated themselves from dependence on the entire malignant apparatus of modern medicine.[52] Less extreme, but in the same vein, the economist Victor Fuchs argued that medical care had contributed to health early in the twentieth century, but that more medical care now would reduce neither mortality nor disease.[53]

Ironically, these conclusions were drawn at a time when America was making exceptional advances in health. From the mid-1950s until 1968, age-adjusted death rates had been relatively stable. The lack of progress in that period seemed to confirm skepticism about the value of medical care. But from 1968 to 1975, death rates dropped 14 percent—or from 747 to 642 people a year in a population of 100,000. As David E. Rogers and Roger J. Blendon have pointed out, "This rate of decrease is as high as we have seen anytime this century."[54] Among the fifteen top causes of death, ten have declined, and as Karen Davis and Cathy Schoen note, those that have declined are more sensitive to medical treatment, while those that have not, such as homicide, suicide, and cirrhosis, are most sensitive to social pathology. Deaths from heart disease fell 23 percent in fifteen years—5 percent from 1963 to 1968 and another 15 percent by 1975. Between 1960 and 1975 infant mortality rates were down 38 percent (from 26 to 16 infant deaths per 1,000 live births), and maternal mortality dropped 71 percent (from 37.1 to 10.8 deaths per 100,000 live births). Studies of specific areas where neighborhood health centers or other programs introduced special efforts to improve prenatal, child, and maternal health showed clear evidence that the services did make a difference.[55] Undoubtedly, some share of this improvement was due to other measures besides medical care, such as pollution controls due to new environmental regulation and better nutrition as a result of the food stamp program. No one has yet teased out the relative effects of different variables. Moreover, much of what medical care provides is not lifesaving, but reduces disability, disfigurement, and confusion about the nature of experience. These restorative and educational functions make up most of physicians' routine work, but the new therapeutic nihilism did not wish to acknowledge that they had any value. Just as medicine used to be uncritically given credit for gains in health that had other causes, so medicine was now disparaged without prudent regard for its benefits.

If the First Revelation of the seventies had been that a "health care crisis" existed, the Second Revelation was that health care hardly affects health. The Second Revelation obviously made the First Revelation seem less important. In other areas, too, the generalization of doubt undermined the generalization of rights. Distributive justice is a morally compelling concern, after all, only when what there is to distribute, or redistribute, is genuinely valuable. If it is irrelevant or harmful to human welfare, the poor would be better off without it. This was Illich's conclusion: To give the lower class greater access to health care, he wrote, "would only equalize the delivery of professional illusions and torts."[56]

The recognition of medical care's limited effects on health did not necessarily favor a conservative political viewpoint. While it encouraged more conservative views of medical care, it also might have encouraged more liberal views of public health. But the most immediate political impact of the new therapeutic nihilism on health policy was to concentrate attention on cost control. If the case for improving access had been weakened, the case for reducing costs was stronger than ever. Thus the change in intellectual fashions complemented the dismal new economic conditions. Together, they set up two formidable roadblocks in the path of national health insurance.

The Liberal Impasse

The politics of health care in the second half of the 1970s mirrored a general political stalemate in the society. In health care, as in energy and economic policy, opposing interests were sufficiently strong to block almost any coherent course of action, conservative or progressive. While liberals could maintain old programs, they lacked the power to initiate new ones or to make old ones work well. Until 1976 the split between a Republican president and a Democratic Congress seemed to retard any effective political response to the nation's social and economic problems, but the election of a Democratic president in 1976 did not end the stalemate. Elected as an outsider, Jimmy Carter was unable to get cooperation on key domestic issues from a Congress controlled by his own party. Despite the Democrats' primacy, the political climate was turning more conservative; in a sense, the situation was exactly the opposite of that of the early seventies, when Republicans had to respond to a liberal consensus. As inflation and energy became larger preoccupations, the Democratic leadership began to regard any further liberal initiatives as impractical. The various movements for civil and social rights were increasingly treated not as just causes but as special interests, like dairy farmers or the shoe industry. Yet the Democrats were wedded to all these interests. Torn by conflicting pressures, under the shadow of rising inflation, the Democrats proved incapable of effective action in health care as in other areas of social policy.

Candidate Jimmy Carter pledged himself to a comprehensive national health insurance plan at a point in his campaign when he was anxiously courting union support. But President Carter was not anxious to press ahead because of budgetary pressures and the risk a program might pose to his anti-inflation effort. In its first two years, the Carter administration let health insurance get backed up behind its proposals for welfare reform and hospital cost containment. Carter's economic advisors, like Ford's, urged that a health plan be postponed or dropped entirely.

Soon after Carter took office, a division opened up between the president and Senator Kennedy. The new HEW secretary, Joseph A. Califano, Jr., indicated that a plan would take at least a year to prepare. "The issue isn't working up a new program," Kennedy told Califano, "We already have a program we've been working on for years. What we need is a political negotiation." Kennedy also strenuously objected to the president's wish to phase in a plan gradually over several years; in Kennedy's view, there had to be a comprehensive reform of the system when national health insurance was inaugurated.[57]

Both the Carter administration and Kennedy recognized that any program for expanded health insurance would simultaneously have to be a program for cost containment. Public and private third-party payers already covered, to varying degrees, 90 percent of the population; a national health plan was now a matter of completing a journey well under way. Nor did it necessarily have to cost any more than America currently spent on medical care. At over 8 percent of GNP, America was already outspending most other countries that had comprehensive national health plans. At the beginning of the 1970s, when Canada introduced a comprehensive plan, it was spending as much as the United States on health care—about 7.3 percent of GNP. At the end of the decade, while health costs approached (and then passed) 9 percent of GNP in the United States, they stabilized at about 7.5 percent in Canada. The United States maintained its fragmented, cost-based reimbursement system, while the Canadian provinces controlled costs by setting rates in negotiations with health care providers.[58]

Yet it was a fixed preconception of public debate in America that national health insurance would mean sizeable new expenditures. And though additional costs were not inherently necessary, they were likely, since Congress may well have been incapable of adopting the structural reforms necessary to control expenditures, which is to say, to control the incomes of all those with interests in the health care industry.

The response to Carter's proposal for hospital cost containment seemed to confirm this estimate. In 1977 the president asked Congress to limit increases in hospital charges to about one and a half times the rate of growth in the consumer price index. Hospital charges in 1977 rose 15.6 percent over 1976 levels, compared to an overall inflation rate of 6 percent; Carter's program would have put a flat cap on hospital rate increases at 9 percent. Though the measure passed the Senate, it died in the House, the victim of a massive lobbying effort by the hospital industry.

By early 1978 Kennedy was becoming increasingly impatient with the administration's progress on national health insurance as well as its performance on other health issues. In July, after a year and a half in office, the president allowed only general principles for a health plan to be released. A legislative proposal was to follow a year later. Sensing that the administration was stalling, labor leaders and other liberals, led by Senator Kennedy, decided to go their own way.

The new proposal they fashioned was a striking departure from earlier liberal programs. Instead of a public system, it called for private health plans (HMOs, independent practice associations, Blue Cross, commercial insurance) to compete for subscribers, who would receive a health insurance card entitling them to hospital and physicians' care and a variety of other basic health services. The cost of the card would vary according to income; employers would bear 65 percent of the cost for their workers, while the government would pick up the cost for the poor. Since the insurance card would not identify the source of payment, the poor would not be channeled through a separate payment system, as they were under Medicaid. To discourage insurers from only enrolling the affluent and the healthy, they would be paid according to the actuarial risk that their subscribers represented (more for the aged, the poor, and so on.). On the other hand, consumers would receive rebates or extra services if they chose to enroll in more efficient plans. Fixed negotiated rates would replace cost-based reimbursement for hospitals and usual and customary fees for doctors. The entire system would be forced to operate within a budget constraint.

The administration regarded the new Kennedy plan as unworkable and politically impractical. Instead, it proposed requiring businesses to provide a minimum package of benefits for their employees, expanding public insurance for the aged and the poor, and creating a new public corporation to sell coverage to the rest of the population. After two and a half years, the Carter administration had succeeded in rewriting the Nixon plan of 1974, which it proposed not go into effect until 1983.

There was a basic difference in outlook between the Kennedy and Carter approaches. Kennedy saw national health insurance as an opportunity to reconstitute the health system on a new framework of incentives and bargaining relationships; improvements in cost control would accompany improvements in access. Hence national health insurance could resolve problems of individual and social cost simultaneously. Carter, on the other hand, regarded national health insurance as an onus the system could bear only if cost controls preceded it and the economy prospered. So the administration approached a plan reluctantly and never aggressively sought its enactment.

Neither program had any chance. In May 1979 a senior HEW official insisted, "We are going to Congress at the outer limits of political possibility."[59] But the Democratic leadership in the House had already told Califano they did not even want a plan submitted. When Kennedy released his program May 14 and Carter his a month later, the press paid more attention to the political rivalry between the two than to their plans for health care. Soon Kennedy was defeated by Carter and Carter by Reagan, and once again national health insurance vanished like a mirage from American politics.

In the fall of 1979, hospital cost containment met the same fate, in what proved to be a turning point in government regulation of the health care industry. In response to the prospect of federal controls, the hospitals had started a voluntary effort to keep down their costs, which rose 12.8 percent in 1978. In early 1979 the administration introduced a modified bill that would have imposed controls on hospitals only if their cost increases exceeded a specified limit. The limit would vary according to the cost of the goods and services a hospital bought, the population it served, and the cost of new technology.

But these concessions to flexibility made the regulations more complex, and the new bill drew quick fire from the growing anti-regulatory forces in Congress. By 1979 the reputation of health care regulation was none too good. Some early evaluations of the PSRO program suggested that it cost more than it saved. A study of the effects of certificate-of-need programs found that they slowed construction of hospital beds, but that other capital expenditures increased and the net effect was negligible.[60] Other studies were more positive about both programs, and an analysis of hospital rate regulation found that after 1975, six states where the programs were given broad authority had held increases in hospital costs 14 percent below the national average.[61] Califano claimed that the administration cost containment measure would save $53 billion over five years. But to its opponents, led by Representative David Stockman of Michigan, the bill was a symbol of overregulation, a blind intrusion by government into the private sector which would penalize hospitals that had been efficient and could only reduce the quality of hospital services. The hospital associations saw to it that congressmen were lobbied by hospital officials from their own districts. The opposition prevailed, and on November 15, 1979, the House voted 234 to 166 to defeat the measure.

To the supporters of regulation, the hospital lobby's opposition epitomized the ability of organized groups with highly concentrated interests to block measures that would benefit the public at large. But the bill itself testified to the limits of the Democrats' capacity to deal with the underlying problems in health care. This was, after all, their major legislative effort in health care, but it would have left unchanged the skewed incentives of the reimbursement system and only superimposed a new layer of controls.

However, the major attempts at structural reform, begun earlier in the decade were not successfully restraining the growth of national medical expenditures. Of all the initiatives, HMOs and health planning had been introduced with the greatest expectations. To their advocates, they were not simply new programs but strategies for changing the fundamental organization of the medical care system.

The HMO program did pick up momentum about 1976. That year Congress reduced the mandatory benefits and other stringent requirements that had been hobbling the program. Then in May 1977—after seeing some routine data on federal employees showing that for every 1,000 people, Kaiser plan subscribers had only 349 days of hospitalization a year, compared to a national average of 1,149—Secretary Califano called for a review to see what needed to be done to revive federal HMO assistance. In 1978 Congress again amended the law to increase federal aid, and in that year HMO enrollment increased 1.4 million over the year before.

By mid-1979, there were 217 HMOs, far less than the 1,700 the Nixon administration originally foresaw. Yet the total enrollment of 7.9 million people was twice as many as in 1970, and HMOs continued to perform well, providing medical care at significantly lower expense mainly because of reduced hospitalization. In California, the upper Midwest, and several cities in the Northeast, HMO development seemed to reach a "take-off" point. Some evidence indicated that in Minneapolis-St. Paul the rapid spread of HMOs had kept down prices in the fee-for-service sector. But HMO enrollment was still only 4 percent of the nation's population, and the administration projections gave them less than 10 percent by 1990.[62]

The new health planning agencies, Congress had said in 1974, were supposed not only to control costs, but also to improve the accessibility, acceptability, continuity, and quality of services. "Scientific planning with teeth" had been the motto, but skeptics argued they would be little different from planning efforts in the past: No matter what the distribution of representatives on HSAs, the providers would still prevail, and there would be little restraint on costs. Critics predicted gullible consumers on the boards would easily be swayed by authoritative doctors and hospital administrators; besides, consumers had no incentive to oppose projects that would bring jobs and services to their communities, while the costs would be spread over the state or the nation.

The new planning programs turned out to be more devoted to cost control than their critics initially expected—or the industry wanted. The early analyses underestimated the commitment to cost containment of both the professional planners on the staff and community activists on the boards. The providers were often split—for example, between public and private institutions, or along geographical lines. Also, many of the nonelite provider representatives, especially the nurses, allied themselves with consumers. So the hospitals and doctors did not dominate the planning process as easily as they had in the past.[63]

Nonetheless, however diligent in reviewing applications, the HSAs had limited impact. Their recommendations could be overturned by the states and often were. In Massachusetts some nursing homes that had been denied certificates of need were able to secure legislative exemptions. Most important, the planning agencies were still scarcely planning at all. They were mainly reacting to the plans of others. Preoccupied with project review, they could not take the initiative, nor did they have the funds to open new health care programs. Though they could review the "appropriateness" of existing facilities, they could do nothing about those they judged unnecessary. They could hold up or veto projects, but the underlying incentives of the reimbursement system were beyond their purview.

Reform had succeeded in many of its original aims to improve access to health services. The concerns of 1970 about a shortage of doctors, particularly family practitioners, were now much alleviated. American medical schools had responded to capitation grants by increasing their enrollments; family practice had grown, faster than expected, into a major specialty.[64] Despite cutbacks, Medicaid and other programs were also continuing to improve access to medical care among the poor.

But by the end of the 1970s, equal access to health care was no longer a governing concern for those who governed. HSAs had been launched both to control costs and to improve access, but the evaluations now paid attention only to their success in cost containment. Other programs, like the PSROs, which were partly aimed at quality control, were also evaluated on the narrow grounds of cost control—and found wanting.

Political roles had switched. By the late seventies, reformers—forced to justify the expansion of bureaucracy and regulation in health care—were on the defensive, while the health care providers denounced the excesses, duplication, and irrationality of government. When the decade began, reformers were criticizing the inefficiency of the health care industry; when it ended, the industry was criticizing the inefficiency of reform.

There remained roughly 26 million people in 1978 who had no insurance protection, public or private, and many more who had limited coverage that would prove inadequate if they fell seriously ill.[65] The corridor between private insurance and welfare medicine was especially wide in the states, many of them in the South, that severely restricted Medicaid eligibility. Despite general agreement about the irrationality of this system, the financial insecurity it created, and its effects on the use of primary and preventive health services, the Democrats were unable while in power from 1976 to 1980 to do anything about it. And, because they also could not deal with the underlying contradictions of accommodation, they put in jeopardy the gains that reform had made. They had succeeded in making health care part of the public household, but they had failed to put the household in order.

THE REPRIVATIZATION OF THE PUBLIC HOUSEHOLD

The redistributive and regulatory reforms of the 1960s and 1970s greatly expanded the boundaries of the political in health care. Once the government assumed a large share of the financial burden for medical services, conservatives cooperated on grounds of fiscal prudence in the expansion of political authority. Initially, the resistance came mainly from physicians, who feared government would restrict their autonomy and income. Their opposition, while influential, was no longer sufficient to hold back state intervention. But by the late 1970s, the opposition assumed more formidable proportions in American politics. A newly revived conservatism sought to throw back the boundaries of the political, to return tax money and government functions to the private sector—in short, to reprivatize much of the public household.

The case for reprivatization rests on several arguments. In the view of its critics, the welfare state has become "overloaded" and Western democracies have become "ungovernable." The increasing role of the state in the allocation of resources and distribution of income has aroused unrealistic expectations. By shedding some of its functions, government can gain respite from the demands for unlimited entitlements and the conflicts that such demands inevitably generate. In addition, these conservative critics say, government is inherently incompetent at certain tasks. The requirements of politics conflict with the demands of efficiency. For example, the government cannot close down an unproductive plant, like an outmoded hospital. The instruments of public policy are also said to be insufficiently sensitive to variations in individual preferences and local conditions. And, finally, government creates a "new class" with an interest in more government, financed by increased taxation, which then becomes a burden to the private economy and dampens the fires of innovation and investment.

This is the by now familiar neoconservative case. Although the public did not exactly understand, much less endorse, the larger program of reprivatization, much of the public—a majority in 1980—clearly shared a general antipathy to government. Inflation gave arguments against deficit spending a seemingly urgent rationale, and interventionist liberal social policies, such as affirmative action and school busing for desegregation, had burned up much of the good will liberalism had inherited from the New Deal. This combination of circumstances gave conservatives an opportunity to carry out broad cutbacks not only in government expenditures but also in government functions.

In medical care, conservative ideas have undergone three important changes over the past two decades. Until the 1970s, conservatives had argued against government intervention in health care mainly on the grounds of voluntarism. Although a few devotees of the free market, notably Milton Friedman, criticized the medical profession as a cartel and called for the abolition of licensing, this was primarily an intellectual amusement. No one seriously tried to carry it out. The health maintenance strategy was the first sign of a shift of emphasis in conservative thought about health policy from voluntarism to competition.

Yet, the HMO program, while initially successful in gaining presidential support, soon became a burden to the advocates of competition. It seemed apparent, as HMO development slowed down in the mid-seventies, that the program would not answer the demand for a comprehensive remedy to rising costs. So the second adaptation of advocates of competition was to generalize the idea beyond HMOs. For example, Clark Havighurst, a law professor at Duke, formulated proposals for expanding antitrust activity in the health care field, which the Federal Trade Commission entered in 1975. Alain Enthoven, an economist at Stanford, developed a competitive model for national health insurance. Though Califano originally sponsored Enthoven's work, the Carter administration did not endorse it. Nonetheless, Enthoven's ideas became widely influential as the most sophisticated statement of a "market" approach to health policy.[66]

By the late 1970s the third adaptation of conservative thought was under way: Nixon's Tory reformism gave way to a new fundamentalism in politics and economics. In health care, the hospital cost-containment battle helped mobilize anti-regulatory sentiment. And now conservatives had their revelation, the Third Revelation of the decade: The problems of health care in America could be cured by relying on competition and incentives, if only government's role were reduced to a minimum. When Ronald Reagan was elected president in 1980, it appeared this view would guide policy. President Reagan chose for top positions two of the leading congressional advocates of a competitive strategy in health care—Representative David Stockman, to be director of the Office of Management and Budget, and Senator Richard Schweiker, to be secretary of Health and Human Services. The administration immediately sought to abolish the HSAs and PSROs, to consolidate federal health programs in "block grants" to the states, and to "cap" federal support for Medicaid.

But conservatives, like liberals, have trouble carrying out an ideologically faithful policy; they, too, have interest groups to worry about. The insurance companies and medical profession have shown relatively little enthusiasm for the conservative program of intensified competition. And while the doctors and hospitals welcomed relief from regulation, they could not be entirely happy about plans to reduce the federal aid that they were now accustomed to receiving. Cutbacks bring constraint, and competition does, too; strong organizations take over the weak. And, as one president of a county medical society said at an AMA meeting soon after Reagan took office, "Our mentor has always been Hippocrates, not Adam Smith."[67] These sources of opposition have blocked any quick action to carry out a serious competitive strategy. Indeed, in its second year, the Reagan administration was backing away from the competitive approach, even as it continued to cut back public regulation, public health services, and public financing for the personal health services of the poor.

The consequences of reprivatization, if it can be carried out, are almost certainly going to be different from the public's expectations. In its rejection of "big government" the public seems to be expressing a desire to return to older and simpler ways. Similarly, the medical profession, in protesting against government regulation, wants a return to the traditional liberties and privileges of private practice. But at least in medical care, the reliance on the private sector is not likely to return America to the status quo, but rather to accelerate the movement toward an entirely new system of corporate medical enterprise.

CHAPTER FIVE

The Coming of
the Corporation

THE INDEPENDENT small businessman is firmly rooted in the American imagination. His misfortune is that he is much less firmly rooted in the American economy. As large corporations have risen to dominate economic life, the myth and the ideal of the entrepreneur have persisted—and not only in the daydreams of men on assembly lines who want a business of their own. Among economists, competition among numerous small firms remains the norm of analysis, from which all other conditions are distressing aberrations. In sociology, the independent practitioner is similarly the point of departure in the study of the professions. Bureaucratic professionals still seem anomalous even though they now represent the overwhelming majority of professionals in the modern world.

In the twentieth century, medicine has been the heroic exception that sustained the waning tradition of independent professionalism. Physicians not only escaped from corporate and bureaucratic control in their own practices; they channeled the development of hospitals, health insurance, and other medical institutions into forms that did not intrude upon their autonomy. But the exception may now be brought into line with the governing rule.

Unless there is a radical turnabout in economic conditions and American politics, the last decades of the twentieth century are likely to be a time of diminishing resources and autonomy for many physicians, voluntary hospitals, and medical schools. Two immediate circumstances cast a shadow over their future: the rapidly increasing supply of physicians and the continued search by government and employers for control over the growth of medical expenditures. These developments promise to create severe strains throughout the medical system. They may prepare the way, moreover, for the acceleration of a third development, the rise of corporate enterprise in health services, which is already having a profound impact on the ethos and politics of medical care as well as its institutions.

Throughout Book One I argued that sovereignty of the medical profession entailed the restriction of competition, the limiting of regulation by government or private organizations, and authority to define and interpret the standards and the understandings that govern medical work. Emerging developments now jeopardize the profession's control of markets, organizations, and standards of judgment. The profession has benefited from state protection and political accommodation of its interests, but government is no longer so sympathetic and physicians are no longer the single, dominating claimant in the medical industry. The rise of the profession required internal cohesiveness and strong collective organization, yet rising pressures now threaten to drive a wedge between different segments of the medical profession. The prospect is not simply for the weakening of professional sovereignty, but for greater disunity, inequality, and conflict throughout the entire health care system.

ZERO-SUM MEDICAL PRACTICE

The Doctor "Surplus" and Competition

While market-oriented policy makers debate how to make health care more competitive, competitive pressures are building up as a result of earlier liberal programs aimed at alleviating the "doctor shortage." Between 1965 and 1980, federal aid succeeded in increasing the number of medical schools from 88 to 126 and raising the number of graduates from 7,409 to 15,135. By 1985 graduates will rise to 17,000 a year.[1] Despite new immigration policies adopted in 1976 to reduce the influx of foreign physicians, doctors in active practice in the United

States increased from 377,000 in 1975 to nearly 450,000 in 1980 and are projected to rise to nearly 600,000 by the end of the decade. This rapid expansion coincides with a slowdown in population growth. For every 100,000 people, the United States had 148 doctors in 1960, 177 in 1975, and 202 in 1980. In 1990 the rate per 100,000 people is expected to jump to 245, making America one of the countries in the world most heavily populated with physicians.[2]

By 1990 the aging of the population will increase demand for only a small proportion of these additional doctors. It is unclear whether other changes, such as in income, insurance coverage, or technology, will lead Americans to use more—or fewer—physicians' services per capita. In 1979 the Bureau of Health Manpower estimated that the demand for physicians would continue to match the supply at the end of the eighties because of a trend toward increased use of medical services that had been evident from 1968 to 1976. However, as the Congressional Office of Technology Assessment pointed out, Medicare and Medicaid produced a rapid and exceptional rise in utilization in the late 1960s. After 1971 demand appears to have stabilized. (It may actually have dropped after 1977, when Medicaid enrollments began to be cut.) If utilization does not increase, according to the Office of Technology Assessment, the "surplus" might be as high as 185,000 in 1990.[3] In 1980, another group, the Graduate Medical Education National Advisory Committee (GMENAC), projected a possible surplus of 70,000 over the "need" for physicians in 1990—and this estimate assumed no socioeconomic barriers to service whatsoever.[4]

Estimating whether a "surplus" will develop is as much a political as a technical assessment. The future demand for physicians will depend on uncertain political developments, such as the fate of national health legislation. Future demand might be stimulated by greater public or private health insurance; or conversely, it might be reduced by cutbacks in public financing or in the tax subsidies to private plans. The demand for doctors' services might also be reduced by the incursions of related professionals and paramedical workers; or increased, if those alternatives are cut off by restrictive licensing and reimbursement practices. It might rise if fee-for-service prevails, or it might drop if prepaid plans succeed. By using paramedical workers, keeping surgeons working full time, and monitoring physician performance, HMOs operate successfully with significantly lower ratios of doctors to patients than did the United States as a whole even before the current surge in physician supply. If economic pressures force greater rationalization of health services, the "surplus" could be significantly greater than projections based on current patterns.

On the other hand, changes in the composition of the medical profession may reduce the impact of its growing numbers. Competitive pressures may be relieved by the women who make up one quarter of new doctors. Some evidence suggests that, on the average, women physicians work fewer hours per week and see fewer patients per hour.[5] In addition, if private practice becomes more competitive, more doctors may move into managerial roles. The growth of administrative and corporate medicine may also provide a convenient "retreat from patients" for cases of professional "burn-out" in clinical practice.[6]

These contingencies, affecting both demand and supply, make any prediction of a "surplus" risky. Medical unemployment is now commonplace in much of Western Europe and Latin America; whether it will reach the United States is uncertain. But there is already evidence of significant slack in the demand for doctors. Between 1970 and 1980, according to AMA data, patient visits per doctor dropped 12 percent from 132.5 to 116.6 a week.[7] This decline may have been due not just to growing numbers of physicians, but to declining per capita use of physicians' services. According to federal surveys, between 1975 and 1979 physician visits per person in America dropped 8 percent from 5.1 to 4.7 per year.[8] A 1979 survey indicated that only 57 percent of office-based practitioners believed they were working at full capacity. While some were satisfied working less, 25 percent wanted to see more patients.[9]

Many economists and policy makers have argued that the peculiar structure of the medical market would allow doctors to compensate for this slack by raising fees and performing additional tests, operations, and other services. Some evidence lends support to this view, but the ability of physicians to induce demand is not unlimited. Between 1971 and 1974, during President Nixon's Economic Stabilization Program, doctors responded to fee controls by increasing volume (especially return visits and diagnostic tests), but they were able only partially to offset losses in income.[10] From 1974 to 1977, when patient visits declined, they increased fees but again only partly compensated for the loss. According to surveys by both the AMA and *Medical Economics*, doctors' incomes fell somewhat, though not seriously, behind inflation in the 1970s.[11] By 1979 recruiters for physician group practices were reporting that it was a buyer's market: More doctors were applying for jobs than there were openings. Some groups had not raised starting salaries for several years in spite of inflation.[12]

The eighties are likely to bring a more serious squeeze. In the postwar decades (1945–1980), medical expenditures, adjusted for inflation, grew more rapidly than the number of physicians. Hence each doctor worked in a world where resources were expanding.[13] In the 1980s the physician supply will grow more rapidly and medical expenditures more slowly. In constant dollars, medical expenditures per physician may not grow at all. In 1975 there were 565 Americans per doctor; by 1990 there will be only 404—a reduction of nearly 30 percent in the potential clientele for the average physician. For 404 people to spend the equivalent of 565 on doctors' bills would require a substantial growth in personal income, a shift of expenditures from other goods and services to health care, or a shift of the "health care dollar" from hospitals and other providers to physicians. The economic and political climate—slow economic growth and growing opposition to higher medical expenditures—makes it difficult to envision either of the first two taking place.

Increasingly, the gains of one physician, or group of physicians, will have to come at the expense of other physicians or other providers. In the language of game theory, medical services in the 1980s will become more of a zero-sum game. New physicians may no longer be able to introduce an additional layer of specialized services into a community on top of what other practitioners offer. They will have to take business away from someone else. One third of the physicians practicing in 1990 will have finished their training in the eighties. Losses of income may fall most heavily on this huge baby-boom generation in the medical profession.* Young doctors, the least attached to current practices, will be under the greatest pressure to break with them.[14]

Some responses to competition may benefit patients. Doctors may hold more convenient office hours, make house calls, locate in rural areas, and take more time with their patients as they try to cultivate a practice. In short, there may be a shift to greater dependence on patients, as in the nineteenth century.

But a zero-sum situation may also mean increasingly bitter competition among groups of physicians allied with different types of health plans. It may pit established insiders against newcomers, as doctors in some communities close ranks. If they follow a protectionist strategy, established doctors may fight to curtail the spread of HMOs, to deny admitting privileges for younger colleagues at local hospitals, and to maintain restrictions on licensing authority and third-party reimbursement for psychologists, optometrists, nurse practitioners, and others competing for medical expenditures.

The doctor "glut" of the eighties will probably contribute to the

---

*The baby boom is hitting medicine later because of the length of medical training and the delay in the expansion of medical schools until years after other forms of graduate education expanded.

growth of organizations in medical care. Many young doctors, coming out of medical school heavily in debt, may find the expense of establishing a practice beyond their means. They will be more inclined to take salaried positions with hospitals, group practices, and HMOs than their forerunners, and they will have less bargaining power because of their numbers.

The rising supply of physicians is likely to affect fee-for-service medicine and HMOs in opposite ways. An increasing supply will raise costs in the fee-for-service sector because of doctors' incentive to create demand. More fee-for-service surgeons will do more surgery and produce higher premiums for health insurance. On the other hand, prepayment plans should be able to hire physicians on more favorable terms. The rising doctor supply may, therefore, increase the price advantage of HMOs over conventional insurance.

Physicians may respond to competitive pressures by forming more group practices. The proportion of doctors in groups has increased steadily. Group physicians, who were only 1.2 percent of the profession in 1940, rose to 2.6 percent in 1946, 5.2 percent in 1959, and 12.8 percent by 1969. Postwar growth of group practice has followed its earlier pattern. Group practices developed most in rural areas and small towns, especially in the West, where hospital development was initially delayed.[15] By 1980 the 88,000 doctors in groups represented a quarter of the doctors in active practice. From the physicians' viewpoint, a major advantage of group practice is that it enables them to capture directly the profits from ancillary services that provide some of the most lucrative sources of hospital revenue. As Jeff Goldsmith, a business consultant, points out, group practices are vertically integrated forms of production with two outputs, physicians' services and ancillary services, such as X-rays and laboratory tests. The economies of scale in physicians' services are limited; the optimal size of a physician group may be only about six doctors. But large groups may generate substantial profits from ancillary services. "Ancillary profits," notes Goldsmith, "are a significant incentive for the formation of groups, one which is likely to become more powerful as market pressures reduce the profitability of the physicians' services component of what a practice produces."[16]

Collision Course

If physicians respond to their growing numbers by trying to garner a larger share of health care expenditures, the effects may ricochet through the medical system. Doctors who develop group practices to capture ancillary profits represent an economic threat to hospitals. So, too, do the doctors who form HMOs that may reduce the demand for inpatient hospital services. On the other hand, hospitals are developing satellite clinics and other outpatient facilities to assure themselves of a steady flow of referrals. As a result, doctors and hospitals may be on a "collision course" as doctors invade institutional services and hospitals invade ambulatory care.

Private doctors have several critical advantages in such a conflict. Their established relations with patients still give them leverage over the hospitals; hospitals that challenge doctors in their own market may risk a boycott. Private practitioners also have less overhead, and because they are not reimbursed on the basis of costs, they can adjust prices more flexibly to compete with hospitals. In addition, doctors have been exempted from certificate-of-need regulation.[17]

Hospitals, on the other hand, may enjoy some advantages because of the growing supply of physicians. Like other organizations, hospitals may find themselves in a stronger bargaining position in negotiations over compensation with staff physicians. Furthermore, if practitioners grow in number while state laws continue to restrict hospital expansion, doctors will be forced to compete for access to hospital beds.

The growing supply of doctors is almost certain to increase tensions between hospitals and their medical staffs. From the administration's viewpoint, any given physician will represent progressively fewer patients. Hence the interest of the hospital will be to expand its medical staff to keep as many beds filled as possible, while the interest of staff physicians will be to restrict privileges to keep down competition. There will be continuing struggles about which doctors will have admitting privileges and permission to do surgery and complicated diagnostic tests.[18]

Teaching hospitals may have especially serious problems. They have been training their own competition. More specialists are dispersing into the suburbs and smaller towns, where they may provide services previously available only in large medical centers. At the same time, closer scrutiny of reimbursement levels by third-party payers may make it harder for teaching hospitals to continue to cross-subsidize education and research out of patient revenues. Cutbacks in Medicaid may hit them especially hard because of the large number of poor patients in inner-city areas where many teaching hospitals are located. Teaching hospitals have already begun to respond by providing more ambulatory care to bring in patients from other neighborhoods. Like physician groups, they are interested in participating in HMOs to "lock in" patient populations. Thus pressures from a rising physician supply are likely, as Paul Ellwood and Linda Ellwein suggest, to "throw teaching hospitals into a more intense, competitive relationship with nonteaching hospitals."[19]

Throughout the medical world, the rising numbers of physicians mean renewed conflict and fragmentation.

The 1960s and 1970s broke down the uniformity and cohesiveness of the profession. The postwar development of medicine opened up divisions among institutionally based academic physicians, office-based private practitioners, and the "Third World of medicine" (older general practitioners and foreign-trained doctors, many in rural or inner-city areas with large Medicaid populations). Oddly enough, as a result of the influx of foreign doctors, medicine is now one of the most ethnically diverse of the upper-income occupations, with large numbers of Koreans, Indians, and others from abroad. Today one fifth of American doctors are immigrants. The 1970s also opened the gates to women and saw growing numbers of doctors go to work for HMOs and other organizations.

To maintain its claim to represent American physicians, the AMA will have to develop "advocacy services" for these groups. Women are a case in point. Forty-eight percent of men in the profession, but only 26.6 percent of women doctors belong to the AMA.[20] An AMA committee recently pointed out that AMA membership will not keep pace with rising number of doctors unless the organization increases its appeal to women doctors. It recommended that the AMA endorse the Equal Rights Amendment, support day care, and vigorously respond to medical issues of concern to women, including unnecessary hysterectomies and the overprescription of tranquilizers and antidepressants.[21] Another AMA committee has recommended policies to attract foreign medical graduates. James Sammons, executive vice president of the AMA, sees the AMA as representing doctors in negotations with hospitals and HMOs.[22] If it assumes the function of bargaining agent, it will obviously become more like a union. The growth of corporate medical organizations may push it in this direction. However, since some of its members are likely to be the owners and managers of such organizations, the AMA will find it difficult to represent both sides in labor negotiations. Of all the forces fragmenting the profession in the 1980s, none promises to introduce more antagonistic divisions than the growing presence of corporations in medical care.

THE GROWTH OF CORPORATE MEDICINE

Elements of the Corporate Transformation

Although physicians and voluntary hospitals have been preoccupied with government regulation, they may be on their way to losing their autonomy to another master. Medical care in America now appears to be in the early stages of a major transformation in its institutional structure, comparable to the rise of professional sovereignty at the opening of the twentieth century. Corporations have begun to integrate a hitherto decentralized hospital system, enter a variety of other health care businesses, and consolidate ownership and control in what may eventually become an industry dominated by huge health care conglomerates.

This transformation—so extraordinary in view of medicine's past, yet so similar to changes in other industries—has been in the making, ironically enough, since the passage of Medicare and Medicaid. By making health care lucrative for providers, public financing made it exceedingly attractive to investors and set in motion the formation of large-scale corporate enterprises. Nursing homes and hospitals had a long history of proprietary ownership, but almost entirely as small, individually owned and operated enterprises. One of the first developments in the corporate transformation was the purchase of these facilities by new corporate chains. This, in a sense, was the first beachhead of for-profit corporations in the delivery of medical care. Paradoxically, the efforts to control expenditures for health services also stimulated corporate development. The conservative appropriation of liberal reform in the early seventies opened up HMOs as a field for business investment. And in ways entirely unexpected, the regulation of hospitals and other efforts to contain costs set off a wave of acquisitions, mergers, and diversification in the nonprofit as well as profit-making sectors of the medical care industry. Pressure for efficient, business-like management of health care has also contributed to the collapse of the barriers that traditionally prevented corporate control of health services.

These are the outlines of a process that has now gone considerably beyond what observers have described, at least since the early 1970s, as the rise of a "medical-industrial complex." In its original sense, the medical-industrial complex referred to the linkages between the doctors, hospitals, and medical schools and the health insurance companies, drug manufacturers, medical equipment suppliers, and other profit-making firms. Their interests seemed so closely interlocked that they constituted a single system, a seamless web of influence, a common front for a particular style, structure, and distribution of medical care. This early usage emphasized the hidden connections between industry and a medical system that was still made up almost entirely of independent practitioners and local, nonprofit institutions. As of the early seventies, profit-making hospital and nursing home chains were visibly on the rise but still marginal to the health care system as a whole.[23]

Ten years later, this is no longer the case: Large health care corporations are becoming a central element in the system. Arnold S. Relman, editor of *The New England Journal of Medicine*, alerted his readers in 1980 that the the rise of a "new medical-industrial complex" was the "most important health-care development of the day." Relman wanted to distinguish the growing businesses that sell health services to patients for a profit, such as chain hospitals, walk-in clinics, dialysis centers, and home care companies, from the "old" complex of firms that sell drugs, equipment, and insurance.[24]

But the change goes beyond the increased penetration of profit-making firms directly into medical services. By the growth of corporate medicine, I refer also to changes in the organization and behavior of nonprofit hospitals and a general movement throughout the health care industry toward higher levels of integrated control. Five separate dimensions need to be distinguished:

1. *Change in type of ownership and control*: the shift from nonprofit and governmental organizations to for-profit companies in health care

2. *Horizontal integration*: the decline of freestanding institutions and rise of multi-institutional systems, and the consequent shift in the locus of control from community boards to regional and national health care corporations

3. *Diversification and corporate restructuring*: the shift from single-unit organizations operating in one market to "polycorporate" and conglomerate enterprises, often organized under holding companies, sometimes with both nonprofit and for-profit subsidiaries involved in a variety of different health care markets

4. *Vertical integration*: the shift from single-level-of-care organizations, such as acute-care hospitals, to organizations that embrace the various phases and levels of care, such as HMOs

5. *Industry concentration*: the increasing concentration of ownership and control of health services in regional markets and the nation as a whole

Although changes are taking place along all these dimensions simultaneously, they vary in their origins and significance. The growth of multi-institutional systems is a distinct issue from the shift from nonprofit to for-profit ownership. The emergence of diversified health care companies is not the same as the spread of vertically integrated HMOs. Each of these developments in the corporate transformation of American medicine has somewhat different implications for the medical profession and medical care.

The Consolidation of the Hospital System

Unquestionably the most dramatic corporate expansion has taken place in hospital care. The traditional freestanding general hospital, governed by its own board, administrators, and medical staff, is now giving way to larger multihospital systems run by àn increasingly powerful corporate management. In 1961 there were only five consolidations of hospitals in the United States; by the early 1970s, the number had grown to about fifty a year.[25] In its 1980 survey of multihospital systems, the trade journal *Modern Healthcare* found 176 systems owning or managing 294,199 beds. Another survey, conducted under the auspices of the American Hospital Association, found 245 multihospital systems with 301,894 beds. These estimates, based on somewhat different definitions, indicate that by 1980 about 30 percent of the nation's 988,000 community hospital beds were in multi-institutional corporations.[26] The distribution ranged from only about 10 percent of hospital beds in New England to about 40 percent in the Far West.[27]

Nonprofit organizations account for the majority of beds in multihospital systems. In 1980 the nonprofits operated 57.6 percent of the beds in multihospital systems, the investor-owned chains 35.1 percent, and public systems (excluding federal hospitals) 7.3 percent. But the for-profit chains account for most of the recent growth. Nearly 65 percent of the 20,000 beds added by multihospital systems in 1980 were added by the for-profit companies.[28]

After their emergence in 1968, the profit-making hospital chains grew faster in the 1970s than the computer industry. In 1970 the largest for-profit chain controlled twenty-three hospitals; by 1981 the same company, Hospital Corporation of America, owned or managed more than three hundred hospitals with 43,000 beds. In 1981 the profit-making chains owned or managed hospitals with 121,741 beds, up 68 percent over the total of 72,282 beds they had held five years earlier.[29]

Not all of these beds were in the United States. Several of the chains have become multinational corporations. American Medical International owns or manages facilities in England, Spain, Switzerland, Singapore, France, and Venezuela as well as the United States. In 1979 Hospi-

tal Corporation of America purchased a prepaid health plan in Brazil
with five hospitals, forty-two clinics, 780 doctors, and an enrollment of
over a half million people.[30]

In the United States, the chain hospitals are concentrated in the
South and Southwest in such states as Florida, Texas, and California.
The hospitals are typically medium in size, ranging from 100 to 200 beds,
and do not have residency programs.

One of the largest chains, Humana, Inc., exemplifies the rise of the
hospital corporations. Humana started out in Louisville in 1968 with a
few nursing homes and $4.8 million in revenues. Shifting to the more
lucrative acute-care business, the company cashed in on its nursing
homes and began buying and building hospitals. According to its president, the firm wanted to provide as uniform and reliable a product as
a MacDonald's hamburger coast to coast. By 1980 it had ninety-two hospitals and $1.4 billion in revenues; an original share, which cost $8 in
1968, was now worth $336.[31]

Most of the early growth of the profit-making chains came as they
bought up individually owned proprietary facilities. Hence the growth
of the for-profit chains has not meant a commensurate expansion of the
proprietary sector. The emergence of the chains arrested a decline in
the proprietary hospital sector that had been continuing steadily over
the previous half century. After dropping from 2,435 in 1928 to 738 in
1972, the number of investor-owned hospitals held steady in the 1970s.
However, the average size of these hospitals increased more than 50
percent. The share of community hospital beds owned by proprietary
hospitals increased from 6.5 to 8.8 percent between 1972 and 1980; the
proportion of beds in hospitals owned by investors or managed by investor-owned companies rose to 12.4 percent.[32]

The statistics understate the significance of the change. The old independent proprietary hospitals were typically small institutions owned
and controlled by physicians. They were not really that different from
many nonprofit hospitals equally dominated by their medical staff. The
rise of the for-profit chains has, for the first time, introduced managerial
capitalism into American medicine on a large scale.

Multihospital systems vary in the degree of centralization across a
spectrum that ranges from fairly loose affiliations to tight management
by corporate headquarters. Strong central management is the pattern
among the for-profit chains. The majority of for-profit companies report
that the power to set hospital budgets, plan capital investments, appoint
chief hospital administrators, and make other key decisions rests with
management at corporate headquarters. The profit-making chains have
also adopted standardized management procedures, standardized ac-

counting, and other uniform practices. These tendencies are, as a rule, less advanced in the nonprofit systems.[33]

There are two distinct aspects to patterns of control: Decisions may be local or centralized; and, if centralized, they may rest with a corporate board or corporate managers. One survey reports that local board responsibility for budgets and other key matters is the modal pattern only in the religious (mainly Catholic) multihospital systems. Among the secular nonprofits, such decisions more commonly rest with corporate boards, but in the for-profit chains, power usually lies with corporate management. The limited role of the boards of for-profit hospital companies suggests that, like most other large corporations, they are controlled by their inside directors.[34]

The greater power of corporate management may reflect how the hospital chains were built. Another reason for greater centralization and standardized management may be size. The average number of hospitals in investor-owned chains in 1980 was 23.5, compared to an average of between 6 and 7 hospitals in nonprofit systems.[35]

However, the differences in size and management may be diminishing. In the late seventies, some nonprofit systems adopted a more aggressively expansionist strategy and began bidding against the for-profits for new acquisitions. In 1981 Fairview Community Hospitals, a nonprofit system founded in 1973 and based in Minneapolis, bought a for-profit chain, A. E. Brim of Portland, Oregon. The purchase gave Fairview a total of 41 hospitals with 2,165 beds. As of 1979, the largest nonprofit was Sisters of Mercy Health Corporation (founded in 1976), with 23 hospitals and 5,584 beds.

Ownership and control are much more highly concentrated in the for-profit sector. By 1981, after several large mergers, nearly three quarters of the beds in for-profit multihospital systems were operated by the top three companies (Hospital Corporation of America, Humana, and American Medical International). On the other hand, the top three nonprofits (Kaiser Foundation Hospitals, Sisters of Mercy Health Corporation, and Sisters of Charity of Houston) operated less than a tenth of the beds in nonprofit systems.[36] The for-profits and nonprofits also differ in their patterns of development. While the leading profit-making chains are national, the nonprofits typically operate in one area or contiguous states. The for-profits show a stronger tendency toward "horizontal" growth through the hospital industry; the nonprofits, toward "vertical" growth through different levels of care in health services. While most of the for-profit chains have restricted themselves to acute care facilities, many of the nonprofits have built satellite clinics and operate nursing homes in their areas.[37]

Some might assume, given their growth, that multihospital systems are more efficient than independent hospitals and that, given their incentives, for-profit hospitals are more efficient than nonprofits. But this is to assume that the incentives facing hospitals reward efficiency.

There are many reasons why multihospital systems might be more efficient. David Starkweather, a professor of hospital administration, points out that the average American hospital is about half the minimum optimal size. As hospitals increase in size up to about 300 beds, their unit costs drop. (However, once past 600 or 700 beds, their costs begin to increase again.) Economies of scale up to 300 beds arise for several reasons: Small hospitals tend to have higher excess capacity, in part because their occupancy rates are less stable; larger size permits cheaper purchasing in volume and makes capital available at lower cost; and the feasibility of using specialized services increases with size.[38]

But while the potential efficiencies are impressive, the evidence of actual savings is not. One study, comparing a matched sample of merging and independent hospitals, found that the merged hospitals actually experienced greater increases in average cost per case and other indicators of expense.[39] Some savings seem to develop over time. Starkweather observes that "research suggests an initial period of inefficiency after a merger, when unit costs are even higher than they would have been otherwise. The period of greater inefficiency can last eight to twelve years."[40] Among the reasons are the costs of buying off opposition. Physicians are rarely displaced if they duplicate services. If one of two merging hospitals has lower standards in physical resources or in pay, the merger will usually require leveling standards up rather than down. These changes are not necessarily bad, but they rarely result in significantly lower costs.

There is even less evidence to suggest that the for-profit companies achieve any savings over nonprofits. A 1981 study by the consulting firm Lewin and Associates covers a matched sample of fifty-three hospitals owned by for-profit chains in California, Florida, and Texas and fifty-three nonprofits in the same states. The authors caution that it is difficult to extrapolate to the country as a whole because these are all states with little hospital regulation; however, since the chains deliberately locate in such states, this is not a limitation that studies can easily overcome.

Lewin and Associates wanted to find whether the for-profits and nonprofits differed in their cost to purchasers of health care and, if so, whether the differences were due to operating costs, markup of charges over costs, or differences in service. They found that the investor-owned hospitals had slightly higher costs, charged considerably more, and had higher revenues per day and per case. For cost payers (Medicare and Medicaid), the for-profit hospitals were only a bit more expensive per day and about the same per hospital admission. But for charge payers (such as subscribers to private health insurance), the for-profits were 23 percent more expensive per day and 17 percent more costly per admission. Routine charges were similar; the big difference was in the for-profits' high markup of such ancillary services as drugs and supplies. "Administrative and general service costs" were also 13 percent greater in the profit-making hospitals, due to higher "home office" costs, such as interest expenses, financial services, and data processing. Contrary to the expectation that the chains would achieve economies of scale, the study concluded that "home office expenses do not produce equivalent savings in individual local hospitals."[41] National data also indicate that, for every bed-size category, for-profit hospitals have higher costs than the overall average for community hospitals.[42]

Even if larger hospital systems, or for-profit hospitals, were to produce hospital care more economically, they would still have the same incentives as freestanding hospitals to admit patients not needing hospitalization. They would still be likely to overuse technological services that receive disproportionately high reimbursement. And they would continue to duplicate expensive equipment available elsewhere in the community because the costs can be recovered through the insurance system. Though they may be exceedingly efficient in maximizing reimbursement rates, this sort of efficiency does not necessarily benefit their patients or the rest of society.

Why, then, have the multihospital systems grown? Expanding private insurance and Medicare gave the initial financial impetus to proprietary chains. Even though multihospital systems may not return savings to the public, their larger size may still give them advantages in the marketplace and the legislatures. They may answer demands for power, profit, and institutional survival that freestanding hospitals cannot satisfy. In recent years, closer regulation, tighter reimbursement, and higher interest rates seem to have stimulated the process of consolidation. Financial straits have obliged a growing number of voluntary and public hospitals to surrender some of their autonomy, look for stronger management, or pursue acquisitions and diversification themselves. Barred by regulatory agencies from expanding, some voluntary hospitals have sought acquisitions and mergers as an alternative. Also, public regulation may have stimulated hospitals to hire planners, lawyers, and financial advisors, who then found new functions for themselves in arranging mergers and acquisitions. Limits on new construction have also restricted competition, making existing hospitals attractive as an investment. And, in addition, the increasing complexity of the regulatory environment gave a growing advantage to large organizations, which can more easily influence and adapt to new regulations. As one hospital expert puts it, "Whenever government mandates a new report or establishes a new regulation, the administration needs better information and is more receptive to joining a chain."[43] As financing became more difficult and complex with high interest rates in the late seventies, the multihospital systems gained a critical advantage because they could secure easier access to debt markets than single hospitals.[44]

Industry experts anticipate rapid growth of multihospital systems, especially the for-profits. Some are predicting that the for-profit chains will double in size in the eighties while the hospital industry as a whole will experience little growth. The gloomy economic forecast for voluntary hospitals is a boon to the multihospital systems. The greater the squeeze in reimbursements, the more pressure there will be on the relatively weak, freestanding institutions to sell out to multihospital systems with greater financial resources. Some local governments, meeting stiff resistance to higher taxes or bond issues, are finding it more attractive to sell public hospitals. A vice president of American Medical International explains, "Where historically government officials felt it was improper to sell their hospitals, many now feel that it's inappropriate for government to be in the business of operating them."[45]

The profit-making chains also have a need to grow. Continued growth is necessary to keep up the price of their stocks and postpone tax liabilities. But they do face some limits. The independent proprietary hospitals that provided the basis for their early growth are becoming more scarce. The chains do not want to own hospitals in depressed areas with large numbers of Medicaid patients. Nor are they likely to buy up teaching hospitals. But there is probably ample room for growth in the medium-size hospitals in the more attractive neighborhoods, if the boards of voluntary hospitals can be convinced to sell.

This may ultimately prove to be the limiting factor. The growth of national hospitals chains promises to withdraw control of a civic institution from local authorities. The chains, as Starkweather points out, "transfer ownership out of the local community, increasing the difficulty of achieving local . . . reorganization of health care delivery."[46] Companies may shut down local services that do not yield enough revenue to the corporation, just as industrial conglomerates sometimes close plants that do not make a "hurdle" (return on investment) that may be as high as 20 to 25 percent.[47] Plant shutdowns have yet to arise in the commercial hospital industry, but they are not hard to imagine. Nor is it hard to imagine the concessions that multinational hospital corporations will be able to extract from local communities by threatening to close down their hospitals.

The implications for the future distribution of hospital care may also arouse opposition. The for-profit chains have an undisguised preference for privately insured patients. As *Fortune* explained in an article on Humana,

> Privately insured patients can be charged what the market will bear. When a hospital has empty beds, Medicare and Medicaid patients are better than cold sheets, and Humana charges off every penny of overhead on them the government will allow. But if it isn't trying to fill a lot of empty beds, Humana treats as few of those patients as possible.
>
> Humana prefers to own facilities in suburbs where young working families are having lots of babies. Though young people use hospitals less than the elderly, they are more likely to be privately insured and in need of surgery, which makes the most money. The babies provide a second generation of customers.[48]

Humana's policy is to treat all emergency cases. However, if a wallet biopsy—one of the procedures in which American hospitals specialize—discloses that the victims are uninsured, it transfers them to public institutions. As a Humana official explained, in regard to a patient who died after being transfered within one day of suffering a heart attack, "These freebies cost $2,000 or $3,000 a day. Who's going to pay for them?"[49] The chains certainly aren't.

The Decomposition of Voluntarism

The 1970s and 1980s have brought harsher times for many public and nonprofit hospitals. The tilt of postwar policy toward the hospital has become a tilt away from hospital care. Funds for capital investment are no longer abundant. Cutbacks in reimbursement rates under government programs threaten the survival of institutions with large numbers of poor patients. New organizations, such as HMOs, reduce the demand for hospital care, and the growing supply of physicians encourages doctors to "invade" services performed by hospitals to capture a larger share of ancillary profits. Hospitals face a more competitive market, and many may not endure.

In response, many voluntary hospitals are diversifying into other health care businesses. Administrators see diversification as a way to generate new revenues and raise additional capital for renovation and expansion. Often they are reorganizing their corporate structures at the same time. In one model, the hospital becomes the parent corporation for a variety of subsidiaries; in another, it establishes a parent holding company, which owns the hospital as well as other subsidiaries. These new legal arrangements protect the hospital's tax-exempt status while it diversifies and ensures that reimbursements for hospital care will not be cut because of revenues from new businesses. The "polycorporate" structure, says an enthusiastic hospital consultant, Montague Brown, makes it possible for hospitals "to build thriving business ventures [to] generate profits that the parent corporation can use wherever it chooses." While the hospital subsidiary continues to operate as in the past, the new holding company can pursue acquisitions and spin off new subsidiaries. "The chief executive officer of the new polycorporate enterprise," writes Brown, "may well be the former president, or even the current president, of the hospital but his or her work will resemble less and less the traditional task of the hospital administrator." It will be more like managing a conglomerate.[50]

Under the umbrella of this new polycorporate enterprise, the tax-exempt, nonprofit hospital can operate taxable, for-profit businesses. In early 1981 the IRS agreed that a voluntary hospital in California did not lose its tax-exempt status after undertaking various profit-making ventures, which included a medical office building, a shopping center, a restaurant, and a contract management consulting firm. It even appears that the profit-making subsidiaries of a nonprofit hospital can sell stock to investors, as long as the tax-exempt and taxable organizations are kept separate.[51]

By early 1981 several hundred corporate reorganizations of hospitals had taken place. In Pittsburgh, Pennsylvania, for example, the non-profit Allegheny General Hospital created a new parent holding company, Allegheny Health Education and Research Corporation, to generate new revenues and capital. Among its subsidiaries is a for-profit company, Allegheny Diagnostic Services, Inc., which sells cardiac rehabilitation, sports medicine, and laboratory services. In Berkeley, California, the nonprofit Alta Bates Hospital created a holding company to operate the hospital, another hospital it had acquired, a management services firm, a foundation, a group of nursing home and retirement centers, and Alta Bates Ambulatory Health Services, Inc., which operates a dialysis center, home care services, a pathology institute, a hospice, and a sports medicine unit.[52]

The ambitions of hospital administrators now go considerably beyond the traditional hospital functions. In Kansas City, Missouri, the 600-bed, nonprofit Research Medical Center operates a profit-making subsidiary, Health Services Management, Inc., which sells assertiveness training, stress management, continuing medical education, and speech and language group therapy for children. After reorganizing, Research Medical's president indicated that among the new ventures being considered were a chain of health food restaurants, retail pharmacies, and hearing aid and eyeglass stores. "We have only about two years in which to do this," explained the company president, since hospitals that fail to diversify "are going to be gobbled up in mergers and acquisitions."[53]

Corporate reorganizations of hospitals often involve what consultants call "unbundling." Suppose a hospital has a laboratory that has been providing services to other hospitals. When unbundled, the department becomes a separate corporation, which can then pursue business on its own. The profits it generates for the parent holding company do not reduce the hospital's reimbursement rates.

Conversely, the hospital may contract out part of its own operations to independent corporations. Voluntary hospitals have long served as nonprofit shelters for the highly profitable businesses operated within them by radiologists and pathologists. Now they are increasingly contracting with physician groups to provide patient care. These groups, organized as professional corporations, may then hire their own employees and expand their operations to other institutions. Some may grow into substantial corporate enterprises. Many hospitals already buy coverage of their emergency rooms from a company that supplies physicians and operates the entire service. As the principle is extended, it may turn the nonprofit hospital into a beehive of corporate activity.

The extension of the voluntary hospital into profit-making businesses and the penetration of other corporations into the hospital signal the breakdown of the traditional boundaries of voluntarism. Increasingly, the polycorporate hospitals are likely to become multihospital systems and competitors with profit-making chains, HMOs, and other health care corporations. The president of one nonprofit multihospital system, which has profit-making subsidiaries, comments that "it may be increasingly difficult to distinguish those chains with voluntary origins from those which have been built with stock ownership."[54] Eventually, it may also be difficult to distinguish those health care conglomerates that began as hospital systems from those that began in other markets.

Corporate activity in other medical services has been considerable. About 77 percent of the nursing homes in the United States are proprietary, and an increasing proportion are being bought up by large corporate chains. The nursing home chains are also going into the "life care" business, constructing retirement apartments next to nursing homes. Other companies provide home care, which involves home-making assistance, physiotherapy, and nursing and medical services. Compared to nursing homes, which generated about $19 billion in revenues in 1980, home care is still a small business, worth perhaps $3 billion, with about a half billion dollars going to ten large companies in 1980.[55]

There are also dozens of other related health care businesses, such as dental care, optical services, weight-control, rehabilitation, CAT scanning, and various kinds of laboratory services. Emergicenters—also called minor emergency centers, convenience clinics, or walk-in clinics—are typical and perhaps the most important. Often located in shopping centers, they provide immediate treatment for any medical problem, generally without an appointment. The owner of two emergicenters in Massachusetts calls them "the fast-food concept applied to medicine." Such centers increased in number from about fifty to over two hundred nationwide between 1978 and 1981. In several states, chains operate clinics often in partnership with physicians; one company has begun to create a national franchise. A vice president of Merrill, Lynch gushes that emergicenters "can attract as much as 25 percent of the approximately $45 billion that Americans spent on physician and hospital outpatient services last year. That's more than $10 billion—bigger than the fast-food industry. And with centralized management and economies of scale, they can prove highly attractive to entrepreneurial capital."[56]

Large, multi-unit corporations are also gaining a major position in the organization of HMOs. At the beginning of the 1970s, the prepayment plans, except for Kaiser, were locally controlled. None were profit-making companies. By 1980 the majority of HMOs were being drawn into several large networks run by Kaiser, Blue Cross, INA, and Prudential. Without extensive government aid for start-up capital, the consumer-run, cooperative organizations are certain to decline, and the surviving HMOs will increasingly become part of large corporate networks.

The Trajectory of Organization

Throughout much of this work I have been concerned with the social selection of organizations. I have asked what explains the forms of medical practice, hospitals, private health plans, and public programs that emerged in America out of the diverse possibilities that were historically available. The reader may wonder, of the many kinds of organization that now exist (or might appear) in medical care, which are likely to prevail in the future? And what effects are they likely to have on the medical profession and the society?

The array of organizational forms in medicine is now extraordinarily complex. On all the dimensions I listed earlier—type of ownership and control; extent of horizontal integration; diversification; vertical integration; and overall levels of concentration in regional health care markets—there is tremendous ferment and variety through the United States. The traditional private practitioner, freestanding voluntary hospital, and indemnity or service-benefit health insurance plan continue to be the norm, but they are losing their former dominance. In the future, more doctors will be in group practice; more hospitals will be in multihospital systems; and more insurance companies will be directly involved in providing medical care through HMOs. The traditional boundaries among these three sectors are being challenged: Doctors are integrating "backward" into institutional services; hospitals are integrating "forward" into ambulatory care; insurance companies are adopting new arrangements with "preferred providers" to create hybrid prepayment plans. No one today could safely predict the outcome of these developments.

However, most observers would agree that the movement toward integrated control will continue. Starkweather suggests that the roughly five thousand different corporations responsible for the nation's hospitals will be reduced to about two thousand by 1990.[57] Another analyst suggests that by the year 2000, health care conglomerates, each with revenues of over $500 million a year, will account for about a fifth of all spending on hospitals and nursing homes.[58] These are relatively modest projections. A radical Reaganite program could accelerate the movement. Before being appointed director of the Office of Management and Budget, David Stockman declared that "under the kind of system that I'm talking about . . . I think most hospitals will become parts of for-profit marketing operations or they will become for-profit on their own."[59]

The long-run question is which form of integration will predominate. Several major types have now appeared: (1) the academic medical "empire," with its extended network of affiliation agreements; (2) the regional, nonprofit multihospital system; (3) the national, for-profit hospital chains; (4) HMOs, both independent and in chains; and (5) the diversified health care "conglomerate" with different lines of business in health care, but not offering comprehensive services to a defined population as in an HMO.

These different forms of corporate health care will be engaged in both economic and political competition with one another. If the financing system for medical care rewarded economic performance, both the academic medical empires and the for-profit chains would be handicapped by their higher costs. But this is not necessarily a fatal disadvantage as long as the reimbursement system permits higher-cost institutions to receive additional funds. The for-profit chains' higher markups on ancillary services, along with their superior access to private capital, actually provide them with funds for expansion. The academic medical centers are in more serious difficulty because of their higher costs, but they may be able to persuade government, perhaps after a few threatened bankruptcies, to accept more of the burden of financing medical education.

As I've already indicated, there is no evidence for significant savings from for-profit over nonprofit organizations and little evidence for savings from multihospital systems over freestanding institutions. Horizontal integration has more advantages for the organizations than for the society. Similarly, corporate restructuring—the emergence of the polycorporate enterprise—has as its main motive the maximization of reimbursement. These are primarily adaptations to an incentive system that continues to be skewed; there is no reason to expect that they will meet the demands of the government or employers for containment of medical costs.

On the other hand, vertical integration—comprehensive prepayment—has the potential to yield significant savings of money and improvements in effectiveness. There is clear and convincing evidence for substantial savings from HMOs; the main reason is the reduction in expensive hospital care—hardly surprising in view of the effects on the rest of the health care system of the long-standing tilt toward hospitals in government policy, private insurance, and relative prices paid physicians for hospital and office services.[60]

Many observers, more confident of the rationality of the medical system than I am, foresee a shift from horizontal to vertical integration. In this view, the regional, nonprofit multihospital systems will be precursors to comprehensive health care plans, and even the for-profit hospital chains will eventually turn toward HMOs.[61]

There is precedent for this view. In his history of the rise of corporate management, Alfred Chandler notes that there were two paths to the modern corporation in America. One was to expand by merger. This was basically a strategy of horizontal integration, aimed at increasing profits by controlling price and output. The other was to combine a system of mass marketing with mass production; this was a strategy of vertical integration aimed at raising profits by cutting costs. In the long run, the first strategy could not succeed alone. "The firms that first grew large by taking the merger route remained profitable only if after consolidating they then adopted a strategy of vertical integration," writes Chandler.[62]

The reasons for the lower costs of vertically integrated health care enterprises are not the same as for vertically integrated manufacturing companies. But if government and employers paying fringe benefits put pressure on American medicine to minimize its costs to society, the movement toward vertical integration (that is, to HMOs) will ultimately predominate. In that event, the likely trajectory of organization will lead increasingly toward corporate HMO networks.

But there is no reason to assume that cost minimization will prevail. Doctors continue to hold strategic position through their established relations with both patients and hospitals. The major block to HMO development is the unwillingness of potential subscribers to break long-standing ties with their doctors. The relations between hospitals and their medical staffs—particularly the fact that doctors have admitting privileges only at certain hospitals and that hospitals draw their patients through their doctors' practices—also tend to block the substantial reduction of hospital capacity that would be the outcome of HMO development.

The competition among types of corporate medical care is extraordinarily sensitive to the vagaries of politics. Changes in the details of reimbursement policy have immense implications for the profitability of different types of organizations. Highly organized lobbies may be able to recover through the manipulation of public policy what they could not otherwise achieve. This is the problem of political feedback: Once powerful organizations become established, they find the political means to sustain themselves.

Kidney dialysis centers provide a particularly graphic example of the rise of a private industry in response to public financing and then the manipulation of public policy by the industry it originally created. In 1972 Congress extended Medicare to one group of patients under age sixty-five: the victims of end-stage renal disease. At the time, about nine thousand patients were receiving long-term renal dialysis, 37 percent at home and almost all through nonprofit programs, which were attempting wherever possible to arrange kidney transplants as a more permanent solution.

By 1976 the proportion on home dialysis dropped to less than 10 percent, as dialysis centers proliferated. According to a 1975 congressional study, dialysis then cost between $4,000 and $6,000 a year if done at home, between $14,000 and $20,000 at a clinic, and about $30,000 at a hospital. Congress had been told in 1972 that four years later the cost of the program would be $200 million; it turned out to be about twice that amount. Among the more benign explanations for the decline of home dialysis was the increased proportion of elderly and very sick patients receiving dialysis as the program expanded. But it was also apparent that Congress had helped create the problem by providing incentives for institutional dialysis to both doctors and patients. Apart from deductibles, the government paid the entire cost of treatment at a clinic or hospital but only about 80 percent of the cost of treatment at home. It had also encouraged doctors who specialized in the field to set up profit-making centers to which they could refer their own patients. Opponents of the centers pointed to the huge disparities in rates of home treatment between different areas of the country. In Seattle, Washington, where the Northwest Kidney Center strongly favored home treatment, 100 percent of the dialysis patients were being treated at home, whereas in Los Angeles, 95 percent of the patients received institutional dialysis. A medical professor from the University of Washington explained that many doctors were reluctant to give their patients the responsibility of self-treatment. "If the physician also happens to own the dialysis center, he's pretty interested in keeping that center full, the motivation is pretty small to get the patients home, and that's essentially what's been happening in Los Angeles County."[63]

In 1976 several Democrats in the House of Representatives sought legislation equalizing government reimbursements for home and institutional dialysis and requiring that by 1980 half of dialysis patients be on home treatment or "self-care" at institutions. However, National Medical Care, Inc., the leading operator of for-profit dialysis centers, weighed into the battle, hiring Reagan's 1976 campaign manager John Sears as its chief lobbyist. On emerging from the House, the 50 percent requirement of home dialysis had become a "goal." When the bill left the Senate, even the goal had disappeared. Congress just expressed its "intent" that as many patients as possible receive home dialysis. "The lobbyists gutted the hell out of [the legislation]," one Social Security official commented.

By 1980 National Medical Care owned 120 dialysis centers and treated 17 percent of the nation's 48,000 dialysis patients. In several cities, including Boston, Washington, and Dallas, it controlled the dialysis market. Very few of its patients are dialyzed at home. The company is vertically integrated: One subsidiary makes dialysis supplies and equipment; another performs the laboratory tests for dialysis patients. NMC has also branched out into obesity control, psychiatric care, and respiratory therapy—another emerging health care conglomerate.[64]

This kind of conglomerate development may well prevail over the development of comprehensive medical care through HMOs. The industrialization of episodic medicine was not the original intent of the market idealists of the early 1970s who favored health maintenance organizations. Many of them regard chain hospitals and emergicenters as the antithesis of what they had in mind. They wanted corporate involvement to change the nature of health care; it seems more likely, in the foreseeable future, to reproduce the defects of the traditional system on a grander scale.

DOCTORS, CORPORATIONS, AND THE STATE

The great illusion of physicians and the hospital industry in the 1970s was that liberal government was causing their troubles. The real threat to their autonomy lay in the demands they were placing upon private health insurance as well as public programs. Private insurers and employers want medical expenditures to be controlled. And though business has become more wary of planning and regulation, it wants medicine put under constraint of some kind.

In the early 1980s, spokesmen for business are calling for control over costs by the private sector. Though this approach has ideological affinities with the competitive model in health policy, the two are not exactly the same. The chief instance of private-sector regulation is the business coalition. In 1974 the Business Roundtable, whose members consist of the chief executive officers (CEOs) of the largest corporations in the United States, created a new organization called the Washington Business Group on Health. The initial purpose was to defeat national health insurance, but the group increasingly became involved in other medical policy issues, particularly cost containment. Local business coalitions to encourage containment of medical costs have been the next step. By early 1982 about eighty such coalitions were in process of formation around the United States. Their agenda includes such issues as utilization review and review of capital spending by medical institutions, not altogether different from the concerns of the PSROs and HSAs that the Reagan administration was intent on dismantling. The attack on regulation may not presage its disappearance but rather a transfer of functions from federally-sponsored organizations to business-sponsored organizations and the states. It is not difficult to imagine a situation in which some corporations (i.e., employers) lean on other corporations (i.e., insurers, HMOs, hospital chains), which, in turn, lean on the professionals to control costs. However, some critics object the employers won't lean hard enough because their stake is too small.[65]

The emergence of corporate enterprise in health services is part of two broad currents in the political economy of contemporary societies. The older of these two movements is the steady expansion of the corporation into sectors of the economy traditionally occupied by self-employed small businessmen or family enterprises. In this respect, the growth of corporate medical care is similar to the growth of corporate agriculture. The second and more recent movement is the transfer of public services to the administrative control or ownership of private corporations—the reprivatization of the public household.

As I've already indicated, liberal and conservative policies, in opposite ways, have both promoted corporate health care. Medicare and Medicaid stimulated the huge growth in proprietary nursing homes and hospitals and later the rise of dialysis clinics, home care businesses, and emergicenters. Cutbacks in financing have encouraged the same developments. This shift was not inevitable. The legal rule against the corporate practice of medicine might conceivably have been steadfastly enforced by the courts. The early liberal programs might have emphasized neighborhood health centers instead of Medicaid and more generally have fostered public facilities instead of public financing for private health care. The great irony is that the opposition of the doctors and hospitals to public control of public programs set in motion entrepreneurial forces that may end up depriving both private doctors and local voluntary hospitals of their traditional autonomy.

The profession was long able to resist corporate competition and corporate control by virtue of its collective organization, authority, and strategic position in mediating the relation of patients to hospitals, pharmaceutical companies, and use of third-party payment. Today, physicians still hold authority and strategic position, but these have eroded. Specialization has diminished the scope of relations between doctors and patients. Although patients who have established satisfactory relationships with private physicians are less likely to enroll in HMOs, HMOs have been developing more rapidly than before partly because ties between doctors and patients are so much weaker. (The rise in malpractice suits against private physicians has the same cause.) Employers and the government have become critical intermediaries in the system because of their financial role, and they are using their power to reorient the system.

In addition, the profession is no longer steadfastly opposed to the growth of corporate medicine. Physicians' commitment to solo practice has been eroding; younger medical school graduates express a preference for practicing in groups. The longer period of residency training may cultivate more group-oriented attitudes. Young doctors may be more interested in freedom *from* the job than freedom *in* the job, and organizations that provide more regular hours can screen out the invasions of private life that come with independent professional practice.

The AMA is no longer as devoted to solo practice either. "We are not opposed to the corporate practice of medicine," says Dr. Sammons of the AMA. "There is no way that we could be," he adds, pointing out that a high proportion of the AMA's members are now involved in corporate practice. According to AMA data, some 26 percent of physicians have contractual relationships with hospitals; three out of five of these doctors are on salary.[66] About half the physicians in private practice have set up professional corporations to take advantage of special tax-sheltering provisions.[67] Many physicians in private practice receive part of their income through independent practice associations, HMOs, and for-profit hospitals and other health care companies. The growth of corporate medicine has simply gone too far for the AMA to oppose it outright. Dr. Sammons explains that the AMA would oppose any interference by organizations in medical decisions, but says that he is satisfied that none of the forms of corporate practice currently threaten professional autonomy.[68] However, at the local level, medical societies often still vigorously oppose HMOs and other forms of integrated control.[69]

Doctors are not likely, as some sociologists have suggested, to become "proletarianized" by corporate medicine. "Proletarianized" suggests a total loss of control over the conditions of work as well as a severe reduction in compensation. Such a radical change is not in prospect. Corporations will require the active cooperation of physicians. Profit-making hospitals require doctors to generate admissions and revenues; prepaid health plans, while having the opposite incentives, still require doctors' cooperation to control hospital admissions and overall costs. Because of their dependence on physicians, the corporations will be generous in granting rewards, including more autonomy than they give to most other workers. The new generation of women physicians may find the new corporate organizations willing to allow more part-time and intermittent work than is possible in solo practice.

Nonetheless, compared with individual practice, corporate work will necessarily entail a profound loss of autonomy. Doctors will no longer have as much control over such basic issues as when they retire. There will be more regulation of the pace and routines of work. And the corporation is likely to require some standard of performance, whether measured in revenues generated or patients treated per hour. To stimulate admissions, Humana offers physicians office space at a discount in buildings next to its hospitals and even guarantees first-year incomes of $60,000. It then keeps track of the revenues each doctor generates.

"They let you know if you're not keeping up to expectations," says one young physician. Humana's president is frank about what happens if they fail to produce: "I'm damn sure I'm not going to renegotiate their office leases. They can practice elsewhere."[70]

Under corporate management, there is also likely to be close scrutiny of mistakes, if only because of corporate liability for malpractice. An enthusiastic management consultant writes that "individual incompetence and sloppy clinical performance will be less tolerated there than in freestanding large voluntary hospitals. . . . The large conglomerate can purchase and/or develop sophisticated quality-of-care control programs managed by statisticians. Working at corporate headquarters, the statisticians will not be concerned about individual physicians' reactions. Their reports, however, will supply individual hospitals with results about physicians who are not measuring up. . . . Senior management at the corporate level will constantly be mindful that the corporation's reputation comes first . . . ."[71] This, of course, may be management fantasy, but unlike PSROs, which this control system resembles, it cannot be denounced as government regulation.

New distinctions will need to be made among owning, managing, employed, and independent physicians. The rise of corporate medicine will restratify the profession. A key question will be the control over the appointment of managing physicians. If the managers are accountable to doctors organized in medical groups, the profession may be able to achieve some collective autonomy within the framework of the corporation (as they do in Kaiser). Another key issue will be the boundary between medical and business decisions; when both medical and economic considerations are relevant, which will prevail and who will decide? Much will depend on the external forces driving the organization. Thus far, conflict has been muted by affluence. A regime of medical austerity will test the limits of professional autonomy in the corporate system.

One reason that there will be a loss of autonomy is that the organizations in which physicians work are themselves likely to become *heteronomous*—that is, the locus of control will be outside the immediate organization. Professional autonomy has been protected by the institutional autonomy of hospitals. In the multihospital systems, centralized planning, budgeting, and personnel decisions will deprive physicians of much of the influence they are accustomed to exercise over institutional policy.

Perhaps the most subtle loss of autonomy for the profession will take place because of increasing corporate influence over the rules and standards of medical work. Corporate management is already thinking about the different techniques for modifying the behavior of physicians, getting them to accept management's outlook and integrate it into their everyday work. That way they do not need to be supervised and do not sense any loss of control. Sociologists have long talked about the "professional socialization" that takes place in medical school as students acquire the values and attitudes of mature physicians. Now they will have to study "corporate socialization" as young doctors learn to do things the way the plan or the company has them done.[72]

The rise of a corporate ethos in medical care is already one of the most significant consequences of the changing structure of medical care. It permeates voluntary hospitals, government agencies, and academic thought as well as profit-making medical care organizations. Those who talked about "health care planning" in the 1970s now talk about "health care marketing." Everywhere one sees the growth of a kind of marketing mentality in health care. And, indeed, business school graduates are displacing graduates of public health schools, hospital administrators, and even doctors in the top echelons of medical care organizations. The organizational culture of medicine used to be dominated by the ideals of professionalism and voluntarism, which softened the underlying acquisitive activity. The restraint exercised by those ideals now grows weaker. The "health center" of one era is the "profit center" of the next.

No less important than its effect on the culture of medical care institutions is the likely political impact of the growth of corporate enterprise. As an interest group, the new health care conglomerates will obviously be a powerful force. In one case—the renal dialysis clinics—the influence of one corporation prevented Congress from adopting legislation that would have cut federal health care costs, which is to say corporate profits. The profit-making hospitals clearly benefit from the structure of private health insurance and can be counted on to oppose any national health program that might threaten to end private reimbursement. The corporate health services industry will also represent a powerful new force resisting public accountability and participation.

A corporate sector in health care is also likely to aggravate inequalities in access to health care. Profit-making enterprises are not interested in treating those who cannot pay. The voluntary hospital may not treat the poor the same as the rich, but they do treat them and often treat them well. A system in which corporate enterprises play a larger part is likely to be more segmented and more stratified. With cutbacks in public financing coming at the same time, the two-class system in medical care is likely to become only more conspicuous.

This turn of events is the fruit of a history of accommodating professional and institutional interests, failing to exercise public control over public programs, then adopting piecemeal regulation to control the inflationary consequences, and, as a final resort, cutting back programs and turning them back to the private sector. The failure to rationalize medical services under public control meant that sooner or later they would be rationalized under private control. Instead of public regulation, there will be private regulation, and instead of public planning, there will be corporate planning. Instead of public financing for prepaid plans that might be managed by the subscribers' chosen representatives, there will be corporate financing for private plans controlled by conglomerates whose interests will be determined by the rate of return on investments. That is the future toward which American medicine now seems to be headed.

But a trend is not necessarily fate. Images of the future are usually only caricatures of the present. Perhaps this picture of the future of medical care will also prove to be a caricature. Whether it does depends on choices that Americans have still to make.

NOTES

BOOK ONE / A SOVEREIGN PROFESSION

Introduction

The Social Origins of Professional Sovereignty

1. M. I. Finley, *The Ancient Economy* (London: Chatto & Windus, 1973), 57; N. D. Jewson, "Medical Knowledge and the Patronage System in 18th Century England," *Sociology* 8 (September 1974), 369–85; Theodore Zeldin, *France 1848–1945*, vol. 1, *Ambition, Love and Politics* (Oxford: The Clarendon Press, 1973), 23–42.

2. David K. Shipler, "Life for Soviet Women All Work, Little Status," *New York Times*, August 9, 1976.

3. "American versus European Medical Science," *Medical Record* 4 (May 15, 1869), 133.

4. See Steven Lukes, "Power and Authority," in *A History of Sociological Analysis*, ed. Robert Nisbet and Tom Bottomore (New York: Basic Books, 1978), 642.

5. Hannah Arendt, "What is Authority?" in *Between Past and Future* (New York: Viking, 1961), 93.

6. Those analysts of authority who follow in the tradition of Max Weber sometimes tend to emphasize legitimacy to the exclusion of dependence. Weber himself notes that subordinates obey authority for many reasons, including helplessness and fear of the power available to authority. But he makes legitimacy the organizing principle of his analysis and specifically excludes other factors, such as helplessness, from his theoretical model of the types of authority. See Max Weber, *Economy and Society*, ed. Guenther Roth and Claus Wittich (New York: Bedminster Press, 1968), I:214. I depart from Weber in bringing dependence into the model and emphasizing the tensions between dependence and legitimacy. Peter Blau suggests the idea of developing an alternative typology of authority on the basis of dependency conditions. See his "Critical Remarks on Weber's Theory of Authority," *American Political Science Review* 57 (June 1963), 305–16.

7. Lukes, "Power and Authority," 640. Lukes here is summarizing the ideas of Carl Friedrich.

8. Ibid., 640.

9. See, in this regard, Marcia Millman, *The Unkindest Cut* (New York: William Morrow, 1977), Chap. 9.

10. By giving as much emphasis to dependence as legitimacy, I mean to call attention to the ambivalence of authority relations, which are often lost in more idealized accounts particularly of traditional or charismatic authority. On the emotional aspects of authority, see Richard Sennett, *Authority* (New York: Knopf, 1980).

11. Much work on the medical profession and doctor-patient relationships concentrates exclusively on therapeutic functions. For an analysis of the administrative role of physicians, see Deborah Stone, "Physicians as Gatekeepers: Illness Certification as a Rationing Device," *Public Policy* 27 (Spring 1979), 227–54.

12. Weber, *Economy and Society*, I:53; see also the editors' discussion of the difficulties in translating *Herrschaft* (ibid., 61–62), as well as Weber's distinction (as they translate it) between domination by authority and domination by virtue of economic power (ibid., III:941).

13. Lukes describes what I have termed "cultural" and "social authority" as "authority over belief" and "authority over conduct." However, he then identifies authority over belief as one of three ways of conceptualizing authority, the other two being authority by convention and authority by imposition. This classification seems unfortunate. Lukes tends to identify different aspects of authority as alternative models.

14. Quoted by Arendt, *Between Past and Future*, 123.

15. This three-fold classification—collegial, cognitive, moral—does not belong to any one author, but it covers, I think, the main elements in what can sometimes become a lengthy list of attributes. For some of the attempts to define the essentials of a profession, see Ernest Greenwood, "Attributes of a Profession," *Social Work* 2 (July 1957), 44–55; Morris L. Cogan, "Toward a Definition of Profession," *Harvard Educational Review* 23 (Winter 1953), 33–50; Talcott Parsons, "The Professions and Social Structure," in *Essays in Sociological Theory*, rev. ed. (Glencoe, Ill.: Free Press, 1954), 34–39. For an influential developmental model, see Harold L. Wilensky, "The Professionalization of Everyone?" *American Journal of Sociology* 70 (September 1964), 137–58. For a critical review, see Terence J. Johnson, *Professions and Power* (London: Macmillan, 1972).

16. Johnson, *Professions and Power*; see also Eliot Freidson, *Profession of Medicine* (New York: Dodd, Mead, 1970).

17. See, for example, Richard H. Shryock, *Medicine in America: Historical Essays* (Baltimore: Johns Hopkins University Press, 1966) and William G. Rothstein, *American Physicians in the Nineteenth Century: From Sects to Science* (Baltimore: Johns Hopkins Press, 1972). In Rosemary Stevens' work *American Medicine and the Public Interest* (New Haven, Conn.: Yale University Press, 1971), science produces specialization, which then becomes the focus of political conflict in the profession. As she tells the story, the failure of the profession to meet the challenge of specialization—that is, the need for more coordinated organization and financing—constitutes its failure to satisfy the public interest.

18. For an excellent account of the struggle for authority and its relation to changing social organization, see Thomas L. Haskell, *The Emergence of Professional Social Science* (Urbana, Ill.: University of Illinois Press, 1977).

19. Eliot Freidson, *Professional Dominance: The Social Structure of Medical Care* (New York: Atherton, 1970), 117.

20. For Parsons' classic statement, see *The Social System* (Glencoe, Ill.: Free Press, 1951), Chap. 10.

21. See Robert K. Merton and Elinor Barber, "Sociological Ambivalence," in *Sociological Theory, Values and Sociocultural Change*, ed. Edward A. Tiryakian (New York: Free Press, 1963), 91–120.

22. See Freidson, *Profession of Medicine*, esp. Chap. 7.

23. Magali Sarfatti Larson, *The Rise of Professionalism* (Berkeley: University of California Press, 1977), 14.

24. Where firms encounter severe information problems in regulating outside contractors, and where they suspect that such contractors have divergent goals or represent an obstacle to reorganizing the labor process, they have a strong incentive to incorporate them directly into their own organization. See Oliver E. Williamson, *Markets and Hierarchies: Analysis and Antitrust Implications* (New York: Free Press, 1975), and Stephen Marglin, "What Do Bosses Do?" *Review of Radical Political Economics* 6 (1974), 60–112.

25. On the role of physicians in the legislation of moral behavior, see James C. Mohr, *Abortion in America: The Origins and Evolution of National Policy, 1800–1900* (New York: Oxford University Press, 1978); James Reed, *From Private Vice to Public Virtue: The Birth Control Movement and American Society Since 1830* (New York: Basic Books, 1978); Linda Gordon, *Women's Body, Women's Right: Birth Control in America* (New York: Penguin, 1977); and David Pivar, *Purity Crusade: Sexual Morality and Social Control* (Westport, Conn.: Greenwood, 1973).

Chapter One

Medicine in a Democratic Culture, 1750–1850

1. Oliver Wendell Holmes, "The Position and Prospects of the Medical Student," in *Currents and Counter Currents in Medical Science* (Boston: Ticknor and Fields, 1861), 316.
2. For evidence on the growing inequalities in wealth, see James A. Henretta, *The Evolution of American Society, 1700–1815* (Lexington, Mass.: Heath, 1973), 103–06, and Edward Pessen, *Riches, Class and Power Before the Civil War* (Lexington, Mass.: Heath, 1973), 31–45. Pessen attempts to disprove Tocqueville's "egalitarian thesis" by showing there were great and stable concentrations of wealth, but his evidence does not address Tocqueville's larger and more complex arguments about American culture.
3. Alexis de Tocqueville, *Democracy in America*, tr. Henry Reeve (New York: Schocken, 1961), II:211. For an extraordinary array of evidence on the decline in deference to age, see David Hackett Fischer, *Growing Old in America* (New York: Oxford University Press, 1977), 77–112. On the general political history of the Jacksonian period, see Arthur M. Schlesinger, Jr., *The Age of Jackson* (Boston: Little, Brown, 1945).
4. William Buchan, *Domestic Medicine, or the Family Physician . . .*, 2nd ed. (Philadelphia, 1771), 171. For the various editions of his work in America, see Francesco Guerra, *American Medical Bibliography, 1639–1783* (New York: Lathrop C. Harper, 1962), 191. Francis Packard, writing in 1931, thought Buchan's work had been used more than any other book of its kind ever had been or ever would be. It was an instant success when published, selling eighty thousand copies in Buchan's lifetime, and was translated into all the major European languages. (*Dictionary of National Biography*, III:180–81). For a detailed account on the background of the book, which indicates that William Smellie probably shared the authorship, see C. J. Lawrence, "William Buchan: Medicine Laid Open," *Medical History* 19 (January 1975), 20–35. John Blake provides an excellent account of the tradition in "From Buchan to Fishbein: The Literature of Domestic Medicine," in *Medicine Without Doctors: Home Health Care in American History*, ed. Guenter B. Risse, Ronald L. Numbers, and Judith Walzer Leavitt (New York: Science History Publications, 1977), 11–30. For a medical advisor predating Buchan, see John Tennant, *Every Man His Own Doctor, or the Poor Planter's Physician* (Williamsburg, 1734), which had four printings. For works after Buchan that show a debt to him, see Alexander Thomson, *The Family Physician: or, Domestic Medical Friend* (New York, 1802); James Ewell, *The Planter's and Mariner's Medical Companion* (Baltimore, 1813); and the discussion in Blake, "From Buchan to Fishbein," 15–18.
5. Buchan, *Domestic Medicine*, x, vii.
6. Bernard Semmel, *The Methodist Revolution* (New York: Basic Books, 1973).
7. John Wesley, *Primitive Physic: Or an Easy and Natural Method of Curing Most Diseases* (1791; reprint ed., London: The Epworth Press, 1960), 6–27.
8. John C. Gunn, *Domestic Medicine. . .* (New York: Saxton, Barker and Co., 1860), 141. Originally published in Knoxville in 1830, Gunn's work went through dozens of editions, by the ninth claiming over 100,000 in sales. See M. E. Pickard and R. C. Buley, *The Midwest Pioneer, His Ills, Cures, and Doctors* (Crawfordsville, Ind.: Banta, 1945).
9. Wesley, *Primitive Physic*, 26; Buchan, *Domestic Medicine*, viii–ix.
10. Buchan, *Domestic Medicine*, 58; Lester King, *The Medical World of the Eighteenth Century* (Chicago: University of Chicago Press, 1958), 318–20.
11. Buchan, *Domestic Medicine*, 328–29; but see Gunn, *Domestic Medicine*, 383–84, who says epileptic fits generally occur during the full moon.
12. Keith Thomas, *Religion and the Decline of Magic* (New York: Scribner, 1971).
13. Ibid., 85.
14. Charles E. Rosenberg, *The Cholera Years* (Chicago: University of Chicago Press, 1962), esp. Chaps. 2 and 7.
15. W. J. Reader, *Professional Men: The Rise of the Professional Classes in Nineteenth-Century England* (New York: Basic Books, 1966), 16–21, 31–43, 48–54; S. W. F. Holloway, "Medical Education in England, 1830–1858: A Sociological Analysis," *History* 49 (1964), 299–324.

16. N. D. Jewson, "Medical Knowledge and the Patronage System in 18th Century England," *Sociology* 8 (September 1974), 369–85; on patronage and professionalism, see Terence J. Johnson, *Professions and Power* (London: Macmillan, 1972).

17. Richard H. Shryock, *Medicine and Society in America: 1660–1860* (New York: New York University Press, 1960), 9–10.

18. Wyndham B. Blanton, *Medicine in Virginia in the Eighteenth Century* (Richmond, Va.: Garrett & Massie, 1931), 36, 20, 24, 49.

19. J. M. Toner, *Contributions to the Annals of Medical Progress in the United States, Before and During the War of Independence* (Washington, 1874), 106. Samuel Haber discusses the "first wave of professionalism" in his essay, "The Professions and Higher Education in America: A Historical View," in *Higher Education and the Labor Market*, ed. Margaret Gordon (New York: McGraw-Hill, 1974).

20. David Cowan, *Medicine and Health in New Jersey: A History* (New York: Van Nostrand, 1964), 6–7.

21. John Morgan, *Discourse on the Institution of Medical Schools in America* (1765; reprint ed., Baltimore: John Hopkins Press, 1937), xvii; Whitfield Bell, *John Morgan, Continental Doctor* (Philadelphia: University of Pennsylvania Press, 1965).

22. Charles Caldwell, *The Autobiography of Charles Caldwell* (Philadelphia: Lippincott, Grambo, 1855), 121–22; on aristocratic versus middle-class styles, see Erving Goffman, *The Presentation of Self in Everyday Life* (Garden City, N.Y.: Doubleday, 1959), 33–34.

23. Benjamin Rush, "Observations on the Duties of a Physician, and the Methods of Improving Medicine; Accommodated to the Present State of Society and Manners in the United States," in *Medical Inquiries and Observations*, 2nd ed. (Philadelphia: J. Conrad, 1805), 390–91.

24. Richard H. Shryock, "Benjamin Rush from the Perspective of the Twentieth Century," in *Medicine in America: Historical Essays* (Baltimore: Johns Hopkins Press, 1966), 237.

25. My discussion of early medical schools relies on William F. Norwood, *Medical Education in the United States Before the Civil War* (Philadelphia: University of Pennsylvania Press, 1944).

26. William Rothstein, *American Physicians of the Nineteenth Century* (Baltimore: Johns Hopkins Press, 1972), 73.

27. Joseph Kett, *The Formation of the American Medical Profession: The Role of Institutions, 1780–1860* (New Haven, Conn.: Yale University Press, 1968), 14–30; Malcolm Sydney Beinfeld, "The Early New England Doctor: An Adaptation to a Provincial Environment," *Yale Journal of Biology and Medicine* 15 (December 1942), 278.

28. John Duffy, *A History of Public Health in New York City, 1625–1866* (New York: Russell Sage Foundation, 1968), 65–66.

29. Rothstein, *American Physicians*, 75–79. Here and in the next several paragraphs I draw on Rothstein's arguments.

30. Henry B. Shafer, *The American Medical Profession, 1783 to 1850* (New York: Columbia University Press), 221–22.

31. Reginald H. Fitz, "The Rise and Fall of the Licensed Physician in Massachusetts, 1781–1860," *Transactions of the Association of American Physicians* 9 (1894), 1–18.

32. Daniel Drake, *Practical Essays on Medical Education and the Medical Profession* (1832; reprint ed., Baltimore: Johns Hopkins Press, 1952), 91–93.

33. Karl Mannheim, *Essays on the Sociology of Knowledge* (London: Routledge and Kegan Paul, 1952), 200; for some examples of folk medical beliefs in America that originated in long forgotten treatises, see Bruno Gebhard, "The Interrelationship of Scientific and Folk Medicine in the United States of America since 1850," in *American Folk Medicine*, ed. Wayland D. Hand (Berkeley: University of California Press, 1976), 87–98.

34. James Still, *Early Recollections and Life of Dr. James Still* (1877; reprint ed., New Brunswick, N.J.: Rutgers University Press, 1973), 77.

35. Pickard and Buley, *The Midwest Pioneer*, 36.

36. Virgil J. Vogel, *American Indian Medicine* (Norman, Okla.: University of Oklahoma Press, 1970), 52–54; Otho T. Beall, Jr. and Richard H. Shryock, *Cotton Mather: First Significant Figure in American Medicine* (Baltimore: Johns Hopkins Press, 1954), 28, 46; Wesley, *Primitive Physic*, 24.

37. Robert J. T. Joy, "The Natural Bonesetters with Special Reference to the Sweet Family of Rhode Island," *Bulletin of the History of Medicine* 28 (September–October 1954), 416–41.

38. Kett, *Formation of the American Medical Profession*, 108.

39. Catherine M. Scholten, " 'On the Importance of the Obstetrick Art': Changing Customs of Childbirth in America, 1760 to 1825," *William and Mary Quarterly* (Summer 1977), 427–45.

40. Gerda Lerner, "The Lady and the Mill Girl: Changes in the Status of Women in the Age of Jackson," in *The Majority Finds Its Past: Placing Women in History* (New York: Oxford University Press, 1979), 15–30.

41. Mary R. Walsh, *"Doctors Wanted: No Women Need Apply"* (New Haven, Conn.: Yale University Press, 1978), xiv, 3–6, 14–16. See also John B. Blake, "Women and Medicine in Ante-Bellum America," *Bulletin of the History of Medicine* 39 (March–April 1965), 99–123.

42. Richard H. Shryock, "Sylvester Graham and the Popular Health Movement, 1830–1870," in *Medicine in America: Historical Essays*, 111–25.

43. Alex Berman, "The Impact of the Nineteenth-Century Botanico-Medical Movement in American Pharmacy and Medicine" (Ph. D. diss., University of Wisconsin, 1954).

44. Samuel Thomson, *Narrative of the Life and Medical Discoveries of Samuel Thomson. . .to which is added An Introduction to his New Guide to Health*, 2nd. ed. (Boston, 1825), 43–44.

45. Ibid., 199–200.

46. *Thomsonian Recorder* 1 (December 15, 1832), 123.

47. Thomson, *Narrative of the Life*, 41–42.

48. *Thomsonian Recorder* 1 (June 1, 1833), 376.

49. Thomson, *Narrative of the Life*, 158; Ronald L. Numbers, "Do-It-Yourself the Sectarian Way," in Risse, Numbers, and Leavitt, eds., *Medicine Without Doctors*, 50.

50. *Thomsonian Recorder* 4 (January 2, 1836), 106–07; (March 12, 1836), 187.

51. Ibid., 188.

52. Kett, *Formation of the American Medical Profession*, 130. The Eclectics, too, had a radical heritage. The founder, Wooster Beach, edited a journal in which he denounced "King-craft, Priest-craft, Lawyer-craft, and Doctor-craft."

53. For some limited quantitative evidence, see Edward C. Atwater, "The Medical Profession in a New Society, Rochester, New York (1811–60)," *Bulletin of the History of Medicine* 47 (May–June 1973), 221–35; on the decline of support particularly in the upper classes, see Rosenberg, *The Cholera Years*, 154–64.

54. Richard H. Shryock, *The Development of Modern Medicine* (New York: Knopf, 1947); Michel Foucault, *The Birth of the Clinic* (New York: Pantheon, 1973); Erwin Ackerknecht, *Medicine at the Paris Hospital, 1794–1848* (Baltimore: Johns Hopkins Press, 1967); Owsei Temkin, "The Role of Surgery in the Rise of Modern Medical Thought," *Bulletin of the History of Medicine* 25 (May–June 1951), 248–59.

55. Shryock, *The Development of Modern Medicine*, 249.

56. On these developments, see George Rosen, *The Specialization of Medicine, with Particular Reference to Ophthalmology* (New York: Froben Press, 1944), and Stanley J. Reiser, *Medicine and the Reign of Technology* (Cambridge: Cambridge University Press, 1978).

57. Ackerknecht, *Medicine at the Paris Hospital*, Chap. 13.

58. Jacob Bigelow, *Modern Inquiries: Classical, Professional and Miscellaneous* (Boston: Little, Brown, 1867), 144, 230–311; Shryock, *Medicine and Society in America*, 131–32; Charles E. Rosenberg, "The Therapeutic Revolution: Medicine, Meaning and Social Change in Nineteenth-Century America," in *The Therapeutic Revolution: Essays in the Social History of American Medicine*, ed. Morris J. Vogel and Charles E. Rosenberg (Philadelphia: University of Pennsylvania Press, 1979), 3–25; John Harley Warner, " 'The Nature-Trusting Heresy': American Physicians and the Concept of the Healing Power of Nature in the 1850's and 1860's," *Perspectives in American History* 11 (1977–78), 291–324.

59. Karl Mannheim, "The Democratization of Culture," in *Essays on the Sociology of Culture* (London: Routledge and Kegan Paul, 1956), 184–85.

60. December 27, 1833; as cited in the *Thomsonian Recorder* 3 (January 17, 1835), 127.

61. Perry Miller, *The Life of the Mind in America* (New York: Harcourt Brace & World, 1965), 102.

62. Henry Steele Commager, *The Era of Reform, 1830–1860* (New York: Van Nostrand, 1960), 71.

63. Lee Benson, *The Concept of Jacksonian Democracy* (Princeton, N.J.: Princeton University Press, 1961). The anti-Masonic movement, writes Benson (24), represented "an impassioned, levelling attack by members of the 'lower classes' against the village and urban 'aristocracy.'" This assault on secret societies had a counterpart in medicine. An exclusive national fraternity called Kappa Lamda, founded in 1820, was charged with monopolizing top medical school and hospital positions. In 1838 *The New York Whig* published an exposé calling it "secret, dark, impalpable." The club declined, finally disappearing in 1862. (Kett, *Formation of the American Medical Profession*, 112)

64. On commercial and middle-class hostility to the law, see Morton J. Horwitz, *The Transformation of American Law, 1780–1860* (Cambridge: Harvard University Press, 1977), 140–59, and Maxwell Bloomfield, *American Lawyers in a Changing Society, 1776–1876* (Cambridge: Harvard University Press, 1976), 44; Matthew A. Crenson, *The Federal Machine: Beginnings of Bureaucracy in Jacksonian America* (Baltimore: Johns Hopkins Press, 1975).

65. Schlesinger, *Age of Jackson*, 134; James Willard Hurst, *The Growth of American Law: The Law Makers* (Boston: Little, Brown, 1950), 280.

66. Cited in Harris L. Coulter, *Divided Legacy: A History of the Schism in Medical Thought* (Washington, D.C.: McGrath Publishing, 1973), III:98.

67. See the appendices in Rothstein, *American Physicians*, 332–43.

68. Cited in Coulter, *Divided Legacy*, 95–96; see also Kett, *Formation of the American Medical Profession*, 21–22.

Chapter Two

The Expansion of the Market

1. Karl Polanyi, *The Great Transformation* (Boston: Beacon Press, 1957).

2. *Judah v. M'Namee*, 3 Blackf. 269 (Ind., 1833).

3. Wyndham B. Blanton, *Medicine in Virginia in the Seventeenth Century* (Richmond, Va.: Garrett & Massie, 1930), 250–59; Wilhelm Moll, "Medical Fee Bills," *Virginia Medical Monthly* 93 (November 1966), 657–64.

4. *Pynchon v. Brewster*, Quincy 224 (Mass. 1776); *Glover v. Le Testue*, Quincy 225 (Mass. 1770).

5. Ruth E. Peters, "Statutory Regulation of Lawyers' Fees in Massachusetts, New York, Pennsylvania, South Carolina, Tennessee, and Virginia from the mid-Seventeenth Century to the mid-Nineteenth Century." (Unpublished paper, Harvard Law School, May 1975).

6. *New England Journal of Medicine and Surgery* 14 (1825), 50–51; cited in George Rosen, *Fees and Fee Bills: Some Economic Aspects of Medical Practice in 19th-Century America* (Baltimore: Johns Hopkins Press, 1946), 6.

7. "Fees and Fee Bills," *Medical and Surgical Reporter* 7 (December 7, 1861), 231–32.

8. *Pray v. Stinson*, 21 Me. (8 Shep) 402; *Peck v. Hutchinson*, 88 Iowa 320, 55 N.W. 511.

9. Barnes Riznik, "Medicine in New England, 1790–1840." (Unpublished manuscript, Old Sturbridge Village, 1963), 78–81. In ascertaining debts, Riznik examined the probate records for thirty-four "typical" physicians from Worcester County, Massachusetts; twenty-six had unsettled debts when they died and more than half owed between $2,500 and $10,000.

10. Riznik, *Medicine in New England, 1790–1840* (Sturbridge, Mass.: Old Sturbridge Village, 1965), 24. This pamphlet is a shorter version of Riznik's 1963 manuscript.

11. Richard H. Shryock, *Medical Licensing in America, 1650–1965* (Baltimore: Johns Hopkins Press, 1967), 31–32.

12. Estimating the necessary investment for medical practice is difficult because so many of the costs are uncertain. Many doctors never attended medical school or, if they attended, remained for only one term or even part of a term; apprenticeships varied in length. Accordingly, I have given a range of costs rather than a single average. The elements are as follows:

1. the fee for three years of apprenticeship or office study;
2. tuition and living costs for two terms (about twenty-six weeks) of medical school;
3. the cost of a horse and buggy;
4. the cost of books, medicines and equipment;
5. the opportunity cost of time invested in an apprenticeship and medical education;
6. the opportunity cost of money invested, assuming a normal rate of return of 10 percent.

My rough estimates of these are as follows: (1) 3 times $50–100 per year; (2) $150–300, depending on whether the school was rural or urban; (3) $200–300; (4) $25–100; (5) $150; (6) $35–125. The low estimate assumes three years of apprenticeship at the lowest fee, no formal medical education, and minimal expenditures for books and medicines (total $560). The high estimate assumes three years of apprenticeship at the higher fee, an urban medical education, and larger expenditures for a library and medicines (total $1,275). Obviously, if one were to include the cost of a house and the need to support a family through the lean early years of practice, the costs would go higher.

The data for apprenticeship and medical school costs come directly from William F. Norwood, *Medical Education in the United States Before the Civil War* (Philadelphia: University of Pennsylvania Press, 1944), 393–95. The estimate of the opportunity cost of time assumes that an unskilled twenty-year-old male would be able to earn no more than $50 a year more than he might receive in kind as an apprentice, or during his weeks in medical school.

13. See Clarence H. Danhof, "Farm-making Costs and the 'Safety Valve': 1850–1860," *Journal of Political Economy* 49 (June 1941), 317–59.

14. U.S. Bureau of the Census, *Historical Statistics of the United States, Colonial Times to 1970* (Washington, D.C.: Department of Commerce, 1975), 76 (1850 only); William Barlow and David O. Powell, "To Find a Stand: New England Physicians on the Western and Southern Frontier, 1790–1840," *Bulletin of the History of Medicine* 54 (Fall 1980), 386.

15. Riznik, *Medicine in New England* (1965), 15.

16. Barlow and Powell, "To Find a Stand," 386–401.

17. Technically, there was another factor—the "indivisibility" of physicians' services due to the limits of contemporary transportation. While a poor rural area might not have been able to support one well-trained doctor, it conceivably could have supported one-eighth, if the physician could have covered eight such areas with the help of modern cars and roads. But because transportation was primitive, communities did not have the opportunity to choose a fraction of a well-trained and more highly priced physician over the full services of a less trained and lower-priced doctor.

18. Benjamin Rush, "Observations on the Duties of a Physician, and the Methods of Improving Medicine; Accommodated to the Present State of Society and Manners in the United States," in *Medical Inquiries and Observations* (Philadelphia: J. Conrad, 1805), 390.

19. Richard Dunlop, *Doctors of the American Frontier* (Garden City, N.Y.: Doubleday, 1962), 129–30.

20. *Boston Medical and Surgical Journal* 15 (November 30, 1836), 273.

21. Ivan Waddington, "The Development of Medicine as a Modern Profession," in *A Social History of the Bio-medical Sciences*, ed. Massimo Piattelli-Palmarini (Milan: Franco Maria Ricci, forthcoming).

22. For a general discussion of indirect prices, see Gary Becker, "A Theory of the Allocation of Time," *The Economic Journal* 75 (September 1965), 493–517.

23. Rolla M. Tryon, *Household Manufactures in the United States, 1640–1860* (Chicago: University of Chicago Press, 1917), 243, 11. See also Stuart Bruchey, *The Roots of American Economic Growth, 1607–1861* (New York: Harper & Row, 1965), 26–31.

24. These data have been culled from Rosen, *Fees and Fee Bills*, 15–16, which contains numerous other fee tables that would make the point equally well.

25. Direct estimates of transportation and opportunity costs indicate that the cost of travel exceeded the basic consultation fee at about two miles. See my calculations in "Medicine, Economy and Society in Nineteenth-Century America," *Journal of Social History* 10 (Summer 1977), 604–05.

26. Samuel C. Busey, *Personal Reminiscenses and Recollections . . .* (Washington, D.C., 1895), 157–58.

27. Thomas N. Bonner, *Medicine in Chicago, 1850–1950* (Madison, Wis.: American Historical Research Center, 1957), 200.

28. Ibid.

29. Rosen, *Fees and Fee Bills*, 30, 41.

30. O. Larsell, *The Doctor in Oregon: A Medical History* (Portland, Ore.: Binsford & Mort, 1947), 160.

31. U.S. Bureau of the Census, *Historical Statistics*, 11–12. See also Adna F. Weber, *The Growth of Cities in the Nineteenth Century* (New York: Macmillan, 1899).

32. American Medical Association, Committee on Social Insurance, *Statistics Regarding the Medical Profession* (Chicago: American Medical Association, 1916), 38–39.

33. Victor C. Vaughan, *A Doctor's Memories* (Indianapolis: Bobbs-Merrill, 1926), 269.

34. On the role of railroads in bringing in patients from a distance, see Helen Clapesattle, *The Doctors Mayo* (Minneapolis: University of Minnesota Press, 1941), 348–53. For further discussion of doctors' relation to railroads, see Chapter 6.

35. Samuel Hays, "Introduction" to *Building the Organizational Society*, ed. Jerry Israel (New York: Free Press, 1972), 9–10. On the subject of changing transportation costs, see George Rogers Taylor, *The Transportation Revolution* (New York: Rinehart, 1951) and especially Allen Pred, *Urban Growth and the Circulation of Information* (Cambridge: Harvard University Press, 1973).

36. John Brooks, *Telephone: The First Hundred Years* (New York: Harper & Row, 1976), 65; Marion May Dilts, *The Telephone in a Changing World* (New York: Longmans Green, 1941), 9.

37. Clapesattle, *The Doctors Mayo*, 135–36.

38. Verlin C. Thomas, *The Successful Physician* (Philadelphia: Saunders, 1923), 146.

39. George Kessel, "Would Not Practice Without an Auto," *Journal of the American Medical Association* [hereafter referred to as *JAMA*] 50 (March 7, 1908), 814.

40. J. A. Bowling, "Testimony from the Southwest," *JAMA* 46 (April 21, 1906), 1179.

41. "A Compilation of Automobile Statistics," *JAMA* 54 (April 9, 1910), 1273–74.

42. H. A. Stalker, "The Automobile as a Physician's Vehicle," *JAMA* 52 (March 7, 1908), 812.

43. C. A. Hibbert, "Transient Flat Life Requires Physician to Cover Wide Territory," *JAMA* 58 (April 6, 1912), 1080. For more on the subject, see Lewis Mayers and Leonard V. Harrison, *The Distribution of Physicians in the United States* (New York: General Education Board, 1924), and Michael L. Berger, "The Influence of the Automobile on Rural Health Care, 1900–1929," *Journal of the History of Medicine and the Allied Sciences* 28 (October 1973), 319–35.

44. Tryon, *Household Manufactures*, 275–76, 291–93.

45. Antonio Ciocco and Isidore Altman, "The Patient Load of Physicians in Private Practice, A Comparative Statistical Study of Three Areas," *Public Health Reports* 58 (September 3, 1943), 1329–51.

46. Gerald N. Grob, *Mental Institutions in America: Social Policy to 1875* (New York: Free Press, 1973). On these developments, see also David J. Rothman, *The Discovery of the Asylum: Social Order and Disorder in the New Republic* (Boston: Little, Brown, 1971), and Andrew T. Scull, *Decarceration: Community Treatment and the Deviant—A Radical View* (Englewood Cliffs, N.J.: Prentice-Hall, 1977), 15–40.

47. Michel Foucault, *Madness and Civilization: A History of Insanity in the Age of Reason* (London: Tavistock Publications, 1967).

48. Grob, *Mental Institutions in America*, 135. Grob cites a complaint by Samuel Woodward that he was taking a large cut in income since he claimed to make $5,000 a year in private practice. But if he did earn that much, it was extremely unusual; by professional standards of the day, these were high-paying positions.

49. The superintendents formed an independent professional society in 1844 and later rebuffed efforts by the AMA for an affiliation. See Grob, *Mental Institutions in America*, 147–50.

50. For 1873 see J. M. Toner, "Statistics of Regular Medical Associations and Hospitals of the United States," *Transactions of the American Medical Association* 24 (1873), 314-33; for the later dates, U.S. Bureau of the Census, *Historical Statistics*, 78; for a state-by-state survey for this period, "Twenty-five Years' Growth of the Hospital Field," *National Hospital Record* 7 (September 1903), 23-27.

51. U.S. Bureau of the Census, *Historical Statistics*, 41. On family structure, see William J. Goode, *World Revolution and Family Patterns* (New York: Free Press, 1963), 70-76; Frank Furstenberg, "Industrialization and the American Family: A Look Backward," *American Sociological Review* 31 (June 1966), 326-37; and Edward Shorter, *The Making of the Modern Family* (New York: Basic Books, 1975).

52. Bernard Farber, *Guardians of Virtue: Salem Families in 1800* (New York: Basic Books, 1972), 46; Richard Sennett, *Families Against the City: Middle Class Homes of Industrial Chicago, 1872-1890* (Cambridge: Harvard University Press, 1970), 79.

53. Henry Hurd, "The Hospital as a Factor in Modern Society," *The Modern Hospital* 1 (September 1913), 33.

54. Morris Vogel, "Boston's Hospitals, 1870-1930: A Social History," (Ph.D. diss., University of Chicago, 1974), 188-99. See also John Modell and Tamara K. Hareven, "Urbanization and the Malleable Household: An Examination of Boarding and Lodging in American Families," *Journal of Marriage and the Family* 35 (1973), 467-79. Modell and Hareven point out that one-person households rose from 3.7 to 20 percent of total households between 1790 and 1970.

For the English case, see Brian Abel-Smith, *The Hospitals, 1800-1948: A Study in Social Administration in England and Wales* (Cambridge: Harvard University Press, 1967), 141.

55. Talcott Parsons and Renée Fox, "Illness, Therapy and the Modern Urban Family," *Journal of Social Issues* 8 (1952), 31-44.

56. *New York Times*, December 31, 1900.

57. Quoted in Scull, *Decarceration*, 15.

58. Dr. Henry B. Hemenway, "Discussion," *Bulletin of the American Academy of Medicine* 10 (1909), 635.

59. S. W. F. Holloway, "Medical Education in England, 1830-1858: A Sociological Analysis," *History* 49 (1964), 299-324.

60. Ibid.

Chapter Three

The Consolidation of Professional Authority, 1850-1930

1. Samuel Gross, *The Autobiography of Samuel Gross* (Philadelphia: Saunders, 1893), I:93.

2. Arpad Gerster, *Recollections of a New York Surgeon* (New York: Paul B. Hoeber, 1917), 162.

3. J. Marion Sims, *The Story of My Life* (New York: Appleton, 1889), 116.

4. Anne R. Burr, *Weir Mitchell: His Life and Letters* (New York: Duffield and Company, 1929), 43.

5. [Worthington Hooker], "Report of the Committee on Medical Education," *Transactions of the American Medical Association* 4 (1851), 420-23. A later study, published in 1882, covering 58 colleges and 39,054 alumni graduating since 1825, gave roughly similar proportions: 9.2 percent went into medicine, 21 percent into divinity, and 19.7 percent into law. As of 1880, fewer students at medical schools had bachelor's degrees than at either law or divinity schools. See Charles McIntyre, "The Percentage of College-Bred Men in the Medical Profession," *Medical Record* 22 (December 16, 1882), 681.

6. Editorial, "American vs. European Medical Science," *Medical Record* 4 (May 15, 1869), 133.

7. Fred B. Rogers, "General John Beatty (1749–1826): Patriot and Physician," *Bulletin of the History of Medicine* 32 (January–February 1958), 39.

8. For the list of physicians serving in Congress, see "Appendix," in James G. Burrow, *AMA: Voice of American Medicine* (Baltimore: Johns Hopkins Press, 1963), 405–07; see also "Doctors in Government," *JAMA* 163 (February 2, 1957), 361–64.

9. "The Pecuniary Condition of the Medical Profession in the United States," *Boston Medical and Surgical Journal* 4 (February 15, 1831), 9, citing an article from the *Christian Examiner*.

10. Sims, *Story of My Life*, 192.

11. Edward C. Atwater, "The Medical Profession in a New Society, Rochester, New York (1811–60)," *Bulletin of the History of Medicine* 47 (May–June 1973), 229.

12. [Lemuel Shattuck, N. P. Banks, Jr., and Jehiel Abbott], *Report of a General Plan for the Promotion of Public and Personal Health* (Boston: Dutton and Wentworth, 1850), 59.

13. Edgar Martin, *The Standard of Living in 1860* (Chicago: University of Chicago Press, 1942), 394. A budget appearing in *The New York Times*, November 8, 1853, for a workingman's family of four, "living moderately," had total expenditures of $600. Martin says lawyers and doctors "seem to have received somewhere in the neighborhood of $1,000 a year in country districts, $2,000 in the cities," but offers no source or documentation. These figures seem high, at least for doctors.

14. U.S. Bureau of the Census, *Historical Statistics of the United States, Colonial Times to 1970* (Washington, D.C.: U.S. Department of Commerce, 1975), 165.

15. Chester Wright, cited in Martin, *Standard of Living in 1860*, 394.

16. M. E. Pickard and R. C. Buley, *The Midwest Pioneer, His Ills, Cures, and Doctors* (Crawfordsville, Ind.: Banta, 1945), 161.

17. "A Legion of Leeches," *Detroit Review of Medicine and Pharmacy* 6 (January 1871), 19.

18. B. Joy Jeffries, "Reestablishment of the Medical Profession [Part 2]," *Boston Medical and Surgical Journal* 118 (June 21, 1888), 613.

19. C. R. Mabee, *The Physician's Business and Financial Adviser*, 5th ed. (Cleveland: Continental Publishing, 1901), 170. On page 185, Mabee cites an unidentified New York journal as saying that average receipts for a doctor did not exceed $900.

20. D. W. Cathell, *The Physician Himself* (Philadelphia: F. A. Davis), 1890 ed., 276; 1905 ed., 379.

21. Editorial, "Does It Pay to Be a Doctor?" *JAMA* 42 (January 23, 1904), 247.

22. U.S. Bureau of the Census, *Historical Statistics*, 168.

23. G. F. Shears, "Making a Choice," *Cosmopolitan* 34 (April 1903), 654. Cited in Gerald E. Markowitz and David Karl Rosner, "Doctors in Crisis: A Study of the Use of Medical Education Reform to Establish Modern Professional Elitism in Medicine," *American Quarterly* 25 (March 1973), 83–107.

24. Cathell, *Physician Himself* (1890), 80, 83.

25. Ibid. (1882), 34.

26. The example is Sartre's. See Erving Goffman, *The Presentation of Self in Everyday Life* (Garden City, N.Y.: Doubleday, 1959), 33.

27. Cathell, *Physician Himself* (1890), 94.

28. Ibid., 97.

29. Ibid., 143.

30. Ibid., 242.

31. Gerster, *Recollections*, 163.

32. Jeffries, "Reestablishment of the Medical Profession [Part 2]," 614; see also, idem, "Reestablishment of the Medical Profession [Part I], *Boston Medical and Surgical Journal* 118 (June 14, 1888), 589–93.

33. Cathell, *Physician Himself* (1890), 148.

34. Charles Rosenberg, "The Practice of Medicine in New York A Century Ago," *Bulletin of the History of Medicine* 41 (May–June 1967), 225–28.

35. John Shaw Billings, *Selected Papers* ([Chicago]: Medical Library Association, 1965), 191; William Rothstein, *American Physicians in the Nineteenth Century* (Baltimore: Johns Hopkins Press, 1972), suggests this line of argument.

36. W. J. Reader, *Professional Men: The Rise of the Professional Classes in Nineteenth-Century England* (New York: Basic Books, 1967), 47.

37. Billings, *Selected Papers*, 191.

38. Nathan Smith Davis, *History of the American Medical Association, from Its Organization to January, 1855* (Philadelphia, 1855), 37–38.

39. S. Oakley Vanderpoel, in Alfred C. Post et al., *An Ethical Symposium* (New York: Putnam, 1883), 37–38.

40. James Howard Means, *The Association of American Physicians* (New York: Blakiston, 1961), 10.

41. Mancur Olson, *The Logic of Collective Action* (Cambridge: Harvard University Press, 1965). I have eschewed the term "public good" here because it would only be confusing, though technically correct.

42. George W. Corner, *Two Centuries of Medicine: A History of the School of Medicine, University of Pennsylvania* (Philadelphia: Lippincott, 1965), 32–34; Cecil K. Drinker, *Not So Long Ago* (New York: Oxford University Press, 1937), 150–51.

43. Rush Van Dyke, *Valedictory Address to Graduates of Philadelphia College of Medicine, 1849* (Philadelphia, 1849), 9–10; cited in Henry B. Shafer, *The American Medical Profession, 1783 to 1850* (New York: Columbia University Press, 1937), 153–54.

44. Harvey Wickes Felter, *History of the Eclectic Medical Institute* (Cincinnati: Published for the Alumni Association, 1902), 39–42.

45. Chauncey D. Leake, ed., *Percival's Medical Ethics* (Baltimore: Williams, 1927), Appendix III, 225–35.

46. Cathell, *Physician Himself* (1890), 184–86.

47. Max Weber, *Economy and Society*, tr. Guenther Roth and Claus Wittich (New York: Bedminster Press, 1968), I:56; III:1164. For a review and analysis of contrasting interpretations, see Peter Berger, "The Sociological Study of Sectarianism," *Social Research* 21 (1954), 467–85.

48. Sidney E. Ahlstrom, *A Religious History of the American People* (New Haven: Yale University Press, 1972). 472–87, 1019–29. See also David Edwin Harrell, Jr., *All Things Are Possible: The Healing and Charismatic Revivals in America* (Bloomington, Ind.: Indiana University Press, 1975).

49. Richard Niebuhr, *The Social Sources of Denominationalism* (New York: Holt, 1929).

50. Bryan R. Wilson, *Sects and Society* (Berkeley: University of California Press, 1961), 354.

51. For an extended exposition of homeopathic doctrine by a sympathizer, see Harris Coulter, *Divided Legacy: A History of the Schism in Medical Thought* (Washington, D.C.: McGrath Publishing Co., 1973), esp. Chap. 1.

52. Martin Kaufman, *Homeopathy in America: The Rise and Fall of a Medical Heresy* (Baltimore: Johns Hopkins Press, 1971); Coulter, *Divided Legacy*, 101–04. Coulter presents some evidence suggesting homeopaths had higher incomes than regular physicians.

53. Joseph Kett, *The Formation of the American Medical Profession* (New Haven, Conn.: Yale University Press, 1968).

54. Coulter, *Divided Legacy*, 204. For the classic critique, originally published in 1842, see Oliver Wendell Holmes, "Homeopathy and its Kindred Delusions" in *Medical Essays, 1842–1882* (Boston: Houghton-Mifflin, 1892).

55. Kaufman, *Homeopathy in America*, 63–92.

56. Kett, *Formation of the American Medical Profession*, 185–86; J. M. Toner, "Tabulated Statistics of the Medical Profession of the United States," *Transactions of the American Medical Association* 22 (1871), 155; *JAMA* 79 (August 23, 1913), 600.

57. H. R. Hopkins, in Post et al., *Ethical Symposium*, 184.

58. Donald E. Konold, *A History of American Medical Ethics, 1847–1912*. (Madison, Wis.: State Historical Society of Wisconsin, 1962), 26.

59. *New York Times*, May 28, 1873.

60. Kaufman, *Homeopathy in America*, 93–109.

61. Coulter, *Divided Legacy*, 328–91.

62. William Ely in Post et al., *Ethical Symposium*, 12.

63. Rothstein, *American Physicians in the Nineteenth Century*, 304.

64. Lawrence M. Friedman, "Freedom of Contract and Occupational Licensing, 1890–1910: a Legal and Social Study," *California Law Review* 53 (May 1965), 494–97.

65. Ibid., 500–12.

66. Bonner, *Medicine in Chicago*, 208.

67. Eleven states required an examination only; ten offered an alternative between passage of an exam and presentation of an acceptable diploma. For a table giving the state-by-state laws, see "Laws Regulating the Practice of Medicine in the Various States and Territories of the United States," *JAMA* 37 (November 16, 1901), 1318.

68. Harold W. Eickhoff, "The Organization and Regulation of Medicine in Missouri, 1883–1901." (Ph.D. diss., University of Missouri, 1964), 36–40, 82, 116–22, 145–48, 274–76.

69. Perry H. Millard, "The Propriety and Necessity of State Regulation of Medical Practice," *JAMA* 9 (October 15, 1887), 491.

70. T. A. Bland, "The Medical Trust," *The Arena* 19 (1898), 520–26; B. O. Flower, "Restrictive Medical Legislation and the Public Weal," ibid., 781–809; Herbert Spencer, *Social Statics* (London: John Chapman, 1851), 372–95; Henry James, ed., *Letters of William James* (Boston: Atlantic Monthly Press, 1920), II:67.

71. 129 U.S. 114. See also Frances P. DeLancy, *The Licensing of Professions in West Virginia* (Chicago: Foundation Press, 1938).

72. 170 U.S. 189; Friedman, "Freedom of Contract and Occupational Licensing," 493ff.

73. John A. Wyeth, "President's Address," *JAMA* 38 (June 14, 1902), 1555.

74. Rothstein, *American Physicians of the Nineteenth Century*, 323.

75. "Medical Education in the United States," *JAMA* 79 (August 19, 1922), 629, 632–33.

76. A. T. Still, *The Autobiography of A. T. Still* (Kirksville, Mo.: self-published, 1897), 286–87; Eickhoff, "The Organization and Regulation of Medicine in Missouri," 185–200.

77. Edwin Franden Dakin, *Mrs. Eddy* (New York: Grosset and Dunlap, 1929), 115.

78. "The Organization of the Medical Profession," *JAMA* 38 (January 11, 1902), 113. See also ibid. (January 25, 1902), 250–51; ibid. (February 1, 1902), 324–25), ibid. (February 8, 1902), 400; ibid. (February 15, 1902), 460–61; ibid. (February 22, 1902), 514–15; ibid. (March 1, 1902), 584–85.

79. "Preliminary Report of the Committee on Organization," *JAMA* 36 (May 25, 1901), 1450.

80. For the state-by-state analysis, see J. N. McCormack, "An Epitome of the History of Medical Organization in the United States," *JAMA* 44 (April 15, 1905), 1213–18.

81. Burrow, *AMA*, 49–51.

82. Richard Hofstadter, *The Age of Reform* (New York: Random House, 1955), 148–64.

83. F. H. Todd, "Organization," *JAMA* 39 (October 25, 1902), 1061.

84. On the increase in malpractice suits, see Andrew A. Sandor, "The History of Professional Liability Suits in the United States," *JAMA* 163 (February 9, 1957), 459–66. Sandor's data refer only to appellate decisions and are consequently quite inconclusive; however, the increased concern of physicians about lawsuits seems to bear him out. On the locality rule, see *Gramm* v. *Boener*, 56 Ind. 497 (1877) and *Small* v. *Howard*, 128 Mass. 131, 35 Am. Rep. 363 (1880). On malpractice defense funds, see "Organized Medical Defense," *JAMA* 38 (January 4, 1902), 37, 43; "The Varied Functions Possible in the County Medical Society," *JAMA* 44 (March 18, 1905), 881–82; Walter L. Burrage, *A History of the Massachusetts Medical Society, 1781–1922* (Norwood, Mass.: private printing, 1923), 452; Oliver Garceau, *The Political Life of the American Medical Association* (Cambridge: Harvard University Press, 1941), 103–04.

85. U.S. Bureau of the Census, *Historical Statistics*, 76.

86. Lawrence Veysey, *The Emergence of the American University* (Chicago: University of Chicago Press, 1965); Joseph Ben-David and Awraham Zloczower, "Universities and Academic Systems in Modern Societies," *Archives of European Sociology* 3 (1962), 71–75.

87. *Annual Report of the President of Harvard College, 1869–70*, 18; *Annual Report of the President of Harvard College, 1871–72*, 25–26.

88. Frederick C. Shattuck and J. Lewis Bremer, "The Medical School, 1869–1929," in *The Development of Harvard University*, ed. Samuel Eliot Morison (Cambridge: Harvard University Press, 1930), 556–57; Hugh Hawkins, *Between Harvard and America: The Educational Leadership of Charles W. Eliot* (New York: Oxford University Press, 1972), 60–61; Henry Bigelow, *Medical Education in America* (Cambridge: Harvard University Press, 1871).

89. *Annual Report of the President of Harvard College, 1870–71*, 20.

90. *Annual Report of the President of Harvard College, 1879–1880*, 25, 33–34; Shattuck and Bremer, "The Medical School," 560–61.

91. Corner, *Two Centuries*, 142–51.

92. Martin Kaufman, *American Medical Education: The Formative Years, 1765–1910* (Westport, Conn.: Greenwood Press, 1976), 155–56.

93. Alan M. Chesney, *The Johns Hopkins Hospital and the Johns Hopkins University School of Medicine*, vol. I, *Early Years, 1867–1893* (Baltimore: Johns Hopkins Press, 1943).

94. Simon Flexner and James Thomas Flexner, *William Henry Welch and the Heroic Age of American Medicine* (New York: Dover, 1966); Donald Fleming, *William H. Welch and the Rise of Modern Medicine* (Boston: Little, Brown, 1954).

95. See Markowitz and Rosner, "Doctors in Crisis," 95.

96. Mary R. Walsh, *"Doctors Wanted: No Women Need Apply"* (New Haven, Conn.: Yale University Press, 1977), 176–93.

97. Arthur Dean Bevan, "Cooperation in Medical Education and Medical Service," *JAMA* 90 (April 14, 1928), 1173–77.

98. See Table I, "Statistics of Medical Colleges in the United States and Canada" in the AMA's annual reports on medical education, *JAMA* 37 (1901), 758–59; 39 (1902), 568–69; 41 (1903), 452–53; 43 (1904), 504–05; 45 (1905), 566–67; 47 (1906), 592–93; 49 (1907), 588–89; 51 (1908), 586–87; 53 (1909), 546–49.

99. Abraham Flexner, *Medical Education in the United States and Canada*, Bulletin no. 4 (New York: Carnegie Foundation for the Advancement of Teaching, 1910).

100. Ibid., 11.

101. "Medical Education—Progress of Twenty-Two Years," *JAMA* 79 (August 19, 1922), 660–61; "State Requirements of Preliminary Education," *JAMA* 79 (August 19, 1922), 658.

102. Ernest V. Hollis, *Philanthropic Foundations and Higher Education* (New York: Columbia University Press, 1938), 211–17. Hollis estimated the total contribution of foundations to medical education and research by 1936 at $154 million. On the role of the General Education Board, see Daniel Fox, "Abraham Flexner's Unpublished Report: Foundations and Medical Education, 1909–1928," *Bulletin of the History of Medicine* 54 (Winter 1980), 475–96.

103. Several Marxists have argued, further, that capitalists had a distinctive interest in the success of scientific medicine because of its ideological functions. See Howard Berliner, "A Larger Perspective on the Flexner Report," *International Journal of Health Services* (1975), 573–92, and E. Richard Brown, *Rockefeller Medicine Men: Medical Care and Capitalism in America* (Berkeley: University of California Press, 1978). Berliner begins his "larger perspective" by stating that scientific medicine conceives of the body as a machine, a conception suspiciously similar to other capitalist ideas. He then associates scientific medicine with "allopathic" remedies, such as bleeding, that preceded the bacteriological revolution, and finally suggests that capitalism had an interest in the triumph of this kind of medicine because it served the indispensable functions of legitimation and capital accumulation. Sad to say, many people consider this Marxism, and sadder still, many Marxists take it seriously. For more on Brown's book, see Chapter 6.

104. Corner, *Two Centuries*, 187. The average value of a chair to a clinical professor was "perhaps" $10,000 "by reason of the practice which it brings with it." Ross V. Patterson to Abraham Flexner, March 31, 1909 (Flexner papers, Box 19, Library of Congress).

105. Fleming, *William H. Welch*, 177–78.

106. Hollis, *Philanthropic Foundations*, 211–12. Brown, *Rockefeller Medicine Men*, treats the full-time requirement as an "entering wedge" of corporate capitalism in medical care; for a less intoxicated discussion, see Fox, "Flexner's Unpublished Report," 484–87.

107. Joseph C. Aub and Ruth K. Hapgood, *Pioneer in Modern Medicine: David Linn Edsall of Harvard* (n.p.: Harvard Medical Alumni Association, 1970), passim.

108. Fox, "Flexner's Unpublished Report," 489–90.

109. Rosemary Stevens, *American Medicine and the Public Interest* (New Haven, Conn.: Yale University Press, 1971), 116–20; J. A. Curran, "Internships and Residencies: Historical Background and Current Trends," *Journal of Medical Education* 34 (September 1959), 878–89.

110. Walsh, *"Doctors Wanted: No Women Need Apply,"* 178–267; Carol Lopate, *Women in Medicine* (Baltimore: Johns Hopkins Press, 1968); Flexner, *Medical Education*, 178–79.

111. Numa P. G. Adam, "Sources of Supply of Negro Health Personnel: Section A: Physicians," *Journal of Negro Education* 6 (July 1937), 468.

112. *Collier's Weekly*, June 11, 1910 (Flexner papers, Box 19, Library of Congress).

113. Flexner, *Medical Education*, 16, 45–46.

114. Raymond Pearl, "Distribution of Physicians in the U.S.," *JAMA* 84 (April 4, 1925), 1024–27.

115. American Medical Association, Committee on Social Insurance, *Statistics Regarding the Medical Profession* (Chicago: American Medical Association, 1916), 38–39.

116. Samuel Hopkins Adams, "The Vanishing Country Doctor," with sequels, *Ladies' Home Journal* 40 (October 1923), 23ff; ibid. (November 1923), 26ff; ibid. 41 (February 1924), 31ff; William Allen Pusey, "The Disappearance of Doctors from Small Towns," *JAMA* 88 (February 12, 1927), 505–06.

117. Lewis Mayers and Leonard V. Harrison, *The Distribution of Physicians in the United States* (New York: General Education Board, 1924), 47–48.

118. U.S. Bureau of the Census, *Historical Statistics*, 76.

119. Louis S. Reed, *The Healing Cults, A Study of Sectarian Medical Practice: Its Extent, Causes, and Control* (Chicago: University of Chicago Press, 1932), 1–4, 24–26, 50–54.

120. Selwyn D. Collins, "Frequency and Volume of Doctors' Calls Among Males and Females in 9,000 Families, Based on Nation-Wide Periodic Canvasses, 1928–31," *Public Health Reports* 55 (November 1, 1940), 1987–88.

121. James Harvey Young, *The Toadstool Millionaires* (Princeton, N.J.: Princeton University Press, 1961), 167–70.

122. Sarah Stage, *Female Complaints: Lydia Pinkham and the Business of Women's Medicine* (New York: Norton, 1979), 89–90, 105–06, 130–31.

123. A[braham] Jacobi, "Proprietary Medicines," *JAMA* 97 (September 29, 1906), 978. See also Richard C. Cabot, "The Physician's Responsibility for the Nostrum Evil," ibid., 982.

124. "Secret Nostrums and the Journal," *JAMA* 34 (June 2, 1900), 1420. See also "Relation of Pharmacy to the Medical Profession," ibid. 34 (April 21, 1900), 986–88; ibid. 34 (April 28, 1900), 1049–51; and sequels.

125. Edward Bok, "The Patent Medicine Curse," *Ladies' Home Journal* 21 (May 1904), 18.

126. Samuel Hopkins Adams, *The Great American Fraud* (n.p.: Collier & Son, 1905 and 1906), 39.

127. Edward Bok, "Pictures that Tell Their Own Stories," *Ladies' Home Journal* 22 (September 1905), 15; Stage, *Female Complaints*, 140, 160–62.

128. Adams, *Great American Fraud*, 60.

129. Ibid., 84.

130. Austin Smith, "The Council on Pharmacy and Chemistry," in Morris Fishbein, *A History of the American Medical Association, 1847 to 1947* (Philadelphia: Saunders, 1947), 876.

131. Editorial, "A Great Paper Attempts the Impossible," *JAMA* 58 (April 13, 1912), 1118.

132. Jacob A. Goldberg, "The Advertising Physician," *Hygeia* 1 (August 1923), 308–11.

133. Stage, *Female Complaints*, 198.

134. R. V. Pierce, *The People's Common Sense Medical Adviser in Plain English; or, Medicine Simplified*, 99th ed. [?] (Buffalo, N.Y.: World's Dispensary Medical Association, 1918), 379.

135. Smith, "Council on Pharmacy and Chemistry," 871.

136. Peter Temin, *Taking Your Medicine: Drug Regulation in the United States* (Cambridge: Harvard University Press, 1979), Chap. 2.

137. This quotation and others that follow are drawn from Rima D. Apple, " 'To Be Used Only Under the Direction of a Physician': Commercial Infant Feeding and Medical Practice, 1870–1940," *Bulletin of the History of Medicine* 54 (Fall 1980), 402–17.

138. Ibid., 412.

139. Erwin H. Ackerknecht, *Therapeutics from the Primitives to the 20th Century* (New York: Hafner Press, 1973), 128–36.

140. Rothstein, *American Physicians of the Nineteenth Century*, 266.

141. Irving Fisher, *Report on National Vitality: Its Wastes and Conservation*, Bulletin no. 30 of the Committee of One Hundred on National Health (Washington, D.C.: U.S. Government Printing Office, 1909), 7, 66.

142. *JAMA* 60 (June 21, 1913), 1996.

143. Stanley J. Reiser, *Medicine and the Reign of Technology* (Cambridge: Cambridge University Press, 1978), 43, 38.

144. Ibid., 68.

145. Shryock, *Development of Modern Medicine*; H.J. Parish, *A History of Immunization* (Edinburgh: E. & S. Livingstone, 1965).

146. John B. McKinlay and Sonja M. McKinlay, "The Questionable Contribution of Medical Measures to the Decline of Mortality in the United States," *Health and Society* 55 (Summer 1977), 405–28. In a listing of the "Year of Medical Intervention (Either Chemotherapy or Prophylaxis)," the McKinlays list 1930 for diphtheria (toxoid) and 1948 for typhoid (chloramphenicol). They write that diphtheria and typhoid "showed negligible declines in their mortality rates subsequent to the date of medical intervention" (421). Have they never heard of diphtheria antitoxin or typhoid vaccine?

147. For the evidence on tetanus and diphtheria, see Parish, *History of Immunization*, 131, 166–69; see also Edgar Sydenstricker, *Health and Environment* (New York: McGraw-Hill, 1933); C.-E. A. Winslow, *Health Survey of New Haven* (New Haven: [Community Chest] 1928), 374–81.

148. John Lovett Morse, "Recollections and Reflections on Forty-Five Years of Artificial Infant Feeding," *Journal of Pediatrics* 7 (September 1935), 324.

149. Thomas E. Cone, Jr., *History of American Pediatrics* (Boston: Little, Brown, 1979), 138.

150. "Discussion," *Minnesota Medicine* 6 (July 1923), 445.

151. These remarks appear in Victor C. Vaughan, "The Promotion of Periodic Health Examinations by the Medical Profession," *AMA Bulletin* 16 (March 15, 1923), 296. Vaughan gives an extended account of these experiences in his autobiography, *A Doctor's Memories* (Indianapolis: Bobbs-Merrill, 1926), 375–79, 397–99.

152. Christopher Lasch, *The Culture of Narcissism* (New York: Norton, 1979), 228–29, and idem, "Life in the Therapeutic State," *The New York Review of Books*, June 12, 1980, 24–32.

153. R. G. Leland, "Income from Medical Practice," *JAMA* 96 (May 16, 1931), 1687–91; U.S. Bureau of the Census, *Historical Statistics*, 176; Maurice Leven, *Incomes of Physicians* (Chicago: University of Chicago Press, 1932), 20, 105–06; Milton Friedman and Simon Kuznets, *Income from Independent Professional Practice* (New York: National Bureau of Economic Research, 1945), 67–68, 84.

154. Friedman and Kuznets, *Income from Independent Professional Practice*, 14–15.

155. George S. Counts, "The Social Status of Occupations: A Problem in Vocational Guidance," *The School Review* 33 (January 1925), 16–27; George W. Hartmann, "The Prestige of Occupations, A Comparison of Educational Occupations and Others," *Personnel Journal* 12 (October 1934), 144–52.

156. Rothstein, *American Physicians in the Nineteenth Century*, argues for the view that demonstrably valid therapies explain the transition of medicine "from sects to science," but provides much persuasive evidence against his own position. The therapeutic innovations seem too little and too late to explain the decline of the sects. Rothstein emphasizes the indifference and resistance of practitioners to bacteriology as late as the 1890s; then comes diphtheria antitoxin, and presto, the profession is transformed. This is hard to swallow. Though Rothstein's book is invaluable for its illuminating analysis of medical societies and medical sects, his analysis of the transformation pays no attention to the broader changes in the society.

For the second view, see Jeffrey L. Berlant, *Profession and Monopoly: A Study of Medicine in the United States and Great Britain* (Berkeley: University of California Press, 1975).

157. Karl Polanyi, *The Great Transformation* (Boston: Beacon Press, 1957), 152.

Chapter Four

The Reconstitution of the Hospital

1. For comparisons of the relations among physicians, patients, and hospitals in America and elsewhere, see Milton I. Roemer and Jay W. Freidman, *Doctors in Hospitals* (Baltimore: John Hopkins Press, 1971), 49–61. For more general comparative studies, which have been of immense use in this chapter, see William Glaser, "American and Foreign Hospitals: Some Sociological Comparisons," in *The Hospital in Modern Society*, ed. Eliot Freidson (New York: Free Press, 1963), 37–72, as well as Glaser's neglected but superb book, *Social Settings and Medical Organization: A Cross-National Study of the Hospital* (New York: Atherton, 1970). For cross-national comparisions as of 1885, see Lewis S. Pilcher, "On the Organization of the Surgical Staff in General Hospitals," *Annals of Surgery* 2 (1885), 389–408.

2. The analysis in this chapter deals with general hospitals rather than mental institutions, except where comparison has seemed instructive.

This chapter appears in virtually the same form as it was written and circulated in 1976–77 and formed part of a doctoral thesis at Harvard submitted in 1977. Since that time, some excellent new work on hospitals has appeared. See, especially, the new books by David Rosner, *A Once Charitable Enterprise* (Cambridge: Cambridge University Press, forthcoming) and Morris Vogel, *The Invention of the Modern Hospital: Boston, 1870–1930* (Chicago: University of Chicago Press, 1980). I saw a part of David Rosner's work in manuscript and the unpublished version of Morris Vogel's thesis; consequently, only those are cited. See also Charles E. Rosenberg, "Inward Vision and Outward Glance: The Shaping of the American Hospital, 1880–1914," in *Social History and Social Policy*, ed. David J. Rothman and Stanton Wheeler (New York: Academic Press, 1981). This was too late in coming to my attention to have been used here.

3. The historical sociology of organizations is a still largely undeveloped, or at least unintegrated, subject. On the changing structure of corporate enterprise, see Alfred Chandler, *The Visible Hand* (Cambridge: Harvard University Press, 1977). On the history of universities, see Lawrence Veysey, *The Emergence of the American University* (Chicago: University of Chicago Press, 1965).

4. "Communal" and "associative" are Parsons' translations of Weber's *Vergemeinschaftung* and *Vergesellschaftung*, which were in turn derived from Tönnies. See Max Weber, *The Theory of Social and Economic Organization* (New York: Oxford University Press, 1947), 136–39.

5. John P. Davis, *Corporations*, ed. Abram Chayes (1905; reprint ed., New York: Capricorn Press, 1961), xix.

6. George Rosen, "The Hospital: Historical Sociology of a Community Institution," in Freidson ed., *The Hospital in Modern Society*, 10. See also Rotha Mary Clay, *The Medieval Hospitals of England* (London: Methuen, 1909), 143–57.

7. David J. Rothman, *The Discovery of the Asylum* (Boston: Little, Brown, 1971), 42–43. The terms "derived" and "designed" are used in John Thompson and Grace Goldin, *The Hospital: A Social and Architectural History* (New Haven, Conn.: Yale University Press, 1973).

8. Henry Sigerist, "An Outline of the Development of the Hospital," *Bulletin of the History of Medicine* 4 (July 1936), 573–81.

9. Rothman, *Discovery of the Asylum*, 3–29, 180–205; for the arguments in favor of shifting from home relief to the almshouse, see Philadelphia Board of Charities, "Report of the Committee . . ." (1827), esp. 23–30; [Josiah Quincy], "Report of the Committee on the Pauper Laws . . ." (1821), 9; and John Yates, "Report of the Secretary of State . . ." (1824), 939–63; reprinted in *The Almshouse Experience: Collected Reports* (New York: Arno Press, 1971). On later reform, see Robert H. Bremner, *From the Depths: The Discov-*

ery of Poverty in the United States (New York: New York University Press, 1956), 46–57.
For the transition from almshouse to city hospital, see Robert John Hunter, *The Origin
of the Philadelphia General Hospital, Blockley Division* (Philadelphia: Rittenhouse
Press, 1955); Douglas Carroll, "History of the Baltimore City Hospitals," *Maryland State
Medical Journal* 15 (January 1966), 87–90; (February 1966), 46–48; (March 1966), 75–
78; (April 1966), 65–68; ((May 1966), 83–85; (June 1966), 101–03; (July 1966), 117–19;
(August 1966), 69–71; (September 1966), 105–08; (October 1966), 89–96; (November
1966), 103–11.

Rothman associates the almshouse with the penitentiary and mental asylum and argues
that the motive force for their growth lay in the zeal of Jacksonian reformers to rehabilitate the dependent, the criminal, and the insane. But as he himself concedes, the shift
to almshouse relief was equally designed to be a deterrent to poverty by denying the
poor relief in their homes. The reports recommending almshouses are plainly concerned
with their effect on the poor *outside* the institutions, rather than on those within. In eliminating home relief, the states were also forcing the immigrant communities to develop
their own institutions for the poor and the sick. The interests in disciplining the poor and
limiting public expenditures would seem adequately to account for the spread of almshouses, and so Rothman's emphasis on rehabilitation as a motive for their development
seems to stretch his argument too far.

10. Leonard K. Eaton, *New England Hospitals, 1790–1837* (Ann Arbor: University of
Michigan Press, 1957).

11. Benjamin Rush, *Medical Inquiries and Observations*, 2d ed. (Philadelphia: J. Conrad, 1805), I:276; John E. Erichsen, *On Hospitalism and the Causes of Death After Operations* (London: Longmans, 1874); James Y. Simpson, "Our Existing System of Hospitalism
and Its Effects," *Edinburgh Medical Journal* 15 (December 1869), 523–32; W. Gill Wylie,
Hospitals: Their History, Organization, and Construction (New York: Appleton, 1877),
57–66.

12. Nathaniel I. Bowditch, *A History of the Massachusetts General Hospital to August
5, 1851*, 2nd. ed. with continuation to 1872 (Boston: The Trustees, 1872), 3–9; Morris Vogel,
"Boston's Hospitals, 1870–1930: A Social History." (Ph.D. diss., University of Chicago,
1974), 12–18. Among patients admitted during 1868 to St. Louis City Hospital, more than
four fifths were either single or widowed; only 17.3 percent were married. Board of
Health, *Second Annual Report* (St. Louis, 1869), 19.

13. Francis R. Packard, *Some Account of the Pennsylvania Hospital* (Philadelphia:
Engle Press, 1938), 9.

14. *History of the Reading Hospital, 1867–1942* ([Reading, Pa.]: The Reading Hospital,
1942), 5.

15. Allan Nevins and Milton Halsey Thomas, eds., *The Diary of George Templeton
Strong: The Turbulent Fifties, 1850–1859* (New York: Macmillan, 1952), 92.

16. Hyman Grinstein, *The Rise of the Jewish Community of New York, 1654–1860* (Philadelphia: Jewish Publication Society of America, 1945), 155–59, 187–88.

17. Robert W. Downie, "Pennsylvania Hospital Admissions, 1751–1850: A Survey,"
Transactions and Studies of the College of Physicians 32 (1964), 25.

18. George Worthington Adams, *Doctors in Blue* (New York: Collier Books, 1961), 101–
51.

19. Elizabeth C. Hobson, *Recollections of a Happy Life* (New York: privately printed,
1914), 77–114; the description of the ladies of the State Charities Aid Association comes
from its first annual report, cited in M. Adelaide Nutting and Lavinia L. Dock, *A History
of Nursing* (New York: Putnam, 1907), II:370.

20. Jo Ann Ashley, *Hospitals, Paternalism, and the Role of the Nurse* (New York:
Teachers College Press, 1976), 20 and passim.

21. Frederick F. Cartwright, *The Development of Modern Surgery* (London: Arthur
Barker, 1967), 12–22.

22. Helen Clapesattle, *The Doctors Mayo* (Minneapolis: University of Minnesota Press,
1941), 297–338, 407, 432.

23. S. E. Crocker, "The Invalid in Home and Hospital," *National Hospital Record* 2
(March 1899), 7–9.

24. Vogel, "Boston's Hospitals," 140. The Bridgeport figures are cited in Commission
on Hospital Care, *Hospital Care in the United States* (New York: Commonwealth Fund,
1947), 545. U.S. Bureau of the Census, *Hospitals and Dispensaries: 1923*, 3.

25. The early history of Lincoln Hospital is recounted in Fitzhugh Mullan, *White Coat, Clenched Fist: The Political Education of an American Physician* (New York: Macmillan, 1976), 117–21.

26. Vogel, "Boston's Hospitals," 36, 115–18; "Children's Hospital, Papers and Clippings, 1869–1879," Countway Library, Harvard Medical School.

27. Florence Nightingale, *Notes on Hospitals*, 3rd ed. (London: Longman, Roberts and Green, 1863), 51–52.

28. Niles Carpenter, *Hospital Service for Patients of Moderate Means* (Washington, D.C.: Committee on the Costs of Medical Care, 1930), 23. The data are based on a survey of architects belonging to the American Hospital Association in which they were asked to report the number of beds in hospitals they had designed in 1908, 1918, and 1928.

29. On the early obligations of patients, see Thomas G. Morton, *A History of the Pennsylvania Hospital, 1751–1895* (Philadelphia: Times Printing House, 1895), 210; Sidney Goldstein, "The Social Function of the Hospital," *Charity and the Commons* 18 (May 4, 1907), 162; Talcott Parsons, *The Social System* (Glencoe, Ill.: Free Press, 1951), 428–47.

30. S. S. Goldwater, "The Cost of Modern Hospitals," *National Hospital Record* 9 (November 1905), 39–48.

31. Frank Tucker, "The Financial Problem of New York's Hospitals," *Charities* 12 (January 2, 1904), 27–32; "What the Managers of the Hospitals Have to Say About Their Financial Problem," ibid., 32–46; "Press Comment . . .," ibid., 83–85.

32. David Rosner, "Bedside Business: The Transformation of Brooklyn's Hospitals During the Progressive Era." (Unpublished manuscript, Harvard University, 1977).

33. E.H. Lewinski-Corwin, *The Hospital Situation in Greater New York* (New York: Putnam, 1924), 121, 130.

34. U. S. Bureau of the Census, *Hospitals and Dispensaries: 1923*, 4.

35. Albert R. Lamb, *The Presbyterian Hospital and the Columbia- Presbyterian Medical Center, 1868–1943* (New York: Columbia University Press, 1955), 22–24; Vogel, "Boston's Hospitals," 126–29.

36. Herbert D. Howard, "The Managers and the Superintendent," *National Hospital Record* 6 (December 1902), 10.

37. J. M. Toner, "Statistics of Regular Medical Associations and Hospitals of the United States," *Transactions of the American Medical Association* 24 (1873), 314–33; E. H. L. Corwin, *The American Hospital* (New York: Commonwealth Fund, 1946), 7.

38. Henry S. Stark, "Hospital Reform in a New Light," *National Hospital Record* 10 (February 1907), 18–19.

39. Lewis S. Pilcher, "On the Organization of the Surgical Staff in General Hospitals," *Annals of Surgery* 2 (1885), 399.

40. For a discussion of the value of hospital appointments, see Michael M. Davis and C. Rufus Rorem, *The Crisis in Hospital Finance* (Chicago: University of Chicago Press, 1932), 78–89.

41. "The Medical Profession and the Hospitals," *Medical Record* 45 (January 6, 1894), 16.

42. Henry C. Burdett, *Pay Hospitals and Paying Wards Throughout the World* (Philadelphia: Presley Blakiston, 1880), 73; George W. Gay, "Abuse of Medical Charity," *Boston Medical and Surgical Journal* 152 (March 16, 1905), 300; E. W. Cushing, "The Physician and the Private Hospital Patient," ibid., 311; "Private Patients' Liability," *National Hospital Record* 8 (October 1904), 6.

43. H. D. Niles, "Our Hospitals," *JAMA* 38 (March 22, 1902), 759–61; Bayard Holmes, "The Hospital Problem," ibid. 47 (August 4, 1906), 320. Holmes was the Socialist candidate for Mayor of Chicago in 1895.

44. A. L. Beahan, "Hospitals in the Smaller Towns," *Buffalo Medical Journal* 41 (1901), 187; Laura Lane, "The Individual Private Hospital," *National Hospital Record* 10 (July 1907), 37ff.

45. "Hospitals and General Practitioners," *National Hospital Record* 10 (March 1907), 9; Arpad G. Gerster, "System of American Hospital Economy," *National Hospital Record* 9 (January 1906), 17–19.

46. "The City Hospital Issue," *Cincinnati Medical News* 1 (November 1914), 326–27; Dr. R. Lincoln Graham, "History of the Decay of Medical Opulence," *The Medical Econo-*

mist, publication of the Federation of Medical Economic Leagues 3 (February 1915), 40; S. S. Goldwater, "The Extension of Hospital Privileges to All Practitioners of Medicine," *JAMA* 84 (March 28, 1925), 933–35.

47. "Article 3—Need for More Hospitals," *National Hospital Record* 8 (November 1904), 26; Albert J. Ochsner and Meyer J. Sturm, *The Organization, Construction and Management of Hospitals* (Chicago: Cleveland Press, 1909), 563.

48. Rosner, "Bedside Business"; Corwin, *Hospital Situation in Greater New York*, 45, 177; Davis and Rorem, *Crisis in Hospital Finance*, 81; "Hospital Service in the United States," *JAMA* 98 (June 11, 1932), 2073; "Hospital Service in the United States," *JAMA* 102 (March 31, 1934), 1014.

49. Roemer and Friedman, *Doctors in Hospitals* 36–39.

50. Cleveland Hospital Council, *Cleveland Hospital and Health Survey* (Cleveland: The Council, 1920), 858, 863; Oswald Hall, "The Stages of a Medical Career," *American Journal of Sociology* 53 (March 1948), 331.

51. Oswald Hall, "The Informal Organization of the Medical Profession," *Canadian Journal of Economics and Political Science* 12 (February 1946), 30–44; Hall, "Stages of a Medical Career," 327–36.

52. Glaser, "American and Foreign Hospitals," 54.

53. "Hospital Service in the United States" *JAMA* 94 (March 29, 1930), 928; Max Sehan, *Blacks and American Medical Care* (Minneapolis: University of Minnesota Press, 1973), 72–73.

54. U.S. Bureau of the Census, *Historical Statistics of the United States: Colonial Times to 1970* (Washington, D.C.: U.S. Department of Commerce, 1975), 78.

55. U.S. Bureau of the Census, *Hospitals and Dispensaries: 1923*, 25–26 (from Tables 5 and 6).

56. Irving Fisher, "Private Patients in General Hospitals," *National Hospital Record* 8 (June 1905), 19–25.

57. "The Hospital Superintendents on the Hospital Situation in New York," *Charities* 12 (February 6, 1904), 157–61.

58. S. S. Goldwater, "The United States Hospital Field," in *Hospital Charities*, ed. Henry Burdett (London: The Scientific Press, 1906).

59. U.S. Bureau of the Census, *Benevolent Institutions, 1904*, 20.

60. George Wilson, "The Hospitals of the National [Capital]," *National Hospital Record* 9 (May 1906), 12.

61. Vogel, "Boston's Hospitals," 83–84.

62. On the exclusion of the Irish, see Vogel, "Boston's Hospitals," 21–22; on Jewish misgivings about non-Jewish hospitals, see Grinstein, *Rise of the Jewish Community of New York*, 155–59; the quotation from a Russian Jew appeared in the *Yidische Gazaetten* (April 1894), cited in Moses Rischin, *The Promised City: New York's Jews 1870–1914* (Cambridge: Harvard University Press, 1962), 104; Richard C. Cabot, *Social Service and the Art of Healing* (New York: Moffat, Yard, 1909), 4–8.

63. Hall, "Stages of a Medical Career," 330.

64. Johan Goudsblom, *Dutch Society* (New York: Random House, 1967), 32, 124.

65. For a discussion of ethnic relations in higher education, with broader reflections, see Christopher Jencks and David Riesman, *The Academic Revolution* (Garden City, N.Y.: Doubleday, 1968), Chaps. 8 and 9.

66. Glaser, *Social Settings and Medical Organization*, 32–38, 74–75.

67. Charles P. Emerson, "The American Hospital Field," in *Hospital Management*, ed. Charlotte A. Aikens (Philadelphia: Saunders, 1911), 22; *American Medicine: Testimony Out of Court* (New York: American Foundation, 1937), II:723–24.

68. Glaser, "American and Foreign Hospitals," 39–50.

69. On the early development of hospital administration, see Michael M. Davis, *Hospital Administration: A Career* (New York, 1929). On the shifting balance between physicians and administrators, see Roemer and Friedman, *Doctors in Hospitals*, 118–20; Robert N. Wilson, "The Physician's Changing Hospital Role," *Human Organization* 18 (Winter 1959–1960), 177–83.

70. Charles Perrow, "Goals and Power Structures: A Historical Case Study," in *The Hospital in Modern Society*, ed. Freidson, 112–46; and idem, "The Analysis of Goals in Complex Organizations," *American Sociological Review* 26 (December 1961), 854–66.

Chapter Five

The Boundaries of Public Health

1. C.-E. A. Winslow, "The Untilled Fields of Public Health," *Science* 51 (January 9, 1920), 30.

2. On the changing orientation of public health, see Charles V. Chapin, "History of State and Municipal Control of Disease," in *A Half Century of Public Health*, ed. Mayzyck P. Ravenal (New York: American Public Health Association, 1921), 135–37; Barbara Gutmann Rosenkrantz, *Public Health and the State: Changing Views in Massachusetts, 1842–1936* (Cambridge: Harvard University Press, 1972); James H. Cassedy, *Charles V. Chapin and the Public Health Movement* (Cambridge: Harvard University Press, 1962); and George Rosen, *A History of Public Health* (New York: MD Publications, 1958), Chap. 7.

3. Charles Rosenberg, "Social Class and Medical Care in Nineteenth-Century America: The Rise and Fall of the Dispensary," *Journal of the History of Medicine and the Allied Sciences* 29 (January 1974), 32–54; Michael M. Davis, *Clinics, Hospitals and Health Centers* (New York: Harper and Brothers, 1927).

4. George F. Shrady, "A Propagator of Pauperism: The Dispensary," *The Forum* 23 (June 1897), 425; Shrady cites the preceding quotation from an article in the *Medical Record*; Agnes C. Vietor, "The Abuse of Medical Charity: The Passing of the 'Charity' Hospital and Dispensary," *Boston Medical and Surgical Journal* 140 (May 4, 1899), 419; Davis, *Clinics, Hospitals and Health Centers*, 80–83.

5. Michael M. Davis, Jr., and Andrew W. Warner, *Dispensaries: Their Management and Development* (New York: Macmillan, 1918), 42.

6. Ibid., 46–58; further studies of dispensary abuse are summarized in Davis, *Clinics, Hospitals and Health Centers*, 53ff; W. S. Thayer, "On Some Functions of the Free Dispensary," *Boston Medical and Surgical Journal* 168 (February 6, 1913), 185–88; Mary Richmond, comments at Fourth Annual Conference of the Association of Hospital Superintendents, *National Hospital Record* 6 (March 1903), 8–10. Unfortunately, we have no estimate of the relative share of medical care provided to the poor by dispensaries and by physicians in their own offices as simple charity or under contract with local government. Therefore, we cannot tell whether the growth of dispensaries meant more free service to the poor or a shift away from subsidized care in offices and homes. If the rise of dispensaries represented an absolute increase in the amount of free service, did it also represent an increase in services per person, or was it only a response to the increased numbers of the poor? Available data do not seem to answer these questions.

7. Committee on Inquiry into the Department of Health, Charities and Bellevue and Allied Hospitals, *Report* (New York, 1913), 532.

8. Editorial, "Too Many Schools," *National Hospital Record* 6 (November 1902), 33; on the growth of clinic fees, see Davis, *Clinics, Hospitals and Health Centers*, 323–38.

9. For a recent review of the developments discussed here, see John Duffy, "The American Medical Profession and Public Health: From Support to Ambivalence," *Bulletin of the History of Medicine* 53 (Spring 1979), 1–22.

10. The following paragraphs, except where other sources are specifically noted, draw on John Duffy, *A History of Public Health in New York City, 1866–1966* (New York: Russell Sage Foundation, 1974); C.-E. A. Winslow, *The Life of Hermann M. Biggs* (Philadelphia: Lea & Febiger, 1929); Wade W. Oliver, *The Man Who Lived for Tomorrow: A Biography of William Hallock Park, M.D.* (New York: Dutton, 1941); Jonathan T. Deland, "Hermann Biggs' Public Health Work and the Medical Profession: New York City and State, 1889–1923." (Unpublished B.A. thesis, Commmittee on History and Science, Harvard University, March 1976).

11. Board of Health, *Annual Report* (New York, 1893), 12–13.

12. W. R. Ingle Dalton, letter, *New York Times*, November 24, 1901. Seven children in St. Louis had just died of tetanus after receiving contaminated diphtheria antitoxin

distributed by the city health department (*New York Times*, November 19, 1901). In 1902 Congress passed the Biologics Control Act, prohibiting the interstate sale of such products without a license from the U.S. Public Health Service.

13. Daniel M. Fox, "Social Policy and City Politics: Tuberculosis Reporting in New York, 1889–1900," *Bulletin of the History of Medicine* 49 (Summer 1975), 169–95; Hermann M. Biggs, "Sanitary Measures for the Prevention of Tuberculosis in New York City and their Results," *JAMA* 39 (December 27, 1902), 1635–38.

14. Samuel Hopkins Adams, "Tuberculosis: The Real Race Suicide," *McClure's* 24 (January 1905), 234–49.

15. Duffy, *Public Health in New York City*, 244.

16. Leonard P. Ayres, "What American Cities Are Doing for the Health of School Children," *The Annals* 37 (March 1911), 250–60; Annette Lynch, "Evaluating School Health Programs," in *Health Services: The Local Perspective*, ed. Arthur Levin (New York: Academy of Political Science, 1977), 89–92; Mary Ross, "Health Inventory: 1934," *Survey Graphic* 23 (January 1934), 38–40.

17. Chapin, "History of State and Municipal Control of Disease," 140.

18. Cassedy, *Chapin and the Public Health Movement*, 96, 100.

19. Charles V. Chapin, *How to Avoid Infection* (Cambridge: Harvard University Press, 1917), 61–62.

20. C.-E. A. Winslow, *The Evolution and Significance of the Modern Public Health Campaign* (New Haven, Conn.: Yale University Press, 1923), 57, 58.

21. Richard H. Shryock, *National Tuberculosis Association 1904–1954* (New York: National Tuberculosis Association, 1957), 130, 157–58, 170.

22. Davis and Warner, *Dispensaries* (1918), 12–17; Davis, *Clinics, Hospitals and Health Centers* (1927), 15–17. Note the change in terminology in the title of Davis' later book.

23. John C. Burnham, "Medical Specialists and Movements Toward Social Control in the Progressive Era: Three Examples," in *Building the Organizational Society*, ed. Jerry Israel (New York: Free Press, 1972), 19–30.

24. Stanley Joel Reiser, "The Emergence of the Concept of Screening for Disease," *Health and Society* 56 (Fall 1978), 403–25.

25. Ibid; James A. Tobey, "The Health Examination Movement," *The Nation's Health* 9 (September 1923), 610–11, 648. For an effusive statement of the creed, see James A. Tobey, "A Layman's View of Health Examinations," *Boston Medical and Surgical Journal* 191 (November 6, 1924), 875–78.

26. J. H. J. Upham, "The State Medical Association and the State Board of Health," *AMA Bulletin* 16 (February 1923), 273.

27. "Like Banquo's Ghost the Chicago Public Health Institute Will Not Down," *Illinois Medical Journal* 58 (November 1930), 313ff; *New York Times*, April 8, 11, and 14, 1929.

28. Davis, *Clinics, Hospitals and Health Centers*, 357; George Rosen, "The First Neighborhood Health Center Movement: Its Rise and Fall," *American Journal of Public Health* 61 (August 1971), 1620–37; John D. Stoeckle and Lucy M. Candib, "The Neighborhood Health Center—Reform Ideas of Yesterday and Today," *New England Journal of Medicine* 280 (June 19, 1969), 1385–90. Stoeckle and Candib, trying to find antecedents for the neighborhood health centers of the 1960s, do not make clear that the earlier health centers were not primarily involved in providing medical care; their sponsors swore they would not compete with local practitioners. On the other hand, the programs of the 1960s attempted to provide comprehensive services in areas where private doctors had virtually disappeared.

29. Hermann M. Biggs, "The State Board of Health," *New York State Journal of Medicine* 21 (January 1921), 7; see also Victor C. Vaughan, "Rural Health Centers as Aids to General Practitioners," *JAMA* 76 (April 9, 1921), 983–85.

30. Milton Terris, "Hermann Biggs' Contribution to the Modern Concept of the Health Center," *Bulletin of the History of Medicine* 20 (October 1946), 387–412.

31. Edward L. Hunt, "The Health Centres Bill of 1920," *New York State Journal of Medicine* 21 (January 1921), 2.

32. Greer Williams, "Schools of Public Health—Their Doing and Undoing," *Health and Society* 54 (Fall 1976), 501–02.

33. Rosenkrantz, *Public Health and the State*, 179, 182.

Chapter Six

Escape from the Corporation, 1900–1930

1. On the development of industrial medicine in the United States, see Henry B. Selleck, with Alfred H. Whittaker, *Occupational Health in America* (Detroit: Wayne State University Press, 1962), and T. Lyle Hazlett and William W. Hummel, *Industrial Medicine in Western Pennsylvania, 1850–1950* (Pittsburgh: University of Pittsburgh Press, 1957).

2. For surveys of the extent of development, see C. D. Selby, "Studies of the Medical and Surgical Care of Industrial Workers," *Public Health Bulletin*, no. 99 (1919); National Industrial Conference Board, *Medical Care of Industrial Workers* (New York: National Industrial Conference Board, 1926); and "Medical and Hospital Service for Industrial Employees," *Monthly Labor Review* 24 (January 1927), 7–19.

3. Interstate Commerce Commission, *Fifteenth Annual Report* (Washington, D.C.: U.S. Government Printing Office, 1902), 58; C. B. Herrick, "The Railway Surgeon and His Work," *Transactions of the Medical Society of the State of New York* (1898), 214–19.

4. I. M. Rubinow, *Social Insurance* (New York: Henry Holt, 1916), 288–89.

5. Pierce Williams, *The Purchase of Medical Care Through Fixed Periodic Payments* (New York: National Bureau of Economic Research, 1932); Jerome Schwartz, "Early History of Prepaid Medical Care Plans," *Bulletin of the History of Medicine* 39 (September–October 1965), 450–75.

6. Stuart D. Brandes, *American Welfare Capitalism, 1880–1920* (Chicago: University of Chicago Press, 1976).

7. Williams, *Purchase of Medical Care*, 1–23.

8. Schwartz, "Early History of Prepaid Medical Care Plans," reports some worker support for company medical plans, but see Brandes, *American Welfare Capitalism* for a more thorough analysis.

9. "Contract Practice," *JAMA* 49 (December 14, 1907), 2028–29; Selleck and Whittaker, *Occupational Health in America*, 61; Alice Hamilton, *Exploring the Dangerous Trades* (Boston: Little, Brown, 1943), 3.

10. National Industrial Conference Board, *Health Services in Industry*, Report no. 34 (New York: National Industrial Conference Board, January 1921), 15.

11. "Medical and Hospital Service for Industrial Employees," *Monthly Labor Review* 24 (January 1927), 7–19; National Industrial Conference Board, *Medical Care of Industrial Workers*; J. D. Hackett, *Health Maintenance in Industry* (Chicago: A. W. Shaw, 1925).

12. Physicians in the AMA often opposed the extension of compensation in cases of occupational diseases because they regarded it "as creeping toward socialized or state medicine." Carey McCord, "The Present Status of Industrial Medicine," *AMA Bulletin* 25 (January 1930), 11–21.

13. On the decline of corporate paternalism, see Brandes, *American Welfare Capitalism*.

14. Schwartz, "Early History of Prepaid Medical Care Plans," 455; Note, "Right of Corporation to Practice Medicine," *Yale Law Journal* 48 (1938), 346–51.

15. Lawrence G. Goldberg and Warren Greenberg, "The Emergence of Physician-Sponsored Health Insurance: A Historical Perspective," in *Competition in the Health Sector: Past, Present and Future*, ed. Warren Greenberg (Washington, D. C.: Federal Trade Commission, 1978), 288–321.

16. John Kenneth Galbraith, *Economics and the Public Purpose* (Boston: Houghton Mifflin, 1973), 73.

17. Rubinow, *Social Insurance*, 293.

18. Charles Henderson, *Industrial Insurance in the United States* (Chicago: University of Chicago Press, 1908), 112–27.

19. In this section, I draw on George Rosen, "Contract or Lodge Practice and Its Influence on Medical Attitudes to Health Insurance," *American Journal of Public Health* 67 (April 1977), 374–78.

20. Anna Kalet, "Voluntary Health Insurance in New York City," *American Labor Legislation Review* 6 (June 1916), 142–54. For a detailed description of fraternal organizations

and benefit societies, see *Report of the Health Insurance Commission of Illinois*, May 1, 1919, 118–24.

21. George S. Mathews, "Contract Practice in Rhode Island," *Bulletin of the American Academy of Medicine* 10 (1909), 599.

22. James G. Burrow, *Organized Medicine in the Progressive Era: The Move Toward Monopoly* (Baltimore: Johns Hopkins University Press, 1977), 120–22.

23. Horace M. Alleman, "Lodge Practice," *Pennsylvania Medical Journal* 15 (December 1911), 223.

24. Mathews, "Contract Practice in Rhode Island," 602.

25. Ibid., 602–03, 604.

26. "Contract Practice," *JAMA* 49 (December 14, 1907), 2028–29; "Contract Practice," *JAMA* 57 (July 8, 1911), 145–46. In 1912 a report of the AMA Judicial Council gave a sympathetic view of lodge practice, but the council at that time was chaired by Alexander Lambert, whose views were not characteristic of the profession. The report was a prelude to the debate over health insurance. See *JAMA* 60 (June 28, 1913), 1997–98.

27. Mathews, "Contract Practice in Rhode Island," 600; Dr. J. K. Weaver, "Discussion," *Bulletin of the American Academy of Medicine* 10 (1909), 630–32. For a later report of medical society actions against doctors working for fraternal orders, see "Lodge Practice and the Medical Society," *AMA Bulletin* 16 (March 15, 1923), 290–92. For a state-by-state survey of medical society responses that emphasizes variations in policy, see Burrow, *Organized Medicine in the Progressive Era*, 124–32.

28. Irving Howe, *World of Our Fathers* (New York: Harcourt Brace Jovanovich, 1976), 188. Cited by Rosen, "Contract or Lodge Practice," 375

29. Henry Keller, "Contract Practice," *The Medical Economist* 1 (December 1913), 143–149.

30. Williams, *Purchase of Medical Care*, 290–91; Schwartz, "Early History of Prepaid Medical Care Plans," 452–54.

31. Howe, *World of Our Fathers*, 188.

32. Weaver, "Discussion," 631.

33. Quotations are from Helen Clapesattle, *The Doctors Mayo* (Minneapolis: University of Minnesota Press, 1941), 388, 392. Other details on the Mayo Clinic are from ibid., 339–535.

34. Ibid.; also C. Rufus Rorem, *Private Group Clinics* (Chicago: University of Chicago Press, 1931), 115–18.

35. Clapesattle, *The Doctors Mayo*, 788; Walker Winslow, *The Menninger Story* (New York: Doubleday, 1956), 13–16.

36. American Medical Association, Bureau of Medical Economics, *Group Practice* (Chicago: American Medical Association, 1933), 13–17.

37. Rorem, *Private Group Clinics*, 15–18.

38. AMA, *Group Practice*, 14.

39. Dr. Russell Lee, personal conversation, Palo Alto, California, August 1975.

40. AMA, *Group Practice*, 15.

41. Rorem, *Private Group Clinics*, 13.

42. Clapesattle, *The Doctors Mayo*, 531, 534.

43. Michael M. Davis, Jr., "Organization of Medical Service," *American Labor Legislation Review* 6 (March 1916), 18.

44. Rorem, *Private Group Clinics*, 102.

45. " 'Group Practice'—A Menace or a Blessing," *JAMA* 76 (February 12, 1921), 452–53.

46. Rorem, *Private Group Clinics*, 19–20.

47. Veader Newton Leonard, "The Significance of Group Practice," *JAMA* 76 (February 12, 1921), 421–26. Leonard mentions two other types—the staffs of closed hospitals and diagnostic groups—but these were excluded in most discussions of group practice.

48. Rorem, *Private Group Clinics*, 26–31.

49. Rexwald Brown, "Group Medicine in Practice," *AMA Bulletin* 18 (December 1923), 443–48.

50. Edward B. Stevens, *The History of the Medical Group Management Association, 1926–1976* (Denver: Medical Group Management Association, 1976), 22.

51. AMA, *Group Practice*, 42.

52. Ibid., 40–42.

53. American Medical Association, *Proceedings of the House of Delegates* (1934), 47.

54. Stephen Marglin, "What Do Bosses Do? The Origins and Functions of Hierarchy in Capitalist Production," *Review of Radical Political Economics* 6 (1974), 62.

55. American Medical Association, Bureau of Medical Economics, *Economics and the Ethics of Medicine* (Chicago: American Medical Association, 1935), 49–50.

56. Alleman, "Lodge Practice," 223; also cited by Burrow, *Organized Medicine in the Progressive Era*, 127.

57. AMA, *Economics and the Ethics of Medicine*, 45.

58. *Annual Report of the President, 1880–81*, 29.

59. Edward Louis Bauer, *Doctors Made in America* (Philadelphia: Lippincott, 1963), 247–49.

60. Bruce Steinwald and Duncan Neuhauser, "The Role of the Proprietary Hospital," *Law and Contemporary Problems* 35 (Autumn 1970), 818–20; E.H.L. Corwin, *The American Hospital* (New York: Commonwealth Fund, 1946), 29.

61. *JAMA* 92 (March 30, 1929), 1050.

62. Rosemary Stevens, *American Medicine and the Public Interest* (New Haven, Conn.: Yale University Press, 1971), 225–31, 238–43.

63. In this discussion of clinical laboratories, I rely entirely on William D. White, *Public Health and Private Gain: The Economics of Licensing Clinical Laboratory Personnel* (Chicago: Maroufa Press, 1979).

64. Ibid., 63.

65. George Unwin, *Industrial Organization in the Sixteenth and Seventeenth Centuries* (Oxford: Clarendon Press, 1904), 96.

66. Judy Barrett Litoff, *American Midwives, 1860 to the Present* (Westport, Conn.: Greenwood Press, 1978), 76.

67. Commission on Graduate Medical Education, *Graduate Medical Education* (Chicago: University of Chicago Press, 1940), 132–33; Abraham Flexner, *Medical Education in the United States and Canada* (New York: Carnegie Foundation for the Advancement of Teaching, 1910).

68. Stevens, *American Medicine and the Public Interest*, 127–28.

69. Kenneth Arrow, "Uncertainty and the Welfare Economics of Medical Care," *American Economic Review* 53 (December 1963), 941–69.

70. E. Richard Brown, *Rockefeller Medicine Men: Capitalism and Medical Care in America* (Berkeley: University of California Press, 1979), 3–4, 119–30, and elsewhere.

71. Ibid., 117–18. Brown cites the National Association of Manufacturers and the National Civic Federation. He evidently mistakes a committee report never adopted by the NAM for its official position. The National Civic Federation was vehement in its denunciations of health insurance. See my discussion in Book Two, Chapter 1.

72. Ibid., 113.

73. Joseph Schumpeter, *Capitalism, Socialism and Democracy* (New York: Harper & Row, 1950), 125–26.

BOOK TWO / THE STRUGGLE FOR MEDICAL CARE
Chapter One

The Mirage of Reform

1. I. M. Rubinow, *Social Insurance* (New York: Henry Holt, 1916), 224–50.

2. Gaston V. Rimlinger, *Welfare Policy and Industrialization in Europe, America and Russia* (New York: Wiley, 1971), Chaps. 2 and 3.

3. Reinhard Bendix, *Nation-Building and Citizenship* (New York: Wiley, 1971), 80–101.

4. Rimlinger, *Welfare Policy and Industrialization*; Peter Flora et al., "On the Development of the Western European Welfare States." (Paper prepared for the International Political Science Association, Edinburgh, August 16–21, 1976).

5. Rimlinger, *Welfare Policy and Industrialization*, 110–12.

6. Bentley B. Gilbert, *British Social Policy, 1914–1939* (London: Batsford, 1970), 15. See also Gilbert's earlier book, *The Evolution of National Insurance in Great Britain* (London: Michael Joseph, 1966), Chaps. 6 and 7.

7. Gilbert, *Evolution of National Insurance*, 165–67; Rubinow, *Social Insurance*, 226.

8. Charles R. Henderson, *Industrial Insurance in the United States* (Chicago: University of Chicago Press, 1909), 112–27; Edgar Sydenstricker, "Existing Agencies for Health Insurance in the United States," in U.S. Department of Labor, *Proceedings of the Conference on Social Insurance, 1916* (Washington, D.C.: U.S. Government Printing Office, 1917), 430–75.

9. James B. Kennedy, *Beneficiary Features of American Trade Unions* (Baltimore: Johns Hopkins University Studies in Historical and Political Science, 1908); *Twenty-Third Annual Report of the Commissioner of Labor 1908* (Washington, D.C.: U.S. Government Printing Office, 1909), 28–30, 205–13.

10. Edwin J. Faulkner, *Health Insurance* (New York: McGraw-Hill, 1960), Chap. 16; Rubinow, *Social Insurance*, 295–96.

11. John F. Dryden, *Addresses and Papers on Life Insurance and Other Subjects* (Newark, N.J.: Prudential Press, 1909), 31–32.

12. *Report of the Health Insurance Commission of Illinois*, (n.p.: May 1, 1919), 108 [henceforth referred to "Illinois commission report"]; Ohio Health and Old Age Insurance Commission, *Health, Health Insurance, Old Age Pensions* (Columbus, Ohio, 1919), 156 [henceforth referred to as "Ohio commission report"]; *Report of the Social Insurance Commission of the State of California, March 1919* (Sacramento: California State Printing Office, 1919), 11. For two earlier overviews, see Rubinow, *Social Insurance*, 281–98 and Sydenstricker, "Existing Agencies for Health Insurance," esp. 431–36.

13. Rubinow, *Social Insurance*, 296, 419–20; Marquis James, *The Metropolitan Life: A Study in Business Growth* (New York: Viking, 1947), 73–93.

14. On the background of the AALL, see Irwin Yellowitz, *Labor and the Progressive Movement in New York State, 1897–1916* (Ithaca, N.Y.: Cornell University Press, 1965), 55–59; John R. Commons and A. J. Altmeyer, "The Health Insurance Movement in the United States," in Ohio commission report, 291–92; and Roy Lubove, *The Struggle for Social Security, 1900–1935* (Cambridge: Harvard University Press, 1970).

15. For the association's model bill, see *American Labor Legislation Review* 6 (June 1916), 239–68.

16. Yellowitz, *Labor and the Progressive Movement*, 85.

17. Illinois commission report, 15–17; Rubinow, *Social Insurance*, 214.

18. Illinois commission report, 15, 18.

19. Ibid., 20–22. The New York Charity Organization Society found three fourths of a sample of five thousand charity cases were caused by sickness. See Hace Sorel Tishler,

Self-Reliance and Social Security, 1870–1917 (Port Washington, N.Y.: Kennikat Press, 1971), 164.

20. Rubinow, *Social Insurance*, 298. On Rubinow's general political views and career, see J. Lee Kreader, "Isaac Max Rubinow: Pioneering Specialist in Social Insurance," *Social Service Review* 50 (September 1976), 402–25.

21. Irving Fisher, "The Need for Health Insurance," *American Labor Legislation Review* 7 (March 1917), 23.

22. B. S. Warren and Edgar Sydenstricker, "Health Insurance: Its Relation to Public Health," *Public Health Bulletin*, no. 76 (March 1916), 6.

23. Ibid., 54.

24. I. M. Rubinow, "Social Insurance" (Chicago: American Medical Association, 1916), 24.

25. Ohio commission report, 136.

26. Ronald L. Numbers, *Almost Persuaded: American Physicians and Compulsory Health Insurance* (Baltimore: Johns Hopkins University Press, 1978) and Tishler, *Self-Reliance and Social Security*, 167–70. I owe a considerable debt to both these studies in this discussion.

27. Numbers, *Almost Persuaded*, 34.

28. Warren and Sydenstricker, "Health Insurance"; "Report of the Standing Committee Adopted by the Conference of State and Territorial Health Authorities with the United States Public Health Service, Washington, D.C., May 13, 1916," *Public Health Reports* 31 (July 21, 1916), 1919–25; Alexander Lambert, "Organization of Medical Benefits Under the Proposed Sickness (Health) Insurance System," in U.S. Department of Labor, *Proceedings of the Conference on Social Insurance, 1916*, 651–53.

29. Michael M. Davis, Jr., to John B. Andrews, July 21, 1915, in *Papers of the American Association for Labor Legislation*, 1905–1945 (Glen Rock, N.J.: Microfilm Corporation of America, 1973), reel 14.

30. Lambert, "Organization of Medical Benefits," 655–59.

31. Numbers, *Almost Persuaded*, 50–51.

32. *American Labor Legislation Review* 7 (March 1917), 51–65; Numbers, *Almost Persuaded*, 84.

33. U.S. Congress, House Committee on Labor, *Hearings Before the Committee on H.J. Resolution 159 . . . April 6 and 11, 1916*, 64th Cong., 1st sess., 36–45, 122–89.

34. Marc Karson, *American Labor Unions and Politics, 1900–1918* (Carbondale, Ill.: Southern Illinois University Press, 1958).

35. Selig Perlman, *A Theory of the Labor Movement* (New York: Macmillan, 1928), 162.

36. Nathan Fine, *Labor and Farmer Parties in the United States, 1828–1928* (New York: Rand School of Social Science, 1928), 129.

37. Bernard Mandel, *Samuel Gompers* (Yellow Springs, Oh.: Antioch Press, 1963), 32.

38. Ibid., 183; see also Samuel Gompers, "Trade Union Health Insurance," *American Federationist* 23 (November 1916), 1072–74; Philip Taft, *The A.F. of L. in the Time of Gompers* (New York: Harper & Row, 1957), 364–65.

39. Commons and Altmeyer, "Health Insurance Movement," 300. Gompers' objections were not insuperable. The New York State Federation supported a bill that would have provided low cash benefits under the compulsory system, thereby leaving room for fraternal and trade union plans to furnish additional cash benefits. Moreover, the German insurance system had stimulated union growth since it provided workers an opportunity to elect representatives.

40. National Association of Manufacturers, *Proceedings of the 21st Annual Convention*, May 15–17, 1916, 33–38; idem, *Proceedings of the 22nd Annual Convention*, May 14–16, 1917, 20–21; Frank F. Dresser, "Suggestions Regarding Social Insurance." (An Address Before the Conference on Social Insurance, Washington, D.C., December 4–9, 1916, NAM Pamphlet 46).

41. National Industrial Conference Board, "Sickness Insurance or Sickness Prevention?" Research Report no. 6 (Boston: National Industrial Conference Board, 1918), and idem, "Is Compulsory Health Insurance Desirable?" Special Report no. 4 (Boston: National Industrial Conference Board, 1919).

42. On the background of the National Civic Federation, see James Weinstein, *The Corporate Ideal in the Liberal State: 1900–1918* (Boston: Beacon Press, 1968).

43. Karson, *American Labor Unions and Politics*; Yellowitz, *Labor and the Progressive Movement*; Robert Wiebe, *Businessmen and Reform* (Cambridge: Harvard University Press, 1962), 158–67.

44. Tishler, *Self-Reliance and Social Security*, 179–89.

45. Ibid.; for a sampler of opinions, see "If Not Compulsory Insurance, What" *National Civic Federation Review* 4 (June 5, 1919).

46. James, *Metropolitan Life*, 171–72.

47. Numbers, *Almost Persuaded*, 78; F. L. Hoffman, *Facts and Fallacies of Compulsory Insurance* (Newark, N.J.: Prudential Press, 1917).

48. Lee K. Frankel, "Some Fundamental Considerations in Health Insurance," in U.S. Department of Labor, *Proceedings of the Conference on Social Insurance 1916*, 598–605.

49. Numbers, *Almost Persuaded*, 67.

50. Ibid., 73.

51. Ibid., 75–77.

52. League for the Conservation of Public Health, "It Shall Not Pass," (n.d., n.p.) and letter to doctors, October 8, 1918, Ray Lyman Wilbur papers, Stanford University, Stanford, Calif.

53. Arthur Viseltear, "Compulsory Health Insurance in California, 1915–1918," *Journal of the History of Medicine and the Allied Sciences* 24 (April 1969), 151–82; Numbers, *Almost Persuaded*, 79–81.

54. Lubove, *The Struggle for Social Security*, 83–84.

55. Illinois commission report, 209.

56. I.M. Rubinow, "Public and Private Interests in Social Insurance," *American Labor Legislation Review* 21 (June 1931), 181–91.

57. Even Lubove's otherwise admirable account in *The Struggle for Social Security* avoids facing the complexities of the problem by ignoring the AMA's early approval of health insurance and treating the doctors' response as an automatic expression of objective interests.

58. Gilbert, *Evolution of National Insurance*, 425–28.

59. Rimlinger, *Welfare Policy and Industrialization*, 112–22.

60. Gilbert, *Evolution of National Insurance*, 356–440.

61. Chester Rowell to Ray Lyman Wilbur, October 7, 1918. Wilbur Papers.

62. Numbers reports that the average income of taxed physicians in Wisconsin rose 41 percent from 1916 to 1919. See *Almost Persuaded*, 113.

63. Lubove, *The Struggle for Social Security*, 45–51; see also Lawrence M. Friedman and Jack Ladinsky, "Social Change and the Law of Industrial Accidents," *Columbia Law Review* 67 (January 1967), 50–82.

64. I. S. Falk, *Security Against Sickness* (Garden City, N.Y.: Doubleday, Doran, 1936), 14–16.

65. Michael M. Davis, Jr., preface to Harry A. Millis, *Sickness and Insurance* (Chicago: University of Chicago Press, 1937), v.

66. Michael M. Davis, Jr., "The American Approach to Health Insurance," *Milbank Memorial Fund Quarterly* 12 (July 1934), 214.

67. Milton Friedman and Simon Kuznets, *Income from Independent Professional Practice* (New York: National Bureau of Economic Research, 1945).

68. Ohio insurance commission, 116.

69. I. S. Falk, C. Rufus Rorem, and Martha D. Ring, *The Cost of Medical Care* (Chicago: University of Chicago Press, 1933), 89. The estimate was only for private expenditures; figuring in tax money spent on hospital care, the proportion of social expenditures going to hospitals was 23 percent (p. 19).

70. Davis, "American Approach," 211.

71. Committee on the Costs of Medical Care, *Medical Care for the American People* (Chicago: University of Chicago Press, 1932), 19.

72. Davis, "American Approach," 214–15.

73. Sheila M. Rothman, *Woman's Proper Place* (New York: Basic Books, 1978), 136–52.

74. Harry H. Moore, *American Medicine and the People's Health* (New York: Appleton, 1927), 21.

75. Paul Kellogg to Edward Filene, November 7, 1927. Wilbur papers.

76. CCMC, *Medical Care for the American People*, Chap. 1. The general summary of findings is presented in Falk, Rorem, and Ring, *Cost of Medical Care*.

77. CCMC, *Medical Care for the American People*, 32–36.

78. Roger I. Lee, Lewis Webster Jones, and Barbara Jones, *The Fundamentals of Good Medical Care* (Chicago: University of Chicago Press, 1933), 12.

79. Ibid.

80. CCMC, *Medical Care for the American People*, 7.

81. Ibid., 41.

82. "Introduction," in Falk, Rorem, and Ring, *Cost of Medical Care*, vi–vii.

83. CCMC, *Medical Care for the American People*, 61, 128–30.

84. Ibid., 94.

85. Ibid., 68.

86. Ibid., 130–32, 189–201.

87. Ibid., 152–83.

88. "The Committee on the Costs of Medical Care," *JAMA* 99 (December 3, 1932), 1950–51.

89. *New York Times*, November 30, 1932.

90. Averaging the order of enactment of compulsory or subsidized voluntary insurance programs in twelve major European countries, Flora and his associates find that industrial accident insurance ranks 1.7; sickness insurance, 2.2; old-age insurance, 2.7; and unemployment insurance, 3.5. See Flora et al., "On the Development of the Western European Welfare States," 22.

91. Paul H. Douglas, *Social Security in the United States* (New York: McGraw-Hill, 1936), 70.

92. Edwin Witte, *The Development of the Social Security Act* (Madison, Wis.: University of Wisconsin Press, 1962), 174–75. On Witte, see Theron F. Schlabach, *Edwin Witte: Cautious Reformer* (Madison, Wis.: State Historical Society of Wisconsin, 1969).

93. Abraham Epstein, "Social Security—Fiction or Fact?" *The American Mercury* 33 (October 1934), 129–38.

94. Witte, *Development of the Social Security Act*, 175–80; Daniel S. Hirshfield, *The Lost Reform* (Cambridge: Harvard University Press, 1970), 44–52.

95. Committee on Economic Security, *Report to the President* (Washington, D.C.: U.S. Government Printing Office, 1935).

96. "Report of the Special Reference Committee," *JAMA* 104 (March 2, 1935), 751–52. This was really no concession at all.

97. Arthur J. Altmeyer, *The Formative Years of Social Security* (Madison, Wis.: University of Wisconsin Press, 1968), 57–58n; Witte, *Development of the Social Security Act*, 185ff, 205–10; Hirshfield, *Lost Reform*, 55–60.

98. Douglas, *Social Security*, 100–01.

99. G. St. J. Perrot, Edgar Sydenstricker, and Selwyn D. Collins, "Medical Care During the Depression," *Milbank Memorial Fund Quarterly* 12 (April 1934), 99–114.

100. *New York Times*, June 12, 1938.

101. Paul A. Dodd, *Economic Aspects of Medical Services* (Washington, D.C.: Graphic Arts Press, 1939), 209; Simon Kuznets and Milton Friedman, "Income from Independent Practice, 1929–1936," *National Bureau of Economic Research Bulletin* (February 5, 1939), 8; George D. Wolf, *The Physician's Business* (Philadelphia: Lippincott, 1938), 112.

102. New York State Legislative Commission on Medical Care, *Medical Care for the People of New York State* (n.p.: February 15, 1946), 171–72; Franz Goldmann, *Public Medical Care* (New York: Columbia University Press, 1945). Even though the federal government appropriated no money for medical care under old-age assistance, its contributions to cash allowances freed up state money to be used for medical care. The state of Washington in 1941 established the right of persons over sixty-five to "more or less complete medical care at public expense" (ibid., 74).

103. Samuel Lubell and Walter Everett, "Rehearsal for State Medicine," *Saturday Evening Post*, December 17, 1938, 23ff.

104. Morris Fishbein, *History of the American Medical Association* (Philadelphia: Saunders, 1947), 407–08.

105. Mary Ross, "California Weighs Health Insurance," *Survey Graphic* 24 (May 1935), 213ff.

106. George A. Shipman, Robert J. Lampman and S. Frank Miyamoto, *Medical Service Corporations in the State of Washington* (Cambridge: Harvard University Press, 1962), 22–23.

107. Walter Bierring, "The Family Doctor and the Changing Order," *JAMA* 102 (June 16, 1934), 1997.

108. Friedman and Kuznets, *Incomes from Independent Professional Practice*, 12–20.

109. Hirshfield, *The Lost Reform*, 76–78.

110. Oliver Garceau, *The Political Life of the American Medical Association* (Cambridge: Harvard University Press, 1941), 132.

111. Ibid., 77

112. George Gallup, "Most Doctors Back Health Insurance," *New York Times*, June 15, 1938; Garceau, *Political Life*, 133–34.

113. Hirshfield, *The Lost Reform*, 128–30; Garceau, *Political Life*, 147–52.

114. Quoted in James Rorty, *American Medicine Mobilizes* (New York: Norton, 1939), 93–94; see also John P. Peters, "Medicine and the Public," *New England Journal of Medicine* 220 (March 23, 1939), 504–10.

115. "The American Foundation Proposals for Medical Care," *JAMA* 109 (October 16, 1937), 1280–81.

116. Hirshfield, *The Lost Reform*, 102–05.

117. "A National Health Program: Report of the Technical Committee on Medical Care," in Interdepartmental Committee to Coordinate Health and Welfare Activities, *Proceedings of the National Health Conference*, July 18, 19, 20, 1938, Washington, D.C. (Washington, D.C.: U.S. Government Printing Office, 1938), 29–63.

118. Altmeyer, *Formative Years*, 96.

119. "Procedings of the Special Session," *JAMA* 111 (September 24, 1938), 1191–1217; Morris Fishbein, "American Medicine and the National Health Plan," *New England Journal of Medicine* 220 (March 23, 1939), 495–504. Fishbein ridicules the national health program.

120. Arthur J. Viseltear, "Emergence of the Medical Care Section of the American Public Health Association, 1926–48," *American Journal of Public Health* 63 (November 1973), 992.

121. Altmeyer, *Formative Years*, 96.

122. Ibid., 115.

123. Robert F. Wagner, "The National Health Bill," *American Labor Legislation Review* 29 (1939), 13–44.

124. Altmeyer, *Formative Years*, 126–27.

125. William Leuchtenberg, *Franklin D. Roosevelt and the New Deal, 1932–1940* (New York: Harper & Row, 1963), 88.

126. Hirshfield, *The Lost Reform,* passim.

127. In the discussion of public opinion, I follow Michael E. Schiltz, *Public Attitudes Toward Social Security 1935–1965* (Washington, D.C.: U.S. Government Printing Office, 1970), 123–50.

128. John Blum, *From the Morgenthau Diaries: Years of War, 1941–1945* (Boston: Houghton Mifflin, 1967), 72.

129. Altmeyer, *Formative Years*, 261.

130. For background on the bill, see Monty M. Poen, *Harry S. Truman Versus the Medical Lobby* (Columbia, Mo.: University of Missouri Press, 1979), 31–36. I am indebted to Poen's account for much of the following discussion.

131. Ibid., 42–43.

132. "A National Health Program: Message from the President," *Social Security Bulletin* (December 1945), 7.

133. Ibid., 8.

134. Ibid., 11.

135. A. J. Altmeyer, "How Can We Assure Adequate Health Service for All the People?" *Social Security Bulletin* (December 1945), 15–16.

136. Poen, *Truman Versus the Medical Lobby*, 85–86.

137. Schiltz, *Public Attitudes Toward Social Security*, 134.

138. Foote, Cone, and Belding, *Survey of Public Relations of the California Medical Profession* (n.p., 1944), 4–5.

139. New York State Legislative Commission, *Medical Care for the People of New York State*, 26–28.

140. Foote, Cone, and Belding, *Survey of Public Relations*; Schiltz, *Public Attitudes Toward Social Security*, 136–39.

141. Richard Harris, *A Sacred Trust* (New York: New American Library, 1966), 31–33.

142. U.S. Senate, *National Health Program*, Hearings Before the Committee on Education and Labor, 77th Cong., 2nd sess., pt. 1, April 2–16, 1946, 47ff.

143. Poen, *Truman Versus the Medical Lobby*, 75–80, 90.

144. Ibid., 96–97.

145. Ibid., 102–06.

146. National Health Assembly, *America's Health: A Report to the Nation* (New York: Harper and Brothers, 1949).

147. Harris, *Sacred Trust*, 44–46.

148. Schiltz, *Public Attitudes Toward Social Security*, 134.

149. Poen, *Truman Versus the Medical Lobby*, 118–22.

150. Altmeyer, *Formative Years*, 261–62.

151. Ibid., 185–86.

152. Poen, *Truman Versus the Medical Lobby*, 181–82.

153. Godfrey Hodgson, *America in Our Time* (New York: Doubleday, 1977), 77.

Chapter Two

The Triumph of Accommodation

1. The idea that indemnity and service-benefit plans represent different approaches to risk is developed in William C. L. Hsiao and Beth Stevens, "Cooptation Versus Isolation: Health Insurance Organizations and Their Relations with Physicians," (unpublished paper, Harvard University School of Public Health, July 15, 1980).

2. Marquis James, *The Metropolitan Life: A Study in Business Growth* (New York: Viking, 1947), 262–64; *Report of the Health Insurance Commission of Illinois* (n.p.: May 1, 1919), 135–40; Edwin J. Faulkner, *Health Insurance* (New York: McGraw-Hill, 1960), Chap. 16.

3. Pierce Williams, *The Purchase of Medical Care Through Fixed Periodic Payment* (New York: National Bureau of Economic Research, 1932), 258–60.

4. Committee on the Costs of Medical Care, *Medical Care for the American People* (Chicago: University of Chicago Press, 1932), 91–92.

5. For the conventional account, see C. Rufus Rorem, *Blue Cross Hospital Service Plans* (Chicago: Hospital Service Plan Commission, 1944), 7; on private promotion, see Michael M. Davis and C. Rufus Rorem, *The Crisis in Hospital Finance* (Chicago: University of Chicago Press, 1932), 211–13; also, Louis S. Reed, *Blue Cross and Medical Service Plans* (Washington, D.C.: Federal Security Agency, 1949), 9–10.

6. "A Statistical Analysis of 2,717 Hospitals," *Bulletin of the American Hospital Association* 4 (July 1930), 68.

7. Davis and Rorem, *Crisis in Hospital Finance*, 5.

8. Ibid., 3.

9. Ibid., 12.

10. Rorem, *Blue Cross Hospital Service Plans*, 7, 12–13.

11. Reed, *Blue Cross and Medical Service Plans*, 13–14, 54–56.

12. Odin W. Anderson, *Blue Cross Since 1929: Accountability and the Public Trust* (Cambridge, Mass.: Ballinger, 1975), 42.

13. Reed, *Blue Cross and Medical Service Plans*, 11–12, 54–58.

14. Rorem, *Blue Cross Hospital Service Plans*, 11.

15. By sustaining hospitals that would have otherwise gone bankrupt through competition, the community-wide plans may be said to have preserved a wider set of alterna-

tive facilities. But they did so at a price people probably did not realize they were paying.

16. C. Rufus Rorem, "Group Hospitalization Plans Forge Ahead," *Hospitals* 10 (April 1936), 62–66; "Group Hospitalization Plans Protect One Million Persons," *Hospitals* 11 (July 1937), 120–22.

17. Anderson, *Blue Cross Since 1929*, 40.

18. Duncan M. MacIntyre, *Voluntary Health Insurance and Rate Making* (Ithaca, N.Y.: Cornell University Press, 1962), 124–25; C. A. Kulp, *Casualty Insurance* (New York: Ronald Press, 1956); U.S. Senate, Committee on Labor and Public Welfare, *Health Insurance Plans in the United States*, Report no. 359, pt. 2, 82d Cong., 1st sess., 1951 (henceforth cited as "1951 Senate Report"), 99.

19. Herman N. Somers and Anne R. Somers, *Doctors, Patients and Health Insurance* (Washington, D.C.: The Brookings Institution, 1961), 548.

20. *JAMA* 104 (May 4, 1935), 1614.

21. *JAMA* 111 (September 24, 1938), 1216.

22. Davis and Rorem, *Crisis in Hospital Finance*, 90–96.

23. E. M. Dunstan and Jo C. Alexander, "Group Hospitalization Plan: Survey of Local Organized Medical Opinion on the Baylor University Hospital," *Hospitals* 10 (August 1936), 75–81.

24. *JAMA* 102 (June 30, 1934), 2200–01. This is this source for the quotations from the ten principles that appear in the following paragraphs.

25. At the 1935 meeting of the AMA House of Delegates, the wording was revised to read: "In whatever way the cost of medical service may be distributed, it should be paid for by the patient in accordance with his income status and in a manner that is mutually satisfactory." *JAMA* 104 (June 29, 1935), 2364.

26. Davis and Rorem, *Crisis in Hospital Finance*, 202–03.

27. George A. Shipman et al., *Medical Service Corporations in the State of Washington* (Cambridge: Harvard University Press, 1962).

28. Mary Ross, "The Case of the Ross-Loos Clinic," *Survey Graphic* 24 (June 1935), 300ff; Arnold I. Kisch and Arthur J. Viseltear, *The Ross-Loos Medical Group*, U.S. Public Health Service, Medical Care Administration Study no. 3 (1967).

29. Paul de Kruif, *Kaiser Wakes the Doctors* (New York: Harcourt Brace, 1943), 20–35.

30. Davis and Rorem, *Crisis in Hospital Finance*, 205–06.

31. "How Prepayment Got Its Start," *Group Practice* 22 (December 1973), 17–19.

32. Jerome Schwartz, "Early History of Prepaid Medical Care Plans," *Bulletin of the History of Medicine* 39 (September–October 1965), 470–75, and idem, "Prepayment Clinics of the Mesabi Iron Range: 1904–1964," *Journal of the History of Medicine and the Allied Sciences* 22 (April 1967), 139–51.

33. Michael Shadid, "Rural Health Projects in Action—II," *American Cooperation, 1946* (Washington, D.C.: American Institute of Cooperation, 1947), 429.

34. Michael Shadid, *A Doctor for the People* (New York: The Vanguard Press, 1939).

35. Ben Swigart, "Rural Health Projects in Action—I," *American Cooperation, 1946,* 423–28; Eugene Butler, "Cooperatives and Rural Health: II. What Texas Has Done," *American Cooperation, 1947,* 420–27.

36. Franz Goldmann, *Voluntary Medical Care Insurance in the United States* (New York: Columbia University Press, 1948), 130, 135.

37. Goldmann, *Voluntary Medical Care Insurance*, 65–66. The following year the CIO suggested that as a "spur" to the adoption of national health insurance, CIO unions assist in forming medical cooperatives in their communities.

38. Shadid, "Rural Health Projects in Action," 432.

39. Michael Shadid, "Cooperative Versus Competitive Medicine," *American Cooperation, 1940,* 83–88.

40. Ross, "Case of the Ross-Loos Clinic"; Andrew and Hannah Biemiller, "Medical Rift in Milwaukee," *Survey Graphic* 27 (August 1938), 418–20; Waldeman Kaempffert, "Group Practice Fight Growing More Bitter," *New York Times*, August 7, 1938; Thomas N. Bonner, *Medicine in Chicago* (Madison, Wis.: American Historical Research Center, 1957), 217–18; James Rorty, *American Medicine Mobilizes* (New York: Norton, 1939), 135ff.

41. *American Medical Association* v. *United States* 110 F 2d 703; Rorty, *American Medical Mobilizes*, 286.

42. 110 F 2d 703.

43. *Washington Post*, December 21, 1938 (emphasis added).

44. *American Medical Association* v. *United States* 317 U.S. 519 (1943).

45. Horace R. Hansen, "Group Health Plans: A Twenty-Year Legal Review," *Minnesota Law Review* 42 (March 1958), 527–48.

46. *JAMA* 111 (July 2, 1938), 59.

47. Ibid., 119 (June 20, 1942), 727–28.

48. Anderson, *Blue Cross Since 1929*, 58n.

49. Reed, *Blue Cross and Medical Service Plans*, 137–41; Joseph W. Garbarino, *Health Plans and Collective Bargaining* (Berkeley: University of California Press, 1960), 89–106.

50. Garbarino, *Health Plans and Collective Bargaining*, 106–11.

51. Anderson, *Blue Cross Since 1929*, 45; Nathan Sinai, Odin W. Anderson, and Melvin L. Dollar, *Health Insurance in the United States* (New York: Commonwealth Fund, 1946), 73, 84–94.

52. Sinai, Anderson, and Dollar, *Health Insurance in the United States*, 64–65.

53. Reed, *Blue Cross and Medical Service Plans*, 81–91.

54. Ibid., 69–71; Cone, Foote, and Belding, "Survey of Public Relations of the California Medical Association," 81. New York Legislative Commission on Medical Care, *Medical Care for the People of New York State* (n.p.: February 15, 1946), 223.

55. Ibid., 81–82.

56. Daniel Hirshfield, *The Lost Reform* (Cambridge: Harvard University Press, 1970), 97.

57. Leon Applebaum, "The Development of Voluntary Health Insurance in the United States," *Journal of Risk and Insurance* (September 1961), 15–23; John T. Dunlop, "Appraisal of the Wage Stabilization Policies," U.S. Department of Labor, Bulletin no. 1009, 166–67.

58. Raymond Munts, *Bargaining for Health* (Madison, Wis.: University of Wisconsin Press, 1960), 7–12.

59. Ibid., 9–10; Garbarino, *Health Plans and Collective Bargaining*, 19.

60. On Taft-Hartley, see Munts, *Bargaining for Health*, 10–12, and Arthur F. McClure, *The Truman Administration and the Problems of Postwar Labor, 1945–1948* (Rutherford, N.J.: Fairleigh Dickinson Press, 1969), 162–84.

61. H. M. Douty, "Post-war Wage Bargaining in the United States," in *Labor and Trade Unionism*, ed. Walter Galenson and Seymour Martin Lipset (New York: Wiley, 1960), 192–202.

62. Garbarino, *Health Plans and Collective Bargaining*, 19–20.

63. Odin W. Anderson and Jacob J. Feldman, *Family Medical Costs and Voluntary Health Insurance: A Nationwide Survey* (New York: McGraw-Hill, 1956), 11.

64. 1951 Senate Report, 98–99.

65. Ibid., 122.

66. Munts, *Bargaining for Health*, 104.

67. Garbarino, *Health Plans and Collective Bargaining*, 280–82.

68. The following analysis relies on Janet E. Ploss, "A History of the Medical Care Program of the United Mine Workers of America Welfare and Retirement Fund" (Master's thesis, Johns Hopkins School of Hygiene and Public Health, 1980). I am much indebted to Ms. Ploss for allowing me to draw upon her excellent study.

69. See Derek C. Bok and John T. Dunlop, *Labor and the American Community* (New York: Simon and Schuster, 1970).

70. Ploss, "History of the Medical Care Program," Chap. 1.

71. U.S. Department of the Interior, *A Medical Survey of the Bituminous-Coal Industry* (Washington, D.C.: U.S. Government Printing Office, 1947), 75–77, 111, 123, 137–64.

72. Ploss, "History of the Medical Care Program," Chap. 2; Leslie Falk, "Group Health Plans in Coal Mining Communities," *Journal of Health and Human Behavior* 4 (Spring 1963), 4–13.

73. Munts, *Bargaining for Health*, 99; see also idem, 61–63, and Garbarino, *Health Plans and Collective Bargaining*, 182.

74. Munts, *Bargaining for Health*, 21.

75. Garbarino, *Health Plans and Collective Bargaining*, 149–57; see also Wallace Croatman, "Are Labor's Health Centers a Threat to Doctors?" *Medical Economics* 31 (October 1954), 109–18.

76. Goldmann, *Voluntary Medical Care Insurance*, 150.

77. Angus McDonald, "Health on the Farm," *The New Republic* 116 (March 3, 1947), 32–33.

78. Jerry Voorhis, *American Cooperatives* (New York: Harpers and Brothers, 1961), 32; Somers and Somers, *Doctors, Patients and Health Insurance*, 348–49. See also Helen L. Johnston, "Rural Health Cooperatives," *Public Health Bulletin* no. 308 (1950).

79. William A. MacColl, "Reflections on the Birth of Group Health," Group Health Cooperative of Puget Sound, February 1972, 4. See also idem, *Group Practice and Prepayment of Medical Care* (Washington, D.C.: Public Affairs Press, 1966), 36–42.

80. On Kaiser's early history, see de Kruif, *Kaiser Wakes the Doctors*, passim; Greer Williams, *Kaiser-Permanente Health Plan: Why It Works* (Oakland, Calif.: Henry J. Kaiser Foundation, 1971), 4–6; Waldemar Nielsen, *The Big Foundations* (New York: Columbia University Press, 1973), 245–49; E. W. Saward et al., "Documentation of Twenty Years of Operation and Growth of a Prepaid Group Practice Plan," *Medical Care* 6 (May–June 1968), 231–44.

81. On HIP, see George Baehr, *A Report of the First Ten Years* (New York: HIP, 1957); Louis L. Feldman, *Organization of a Medical Group Practice Prepayment Program in New York City* (New York: HIP, 1953) and idem, "Legislation and Prepayment for Group Practice," *Bulletin of the New York Academy of Medicine* 47 (April 1971), 411–22.

82. "The Patient's Dilemma," *San Francisco Chronicle*, February 22, 1949, reprinted in U.S. Senate, *National Health Program, 1949*, Hearings Before a Subcommittee of the Committee on Labor and Public Welfare, pt. 1, May 23–June 2, 1949, 81 Cong., 1st sess., 271–76; Garbarino, *Health Plans and Collective Bargaining*, 125–27.

83. Garbarino, *Health Plans and Collective Bargaining*, 205–23.

84. Kenneth P. Andrews, "How They're Fighting the Kaiser Plan," *Medical Economics* 31 (September 1954), 126–31.

85. *Group Health Cooperative of Puget Sound* v. *King County Medical Society*, 39 Wash. 2d 586, 237 Pac 2d 737 (1951); see also Claron Oakley, "Closed Panel Plans are Hard to Beat in Court," *Medical Economics* 32 (May 1955), 103–07.

86. Claron Oakley, "They Met the Challenge of Panel Medicine," *Medical Economics* 32 (February 1955), 122–30.

87. Garbarino, *Health Plans and Collective Bargaining*, 191–96.

88. Commission on Medical Care Plans, Report, pt. 1., *JAMA* (January 17, 1959), 34–42, 63.

89. However, group enrollees in the cooperative (about 60 percent of the membership as of 1973) did not have voting rights as members; they were represented by their bargaining agents in periodic negotiations. The dual structure of the plan originated in 1945 when the cooperative purchased the Medical Security Clinic, which had several industrial contracts among its assets. For a discussion, see "Who Should Run Group Health?" *View* (Group Health Cooperative), January–February 1973, 4–6. See also Jerome L. Schwartz, "Participation of Consumers in Prepaid Health Plans," *Journal of Health and Human Behavior* 5 (Summer and Fall 1964), 74–84.

90. 1951 Senate Report, 80–81; Odin W. Anderson, Patricia Collette, and Jacob J. Feldman, *Changes in Family Medical Expenditures and Voluntary Health Insurance: A Five-Year Resurvey*, (Cambridge: Harvard University Press, 1963), 8–9. The relative standings of the commercial insurers, Blue Cross, and the independent plans stayed about the same between 1953 and 1958. Howevever, Blue Shield increased its share of the market significantly.

91. 1951 Senate Report, 74–79, 99–106.

92. MacIntyre, *Voluntary Health Insurance and Rate Making* 58. The data refer to 1959, but the pattern was the same earlier. See 1951 Senate Report, 110–11, and Somers and Somers, *Doctors, Patients and Health Insurance*, 300, 326–27.

93. MacIntyre, *Voluntary Health Insurance and Rate Making*, 26–49; Somers and Somers, *Doctors, Patients and Health Insurance*, 309–11.

94. Ibid., 155–61.

95. Garbarino, *Health Plans and Collective Bargaining*, 228.

96. Somers and Somers, *Doctors, Patients and Health Insurance*, 304.

97. Ibid., 261–62, citing C. A. Kulp.

98. Other factors, such as per-capita income, were positively related to Blue Cross development. But in the Pacific states, as Reed pointed out, per capita income was high, but the hospitals were not "strongly voluntary," many having recently converted from

proprietary status. Blue Cross had made relatively slow progress there. See Reed, *Blue Cross and Medical Service Plans*, 28–30.

99. Somers and Somers, *Doctors, Patients and Health Insurance*, 300.

100. Anderson, Collette, and Feldman, *Changes in Family Medical Expenditures*, 4–6, 171.

101. Garbarino, *Health Plans and Collective Bargaining*, 22.

Chapter Three

The Liberal Years

1. U.S. Public Health Service, Office of Research, Statistics and Technology, *Health: United States 1981* (Hyattsville, Md.: U.S. Department of Health and Human Services, 1981), 263; Maryland Y. Pennell and David B. Hoover, *Health Manpower Source Book 21: Allied Health Manpower Supply and Requirements: 1950–1980* (Bethesda, Md.: U.S. Department of Health, Edcuation and Welfare, 1970), 4.

2. "Report of the Medical Advisory Committee," in Vannevar Bush, *Science: The Endless Frontier* (1945; reprint ed., Washington, D.C.: National Science Foundation, 1960), 49.

3. Godfrey Hodgson, *America in Our Time* (New York: Doubleday, 1976), 19.

4. See, for example, Harry Stack Sullivan, "Remobilization for Enduring Peace and Social Progress," *Psychiatry* 10 (August 1947), 239–52; and, for a critical review, Christopher Lasch, *Haven in a Heartless World: The Family Besieged* (New York: Basic Books, 1977), 97–99.

5. A. Hunter Dupree, "Central Scientific Organization in the United States Government," *Minerva* 1 (Summer 1963), 453–69.

6. Richard H. Shryock, *American Medical Research* (New York: Commonwealth Fund 1947), 91–98. The following paragraphs draw frequently on Shryock.

7. Cited in ibid., 135–36.

8. On the scientific role of the Department of Agriculture, see Dupree, "Central Scientific Organization"; in relation to environmental toxicology, see James Whorton, *Before Silent Spring: Pesticides and Public Health in Pre-DDT America* (Princeton, N. J.: Princeton University Press, 1974); on antibiotics, Selman A. Waksman, "The Microbiology of the Soil and the Antibiotics," in *The Impact of the Antibiotics on Medicine and Society*, ed. Iago Galdston (New York: International Universities Press, 1958), 3–7.

9. Stephen Strickland, *Politics, Science and Dread Disease: A Short History of United States Medical Research Policy* (Cambridge: Harvard University Press, 1972), 1–14. For the basic history, see Ralph C. Williams, *The United States Public Health Service, 1798–1950* (Richmond, Va.: Whittet & Shepperson, 1951).

10. Shryock, *American Medical Research*, 277. On the history of the National Cancer Institute, see [Devra M. Breslow], *A History of Cancer Control in the United States, 1946–1971*, II, *A History of Programmatic Developments in Cancer Control*, U.S. Department of Health, Education and Welfare, National Cancer Institute, Publication no. (NIH) 79-1518; and Richard A. Rettig, *Cancer Crusade: The Story of the National Cancer Act of 1971* (Princeton, N.J.: Princeton University Press, 1977).

11. A. N. Richards, "The Impact of the War on Medicine," *Science* 103 (May 10, 1946), 578.

12. Bush, *Science: The Endless Frontier*, 6, 10–12, 31–40. For background on the report, see J. M. England, "Dr. Bush Writes a Report: 'Science—the Endless Frontier,'" *Science* 191 (January 9, 1976), 41–47; also, more generally, Daniel S. Greenberg, *The Politics of Pure Science* (New York: New American Library, 1967).

13. For a summary of PHS activities and postwar developments, see Congressional Quarterly Service, *Congress and the Nation, 1945–64: A Review of Government and Politics in the Postwar Years* (Washington, D.C.: Congressional Quarterly Service, 1965), 1126–

33; also, Williams, *United States Public Health Service*. The budget figures come from Strickland, *Politics, Science and Dread Disease*, 29.

14. On the Lasker lobby, see Strickland, *Politics, Science and Dread Disease*, 32–54, and Elizabeth Brenner Drew, "The Health Syndicate: Washington's Noble Conspirators," *Atlantic Monthly* 220 (December 1967), 75–82.

15. Kenneth M. Endicott and Ernest M. Allen, "The Growth of Medical Research 1941–1953 and the Role of the Public Health Service Research Grants," *Science* 118 (September 25, 1953), 337. See also Thomas B. Turner, "The Medical Schools Twenty Years Afterwards: Impact of the Extramural Research Support of the National Institutes of Health," *Journal of Medical Education* 42 (February 1967), 109–18.

16. Endicott and Allen, "Growth of Medical Research," 341.

17. Morris Janowitz, *The Professional Soldier* (New York: Free Press, 1960).

18. William Menninger, *Psychiatry in a Troubled World: Yesterday's War and Today's Challenge* (New York: Macmillan, 1948).

19. William Menninger, *Psychiatry: Its Evolution and Present Status* (Ithaca, N.Y.: Cornell University Press, 1948), 2. On the earlier development of psychiatry, see Nathan G. Hale, Jr., *Freud and the Americans* (New York: Oxford University Press, 1971).

20. Albert Deutsch, *The Shame of the States* (New York: Harcourt Brace, 1948), 138–39. See also idem, *The Mentally Ill in America* (New York: Columbia University Press, 1949), 448–49.

21. On the background of the legislation, see Jeanne L. Brand, "The National Mental Health Act of 1946: A Retrospect," *Bulletin of the History of Medicine* 39 (May–June 1965), 231–44. For an account of the rise of NIMH, see Robert H. Connery et al., *The Politics of Mental Health* (New York: Columbia University Press, 1968).

22. Richard Carter, *Breakthrough: The Saga of Jonas Salk* (New York: Trident Press, 1966), 1. See also David Sills, *The Volunteers* (Glencoe, Ill.: Free Press, 1957), esp. 176–99, and John R. Paul, *A History of Poliomyelitis* (New Haven, Conn.: Yale University Press, 1971).

23. For a budget chart, see Congressional Quarterly Service, *Congress and the Nation*, 1132. On the congressional backing, see Strickland, *Politics, Science and Dread Disease*, 75–183; and for a general review by the director of NIH in its golden age, see James A. Shannon, "The Advancement of Medical Research: A Twenty Year View of the Role of the National Institutes of Health," *Journal of Medical Education* 42 (February 1967), 97–108.

24. Strickland, *Politics, Science and Dread Disease*, 55–74.

25. I have written at length on the background and problems of the VA hospitals in my book *The Discarded Army: Veterans After Vietnam* (New York: Charterhouse, 1974), 71–112.

26. Dan Feshbach, "What's Inside the Black Box: A Case Study of Allocative Politics in the Hill-Burton Program," *International Journal of Health Services* 9 (1979), 313–39.

27. Commission on Hospital Care, *Hospital Care in the United States* (New York: Commonwealth Fund, 1947), 411.

28. Feshbach, "What's Inside the Black Box"; Herbert Klarman, "Planning for Facilities," in *Regionalization and Health Policy*, ed. Eli Ginzburg (Washington, D.C.: U.S. Government Printing Office, 1973), 27. See also Frank J. Thomson, *Health Politics and the Bureaucracy: Politics and Implementation* (Cambridge, Mass.: MIT Press, 1981), 29–38. A case study by Ray Elling suggests that, beneath the surface of consensus described by Thomson, the political conflicts were intense; see Ray H. Elling, "The Hospital-Support Game in Urban Center," in *The Hospital in Modern Society*, ed. Eliot Freidson (New York: Free Press, 1963), 73–111.

29. U.S. Department of Health, Education and Welfare, *Facts About the Hill-Burton Program, July 1, 1947–June, 30, 1971*; Judith R. Lave and Lester B. Lave, *The Hospital Construction Act: An Evaluation of the Hill-Burton Program, 1948–1973* (Washington, D.C.: American Enterprise Institute, 1974)

30. However, the program did not succeed in attracting doctors to low-income states, as its supporters originally predicted. See Lawrence J. Clark et al., "The Impact of Hill-Burton: An Analysis of Hospital Bed and Physician Distribution in the United States, 1950–1970," *Medical Care* 18 (May 1980), 532–50. Nor did it redistribute doctors within states. See William A. Rushing, *Community, Physicians and Inequality* (Lexington, Mass.: Lexington Books, 1975), 200–03.

31. On the distribution of funds by community, see Lave and Lave, *Hospital Construction Act*, 19–21; and Jacquelyn Hochban et al., "The Hill-Burton Program and Changes in Health Services Delivery," *Inquiry* 8 (Spring 1981), 61–69. De Vise notes that in twenty-five years of the Hill-Burton program not one inner-city hospital in Chicago received aid, while two dozen in the suburbs were built or expanded with federal assistance. See Pierre de Vise, *Misused and Misplaced Hospitals and Doctors: A Locational Analysis of the Urban Health Care Crisis* (Washington, D.C.: Association of American Geographers, 1973), 76.

32. In 1949 the law was revised to vary the proportion of local funds required from two thirds in high-income states to one third in low-income states. Thus state per capita income entered the process twice—first, in allocating funds among the states; second, in determining what proportion of the cost local sponsors would have to raise.

33. Quoted in Feshbach, "What's Inside the Black Box," 326.

34. For a review of the legal history, see Rand E. Rosenblatt, "Health Care Reform and Administrative Law: A Structural Approach," *Yale Law Journal* 88 (December 1978), 264–86.

35. Don K. Price, "A Political Hypochondriac Looks at the Future of Medicine" (National Academy of Sciences, Washington, D.C., May 9, 1973).

36. Edward A. Shils, "The Autonomy of Science," in *The Sociology of Science*, ed. Bernard Barber and Walter Hirsch (New York: Free Press, 1962), 610–14.

37. Stevens, *American Medicine and the Public Interest*, 350–51.

38. John E. Deitrick and Robert C. Berson, *Medical Schools in the United States at Midcentury* (New York: McGraw-Hill, 1953), 195; Patricia L. Kendall, *The Relationship Between Medical Educators and Medical Practitioners* (Evanston, Ill.: Association of American Medical Colleges, 1965), 32.

39. Robert G. Petersdorf, "The Evolution of Departments of Medicine," *New England Journal of Medicine* 303 (August 28, 1980), 491.

40. Vernon W. Lippard, *A Half Century of Medical Education: 1920–1970* (New York: Josiah Macy, Jr., Foundation, 1974), 42–43.

41. Kendall, *Relationship Between Medical Educators and Medical Practitioners*, 36, 42, 57.

42. Marcus S. Goldstein, *Income of Physicians, Osteopaths and Dentists from Professional Practice* (Washington, D.C.: Social Security Administration, Office of Research and Statistics, 1972).

43. Kendall, *Relationship Between Medical Educators and Medical Practitioners*, 82.

44. Lippard, *Half Century*, 47–48.

45. Quoted in Robert K. Merton, "Some Preliminaries to a Sociology of Medical Education," in *The Student Physician*, ed. Robert K. Merton, George G. Reader, and Patricia L. Kendall (Cambridge: Harvard University Press, 1957), 24.

46. Patricia L. Kendall and Hanan C. Selvin, "Tendencies Toward Specialization in Medical Training," in ibid., 153–74; student quoted, ibid., 163.

A survey of graduates of six public and six private medical schools from the classes of 1950 and 1954 indicates the tendency toward specialization was more pronounced at the private institutions. Fremont J. Lyden, H. Jack Geiger, and Osler L. Peterson, *The Training of Good Physicians: Critical Factors in Career Choices* (Cambridge: Harvard University Press, 1968).

In the late fifties, at least at Harvard Medical School, there seems also to have been a shift from emphasis on private specialty practice to scientic work; this was at the height of public support for medical research and may also have reflected the general post-Sputnik climate. See Daniel H. Funkenstein, *Medical Students, Medical Schools and Society During Five Eras: Factors Affecting the Career Choice of Physicians 1958–1976* (Cambridge, Mass.: Ballinger, 1978).

47. Stevens, *American Medicine and the Public Interest*, 203, 244–57. See also Patricia L. Kendall, "Medical Specialization: Trends and Contributing Factors" in *Psychosocial Aspects of Medical Training*, ed. R. H. Coombs and C. E. Vincent (Springfield, Ill.: C. C Thomas, 1971), 449–97.

48. For discussions of these developments, see Stevens, *American Medicine and the Public Interest*, 208–17, 258–66; and Lippard, *Half Century*, 93–95.

49. Stevens, *American Medicine and the Public Interest*, 279–80.

50. J. A. Curran. "Internships and Residencies· Historical Backgrounds and Current Trends," *Journal of Medical Education* 34 (September 1959), 873–84.

51. For supporting data on these points, see Roy Penchansky and Gerald Rosenthal, "Productivity, Price and Income Behaviour in the Physicians' Services Market—a Tentative Hypothesis," *Medical Care* 3 (October–December 1965), 240–44.

52. Mark S. Blumberg, "Physicians Fees as Incentives," in *Changing the Behavior of the Physician: A Management Perspective* (Proceedings of the Twenty-First Annual Symposium on Hospital Affairs, Graduate Program in Hospital Administration and Center for Health Administration Studies, Graduate School of Business, University of Chicago, June 1979), 29–30.

53. Penchansky and Rosenthal, "Productivity, Price and Income Behavior."

54. Kendall, "Medical Specialization: Trends and Contributing Factors," 460. For an interesting interpretation that relates specialty prestige to variations in doctor-patient relations, see Stephen M. Shortell, "Occupational Prestige Differences Within the Medical and Allied Health Professions," *Social Science and Medicine* 8 (January 1974), 1–9.

55. Surgeon General's Consultant Group on Medical Education, *Physicians for a Growing America* (Washington, D.C.: U.S. Government Printing Office, 1959), 8–11.

56. U.S. Department of Health Education and Welfare, Division of Public Health Methods, *Health Manpower Source Book*, vol. 9, *Physicians, Dentists and Professional Nurses*, 27.

57. Selwyn D. Collins, "Frequency and Volume of Doctors' Calls Among Males and Females in 9,000 Families, Based on Nationwide Periodic Canvasses, 1928–31," *Public Health Reports* 55 (November 1, 1940), 1977–2020; Antonio Ciocco, Isidore Altman and T. David Truan, "Patient Load and Volume of Medical Services," *Public Health Reports* 67 (June 1952), 533. See also Bernhard J. Stern, *American Medical Practice in the Perspectives of a Century* (New York: Commonwealth Fund, 1945).

58. Raymond S. Duff and August B. Hollingshead, *Sickness and Society* (New York: Harper Row, 1968), 58.

59. U.S. Department of Health, Education and Welfare, *Health Manpower Source Book*, 9:18, 25.

60. Rosemary Stevens and Joan Vermeulen, *Foreign Trained Physicians and American Medicine* (U.S. Department of Health Education and Welfare, 1972), 112.

61. John C. Nunemaker et al., "Graduate Medical Education in the United States," *JAMA* 174 (October 8, 1960), 578.

62. Alice M. Yohalem and Charles M. Brecher, "The University Medical Center and the Metropolis: A Working Paper," in *The University Medical Center and the Metropolis*, eds. Eli Ginzburg and Alice M. Yohalem (New York: Josiah Macy, Jr., Foundation, 1974), 10–13; "Graduate Medical Education: Annual Report on Graduate Medical Education in the United States," *JAMA* 226 (November 19, 1973), 930.

The term "empire" comes from John Ehrenreich and Barbara Ehrenreich, *The American Health Empire: Power, Politics and Profits* (New York: Random House, 1970). More than any other single book, this focused attention on the growing power of medical schools and their relation to the larger system. But perhaps because they were writing from the perspective of New York City, the authors did not, I think, see the historical and economic limits of the phenomenon.

63. Willard C. Rappleye, *The Current Era of the Faculty of Medicine, Columbia University, 1910–1958* (New York: Columbia University Press, 1958).

64. Duff and Hollingshead, *Sickness and Society*, 46.

65. American Hospital Association, *Hospital Statistics, 1972* (Chicago: American Hospital Association, 1972), 190; see also Cecil G. Sheps et al., *Medical Schools and Hospitals: Interdependence for Education and Service* (Evanston, Ill.: Association of American Medical Colleges, 1965) in *Journal of Medical Education* 40 (September 1965), pt. II, 12.

66. For this schema, I am indebted to Alfred E. Miller, "The Changing Structure of the Medical Profession in Urban and Suburban Settings," *Social Science and Medicine* 11 (March 1977), 233–43.

67. Hodgson, *America in Our Time*, 7.

68. Surgeon General's Consultant Group on Medical Education, *Physicians for a Growing America* (Washington, D.C.: U.S. Government Printing Office, 1959).

69. Milton I. Roemer and Max Shain, "Hospital Utilization Under Insurance," mimeographed (Ithaca, N.Y.: Cornell University School of Business and Public Administration, 1959), 17–18, 51.

70. U.S. Bureau of the Census, *Historical Statistics of the United States, Colonial Times to 1970* (Washington, D.C.: U.S. Department of Commerce, 1975), 84.

71. For a review of the debate, see Andrew T. Scull, *Decarceration* (Englewood Cliffs, N.J.: Spectrum, 1977).

72. Joint Commission on Mental Illness and Health, *Action for Mental Health* (New York: Basic Books, 1961). For the historical background, see Connery et al., *Politics of Mental Health*, 37–47.

73. "Special Message to the Congress on Mental Illness and Mental Retardation, February 5, 1963," *Public Papers of the President, John F. Kennedy, 1963*, 126, 128. For studies of the program, see Franklin D. Chu and Sharland Trotter, *The Madness Establishment* (New York: Grossman, 1974) and Connery et al., *Politics of Mental Health*.

74. James L. Sundquist, *Politics and Policy: The Eisenhower, Kennedy and Johnson Years* (Washington, D.C.: Brookings Institution, 1968), 13–56.

75. Daniel P. Moynihan, *Maximum Feasible Misunderstanding: Community Action in the War on Poverty* (New York: Free Press, 1969).

76. For the story of Medicare, see Theodore R. Marmor, *The Politics of Medicare* (Chicago: Aldine, 1973); Richard Harris, *A Sacred Trust* (New York: New American Library, 1966); and Sundquist, *Politics and Policy*, 287–321.

77. Harris, *Sacred Trust*, 110–15, 144; Marmor, *Politics of Medicare*, 35–38.

78. Robert Stevens and Rosemary Stevens, *Welfare Medicine in America: A Case Study of Medicaid* (New York: Free Press, 1974).

79. President's Commission on Heart Disease, Cancer and Stroke, *Report to the President: A National Program to Conquer Heart Disease, Cancer and Stroke* (Washington, D.C.: U.S. Government Printing Office, 1964), v. 1, viii.

80. Drew, "Health Syndicate."

81. H. Jack Geiger, "Community Control—or Community Conflict," in *Neighborhood Health Centers*, ed. Robert M. Hollister, Bernard M. Kramer, and Seymour S. Bellin (Lexington, Mass.: Lexington Books, 1974), 140. On the origins of the health centers, see Sar Levitan, *The Great Society's Poor Law: A New Approach to Poverty* (Baltimore: Johns Hopkins Press, 1969), 191–205; Lisbeth Bamberger Schorr and Joseph T. English, "Background, Context and Significant Issues in Neighborhood Health Center Programs," *Milbank Memorial Fund Quarterly* 66 (July 1968), 289–96, reprinted in Hollister et al., eds., *Neighborhood Health Centers*, 45–50; and Daniel I. Zwick, "Some Accomplishments and Findings of Neighborhood Health Centers," in ibid., 69–90.

82. Karen Davis and Cathy Schoen, *Health and the War on Poverty* (Washington, D.C.: Brookings Institution, 1978), 164.

83. Ibid., 173–200.

84. For subsequent developments, see "Community Health Centers—Fifteen Years Later," *Urban Health* (April 1980), 34–40.

85. Davis and Schoen, *Health and the War on Poverty*, 41–48.

86. Karen Davis and Roger Reynolds, "The Impact of Medicare and Medicaid on Access to Medical Care," in *The Role of Health Insurance in the Health Services Sector*, ed. Roger N. Rosett (New York: National Bureau of Economic Research, 1976). For a survey of programs and their effects, see Charles E. Lewis, Rashi Fein, and David Mechanic, *A Right to Health: The Problem of Access to Primary Medical Care* (New York: Wiley, 1976).

87. U.S. Bureau of the Census, *Characteristics of the Population Below the Poverty Level: 1978*, Series P-60, no. 124, June 1980, 16. The proportion of the poor with a working head of household dropped from 68 to 48 percent between 1959 and 1976 (ibid., 28). Even excluding female-headed households, the decline was from 75 to 60 percent (ibid., 34).

88. Compare National Center for Health Statistics, *Bed Disability Among the Chronically Limited, United States July 1957–June 1961*, Series 10, no. 12, and U.S. Department of Health, Education and Welfare, *Health: United States, 1979*, 117–18. Low-income persons had 66 percent more "bed disability" days per person than high-income persons in 1957–61, but in 1972 they had 123 percent more such days. See also Harold S. Luft, *Poverty*

and Health: Economic Causes and Consequences of Health Problems (Cambridge, Mass.: Ballinger, 1978). About 65 percent of poor families consisting of at least a husband and wife include a disabled adult, and at least 30 percent of the disabled who are currently poor are poor because of their health problems.

89. Aday and her colleagues, adjusting use of physicians' services by number of days of disability, find that by 1976 no differences existed between different levels of income. However, Kleinman, using a much larger survey for 1978, finds that high-income people were seeing physicians 73 percent more often in relation to a somewhat different index of need—bed disability days. The bed-disability index may reflect the differences in health more accurately. Ordinary disability days show less variation by income, perhaps because higher-income people include illnesses of lesser severity. See LuAnn Aday, Ronald Andersen, and Gretchen V. Fleming, *Health Care in the U.S.: Equitable for Whom?* (Beverly Hills, Calif.: Sage Publications, 1980); Kleinman's data are presented in Karen Davis, Marsha Gold and Diane Makuc, "Access to Health Care for the Poor: Does the Gap Remain?" *Annual Review of Public Health* 2 (1981), 159–82.

For evidence on the continuing differences in waiting time and other indicators of access, see Frank Sloan and Judith K. Bentkover, *Access to Ambulatory Care and the U.S. Economy* (Lexington, Mass.: Lexington Books, 1979).

90. Davis, Gold, and Makuc, "Access to Health Care for the Poor."

91. Davis and Schoen, *Health and the War on Poverty*, 52–56.

92. Judith M. Feder, *Medicare: The Politics of Federal Hospital Insurance* (Lexington, Mass.: Lexington Books, 1977). For an earlier study, see Herman Miles Somers and Anne Ramsay Somers, *Medicare and the Hospitals: Issues and Prospects* (Washington, D.C.: Brookings Institution, 1966), 154–96.

93. Klarman, "Planning for Facilities," 25–36.

94. For another view of the limits of planning and reform, see Robert Alford, *Health Care Politics: Ideological and Interest Group Barriers to Reform* (Chicago: University of Chicago Press, 1975).

Alford proposes a theory of "structural interests" to explain what he regards as the negligible results of health reform. The key structural interests are (1) professional monopoly, the interest of physicians and the "dominant interest" of the system; (2) corporate rationalization, a "challenging interest" shared by medical school faculties, hospital administrators, health planners, and others associated with institutions; and (3) health equality, a "repressed" interest shared by the poor and other neglected people. Alford's argument is that the failure of health reform has stemmed from a deadlock between professional monopoly and corporate rationalization.

This analysis—or at least the vocabulary Alford introduced—has proved highly persuasive to sociologists and political scientists studying American medicine. The approach represents an important contribution, but for several reasons I have chosen not to use it.

First of all, the concept of "stuctural interests" is almost metaphysical in its abstraction. Alford insists that structural interests are not to be confused with interest groups: "This concept [structural interests] leaves empirically open the extent to which and the conditions under which coalitions form and constitute interest groups in the usual sense. The central idea is that existing institutions function for all occupations, groups, or organizations which have the *common interest* signified by the classifying term." (Ibid., 14–15; italics mine.) But can occupations, groups, and organizations be classifed unambiguously by the common structural interests Alford imputes to them? A major difficulty arises with the classification of hospital administrators as having interests structurally opposed to those of private physicians. For as I have argued earlier in this chapter, the interests of community hospitals and their doctors were intimately linked. Alford presumes that the support of some administrators for regionalization and other "corporate rationalist" reforms indicated a deep-seated interest of all administrators—or perhaps I should say, a structural interest of administration in its pure, Platonic sense.

The difficulty goes deeper. Alford hypothesizes the existence of structural interests, but he actually writes about the beliefs of the groups and their representatives. The book is largely an account of the various reports recommending reorganization of health services in New York City. Alford has little to say about the actual economic relations of the system, even in New York; the book is missing any sustained historical analysis of institutional structure. Consequently, the categories used to describe structural interests are drawn from an analysis of ideological differences, not of institutional arrangements.

Furthermore, the account does not persuasively explain why the hypothesized structural interests were deadlocked. Alford writes, "Rather than a societal consensus giving the doctors power, it is the doctors' power which generates the societal consensus." (Ibid., 17.) But where did the doctors' power come from? We are left with the impression that it was always there, a kind of prime mover. On the other hand, the approach I have taken attempts to explain how the institutional structure of the medical system was historically produced, including how the power of the medical profession was generated. I do not take the interests of physicians as structurally unambiguous (see my discussion of the defeat of health insurance during the Progressive era), and I emphasize the decisive importance of political decisions in shaping the evolution of the system. The failure of reform cannot be understood primarily on the basis of divided interests within medicine; it is traceable to a more general pattern of political accommodation. (For a more extended discussion, see Paul Starr and Gösta Esping-Andersen, "Passive Intervention," *Working Papers for a New Society* 7 [July–August 1979], 15–25.)

Finally, Alford's notion of "corporate rationalization" was plainly derived from New Left theories of "corporate liberalism" that were popular in the late 1960s. The latent function of such theories was to discredit the redistributive reforms proposed by liberals. The theories sought to associate such reforms with the hidden interests of established institutions, which could then be demonstrated to have caused the problems of inequality or alienation in the first place. Like other radical theories of the period, Alford's minimizes and disparages the significance of liberal reforms by describing them as mere efforts to rationalize the corporate order. In his account, these reforms, by definition, do not satisfy the interests of poor people and others in need of medical care; what ought to be subject to empirical confirmation is written into his classification of structural interests. The term "corporate rationalization" does have a use in regard to medicine— specifically to describe the kinds of rationalization that health care corporations may bring about. (On those developments, see the final chapter of this book.)

95. For an interpretation that emphasizes correspondences between medicine and class structure in the United States, see Vicente Navarro, *Medicine Under Capitalism* (New York: Prodist, 1976).

96. On the concept of "structural power," see Steven Lukes, *Power: A Radical View* (New York: Macmillan, 1974).

Chapter Four

End of a Mandate

1. U.S. Public Health Service, Office of Research, Statistics and Technology, *Health: United States, 1981* (Hyattsville, Md.: U.S. Department of Health and Human Services, 1981), 263.

2. *New York Times*, July 11, 1969.

3. "$60-Billion Crisis in Health Care," *Business Week* (January 17, 1970), 50–64.

4. "It's Time to Operate," *Fortune* 81 (January 1970), 79.

5. Ronald Andersen, Joanna Kravits and Odin W. Anderson, "The Public's View of the Crisis in Medical Care: an Impetus for Changing Delivery Systems?" *Economic and Business Bulletin* 24 (1971), 44–52.

6. Godfrey Hodgson, "The Politics of American Health Care," *Atlantic* 232 (October 1973), 55.

7. U.S. Public Health Service, *Health: United States, 1981*, 268–69.

8. Victor R. Fuchs, *Who Shall Live?* (New York: Basic Books, 1974), 92–95. More recent calculations of national health expenditures for these years are slightly higher. See U.S. Public Health Service, *Health: United States, 1981*, 263.

9. Martin S. Feldstein, "Hospital Cost Inflation: A Study of Nonprofit Price Dynamics," *American Economic Review* 61 (December 1971), 853–72.

10. U.S. Public Health Service, *Health: United States, 1981*, 270.

11. Thomas L. Delbanco, Katherine C. Meyers, and Elliot A. Segal, "Paying the Physician's Fee: Blue Shield and the Reasonable Charge," *New England Journal of Medicine* 301 (December 13, 1979), 1314–20.

12. Mark S. Blumberg, "Physicians Fees as Incentives," in *Changing the Behavior of the Physician: A Management Perspective* (Proceedings of the Twenty-First Annual Symposium on Hospital Affairs, Graduate Program in Hospital Administration and Center for Health Administration Studies, Graduate School of Business, University of Chicago, June 1979), 20–32.

13. Benson B. Roe, "The UCR Boondoggle: A Death Knell for Private Practice?" *New England Journal of Medicine* 305 (July 2, 1981), 41–45, and correspondence, ibid. 30 (November 19, 1981), 1287–88.

14. Louis A. Orsini, "Hospital Financing: PUBLIC ACCOUNTABILITY—The Case of Rates Prospectively Determined by State Agencies for All Patients," *Viewpoint*, Health Insurance Association of America (January 1974).

15. Alan A. Stone, *Mental Health and the Law: A System in Transition* (Rockville, Md.: National Institute of Mental Health, 1975), 83–96; George J. Annas, *The Rights of Hospital Patients* (New York: Discus Books, 1975), 3–9.

16. Annas, *Rights of Hospital Patients*, 57–78.

17. William J. Curran, "The Patients' Bill of Rights Becomes Law," *New England Journal of Medicine* 290 (January 6, 1974), 32–33.

18. Jean Hamburger, *The Power and the Frailty: The Future of Medicine and the Future of Man* (New York: Macmillan, 1973), 83.

19. Sue Sprecher, "Psychosurgery Policy Soon to be Set," *Real Paper*, January 21, 1978.

20. David J. Rothman, "The State as Parent: Social Policy in the Progressive Era," in Willard Gaylin et al., *Doing Good: The Limits of Benevolence* (New York: Pantheon, 1978), 69–95.

21. "Medical Education in the United States, 1979–1980," *JAMA* 244 (December 26, 1980), 2814. For a review of the evidence of changes among women doctors, see Naomi Bluestone, "The Future Impact of Women on American Medicine," *American Journal of Public Health* 68 (August 1978), 760–63.

22. Sheryl Burt Ruzek, *The Women's Health Movement: Feminist Alternatives to Medical Control* (New York: Praeger, 1978).

23. George J. Annas, "Homebirth: Autonomy vs. Safety," *Hastings Center Report* 8 (August 1978), 19–20.

24. Dan Cordtz, "Change Begins in the Doctor's Office," *Fortune* (January 1970), 84.

25. Quoted in John K. Iglehart, "Prepaid Group Medical Practice Emerges as Likely Federal Approach to Health Care," *National Journal* 3 (July 10, 1971), 1444.

26. For a review of the various national health insurance proposals, see Karen Davis, *National Health Insurance: Benefits, Costs and Consequences* (Washington, D.C.: Brookings Institution, 1975).

27. Joseph Falkson, *HMOs and the Politics of Health System Reform* (Chicago: American Hospital Association, 1980), 10. The following discussion draws frequently on Falkson and interviews of my own with Paul Ellwood and others while I was writing, "The Undelivered Health System," *The Public Interest*, no. 42 (Winter 1976), 66–85. Some of the passages on HMOs in this chapter originally appeared in that article.

28. This was later published as Paul M. Ellwood, Jr., et al., "The Health Maintenance Strategy," *Medical Care* 9 (June 1971), 291–98.

29. *New York Times*, February 19, 1971.

30. Carnegie Commission on Higher Education, *Higher Education and the Nation's Health* (New York: McGraw-Hill, 1970).

31. *New York Times*, September 4, 1971.

32. "Can the A.M.A. recover from its political mistakes? *Medical Economics* (January 5, 1970), 27–39.

33. Walter C. Bornemeier, "Blueprint for the Future," *JAMA* 217 (July 19, 1971), 324. On the AMA's troubles in the mid-1970s, see John Carlova, "Going, Going . . . AMA's Grip on State Societies," *Medical Economics* 52 (February 3, 1975), 33–42; *New York Times*,

June 19, 1975; and John K. Iglehart, "No More Dr. Nice Guy," *National Journal* 8 (March 6, 1976), 313.

34. William J. Curran, *National Survey and Analysis of Certificate of Need Laws: Health Planning and Regulation in State Legislatures* (Chicago: American Hospital Association, 1973).

35. American Hospital Association, *Hospital Regulation: Report of the Special Committee on the Regulatory Process* (Chicago: American Hospital Association, 1977).

36. *New York Times*, December 16, 1972; Paul B. Ginsburg, "Inflation and the Economic Stabilization Program," in *Health: A Victim or Cause of Inflation*, ed. Michael Zubkoff (New York: Prodist, 1976), 31–51.

37. Barbara Isenberg, "Physician Panels are Used Increasingly to Police Skyrocketing Costs of Treating the Aged, Needy," *Wall Street Journal*, April 7, 1972.

38. George Maddaloni, "PSRO—Relationships of Organized Medicine in PSRO [*sic*]" in *Public Control of Medical Care: History, Practices and Problems of the Federal Professional Standards Review Organization*, ed. Nathan Goldfarb, Hofstra University Yearbook of Business, Series 13, vol. 2, 121–89; Judith Axler Turner, "HEW Begins Medical Review; AMA, Hospitals Mount Opposition," *National Journal Reports* 6 (January 19, 1974), 90–102.

39. John K. Iglehart, "Executive-legislative Conflict Looms over Continuation of Health Care Subsidies," *National Journal* 5 (May 5, 1973), 645–52; "Executive-Congressional Coalition Seeks Tighter Regulation for Medical-Services Industry," *National Journal Reports* 5 (November 10, 1973), 1684–92.

40. Leonard S. Rosenfeld and Irene Rosenfeld, "National Health Planning in the United States: Prospects and Portents," *International Journal of Health Services* 5 (1975), 441–53.

41. Russell B. Roth, M.D., "A Bankrupt Law," *American Medical News* (November 22, 1976), 10.

42. American Hospital Association, *Hospital Regulation*, 15.

43. *New York Times*, February 8, 1974.

44. "Insuring the Nation's Health," *Newsweek*, June 3, 1974.

45. John K. Iglehart, "National Insurance Plan Tops Ways and Means Agenda," *National Journal Reports* 6 (March 16, 1974), 383.

46. Alice M. Rivlin, "Agreed: Here Comes National Health Insurance," *New York Times Magazine*, July 21, 1974. See also John K. Iglehart, "Consensus Forms for National Insurance Plan, Proposals Vary Widely in Scope," *National Journal Reports* 5 (December 12, 1973), 1855–63; and idem, "Compromise Seems Unlikely on Three Major Insurance Plans," *National Journal Reports* 6 (May 11, 1974), 700–07.

47. Executive Office of the President, Council on Wage and Price Stability, *The Problem of Rising Health Care Costs* (April 1976).

48. *National Journal* 8 (October 16, 1976), 1460.

49. John K. Iglehart, "The Rising Costs of Health Care—Something Must be Done, but What?" *National Journal* 8 (October 16, 1976),

50. Some of the following is taken from my article, "The Politics of Therapeutic Nihilism," *Working Papers for a New Society* 3 (Summer 1976), 48–55.

51. Aaron Wildavsky, "Doing Better and Feeling Worse: The Political Pathology of Health Policy," *Daedalus* 106 (Winter 1977), 105, and John H. Knowles, "The Responsibility of the Individual," ibid., 57–80.

52. Ivan Illich, *Medical Nemesis: The Expropriation of Health* (New York: Patheon, 1976).

53. Victor R. Fuchs, *Who Shall Live? Health, Economics and Social Choice* (New York: Basic Books, 1974).

54. David E. Rogers and Robert J. Blendon, "The Changing American Health Scene: Sometimes Things Get Better," *JAMA* 237 (April 18, 1977), 1710–14.

55. Karen Davis and Cathy Schoen, *Health and the War on Poverty* (Washington, D.C.: Brookings Institution, 1978), 26–35, 184–85, 219–24.

56. Illich, *Medical Nemesis*, 242.

57. Joseph A. Califano, Jr., *Governing America* (New York: Simon and Schuster, 1981), 97.

58. Theodore Marmor and Edward Tenner, "National Health Insurance: Canada's Path, America's Choice," *Challenge* 20 (May–June 1977), 13–21.

59. Interview with Ben Heineman, Jr., May 1979. At the time I was writing an article for *The New Republic*.

60. David S. Salkever and Thomas W. Bice, "The Impact of Certificate of Need Controls on Hospital Investment," *Milbank Memorial Fund Quarterly* 54 (Spring 1976), 185–214.

61. Brian Biles, Carl J. Schramm, and J. Graham Atkinson, "Hospital Cost Inflation Under State Rate Setting Programs," *New England Journal of Medicine* 303 (September 18, 1980), 664–67.

62. Califano, *Governing America*, 166–67; Falkson, *HMO's*, 184–208.

63. For two studies of the HSA's, see Drew Altman, Richard Greene, and Harvey M. Sapolsky, *Health Planning and Regulation: The Decision-Making Process* (Washington, D.C.: AUPHA Press, 1981); and James A. Morone, "The Dilemma of Citizen Representation: Democracy, Planning and Bureaucracy in Local Health Politics." (Ph.D. diss., University of Chicago, 1981).

64. Alan Blum, "Family Practice On and Off the Campus," *JAMA* 245 (April 17, 1981), 1560–61.

65. U.S. Department of Health and Human Services, National Center for Health Services Research, "Who Are the Uninsured?" *Data Preview* 1 (1980). The statistics are for 1977–78.

66. Clark C. Havighurst, "Competition in Health Services: Overview, Issues and Answers," *Vanderbilt Law Review* 34 (May 1981), 1115–78. Alain C. Enthoven, *Health Plan: The Only Practical Solution to Soaring Health Costs* (Reading, Mass.: Addison-Wesley, 1980). See also, Alain C. Enthoven, "How Interested Groups have Responded to a Proposal for Economic Competition in Health Services," *American Economic Review* 70 (May 1980), 142–48.

67. *New York Times*, February 16, 1981.

Chapter Five

The Coming of the Corporation

1. "Medical Education in the United States, 1979–1980," *JAMA* 244 (December 26, 1980), 2813.

2. Congress of the United States, Office of Technology Assessment, *Forecast of Physician Supply and Requirements* (Washington, D.C.: U.S. Government Printing Office, April 1980), 22.

3. Ibid., 7–12.

4. U.S. Dept. of Health and Human Services, *Summary Report of the Graduate Medical Educational National Advisory Committee* (Washington, D.C.: U.S. Government Printing Office, 1980), I:3, 67.

5. See data from an as yet unpublished study by Kathryn Langwell, with accompanying caveats, in Uwe E. Reinhardt, "The GMENAC Forecast: An Alternative View," *American Journal of Public Health* 71 (October 1981), 1151–52.

6. On "burn-out" and the "retreat from patients," see Martin R. Lipp, *The Bitter Pill* (New York: Harper Row, 1980), Chaps. 1, 11–15.

7. Gerald L. Glandon and Jack L. Werner, "Physicians' Practice Experience During the Decade of the 1970s," *JAMA* 244 (December 5, 1980), 2518.

8. National Center for Health Statistics, *Current Estimates from the Health Interview Survey: United States–1979*, Series 10, no. 136 (Hyattsville, Md.: U.S. Department of Health, Education and Welfare, 1981), 4.

9. Arthur Owens, "Working at Full Capacity? A Lot of Your Colleagues Aren't," *Medical Economics* 56 (April 2, 1979), 63 ff.

10. Jack Hadley et al., "Can Fee-for-Service Coexist with Demand Creation?" *Inquiry* 16 (Fall 1979), 247–58.

11. Gerald L. Glandon and Roberta J. Shapiro, "Trends in Physicians' Incomes, Expenses and Fees: 1970–1979," in *Profile of Medical Practice 1980*, ed. Gerald L. Glandon and Roberta J. Shapiro (Chicago: American Medical Association, 1980), 39–49; "Earnings Survey," *Medical Economics* 57 (September 15, 1980), 120–21.

12. Harry T. Paxton, "Group Practice Jobs: Suddenly It's a Buyer's Market," *Medical Economics* 56 (November 26,1979), 27–34.

13. Victor R. Fuchs, "The Coming Challenge to American Physicians," *New England Journal of Medicine* 304 (June 11, 1981), 1487–90.

14. For some reports on cities where doctors are plentiful, see John H. Lavin, "Doctor Surplus: Close-Up of a Town that's Feeling the Crunch," *Medical Economics* (September 29, 1980), 69–80; and Marilyn Chase, "City of Doctors: Will Surplus of M.D.'s Be Good for Patients? Look at San Francisco," *Wall Street Journal*, March 13, 1980.

15. Milton I. Roemer, Jorge A. Mera, and William Shonick, "The Ecology of Group Medical Practice in the United States," *Medical Care* 12 (August 1974), 627–37. On the early development of groups, see Book One, Chapter 6.

16. Jeff Charles Goldsmith, *Can Hospitals Survive? The New Competitive Health Care Market* (Homewood, Ill.: Dow Jones-Irwin, 1981), 35–36.

17. Ibid., 46, 136–44.

18. Paul M. Ellwood and Linda Krane Ellwein, "Physician Glut Will Force Hospitals to Look Outward," *Hospitals* (January 16, 1981), 81–85.

19. Ibid., 83–84. See also Marla Salmon White and Richard A. Culbertson, "The Oversupply of Physicians: Implications for Hospital Planning," *Hospital Progress* 62 (February 1981), 28–31.

20. American Medical Association, "Federal and Non-Federal Physicians, By AMA Membership, Sex and State," November 23, 1981 (courtesy of AMA).

21. "Report of the Ad Hoc Committee on Women Physicians in Organized Medicine," American Medical Association, 1980.

22. Interview, Chicago, Ill., January 15, 1981.

23. The term was used by both *Fortune* and the radical Health Policy Advisory Committee (Health-PAC). See Harold B. Meyers, "The Medical Industrial Complex," *Fortune* 81 (January 1970), 90ff, and John Ehrenreich and Barbara Ehrenreich, *The American Health Empire* (New York: Random House, 1970), 95–123.

24. Arnold S. Relman, "The New Medical-Industrial Complex," *New England Journal of Medicine* 303 (October 23, 1980), 963–70.

25. David B. Starkweather, *Hospital Mergers in the Making* (Ann Arbor, Mich.: Health Administration Press, 1981), 5.

26. Donald E. L. Johnson and Vince diPaolo, "Multihospital System Survey," *Modern Healthcare* 11 (April 1981), 80. Montague Brown et al., "Trends in Multihospital Systems: A Multiyear Comparison," *Health Care Management Review* 6 (Fall 1980), 9–22.

Although both found about 300,000 beds in multihospital systems, the two surveys were actually measuring somewhat different statistics. The *Modern Healthcare* survey was limited to centrally managed systems, whereas the AHA survey included many systems whose hospitals were only loosely affiliated. However, *Modern Healthcare* included hospitals that were managed but not owned by chains, whereas the AHA survey seems to have been limited to owned hospitals. These differences in definition apparently cancelled themselves out in the total beds counted. However, they yield different estimates of the composition of the multihospital sector since the for-profits are more often centrally managed and since they also account for most of the hospitals under contract management.

27. Brown et al., "Trends in Multihospital Systems," 21.

28. Johnson and diPaolo, "Multihospital System Survey," 96.

29. "Management Company Expansion Spurs Investor-Owned Growth," *Federation of American Hospitals Review* 14 (November–December 1981), 54–55.

30. Marilyn Mannisto, "Hospital Management Companies Expand Foreign Operations," *Hospitals* 55 (February 1, 1981), 52–56. Hospital Corporation of America, *Annual Report, 1980*.

31. Gwen Kinkead, "Humana's Hard-Sell Hospitals," *Fortune* (November 17, 1980), 68–81.

32. American Hospital Association, *Hospital Statistics, 1981* (Chicago: American Hospital Association, 1981), 6–7; Johnson and diPaolo, "Multihospital System Survey," 96; Bruce Steinwald and Duncan Neuhauser, "The Role of the Proprietary Hospital," *Law and Contemporary Problems* 35 (Autumn 1970), 824.

33. Janet Bly and William P. Pierskalla, "Religious Systems' Local Boards Have More Decision-making Power," *Modern Healthcare* 11 (April 1981), 88–89, 91. The AHA survey, which classified systems according to degree of centralization, found that "managed" systems accounted for 21 percent of all community hospital beds, while "affiliated" systems accounted for only 10 percent. The growth in multihospital systems between 1975 and 1979 had occurred primarily in the managed systems. Brown et al., "Trends in Multihospital Systems," 15–16.

34. Bly and Pierskalla, "Religious Systems' Local Boards Have More Decision-making Power." On control by inside directors, see Edward Herman, *Corporate Power, Corporate Control* (New York: Cambridge University Press, 1981).

Managerial control does not necessarily mean, as some theorists of the managerial revolution argue, that the companies are more devoted to growth than to profits. The inside directors typically hold substantial investments in company stock; their success as managers depends on keeping up the company's price-earnings ratio. Consequently, even when managers control corporations, they are no less devoted to ownership interests.

35. Johnson and diPaolo, "Multihospital System Survey."

36. Ibid., 81.

37. Robert Derzon, Lawrence S. Lewin, and J. Michael Watt, "Not-for-profit Chains Share in Multihospital System Boom," *Hospitals* (May 16, 1981), 65–71.

38. Starkweather, *Hospital Mergers*, 12–17.

39. Thomas F. Treat, "The Performance of Merging Hospitals," *Medical Care* 14 (March 1976), 199–209.

40. David B. Starkweather, "U.S. Hospitals: Corporate Concentration vs. Local Community Control," *Public Affairs Report*, Bulletin of the Institute of Governmental Studies, University of California, Berkeley, 22 (April 1981), 6.

41. Lawrence S. Lewin, Robert A. Derzon, and Rhea Margulies, "Investor-owneds and Nonprofits Differ in Economic Performance," *Hospitals* (July 1, 1981), 52–58. For some weak evidence favoring for-profit hospitals, see Carson W. Bays, "Cost Comparisons of Forprofit and Nonprofit Hospitals," *Social Science and Medicine* 13C (December 1979), 219–25.

42. Brown et al., "Trends in Multihospital Systems," 17–20.

43. S. David Pomrinse, "Voluntary Planning Forestalls Excessive Competition, Regulation," *Hospital Progress* 62 (March 1981), 37.

44. Derzon, Lewin, and Watt, "Not-for-profit Chains," 66–67.

45. Vince diPaolo, "Gloomy Economic Prospects Will Spur Hospital Acquisition Market," *Modern Healthcare* 11 (January 1981), 70.

46. Starkweather, "U.S. Hospitals: Corporate Concentration vs. Community Control," 6.

47. Barry Bluestone and Bennett Harrison, "Why Corporations Close Profitable Plants," *Working Papers for a New Society* 7 (June 1980), 15–23.

48. Kinkead, "Humana's Hard-Sell Hospitals," 70.

49. Ibid., 81.

50. Montague Brown, "Systems Diversify with Ventures Outside the Hospital," *Hospitals* (April 1, 1981), 147–53.

51. Donald E. L. Johnson, "Nonprofit's Taxed Unit Can Sell Stock," *Modern Healthcare* 11 (June 1981), 90–92. Sally Berger, "Innovative Backround Triggered Trustees' Interest in Conglomerate," *Modern Healthcare* 11 (February 1981), 108, 110.

52. Sheila L. Simler, "Leading Hospitals Restructure, Even Though Benefits May Be Short-lived," *Modern Healthcare* 11 (March 1981), 68–73.

53. Dan Ruck, "Young System Races into Growth Program," *Modern Healthcare* 11 (June 1981), 60–64.

54. Paul A. Teslow, quoted in Donald E.L. Johnson, "Nonprofits Will Merge, Add Services in the 1980's," *Modern Healthcare* 11 (May 1981), 66.

55. Esther Fritz Kuntz, "Nursing Home Chains Buy Up Smaller Groups," *Modern Healthcare* 11 (June 1981), 68–74; Relman, "New Medical-Industrial Complex," 964.

56. Eleanor Siegel, "Emergence of Emergicenters," *Boston Globe*, June 8, 1981. Howard Eisenberg, " 'Convenience Clinics': Your Newest Rival for Patients?" *Medical Eco-

nomics (November 24 1980), 71–84; Linda A. Burns and Mindy S. Ferber, "Freestanding Emergency Care Centers Create Public Policy Issues," *Hospitals* (May 16, 1981), 73–76.

57. Starkweather, "U.S. Hospitals: Corporate Concentration vs. Local Community Control," 1.

58. Richard L. Johnson, "Health Care 2000 A.D.: The Impact of Conglomerates," *Hospital Progress* 62 (April 1981), 48–53.

59. David A. Stockman, "Premises for a Medical Market Place: A Neoconservative's Vision of How to Transform the Health System," *Health Affairs* 1 (Winter 1981), 16.

60. For a scrupulous analysis of the evidence, see Harold S. Luft, *Health Maintenance Organizations: Dimensions of Performance* (New York: Wiley, 1981). For some further evidence of HMOs competitive impact, see Jon B. Christianson, "The Impact of HMOs: Evidence and Research Issues," *Journal of Health Politics, Policy and Law* 5 (Summer 1980), 354–57.

61. Stephen Shortell, "The Researcher's View," in *Hospitals in the 1980s: Nine Views* (Chicago: American Hospital Association, 1977).

62. Alfred Chandler, *The Visible Hand: The Managerial Revolution in American Business* (Cambridge: Harvard University Press, 1977), 315.

63. Daniel S. Greenberg, "Renal Politics," *New England Journal of Medicine* 298 (June 22, 1978), 1427–28; medical professor quoted in John K. Iglehart, "Kidney Treatment Problem Readies HEW for National Health Insurance," *National Journal* (June 26, 1976), 900.

64. Gina Bari Kolata, "NMC Thrives Selling Dialysis," *Science* 208 (April 25, 1980), 379–82.

65. Paul W. Earle, "Business Coalitions—A New Approach to Health Care Cost Containment." (American Medical Association, January 1982); for two reports on business views, see John Iglehart, "Health Care and American Business," *New England Journal of Medicine* 306 (January 14, 1982), 120–24, and idem, "Drawing the Lines for the Debate on Competition," *New England Journal of Medicine* 305 (July 30, 1981), 291–96. For a skeptical view that business is not really that much interested in health costs, see Harvey M. Sapolsky, "Corporate Attitudes toward Health Care Costs," *Milbank Memorial Fund Quarterly* 59 (Fall 1981), 561–85.

66. American Medical Association, *SMS Report* [Sociomedical Monitoring System] (February 1982), 1.

67. Goldsmith, *Can Hospitals Survive?*, 33–34.

68. Interview, January 15, 1982.

69. Clark Havighurst, "Professional Restraints on Innovation in Health Care Financing," *Duke Law Journal* (May 1978), 303–87.

70. Kinkhead, "Humana's Hard-Sell Hospitals," 76.

71. Johnson, "Health Care 2000 A.D," 49–50.

72. Freidson distinguishes between physicians' "technical" autonomy in defining the "content" of their work and their social and economic autonomy in controlling the organization or "terms" of work. Eliot Freidson, *Profession of Medicine* (New York: Dodd, Mead, 1970), 373. This distinction may become increasingly untenable as corporate organizations make the technical standards an object of modification.

INDEX